Error-Control Coding for Computer Systems

Prentice Hall Series in

Computer Engineering

Edward J. McCluskey, Series Editor

McCluskey	*Logic Design Principles*
Rao & Fujiwara	*Error-Control Coding for Computer Systems*
Wakerly	*Digital Design Principles and Practices*

Error-Control Coding for Computer Systems

T. R. N. Rao

Z. L. Loflin Chair Professor of Computer Science
Center for Advanced Computer Studies
University of Southwestern Louisiana
Lafayette, Louisiana

E. Fujiwara

Senior Research Engineer
Nippon Telegraph and Telephone Corporation
Tokyo

Prentice Hall
Englewood Cliffs, New Jersey 07632

LIBRARY OF CONGRESS
Library of Congress Cataloging-in-Publication Data

Rao, T. R. N. (Thammavarapu R. N.)
Error-control coding for computer systems / T.R.N. Rao, E. Fujiwara.
p. cm. -- (Prentice Hall series in computer engineering)
Bibliography: p.
Includes index.
ISBN 0-13-283953-9
1. Error-correcting codes (Information theory) 2. Computer arithmetic and logic units. I. Fujiwara, E. (Eiji) II. Title. III. Series.
QA268.R363 1989
005.7'2--dc19 88-17892
CIP

Editorial/production supervision and
interior design: Cracom Corporation
Cover design: Joel Mitnick Design, Inc.
Manufacturing buyer: Mary Noonan

Published by Prentice-Hall, Inc.
A Division of Simon & Schuster
Englewood Cliffs, New Jersey 07632

Printed in the United States of America
10 9 8 7 6 5 4 3 2 1

ISBN 0-13-283953-9

Prentice-Hall International (UK) Limited, *London*
Prentice-Hall of Australia Pty. Limited, *Sydney*
Prentice-Hall Canada Inc., *Toronto*
Prentice-Hall Hispanoamericana, S.A., *Mexico*
Prentice-Hall of India Private Limited, *New Delhi*
Prentice-Hall of Japan, Inc., *Tokyo*
Simon & Schuster Asia Pte. Ltd., *Singapore*
Editora Prentice-Hall do Brasil, Ltda., *Rio de Janeiro*

To

Late Sri Thammavaram Ramakrishnaiah
Late Smt Thammavaram Laxmamma
Ranjana Mala and Charu Krishna

and

Hideo Fujiwara
Late Hideko Fujiwara
Sachiko and Sayaka

Contents

Preface

Error-control coding theory has been an established field of study for over 30 years, and many applications have sprung up in communications and, more recently, in computer systems. This book concentrates specifically on codes for computer systems' applications.

Many types of error-control codes have been applied to memory systems and arithmetic processors, and error-checking techniques have been extensively used for logic circuits and programmable logic arrays (PLA). Every memory designer has adopted some form of error-control code to enhance reliability. Built-in error-checking and -correcting features have been found essential for megabit-level chip designs. On-the-chip codes have also been developed to improve yields and enhance testability of semiconductor chips. A comprehensive study of all such applications can be found in this text.

The book has been developed primarily from the notes for a graduate-level class, Coding Theory and Applications to Computer Systems, offered at The Center for Advanced Computer Studies of the University of Southwestern Louisiana. The fundamentals of coding theory and the mathematical background necessary for understanding the applications to computer systems are comprehensively detailed in the early chapters. Discussions of the codes for high-speed memories (the bit-correcting and byte-correcting types) and mass memories (the multiple-random-errors and burst correcting types), the asymmetric, unidirectional, and semidistance coding theory, and the applications to logic design are unique features of this book. Many state-of-the-art coding techniques applicable to computer systems are presented in a comprehensive manner.

Chapter 1 provides background and a preview of what is to come in the following chapters. It introduces various channel models, namely, the binary symmetric channel, erasure channel, the asymmetric channel (Z-channel), the burst error channel, and the arithmetic channel. These models are intended to illustrate the types of errors occurring in various computer elements or subsystems. Chapter 2 is a review of the mathematics of groups, fields, vector spaces, polynomial algebras, and number theory used throughout the text.

Chapter 3 begins with the theory of linear codes and cyclic codes and ends with a brief section on arithmetic codes. It contains encoder decoder logics for parallel (high-speed) implementations and for serial (linear feedback shift register) implementations as well. Important classes of codes, namely BCH codes, Reed-Solomon codes, and Fire codes are described and explained in this chapter.

Chapters 4 and 5 cover coding techniques for high-speed semiconductor memories, the former in terms of bit-error correction/detection and the latter in terms of byte-error correcting codes and techniques. Modified Hamming SEC-DED codes, memory chip codes, double-bit-error correcting codes, code design techniques for high-speed memories, and test patterns for semiconductor memories are presented in Chapter 4. Single-byte-error correcting (SbEC) codes, single-byte-error correcting and double-byte-error detecting (SbEC-DbED) codes, and byte/burst-error detecting SEC-DED codes are subjects of Chapter 5.

Chapter 6 is on various codes for mass memories, such as magnetic tapes and discs, bubble memories, and optical discs. For magnetic tapes, single- and multiple-track error detection/correction codes are detailed. Interleaved Reed-Solomon codes for correcting large burst errors and multiple small bursts are derived for mass storage systems. Other topics, such as, two-dimensional encoding and multiple encoding schemes suitable for optical discs and digital audio systems are included here.

Chapter 7 provides theory on classes of asymmetric, unidirectional error codes. The theory leading to t-error correcting and All-Unidirectional-Error Detecting (tEC-AUED) codes is presented and illustrated by means of examples. A class of unordered codes, defined here as semidistance codes, find interesting practical application to error-tolerant memory address decoder logic.

Chapters 8 and 9 are on the theory and practical methods for coding for logic design, that is, for designing self-checking circuits. The various concepts of self-checking circuits, such as fault-secure, self-testing, totally self-checking, strongly fault-secure, and error-secure/error-propagating circuits, are explained. This leads to the discussion of self-checking combinational and sequential circuits in Chapter 8. Finally, in Chapter 9 the design of self-checking checkers based on the checker concepts mentioned in Chapter 8 is discussed, along with self-checking processors and error masking for yield improvement using error correcting codes.

The introductory portions of the book (Chapters 1 through 4) and parts of Chapters 5, 6, and 8 can be used as a text for a course at an advanced undergraduate level or for an introductory one-semester course at the graduate level. For graduate classes and advanced students who have a background in mathematics and logic circuits and some rudimentary knowledge of codes, the book can be used as a whole with selection of topics from each of the chapters. The practicing engineer/designer will find the latter chapters of the book a practical guide and useful reference.

We have collaborated closely and have prepared together all chapters of the manuscript; however, it is only fair to mention here that Chapters 1, 2, 3, and 7 are largely the contributions of Rao, while the remaining text, Chapters 4, 5, 6, 8, and 9, are written by Fujiwara. The two authors have worked to unify the different terminologies and notations used in the United States and Japan.

We are grateful to Prentice Hall's many anonymous reviewers who provided excellent suggestions and comments for revising the manuscript. Many faculty colleagues have also had valuable suggestions. Among them we acknowledge professors Terry M. Walker of the University of Southwestern Lousiana and Yoshihiro Tohma of the Tokyo Institute of Technology, who encouraged us to write this book and lent support during the preparation of the manuscript. Help and guidance were given us by associate professors Takashi Nanya and Kohichi Sakaniwa of the Tokyo Institute of Technology on the topics of self-checking concepts and unidirectional codes. Many graduate students who have taken the graduate course from the preliminary drafts of the book, particularly T. N. Ahn, T. Hwang, J. Kelkar, S. Y. Lee, and S. M. Liu, helped us in editing and corrections. Joan Heine and Rita Landry, our secretaries, helped type the manuscripts. We wish to express our gratitude and thanks to all these people and to our wives, Mala Rao and Sachiko Fujiwara, for their support and encouragement, which made this project possible.

T. R. N. Rao
E. Fujiwara

About the Authors

T. R. N. Rao (also known as N. Rao Thammavaram) received his undergraduate education in India and his M.S. and Ph.D. degrees in Electrical Engineering from the University of Michigan, Ann Arbor, in 1961 and 1964, respectively. He was a member of the Technical Staff of Bell Telephone Laboratories, Holmdel, New Jersey, from 1964 to 1966. He was with the Department of Electrical Engineering, University of Maryland, College Park, Maryland, from 1966 to 1975 and was Professor of Computer Science, Southern Methodist University, Dallas, from 1975 to 1980.

Dr. Rao is presently the Loflin Chair Professor of Computer Science at the Center for Advanced Computer Studies, University of Southwestern Louisiana, Lafayette. His interests are in computer arithmetic, fault-tolerant computing, coding theory, and cryptology. In addition to this book, he is the author of over 50 technical papers and a textbook, *Error Coding for Arithmetic Processors*. He has received the *IEEE Fellow* award for contributions to "Arithmetic Codes, Fault-Tolerant Computing and Unidirectional Error Codes," also the Distinguished Professor award from the USL Foundation in 1984, and the Outstanding Researcher award from USL Sigma Chi chapter in 1985, and he has served as ACM lecturer since 1984 and as IEEE CS distinguished visitor for several years. Rao also served as Fulbright lecturer to India during 1986–1987.

E. Fujiwara received his B.S. and M.S. degrees in electronic engineering in 1968 and 1970, respectively, and his Ph.D. in 1981, all from the Tokyo Institute of Technology, Tokyo, Japan.

Since joining the NTT Electrical Communication Laboratories, Japan, in 1970, Dr. Fujiwara has been engaged in developing DIPS-1 and DIPS-11 computer systems and in research on fault-tolerant computing. He is now a senior research engineer of NTT Communications and Information Processing Laboratories. From June 1985 to July 1986 he was a visiting associate professor at the Center for Advanced Computer Studies of the University of Southwestern Louisiana. His current research interests include error-correcting codes, fault-tolerant memory, self-checking logic, VLSI testing, and VLSI defect-tolerant techniques.

Dr. Fujiwara received the Young Engineer Award from the Institute of Electronics, Information and Communication Engineers of Japan in 1978. He is the author of over 30 technical papers in the area of application of error-correcting codes to computer systems and is a coauthor of *Essentials of Error-Correcting Coding Techniques*.

Error-Control Coding for Computer Systems

1

Introduction

In computer systems, large amounts of data move between various subsystems. For instance, the data traffic between the CPU and main memory may be of the order of 100 million bits every second. Even though the systems are designed for very high reliability, there are bound to be a few errors in these communications caused by such things as atmospherics, electrical noise, component or device malfunctions, or sometimes design or program faults. It is important that the system detect these errors as and when they occur. Some remedial action such as *error correction* or *error recovery* must take place before a more serious situation like a *system crash* arises. We will formally define such terms as malfunction, failure, faults, and errors in a later section, but for now we will discuss errors simply as incorrect values (e.g., a "1" becoming a "0" or a "0" becoming a "1") in a register or a word of data.

Let A be a binary register of n bits, and its value represented by $A = (a_0, a_1, \ldots, a_{n-1})$ where $a_i \in \{0, 1\} = GF(2)$ ($GF(2)$ is read as Galois field of two elements). A is considered to be a word or vector of dimension n over $GF(2)$. We consider some errors (or faults) occurring in the register A to alter its value to $A' = (a'_0, a'_1, \ldots, a'_{n-1})$, $a'_i \in GF(2)$. The errors in the register are characterized by the error vector $E = (e_0, e_1, \ldots, e_{n-1})$ where $e_i = a'_i - a_i$ for $i = 0, 1, \ldots, n - 1$. The subtraction $a'_i - a_i$ is simply the operation in $GF(2)$ that is the same as addition ($1 + 1 = 0 = 1 - 1$ and $0 - 1 = 1$). We will study $GF(2)$ and other finite field structures in detail in Chapter 2.

Consider the example:

Correct word A $=1011010$
Erroneous word A' $=1101000$
Error word $E = A' - A = 0110010$

Clearly, errors have occurred in three different components of A to result in A'. This is called a triple-error in word A', and E is an error word of (*Hamming*) *weight* 3.

Another way to interpret register A, as we do in arithmetic units, would be to consider it as an integer or number; $(A)_2 = (a_0, a_1, \ldots, a_{n-1})_2 = \sum_{i=0}^{n-1} a_i 2^i$. Then we consider the errors to be arithmetic errors, in which case we have a different interpretation for deriving the error word; the number of errors is instead expressed by its *arithmetic weight* (also called the *Peterson weight*). These errors will be formally defined in Section 3.4. Thus, we come to an important question: *How do we classify errors?* Based on the communication channel, memory type or memory characteristics, and operation (arithmetic, logical, memory, etc.), we will classify errors as *symmetric*, *asymmetric*, *unidirectional*, or *arithmetic* and so on in the following section.

1.1 CHANNEL MODELS AND ERRORS

First, we define some simple channel models and proceed from these to define the classes of errors. A communication channel is shown in Fig. 1.1. The transmitted word X is corrupted by the noise of the channel or medium to change it to X'. The error word E is characterized by $E = X' - X$. The *binary symmetric channel* (BSC) is a practical and simple model for random errors that occur over a transmitted word with equal probability of a 1 to 0 error (1-error) and a 0 to 1 error (0-error) (see Fig. 1.2). Also, the noise is random in the sense that it affects each bit

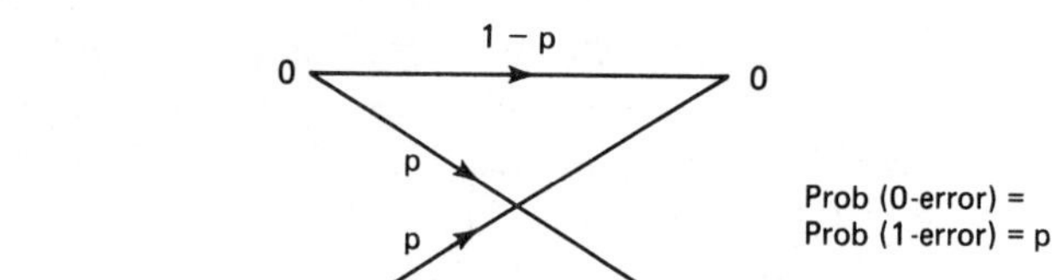

Figure 1.1 Communication channel.

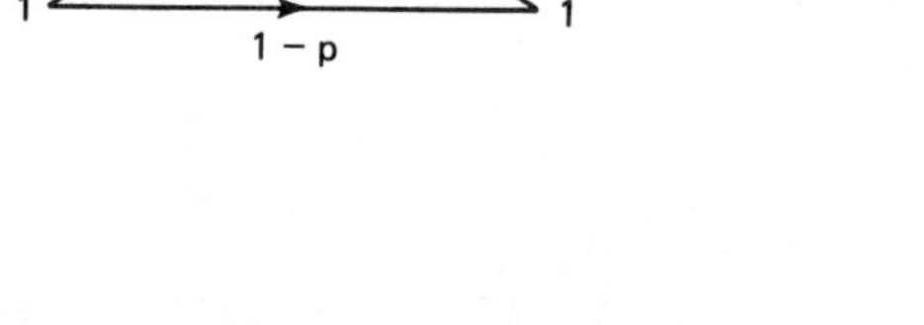

Figure 1.2 Binary symmetric channel model.

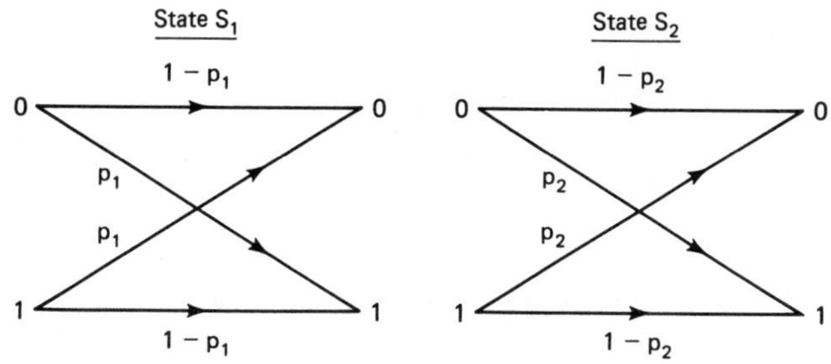

Figure 1.3 A simple model of a burst channel.

independently in the transmitted word. That is the reason for also characterizing this channel as a *discrete memoryless channel* (DMC).

Definition 1-1. If the errors in a word (or vector) are independent of each other and both 1-errors and 0-errors are equally probable, then these errors are said to be *symmetric errors* or *random (symmetric) errors.*

On the other hand, if the channel has states with varying noise levels in time and extreme noise states, there could be a sequence of errors during a particular string or portion of the received word. These errors are classified as *burst* errors and the channel is said to be modeled as a *channel with memory* or a *burst channel.* A simple burst channel is characterized by two states: S_1, a low-noise state; and S_2, a high-noise state (see Fig. 1.3). This channel shifts from one state to the other in time when noise conditions change or because of malfunctions in the memory medium. The transition probability (or error rate) p_2 is usually several orders of magnitude greater than p_1. Typically in a low-noise state, $p_1 \approx 10^{-10}$, whereas in a high-noise state, $p_2 \approx 10^{-2}$. If the channel stays in state S_2 for a period of time t (b bits long), then errors will be confined to a b-bit portion of the word. These errors are formally stated as follows.

Definition 1-2. If the errors in a word are confined to a b-bit portion of the word, then a *burst* of length b is said to have occurred.

A burst of length b can also be called b-adjacent errors, although not all b bits are in error. To illustrate this, consider the error patterns in the following 12-bit words.

$$E_1 = 000110100000$$
$$E_2 = 010110000000$$
$$E_3 = 000010100000$$
$$E_4 = 011000000000$$

E_1 and E_2 are bursts of length 4; E_3 and E_4 are bursts of length 3 and 2, respectively.

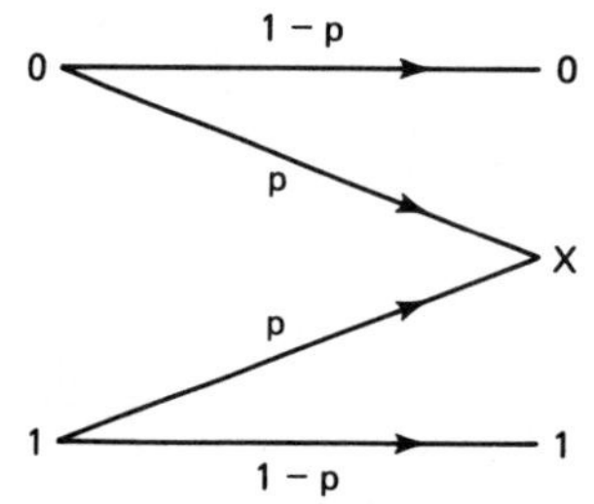

Figure 1.4 Binary erasure channel (BEC).

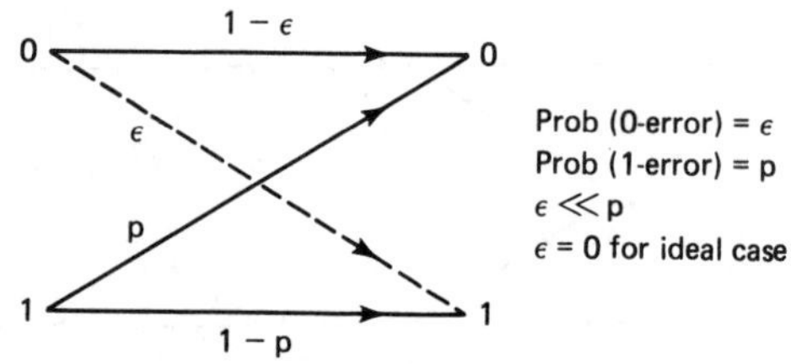

Figure 1.5 Binary asymmetric channel (BAC).

In Chapter 5, we discuss *byte* errors and give several types of byte error detecting/correcting codes. A word of N bits will be composed of n bytes, where each byte is of b bits, and $N = nb$. If the errors in a word are confined to one byte only, then the error pattern is called a *single-byte error*. For the foregoing examples, assume that byte length $b = 4$. Then each word consists of 3 bytes. E_1 and E_2 are not single-byte errors but are double-byte errors, whereas E_3 and E_4 are single-byte errors.

Another channel of importance to both communication and memories is the *binary erasure channel* (BEC) (see Fig. 1.4).

In the BEC, errors do not occur, but there will be *erasures*, denoted by x. The 0's and 1's received are considered to be correct, and the x's received are erasure symbols. Because the positions of the erasures are known, the correction of erasures in a received word will be simpler than the correction of errors. Thus, a given code that is used for error correction can be employed more efficiently to correct erasures. For instance, a *single-error correcting* (SEC) code can be used to correct double erasures; this is explained in detail in a later section.

Binary asymmetric channel (BAC). The binary asymmetric channel is modeled in Fig. 1.5, and it is nearly error free for 0's (totally error-free for the ideal BAC) and noisy for 1's [RAO 75]. The probability of a 0-error is ϵ, and the probability of a 1-error is p with $p \gg \epsilon$. In an ideal BAC (also called the z-channel), only one type of error (0-errors or 1-errors) can occur in the received word. This error type is known *a priori* at the receiver because the channel characteristics are known. Also, the error category is known in certain error-tolerant or defect-tolerant designs. The device is most likely to fail in only one direction. Therefore, we have the following definition.

Definition 1-3. In an ideal BAC, only one type of error (1-errors or 0-errors) can occur, and the error type is known *a priori*. That is, either 0-errors or 1-errors can occur but not both. These errors are called *asymmetric errors*.

Definition 1-4. Both 1-errors and 0-errors can occur in the received words, but in any particular received word, all errors shall be of one type; these errors are characterized as *unidirectional errors*. That is, if multiple errors occur in a given word, then all these errors are 1-errors or 0-errors.

In the symmetric error model (BSC), both 0-errors and 1-errors may occur in a received word. In a BAC, if there are multiple errors, their type is known. A metric that is useful for a BAC is *asymmetric distance*. Theory and practical examples of asymmetric codes and unidirectional codes are presented in Chapter 7.

Arithmetic channels or arithmetic processors. Another model of importance in computer systems is the arithmetic channel. In this classification, we consider the register A to represent a number N in radix r. For the binary radix ($r = 2$) we have

$$N = (A)_2 = \sum_{i=0}^{n-1} a_i 2^i$$

The erroneous number N' is given by

$$N' = (A')_2 = \sum_{i=0}^{n-1} a_i' 2^i$$

Note that a_i' does not denote the complement of a_i here. The error E is given by the arithmetic difference $N' - N$. The subtraction is carried out as in the set of integers, Z. The number of errors in N' is given by the arithmetic weight (also called Peterson weight) of E and is defined in Section 3.4.

Failures, faults, and errors. A *failure* in a logic circuit refers to a physical malfunction that causes an undesired event. The physical malfunction may be due to a line (representing a logic variable) shorted to the ground, two lines shorted together, or a broken line, and so on. The effect of such failures is sometimes called a *fault* (or *logic fault*), an example of which is a logic variable, such as a_i *stuck-at-one* in a vector $(a_0, a_1, \ldots, a_{n-1})$. The effect of logic faults is the introduction of *errors* in the value of registers (or vectors or numbers as the case may be). Therefore, failures, malfunctions, and errors are all undesired events in a computer, but by context they refer to different domains. The failures and malfunctions refer to the physical or device domain, faults refer to the logical (or Boolean) level of abstraction, and errors refer to the informational level (values attached to the registers). These registers can be single-bit or multibit registers, and they can represent vectors (or words, such as op code) or numbers (e.g., operand values). In this book, we are concerned mainly with the informational level and with errors as characterized by the register values. We do not deal with faults, failures, malfunctions, or system crashes. For a detailed treatment of this terminology, the reader may refer to the literature on this subject [AVIZ 82, KOPE 82, ANDE 82].

In computer systems, we also classify errors as hard and soft errors (see Definition 1-5).

Definition 1-5. If the error in any position of a word is permanent in nature (e.g., a_i stuck-at-zero), then it is called a *hard error*. On the other hand, if the error is of a transient type (e.g., α particle damage of a bit), then it is called a *soft error*.

Later on, we consider codes and decoding techniques to correct hard or soft errors and combinations of both types of errors in a word.

1.2 BLOCK CODES, LINEAR CODES, AND DISTANCE METRICS

Codes are designed to detect and/or correct errors occurring in the channels (channels also refer to storage media). A block code consists of a set of codewords of fixed length n, with each codeword being an n-tuple over a finite field, $GF(q)$ of q symbols. (In arithmetic codes, the n-tuples are over a digit set $D = \{0, 1, \ldots, r-1\}$ where r is called the radix of the number system; these are defined in Section 3.4). The set of all n-tuples over $GF(q)$ is a vector space $\mathbf{V}$ (as defined in Chapter 2), and a block code can be a subset $\mathbf{S}$ of $\mathbf{V}$. If this subset $\mathbf{S}$ is a subspace of $\mathbf{V}$, then $\mathbf{S}$ is called a linear (block) code. The finite field $GF(q)$, refers to the Galois field of q elements, and q must be a power of a prime. Most examples we study in this book will be for cases $q = 2$ or 2^b. The symbols from $GF(2^b)$ will be called bytes, and each symbol is represented by b bits. Byte error codes are of importance to byte-organized memory systems and processors. If a symbol from $GF(2^b)$ is in error, then it is called a *byte error*. A byte error is like a burst error; the difference is that each byte error is confined to the b-bit portion corresponding to a symbol from $GF(2^b)$, whereas a burst error can begin from any position of the word.

For a linear code $\mathbf{C}$, the sum of (and the difference between) two codewords is also a codeword. The theory of linear codes has been very extensively studied and there exist many important classes of linear codes. The linear codes that can correct single or multiple errors can also be used in a *detect-only mode* or a *detect-and-correct mode*. Thus, an error-correcting code refers to both an error-detecting code as well as an error-correcting code.

We introduce here the concepts of *Hamming weight* and *Hamming distance* and illustrate by simple examples the relationship of distance to error detection and correction [HAMM 50, PETE 72].

Definition 1-6. The *Hamming weight* of a vector $X = (x_1, x_2, \ldots, x_n)$, denoted by $w(X)$, is the number of nonzero components of X. Each component x_i is an element of $GF(q)$ and the vector X is also called an n-tuple or a word.

Definition 1-7. The *Hamming distance* between two vectors X and Y, denoted by $d(X, Y)$, is the Hamming weight of $X - Y$. It also equals the number of positions in which the two vectors differ. That is,

$$d(X, Y) = w(X - Y) = w(Y - X)$$

$$= \text{the number of positions that } X \text{ and } Y \text{ differ.}$$

Example 1-1 illustrates the distance and weight over any field $GF(q)$.

Example Set 1-1

1. Let $X = (10011)$ and $Y = (01010)$ over $GF(2)$, then $w(X) = 3$, $w(Y) = 2$, and $d(X, Y) = 3$.
2. Let $X = (20120)$ and $Y = (10221)$ over $GF(3)$, then $w(X) = 3$, $w(Y) = 4$, and $d(X, Y) = 3 = w(X - Y) = w(10202)$.

The Hamming distance is a *metric* in the sense that it is a real number satisfying the following.

1. $d(X, Y) > 0$ for $X \neq Y$
   $= 0$ for $X = Y$, (Positive definiteness)
2. $d(X, Y) = d(Y, X)$, (Symmetry)
3. $d(X, Y) + d(Y, Z) \geq d(X, Z)$. (Triangle inequality)

Definition 1-8. The *minimum distance* (often simply called distance) $d_{\min}$ of a code **C** is the minimum of the distances between all pairs of codewords.

A linear code, which will be defined later, is a code in which the difference between (and sum of) two codewords is also a codeword. Therefore, the minimum distance of a linear code is also the minimum weight of codewords excluding the zero vector. Note that every linear code contains the zero vector.

Consider **U**, the set of all n-tuples over $GF(2)$, and let a subset $\mathbf{C} \subset \mathbf{U}$ be a code with a minimum distance d. Only codewords are used for transmission over a channel. At the receiver, the received word is checked to see whether or not it is a codeword. If it is a codeword, then it is accepted; otherwise, it is considered to be an erroneous word, and errors are detected.

Theorem 1-1. *It is necessary and sufficient that the distance* ($d_{\min}$) *of a code is at least d in order to detect any error pattern of weight* $d - 1$ *or less.*

Proof. Since $d_{\min}$ is d, no pattern of $d - 1$ or fewer errors can change the transmitted codeword into another codeword, and therefore such errors are detected. Because there exists at least one pair of codewords with distance d, there exists a particular pattern of d errors for which one codeword can be changed to another codeword, and, accordingly, it is not detected. Q.E.D.

This theorem states that $d_{\min} = d$ guarantees detection of $d - 1$ or fewer errors. On the other hand, if d or more errors occur, they may still be detectable, but it is not always guaranteed.

Theorem 1-2. *A code C can detect and correct all patterns of t or fewer errors if and only if the code has minimum distance* $\geq 2t + 1$.

Proof. Any received word with $t' \leq t$ errors differs from the transmitted word in t' positions, but differs from any other codeword in more than t' positions. This is because every pair of codewords differs in at least $2t + 1$ positions and because of the triangle inequality property of the distance. We can also obtain the same result by constructing (n-dimensional) spheres of radius t for each codeword as its center. These spheres are all disjoint, and for any t or fewer errors from a codeword, the erroneous words will be within the bounds of the respective sphere. Alternately, if the minimum distance is less than $2t + 1$, one can construct a case where a t-error pattern results in a received word at least as close to an incorrect codeword as it is to the correct codeword. Q.E.D.

A more general theorem on error detection and correction can be stated as follows.

Theorem 1-3. *A code can correct any combination of t errors and detect up to d errors* ($d \geq t$) *if and only if the* d_{min} *of the code is* $\geq t + d + 1$.

We illustrate the validity of this theorem by considering again spheres of radius t from each codeword as its center (see Fig. 1.6). It is easy to see that for a codeword, say X_1, t or fewer errors will cause the received word to fall within its own sphere (or domain). Any errors greater than t but less than d in number are detected because the received words will be outside of all these spheres. Fig. 1.6 graphically illustrates this concept. The spheres are all disjoint, because if there is an intersection containing a word, then that word is at the most distance t from two codewords, whereas the two codewords are apart by more than $2t + 1$. That violates triangle inequality and is, therefore, impossible. Similarly, we can show that if the number of errors are greater than t but no greater than d, then the received word will be outside these spheres, so that errors are detected but not corrected.

Some simple examples (replication codes) and graphic illustrations will be helpful here. Hamming codes and more sophisticated classes of codes are covered in Chapter 3.

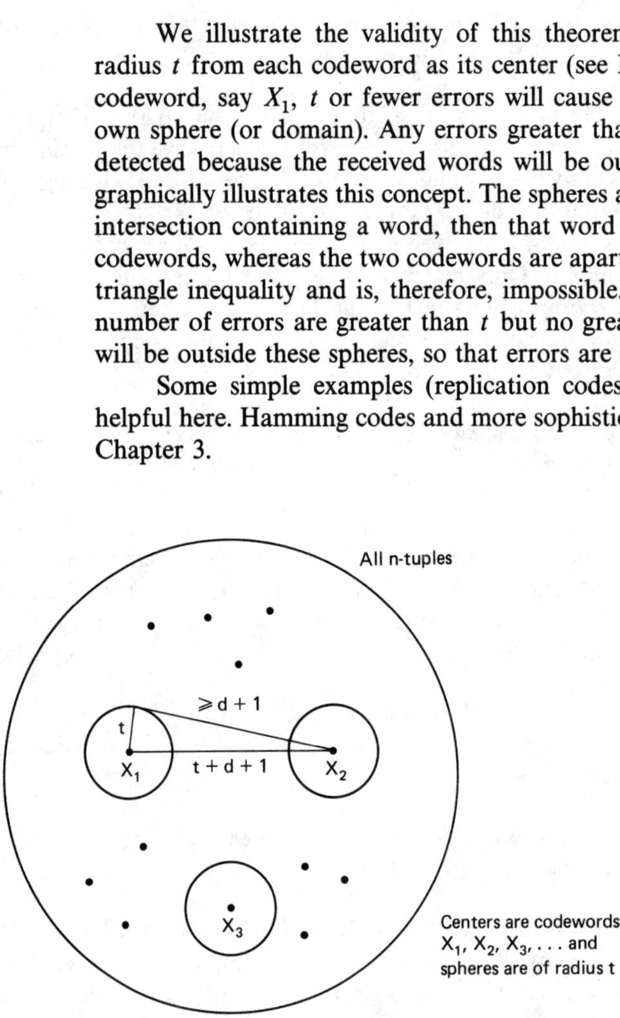

Figure 1.6 Illustration of error detection/correction using spheres around codewords.

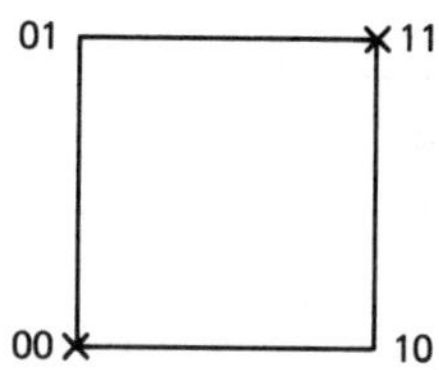

Figure 1.7 A simple distance-2 code.

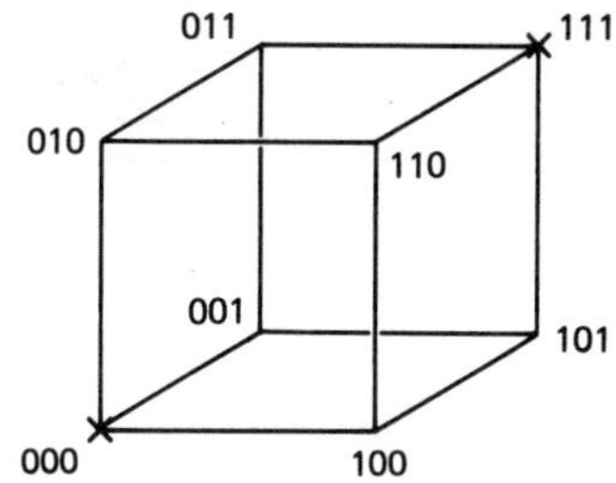

Figure 1.8 A simple distance-3 code.

Distance-2 code. The codewords are $\{00, 11\}$ as shown in Fig. 1.7. If one error occurs, the received word will be 01 or 10, and the error is detected. However, if two errors occur, then one codeword becomes another, and the errors will not be detected. This is a single-error detecting (SED) code.

Distance-3 code. The codewords are $\{000, 111\}$ as shown in Fig. 1.8. The two codewords 000, 111 are at the two extreme corners of a cube. If one error occurs in a transmitted word, it can be corrected by a majority decoding. If two errors occur, say for codeword 000, the received word will be closer to 111 and therefore will be decoded incorrectly, and the majority decoding fails. However, if no correction is attempted but the *detect-only* mode is employed, then double errors can also be detected. Therefore, we have to choose one of two distinct strategies for distance-3 codes:

1. *Error-correction mode:* single error correction (SEC).
2. *Detect-only mode:* double error detection (DED).

The distance-3 code is, therefore, a SEC or DED code depending on the mode of decoding. In one-way communication channels (or memory systems with permanent stuck-at type errors), error correction is more appropriate because a request for retransmission (or instruction retry) would not be helpful. On the other hand, if the channel is a two-way channel (or the memory errors are transient), a repeat transmission request (or instruction retry) would be successful in preventing errors. Therefore, depending on the channel (or medium) and noise environment, the error-correction mode or the detect-and-retry mode is to be adopted.

Distance-4 code. The codewords are $\{0000, 1111\}$. In general, the distance-4 codes can be used as single-error correcting and double-error detecting (SEC-DED) or triple-error detecting (TED) codes, whereas the distance-3 codes are SEC or DED codes. In memory applications, distance-3 codes are referred to as SEC codes and distance-4 codes are referred to as SEC-DED codes. The following table illustrates the SEC-DED property of the code. As a TED code, any received word that is not a codeword is not accepted. But as a SEC-DED code, the received words of weight 2 are detected as double errors.

Code words	0000		1111
SEC	1000		0111
	0100		1011
	0010		1101
	0001		1110
DED		1100	
		1010	
		1001	
		0110	
		0101	
		0011	

Distance-6 code. The codewords are $\{000000, 111111\}$. This code gives a number of decoding choices. By using Theorem 1-3, these choices are to detect d errors and correct t errors ($d \geq t$). The number of choices for the decoders thus increases with the $d_{\min}$.

Choice	d	t
1	3	2
2	4	1
3	5	0

Erasure correction. A note here is appropriate on correcting erasures using the BEC model. As stated earlier, since the erasure positions are known, and the 0's and 1's received are assumed to be correct, the erasure channel model enables codes with $d_{\min} = d$ to correct up to $d - 1$ erasures. To illustrate this, consider the distance-3 code example: $\mathbf{C} = \{000, 111\}$. This code can correct up to two erasures by using Fig. 1.9. Any received word in a column can be decoded by simply going to the top of its column.

000	111
x00	x11
0x0	1x1
00x	11x
xx0	xx1
x0x	x1x
0xx	1xx

Figure 1.9 Decoding of single and double erasures.

1.3 ARRAY DECODING OF BLOCK CODES

The decoding of block codes can be illustrated by means of a table called *array decoding*. Array decoding helps in the understanding of code properties. However, for large block lengths, the array will be too large and impractical. The top row consists of all codewords, namely 0000, 0011, 1100, and 1111 (see Fig. 1.10).

0000	0011	1100	1111
1000	1011	0100	0111
0010	0001	1110	1101
0110	0101	1010	1001

Figure 1.10(a) Array decoding for the BSC model.

0000	0011	1100	1111
x000	x011	x100	x111
0x00	0x11	1x00	1x11
00x0	00x1	11x0	11x1
000x	001x	110x	111x
0xx0	0xx1	1xx0	1xx1
x00x	x01x	x10x	x11x
0x0x	0x1x	1x0x	1x1x
x0x0	x0x1	x1x0	x1x1

Figure 1.10(b) Array decoding for the BEC model.

0000	0011	1100	1111
		0100	0111
		1000	1011
	0001		1101
	0010		1110
			1001
			0110
			1010
			0101

Figure 1.10(c) Array decoding for the BAC model.

If a codeword is received, it is most probably the word transmitted, and it is so assumed. The minimum distance of the code in Fig. 1.10 is 2, and the probability of two errors is of the order of p^2, which is very small compared with the probability of no error, which is $(1-p)^4$, where p is crossover probability in the BSC. If a noncodeword is received, then it is looked up in the table to determine the most probable codeword transmitted. The words are arranged in the table in such a way that any received word in the table is in the column headed by a codeword closest to it, or at least as close to it as any other codeword. Therefore, decoding is performed by looking for the column in which the received word lies and going straight to the top of the column for the closest codeword. This would minimize the probability of erroneous decoding under the assumption that all codewords are equally likely. Such a decoding is also called *maximum-likelihood decoding* (MLD).

The following comments and analyses are in order regarding Fig. 1.10(a). The code is merely a distance-2 code that can detect only single errors. However, under certain circumstances (e.g., a one-way channel), it can be used to correct two particular single errors and one double error by using the decoding table. The probability of correct decoding under error correction mode is given by the following.

$$P_C = (1-p)^4 + 2p(1-p)^3 + p^2(1-p)^2 = Q^4 + 2pQ^3 + p^2Q^2$$

The probability of erroneous decoding is given by

$$P_E = 1 - P_C = 2pQ^3 + 5p^2Q^2 + 4p^3Q + p^4$$

On the other hand, if the channel is a two-way channel and the decoding mode is detect and retry, only the top row of the array is utilized. Then the probability of correct reception is given by

$$P_{CR} = \text{Prob}\,(\textit{correct reception}) = Q^4$$

Also, the other probabilities are given by

$$P_E = \text{Prob}\,(\textit{erroneous decoding}) = 2p^2Q^2 + p^4,$$

$$P_{ARQ} = \text{Prob}\,(\textit{repeat request}) = 1 - P_{CR} - P_E = 1 - Q^4 - (2p^2Q^2 + p^4)$$

$$= 4pQ^3 + 4p^2Q^2 + 4p^3Q$$

Note that the probability of erroneous decoding is much smaller when the detect-and-retry mode is employed, compared with the error-correction mode.

For the binary erasure channel (Fig. 1.10(b)), the array lists all single erasures and only four of the six possible double erasures. One could extend the table further to include the remaining two double erasures and the triple and quadruple erasures. The two remaining double erasures and the triple erasures, if corrected under the error-correction mode, will have a 50% chance of incorrect decoding; the quadruple erasures, if corrected, will have 75% chance of incorrect decoding. If the entire table is used for decoding, the probability of successful decoding with or without erasures is given by

$$P_C = Q^4 + 4pQ^3 + 4p^2Q^2$$

$$\text{Prob}\,(\textit{erasures not correctable}) = 1 - P_C = 2p^2Q^2 + 4p^3Q + p^4$$

For Fig. 1.10(c), the ideal binary asymmetric channel model is assumed, and it is also assumed that the channel is a *1-error* channel (i.e., 0-errors are not possible). Under those assumptions, the array is constructed. Obviously, the codeword 0000 will always be received correctly, and only two single asymmetric errors are possible for the codewords 0011 and 1100, and those are correctable. Double asymmetric errors occurring for these two codewords would result in 0000 (a wrong codeword) and hence cannot be corrected. However, if the transmitted codeword is 1111, *all* single asymmetric errors and *only four* of the double asymmetric errors are correctable. The probability of erroneous decoding under BAC is therefore more complicated than the two previous channel models, but it can be determined with some effort. A thorough treatment of array decoding for linear codes can be found in [PETE 72]. Chapter 3 covers this subject and various code classes in greater detail.

EXERCISES

1.1. Assuming a block length $n = 12$, give examples of error vectors E_1, E_2, E_3, and E_4 as follows.

(a) $W(E_1) = 3$ and E_1 is a burst of length 5.

(b) $W(E_2) = 2$ and E_2 is a burst of length 6.

(c) E_3 and E_4 are single-byte errors with a byte length of 4.

1.2. Show that the Hamming distance is a metric.

1.3. The Lee weight and Lee distance of a vector $X = (x_1, \ldots, x_n)$ over $GF(p)$ are defined as follows [PETE 72].

$$W_L(X) = \sum_{i=1}^{n} f(x_i), \qquad f(x_i) = x_i \qquad \text{for } x_i \le (p-1)/2$$

$$= p - x_i \qquad \text{for } x_i > (p-1)/2$$

$$D_L(X, Y) = W_L(X - Y)$$

(a) Construct vectors X and Y of length 5 over $GF(5)$ and give their Lee weight and Lee distance.

(b) Show that the Lee distance is a metric.

1.4. Given that $d_{\min}$ of a block code is 7, obtain all the decoding choices available for the code if

(a) a BSC model is assumed for errors.

(b) a BEC model is assumed.

(c) both errors and erasures are assumed to occur.

1.5. Assume the crossover probability $p = 10^{-3}$.

(a) If the array given in Fig. 1.10(a) is used for decoding, obtain the P_e, the probability of erroneous decoding.

(b) If the array is used to correct the two single errors but not the double error, determine the probability of erroneous decoding and the probability of errors detected but not corrected.

1.6. A block code uses the following codewords: 00000, 01110, 10101, 11011. Assuming a binary symmetric channel model with crossover probability $p = 10^{-3}$, determine the probability of erroneous decoding if the code is used

(a) as an error detecting code.

(b) for correction of single errors only.

(c) for correction of all possible errors.

1.7. For the cases (a) and (b) of Problem 1.6, determine the probability that errors are detected but not corrected. Give a complete standard array decoding table for the code.

REFERENCES

[ANDE 82] T. Anderson and P. A. Lee. "Fault Tolerance Terminology Proposals." *Dig., 12th Annual Int. Symposium Fault-Tolerant Comput.* (June 1982): 29–33.

[AVIZ 82] A. Avizienis. "The Four-Universe Information System Model for the Study of Fault-Tolerance." *Dig., 12th Annual Int. Symposium Fault-Tolerant Comput.* (June 1982): 6–13.

[HAMM 50] R. W. Hamming. "Error Detecting and Error Correcting Codes." *Bell Sys. Tech. Journal* 26(April 1950): 147–60.

[KOPE 82] H. Kopetz. "The Failure Fault (FF) Model." *Dig., 12th Annual Int. Symposium Fault-Tolerant Comput.* (June 1982): 14–17.

[PETE 72] W. W. Peterson and E. J. Weldon, Jr. *Error Correcting Codes*, 2d. ed. Cambridge: MIT Press, 1972.

[RAO 75] T. R. N. Rao and A. S. Chawla. "Asymmetric Error Codes for Some LSI Semiconductor Memories." *Proc. Annual Southeastern Symposium on Syst. Theory* (March 1975): 170–71.

2 Mathematical Background

This chapter provides a minimal mathematical background necessary to understand subsequent chapters. The mathematical structures of *groups*, *subgroups*, *rings*, *fields*, *vector spaces*, and *subspaces* will be covered at an introductory level. The treatment here will not be rigorous, and most concepts are simply illustrated by means of examples. For a thorough understanding, the reader will be advised to refer to any of the classic texts provided in the bibliography (e.g., [JACO 51] and [BIRK 70]).

In Section 2.3, we provide some elementary concepts of number theory as useful background. Finally, in Section 2.4, *polynomial algebras* and *Galois fields* are covered.

2.1 ALGEBRAIC STRUCTURES

Algebraic structures are necessary to understand codes. The structure enables understanding of the code properties and implementation considerations. Extending codes to fit practical considerations as well as designing new codes requires a good understanding of this material.

Groups. A *group* is a set of elements for which an operation is defined and for which the following four axioms (G1–G4) hold. Let a, b and c be the elements of the group and let $\cdot$ denote the operation in G. The group operation can be any of $+, \cdot, *$, etc., but we will use $\cdot$ for convenience.

(G1) *Closure:* For any $a, b \in G$, $a \cdot b \in G$.

(G2) *Associativity:* For any $a, b, c \in G$, $a \cdot (b \cdot c) = (a \cdot b) \cdot c$. The associativity implies that the order of operation is not important and parentheses are not required.

(G3) *Identity:* There is an identity element $e \in G$ such that for all $a \in G$, $a \cdot e = e \cdot a = a$. If the group operation is $+$ (which is addition), then we use 0 for the identity; if it is $\cdot$ (multiplication), then we use 1 for the identity. It is easy to show that the identity in G is unique.

(G4) *Inverse:* For any $a \in G$, there exists an inverse, $a^{-1} \in G$, such that $a \cdot a^{-1} = a^{-1} \cdot a = e$. Again, it is simple to show that for any a, its inverse a^{-1} is unique. Also, for a group with an addition operation (i.e., for an additive group), the inverse of a is denoted $-a$ and $a + (-a) = (-a) + a = 0$. The group operation is not always explicitly specified, but it is to be understood based on the context of the set. Occasionally we use a notation such as $\{G, +\}, \{H, \cdot\}$ to specify the operation.

In addition to the four axioms, a group may satisfy the commutative law (G5) given as follows. If it does satisfy, the group is called an Abelian group or commutative group.

(G5) *Commutativity:* For any $a, b \in G$, $a \cdot b = b \cdot a$. We will consider mostly Abelian groups in this book. Most structures of codes covered are commutative. Some simple examples of groups are as follows.

Example Set 2-1

1. The set of all integers Z under the addition operation is an Abelian group.
2. The set of integers $Z_4 = \{0, 1, 2, 3\}$ under addition modulo 4 operation is an Abelian group. The addition table in Z_4 is given below.

+	0	1	2	3
0	0	1	2	3
1	1	2	3	0
2	2	3	0	1
3	3	0	1	2

3. The set of all real numbers excluding zero under multiplication is an Abelian group.
4. The set of all nonsingular $(n \times n)$ matrices over real numbers under matrix multiplication is a non-Abelian group.
5. The set of all $(n \times n)$ matrices under addition of matrices is an Abelian group.
6. The set **A(x)** of all polynomials of the form $a(x) = a_0 + a_1x + a_2x^2 + \cdots$ in an indeterminate x where $a_i \in \{0, 1\}$, with $a_i + a_i = 0$ is a group under addition. Here, $f(x) + f(x) = 0$, the identity polynomial, and $f(x)$ is its own inverse.
7. The set $G = \{1, 2, 3, 4\}$ under multiplication modulo 5 is an Abelian group.

To understand these concepts better, the reader may work several problems at the end of the chapter or from other texts ([BIRK 70, JOHN 66]). The following lemmas will also be useful for this understanding.

Lemma 2-1. *The identity element in a group G is unique, and the inverse of each element is unique.*

Proof. If there are two identities in G, denote them by e_1 and e_2. From the identity axiom we get $e_1 = e_1 \cdot e_2 = e_2$. Similarly, if a has two inverses a^{-1} and a_1^{-1}, then

$$a^{-1} = a^{-1} \cdot e = a^{-1}(a \cdot a_1^{-1}) = (a^{-1} \cdot a) \cdot a_1^{-1} = e \cdot a_1^{-1} = a_1^{-1}$$

Therefore, $a^{-1} = a_1^{-1}$ and the inverse of a is unique.

Lemma 2-2. *In a group the cancellation laws hold. That is, for any $a, b, c \in G$,*

$$a \cdot b = a \cdot c \to b = c \qquad \textit{(left cancellation)}$$

$$a \cdot b = c \cdot b \to a = c \qquad \textit{(right cancellation)}$$

(" $\to$ " *is to be read as* "*implies*".)

Proof. Let $a \cdot b = a \cdot c$, then $(a^{-1}) \cdot (a \cdot b) = a^{-1}(a \cdot c)$. By associativity, $(a^{-1} \cdot a) \cdot b = (a^{-1} \cdot a) \cdot c$, $e \cdot b = e \cdot c$. Therefore, $b = c$, and this proves left cancellation. Similarly, we can prove right cancellation. Q.E.D.

An element a is said to *generate* a group G if $a \cdot a = a^2$, $a \cdot a \cdot a = a^3, \ldots$, and so on to exhaust the group. Then, a is said to be a generator and G is called a *cyclic* group. For instance in Z_4, $1 + 1 = 2$, $1 + 1 + 1 = 3$, $1 + 1 + 1 + 1 = 0$ so that 1 generates the entire group. Therefore, 1 is a generator of the cyclic group Z_4.

The *order* of an element a is n, the smallest positive integer such that

$$a^n = 1$$

In the multiplicative group $G = \{1, 2, 3, 4\}$ under mod 5 multiplication, we have $\{2, 2^2 = 4, 2^3 = 3, 2^4 = 1\}$. Therefore, 2 is a generator of the cyclic group G and its order is 4. This has the same structure as $Z_4 = \{0, 1, 2, 3\}$. The number of elements in a group is said to be the *order* of the group. If a generates a group, then the order of a is the same as the order of the group. Every cyclic group of order n has the same structure as $Z_n = \{0, 1, \ldots, n - 1\}$ under addition modulo n. Two groups $\{\mathbf{A}, \cdot\}$ and $\{\mathbf{X}, +\}$ have the same structure (we also say that A and X are *isomorphic* groups) if there is a mapping $f: A \to X$ such that for all $a, b \in A$,

$$f(a \cdot b) = f(a) + f(b); \qquad \text{(morphism)}$$

$$f(a) = f(b) \ \text{ iff } a = b; \qquad \text{(one-to-one)}$$

for any $x \in X$, there exists some $a \in A$ such that

$$f(a) = x \qquad \text{(onto)}$$

A *morphism* is a mapping that preserves structure on the sets. A morphism that is *one to one* and *onto* is called an isomorphism. The reader will be advised to find an isomorphism between Z_4 and G discussed above.

Subgroups. A subset H of a group G is a *subgroup* if it satisfies all the axioms of a group. The operation of the subgroup must, of course, be the same as the group. To determine whether a subset H is a subgroup, one need not verify all the axioms. The following two axioms are sufficient.

(S1) For all $a, b \in H$, $a \cdot b \in H$.
(S2) For any $a \in H$, $a^{-1} \in H$.

Associativity holds in H by virtue that every element of H is also in G. From (S1) and (S2) we can show that identity exists in H.

Example Set 2-2

1. In the group of integers Z, the set of all integers that are multiples of 3 form a subgroup. This subgroup is denoted $3Z = \{0, 3, -3, 6, -6 \cdots\}$.
2. In $Z_4 = \{0,1,2,3\}$ under modulo 4 addition, the subset $H = \{0,2\}$ is a subgroup of Z_4. Integer 1 generates the cyclic group Z_4 and 2 generates the subgroup H. Also, 3 generates Z_4.
3. $G = \{1,2,3,4\}$ is a group under multiplication modulo 5. Note $2 \cdot 3 = 1$, $2 \cdot 4 = 3$, $3 \cdot 4 = 2$, $4 \cdot 4 = 1$, etc. $H = \{1,4\}$ is a subgroup of G. Integers 2 as well as 3 generate G. Only 4 generates the cyclic subgroup H.
4. Consider the group of polynomials given in Example 2-1, that is, $\mathbf{A}(x)$ is the set of all polynomials of the form

   $$a(x) = a_0 + a_1 x + a_2 x^2 + \cdots, \quad a_i \in \{0,1\}.$$

   For this group $\mathbf{A}$, we can find many subgroups. The subset $\mathbf{B}$ of polynomials of degree 1 or less is a subgroup. That is, $\mathbf{B} = \{0, 1, x, x+1\}$ is a subgroup. There is no generator in B and it is not a cyclic group.

There are always two trivial subgroups for any group G: (1) G is a subgroup of G; (2) the identity, $\{e\}$, is a subgroup of G. When we consider subgroups we give only nontrivial ones (i.e., proper subsets of G satisfying the axioms).

Factor groups. Consider the group, the set of all integers Z under addition. The subgroup, $3Z = \{0, 3, -3, 6, -6, 9, \dots\}$ can be used to factor Z into *cosets* as follows.

$$\begin{aligned} 3Z &= \{0, 3, -3, 6, -6, 9, \dots\} \\ 1 + 3Z &= \{1, 4, -2, 7, -5, \dots\} \\ 2 + 3Z &= \{2, 5, -1, 8, -4, \dots\} \end{aligned}$$

If we write the coset $\{5 + 3Z\}$, it is a permutation of $2 + 3Z$, and therefore it is to be the same coset. Under that assumption, there can be only three cosets of $3Z$. These three cosets can be considered as elements of a group under an appropriate operation. $(1 + 3Z) + 3Z = 1 + 3Z$, $(1 + 3Z) + (2 + 3Z) = 3Z$, $(2 + 3Z) + (2 + 3Z) = 1 + 3Z$, etc. Clearly, the set $\{3Z, 1 + 3Z, 2 + 3Z\}$ forms a group under the addition so defined. $3Z$ is the identity element of this group. This factor group will be denoted as $Z/3Z$. However, it can easily be seen that its structure is the same as $Z_3 = \{0, 1, 2\}$ under addition modulo 3. This method of factorization into cosets takes on a greater importance when we study residue classes in rings and fields.

Rings and fields. The group as we have studied it so far is an algebra with one operation. We now consider algebras with two operations—addition and multiplication. A set R is a *ring* if it satisfies the following.

(R1) R is an Abelian group under addition.

(R2) R is closed under multiplication.

(R3) R is associative under multiplication.

(R4) Multiplication is distributive with respect to addition, that is, for any $a, b, c \in R$

$$a \cdot (b + c) = a \cdot b + a \cdot c$$
$$(a + b) \cdot c = a \cdot c + b \cdot c$$

(R5) There is a multiplicative identity (also called *unit*), denoted $1 \in R$, such that

$$\text{for any } a \in R,\ a \cdot 1 = 1 \cdot a = a$$

In some books, (R5) is not included in the axioms, but in others it is included. We choose to include (R5) because the structures we consider in this book have units. The unit element can be shown to be unique in any ring.

A ring R may satisfy (but not necessarily) additional properties as follows.

(R6) *Commutativity:* For any $a, b \in R$, $a \cdot b = b \cdot a \in R$

(R7) *Multiplicative Inverse:* For any $a \in R$, $a \neq 0$, there exists $a^{-1} \in R$ such that

$$a \cdot a^{-1} = a^{-1} \cdot a = 1$$

A ring R satisfying (R6) is called a *commutative ring*. A ring R satisfying (R6) and (R7) is called a *field*. Another way to explain fields is as follows. A field F has two group structures. $\{F, +\}$ is an additive group and $\{F', \cdot\}$, where F' is the set F excluding 0, is a multiplicative group. Also, distributive laws given by (R4) hold in F. Quite often we write ab for $a \cdot b$ in rings and the "$\cdot$" is omitted.

Example Set 2-3 (rings and fields)

1. The set of integers Z is a commutative ring but is not a field.
2. $Z_2 = \{0, 1\}$ under addition modulo 2 and multiplication modulo 2 is a field. This will be denoted $GF(2)$, the Galois field of two elements. Furthermore, it can be

shown that $Z_m = \{0, 1, \ldots, m-1\}$ is a ring, and that it is a field iff m is a prime. Z_p, for a prime p, is called a *prime field* and is denoted $GF(p)$—the Galois field of p elements. The addition and multiplication tables for $GF(2)$ and $GF(3)$ are given as follows.

TABLE FOR $GF(2)$

Addition				Multiplication		
+	0	1		·	0	1
0	0	1		0	0	0
1	1	0		1	0	1

TABLE FOR $GF(3)$

Addition					Multiplication			
+	0	1	2		·	0	1	2
0	0	1	2		0	0	0	0
1	1	2	0		1	0	1	2
2	2	0	1		2	0	2	1

3. The set **A(x)** of all polynomials of the form

$$a(x) = a_0 + a_1 x + a_2 x^2 + \cdots, \qquad (a_i \in GF(2))$$

under addition and multiplication of polynomials is a commutative ring and is not a field. The addition and multiplication in **A(X)** is illustrated below.

Let

$$\begin{aligned} a(x) &= 1 + x^2 + x^3 \\ b(x) &= 1 + x + x^4 \\ \hline a(x) + b(x) &= x + x^2 + x^3 + x^4 \\ a(x) \cdot b(x) &= 1 + x + x^2 + x^6 + x^7 \end{aligned}$$

The reader should carefully verify all the properties for the above examples and also work on the problems at the end of the chapter to become familiar with these structures. Some properties must be of interest here.

Theorem 2-1. *In a ring R, and for all $a, b \in R$, we have $a \cdot 0 = 0 \cdot a = 0$, for all $a \in R$ and $(-a) \cdot b = -(a \cdot b) = a \cdot (-b)$, for all $a, b \in R$.*

Proof. $a \cdot 0 + a \cdot 0 = a \cdot (0 + 0) = a \cdot 0 = a \cdot 0 + 0$. By a left cancellation we get $a \cdot 0 = 0$. Similarly, we can show $0 \cdot a = 0$. Also in R,

$$0 = a \cdot 0 = a \cdot (b + (-b)) = a \cdot b + a(-b)$$

Therefore, $a(-b)$ is the additive inverse of $a \cdot b$. Similarly, we can show that $(-a) \cdot b = a \cdot (-b) = -(a \cdot b)$. Q.E.D.

Definition 2-1. A subset S of a ring R is an *ideal* if it satisfies

(I1) S is a subgroup of R under addition;
(I2) For any $s \in S$ and $r \in R$, $s \cdot r \in S$.

The type of ideals we study here are those that have a generator. As an example, in the ring of integer Z, all multiples of an integer, say 4, comprise an ideal. This ideal is

$$S = 4Z = \{\ldots -8, -4, 0, 4, 8, 12, \ldots\}$$

Its generator is the smallest positive integer in it, which is 4. Similarly, in the ring of polynomials $\mathbf{A}(\mathbf{x})$ over $GF(2)$, an ideal S is the subset of all multiples of a generator polynomial, say $\mathbf{g}(x)$. By definition, the generator is a polynomial of the smallest degree in S. Clearly, there can be only one monic polynomial of the smallest degree in S, and the generator is unique in S. As a further consideration of ideals, we will study these structures in $\mathbf{A}_n(\mathbf{x})$, the algebra of polynomials modulo $x^n - 1$. The generator $\mathbf{g}(x)$ of an ideal in $\mathbf{A}_n(\mathbf{x})$ must, in addition to the other condition, also be a divisor of $x^n - 1$. We will study these structures in Section 3.2 as *cyclic codes*. Also, one can factor a ring R by forming cosets with respect to an ideal in a manner similar to factor groups.

We can define addition and multiplication operations on this set of cosets to obtain a ring structure. As an example, consider the cosets of the ideal $4Z$ given as follows.

$$\begin{aligned} 4Z &= \{\ldots -8, -4, 0, 4, 8, \ldots\} \\ 1 + 4Z &= \{\ldots -7, -3, 1, 5, 9, \ldots\} \\ 2 + 4Z &= \{\ldots -6, -2, 2, 6, 10, \ldots\} \\ 3 + 4Z &= \{\ldots -5, -1, 3, 7, 11, \ldots\} \end{aligned}$$

In the set of cosets, $S = \{4Z, 1 + 4Z, 2 + 4Z, 3 + 4Z\}$, we can define addition and multiplication. This set S and operations are similar to $Z_4 = \{0, 1, 2, 3\}$ under addition and multiplication modulo 4. In fact, S is isomorphic to Z_4. For instance, we have $(2 + 4Z) + (2 + 4Z) = 4Z$, $(1 + 4Z) + (2 + 4Z) = 3 + 4Z$, $(3 + 4Z)(3 + 4Z) = 1 + 4Z$ and $(2 + 4Z)(2 + 4Z) = 4Z$, and so on.

A field F has two group structures. One is that F is an Abelian group under addition. Also, since all nonzero elements in F have multiplicative inverses, F excluding zero, denoted by F', is a multiplicative group. The multiplicative group F' in a finite field can be shown to be a cyclic group and thus has a generator. The element in F that generates F' is called a *primitive element* in F.

A field with a finite number of elements is called a *Galois field*. In Example 2-3, we have already seen $GF(p)$, the field of p elements. In addition to prime fields, there are other finite fields that are called extension fields. An mth degree extension of $GF(p)$ is denoted $GF(p^m)$. For now, we illustrate these fields by examples, and formal theory will be developed in a later section. A degree 2 extension of $GF(2)$ gives $GF(2^2)$, which is also written as $GF(4) = \{0, 1, a, b\}$. The addition and

TABLE 2.1 ADDITION AND MULTIPLICATION IN $GF(4)$

$+$	0	1	a	b
0	0	1	a	b
1	1	0	b	a
a	a	b	0	1
b	b	a	1	0

$\cdot$	0	1	a	b
0	0	0	0	0
1	0	1	a	b
a	0	a	b	1
b	0	b	1	a

multiplication for $GF(4)$ are given in Table 2.1. In this example, $1 + 1 = 0$ and $a + a = 0 = b + b$. Since $a + a = 2a = 0$ for all $a \in GF(4)$, 2 is said to be the *characteristic* of the field. The field $GF(p)$ and all its extensions $GF(p^m)$ have the same characteristic p. The reader should carefully distinguish $GF(4)$ from Z_4, the set of integers modulo 4. In Z_4, $1 + 1 = 2 \neq 0$, whereas in $GF(4)$, $1 + 1 = 0$.

2.2 VECTOR SPACE AND SUBSPACES

A vector space $\mathbf{V}$ is a set of elements (called vectors) over a field F satisfying the following axioms. The elements of F are called scalars.

(V1) $\mathbf{V}$ is an Abelian group under addition.

(V2) For any $\mathbf{u} \in \mathbf{V}$ and any $a \in F$, $a\mathbf{u} \in \mathbf{V}$.

(V3) For any $\mathbf{u}, \mathbf{v} \in \mathbf{V}$ and any $a, b \in F$

$$a(\mathbf{u} + \mathbf{v}) = a\mathbf{u} + a\mathbf{v}$$

$$(a + b)\mathbf{u} = a\mathbf{u} + b\mathbf{u}$$

$$(ab)\mathbf{u} = a(b\mathbf{u}) \text{ and } 1 \cdot \mathbf{u} = \mathbf{u}, 0 \cdot \mathbf{u} = 0$$

A subset $\mathbf{S}$ of a vector space $\mathbf{V}$ (over a field F) is called a subspace if it satisfies all the axioms of a vector space. However, for a subset $\mathbf{S}$ of $\mathbf{V}$ to be a subspace, we need only to verify the following two axioms.

(S1) For any $\mathbf{v}, \mathbf{u} \in \mathbf{S}$, $\mathbf{v} + \mathbf{u} \in \mathbf{S}$.

(S2) For any $\mathbf{v} \in \mathbf{S}$, $a \in F$, $a\mathbf{v} \in \mathbf{S}$.

The other axioms of a vector space are easily verified for $\mathbf{S}$ since it is a subset of $\mathbf{V}$. From (S2), $0 \cdot \mathbf{u} = 0 \in \mathbf{S}$. Also $(-1)\mathbf{v} = -\mathbf{v}$ is in $\mathbf{S}$ for all $\mathbf{v} \in \mathbf{S}$. The distributive and associative laws hold naturally in $\mathbf{S}$. It is necessary to distinguish between vector 0, which is the vector identity and the scalar 0.

Example Set 2-4 (Vector Spaces and Subspaces)

1. The set of all n-tuples over $GF(2)$ can be written as $\mathbf{V} = \{\mathbf{v} | \mathbf{v} = (a_0, a_1, \ldots, a_{n-1}),\ a_i \in GF(2)\}$. The addition in $\mathbf{V}$ is componentwise. That is, if $\mathbf{v} = (a_0, a_1, \ldots, a_{n-1})$ $\mathbf{u} = (b_0, b_1, \ldots, b_{n-1})$, $\mathbf{v} + \mathbf{u} = (a_0 + b_0, a_1 + b_1, \ldots, a_{n-1} + b_{n-1})$. Also for $a \in GF(2)$, $a \cdot \mathbf{u} = (ab_0, ab_1, \ldots, ab_{n-1}) = \mathbf{u}$ if $a = 1$ and $a \cdot \mathbf{u} = (0, 0, \ldots, 0) = 0$ if $a = 0$.

2. The set of all polynomials of degree 3 or less with coefficients from $GF(2)$ can be written as $\mathbf{V}_3(x) = \{\mathbf{v(x)} | \mathbf{v(x)} = a_0 + a_1x + a_2x^2,\ a_i \in GF(2)\}$. This is a vector space over $GF(2)$ as can easily be verified.

A linear combination of m vectors $\mathbf{v}_1, \mathbf{v}_2, \ldots, \mathbf{v}_m$ in $\mathbf{V}$ over F is a sum of the form

$$\mathbf{u} = a_1\mathbf{v}_1 + a_2\mathbf{v}_2 + \cdots + a_m\mathbf{v}_m,\ a_i \in F$$

Clearly, $\mathbf{u} \in \mathbf{V}$.

Theorem 2-2. *The set* $\mathbf{S}$ *of all linear combination of m vectors* $\mathbf{v}_1, \mathbf{v}_2, \ldots, \mathbf{v}_m$ *in* $\mathbf{V}$ *over F is a subspace.*

Proof. If $\mathbf{u}, \mathbf{w}$ are two linear combinations in $\mathbf{S}$, these can be written as

$$\mathbf{u} = a_1\mathbf{v}_1 + \cdots + a_m\mathbf{v}_m \qquad \text{for } a_i \in F$$

$$\mathbf{w} = b_1\mathbf{v}_1 + \cdots + b_m\mathbf{v}_m \qquad \text{for } b_i \in F$$

Then $\mathbf{u} + \mathbf{w} = (a_1 + b_1)\mathbf{v}_1 + \cdots + (a_m + b_m)\mathbf{v}_m$ is also a linear combination vector in $\mathbf{V}$. Also, for any $c \in F$, $c\mathbf{u} = ca_1\mathbf{v}_1 + ca_2\mathbf{v}_2 + \cdots + ca_m\mathbf{v}_m$ is also a linear combination vector. Therefore, the set of all linear combinations (of m vectors) in $\mathbf{V}$ satisfy (S1) and (S2), and it is a subspace.

Definition 2-2. A set of nonzero vectors $\mathbf{v}_1, \mathbf{v}_2, \ldots \mathbf{v}_m$ is *linearly dependent* if and only if there are scalars $c_1, c_2, \ldots c_m$, at least one of them nonzero, such that

$$c_1\mathbf{v}_1 + c_2\mathbf{v}_2 + \cdots + c_m\mathbf{v}_m = 0 \qquad \textit{at least one } c_i \neq 0 \tag{2.1}$$

Clearly, if the set is linearly dependent, then one of these vectors can be obtained as a linear combination of the others. For instance, from (2.1), if $c_m \neq 0$ then we have

$$\mathbf{v}_m = c_m^{-1}(c_1\mathbf{v}_1 + c_2\mathbf{v}_2 + \cdots + c_{m-1}\mathbf{v}_{m-1})$$

$$= d_1\mathbf{v}_1 + d_2\mathbf{v}_2 + \cdots + d_{m-1}\mathbf{v}_{m-1},\ d_i = c_m^{-1}c_i$$

If a set of vectors is not linearly dependent, then it is called *linearly independent*. In such a set, any one of those cannot be obtained as a linear combination of the others.

Definition 2-3. A set of vectors $\mathbf{v}_1, \mathbf{v}_2, \ldots, \mathbf{v}_m$ is said to *span* a vector space $\mathbf{V}$ if and only if every vector in $\mathbf{V}$ is a linear combination of the set.

Theorem 2-3. *Let a set* $\mathbf{v}_1, \mathbf{v}_2, \ldots, \mathbf{v}_m$ *span* $\mathbf{V}$. *Then, any set that is linearly independent in* $\mathbf{V}$ *can have at most m vectors.*

Proof. If a set of k vectors, $\mathbf{u}_1, \mathbf{u}_2, \ldots \mathbf{u}_k$ in $\mathbf{V}$ are linearly independent and $k > m$, then we can readily obtain a contradiction as follows. Since $\mathbf{v}_1, \mathbf{v}_2, \ldots, \mathbf{v}_m$

span $\mathbf{V}$ each of the $\mathbf{u}_i$ $(i = 1, 2, \ldots, k)$ is a linear combination of $\mathbf{v}_1, \mathbf{v}_2, \ldots, \mathbf{v}_m$.

$$\mathbf{u}_1 = a_{11}\mathbf{v}_1 + a_{12}\mathbf{v}_2 + \cdots + a_{1m}\mathbf{v}_m$$
$$\mathbf{u}_2 = a_{21}\mathbf{v}_1 + a_{22}\mathbf{v}_2 + \cdots + a_{2m}\mathbf{v}_m$$
$$\vdots$$
$$\mathbf{u}_k = a_{k1}\mathbf{v}_1 + a_{k2}\mathbf{v}_2 + \cdots + a_{km}\mathbf{v}_m$$

These are k equations over m variables (vectors) with $k > m$. From the first equation, $\mathbf{v}_1$ can be expressed as a linear combination of $\mathbf{u}_1, \mathbf{v}_2, \ldots, \mathbf{v}_m$. Substituting for $\mathbf{v}_1$ in the second equation, we can get $\mathbf{v}_2$ as a linear combination of $\mathbf{u}_1, \mathbf{u}_2, \mathbf{v}_3, \ldots, \mathbf{v}_m$. Proceeding in those lines we can get $\mathbf{u}_{m+1}$ as a linear combination of $\mathbf{u}_1, \mathbf{u}_2, \ldots, \mathbf{u}_m$. That means that $\mathbf{u}_1, \mathbf{u}_2, \ldots, \mathbf{u}_m, \mathbf{u}_{m+1}$ are linearly dependent.

Q.E.D.

Theorem 2-3 states that there can be at most m linearly independent vectors in a vector space that is spanned by m vectors. Therefore, if m linearly independent vectors $\mathbf{v}_1, \mathbf{v}_2, \ldots, \mathbf{v}_m$ span $\mathbf{V}$, then m is said to be the *dimension* of $\mathbf{V}$ and the set $\mathbf{v}_1, \mathbf{v}_2, \ldots, \mathbf{v}_m$ is a *basis* of $\mathbf{V}$. Also, in an m-dimensional space, any basis must be exactly of m vectors, and they are linearly independent. Furthermore, if $\mathbf{V}$ is any m-dimensional vector space, then any set of m linearly independent vectors is a basis of $\mathbf{V}$.

Example. The set $\mathbf{V}$ of all 5-tuples over a binary field is a vector space. A basis for $\mathbf{V}$ can be given by the five vectors that are the row vectors of the (5×5) identity matrix,

$$\mathbf{I}_5 = \begin{bmatrix} 1 & 0 & 0 & 0 & 0 \\ 0 & 1 & 0 & 0 & 0 \\ 0 & 0 & 1 & 0 & 0 \\ 0 & 0 & 0 & 1 & 0 \\ 0 & 0 & 0 & 0 & 1 \end{bmatrix}$$

Consider the vectors $\mathbf{v}_1 = 11010$, $\mathbf{v}_2 = 01101$ in $\mathbf{V}$. The set $\mathbf{S}$ of all linear combination of vectors $\mathbf{v}_1$ and $\mathbf{v}_2$ are the following.

$$0 = 00000$$
$$\mathbf{v}_1 = 11010$$
$$\mathbf{v}_2 = 01101$$
$$\mathbf{v}_1 + \mathbf{v}_2 = 10111$$

One can see that $\mathbf{V}$ is of dimension 5 and the subspace $\mathbf{S}$ spanned by $\mathbf{v}_1$ and $\mathbf{v}_2$ is of dimension 2.

Matrices. This section presents some linear algebra and matrix theory that apply to codes studied in this book. The proofs are given for the most part, and a review of the material is presented, but for a more complete treatment the reader may seek standard texts such as [JACO 51] and [BIRK 70].

A $(k \times n)$ matrix $\mathbf{G}$ is an array of elements from a finite field $GF(q)$ as shown:

$$\mathbf{G} = [g_{ij}] = \begin{bmatrix} g_{00} & g_{01} & \cdots & g_{0,n-1} \\ g_{10} & g_{11} & \cdots & g_{1,n-1} \\ \vdots & \vdots & & \vdots \\ g_{k-1,0} & g_{k-1,1} & \cdots & g_{k-1,n-1} \end{bmatrix} = \begin{bmatrix} \mathbf{g}_1 \\ \mathbf{g}_2 \\ \vdots \\ \mathbf{g}_k \end{bmatrix}$$

$$\textit{with } g_{ij} \in GF(q),\ i \in [0, k-1], \text{ and } j \in [0, n-1].$$

$\mathbf{g}_1, \mathbf{g}_2, \ldots, \mathbf{g}_k$ are rows of $\mathbf{G}$ and are called row vectors of $\mathbf{G}$. Also, the n columns of $\mathbf{G}$ are k-tuples and are called column vectors. Scalars $g_{00}, g_{11}, \ldots, g_{ii}$ are elements of the main diagonal. We can now consider the set of all n-tuples over $GF(q)$ as a vector space $\mathbf{V}$. The rows of $\mathbf{G}$ are vectors in $\mathbf{V}$ and the subspace spanned by the row vectors $\mathbf{g}_0, \mathbf{g}_1, \ldots, \mathbf{g}_{k-1}$ is called the *row space* of $\mathbf{G}$. Similarly, the subspace spanned by the column vectors of $\mathbf{G}$ is called the column space of $\mathbf{G}$. If the k-row vectors are linearly independent, then the dimension of the row space is k. The dimension of the row space of $\mathbf{G}$ is called the *row rank* of $\mathbf{G}$, and so the dimension of column space of $\mathbf{G}$ is the *column rank* of $\mathbf{G}$.

It can be shown that row rank of a matrix must equal the column rank and therefore the *rank* of a matrix refers to the dimension of its row space (as well as column space).

We consider here *elementary row operations* on a matrix $\mathbf{G}$ that do not alter the row space. Similarly, column operations can be defined.

$\mathbf{E}_1$: Interchanging any two rows.

$\mathbf{E}_2$: Multiplication of any row by a nonzero scalar.

$\mathbf{E}_3$: Addition of a scalar multiple of one row to another.

Each of these elementary operations on a $(k \times n)$ matrix $\mathbf{G}$ amounts to a multiplication on the left by an *elementary matrix* illustrated as follows.

$$\begin{array}{ccccc} & \mathbf{E}_1 & \times \quad \mathbf{G} & = & \mathbf{G}_1 \end{array}$$

$$\mathbf{EG} = \begin{bmatrix} 1 & 0 & 0 \\ 0 & 0 & 1 \\ 0 & 1 & 0 \end{bmatrix} \begin{bmatrix} 1 & 0 & 1 & 1 & 0 \\ 1 & 1 & 0 & 1 & 1 \\ 0 & 1 & 0 & 1 & 0 \end{bmatrix} = \begin{bmatrix} 1 & 0 & 1 & 1 & 0 \\ 0 & 1 & 0 & 1 & 0 \\ 1 & 1 & 0 & 1 & 1 \end{bmatrix} = \mathbf{G}_1$$

$\mathbf{E}_1$ is an elementary matrix that is used here to multiply $\mathbf{G}$ on the left to obtain $\mathbf{G}_1$. The second and third rows of $\mathbf{G}$ are interchanged to obtain $\mathbf{G}_1$. Note that the same interchange once again will result in the original matrix (i.e., $\mathbf{E}_1\mathbf{E}_1\mathbf{G} = \mathbf{G}$), and $\mathbf{E}_1$ is its own inverse.

The elementary matrix $\mathbf{E}_2$ is a diagonal matrix with all 1's on the diagonal except for the ith element which is $a \neq 0$. Then, $\mathbf{E}_2\mathbf{G} = \mathbf{G}_1$ is a matrix whose ith row is multiplied by a. Consider the following example of matrix $\mathbf{G}$ over $GF(3)$.

A general form of the elementary matrix $\mathbf{E}_1$ is a modification of the identity matrix in ith and jth rows as shown:

$$\mathbf{E}_1 = \begin{bmatrix} 1 & & & & & & \\ & 1 & & & & & \\ & & \ddots & & & & \\ & & & 0 & \cdots & 1 & & \\ & & & & \cdots & & & \\ & & & 1 & \cdots & 0 & & \\ & & & & & & \ddots & \\ & & & & & & & 1 \end{bmatrix}$$

$\mathbf{E}_2$ is an identity matrix with the ith element modified to $a \neq 0$ and $a \neq 1$ as shown:

$$\mathbf{E}_2 = \begin{bmatrix} 1 & & & & & \\ & 1 & & & & \\ & & \ddots & & & \\ & & & a & & \\ & & & & \ddots & \\ & & & & & 1 \end{bmatrix}$$

$\mathbf{E}_3$ is an identity matrix additionally with an $a \in F$ in one of the rows as shown:

$$\mathbf{E}_3 = \begin{bmatrix} 1 & & & & & \\ & 1 & & & & \\ & \vdots & \ddots & & & \\ & a & \cdots & 1 & & \\ & & & & \ddots & \\ & & & & & 1 \end{bmatrix}$$

To illustrate $\mathbf{E}_2$, we given the following.

$$\begin{matrix} \mathbf{E}_2 & \mathbf{G} & = & \mathbf{G}_1 \\ \begin{bmatrix} 1 & 0 & 0 \\ 0 & 2 & 0 \\ 0 & 0 & 1 \end{bmatrix} & \begin{bmatrix} 2 & 1 & 2 & 1 \\ 1 & 2 & 0 & 2 \\ 1 & 1 & 2 & 0 \end{bmatrix} & = & \begin{bmatrix} 2 & 1 & 2 & 1 \\ 2 & 1 & 0 & 1 \\ 1 & 1 & 2 & 0 \end{bmatrix} \end{matrix}$$

$\mathbf{E}_2^{-1}$, the inverse of $\mathbf{E}_2$, is of the same form as $\mathbf{E}_2$ except a^{-1} replaces a on the diagonal. The third type of elementary matrix $\mathbf{E}_3$ is illustrated as follows. Here, $2 \times$ the third row is added to the second row of $\mathbf{G}$ to obtain $\mathbf{G}_1$.

$$\begin{matrix} \mathbf{E}_3 & \mathbf{G} & = & \mathbf{G}_1 \\ \begin{bmatrix} 1 & 0 & 0 \\ 0 & 1 & 2 \\ 0 & 0 & 1 \end{bmatrix} & \begin{bmatrix} 2 & 1 & 2 & 1 \\ 1 & 2 & 0 & 2 \\ 1 & 1 & 2 & 0 \end{bmatrix} & = & \begin{bmatrix} 2 & 1 & 2 & 1 \\ 0 & 1 & 1 & 2 \\ 1 & 1 & 2 & 0 \end{bmatrix} \end{matrix}$$

The important point to note here is that the row space of $\mathbf{G}$ is the same as the row space of $\mathbf{G}_1$. The inverse of $\mathbf{E}_3$ is also of the same form as $\mathbf{E}_3$, except the nondiagonal element a is replaced by $-a$ to obtain $\mathbf{E}_3^{-1}$. For the foregoing example, we have

$$\begin{matrix} \mathbf{E}_3^{-1} & \mathbf{G}_1 & = & \mathbf{G} \\ \begin{bmatrix} 1 & 0 & 0 \\ 0 & 1 & 1 \\ 0 & 0 & 1 \end{bmatrix} & \begin{bmatrix} 2 & 1 & 2 & 1 \\ 0 & 1 & 1 & 2 \\ 1 & 1 & 2 & 0 \end{bmatrix} & = & \begin{bmatrix} 2 & 1 & 2 & 1 \\ 1 & 2 & 0 & 2 \\ 1 & 1 & 2 & 0 \end{bmatrix} \end{matrix}$$

Similarly, one can define column operations on $\mathbf{G}$ that do not alter the column space of $\mathbf{G}$.

Once again, it is important to remember that row operations on a matrix do not alter its row space. Two matrices are said to be *row equivalent* if their row spaces are the same. The purpose of row operations on a matrix $\mathbf{G}$ is to reduce it to a standard form called *row-reduced canonical form*, which is defined as follows.

Definition 2-4. A matrix $\mathbf{G}$ is said to be in *row-reduced canonical form* (also called the *echelon canonical form* [PETE 72]) if it satisfies the following.

1. The very first nonzero element of each row vector, called the *leading element*, is a 1.
2. Every column containing a leading element has all 0's except that element.
3. The leading element in any row is to the right of the leading elements in every preceding row. All zero rows (if any) are the bottom rows.

The row reduction procedure is similar to the *Gaussian elimination* used to solve linear equations. This procedure also enables one to eliminate rows that are linearly dependent on the previous rows and to determine its row rank. Example 2-6 illustrates a row-reduction procedure on a matrix over $GF(3)$.

Orthogonality and null spaces. Let $\mathbf{V}_n$ denote the vector space of all n-tuples over $GF(q)$; also let $\mathbf{u} = (u_0, u_1, \ldots, u_{n-1})$ and $\mathbf{v} = (v_0, v_1, \ldots, v_{n-1})$ be vectors in $\mathbf{V}_n$. The *inner product* (*dot product* or *scalar product*) of $\mathbf{u}$ and $\mathbf{v}$ is defined by the scalar

$$\mathbf{u} \cdot \mathbf{v} = u_0 v_0 + u_1 v_1 + \cdots + u_{n-1} v_{n-1}$$

As an example, for vectors $\mathbf{u} = (2,1,2)$ and $\mathbf{v} = (0,2,1)$ over $GF(3)$, $\mathbf{u} \cdot \mathbf{v} = 2 \cdot 0 + 1 \cdot 2 + 2 \cdot 1 = 1$. It is easy to verify the following properties.

$$\begin{aligned} \mathbf{u} \cdot \mathbf{v} &= \mathbf{v} \cdot \mathbf{u} \\ \mathbf{u} \cdot (\mathbf{v} + \mathbf{w}) &= \mathbf{u} \cdot \mathbf{v} + \mathbf{u} \cdot \mathbf{w} \\ (a\mathbf{v}) \cdot \mathbf{w} &= a(\mathbf{v} \cdot \mathbf{w}) \end{aligned} \tag{2.2}$$

If $\mathbf{u} \cdot \mathbf{v} = 0$ then $\mathbf{u}$ is said to be *orthogonal* to $\mathbf{v}$ and is written as $\mathbf{u} \perp \mathbf{v}$. Let $\mathbf{S}_1$ be a k-dimensional subspace of $\mathbf{V}_n$. Let $\mathbf{S}_2$ be the set of all vectors in $\mathbf{V}_n$ such that for any $\mathbf{u} \in \mathbf{S}_2$, $\mathbf{u}$ is orthogonal to every vector in $\mathbf{S}_1$. Then we can state the following.

Theorem 2-4. *The set of vectors $\mathbf{S}_2$ orthogonal to every vector in subspace $\mathbf{S}_1$ of the vector space $\mathbf{V}_n$ is also a subspace. $\mathbf{S}_2$ is called the null space of $\mathbf{S}_1$.*

Proof. If $\mathbf{v}$ and $\mathbf{w}$ are two vectors in $\mathbf{S}_2$ orthogonal to every vector in $\mathbf{S}_1$, then $\mathbf{v} + \mathbf{w}$ is also orthogonal to every vector in $\mathbf{S}_1$ and therefore $\mathbf{v} + \mathbf{w} \in \mathbf{S}_2$. Also, $a\mathbf{u} \in \mathbf{S}_2$ for all $a \in GF(q)$ and $\mathbf{u} \in \mathbf{S}_2$. These are proved using properties (2.2) of the inner product. Therefore, $\mathbf{S}_2$ is a subspace. Q.E.D.

If $\mathbf{S}_2$ is the null space of $\mathbf{S}_1$, then it is easy to see that $\mathbf{S}_1$ is the null space of $\mathbf{S}_2$. The dimension of $\mathbf{S}_2$ is given by the following theorem.

Theorem 2-5. *If $\mathbf{S}_2$ is the null space of a subspace $\mathbf{S}_1$ of dimension k in $\mathbf{V}_n$, then $\mathbf{S}_2$ has dimension $n - k$.*

The proof of this theorem is rather long and is not required for understanding the rest of the material and hence is omitted.

Example 2-5

Let $\mathbf{S}_1$ be the row space of $\mathbf{G}$,

$$\mathbf{G} = \begin{bmatrix} 1 & 1 & 0 & 1 & 0 \\ 1 & 0 & 1 & 0 & 1 \end{bmatrix} = \begin{bmatrix} \mathbf{g}_0 \\ \mathbf{g}_1 \end{bmatrix}$$

$\mathbf{S}_1$ consists of four vectors (0 0 0 0 0), (1 1 0 1 0), (1 0 1 0 1), and (0 1 1 1 1). $\mathbf{S}_2$ is the null space of $\mathbf{S}_1$ and can be given as the row space of $\mathbf{H}$,

$$\mathbf{H} = \begin{bmatrix} 1 & 0 & 0 & 1 & 1 \\ 0 & 1 & 0 & 1 & 0 \\ 0 & 0 & 1 & 0 & 1 \end{bmatrix}$$

$\mathbf{S}_2$ will consist of eight vectors that are the linear combinations of the three row vectors of $\mathbf{H}$. It is sufficient to check that each row of $\mathbf{G}$ is orthogonal to each row of $\mathbf{H}$ and that the rows of each matrix are linearly independent. $\mathbf{S}_2$ is also called the null space of $\mathbf{G}$, and $\mathbf{S}_1$ is the null space of $\mathbf{H}$.

A procedure that can be conveniently used to obtain the null space of a given subspace $\mathbf{S}_1$ of $\mathbf{V}_n$ is first to reduce the basis vectors of $\mathbf{S}_1$ to a desired form as shown in Example 2-6.

Example 2-6

Let $\mathbf{S}_1$ be a row space of $\mathbf{G}$,

$$\mathbf{G} = \begin{bmatrix} 2 & 0 & 2 & 2 & 2 \\ 1 & 2 & 2 & 1 & 0 \\ 0 & 1 & 2 & 2 & 2 \end{bmatrix} = \begin{bmatrix} \mathbf{g}_0 \\ \mathbf{g}_1 \\ \mathbf{g}_2 \end{bmatrix}$$

In order to obtain **G** in row-reduced canonical form, we go through the following elementary row operations.

1. Multiplying the first row ($\mathbf{g}_0$) by 2, we get

$$\begin{bmatrix} 1 & 0 & 1 & 1 & 1 \\ 1 & 2 & 2 & 1 & 0 \\ 0 & 1 & 2 & 2 & 2 \end{bmatrix}$$

2. Adding 2 times the first row to the second, we get

$$\begin{bmatrix} 1 & 0 & 1 & 1 & 1 \\ 0 & 2 & 1 & 0 & 2 \\ 0 & 1 & 2 & 2 & 2 \end{bmatrix}$$

3. Multiplying the second row by 2, we get

$$\begin{bmatrix} 1 & 0 & 1 & 1 & 1 \\ 0 & 1 & 2 & 0 & 1 \\ 0 & 1 & 2 & 2 & 2 \end{bmatrix}$$

4. Adding 2 times the second row to the third row, we get

$$\begin{bmatrix} 1 & 0 & 1 & 1 & 1 \\ 0 & 1 & 2 & 0 & 1 \\ 0 & 0 & 0 & 2 & 1 \end{bmatrix}$$

5. Multiplying row 3 by 2, we get

$$\begin{bmatrix} 1 & 0 & 1 & 1 & 1 \\ 0 & 1 & 2 & 0 & 1 \\ 0 & 0 & 0 & 1 & 2 \end{bmatrix}$$

6. As a last step, we add 2 times the third row to the first to get the row-reduced canonical form **G′**,

$$\mathbf{G}' = \begin{bmatrix} 1 & 0 & 1 & 0 & 2 \\ 0 & 1 & 2 & 0 & 1 \\ 0 & 0 & 0 & 1 & 2 \end{bmatrix}$$

Since there are no zero vectors in **G′**, the dimension of $\mathbf{S}_1$ is 3. The leading terms of **G′** are in position 1, 2, and 4. In order to obtain an identity matrix on the left, columns 3 and 4 are exchanged to yield

$$\mathbf{G}'' = \begin{bmatrix} 1 & 0 & 0 & 1 & 2 \\ 0 & 1 & 0 & 2 & 1 \\ 0 & 0 & 1 & 0 & 2 \end{bmatrix} = [\mathbf{I}_3 \quad \mathbf{P}]$$

where $\mathbf{I}_3$ is a (3×3) identity matrix and **P** is a 3×2 matrix. This form of matrix is called *reduced-echelon* form [PETE 72] or *systematic form*. Here $\mathbf{G}'' = \mathbf{G}' \cdot \mathbf{R}$, where **R** is a column permutator matrix (i.e., **R** is a product of elementary column matrices). Note that row operations alone may not always result in a systematic form. Sometimes column permutations also may be required to obtain a systematic form.

Definition 2-5. A $(k \times n)$ matrix $\mathbf{G}$ is said to be in *systematic form* if

$$\mathbf{G} = [\mathbf{I}_k \quad \mathbf{P}] \qquad \text{or} \qquad \mathbf{G} = [\mathbf{P} \quad \mathbf{I}_k] \text{ form.}$$

Theorem 2-6. *Let a $(k \times n)$ matrix $\mathbf{G}$ be given in systematic form as*

$$\mathbf{G} = [\mathbf{I}_k \quad \mathbf{P}] \tag{2.3}$$

Then its null space is given by the row space of $\mathbf{H}$,

$$\mathbf{H} = [-\mathbf{P}^T \quad \mathbf{I}_{n-k}] \tag{2.4}$$

where $\mathbf{P}^T$ is the transpose of matrix $\mathbf{P}$ and $\mathbf{I}_{n-k}$ is the identity matrix of rank $n-k$. By negating each term of $\mathbf{P}^T$, we get $-\mathbf{P}^T$.

Proof. We can expand $\mathbf{G}$ and $\mathbf{H}$ and write

$$\mathbf{G} = \begin{bmatrix} 1 & 0 & 0 & \cdots & 0 & p_{1,1} & p_{1,2} & \cdots & p_{1,n-k} \\ 0 & 1 & 0 & \cdots & 0 & p_{2,1} & p_{2,2} & \cdots & p_{2,n-k} \\ & \vdots & & & & \vdots & & & \vdots \\ 0 & 0 & 0 & \cdots & 1 & p_{k,1} & p_{k,2} & & p_{k,n-k} \end{bmatrix} = \begin{bmatrix} \mathbf{g}_1 \\ \mathbf{g}_2 \\ \vdots \\ \mathbf{g}_k \end{bmatrix},$$

$$\mathbf{H} = \begin{bmatrix} -p_{1,1} & -p_{2,1} & \cdots & -p_{k,1} & 1 & 0 & 0 & \cdots & 0 \\ -p_{1,2} & -p_{2,2} & \cdots & -p_{k,2} & 0 & 1 & 0 & \cdots & 0 \\ \vdots & \vdots & & \vdots & & \vdots & & & \vdots \\ -p_{1,n-k} & -p_{2,n-k} & \cdots & -p_{k,n-k} & 0 & 0 & 0 & \cdots & 1 \end{bmatrix} = \begin{bmatrix} \mathbf{h}_1 \\ \mathbf{h}_2 \\ \vdots \\ \mathbf{h}_{n-k} \end{bmatrix}$$

In the above form, we can evaluate $\mathbf{g}_i \cdot \mathbf{h}_j$, for all i, j and can find each to be zero. Thus, every row vector of $\mathbf{G}$ is orthogonal to every row vector of $\mathbf{H}$, as required for the proof. Q.E.D.

In Theorem 2-6, $\mathbf{G}$ and $\mathbf{H}$ are both in systematic form and the result of this theorem is expressed as

$$\mathbf{G} \cdot \mathbf{H}^T = \mathbf{0} \tag{2.5}$$

To obtain the null space of a given matrix $\mathbf{G}$, the steps used in Example 2-6 are required. That is to reduce $\mathbf{G}$ to its systematic form $\mathbf{G}''$. Note here that the row space of $\mathbf{G}''$ is not always the same as $\mathbf{G}$ because of the column operations that may be required on $\mathbf{G}$ to obtain $\mathbf{G}''$, its systematic form. From $\mathbf{G}''$, its null matrix $\mathbf{H}''$ is obtained using Theorem 2-6. By applying the reverse permutation on $\mathbf{H}''$, we can get $\mathbf{H}$ to satisfy $\mathbf{G} \cdot \mathbf{H}^T = 0$. The row space of matrix $\mathbf{H}$ so obtained is the null space of $\mathbf{G}$. To illustrate this, we go back to Example 2-6 and continue the procedure as follows.

Example 2-7

We have started in Example 2-6 with

$$\mathbf{G} = \begin{bmatrix} 2 & 0 & 2 & 2 & 2 \\ 1 & 2 & 2 & 1 & 0 \\ 0 & 1 & 2 & 2 & 2 \end{bmatrix} \quad \text{over } GF(3)$$

and obtained its echelon-canonical form $\mathbf{G}'$ and its systematic form $\mathbf{G}''$ as follows.

$$\mathbf{G}' = \begin{bmatrix} 1 & 0 & 1 & 0 & 2 \\ 0 & 1 & 2 & 0 & 1 \\ 0 & 0 & 0 & 1 & 2 \end{bmatrix},$$

$$\mathbf{G}'' = \begin{bmatrix} 1 & 0 & 0 & 1 & 2 \\ 0 & 1 & 0 & 2 & 1 \\ 0 & 0 & 1 & 0 & 2 \end{bmatrix} = [\mathbf{I}_3 \quad \mathbf{P}]$$

From Theorem 2-6, we obtain

$$\mathbf{H}'' = [-\mathbf{P}^T \quad \mathbf{I}_2] = \begin{bmatrix} 2 & 1 & 0 & 1 & 0 \\ 1 & 2 & 1 & 0 & 1 \end{bmatrix}$$

To get the null matrix **H**, we transpose columns 3 and 4 as required, thus we have

$$\mathbf{H} = \begin{bmatrix} 2 & 1 & 1 & 0 & 0 \\ 1 & 2 & 0 & 1 & 1 \end{bmatrix}$$

It is easy to verify that $\mathbf{G} \cdot \mathbf{H}^T = 0$, and the row space of **H** is the null space of **G** and vice versa.

2.3 DIVISIBILITY, CONGRUENCES, AND RESIDUES

The theory presented here is to understand the codes presented in this book and is to be supplemented by appropriate reference material. This section is derived from introductory material from standard books on number theory, particularly [VINO 54] and [LEVE 54], and books on coding theory particularly [PETE 72] and [RAO 74]. The proofs are given where necessary for understanding of the topics and are omitted otherwise.

The set of all integers $\{\ldots, -2, -1, 0, 1, 2, 3, \ldots\}$ is denoted by Z. As stated in the previous section, under the addition and multiplication operations, it is a ring. Subtraction in Z can be considered as

$$a - b = a + (-b)$$

where $-b$ is the additive inverse of b. The division operation cannot be defined as the inverse of multiplication as a^{-1} is not always an integer. However, if $a/b = c$ for some integer c, then we say b *divides* a and b is a *divisor* (or *factor*) of a and denote this by $b \mid a$. Also, a is called a *multiple* of b. When b is not a divisor of a (i.e., $b \nmid a$), we can still define division as follows.

2.3.1 Divisibility Theory

Theorem 2-7 (Euclidean Division). *Any integer a can be divided by a positive integer d to obtain a quotient q and remainder r such that*

$$a = qd + r, \qquad \text{for } 0 \le r < d \tag{2.6}$$

In Equation (2.6), r is the least nonnegative remainder, called the *residue* of a modulo d, and it will be denoted also as

$$r = a \bmod d = |a|_d \tag{2.7}$$

Greatest common divisor. We consider here only positive divisors of integers. An integer that divides each one of $a, b, \ldots$ is said to be a *common divisor* of them. The *greatest common divisor* (*gcd*) of $a, b, \ldots$ is written

$$gcd\,(a, b, \ldots) \text{ or simply } (a, b, \ldots)$$

If $gcd\,(a, b) = 1$ then a and b are said to be *relatively prime*. It can be shown that any divisor of a and b also divides $gcd\,(a, b)$. If every pair of $\{a, b, \ldots, m\}$ are relatively prime, then they are said to be *pairwise prime*.

Example. Integers 5 and 15 are common divisors of $\{30, 45\}$ and $gcd\,(30, 45) = 15$. The set $\{10, 12, 15\}$ is relatively prime but is not pairwise prime. The set $\{6, 7, 11\}$ is pairwise prime.

To obtain the gcd of two integers a and b, the division defined by Equation (2.6) is repeatedly employed as follows (this is called Euclid's algorithm).

$$\begin{aligned}
a &= bq_1 + r_1 & 0 &\le r_1 < b \\
b &= r_1 q_2 + r_2 & 0 &\le r_2 < r_1 \\
r_1 &= r_2 q_3 + r_3 & 0 &\le r_3 < r_2 \\
&\vdots \\
r_{n-2} &= r_{n-1} q_n + r_n & 0 &\le r_n < r_{n-1} \\
r_{n-1} &= r_n q_{n+1} & r_{n+1} &= 0
\end{aligned}$$

This algorithm terminates when some $r_{n+1} = 0$. This termination must occur in a finite number of steps, since the sequence $r_1, r_2, r_3, \ldots$ is a decreasing sequence of positive integers and a and b are finite. Also, we have

$$gcd\,(a, b) = gcd\,(b, r_1) = gcd\,(r_1, r_2) = \cdots = (r_{n-1}, r_n) = r_n$$

Therefore, $gcd\,(a, b)$ is given by the smallest positive integer in the sequence $r_1, r_2, \ldots, r_n$. Consider as an example 99 and 279. We write

$$\begin{aligned}
279 &= 99 \times 2 + 81 \\
99 &= 81 \times 1 + 18 \\
81 &= 18 \times 4 + 9 \\
18 &= 9 \times 2 + 0
\end{aligned}$$

This gives us $(279, 99) = 9$. From the foregoing,

$$\begin{aligned} 9 &= 81 - 18 \times 4 \\ &= 81 - (99 - 81)4 \\ &= 5 \times 81 - 4 \times 99 \\ &= 5(279 - 99 \times 2) - 4 \times 99 \\ &= 5 \times 279 - 14 \times 99 \end{aligned}$$

This result can be generalized as follows. If $gcd\,(a, b) = d$, then d can be expressed as

$$d = ar + bs \tag{2.8}$$

for some two integers r and s. This result as expressed in (2.8) is useful in proving several theorems given as follows.

Theorem 2-8. *The integers modulo m, $Z_m = \{0, 1, \ldots, m - 1\}$ form a commutative ring. It is a field if and only if m is a prime.*

Proof. It is easy to show that Z_m under addition and multiplication modulo m is a commutative ring. Assume that m is composite (i.e., it is not a prime), then $m = ab$ for some nonzero $a, b \in Z_m$. Also, $ab = 0$ in Z_m. If a has an inverse, say r, then $ar = ra = 1$. Then $b = 1 \cdot b = (ra)b = r(ab) = r \cdot 0 = 0$, which is contradictory. Therefore, a cannot have an inverse in Z_m, and Z_m is not a field.

Assume that m is a prime. For nonzero $a \in Z_m$, we have $gcd\,(a, m) = 1$, and from (2.8) we have some r, s such that

$$1 = ar + ms$$

The preceding equation implies that $a \cdot r = 1$ in Z_m. If r is in Z_m, then it is the inverse of a in Z_m. If r is not in Z_m, then its residue $r' = r \bmod m$ is in Z_m, and r' is the inverse of a. Therefore, Z_m is a field. Q.E.D.

Lemma 2-3. *If $gcd\,(a, b) = d$, then $gcd\,(a/d, b/d) = 1$.*

Proof. Assume that $(a/d, b/d) = t$. Then t divides both a/d and b/d or td divides both a and b. That is, td is a common divisor of a and b, and therefore must divide d, which is impossible unless $t = 1$, as was to be proved.

Lemma 2-4. *If a divides bc and $gcd\,(a, b) = 1$, then a divides c.*

Proof. If $gcd\,(a, b) = 1$, there are integers r, s such that $ar + bs = 1$. Multiplying the latter by c, we have $acr + bcs = c$. Since a divides bc and also the left-hand side, therefore a must also divide c.

Another theorem that will be useful here is given as follows without proof.

Unique factorization theorem. *Every integer $a > 1$ can be expressed as a product of one or more primes. Furthermore, this expression as a product of primes is unique up to the order of the factors.*

For the proof, see any text on number theory, such as [VINO 54].

The least common multiple. An integer that is a multiple of each one of the integers from the set $a, b, \ldots$ is said to be their *common multiple*. The smallest positive common multiple is called the *least common multiple* (*lcm*), and it is written *lcm* $(a, b, \ldots)$. The following theorem is given here without proof.

Theorem 2-9. *If a and b are divisors of m, then lcm (a, b) also divides m. Furthermore,*

$$lcm\,(a, b) = ab/d \tag{2.9}$$

where d is gcd (a, b).

2.3.2 Linear Congruences and Residues

Definition 2-6. We say that *a is congruent to b modulo m* and write

$$a \equiv b \pmod{m}$$

if and only if m divides $a - b$. We can also write $a = b + km$ for some integer k.

Theorem 2-10. *The congruence defined above satisfies the properties:*

$$\begin{array}{ll} a \equiv a \pmod{m} & (\textit{reflexive}) \\ \textit{If } a \equiv b \pmod{m}, \textit{ then } b \equiv a \pmod{m} & (\textit{symmetric}) \\ \textit{If } a \equiv b \pmod{m} \textit{ and } b \equiv c \pmod{m}, & \\ \textit{then } a \equiv c \pmod{m} & (\textit{transitive}) \end{array}$$

Proof. Since m divides $a - a = 0$, $a \equiv a \pmod{m}$. If m divides $a - b$, m divides $b - a$, and therefore we have the symmetric property. If $a \equiv b \pmod{m}$, $b \equiv c \pmod{m}$, then $a = b + mk_1$ and $b = c + mk_2$ for some k_1 and k_2. Therefore, $a = c + mk_2 + mk_1 = c + m(k_1 + k_2)$, and hence $a \equiv c \pmod{m}$, proving transitivity. Q.E.D.

As a consequence of Theorem 2-10, the congruence is an equivalence relation on integers.

Example 2-8

To illustrate congruence and residue notation we have:

$$23 \equiv -5 \pmod{7}, \qquad 8^2 \equiv 9 \pmod{5},$$

$$23 \bmod 7 = |23|_7 = 2, \qquad |8^2|_5 = 4,$$

$$10 \equiv 7 \pmod{3}, \qquad 10 \bmod 3 = |10|_3 = 1$$

Be careful to note the difference between congruence ($\equiv$) and equality ($=$) symbols as used in the preceding examples. Also note the difference when parentheses are used around *mod* and when they are not used in these examples.

Theorem 2-11. *Given* $a \equiv x \pmod{m}$ *and* $b \equiv y \pmod{m}$, *we have*

$$\begin{aligned} a + b &\equiv x + y \pmod{m} \\ a - b &\equiv x - y \pmod{m} \\ a \cdot b &\equiv x \cdot y \pmod{m} \end{aligned} \tag{2.10}$$

Proof. From the hypothesis, we have that m divides $a - x$ and $b - y$. Therefore, m divides $(a - x) + (b - y) = (a + b) - (x + y)$, which clearly means that $a + b \equiv x + y \pmod{m}$. Also, m divides $(a - x) - (b - y)$. This means that m divides $(a - b) - (x - y)$; and $a - b \equiv x - y \pmod{m}$. From the hypothesis, we have $a = x + k_1 m$, $b = y + k_2 m$ for some k_1, and k_2. Therefore,

$$a \cdot b = (x + k_1 m)(y + k_2 m) = xy + (xk_2 + yk_1 + k_1 k_2 m)m = xy + k_3 m$$

and this proves the last part and completes the proof. Q.E.D.

The following corollary follows easily from the foregoing theorem by setting $b = y = t$.

Corollary 2-1. *Given* $a \equiv b \pmod{m}$, *we have the following for any* t

$$\begin{aligned} a + t &\equiv b + t \pmod{m} \\ a - t &\equiv b - t \pmod{m} \\ at &\equiv bt \qquad \pmod{m} \end{aligned} \tag{2.11}$$

This corollary shows that we can add, subtract, or multiply both sides of a congruence by a constant. But it is not always legitimate to cancel a factor from a congruence. For example, consider $25 \equiv -5 \pmod{10}$. By cancellation of the factor 5 from the numbers 25 and -5, we get the false result $5 \equiv -1 \pmod{10}$. The cancellation of a factor from a congruence is legitimate if the factor is relatively prime to the modulus m. That is, $ka \equiv kb \pmod{m}$ states that m divides $ka - kb = k(a - b)$. If m, k are relatively prime, then from Lemma 2-4 m must divide $a - b$, or $a \equiv b \pmod{m}$, and cancellation holds. As a general result, we have the following.

Theorem 2-12. *Given* $(t, m) = d$, *we have* $ta \equiv tb \pmod{m}$ *if and only if* $a \equiv b \pmod{(m/d)}$.

Proof. Let $a \equiv b \pmod{(m/d)}$. Then m/d divides $a - b$, which means that m divides $d(a - b)$. Since $(t, m) = d$, t/d is an integer, and m must also divide $(t/d)d(a - b) = t(a - b) \pmod{m}$. This gives us $ta \equiv tb \pmod{m}$.

Conversely, let $ta \equiv tb \pmod{m}$. This means that m divides $ta - tb = t(a - b)$, and m/d divides $(t/d)(a - b)$. From Lemma 2-3 $(m/d, t/d) = 1$, and from Lemma 2-4 we have that m/d must divide $a - b$. This gives us $a \equiv b \pmod{(m/d)}$. Q.E.D.

Congruences. Consider a congruence in one unknown x

$$ax \equiv b \pmod{m}$$

This has a unique solution modulo m provided that a is relatively prime to m. The proof of the above is as follows. If $gcd(a, m) = 1$, then from (2.8) there exist integers r, s such that $ar + ms = 1$ or $ar \equiv 1 \pmod{m}$. Multiplying by b we get the congruence $arb \equiv b \pmod{m}$. This gives us $arb \equiv ax \pmod{m}$ or $x = |rb|_m$, the desired solution.

In the foregoing result, r is a multiplicative inverse of a in Z_m and dividing the congruence by a is equivalent to multiplying by r. This we can write as

$$|a^{-1}|_m = r$$

and

$$x = |br|_m$$

Now consider the congruence when $(a, m) = d > 1$. This means that $ax - mk = b$ for some k. Since d divides both a and m, it must divide b. In other words, the congruence is solvable only if d divides b.

The following theorem, given without proof, applies to the general case.

Theorem 2-13. *Given $gcd(a, m) = d$, the congruence*

$$ax \equiv b \pmod{m} \tag{2.12}$$

is solvable for x in Z_m if and only if d divides b. If it is solvable, there are exactly d solutions for x in Z_m.

For proof, see [VINO 54] or [RAO 74].

Example 2-9

Consider the congruence

$$18x \equiv 6 \pmod{21} \tag{2.13}$$

Both sides of the congruence are divided by 2, and $gcd(2, 21) = 1$. Therefore, we can divide (2.13) by 2 and get

$$9x \equiv 3 \pmod{21} \tag{2.14}$$

Since 3 divides both side of the congruence and $3|21$, from Theorem 2-12 we can get

$$3x \equiv 1 \pmod{7} \tag{2.15}$$

This can be solved uniquely for $x = |3^{-1}|_7 = 5$ in Z_7. This solution can be verified by substitution in (2.13). Also, $5 + 7 = 12$, and $5 + 2 \times 7 = 19$ are solutions of (2.13). From Theorem 2-13, these are the only solutions modulo 21.

Consider the two congruences in one unknown

$$x \equiv a \pmod{m_1}, \qquad x \equiv b \pmod{m_2} \tag{2.16}$$

Then $x = a + m_1 y \equiv b \pmod{m_2}$ or $m_1 y \equiv b - a \pmod{m_2}$.

From Theorem 2-13, this congruence is solvable only if $gcd\,(m_1, m_2)$ divides $b - a$. From Theorem 2-12, we can divide this congruence by $(m_1, m_2) = d$ and obtain

$$\frac{m_1}{d} y \equiv \frac{(b-a)}{d} \left(\bmod \frac{m_2}{d}\right)$$

The foregoing has a unique solution for y modulo m_2/d, and therefore $x = a + m_1 y$ has a unique solution modulo $m_1 m_2/d$. Also, y has exactly d solutions modulo m_2, and x will have the same number of solutions modulo $m_1 m_2$. This gives the following.

Theorem 2-14. *Consider the two congruences in one unknown with respect to moduli m_1 and m_2.*

$$x \equiv a \pmod{m_1}, \qquad x \equiv b \pmod{m_2} \tag{2.17}$$

These are solvable only if $d = gcd\,(m_1, m_2)$ divides $a - b$. If they are solvable, then there is a unique solution modulo $lcm(m_1, m_2)$, and exactly d solutions modulo $m_1 m_2$.

Theorem 2-14 can be generalized to any arbitrary number of moduli. However, the case when moduli are pairwise prime will be of most interest and is stated as the Chinese remainder theorem (CRT).

Theorem 2-15 (CRT). *The set of congruences $x \equiv a_i \pmod{m_i}$ for $(i = 1, 2, \ldots, n)$, in which the moduli $m_1, m_2, \ldots, m_n$ are pairwise prime, is solvable, the solution being unique modulo the product $m_1 \cdot m_2 \cdots m_n$.*

Example 2-10

We solve the following congruences using the CRT.

$$x \equiv 2 \pmod 3 \tag{2.18}$$

$$x \equiv 3 \pmod 4 \tag{2.19}$$

$$x \equiv 2 \pmod 5 \tag{2.20}$$

These have a unique solution modulo $3 \cdot 4 \cdot 5 = 60$. To find that solution, we solve the first two congruences, which gives a unique solution modulo $3 \cdot 4 = 12$ and use this with the third congruence to obtain the answer. From (2.18), $x = 3y + 2$, and substituting this into (2.19) we get

$$3y + 2 \equiv 3 \pmod 4$$

$$3y \equiv 1 \pmod 4$$

or

$$y = |3^{-1}|_4 = 3$$

Therefore, $x = 3y + 2 = 3 \cdot 3 + 2 = 11$ in Z_{12}, and we write

$$x \equiv 11 \pmod{12} \tag{2.21}$$

The next step is to solve (2.20) and (2.21) simultaneously. From (2.20), $x = 2 + 5w$ for some w, and substituting into (2.21) we get

$$2 + 5w \equiv 11 \bmod 12$$

$$5w \equiv 9 \bmod 12$$

$$w \equiv |9 \times 5^{-1}|_{12} = 9$$

Therefore, we have the solution $x = 2 + 5 \times 9 = 47$. It is easy to verify the answer.

Table 2.2 illustrates the one-to-one correspondence between $x \in Z_{30}$ and the residues of x with respect to moduli 2, 3, and 5. This system of representation is called the *residue number system* (RNS) or modular arithmetic [RAO 74, GARN 59].

A residue number system (RNS) uses n residues with respect to moduli $m_1, m_2, \ldots, m_n$ that are pairwise prime and represents nonredundantly (i.e., on a one-to-one basis) the set of integers modulo $M = m_1 \cdot m_2 \cdot \cdots m_n$. Let two numbers $x, y \in Z_M$ be represented as n residues (or n-tuples) as follows.

$$x = (x_1, x_2, \ldots, x_n), \qquad x_i = |x|_{m_i} \ (i = 1, 2, \ldots n)$$

$$y = (y_1, y_2, \ldots, y_n), \qquad y_i = |y|_{m_i} \ (i = 1, 2, \ldots n)$$

TABLE 2.2 RNS REPRESENTING Z_{30} [RAO 74]

x	$\|x\|_2$	$\|x\|_3$	$\|x\|_5$	x	$\|x\|_2$	$\|x\|_3$	$\|x\|_5$
0	0	0	0	15	1	0	0
1	1	1	1	16	0	1	1
2	0	2	2	17	1	2	2
3	1	0	3	18	0	0	3
4	0	1	4	19	1	1	4
5	1	2	0	20	0	2	0
6	0	0	1	21	1	0	1
7	1	1	2	22	0	1	2
8	0	2	3	23	1	2	3
9	1	0	4	24	0	0	4
10	0	1	0	25	1	1	0
11	1	2	1	26	0	2	1
12	0	0	2	27	1	0	2
13	1	1	3	28	0	1	3
14	0	2	4	29	1	2	4

It follows from the theory of residues that the sum $S = |x + y|_M$ is given by

$$S = \left(|x_1 + y_1|_{m_1}, |x_2 + y_2|_{m_2}, \ldots, |x_n + y_n|_{m_n}\right) \tag{2.22}$$

Also, the product $P = |x \cdot y|_M$ is given by

$$P = \left(|x_1 \cdot y_1|_{m_1}, |x_2 \cdot y_2|_{m_2}, \ldots, |x_n \cdot y_n|_{m_n}\right) \tag{2.23}$$

The corresponding residues are added or multiplied, and there are no carries between the residue positions. These properties give the advantage of fast addition and multiplication operations and have received considerable attention from computer designers and researchers [SZAB 67]. The RNS suffers from a major disadvantage in sign determination and therefore is used only for special applications. The residue error codes, which are derived from the same theory as RNS, have been useful as codes for arithmetic processors [RAO 74].

2.4 POLYNOMIAL ALGEBRAS

A *polynomial* over a field $GF(q)$ is an expression

$$\mathbf{f}(x) = f_0 + f_1 x + f_2 x^2 + \cdots$$

where x is called an *indeterminate* and the *coefficients* $f_0, f_1, \ldots,$ are in $GF(q)$. The *degree* of $\mathbf{f}(x)$ is the highest *index* of the terms with a nonzero coefficient. The degree of $\mathbf{f}(x) = 1 + x + x^5$ over $GF(2)$ is 5; x^5 will be called the highest index term of $\mathbf{f}(x)$. If $\mathbf{f}(x) = a$, $(a \in GF(q))$, then its degree is zero. If the highest index term in $\mathbf{f}(x)$ has a coefficient 1, then $\mathbf{f}(x)$ is said to be *monic*.

Let $\mathbf{A(x)}$ denote the set of all polynomials in one indeterminate over $GF(q)$. $\mathbf{A(x)}$ can be shown to obey all the axioms of a ring under polynomial addition and multiplication. The $\mathbf{f}(x) = 0$ is the additive identity, and $\mathbf{f}(x) = 1$ is the multiplicative identity. $\mathbf{A(x)}$ also satisfies all the axioms of a vector space. The set of all polynomials of degree $n - 1$ or less over $GF(q)$ will be denoted $\mathbf{A}_n\mathbf{(x)}$. This has a structure identical to $\mathbf{V}_n$. Thus, $\mathbf{A}_n\mathbf{(x)}$ is a vector space of dimension n and can have a basis $\{1, x, x^2, \ldots, x^{n-1}\}$. The notation here will be to write every polynomial

$$\mathbf{f}(x) = f_0 + f_1 x + \cdots + f_{n-1} x^{n-1}$$

of degree $n - 1$ or less by a corresponding n-tuple (or vector) $(f_0, f_1, \ldots, f_{n-1})$. This correspondence is illustrated as follows.

Example 2-11

We consider here $\mathbf{A}_4\mathbf{(x)}$ over $GF(3)$

$$\mathbf{f}(x) = 1 + 2x + x^3 \leftrightarrow \mathbf{f} = (1,2,0,1)$$

$$\mathbf{g}(x) = 2 + 2x + 2x^2 \leftrightarrow \mathbf{g} = (2,2,2,0)$$

$$\mathbf{f}(x) + \mathbf{g}(x) = x + 2x^2 + x^3 \leftrightarrow \mathbf{f} + \mathbf{g} = (0,1,2,1)$$

In the ring of polynomials **A(x)**, we can also define polynomial multiplication. For instance,

$$\mathbf{f}(x) \cdot \mathbf{g}(x) = (1 + 2x + x^3)(2 + 2x + 2x^2) = 2 + 2x^4 + 2x^5 \in \mathbf{A}(x)$$

but the product is not defined in $\mathbf{A}_4(\mathbf{x})$. The degree of the product is the sum of the degrees of the factors. The polynomial ring $\mathbf{A}(x)$ has a structure very much similar to the ring of integers Z. We can add, subtract, and multiply polynomials in a straightforward manner.

A polynomial $\mathbf{b}(x)$ is *divisible* by $\mathbf{d}(x)$ and that $\mathbf{d}(x)$ is a *factor* of $\mathbf{b}(x)$ if there is a polynomial $\mathbf{q}(x)$ such that

$$\mathbf{b}(x) = \mathbf{q}(x) \cdot \mathbf{d}(x)$$

Also, $\mathbf{b}(x)$ is called a *multiple* of $\mathbf{d}(x)$. If $\mathbf{d}(x)$ is a factor of $\mathbf{b}(x)$, then $c\mathbf{d}(x)$ is also a factor for any nonzero scalar c. Therefore, when we consider factors, we need only to state monic polynomial factors. A monic polynomial $\mathbf{f}(x)$ is called *irreducible* or a *prime* polynomial if it has no factors of degree greater than zero other than $\mathbf{f}(x)$ itself.

The *greatest common divisor* (*gcd*) of two polynomials $\mathbf{a}(x)$ and $\mathbf{b}(x)$, denoted as $\gcd(\mathbf{a}(x), \mathbf{b}(x))$, is the greatest degree monic polynomial that divides both $\mathbf{a}(x)$ and $\mathbf{b}(x)$. Also, $\operatorname{lcm}(\mathbf{a}(x), \mathbf{b}(x))$ denotes the *least common multiple* of $\mathbf{a}(x)$ and $\mathbf{b}(x)$ and is given as the smallest degree monic polynomial such that both $\mathbf{a}(x)$ and $\mathbf{b}(x)$ divide it. If the gcd of two polynomials is 1, then they are said to be *relatively prime*. A set $\{\mathbf{a}_1(x), \mathbf{a}_2(x), \ldots, \mathbf{a}_m(x)\}$ are said to be *pairwise prime* if $\gcd(\mathbf{a}_i(x), \mathbf{a}_j(x)) = 1$ *for all* $i \neq j$. An important theorem pertaining to the gcd of polynomials is given here without proof.

Theorem 2-16. *If* $\mathbf{a}(x)$ *and* $\mathbf{b}(x)$ *are two polynomials with* $\gcd(\mathbf{a}(x), \mathbf{b}(x)) = \mathbf{d}(x)$, *then there exists polynomials* $\mathbf{r}(x)$ *and* $\mathbf{s}(x)$ *such that*

$$\mathbf{a}(x) \cdot \mathbf{r}(x) + \mathbf{b}(x) \cdot \mathbf{s}(x) = \mathbf{d}(x) \tag{2.24}$$

Equation (2.24) is analogous to Equation (2.8) given for integers.

Theorem 2-16 and Equation (2.24) will be used to explain and prove several results here. Students are well advised to work a few examples on their own to verify Theorem 2-16.

A polynomial $\mathbf{b}(x)$ can be divided by a polynomial $\mathbf{d}(x)$ to obtain a quotient $\mathbf{q}(x)$ and a remainder $\mathbf{r}(x)$, such that

$$\mathbf{b}(x) = \mathbf{q}(x)\,\mathbf{d}(x) + \mathbf{r}(x) \qquad \text{and} \qquad \deg.\mathbf{r}(x) < \deg.\mathbf{d}(x) \tag{2.25}$$

This again is analogous to Equation (2.6) stated for integers. It is easy to prove that for any $\mathbf{b}(x)$ and $\mathbf{d}(x)$ in (2.25) the quotient and remainder polynomials are unique; and (2.25) is referred to as the *division algorithm* for polynomials. Note that this division algorithm is very much similar to the Euclidean division algorithm in the ring of integers Z. The *residue* of $\mathbf{b}(x)$ modulo $\mathbf{d}(x)$ is the unique remainder obtained by the division algorithm (2.25). We write this as

$$\mathbf{b}(x) \bmod \mathbf{d}(x) = \mathbf{r}(x) = |\mathbf{b}(x)|_{d(x)} \tag{2.26}$$

Another form for Equation (2.26) is

$$\mathbf{b}(x) \equiv \mathbf{r}(x) \pmod{\mathbf{d}(x)} \tag{2.27}$$

where $\equiv$ is read as *congruent to*. If two polynomials are congruent to each other modulo $\mathbf{d}(x)$, then their difference is a multiple of $\mathbf{d}(x)$. It is important to distinguish Equations (2.26) and (2.27). In the form (2.26), where we use $=$, $\mathbf{r}(x)$ is called the residue, and its degree is less than the degree of $\mathbf{b}(x)$. When $\equiv$ is used, as in (2.27), there is no such restriction on the degree of $\mathbf{r}(x)$.

Let $\mathbf{f}(x)$ be a polynomial of degree m over $GF(q)$ for $m \geq 2$. If $(x - a)$ is a factor of $\mathbf{f}(x)$ for $a \in GF(q)$, then a is a *root* (also called *zero*) of $\mathbf{f}(x)$ and $\mathbf{f}(a) = 0$. Also, if $\mathbf{f}(x)$ has m degree 1 factors, then all its roots are in $GF(q)$. An irreducible polynomial $\mathbf{f}(x)$ (of degree $m \geq 2$) has no roots in $GF(q)$, but then its roots are in an extension field of $GF(q)$. Also, an mth degree extension of $GF(q)$ can be obtained by using such an irreducible $\mathbf{f}(x)$. This theory is given in the next section.

Example Set 2-12

Consider $\mathbf{b}(x) = x^3 + x + 1$ over $GF(2)$. This is an irreducible polynomial since it has no factors of degree greater than zero other than itself. To check for factors of degree 1, one needs to verify $b(0) = 0 + 0 + 1 = 1 \neq 0$ and $b(1) = 1 + 1 + 1 = 1 \neq 0$. Since $b(0) \neq 0$, x is not a factor and $b(1) \neq 0$ implies that $x + 1$ is not a factor.

As another example, consider $\mathbf{c}(x) = x^2 + 1$ over $GF(2)$. Since $c(1) = 1 + 1 = 0$, $x + 1$ is a factor and $\mathbf{c}(x) = (x + 1)(x + 1)$. In this case, $\mathbf{c}(x)$ has a double zero of 1.

As another example, let $\mathbf{b}(x) = x^3 + x + 2$ over $GF(3)$, we have $b(0) = 2$, $b(1) = 1$, and $b(2) = 0$. Therefore, 2 is a zero; and $x - 2 = x + 1$ is a factor of $\mathbf{b}(x)$. By dividing, we have $\mathbf{b}(x) = (x + 1)(x^2 + 2x + 2)$. We cannot factor any further because $x^2 + 2x + 2$ is irreducible.

As examples of residues for polynomials over $GF(3)$, we have

$$x^3 + x + 2 \pmod{x + 2} = 1$$

$$x^3 + 2x + 2 \left(\text{mod } x^2 + 1\right) = x + 2$$

These residues are obtained by actual division.

2.4.1 Polynomials Modulo $\mathbf{f}(x)$

Let $\mathbf{f}(x)$ be a polynomial of degree n in $\mathbf{A}(x)$. By using the *modulus* $\mathbf{f}(x)$ in the set $\mathbf{A}(x)$, we can define the *set of polynomials modulo* $\mathbf{f}(x)$. For any polynomial $\mathbf{b}(x)$ in $\mathbf{A}(x)$, there is a unique residue modulo $\mathbf{f}(x)$. For all $\mathbf{A}(x)$, these residues modulo $\mathbf{f}(x)$ cover the set $\mathbf{A}_n(\mathbf{x})$ of polynomials of degree less than n. Therefore, $\mathbf{A}_n(\mathbf{x})$ can also be considered as the set of polynomials modulo $\mathbf{f}(x)$. Of particular interest will be two cases: (1) when $\mathbf{f}(x) = x^n - 1$; and (2) when $\mathbf{f}(x)$ is an irreducible polynomial. These two cases will be studied in detail in the following sections.

The algebra of polynomials modulo $x^n - 1$. The set of polynomials modulo $\mathbf{f}(x)$, for $\mathbf{f}(x) = x^n - 1$ is an important structure useful for *cyclic codes* and will be studied in detail in Chapter 3. Here we see this algebra as the set

$$\mathbf{A}_n(\mathbf{x}) = \{\mathbf{b}(x) | \mathbf{b}(x) \text{ is of degree} < n \textit{ over } GF(q)\}$$

As stated before, $\mathbf{A}_n(\mathbf{x})$ is a vector space over $GF(q)$. In addition, we can define multiplication of polynomials modulo $x^n - 1$ as an operation. Then, $\mathbf{A}_n(\mathbf{x})$ can be easily shown to be a ring under polynomial addition and polynomial multiplication. In this multiplication, any term of degree $\geq n$ can be reduced to a degree smaller than n as follows.

$$\begin{aligned} x^n \,(\text{mod}\, x^n - 1) &= 1 \\ x^{n+1} \,(\text{mod}\, x^n - 1) &= x \\ &\vdots \\ x^{n+j} \,(\text{mod}\, x^n - 1) &= x^j \end{aligned} \tag{2.28}$$

Consider $\mathbf{b}(x) = b_0 - b_1 x + \cdots + b_{n-1}x^{n-1} \in \mathbf{A}_n(\mathbf{x})$. In $\mathbf{A}_n(\mathbf{x})$

$$x \cdot \mathbf{b}(x) = \mathbf{b}^{(1)}(x) = b_{n-1} + b_0 x + \cdots + b_{n-2}x^{n-1} \tag{2.29}$$

and

$$x^2 \mathbf{b}(x) = \mathbf{b}^{(2)}(x) = b_{n-2} + b_{n-1}x + b_0 x^2 + \cdots + b_{n-3}x^{n-1}$$

From (2.29), we see that multiplying x^j of a polynomial is like shifting its coefficients cyclically to the right by j places.

Let $\mathbf{g}(x)$ of degree r (for $r < n - 1$) divide $x^n - 1$. Then the subset of all multiples of $\mathbf{g}(x)$ in $\mathbf{A}_n(\mathbf{x})$ has an important structure, and it will be studied extensively. This structure is a subspace of $\mathbf{A}_n(\mathbf{x})$ and is also an ideal in the ring $\mathbf{A}_n(\mathbf{x})$.

Galois fields. Let $\mathbf{p}(x)$ denote an irreducible polynomial of degree m over $GF(q)$. We consider as before the set $\mathbf{S}$ of polynomials modulo $\mathbf{p}(x)$ in $\mathbf{A}(x)$ as

$$\mathbf{S} = \{\mathbf{b}(x) | \deg . \mathbf{b}(x) < m\} \tag{2.30}$$

Under addition of polynomials and multiplication modulo $\mathbf{p}(x)$, it is easy to show that $\mathbf{S}$ satisfies all the axioms of a commutative ring. In addition, we have the following.

Theorem 2-17. *The set* $\mathbf{S}$ *of polynomials modulo* $\mathbf{p}(x)$, *an irreducible polynomial, is a field.*

Proof. The set $\mathbf{S}$ is given by Equation (2.30). It is a commutative ring under addition and multiplication of polynomials modulo $\mathbf{p}(x)$. The only requirement to prove the theorem is to show that every $\mathbf{a}(x) \in \mathbf{S}$ has an inverse. Since $\mathbf{p}(x)$ is irreducible of degree m and $\mathbf{a}(x)$ of degree less than m, we have $\gcd(\mathbf{a}(x), \mathbf{p}(x)) = 1$.

By Theorem 2-16, there exist $\mathbf{r}(x)$ and $\mathbf{s}(x)$ in $\mathbf{A(x)}$ such that

$$\mathbf{a}(x)\mathbf{r}(x) + \mathbf{p}(x)\mathbf{s}(x) = 1 \tag{2.31}$$

Equation (2.31) can be written as

$$(\mathbf{a}(x)\mathbf{r}(x)) \bmod \mathbf{p}(x) = 1$$

and $\mathbf{r}(x)$ is the inverse of $\mathbf{a}(x)$ modulo $\mathbf{p}(x)$. If the degree of $\mathbf{r}(x)$ is greater than m, $\mathbf{r}'(x) = \mathbf{r}(x) \bmod \mathbf{p}(x)$ can be substituted in (2.31) to obtain

$$(\mathbf{a}(x) \cdot (\mathbf{r}(x) \bmod \mathbf{p}(x))) \bmod \mathbf{p}(x) = 1$$

$$(\mathbf{a}(x) \cdot \mathbf{r}'(x)) \bmod \mathbf{p}(x) = 1, \text{deg.}\, \mathbf{r}'(x) < m \tag{2.32}$$

In Equation (2.32), $\mathbf{r}'(x)$ is an inverse of $\mathbf{a}(x)$ in $\mathbf{S}$. Q.E.D.

Theorem 2-18. *If $p(x)$ is reducible in Theorem 2-17, then* **S** *is a commutative ring but not a field.*

Proof. Since $\mathbf{p}(x)$ is reducible, let $\mathbf{a}(x) \cdot \mathbf{b}(x) = \mathbf{p}(x)$. Then in $\mathbf{S}$, $\mathbf{a}(x)\mathbf{b}(x) = 0$ for nonzero $\mathbf{a}(x)$ and $\mathbf{b}(x)$. If $\mathbf{a}(x)$ has an inverse, say $\mathbf{r}(x)$, then $\mathbf{r}(x)\mathbf{a}(x) = 1$. Then $\mathbf{b}(x) = 1 \cdot \mathbf{b}(x) = \mathbf{r}(x) \cdot \mathbf{a}(x) \cdot \mathbf{b}(x) = \mathbf{r}(x) \cdot 0 = 0$, which is a contradiction. Therefore, $\mathbf{a}(x)$ cannot have an inverse; and $\mathbf{S}$ is not a field. Q.E.D.

Theorems 2-17 and 2-18 together give us the following.

Theorem 2-19. *The set of polynomials modulo* $\mathbf{m}(x)$ *is a commutative ring. It is a field if and only if* $\mathbf{m}(x)$ *is irreducible.*

Example Set 2-13

1. Consider $\mathbf{p}(x) = x^2 + x + 1$ over $GF(2)$. It is irreducible and the set of polynomials modulo the $\mathbf{p}(x)$ is a field denoted

$$GF(2^2) = \{0, 1, x, x + 1\}$$

The addition and multiplication tables are given below. This structure is the same as given in Table 2.1.

2. The set of polynomial modulo the irreducible polynomial $\mathbf{p}(x) = x^2 + 2x + 2$ over $GF(3)$ is a degree 2 extension and gives

$$GF(3^2) = \{0, 1, 2, x, x + 1, x + 2, 2x, 2x + 1, 2x + 2\}$$

TABLE 2.3 $GF(2^2)$ ADDITION AND MULTIPLICATION

+	0	1	x	$x+1$
0	0	1	x	$x+1$
1	1	0	$x+1$	x
x	x	$x+1$	0	1
$x+1$	$x+1$	x	1	0

	0	1	x	$x+1$
0	0	0	0	0
1	0	1	x	$x+1$
x	0	x	$x+1$	1
$x+1$	0	$x+1$	1	x

The addition in $GF(3^2)$ is polynomial addition with the characteristic 3 (i.e., $1 + 2 = 0, 2 + 2 = 1, 2x + x = 0, 2x + 2x = x$, and so on). The multiplication of polynomials is modulo $x^2 + 2x + 2$. A few examples illustrate these.

$$x \cdot x = x^2 = -2x - 2 = x + 1$$
$$x \cdot (x + 1) = x^2 + x = 2x + 1$$
$$(x + 1)(x + 2) = x^2 + 2 = x + 1 + 2 = x$$

The student is advised to prepare a table for addition and multiplication in $GF(3^2)$ as an exercise and answer the related problems at the end of the chapter.

We consider here another method of representation for extension fields. In this method we use α, the zero of an irreducible polynomial, to generate these fields. This theory is illustrated by means of examples.

Example Set 2-14

1. Let α be a zero of the irreducible polynomial $\mathbf{p}(x) = x^2 + x + 1$ over $GF(2)$. Then,

$$\mathbf{p}(\alpha) = \alpha^2 + \alpha + 1 = 0$$
$$\text{or} \quad \alpha^2 = \alpha + 1 \tag{2.33}$$

Equation (2.33) will be called the *characteristic equation* and will be a basis for the structure of the extension field. Multiplying by α on both sides of Equation (2.33) we get

$$\alpha^3 = \alpha \cdot \alpha^2 = \alpha(\alpha + 1) = \alpha^2 + \alpha = \alpha + 1 + \alpha = 1$$

Now we consider the set $\{\alpha, \alpha^2, \alpha^3 = 1\}$. This is a multiplicative cyclic group generated by α. We can now introduce another form for $GF(2^2) = \{0, 1, \alpha, \alpha^2\} = \{0, 1, \alpha, \alpha + 1\}$. The addition and multiplication tables for this structure are the same as in Table 2.3, if α replaces x and $\alpha^2 = \alpha + 1$ replaces $x + 1$.

2. Let α be a root of $\mathbf{p}(x) = x^2 + 2x + 2$ over $GF(3)$. Then $\mathbf{p}(\alpha) = \alpha^2 + 2\alpha + 2 = 0$, which means

$$\alpha^2 = \alpha + 1 \tag{2.34}$$

Equation (2.34) is the characteristic equation for the extension field. We can generate successive powers of α as follows.

$$\alpha^3 = \alpha \cdot \alpha^2 = \alpha(\alpha + 1) = \alpha^2 + \alpha = \alpha + 1 + \alpha = 2\alpha + 1$$
$$\alpha^4 = \alpha \cdot \alpha^3 = \alpha(2\alpha + 1) = 2\alpha^2 + \alpha = 2$$
$$\alpha^5 = \alpha \cdot \alpha^4 = \alpha \cdot 2 = 2\alpha$$
$$\alpha^6 = \alpha \cdot \alpha^5 = \alpha \cdot (2\alpha) = 2\alpha + 2$$
$$\alpha^7 = \alpha \cdot \alpha^6 = \alpha \cdot (2\alpha + 2) = 2\alpha^2 + 2\alpha = \alpha + 2$$
$$\alpha^8 = \alpha \cdot \alpha^7 = \alpha(\alpha + 2) = \alpha^2 + 2\alpha = 1$$

TABLE 2.4 POWERS OF α IN $GF(3^2)$

	α	1
$\alpha =$	1	0
$\alpha^2 =$	1	1
$\alpha^3 =$	2	1
$\alpha^4 =$	0	2
$\alpha^5 =$	2	0
$\alpha^6 =$	2	2
$\alpha^7 =$	1	2
$\alpha^8 =$	0	1

Thus $\{\alpha, \alpha^2, \alpha^3, \ldots, \alpha^7, \alpha^8 = 1\}$ is a multiplicative cyclic group and $\{0, \alpha, \alpha^2, \ldots, \alpha^8 = 1\}$ is another representation for $GF(3^2)$.

Sometimes it is useful to have the above equations in a tabular form as shown in Table 2.4.

Definition 2-7. Let α be a root of $\mathbf{p}(x)$, an irreducible polynomial of degree m over $GF(q)$. If α generates all the nonzero elements of $GF(q^m)$, then, as defined before, α is a *primitive element* of $GF(q^m)$, and $\mathbf{p}(x)$ is called a *primitive polynomial.* α is also called a *primitive root.*

By definition 2-7, and from Example 2-14, we have that both $x^2 + x + 1$ over $GF(2)$ and $x^2 + 2x + 2$ over $GF(3)$ are primitive polynomials. To obtain a better insight into these concepts, we may want to study irreducible polynomials that are not primitive.

Example 2-15

Consider the irreducible polynomial $\mathbf{p}(x) = x^2 + 1$ over $GF(3)$, and let α be its zero. Clearly, $\alpha \notin GF(3)$. We have $\mathbf{p}(\alpha) = \alpha^2 + 1 = 0$ and

$$\alpha^2 = 2$$

$$\alpha^3 = \alpha \cdot \alpha^2 = 2\alpha$$

$$\alpha^4 = \alpha \cdot (2\alpha) = 2\alpha^2 = 1$$

The cyclic group generated by α is $\{\alpha, \alpha^2, \alpha^3, \alpha^4 = 1\}$, and α has order 4. Since α does not generate all the nonzero elements $GF(3^2)$, it is not a primitive element in $GF(3^2)$. However, the set

$$\mathbf{S} = \{0, 1, 2, \alpha, \alpha + 1, \alpha + 2, 2\alpha, 2\alpha + 1, 2\alpha + 2\} \tag{2.35}$$

under addition and multiplication modulo $\alpha^2 + 1$ is a field. It has the same structure as $GF(3^2)$. It would be an interesting exercise for the student to find primitive elements in (2.35).

EXERCISES

2.1. Which of the properties of Abelian groups are satisfied by each of the following algebraic systems?

(a) $\{Z^+, +\}$ Z^+ is the set of positive integers
(b) $\{Z, *\}$ where $a * b = a + b + a \cdot b$
(c) $\{R, *\}$ R is Real field, $a * b = |a + b|$
(d) $\{Z, -\}$ Z is integers, $-$ is subtraction

2.2. Let $\{G, +\}$ be an Abelian group and let

$$G \times G = \{(a, b) | a, b \in G\}$$

with operation $*$ in $G \times G$ defined as follows

$$(a_1, a_2) * (b_1, b_2) = (a_1 + b_1, a_2 + b_2)$$

Prove whether $\{G \times G, *\}$ is or is not an Abelian group.

2.3. Give all subgroups of (a) Z_6, (b) $Z_2 \times Z_2$.

2.4. Pick a proper subgroup of each group in Exercise 2.3 and form its cosets to obtain a factor group. Find out their structures.

2.5. Find all primitive elements in $GF(7)$, $GF(4)$, and $GF(11)$.

2.6. Obtain all irreducible polynomials of degree 2 over $GF(3)$ and determine which of these are primitive.

2.7. Find all primitive polynomials of degree 2 over $GF(4)$.

2.8. For the polynomials below, find their factors, and give all zeros.

(a) $x^4 + x^3 + x^2 + 1$ over $GF(2)$
(b) $x^2 + 2x + 2$ over $GF(3)$
(c) $x^2 + ax + b$ over $GF(4)$

2.9. Reduce the matrices below to a systematic form.

(a) $\mathbf{G}_1 = \begin{bmatrix} 1 & 1 & 0 & 1 & 1 & 1 \\ 0 & 1 & 1 & 1 & 0 & 1 \\ 1 & 1 & 0 & 0 & 1 & 0 \end{bmatrix}$ over $GF(2)$

(b) $\mathbf{G}_2 = \begin{bmatrix} a & 1 & b & 0 & 1 \\ b & 0 & 1 & a & b \\ 0 & b & a & 1 & 0 \end{bmatrix}$ over $GF(4)$

2.10. Let $\mathbf{S}_1$ and $\mathbf{S}_2$ be subspaces of a vector space $\mathbf{V}$. Prove whether $\mathbf{S}_1 \cap \mathbf{S}_2$ and $\mathbf{S}_1 \cup \mathbf{S}_2$ are or are not subspaces of $\mathbf{V}$ ($\cap$ and $\cup$ are intersection and union, respectively).

2.11. Let $\mathbf{S}$ be a subset of $\mathbf{V}_n$, the vector space of all n-tuples over $GF(2)$. Prove that $\mathbf{S}$ is a subspace of $\mathbf{V}_n$ if for all $\mathbf{u}, \mathbf{v} \in S$, $\mathbf{u} + \mathbf{v} \in \mathbf{S}$.

REFERENCES

[BIRK 70] G. Birkhoff and T. C. Bartee. *Modern Applied Algebra*. New York: McGraw-Hill, 1970.

[GARN 59] H. L. Garner. "The Residue Number System." *IRE Transactions on Elec. Comput.* (September 1959): 140–47.

[JACO 51] N. Jacobson. *Lectures in Abstract Algebra*, New York: Van Nostrand, 1951.

[JOHN 66] R. E. Johnson. *University Algebra*. Englewood Cliffs, N.J.: Prentice-Hall, 1966.

[LEVE 56] W. J. LeVeque. *Topics in Number Theory*. Vol. 1. Reading, Mass.: Addison-Wesley, 1956.

[PETE 72] W. W. Peterson and E. J. Weldon, Jr. *Error Correcting Codes*, 2d. ed. Cambridge: MIT Press, 1972.

[RAO 74] T. R. N. Rao. *Error Coding for Arithmetic Processors*. New York: Academic Press, 1974.

[SZAB 67] N. S. Szabo and R. I. Tanaka. *Residue Arithmetic and its Application to Computer Technology*. New York: McGraw-Hill, 1967.

[VINO 54] I. M. Vinogradov. *Elements of Number Theory*. New York: Dover, 1954.

3

Linear Codes

Linear block codes are the subject of this chapter. The codes are *linear* in the sense that if u and v are two codewords, $u + v$ is also a codeword. Each codeword in a *block code* has n symbols from $GF(q)$, where n is called the *block length* (or *code length*). Another class of codes are tree codes [PETE 72, LIN 83], which are not studied in this book. We study only block codes, and therefore we use linear codes to refer to linear block codes. In Section 3.1, we study linear (block) codes as a vector space, and subspaces over $GF(q)$. These are described by *generator* and *parity matrices*. In Section 3.2, these codes are studied as *polynomial codes* and as *cyclic codes*. The cyclic codes are efficiently implemented by *linear feedback shift register* (LFSR) logic and several classes of cyclic codes; namely, *BCH codes*, *RS codes*, and *Fire codes* are introduced. In the final section, we present some introductory material on arithmetic codes. This chapter contains only introductory material on various classes of linear codes; for a comprehensive treatment, the reader is advised to refer to standard texts on coding theory [PETE 72, RAO 74, LIN 83, BLAH 83].

Most codes for computer systems are over $GF(2)$ and $GF(2^b)$; and these will receive our attention. However, to illustrate the theory and for better understanding, we also give several examples of codes over $GF(3)$ and $GF(4)$.

3.1 LINEAR CODES AS VECTOR SPACES

We start here with the vector space $\mathbf{V}_n$ of all n-tuples over $GF(q)$, that is,

$$\mathbf{V}_n = \{(a_0, a_1, \ldots, a_{n-1}) | a_i \in GF(q)\} \tag{3.1}$$

We define linear codes as follows.

Definition 3-1. A subset $\mathbf{C}$ of $\mathbf{V}_n$ is a *linear code* if and only if it is a subspace.

Since $\mathbf{C}$ is a subspace, we can conveniently represent all the code vectors (codewords) of $\mathbf{C}$ as the row space of a $(k \times n)$ matrix $\mathbf{G}$, called the generator matrix or $\mathbf{G}$ matrix of $\mathbf{C}$.

$$\mathbf{G} = \begin{bmatrix} g_{00} & g_{01} & \cdots & g_{0,n-1} \\ g_{10} & g_{11} & \cdots & g_{1,n-1} \\ \vdots & \vdots & & \vdots \\ g_{k-1,0} & g_{k-1,1} & \cdots & g_{k-1,n-1} \end{bmatrix} = \begin{bmatrix} \mathbf{g}_0 \\ \mathbf{g}_1 \\ \vdots \\ \mathbf{g}_{k-1} \end{bmatrix} \tag{3.2}$$

The row vectors $\mathbf{g}_0, \mathbf{g}_1, \ldots, \mathbf{g}_{k-1}$ span the code space $\mathbf{C}$. Also, if the row vectors of $\mathbf{G}$ are linearly independent (LI), then $\mathbf{C}$ has dimension (or rank) k. As a convention we adopt here, the rows of $\mathbf{G}$ matrix are linearly independent. Therefore, $\mathbf{C}$ has exactly q^k codewords in it, and $\mathbf{C}$ is denoted as an (n, k) code.

Example Set 3-1

1. Let $\mathbf{G}$ matrix of a (5, 3) linear code $\mathbf{C}_1$ be given as follows.

$$\mathbf{G}_1 = \begin{bmatrix} 1 & 0 & 1 & 1 & 0 \\ 1 & 1 & 0 & 1 & 1 \\ 0 & 1 & 0 & 1 & 0 \end{bmatrix} \qquad \text{over } GF(2)$$

Then $\mathbf{C}_1$ consists of all vectors in the row space of $\mathbf{G}_1$. The row vectors of $\mathbf{G}$ are linearly independent, and the number of codewords are $q^k = 2^3 = 8$. The codewords of $\mathbf{C}_1$ are

$$\{00000, 10110, 11011, 01010, 01101, 11100, 10001, 00111\}.$$

2. Consider the following $\mathbf{G}$ matrix of a (4, 2) linear code $\mathbf{C}_2$ over $GF(3)$.

$$\mathbf{G} = \begin{bmatrix} 1 & 0 & 2 & 1 \\ 1 & 2 & 0 & 2 \end{bmatrix} = \begin{bmatrix} \mathbf{g}_0 \\ \mathbf{g}_1 \end{bmatrix} \qquad \text{over } GF(3)$$

The code $\mathbf{C}_2$ is the row space of $\mathbf{G}$ and has the $3^2 = 9$ linear combinations of $\mathbf{g}_0$ and $\mathbf{g}_1$ as shown in Table 3.1.

These code examples $\mathbf{C}_1$ and $\mathbf{C}_2$ will be used throughout this section. The error control properties of a linear code are based on the concept of *Hamming weight* and *Hamming distance*, which were defined in Chapter 1. The Hamming weight of a vector $\mathbf{v}$, denoted $w(\mathbf{v})$, is the number of nonzero symbols in $\mathbf{v}$. The Hamming distance between vectors $\mathbf{v}$ and $\mathbf{u}$, denoted $d(\mathbf{v}, \mathbf{u})$, is given by the number of positions in which $\mathbf{v}$ and $\mathbf{u}$ differ. Also, $d(\mathbf{v}, \mathbf{u}) = w(\mathbf{v} - \mathbf{u})$. For code $\mathbf{C}_2$ (of Example set 3-1), the Hamming weight of any nonzero codeword is at least 3. Also, since $\mathbf{C}_2$ is a subspace, the difference $\mathbf{v}_i - \mathbf{v}_j$ of two codewords is also a codeword, the Hamming distance between two codewords is the Hamming weight of another codeword. The *minimum distance* (also $d_{\min}$ and *distance*) of a code $\mathbf{C}$ is the

TABLE 3.1 CODEWORDS FOR THE (4, 2) CODE OVER *GF*(3)

$\mathbf{v}_0 = \mathbf{0}$	$= 0000$
$\mathbf{v}_1 = \mathbf{g}_0$	$= 1021$
$\mathbf{v}_2 = 2\mathbf{g}_0$	$= 2012$
$\mathbf{v}_3 = \mathbf{g}_1$	$= 1202$
$\mathbf{v}_4 = 2\mathbf{g}_1$	$= 2101$
$\mathbf{v}_5 = \mathbf{g}_0 + \mathbf{g}_1$	$= 2220$
$\mathbf{v}_6 = 2\mathbf{g}_0 + \mathbf{g}_1$	$= 0211$
$\mathbf{v}_7 = \mathbf{g}_0 + 2\mathbf{g}_1$	$= 0122$
$\mathbf{v}_8 = 2\mathbf{g}_0 + 2\mathbf{g}_1$	$= 1110$

minimum of distances between all distinct pairs of codewords. The distance of a linear code therefore is also the minimum weight of (nonzero) codewords. As a convention we adopt that *distance* of a code to mean its minimum distance and minimum weight.

The parity matrix (or H matrix). Previously, a linear code **C** was defined as the row space of its **G** matrix. Alternately, **C** can be defined as the null space of a matrix

$$\mathbf{H} = \begin{bmatrix} \mathbf{h}_0 \\ \mathbf{h}_1 \\ \vdots \\ \mathbf{h}_{r-1} \end{bmatrix} = \begin{bmatrix} h_{00} & h_{01} & \cdots & h_{0,n-1} \\ h_{10} & h_{11} & \cdots & h_{1,n-1} \\ \vdots & \vdots & & \vdots \\ h_{r-1,0} & h_{r-1,1} & \cdots & h_{r-1,n-1} \end{bmatrix} \tag{3.3}$$

H is called the *parity matrix* and also the **H** matrix of the code. By convention again, the r vectors of **H** are linearly independent, and thus **H** has a rank r and its null space (Theorem 2-6) has dimension $n - k$. Since we adopt k as the dimension of **C**, we have the row rank r of **H** matrix of an (n, k) code to satisfy

$$r = n - k \tag{3.4}$$

By definition, we have that any n-tuple is a codeword in **C** if and only if it is in the null space of its **H** matrix. This means that for any $\mathbf{u} \in \mathbf{C}$

$$\mathbf{u} \cdot \mathbf{H}^T = \mathbf{0} \tag{3.5}$$

Equation (3.5) follows from the theory of vector spaces given in Section 2.2 and specifically from Equation (2.5).

Example 3-2

For the **G** matrices (of Example set 3-1), we can obtain their **H** matrices.

$$\mathbf{G}_1 = \begin{bmatrix} 1 & 0 & 1 & 1 & 0 \\ 1 & 1 & 0 & 1 & 1 \\ 0 & 1 & 0 & 1 & 0 \end{bmatrix} \quad \text{over } GF(2)$$

By canonical reduction we can put $\mathbf{G}_1$ in its systematic form as

$$\mathbf{G} = \begin{bmatrix} 1 & 0 & 0 & 0 & 1 \\ 0 & 1 & 0 & 1 & 0 \\ 0 & 0 & 1 & 1 & 1 \end{bmatrix} = [\mathbf{I}_3 \quad \mathbf{P}]$$

From Theorem 2-6, the corresponding $\mathbf{H}$ matrix satisfying (3.5) is given by

$$\mathbf{H} = \begin{bmatrix} -\mathbf{P}^T & \mathbf{I}_2 \end{bmatrix} = \begin{bmatrix} 0 & 1 & 1 & 1 & 0 \\ 1 & 0 & 1 & 0 & 1 \end{bmatrix}$$

$\mathbf{H}$ is the parity matrix of $\mathbf{C}_1$. For code $\mathbf{C}_2$ (Example set 3-1) given by its $\mathbf{G}$ matrix,

$$\mathbf{G}_2 = \begin{bmatrix} 1 & 0 & 2 & 1 \\ 1 & 2 & 0 & 2 \end{bmatrix} \quad \text{over } GF(3)$$

its systematic form is given as

$$\mathbf{G} = \begin{bmatrix} 1 & 0 & 2 & 1 \\ 0 & 1 & 2 & 2 \end{bmatrix} = [\mathbf{I}_2 \quad \mathbf{P}]$$

Therefore, the $\mathbf{H}$ matrix of $\mathbf{C}_2$ is given by

$$\mathbf{H} = \begin{bmatrix} -\mathbf{P}^T & \mathbf{I}_2 \end{bmatrix} = \begin{bmatrix} 1 & 1 & 1 & 0 \\ 2 & 1 & 0 & 1 \end{bmatrix}$$

The student is advised to verify that each row of $\mathbf{G}$ is orthogonal to each row of $\mathbf{H}$. That is, $g_i h_j = 0$ for all i, j in these examples.

Dual codes. The null space of a linear code $\mathbf{C}$ is the row space of its $\mathbf{H}$ matrix. The null space of $\mathbf{C}$ is also a subspace and is of dimension $n - k$; therefore, by definition it is an $(n, n - k)$ linear code. Thus, for every linear code $\mathbf{C}$, its null space $\mathbf{C}'$ is called the *dual code* of $\mathbf{C}$. For code $\mathbf{C}'$, its dual code is $\mathbf{C}$. The codes $\mathbf{C}$ and $\mathbf{C}'$ are also called dual codes.

3.1.1 Encoding and Decoding Logic

Consider a data (or message) of k symbols $(d_0, d_1, \ldots, d_{k-1})$. Let $\mathbf{C}$ be an (n, k) linear code over $GF(q)$. The codeword in $\mathbf{C}$ for $(d_0, \ldots, d_{k-1})$ will be an n-tuple $\mathbf{u} = (u_0, u_1, \ldots, u_{n-1})$.

Definition 3-2. If the data symbols $d_0, d_1, \ldots, d_{k-1}$ of every message $\mathbf{d}$ are unchanged and appear in its codeword $\mathbf{u} = (u_0, \ldots, u_{n-1})$, then the code is said to be a *systematic code*.

Consider, for instance, a **G** matrix for **C** in a systematic form.

$$\mathbf{G} = \begin{bmatrix} 1 & 0 & 0 & \cdots & 0 & p_{0,0} & p_{0,1} & \cdots & p_{0,n-k-1} \\ 0 & 1 & 0 & \cdots & 0 & p_{1,0} & p_{1,1} & \cdots & p_{1,n-k-1} \\ & \vdots & & & \vdots & \vdots & \vdots & & \vdots \\ 0 & 0 & 0 & \cdots & 1 & p_{k-1,0} & p_{k-1,1} & \cdots & p_{k-1,n-k-1} \end{bmatrix} = [\mathbf{I}_k \quad \mathbf{P}] \tag{3.6}$$

Then, to encode a data $\mathbf{d} = (d_0, \ldots, d_{k-1})$ is to obtain its codeword **u**,

$$\mathbf{u} = \mathbf{d} \cdot \mathbf{G} = (d_0, \ldots, d_{k-1})[\mathbf{I}_k \quad \mathbf{P}] = (\underbrace{d_0, \ldots, d_{k-1}}_{\text{Data symbols}}, \underbrace{p_k, \ldots, p_{n-1}}_{\text{Parity symbols}})$$

where the parities are given by the following.

$$\begin{aligned} p_k &= d_0 p_{0,0} + d_1 p_{1,0} \cdots d_{k-1} p_{k-1,0} \\ p_{k+1} &= d_0 p_{0,1} + d_1 p_{1,1} \cdots d_{k-1} p_{k-1,1} \\ &\vdots \\ p_{n-1} &= d_0 p_{0,n-k-1} + d_1 p_{1,n-k-1} \cdots d_{k-1} p_{k-1,n-k-1} \end{aligned} \tag{3.7}$$

Thus, the codeword **u** for data **d** consists of data followed by the $n - k$ parity symbols, $p_k, \ldots, p_{n-1}$. The equation set of (3.7) is called *encoding* or *parity generation* equations. Fig. 3.1 shows the logic for generating parities for data $(d_0, d_1, \ldots, d_{k-1})$ to obtain a systematic codeword.

If **G** is not in a systematic form, then $\mathbf{u} = \mathbf{dG}$ will be such that the data symbols are not identifiable in **C** (but are diffused in **u**). The code **C** is then *nonsystematic*. It is often very important in computer systems that the codewords are in systematic form for speed, cost, and convenience in decoding and processing data.

Example 3-3

Let **C** be a (4, 2) code over $GF(3)$ and $\mathbf{G}_1$ and $\mathbf{G}_2$ be **G** matrices in systematic and nonsystematic forms, respectively, given as follows ($\mathbf{G}_1$ and $\mathbf{G}_2$ have the same row space).

$$\mathbf{G}_1 = \begin{bmatrix} 1 & 0 & 2 & 1 \\ 0 & 1 & 2 & 2 \end{bmatrix}, \qquad \mathbf{G}_2 = \begin{bmatrix} 1 & 0 & 2 & 1 \\ 1 & 2 & 0 & 2 \end{bmatrix}$$

The data and corresponding codewords are given in Table 3.2.

Fig. 3.2 is a parallel systematic encoder circuit using $\mathbf{G}_1$ for this code. In this circuit, the rectangular boxes, →□→ , are cells to store ternary data and parity symbols. The circular element, →ⓐ→, represents multiplier by the scalar a in $GF(3)$. The ⇉⊕→ represents adder modulo 3 of the inputs. These same symbols are used for all $GF(q)$.

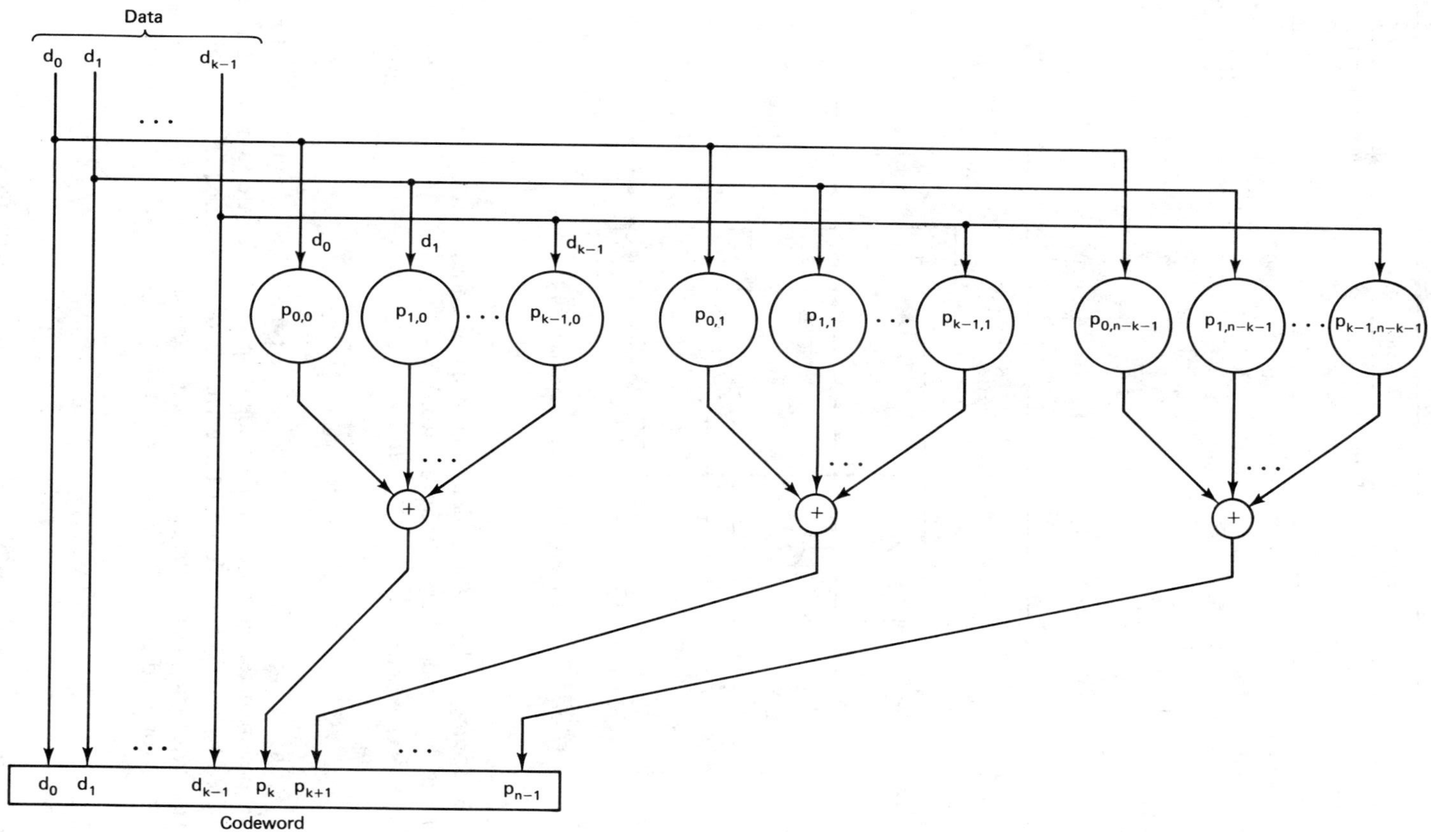

Figure 3.1 Parallel systematic encoder for (n, k) systematic code.

TABLE 3.2 SYSTEMATIC AND NONSYSTEMATIC CODE FORMS

Data		Codewords of **C**							
		Systematic Form				Nonsystematic Form			
d_0	d_1	u_0	u_1	u_2	u_3	u_0	u_1	u_2	u_3
0	0	0	0	0	0	0	0	0	0
1	0	1	0	2	1	1	0	2	1
2	0	2	0	1	2	2	0	1	2
0	1	0	1	2	2	1	2	0	2
0	2	0	2	1	1	2	1	0	1
1	1	1	1	1	0	2	2	2	0
2	1	2	1	0	1	0	2	1	1
1	2	1	2	0	2	0	1	2	2
2	2	2	2	2	0	1	1	1	0

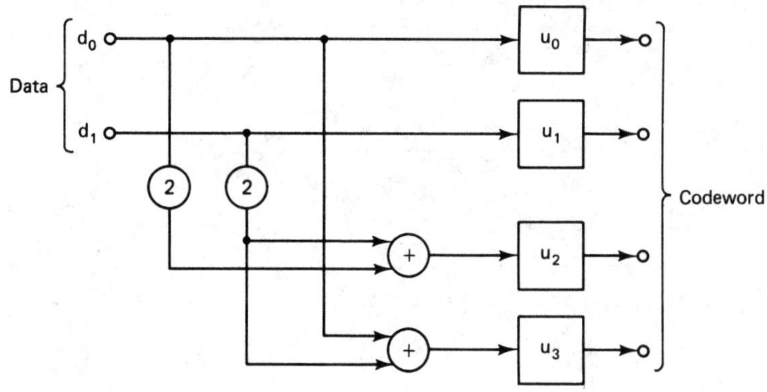

Figure 3.2 A parallel systematic encoder circuit for (4, 2) code over $GF(3)$.

Decoding. The parallel decoding of linear codes is usually based on the **H** matrix of the code. For a received word $\mathbf{v} = (v_0, v_1, \ldots, v_{n-1})$, we define its *syndrome* $\mathbf{s}(\mathbf{v}) = (s_0, s_1, \ldots, s_{n-k})$, given by

$$\mathbf{s}(\mathbf{v}) = \mathbf{v} \cdot \mathbf{H}^T \tag{3.8}$$

If $\mathbf{s} = \mathbf{0}$, then $\mathbf{v}$ is a codeword and it is assumed that there are no errors. If $\mathbf{s} \neq \mathbf{0}$, then errors are detected. Based on the code properties, the detection and correction is handled by the decoder. Also, if the correct codeword stored (or transmitted) is $\mathbf{u} = (u_0, u_1, \ldots, u_{n-1})$, and the corresponding received word is $\mathbf{v} = (v_0, v_1, \ldots, v_{n-1})$, then the error word is $e = (e_0, e_1, \ldots, e_{n-1})$ such that

$$\mathbf{v} = \mathbf{u} + \mathbf{e}$$

and

$$\mathbf{e} = \mathbf{v} - \mathbf{u} = (e_0, e_1, \ldots, e_{n-1}), \quad e_i = v_i - u_i \quad \text{for } i = 0, 1, \ldots, n-1. \tag{3.9}$$

Then we have

$$\mathbf{s(v)} = \mathbf{v} \cdot \mathbf{H}^T = \mathbf{u} \cdot \mathbf{H}^T + \mathbf{e} \cdot \mathbf{H}^T = \mathbf{0} + \mathbf{e} \cdot \mathbf{H}^T = \mathbf{e} \cdot \mathbf{H}^T = \mathbf{s(e)}. \qquad (3.10)$$

To generate the syndrome of a received word, one needs to apply the parity equations defined by the **H** matrix. Therefore, we consider the **H** matrix corresponding to the **G** matrix given in (3.6) as follows.

$$\mathbf{H} = \begin{bmatrix} -p_{0,0} & -p_{1,0} & \cdots & -p_{k-1,1} & 1 & 0 & 0 & \cdots & 0 \\ -p_{0,1} & -p_{1,1} & \cdots & -p_{k-1,2} & 0 & 1 & 0 & \cdots & 0 \\ \vdots & \vdots & & \vdots & & \vdots & & & \vdots \\ -p_{0,n-k-1} & -p_{1,n-k-1} & \cdots & -p_{k-1,n-k-1} & 0 & 0 & 0 & \cdots & 1 \end{bmatrix} \qquad (3.11)$$

Also, $\mathbf{H} = (\mathbf{h}_0, \mathbf{h}_1, \ldots, \mathbf{h}_{n-1})$, where $\mathbf{h}_i$ is the ith column vector of **H** in (3.11). For a received vector $\mathbf{v} = (v_0, v_1, \ldots, v_{n-1})$, its syndrome is

$$\mathbf{s(v)} = \mathbf{v} \cdot \mathbf{H}^T = (v_0, v_1, \ldots, v_{n-1}) \begin{bmatrix} \mathbf{h}_0 \\ \mathbf{h}_1 \\ \vdots \\ \mathbf{h}_{n-1} \end{bmatrix} = (v_0\mathbf{h}_0 + v_1\mathbf{h}_1 + \cdots + v_{n-1}\mathbf{h}_{n-1})$$

From Equation (3.10) we have $\mathbf{v} \cdot \mathbf{H}^T = \mathbf{e} \cdot \mathbf{H}^T$, and

$$\mathbf{s(v)} = \mathbf{s(e)} = e_0\mathbf{h}_0 + e_1\mathbf{h}_1 + \cdots + e_{n-1}\mathbf{h}_{n-1} \qquad (3.12)$$

Thus, the syndrome of **v** is a linear combination of column vectors $\{\mathbf{h}_0, \mathbf{h}_1, \ldots, \mathbf{h}_{n-1}\}$. Equation (3.12) is used in decoding (and correcting errors).

Example Set 3-4

1. For a codeword $\mathbf{u} = 11011$ in $\mathbf{C}_1$ of Example 3-2, consider an error in position 4. That is, $\mathbf{e} = (00010)$, and the corresponding received word is

$$\mathbf{v} = \mathbf{u} + \mathbf{e} = (11001).$$

The **H** matrix of $\mathbf{C}_1$ is

$$\mathbf{H} = \begin{bmatrix} 0 & 1 & 1 & 1 & 0 \\ 1 & 0 & 1 & 0 & 1 \end{bmatrix} = (\mathbf{h}_0, \mathbf{h}_1, \ldots, \mathbf{h}_4)$$

where $\mathbf{h}_i$ (for $i = 0, 1, \ldots, 4$) are column vectors of **H**. The syndrome is

$$\mathbf{s(v)} = \mathbf{v} \cdot \mathbf{H}^T = (11001) \begin{bmatrix} \mathbf{h}_0 \\ \mathbf{h}_1 \\ \vdots \\ \mathbf{h}_4 \end{bmatrix} = \mathbf{h}_0 + \mathbf{h}_1 + \mathbf{h}_4 = (1,0)$$

$$\mathbf{e} \cdot \mathbf{H}^T = (00010) \cdot \mathbf{H}^T = \mathbf{h}_3 = (1,0)$$

2. For code $\mathbf{C}_2$, the **H** matrix is given as

$$\mathbf{H} = \begin{bmatrix} 1 & 1 & 1 & 0 \\ 2 & 1 & 0 & 1 \end{bmatrix} \qquad \text{over } GF(3)$$

If $\mathbf{v} = (0101)$ is received, its syndrome is $\mathbf{v} \cdot \mathbf{H}^T = (0101) \cdot \mathbf{H}^T = (1,1) + (0,1) = (1,2)$. This syndrome is the same as for the single error $\mathbf{e} = (1000)$, since $\mathbf{e} \cdot \mathbf{H}^T = (1000) \cdot \mathbf{H}^T = (1,2)$.

3.1.2 Distance and Error Control

The distance of a linear code can be determined by obtaining all nonzero codewords and finding their minimum weight. Since there are q^k codewords, this method obviously could be very tedious. There is a simpler way to determine the distance from its $\mathbf{H}$ matrix, particularly if the distance is small. This method is based on the following.

Theorem 3-1. *For any codeword* $\mathbf{u}$ *of weight* d *in a linear code* $\mathbf{C}$, d *columns of its* $\mathbf{H}$ *matrix are linearly dependent.*

Proof. Let $\mathbf{u} = (u_0, u_1, \ldots, u_{n-1}) \in \mathbf{C}$ and $w(\mathbf{u}) = d$. That means some d symbols of $\mathbf{u}$ are nonzero and the other $n - d$ symbols are 0's. Since $\mathbf{u}$ is a codeword, $\mathbf{u} \cdot \mathbf{H}^T = 0$ and

$$\begin{aligned} \mathbf{u} \cdot \mathbf{H}^T &= (u_0, u_1, \ldots, u_{n-1}) \cdot (\mathbf{h}_0, \mathbf{h}_1, \ldots, \mathbf{h}_{n-1}) \\ &= u_0\mathbf{h}_0 + u_1\mathbf{h}_1 + \cdots + u_{n-1}\mathbf{h}_{n-1} = 0 \end{aligned} \tag{3.13}$$

where $\mathbf{h}_i$ is the ith column vector of $\mathbf{H}$. Since only d of the u_i are nonzero in (3.13), d-column vectors of $\mathbf{H}$ are linearly dependent. Q.E.D.

Theorem 3-2. *A linear code* $\mathbf{C}$ *has distance at least* d *if and only if every* $d - 1$ *or fewer column vectors of its* $\mathbf{H}$ *matrix are linearly independent.*

Proof. The proof is simple and follows from Theorem 3-1. First, we note that the distance of the code is also its minimum weight and that $\mathbf{h}_i \neq 0$ for all i. The minimum weight is d if and only if no $d - 1$ or fewer columns of $\mathbf{H}$ are linearly dependent. Q.E.D.

Theorem 3-2 is very important not only in determining the distance of a code but also in constructing codes of distance d. To illustrate this, we go back to the $\mathbf{H}$ matrix of $\mathbf{C}_2$.

Example 3-5

Consider

$$\mathbf{H} = \begin{bmatrix} 1 & 1 & 1 & 0 \\ 2 & 1 & 0 & 1 \end{bmatrix} = [\mathbf{h}_0, \mathbf{h}_1, \mathbf{h}_2, \mathbf{h}_3] \qquad \text{of code } \mathbf{C}_2$$

First, we note $\mathbf{h}_i \neq 0$ for all i. If $\mathbf{v}$ is of weight 1, then $\mathbf{v} \cdot \mathbf{H}^T = v_i\mathbf{h}_i$ for some i, and it is nonzero. Therefore, $\mathbf{v}$ is not a codeword. Consider $\mathbf{v} = (1020)$ of weight 2 (i.e., $w(\mathbf{v}) = 2$). Then, $\mathbf{v} \cdot \mathbf{H}^T = (1,2) + 2(1,0) = (0,2) \neq (0,0)$. Therefore, $\mathbf{v}$ is not a codeword. If two columns $\mathbf{h}_i, \mathbf{h}_j$ are linearly dependent, then $\mathbf{h}_i$ is a multiple of $\mathbf{h}_j$; that is not the case in this $\mathbf{H}$ matrix. Therefore, there cannot be a codeword of weight 2. If $\mathbf{v} = (1110)$, then $\mathbf{v} \cdot \mathbf{H}^T = \mathbf{h}_0 + \mathbf{h}_1 + \mathbf{h}_2 = (0,0)$ and $\mathbf{v}$ is a codeword. The first three columns of $\mathbf{H}$ are linearly dependent. Therefore, we conclude that the distance of the code is 3. The important result of this exercise is that for a distance-3 code $\mathbf{C}$, its $\mathbf{H}$ matrix is such that none of its columns is a multiple of another column. This gives us a method of deriving distance-3 codes in a constructive manner.

Example Set 3-6

1. To construct a distance-3 code over $GF(2)$, we can start its $\mathbf{H}$ matrix to have all distinct columns. If $n - k = r = 4$, we can get

$$\mathbf{H}_3 = \begin{bmatrix} 0 & 0 & 0 & 0 & 0 & 0 & 0 & 1 & 1 & 1 & 1 & 1 & 1 & 1 & 1 \\ 0 & 0 & 0 & 1 & 1 & 1 & 1 & 0 & 0 & 0 & 0 & 1 & 1 & 1 & 1 \\ 0 & 1 & 1 & 0 & 0 & 1 & 1 & 0 & 0 & 1 & 1 & 0 & 0 & 1 & 1 \\ 1 & 0 & 1 & 0 & 1 & 0 & 1 & 0 & 1 & 0 & 1 & 0 & 1 & 0 & 1 \end{bmatrix} \tag{3.14}$$

For this $\mathbf{H}$ matrix, no two columns are the same, and hence the distance is at least 3. In fact, it is easy to check that there are three columns that add to 0. Therefore, the distance is 3. This is a $(15,11)$ distance-3 code.

We adopt herein the notation (n, k, d) for linear codes, where d is the distance of the code; n and k are as before. The $\mathbf{H}$ matrix of (3.14) is for a $(15,11,3)$ code. We denote this code as $\mathbf{C}_3$ for future reference.

2. We construct the $\mathbf{H}$ matrix of a distance-3 code over $GF(3)$ with $r = 3$ parity symbols. Each following column must be not only distinct, but also it must not be a multiple of the previous ones. This can be easily accomplished by selecting a column distinct from the previous ones with a leading element 1. This code is a $(13,10,3)$ code over $GF(3)$ and will be denoted as $\mathbf{C}_4$.

$$\mathbf{H}_4 = \begin{bmatrix} 0 & 0 & 0 & 0 & 1 & 1 & 1 & 1 & 1 & 1 & 1 & 1 & 1 \\ 0 & 1 & 1 & 1 & 0 & 0 & 0 & 1 & 1 & 1 & 2 & 2 & 2 \\ 1 & 0 & 1 & 2 & 0 & 1 & 2 & 0 & 1 & 2 & 0 & 1 & 2 \end{bmatrix} \quad \text{over } GF(3) \tag{3.15}$$

3. As another example, an $(n, k, 3)$ code over $GF(4)$ with $r = 2$ check symbols is given by the matrix

$$\mathbf{H}_5 = \begin{bmatrix} 0 & 1 & 1 & 1 & 1 \\ 1 & 0 & 1 & a & b \end{bmatrix} \quad \text{over } GF(4) \tag{3.16}$$

This code will be denoted as $\mathbf{C}_5$ for future reference.

These examples show how distance-3 codes can be constructed over any $GF(q)$. The maximum number of columns (r-tuples) that we can obtain with r parity symbols in a distance-3 $\mathbf{H}$ matrix is called the $n_{\max}$ and is given by

$$n_{\max} = \frac{q^r - 1}{q - 1} \tag{3.17}$$

The codes $\mathbf{C}_3$, $\mathbf{C}_4$, and $\mathbf{C}_5$ of Example Set 3-6 satisfy (3.17). The next step would be to show that these codes correct all single errors. First, we characterize the set of single-error vectors as

$$\mathbf{E}_1 = \{\mathbf{e} \in \mathbf{V}_n | w(\mathbf{e}) = 1\} \tag{3.18}$$

The subscript 1 denotes the weight of error vectors. For example, in code $\mathbf{C}_5$, which is a (5, 3, 3) code over $GF(4)$, the set $\mathbf{E}_1$ consists of

$$\mathbf{E}_1 = \left\{ \left| \begin{pmatrix} \alpha & 0 & 0 & 0 & 0 \\ 0 & \alpha & 0 & 0 & 0 \\ 0 & 0 & \alpha & 0 & 0 \\ 0 & 0 & 0 & \alpha & 0 \\ 0 & 0 & 0 & 0 & \alpha \end{pmatrix} \right| \text{for any nonzero } \alpha \in GF(4) \right\}$$

Since there are three nonzero values for α in $GF(4)$, there are exactly $5 \times 3 = 15$ single-error vectors (or errors) in this code. For the code $\mathbf{C}_3$, which is (15, 11, 3) code over $GF(2)$, the error set $\mathbf{E}_1$ consists of vectors of the form

$$\mathbf{e}_i = (00 \cdots \underset{\substack{\uparrow \\ i\text{th position}}}{0}\!\!10 \cdots 0) \quad \text{for } i = 0, 1, \ldots, 14$$

After this characterization of set $\mathbf{E}_1$, our next step will be to show that for a distance-3 code, there is a unique syndrome for each error vector in $\mathbf{E}_1$. Then, any single error can be determined from the syndrome, and a correction can be made. For code $\mathbf{C}_3$, given by the $\mathbf{H}$ matrix in (3.14), and from Equation (3.10), the syndrome is

$$\mathbf{s}(\mathbf{e}_i) = \mathbf{e}_i \cdot \mathbf{H}^T = \mathbf{h}_i$$

TABLE 3.3 SYNDROME-ERROR TABLE FOR (5, 3) CODE OVER *GF*(4)

Error $\in \mathbf{E}_1$					Syndrome	
1	0	0	0	0	0	1
a	0	0	0	0	0	*a*
b	0	0	0	0	0	*b*
0	1	0	0	0	1	0
0	*a*	0	0	0	*a*	0
0	*b*	0	0	0	*b*	0
0	0	1	0	0	1	1
0	0	*a*	0	0	*a*	*a*
0	0	*b*	0	0	*b*	*b*
0	0	0	1	0	1	*a*
0	0	0	*a*	0	*a*	*b*
0	0	0	*b*	0	*b*	1
0	0	0	0	1	1	*b*
0	0	0	0	*a*	*a*	1
0	0	0	0	*b*	*b*	*a*

The column vector $\mathbf{h}_i$ in (3.14) has value i as a binary number. A simple (4×16) decoder will identify the error position i. This decoder is illustrated in Fig. 3.3 on page 63 as a Hamming (15, 11, 3) code decoder.

As a further illustration of single-error correction (or decoding), we consider the code $\mathbf{C}_5$, which is a (5, 3, 3) code over $GF(4)$. Here, the errors and their corresponding syndrome are given in Table 3.3.

In Table 3.3, there are 15 single errors in $\mathbf{C}_5$, and there are also exactly 15 nonzero syndromes possible (for $r = 2$ and $q = 4$). There is a perfect one-to-one match of errors in $\mathbf{E}_1$ and the nonzero syndromes of the code. This is an example of a *perfect* code, which will be defined in a later section.

3.1.3 Standard Array Decoding

Array decoding was introduced in Chapter 1 with a few examples. Here we study the principles that apply to linear codes under the heading of *Standard Array Decoding*.

Let $\mathbf{C}$ be an (n, k) linear code over $GF(q)$, $\mathbf{u}_0$ denote the $\mathbf{0}$ code vector, and $\mathbf{u}_1, \mathbf{u}_2, \ldots$ be the other code vectors in $\mathbf{C}$. There are q^k code vectors in $\mathbf{C}$. A standard array for decoding can be formed as follows.

The first row consists of all code vectors with $\mathbf{u}_0$ as the first element. In the second row we start with a noncode vector, say $\mathbf{z}_1$, of the smallest possible weight and form a coset with respect to $\mathbf{C}$. That is, we can rightfully call this a coset because $\mathbf{C}$ is, after all, a subgroup of $\mathbf{V}_n$. If $\mathbf{C}$ is a distance d code $d \geq 2$, then there is no code vector of weight 1, and therefore any vector of weight 1 can be a leader for the second row. Similarly, a second vector $\mathbf{z}_2$ of smallest possible weight, and one that has not appeared in the foregoing cosets, is used as the leader for the third row and so on until all vectors in $\mathbf{V}_n$ are exhausted (see Table 3.4).

The standard array thus formed will have all its coset leaders of the smallest possible weight. Also, the coset leaders will be the most possible words received when $\mathbf{0}$ codeword is transmitted.

The theory of factor groups tells us that every vector $\mathbf{v} \in \mathbf{V}_n$ appears in some coset and exactly once only in the array. Therefore, the number of cosets is $l = q^n/q^k = q^{n-k} = q^r$. Based on the theory of standard arrays, the decoding will identify any received vector $\mathbf{v} = \mathbf{u}_i + \mathbf{z}_j$ to its coset leader $\mathbf{z}_j$ as the most likely error or to the column header $(\mathbf{u}_i)$ that is the most likely transmitted code vector [PETE 72].

TABLE 3.4 STANDARD ARRAY FOR LINEAR CODES

$\mathbf{u}_0 = 0$	$\mathbf{u}_1$	$\mathbf{u}_2$	$\cdots$	$\mathbf{u}_i$	$\cdots$	$\mathbf{u}_{q^k-1}$
$\mathbf{z}_1$	$\mathbf{u}_1 + \mathbf{z}_1$	$\mathbf{u}_2 + \mathbf{z}_1$	$\cdots$	$\mathbf{u}_i + \mathbf{z}_1$	$\cdots$	$\mathbf{u}_{q^k-1} + \mathbf{z}_1$
$\mathbf{z}_2$	$\mathbf{u}_1 + \mathbf{z}_2$	$\mathbf{u}_2 + \mathbf{z}_2$	$\cdots$	$\mathbf{u}_i + \mathbf{z}_2$	$\cdots$	$\mathbf{u}_{q^k-1} + \mathbf{z}_2$
$\vdots$	$\vdots$	$\vdots$		$\vdots$		$\vdots$
$\mathbf{z}_{l-1}$	$\mathbf{u}_1 + \mathbf{z}_{l-1}$	$\mathbf{u}_2 + \mathbf{z}_{l-1}$	$\cdots$	$\mathbf{u}_i + \mathbf{z}_{l-1}$	$\cdots$	$\mathbf{u}_{q^k-1} + \mathbf{z}_{l-1}$

A further two vectors, $\mathbf{v}_1$ and $\mathbf{v}_2$, are in the same coset or have the same coset leader, say $\mathbf{z}_j$, if and only if their syndromes are equal to the syndrome of $\mathbf{z}_j$. That means there is a unique syndrome for each coset, and the number of possible syndromes equals the number of cosets.

For an (n, k) code over $GF(q)$, the standard array will have all q^n vectors, and hence the array requires a very large table. For $q = 2$ and $n = 72$, the table requires a storage of $2^{72} \times 72$ bits and hence is totally impractical. But the theory based on standard arrays is useful in understanding codes and developing practical decoding methods.

Since each coset has a unique syndrome, a table of coset leaders vs. syndromes will reduce the table by a big factor. Table 3.3 is indeed one such example. For some codes, even that can be an enormous size. Therefore, other algebraic techniques are developed for decoding.

The **H** matrix of a (6, 3, 3) code over $GF(2)$ is given in Table 3.5. Also shown in the table are its standard array and the syndromes corresponding to each coset. The coset leaders consist of all single errors and one of weight 2, and therefore this code can be used to correct all single errors and one (particular) double error.

$$\mathbf{H} = \begin{vmatrix} 0 & 1 & 1 & 1 & 0 & 0 \\ 1 & 0 & 1 & 0 & 1 & 0 \\ 1 & 1 & 0 & 0 & 0 & 1 \end{vmatrix} \tag{3.19}$$

We denote the number of coset leaders of weight i to be α_i. Then, for this (6, 3, 3) code, $\alpha_0 = 1$, $\alpha_1 = 6$, and $\alpha_2 = 1$. The probability of correct decoding under the assumption of a binary symmetric channel (BSC, see Chapter 1) is given by

$$P \text{ (correct decoding)} = Q^6 + 6Q^5P + Q^4P^2$$

$$P \text{ (incorrect decoding)} = 1 - P \text{ (correct decoding)} \approx 14Q^4P^2 \approx \mathcal{O}(P^2)$$

The probability of incorrect decoding is given under the assumption that $Q \gg P$, and therefore the probability of three or more errors is much smaller than two errors.

TABLE 3.5 STANDARD ARRAY FOR THE (6, 3, 3) CODE

Coset Leader 000000	001110	010101	100011	011011	101101	110110	111000	Syndrome 000
000001	001111	010100	100010	011010	101100	110111	111001	001
000010	001100	010111	100001	011001	101111	110100	111010	010
000100	001010	010001	100111	011111	101001	110010	111100	100
001000	000110	011101	101011	010011	100101	111110	110000	110
010000	011110	000101	110011	001011	111101	100110	101000	101
100000	101110	110101	000011	111011	001101	010110	011000	011
001001	000111	011100	101010	010010	100100	111111	110001	111

Coset codes. Consider an (n, k, d) linear code $\mathbf{C}$ and its standard array. The top row of the standard array is the code $\mathbf{C}$ itself. A coset of $\mathbf{C}$ with coset leader $\mathbf{z}_i$ is designated $\{\mathbf{C} + \mathbf{z}_i\}$. Consider the distance between any two vectors in the coset $\{\mathbf{C} + \mathbf{z}_i\}$. If these vectors are $\mathbf{u}_r + \mathbf{z}_i$ and $\mathbf{u}_s + \mathbf{z}_i$, then

$$d(\mathbf{u}_r + \mathbf{z}_i, \mathbf{u}_s + \mathbf{z}_i) = w(\mathbf{u}_r + \mathbf{z}_i - \mathbf{u}_s - \mathbf{z}_i)$$
$$= w(\mathbf{u}_r - \mathbf{u}_s) = d(\mathbf{u}_r, \mathbf{u}_s)$$

Therefore, the minimum distance between all pairs of vectors in a coset is the minimum distance of the code $\mathbf{C}$. Each of the cosets, thus, is an (n, k, d) nonlinear code, called a *coset code*. There are $q^r - 1$ coset codes for any linear code $\mathbf{C}$.

3.1.4 Perfect and Quasi-Perfect Codes

Definition 3-3. If a code $\mathbf{C}$ can have a standard array such that *all* vectors of weight $\leq t$ are its coset leaders and none of the coset leaders are of weight $> t$, then $\mathbf{C}$ is said to be a *perfect* code. If the standard array of a code has *all* vectors of weight $\leq t$, some but not all vectors of weight $t + 1$ but none of weight greater than $t + 1$ as coset leaders, then that code is said to be a *quasi-perfect* code.

This discussion is for the purpose of understanding how well a code can be utilized to correct errors in an optimum way. For instance, the (6, 3, 3) code of the last example can correct all single errors and one (not all) double error and no errors of weight greater than 2. Hence, it is quasi-perfect.

The column $\begin{bmatrix} 1 \\ 1 \\ 1 \end{bmatrix}$ is missing in $\mathbf{H}$ of (3.19). If we include that column, then we will have a (7, 4, 3) code, which is a perfect single-error correcting code. One more example to illustrate perfect codes is code $\mathbf{C}_2$, whose $\mathbf{H}$ matrix is

$$\mathbf{H} = \begin{bmatrix} 1 & 1 & 1 & 0 \\ 2 & 1 & 0 & 1 \end{bmatrix} \qquad \text{over } GF(3)$$

The standard array of $\mathbf{C}_2$ has $3^2 = 9$ cosets. The coset leaders can be one of weight 0, and the other eight are of weight 1 (i.e., $\alpha_0 = 1$, $\alpha_1 = 8$, $\alpha_2 = \alpha_3 = \alpha_4 = 0$). There are exactly eight single errors for this code. Therefore, $\mathbf{C}_2$ is a perfect SEC code.

A decoder for this code consists of obtaining the syndrome $\mathbf{s}$ for the received word $\mathbf{v}$ and identifying it as a multiple of one of the four columns. Suppose $\mathbf{v} = (1\ 1\ 0\ 2)$ is received. Its syndrome is

$$\mathbf{s}(\mathbf{v}) = (1\ 1\ 0\ 2)\begin{bmatrix} 1 & 2 \\ 1 & 1 \\ 1 & 0 \\ 0 & 1 \end{bmatrix} = (1\ 2) + (1\ 1) + (0\ 0) + (0\ 2) = (2\ 2)$$

Since the leading coefficient ($\mathbf{s}_0$) is 2, the error value is 2. To obtain the error position, we divide $\mathbf{s}(\mathbf{v})$ by 2. This is the same as multiplying by 2 in $GF(3)$, and the result is (1 1). The error position is identified by this vector as the second column of $\mathbf{H}$. The error vector $\mathbf{e}$ is (0 2 0 0), which should be subtracted from $\mathbf{v}$ to get the corrected vector $\hat{\mathbf{v}}$. That corrected vector and its syndrome $\mathbf{s}(\hat{\mathbf{v}})$ are

$$\hat{\mathbf{v}} = \mathbf{v} - \mathbf{e} = (1102) - (0200) = (1202), \mathbf{s}(\hat{\mathbf{v}}) = (00)$$

3.1.5 Hamming Codes

There are two types of Hamming codes over $GF(2)$: (1) distance-3 and (2) distance-4 codes. The distance-3 codes are typified by the $(15, 11, 3)$ code $\mathbf{C}_3$ given in Section 3.1.2. Generally, these parameters apply for distance-3 Hamming codes over $GF(2)$:

number of parities: r
block length : $n = 2^r - 1$
data length : $k = 2^r - 1 - r$

The distance-3 codes can be used either (1) as single-error correcting (SEC) codes or (2) as double-error detecting (DED) codes. We refer to distance-3 codes over $GF(2)$ as SEC codes. The parity matrix for the Hamming code example ($\mathbf{C}_3$) as given by (3.14) is as follows.

$$\begin{array}{rccccccccccccccc} \textit{position} \rightarrow & p_1 & p_2 & d_3 & p_4 & d_5 & d_6 & d_7 & p_8 & d_9 & d_{10} & d_{11} & d_{12} & d_{13} & d_{14} & d_{15} \end{array}$$

$$H = \begin{bmatrix} 0 & 0 & 0 & 0 & 0 & 0 & 0 & 1 & 1 & 1 & 1 & 1 & 1 & 1 & 1 \\ 0 & 0 & 0 & 1 & 1 & 1 & 1 & 0 & 0 & 0 & 0 & 1 & 1 & 1 & 1 \\ 0 & 1 & 1 & 0 & 0 & 1 & 1 & 0 & 0 & 1 & 1 & 0 & 0 & 1 & 1 \\ 1 & 0 & 1 & 0 & 1 & 0 & 1 & 0 & 1 & 0 & 1 & 0 & 1 & 0 & 1 \end{bmatrix}$$

A typical codeword $\mathbf{u} = (p_1 p_2 d_3 p_4 d_5 d_6 d_7 p_8 d_9 d_{10} \cdots d_{15})$ has parities in position 1, 2, 4, and 8, for example, and data bits elsewhere. The parities are computed by the parity equations given as follows.

$$\left.\begin{aligned} p_1 &= d_3 + d_5 + d_7 + d_9 + d_{11} + d_{13} + d_{15} \\ p_2 &= d_3 + d_6 + d_7 + d_{10} + d_{11} + d_{14} + d_{15} \\ p_4 &= d_5 + d_6 + d_7 + d_{12} + d_{13} + d_{14} + d_{15} \\ p_8 &= d_9 + d_{10} + d_{11} + d_{12} + d_{13} + d_{14} + d_{15} \end{aligned}\right\} \tag{3.20}$$

The decoding of a received vector $\mathbf{v} = (v_1, v_2, \ldots, v_{15})$ uses the syndrome equations, which are based on (3.20) and are given as follows.

$$\left.\begin{aligned} s_1 &= v_1 + v_3 + v_5 + v_7 + v_9 + v_{11} + v_{13} + v_{15} \\ s_2 &= v_2 + v_3 + v_6 + v_7 + v_{10} + v_{11} + v_{14} + v_{15} \\ s_3 &= v_4 + v_5 + v_6 + v_7 + v_{12} + v_{13} + v_{14} + v_{15} \\ s_4 &= v_8 + v_9 + v_{10} + v_{11} + v_{12} + v_{13} + v_{14} + v_{15} \end{aligned}\right\} \quad (3.21)$$

The syndrome obtained by using (3.21) written as $\mathbf{s} = (s_4, s_3, s_2, s_1)$ will identify the error position if single errors occur. The (15, 11, 3) Hamming SEC code parallel decoder is shown in Fig. 3.3. For instance, if $\mathbf{s} = (s_4, s_3, s_2, s_1) = 0111$, then position 7 is in error; d_7 output of the 4×16 decoder will be a 1 and $\hat{v}_7 = v_7 \oplus 1 = v_7'$ will be the corrected output bit.

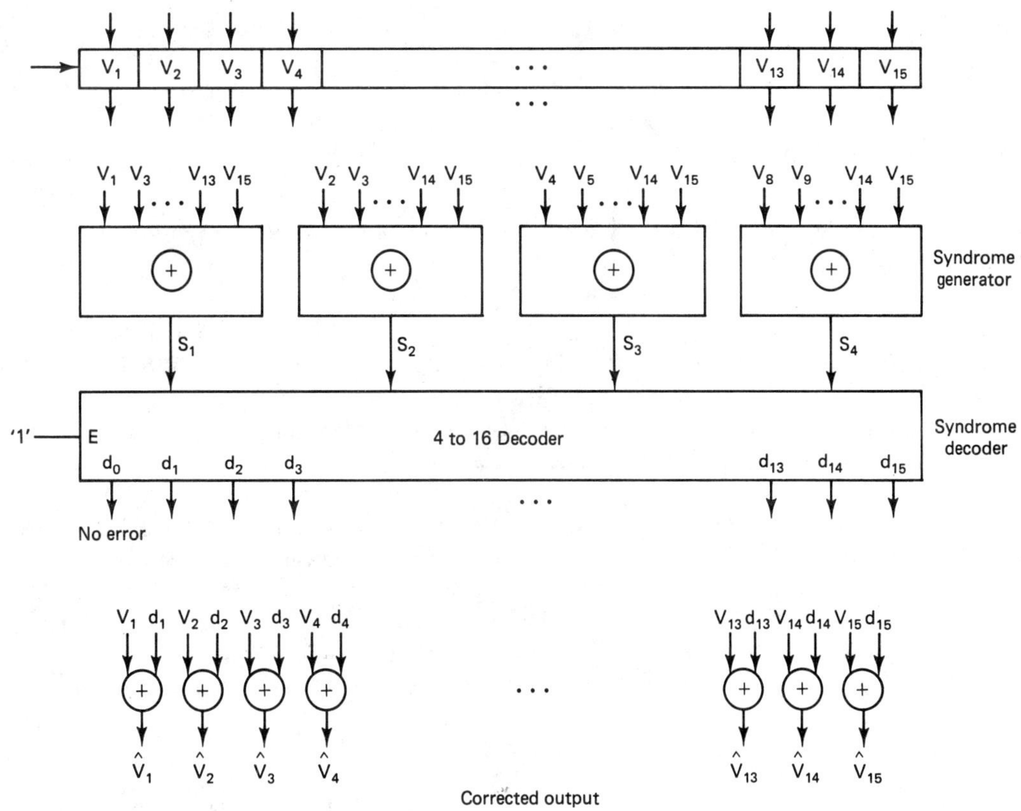

Figure 3.3 Hamming (15, 11, 3) SEC code decoder.

However, if double errors occur, say in positions 3 and 7, the syndrome is $\mathbf{s} = (0011) + (0111) = (0100)$. This would lead to a *miscorrection* in position 4. To prevent miscorrection due to double errors, a Hamming distance-4 code can be employed by adding one more parity check, called the overall parity check (p_{ov}), to the **H** matrix of (3.14). It is given in Equation (3.22).

The distance-4 code is single-error correcting and double-error detecting, and therefore it is called an SEC–DED code.

$$\begin{array}{ll} \textit{positions} \rightarrow & \begin{array}{cccccccccccccccc} p_{ov} & p_1 & p_2 & d_3 & p_4 & d_5 & d_6 & d_7 & p_8 & d_9 & d_{10} & d_{11} & d_{12} & d_{13} & d_{14} & d_{15} \end{array} \\ \mathbf{H} = & \begin{bmatrix} 0 & 0 & 0 & 0 & 0 & 0 & 0 & 0 & 1 & 1 & 1 & 1 & 1 & 1 & 1 & 1 \\ 0 & 0 & 0 & 0 & 1 & 1 & 1 & 1 & 0 & 0 & 0 & 0 & 1 & 1 & 1 & 1 \\ 0 & 0 & 1 & 1 & 0 & 0 & 1 & 1 & 0 & 0 & 1 & 1 & 0 & 0 & 1 & 1 \\ 0 & 1 & 0 & 1 & 0 & 1 & 0 & 1 & 0 & 1 & 0 & 1 & 0 & 1 & 0 & 1 \\ 1 & 1 & 1 & 1 & 1 & 1 & 1 & 1 & 1 & 1 & 1 & 1 & 1 & 1 & 1 & 1 \end{bmatrix} \end{array} \tag{3.22}$$

This is a (16, 11, 4) SEC–DED Hamming code; the encoding requires an overall parity equation (3.23), which is added on to the set (3.20).

$$p_{ov} = p_1 + p_2 + d_3 + \cdots + d_{15} \tag{3.23}$$

The syndrome generation requires one more equation, (3.24), in addition to the set (3.21).

$$s_{ov} = v_0 + v_1 + \cdots + v_{15} \tag{3.24}$$

The syndrome $\mathbf{s} = (s_{ov}, s_4, s_3, s_2, s_1)$ is to be interpreted as follows:

1. If $\mathbf{s} = \mathbf{0}$, then errors are assumed to be 0.
2. If $s_{ov} = 1$, then a single error is assumed to have occurred. The error position is given by the binary number (s_4, s_3, s_2, s_1) (e.g., if $(s_4, s_3, s_2, s_1) = 0101$ then position 5 is in error).
3. If $s_{ov} = 0$, $(s_4, s_3, s_2, s_1) \neq \mathbf{0}$, then a double error (or even number of errors) is detected. This is an uncorrectable error.

For the (16, 11, 4) code represented by the **H** matrix (3.22), a parallel decoder is shown in Fig. 3.4. The syndrome bit $s_{ov} = 1$ indicates a single error and therefore enables the (4×16) decoder to generate the error position indicator d_i. If the single error in the received word is in bit v_0, then d_0 will be a 1 and $\hat{v}_0 = v_0'$ will be the corrected bit. A no error is indicated when all syndrome bits are 0; a double error is indicated when $s_{ov} = 0$, but at least one of the other syndrome bits are nonzero. To have a better understanding, the student is advised to do several exercises from the problem set at the end of the chapter.

Shortened Hamming codes. The distance-3 and distance-4 Hamming codes studied so far have been for the case when the block length is the maximum for a given number of parity checks. That is, if $r = 4$, we have

$$n_{\max} = 2^r - 1 = 15,\ k_{\max} = n_{\max} - r = 11 \text{ (distance-3 code)} \Rightarrow (15, 11, 3) \text{ code}$$

$$= 2^{r-1} = 8,\ k_{\max} = 4 \text{ (distance-4 code)} \Rightarrow (8, 4, 4) \text{ code}$$

However, if the data are only 8 bits, the distance-3 code can be obtained by just deleting any three columns of (3.14), resulting in a (12, 8, 3) code, which is called a shortened Hamming code. Similarly, the **H** matrix of a distance-4 code will result by deleting any three columns of (3.22), giving a (13, 8, 4) code. For convenience in encoding and decoding logic, it is better to delete the rightmost three columns of the **H** matrix.

3.1.6 Other Linear Codes

Modified Hamming SEC–DED code. In the **H** matrix (3.22) of the distance-4 Hamming code, each row except the last one has exactly eight 1's. The syndrome computation requires an EXOR sum of the eight positions as given by (3.21). The syndrome bit s_{ov} is an EXOR sum of all 16 positions (Fig. 3.4). Thus, generating p_{ov} will require a longer time compared to other parity bits. In a parallel encoding, this is unsatisfactory. However, the **H** matrix of (3.22) can be modified by *row operations* in which we add the first four rows to the last row to obtain the following form.

$$\mathbf{H}' = \begin{bmatrix} 0 & 0 & 0 & 0 & 0 & 0 & 0 & 0 & 1 & 1 & 1 & 1 & 1 & 1 & 1 & 1 \\ 0 & 0 & 0 & 0 & 1 & 1 & 1 & 1 & 0 & 0 & 0 & 0 & 1 & 1 & 1 & 1 \\ 0 & 0 & 1 & 1 & 0 & 0 & 1 & 1 & 0 & 0 & 1 & 1 & 0 & 0 & 1 & 1 \\ 0 & 1 & 0 & 1 & 0 & 1 & 0 & 1 & 0 & 1 & 0 & 1 & 0 & 1 & 0 & 1 \\ 1 & 0 & 0 & 1 & 0 & 1 & 1 & 0 & 0 & 1 & 1 & 0 & 1 & 0 & 0 & 1 \end{bmatrix} \tag{3.25}$$

The row space of **H'** is the same as **H**, and the code is not altered by this modification. The last row now has eight 1's as in the other rows, and the encoding and decoding will be substantially faster because of this alteration. In the encoding, the equation for p_{ov}, now with this modification, does not involve the other parities, and therefore its generation is truly parallel.

Also to be noted is that each column of **H'** has exactly an odd number of 1's. Therefore, single errors are detected when the sum of the syndrome components equals an odd number. If the sum is even and nonzero, then a double error is detected. Also, when the sum is odd, the same 4×16 decoder as before can detect the error position. This modified SEC–DED code, therefore, comes under the class of odd-column-parity matrix codes [HSIA 70a], which has many interesting properties and is studied in detail in Chapter 4.

The cross-parity code. An SEC–DED code that is easier to implement than the Hamming code is the *cross-parity code*. In a two-dimensional cross-parity code, horizontal and vertical parity bits are appended to a two-dimensional array of data bits (see Fig. 3.5). Any single error in the array is checked by the horizontal

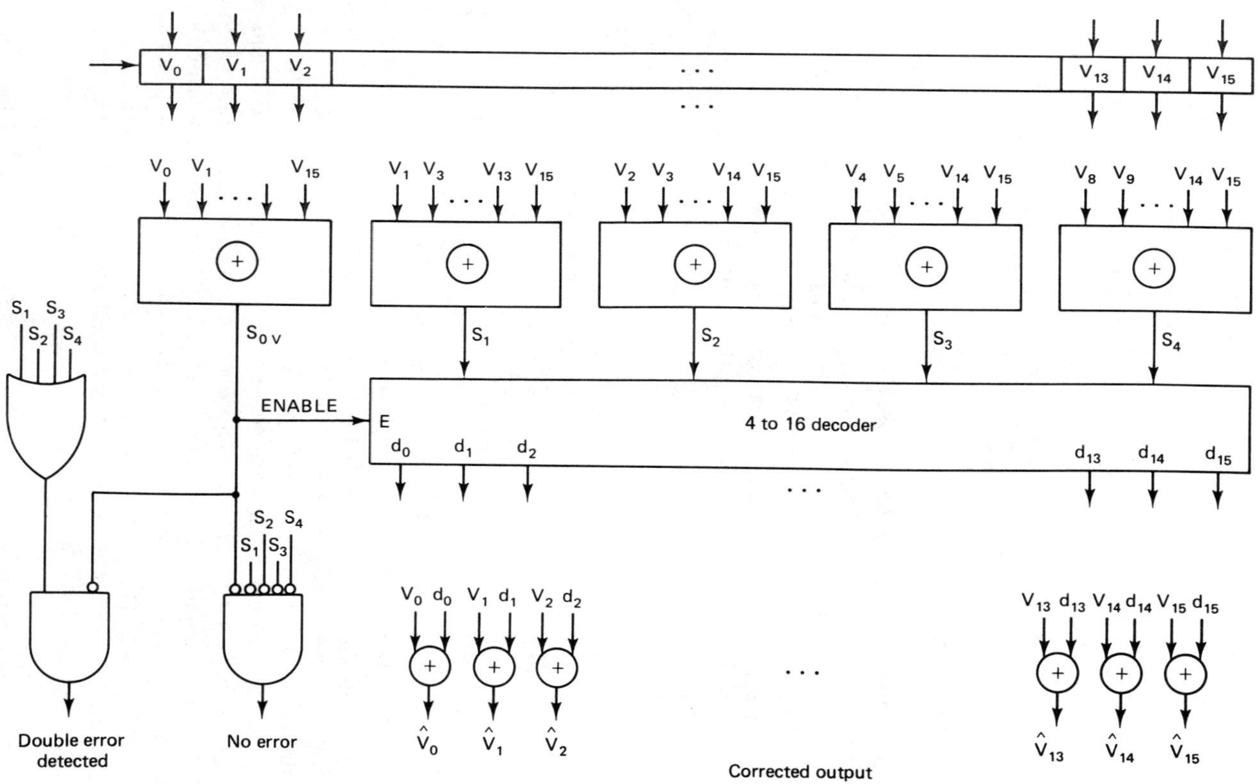

Figure 3.4 Hamming (16, 11, 4) SEC–DED code decoder.

d_0	d_1	d_2	d_3	p_1
d_4	d_5	d_6	d_7	p_2
d_8	d_9	d_{10}	d_{11}	p_3
d_{12}	d_{13}	d_{14}	d_{15}	p_4
p_5	p_6	p_7	p_8	p_9

Figure 3.5 A two-dimensional (25,16,4) cross-parity code.

and vertical parity lines and is therefore detected and corrected. For instance, if d_6 is in error, then the horizontal parity p_2 and vertical parity p_7 detect this error.

Any two errors along a horizontal line are detected by two vertical parity failures and therefore are detected but not corrected. This code has an information rate lower than the Hamming SEC–DED code, but it has a simpler encoding and decoding logic and hence is suited well as a memory-chip code to improve yields. For further details, see Section 4.3 of this book on memory-chip codes.

The cross-parity code is a simple example of the class called *product codes*. If a product code has a horizontal and vertical distance of d_h and d_v, respectively, then the product code has a distance $d_h d_v$. Thus, if the Hamming distance-3 code is employed as a horizontal code and even parity (distance 2) is used vertically, then the product code has distance 6. In addition to the random error correction, the product codes can also correct burst errors, and the reader may refer to [BURT 65, 71a] and [PETE 72].

3.2 CYCLIC CODES

Cyclic codes are an important class of linear codes. These codes have a very nice algebraic structure that is suited well for implementation and construction of many subclasses of codes. There are efficient cyclic codes for detection/correction of multiple random errors, byte errors, and burst errors. These codes can be implemented efficiently by *linear feedback shift register* (LFSR) circuits for serial encoding and decoding operations. They can also be implemented in parallel as linear codes for high-speed memories. First, we study cyclic code structure and SEC, SEC–DED codes. Just as in the previous chapter, we explain the theory and codes by means of examples and illustrations. For a rigorous theory on cyclic codes, the reader is advised to refer to [PETE 72], [BLAH 83], [MACW 77], and [LIN 83].

3.2.1 Polynomial Algebras and Cyclic Code Definition

We review briefly definitions and theory from the last chapter of the algebra of polynomials **A(x)**. This algebra consists of all polynomials of the form

$$\mathbf{f}(x) = f_0 + f_1 x + f_2 x^2 + \cdots, \qquad f_i \in GF(q)$$

A(x) is a ring and has a structure very much analogous to the ring of integers Z. Also, **A(x)** is a vector space over $GF(q)$. Just as we consider $Z_m = \{0, 1, \ldots, m-1\}$, the integer modulo m, we can also consider the set of polynomials modulo $\mathbf{f}(x)$, where $\mathbf{f}(x)$ is a polynomial of degree n in $\mathbf{A}(x)$. The analogy of these structures with integers makes the understanding easier, and therefore we make use of this quite often here.

Let $\mathbf{f}(x)$ be a monic polynomial of degree n,

$$\mathbf{f}(x) = f_0 + f_1 x + \cdots + f_n x^n, \qquad f_i \in GF(q)$$

The algebra of polynomials modulo $\mathbf{f}(x)$ can be denoted as

$$\mathbf{A}_n(\mathbf{x}) = \{a(x) | \text{degree } a(x) < n\}$$

The addition of polynomials in $\mathbf{A}(\mathbf{x})$ is straightforward. The multiplication of polynomials in $\mathbf{A}_n(\mathbf{x})$ is modulo $\mathbf{f}(x)$. The modulo $\mathbf{f}(x)$ is to be understood as similar to integers modulo m. $\mathbf{A}_n(\mathbf{x})$ is a ring, and it is a field if and only if $\mathbf{f}(x)$ is an irreducible (or prime) polynomial. This is analogous to the result that Z_m is a ring, and it is a field if and only if m is a prime. (For details, see Sections 2.3 and 2.4.)

Example Set 3-7

1. Consider $\mathbf{A}(\mathbf{x})$ the set of all polynomials over $GF(2)$ and $\mathbf{A}_3(\mathbf{x})$ the set of polynomials modulo $x^3 + x + 1$ over $GF(2)$. Then, $\mathbf{A}_3(\mathbf{x})$ is given as

$$\mathbf{A}_3(\mathbf{x}) = \{a(x) | a(x) = a_0 + a_1 x + a_2 x^2\}$$

For illustration, the addition and multiplication in $\mathbf{A}_3(\mathbf{x})$ are as follows.

$$(x^2 + 1) + (x + 1) = x^2 + x$$
$$(x^2 + 1) \cdot (x + 1) = x^3 + x^2 + x + 1 = x^2$$
$$x^2 \cdot x^2 = x \cdot x^3 = x(x + 1) = x^2 + x$$

Since $x^3 + x + 1$ is a prime polynomial, $\mathbf{A}_3(\mathbf{x})$ is a field of eight elements. It is just another form of $GF(2^3)$.

2. Consider the set of polynomials modulo $x^2 - 1$ over $GF(3)$. This algebra is

$$\mathbf{A}_2(\mathbf{x}) = \{a(x) | a(X) = a_0 + a_1 x, a_0, a_1 \in GF(3)\}.$$

The addition and multiplication are illustrated by examples as follows.

$$(x + 2) + (2x + 2) = 1$$
$$(x + 1) + (x + 2) = 2x$$
$$(x + 2) \cdot (2x + 2) = 2x^2 + 1 = 0$$
$$x \cdot (2x + 1) = x + 2$$
$$x \cdot (x + 2) = 2x + 1$$
$$x \cdot x = 1$$

Since $x^2 - 1$ is reducible, $\mathbf{A}_2(\mathbf{x})$ is a commutative ring but not a field.

3. Consider the set $\mathbf{A}_n(\mathbf{x})$ of polynomials modulo $x^n - 1$ over $GF(q)$. In this algebra, which is a ring, every polynomial $\mathbf{a}(x)$ is of the form

$$\mathbf{a}(x) = a_0 + a_1 x + \cdots + a_{n-1} x^{n-1}, \qquad a_i \in GF(q)$$

Since $x^n \equiv 1 \ (mod\, x^n - 1)$, we can write $x \cdot x^{n-1} = x^n = 1$ in $\mathbf{A}_n(\mathbf{x})$. Therefore, we have

$$x \cdot \mathbf{a}(x) = a_0x + a_1x^2 + \cdots + a_{n-2}x^{n-1} + a_{n-1}x^n$$
$$= a_{n-1} + a_0x + a_1x^2 + \cdots + a_{n-2}x^{n-1} \tag{3.26}$$

Multiplying a polynomial $\mathbf{a}(x)$ by x^j amounts to shifting the coefficients to the right cyclically by j places. This is an important starting point for understanding cyclic codes. Also note that in $GF(2)$, $-1 = +1$, and therefore $\mathbf{A}_n(\mathbf{x})$ is also called the algebra of polynomials modulo $x^n + 1$.

From here on, $\mathbf{A}_n(\mathbf{x})$ denotes the algebra of polynomial modulo $x^n - 1$ over $GF(q)$.

Definition 3-4. A linear code $\mathbf{C}$ is said to be a *cyclic code* if for any code vector $\mathbf{u} = (u_0, \ldots, u_{n-1}) \in \mathbf{C}$, the vector $\mathbf{u}' = (u_{n-1}, u_0, \ldots, u_{n-2})$ obtained by a shift of the components to the right cyclically (i.e., end-around) is also a code vector in $\mathbf{C}$.

By this definition, any cyclic shift by j places to the left (or right) of a code vector will also be a code vector.

In this chapter, any vector $\mathbf{v} \in \mathbf{V}_n$ will be considered as a polynomial $\mathbf{v}(\mathbf{x}) \in \mathbf{A}_n(\mathbf{x})$, the algebra of polynomials modulo $x^n - 1$. A code vector $\mathbf{u} \in \mathbf{C}$ will be called a code polynomial $\mathbf{u}(x) \in \mathbf{A}_n(\mathbf{x})$. Under this consideration, $\mathbf{u}'$ (the right cyclic shift of $\mathbf{u}$) will be $\mathbf{u}'(x) = x\mathbf{u}(x)$ in $\mathbf{A}_n(\mathbf{x})$. This correspondence is illustrated as follows.

$$\mathbf{C} \subset \mathbf{V}_n \leftrightarrow \mathbf{C} \subset \mathbf{A}_n(\mathbf{x})$$
$$\mathbf{u} = (u_0, u_1, u_2, \ldots, u_{n-1}) \leftrightarrow \mathbf{u}(x) = u_0 + u_1x + \cdots + u_{n-1}x^{n-1}$$
$$\mathbf{u}' = (u_{n-1}, u_0, u_1, \ldots, u_{n-2}) \leftrightarrow \mathbf{u}'(x) = x\mathbf{u}(x) = u_{n-1} + u_0x + \cdots + u_{n-2}x^{n-1}$$

Therefore, the words *vector*, *word*, and *polynomial* are used interchangeably in this section. Let $\mathbf{C}$ be a cyclic code in $\mathbf{A}_n(\mathbf{x})$. Then $\mathbf{C}$ is a linear code, and therefore is a subspace. Trivially, then, $\mathbf{C}$ is a subgroup in $\mathbf{A}_n(\mathbf{x})$. Also, for any code polynomial, $\mathbf{u}(x) \in \mathbf{C}$, $x\mathbf{u}(x)$ is also a code polynomial. Since $x\mathbf{u}(x) \in \mathbf{C}$, $xx\mathbf{u}(x) = x^2\mathbf{u}(x)$ is also in $\mathbf{C}$. Since $\mathbf{C}$ is linear, any linear combination of these code polynomials is a code polynomial. That is, for any $\mathbf{u}(x) \in \mathbf{C}$

$$(a_0 + a_1x + \cdots)\mathbf{u}(x) = \mathbf{a}(x)\mathbf{u}(x) \in \mathbf{C}, \qquad \text{for any } \mathbf{a}(x) \in \mathbf{A}_n(\mathbf{x})$$

Therefore, by Definition 2-1, $\mathbf{C}$ is an ideal in (the ring) $\mathbf{A}_n(\mathbf{x})$. Conversely, let $\mathbf{C}$ be an ideal in $\mathbf{A}_n(\mathbf{x})$. Then, by definition, $\mathbf{C}$ is a subgroup and for all $\mathbf{u}(x) \in \mathbf{C}$,

$$\mathbf{a}(x) \in \mathbf{A}_n(\mathbf{x}), \ \ \mathbf{a}(x)\mathbf{u}(x) \in \mathbf{C} \tag{3.27}$$

By setting $\mathbf{a}(x) = \alpha \in GF(q)$ in (3.27), and combining this with the fact that $\mathbf{C}$ is a subgroup, we get that $\mathbf{C}$ is a linear code. In addition, by setting $\mathbf{a}(x) = x$ in (3.27) for all $\mathbf{u}(x) \in \mathbf{C}$,

$$x\mathbf{u}(x) = \mathbf{u}'(x) \in \mathbf{C} \tag{3.28}$$

Therefore, $\mathbf{C}$ is a cyclic code. Thus, we have proved the following.

Theorem 3-3. *A subset* **C** *of polynomials in* $\mathbf{A}_n(\mathbf{x})$ *is a cyclic code if and only if it is an ideal.*

As an ideal, a cyclic code **C** in $\mathbf{A}_n(x)$ must have a generator (see Section 2.1). That is, every code polynomial in **C** is a multiple of the *generator* polynomial $\mathbf{g}(x)$. Also, $\mathbf{g}(x)$ is the smallest degree monic polynomial in **C** and $\mathbf{g}(x)$ must divide $x^n - 1$. Besides, every factor of $x^n - 1$ generates an ideal in $\mathbf{A}_n(x)$.

Example Set 3-8

1. Let **C** be a cyclic code in $\mathbf{A}_7(\mathbf{x})$, the algebra of polynomial modulo $x^7 - 1$ over $GF(2)$. Then, **C** has a generator $\mathbf{g}(x)$ that is a divisor of $x^7 - 1$. We can factor $x^7 - 1$ into irreducible factors as

$$x^7 - 1 = (x - 1)(x^3 + x + 1)(x^3 + x^2 + 1) \tag{3.29}$$

Any factor of $x^7 - 1$ can be a generator of a cyclic code in $\mathbf{A}_7(x)$. Assume that **C** is generated by $\mathbf{g}(\mathbf{x}) = x^3 + x + 1$. Then the code polynomials are given as follows as multiples of $\mathbf{g}(\mathbf{x})$.

	Code Polynomials in $\mathbf{A}_7(x)$	*Code Vectors in* $\mathbf{V}_7$
$0 \cdot \mathbf{g}(x)$	$= 0$	0000000
$1 \cdot \mathbf{g}(x)$	$= x^3 + x + 1$	0001011
$x \cdot \mathbf{g}(x)$	$= x^4 + x^2 + x$	0010110
$(x + 1) \cdot \mathbf{g}(x)$	$= x^4 + x^3 + x^2 + 1$	0011101
$x^2 \cdot \mathbf{g}(x)$	$= x^5 + x^3 + x^2$	0101100
$(x^2 + 1) \cdot \mathbf{g}(x)$	$= x^5 + x^2 + x + 1$	0100111
$(x^2 + x) \cdot \mathbf{g}(x)$	$= x^5 + x^4 + x^3 + x$	0111010
$(x^2 + x + 1) \cdot \mathbf{g}(x)$	$= x^5 + x^4 + 1$	0110001
$x^3 \cdot \mathbf{g}(x)$	$= x^6 + x^4 + x^3$	1011000
$(x^3 + 1) \cdot \mathbf{g}(x)$	$= x^6 + x^4 + x + 1$	1010011
$(x^3 + x) \cdot \mathbf{g}(x)$	$= x^6 + x^3 + x^2 + x$	1001110
$(x^3 + x + 1) \cdot \mathbf{g}(x)$	$= x^6 + x^2 + 1$	1000101
$(x^3 + x^2) \cdot \mathbf{g}(x)$	$= x^6 + x^5 + x^4 + x^2$	1110100
$(x^3 + x^2 + 1) \cdot \mathbf{g}(x)$	$= x^6 + x^5 + x^4 + x^3 + x^2 + x + 1$	1111111
$(x^3 + x^2 + x) \cdot \mathbf{g}(x)$	$= x^6 + x^5 + x$	1100010
$(x^3 + x^2 + x + 1) \cdot \mathbf{g}(x)$	$= x^6 + x^5 + x^3 + 1$	1101001

It is easily observed from the table that for any code vector, all its cyclic shifts are also in **C**. Furthermore, since every code polynomial $\mathbf{u}(x) = \mathbf{g}(x)\mathbf{d}(x)$ for some $\mathbf{d}(x)$ of degree ≤ 3, it is of the form

$$\mathbf{d}(x) = d_3x^3 + d_2x^2 + d_1x + d_0$$

Thus, there can be only 2^4 distinct polynomials for $\mathbf{d}(x)$, and there are 16 code polynomials. This code is a (7, 4) code. As a general case, the code is an $(n, n - r)$ code where r is the degree of $\mathbf{g}(x)$.

2. As another example, we consider $\mathbf{A}_4(x)$, the algebra of polynomials modulo $x^4 - 1$ over $GF(3)$, and let

$$\mathbf{g}(x) = x^2 + 2$$

be the generator of a cyclic code. We note that $\mathbf{g}(x)$ divides $x^4 - 1$ and every code polynomial is of degree less than 4. The data and code polynomials and vectors are given as follows.

Data		Code	
$\mathbf{d}(x)$	$\mathbf{d}$	$\mathbf{u}(x) = \mathbf{d}(x) \cdot \mathbf{g}(x)$	$\mathbf{u}$
0	00	0	0000
1	01	$x^2 + 2$	0102
2	02	$2x^2 + 1$	0201
x	10	$x^3 + 2x$	1020
$x + 1$	11	$x^3 + x^2 + 2x + 2$	1122
$x + 2$	12	$x^3 + 2x^2 + 2x + 1$	1221
$2x$	20	$2x^3 + x$	2010
$2x + 1$	21	$2x^3 + x^2 + x + 2$	2112
$2x + 2$	22	$2x^3 + 2x^2 + x + 1$	2211

Each codeword $\mathbf{u}$ contains data $\mathbf{d}$ followed by a check that is a complement of $\mathbf{d}$. Thus, $\mathbf{u} = (\mathbf{d}, \bar{\mathbf{d}})$, as can be observed in the foregoing table.

To summarize the results so far of an (n, k) cyclic code $\mathbf{C}$ in $\mathbf{A}(x)$, the generator $\mathbf{g}(x)$ satisfies the following properties.

(C1) $\mathbf{g}(x)$ generates $\mathbf{C}$. That is, every code polynomial is a multiple of $\mathbf{g}(x)$.

(C2) $\mathbf{g}(x)$ is the smallest degree monic polynomial in $\mathbf{C}$.

(C3) $\mathbf{g}(x)$ divides $x^n - 1$.

(C4) The degree of $\mathbf{g}(x)$ is $r = n - k$.

(C5) $g_0 \neq 0$.

(C6) Every proper divisor $\mathbf{g}(x)$ of $x^n - 1$ generates an (n, k) cyclic code, where $r = n - k$ is the degree of $\mathbf{g}(x)$.

3.2.2 Generator and Parity Matrices

Let $\mathbf{g}(x) = x^r + g_{r-1}x^{r-1} + \cdots + g_0$ be the generator of an (n, k) cyclic code $\mathbf{C}$. Then, $x\mathbf{g}(x), x^2\mathbf{g}(x), \ldots, x^{n-r-1}\mathbf{g}(x)$ are code polynomials. Putting them in vector form, we have

$$\mathbf{G} = \begin{bmatrix} 0 & 0 & \cdots & 0 & 1 & g_{r-1} & \cdots & g_2 & g_1 & g_0 \\ 0 & 0 & \cdots & 1 & g_{r-1} & g_{r-2} & \cdots & g_1 & g_0 & 0 \\ & \vdots & & & \vdots & \vdots & & \vdots & \vdots & \vdots \\ 1 & g_{r-1} & \cdots & & g_1 & g_0 & \cdots & & 0 & 0 \end{bmatrix} \tag{3.30}$$

The rows of $\mathbf{G}$ are linearly independent, and $\mathbf{G}$ has a (row) rank of $n - r$. Consequently, $\mathbf{G}$ is a generator matrix of a linear code of dimension $k = n - r$. Since every vector in the row space of $\mathbf{G}$ corresponds to a polynomial that is a multiple of $\mathbf{g}(x)$, the code generated by $\mathbf{G}$ is the same as the cyclic code generated by $\mathbf{g}(x)$. Thus, the $\mathbf{G}$ matrix as just given represents the cyclic code $\mathbf{C}$. To obtain an $\mathbf{H}$ matrix of $\mathbf{C}$, we factor $x^n - 1$ as

$$x^n - 1 = \mathbf{g}(x)\mathbf{h}(x)$$

Clearly, the degree of $\mathbf{h}(x)$ is $n - r = k$. In $\mathbf{A}_n(\mathbf{x})$, we also have, for every code polynomial $\mathbf{u}(x)$,

$$\mathbf{u}(x) = \mathbf{q}(x)\mathbf{g}(x), \quad \text{for some } \mathbf{q}(x)$$

and

$$\mathbf{u}(x)\mathbf{h}(x) = \mathbf{q}(x)\mathbf{g}(x)\mathbf{h}(x) = \mathbf{0} \tag{3.31}$$

Equation (3.31) is analogous to Equation (3.5) given for linear codes, which is $\mathbf{uH}^T = 0$ for any codeword $\mathbf{u}$. Also, $\mathbf{u}(x)x^j\mathbf{h}(x) = 0$ for all j, and therefore we write an $\mathbf{H}$ matrix as follows.

$$\mathbf{H} = \begin{bmatrix} h_0 & h_1 & \cdots & & h_k & 0 & \cdots & 0 \\ 0 & h_0 & h_1 & & \cdots & h_k & \cdots & 0 \\ & \vdots & & & & \vdots & & \vdots \\ 0 & 0 & 0 & \cdots & h_0 & h_1 & \cdots & h_k \end{bmatrix} \tag{3.32}$$

There is an important difference to be noted here about $\mathbf{G}$ and $\mathbf{H}$. The order of coefficient in $\mathbf{H}$ and $\mathbf{G}$ is reversed. This is necessary because polynomial multiplication (for $\mathbf{g}(x)\mathbf{h}(x) = \mathbf{0}$) and the inner product of vectors ($\mathbf{g} \cdot \mathbf{h} = 0$) are different. Any row of the $\mathbf{G}$ matrix is orthogonal to every row of $\mathbf{H}$, coming from the fact that every term of the product $\mathbf{g}(x)\mathbf{h}(x)$ equals $\mathbf{0}$. The linear code $\mathbf{C}'$ generated by $\mathbf{H}$ is the dual code of $\mathbf{C}$. Since the order of the coefficients of $\mathbf{h}(x)$ are reversed in $\mathbf{H}$, the cyclic code represented by $\mathbf{H}$ is generated by the polynomial

$$\mathbf{h}^*(x) = h_0x^k + h_1x^{k-1} + \cdots + h_k \tag{3.33}$$

$\mathbf{h}^*(x)$ has the same coefficients as $\mathbf{h}(x)$ in a reverse order and is called the reciprocal polynomial. Also, $\mathbf{h}^*(x) = x^k\mathbf{h}(1/x)$, and therefore if α is a zero of $\mathbf{h}(x)$, α^{-1} is a zero of $\mathbf{h}^*(x)$. The following can be proved for reciprocal polynomials.

1. $\mathbf{h}^{**}(x) = \mathbf{h}(x)$.
2. If $\mathbf{h}(x)$ is irreducible, so also is $\mathbf{h}^*(x)$.
3. If α, a zero of $\mathbf{h}(x)$, has order n, then α^{-1}, the zero of $\mathbf{h}^*(x)$, also has order n. (3.34)

Systematic forms for cyclic codes. The $\mathbf{G}$ and $\mathbf{H}$ matrices of cyclic codes given before in the form of (3.30) and (3.32) are not in systematic form. The code vectors obtained as

$$\mathbf{u}(x) = \mathbf{d}(x)\mathbf{g}(x)$$

for data $\mathbf{d}(x)$ are nonsystematic in general. There are some exceptions to this, however, as can be seen from Example 2 of Set 3-8. Therefore, the following encoding algorithm is used to obtain systematic cyclic codes. Let $\mathbf{d}(x)$ be a data polynomial to be encoded in an (n, k) cyclic code $\mathbf{C}$, whose generator is $\mathbf{g}(x)$ of degree r. Then we take $\mathbf{d}(x)x^r$ and divide it by $\mathbf{g}(x)$ to obtain a remainder $\mathbf{r}(x)$ using Euclidean division as follows.

$$\mathbf{d}(x)x^r = \mathbf{g}(x)\mathbf{q}(x) + \mathbf{r}(x), \qquad \text{degree } \mathbf{r}(x) < r$$

By moving the remainder $\mathbf{r}(x)$ to the left side, we get a systematic codeword $\mathbf{u}(x)$ for $\mathbf{d}(x)$ shown as follows.

$$\mathbf{u}(x) = \underbrace{\mathbf{d}(x)x^r}_{\text{data symbols}} - \underbrace{\mathbf{r}(x)}_{\text{parity symbols}} = \mathbf{g}(x)\mathbf{q}(x)$$

By this, $\mathbf{u}(x)$ is a multiple of $\mathbf{g}(x)$, and therefore it is a code polynomial. Also, $\mathbf{d}(x) \cdot x^r$ form the higher order terms of $\mathbf{u}(x)$, and $-\mathbf{r}(x)$ will be the r parity symbols that occupy the low order positions of $\mathbf{u}(x)$, thus making it a systematic codeword. By this approach, we can get systematic codewords for Example 1 of Set 3-8.

$\mathbf{d}(x)$	d	$\mathbf{u}(x) = \mathbf{d}(x)x^3 - \mathbf{r}(x)$	$\mathbf{u}$
$\mathbf{0}$	0000	$\mathbf{0}$	0000000
1	0001	$(1)x^3 + x + 1$	0001011
x	0010	$(x)x^3 + x^2 + x$	0010110
$x + 1$	0011	$(x + 1)x^3 + x^2 + 1$	0011101
x^2	0100	$(x^2)x^3 + x^2 + x + 1$	0100111
$x^2 + 1$	0101	$(x^2 + 1)x^3 + x^2$	0101100
$x^2 + x$	0110	$(x^2 + x)x^3 + 1$	0110001
$x^2 + x + 1$	0111	$(x^2 + x + 1)x^3 + x$	0111010
x^3	1000	$(x^3)x^3 + x^2 + 1$	1000101
$x^3 + 1$	1001	$(x^3 + 1)x^3 + x^2 + x$	1001110
$x^3 + x$	1010	$(x^3 + x)x^3 + x + 1$	1010011
$x^3 + x + 1$	1011	$(x^3 + x + 1)x^3 + 0$	1011000
$x^3 + x^2$	1100	$(x^3 + x^2)x^3 + x$	1100010
$x^3 + x^2 + 1$	1101	$(x^3 + x^2 + 1)x^3 + 1$	1101001
$x^3 + x^2 + x$	1110	$(x^3 + x^2 + x)x^3 + x^2$	1110100
$x^3 + x^2 + x + 1$	1111	$(x^3 + x^2 + x + 1)x^3 + x^2 + x + 1$	1111111

In the systematic form, the generator matrix of the code is given by

$$\mathbf{G} = \begin{bmatrix} 1 & 0 & 0 & 0 & 1 & 0 & 1 \\ 0 & 1 & 0 & 0 & 1 & 1 & 1 \\ 0 & 0 & 1 & 0 & 1 & 1 & 0 \\ 0 & 0 & 0 & 1 & 0 & 1 & 1 \end{bmatrix} \tag{3.35}$$

The first row of (3.35) corresponds to data, $\mathbf{d}(x) = x^3$, and its codeword is $x^3 \cdot x^3 + (x^2 + 1)$ in the systematic form. Similarly, the other rows correspond to $\mathbf{d}(x) = x^2$, x, and 1 in that order. The (serial) encoder logic circuit for this systematic code requires a division logic that uses a linear feedback shift register (LFSR).

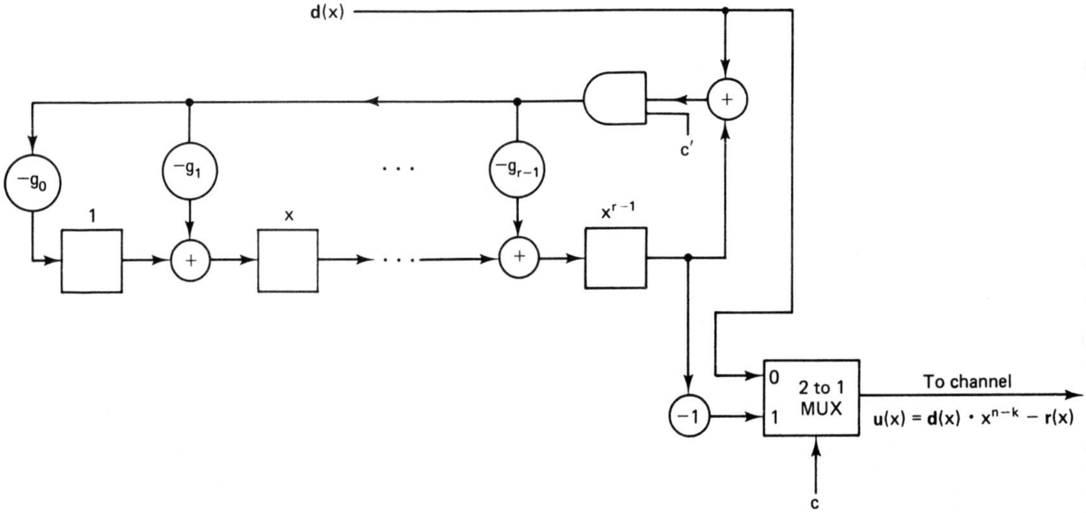

Figure 3.6 LFSR encoder for cyclic codes.

3.2.3 Encoding/Decoding Using LFSR's

The first step in encoding/decoding would be to divide by $\mathbf{g}(x)$ the data polynomial $\mathbf{d}(x)$ premultiplied by x^r and collect the remainder polynomial in a register as shown in Fig. 3.6. The remainder modulo $\mathbf{g}(x)$ of an input term is obtained by the characteristic equation below.

$$-x^r \bmod \mathbf{g}(\mathbf{x}) = g_{r-1}x^{r-1} + g_{r-2}x^{r-2} + \cdots + g_1 x + g_0 \tag{3.36}$$

The point of LFSR where the data is applied has a value of x^r and therefore returns (as feedback) into the shift register as terms shown in Fig. 3.6.

Initially, the shift register cells contain all 0's. The $\mathbf{d}(x)$ to be encoded is applied serially with higher order terms first. With each new input the register is shifted once. After k cycles, the remainder of $(-\mathbf{d}(x) \cdot x^r)$ is accumulated into the register; and this remainder is inverted and passed on to the channel as the check symbols of the codeword. The multiplexer control c stays 0 for $t = 0, 1, \ldots, k-1$ cycles and then changes to $c = 1$ for cycles $t = k, k+1, \ldots, n-1$. The AND gate in the feedback portion enables the LFSR to compute the remainder logic during the first k cycles and then turns off the feedbacks so that the remainder polynomial is passed on to the channel following the data polynomial. This encoding logic is illustrated further by means of examples.

Example Set 3-9

1. The encoder for the binary (7, 4) cyclic code, whose generator is $\mathbf{g}(x) = x^3 + x + 1$, is given as follows (Fig. 3.7).

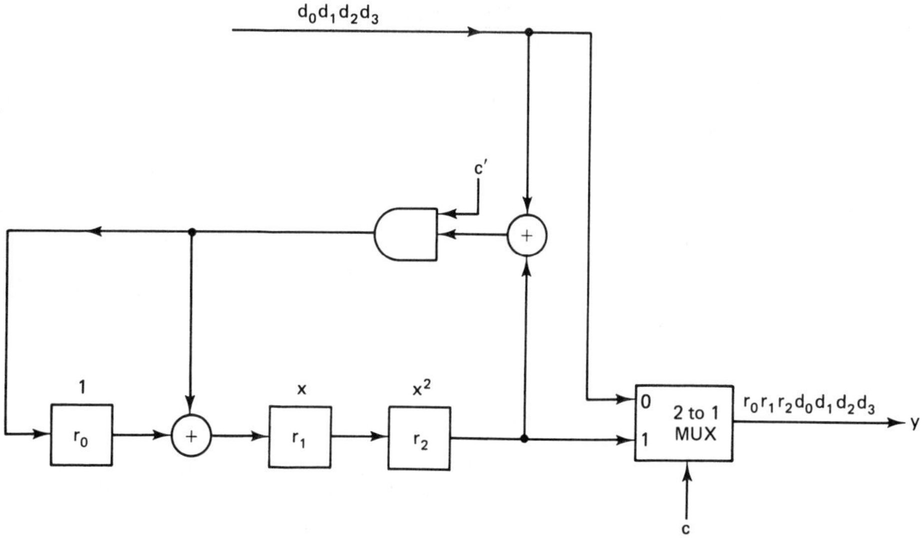

Figure 3.7 The systematic code encoder for (7, 4) cyclic code with generator $\mathbf{g}(x) = x^3 + x + 1$.

Initially, the control variable $c = 0$ for the first 4 cycles, $t = 0, 1, 2$, and 3. The input is serially applied to the LFSR and to the multiplexer with d_3, followed by d_2, d_1, and d_0. By the end of four cycles ($t = 0, 1, 2, 3$), the register will have the residue polynomial formed in the shift register. For the duration of cycles $t = 4, 5, 6$, the control variable c is in state 1 and the multiplexer gates the parity symbols to the output terminal. If the input $\mathbf{d}(x) = x^3 + x^2 + 1$ is applied, then the contents at each cycle are shown as follows. The codeword emerging at the output is 1101001, which represents the code polynomial $\mathbf{u}(x) = x^6 + x^5 + x^3 + 1$.

Cycle	Control	Input	Register			Output
t	c	d	r_0	r_1	r_2	y
0	0	1	0	0	0	1
1	0	1	1	1	0	1
2	0	0	1	0	1	0
3	0	1	1	0	0	1
4	1	x	1	0	0	0
5	1	x	0	1	0	0
6	1	x	0	0	1	1

x: don't care

2. As another example, we consider the (8, 6) code over $GF(3)$ with generator $\mathbf{g}(x) = x^2 + x + 2$. Note that $\mathbf{g}(x)$ is a divisor of $x^8 - 1$.

   For the input $\mathbf{d}(x) = x^4 + 2x^2 + 2$, its code polynomial is generated step by step as follows.

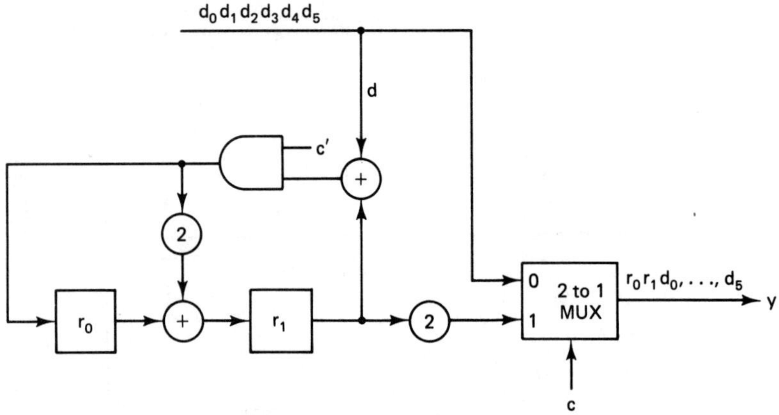

Cycle	Control	Input	Register		Output
t	c	d	r_0	r_1	y
0	0	0	0	0	0
1	0	1	0	0	1
2	0	0	1	2	0
3	0	2	2	2	2
4	0	0	1	1	0
5	0	2	1	0	2
6	1	x	2	2	1
7	1	x	0	2	1

x: don't care

The output code polynomial is $\mathbf{u}(x) = x^6 + 2x^4 + 2x^2 + x + 1$. Also, it is important to note that $\mathbf{u}(x) = \mathbf{d}(x) \cdot x^r - \mathbf{r}(x)$, where

$$\mathbf{r}(x) = \mathbf{d}(x) \cdot x^r \bmod \mathbf{g}(x)$$

To append $-\mathbf{r}(x)$ to the data, a multiplier ② is inserted between the shift register and the multiplexer. To verify that $\mathbf{u}(x)$ is a code polynomial, a formal division here will be appropriate.

$$\begin{array}{r l}
 & x^4 + 2x^3 + x^2 + x + 2 \\
x^2 + x + 2 \,\big) & x^6 \quad +2x^4 \quad +2x^2 + x + 1 \\
 & x^6 + x^5 + 2x^4 \\
\hline
 & 2x^5 \quad +2x^2 + x + 1 \\
 & 2x^5 + 2x^4 + x^3 \\
\hline
 & x^4 + 2x^3 + 2x^2 + x + 1 \\
 & x^4 + x^3 + 2x^2 \\
\hline
 & x^3 \quad + x + 1 \\
 & x^3 + x^2 + 2x \\
\hline
 & 2x^2 + 2x + 1 \\
 & 2x^2 + 2x + 1 \\
\hline
 & 0
\end{array}$$

The division shows that

$$\mathbf{u}(x) = x^6 + 2x^4 + 2x^2 + x + 1 = (x^2 + x + 2)(x^4 + 2x^3 + x^2 + x + 2)$$

and it is a multiple of the generator polynomial. Another encoding method uses the parity polynomial, $\mathbf{h}(x)$, instead of $\mathbf{g}(x)$. Let $\mathbf{u}(x) = u_{n-1}x^{n-1} + \cdots + u_0$ be a code polynomial (with $u_{n-1}, u_{n-2}, \ldots, u_{n-k}$ being information symbols). Then, $\mathbf{u}(x) \cdot \mathbf{h}(x) = 0$, and the coefficient of x^j term (for $j = 0, 1, \ldots, n-1$) in the product $\mathbf{u}(x)\mathbf{h}(x)$ is zero, and therefore we have

$$h_0 u_j + h_1 u_{j-1} + h_2 u_{j-2} + \cdots + h_{k-1} u_{j-k+1} + h_k u_{j-k} = 0 \tag{3.37}$$

The subscript $j - k$ is taken as the residue modulo n. Note also that $\mathbf{h}(x)$ is monic (i.e., $h_k = 1$). Therefore, Equation (3.37) can be written as

$$u_{j-k} = -(h_0 u_j + h_1 u_{j-1} + \cdots + h_{k-1} u_{j-k+1}) \tag{3.38}$$

Equation (3.38) is called a *difference equation* and holds for all $j = 0, 1, \ldots, n-1$. Setting $j = n - 1$ in (3.38), we have

$$u_{n-k-1} = -(h_0 u_{n-1} + h_1 u_{n-2} + \cdots + h_{k-1} u_{n-k}) \tag{3.39}$$

That means that given $u_{n-1}, u_{n-2}, \ldots, u_{n-k}$, we can obtain the next symbol u_{n-k-1} by using (3.39). Then, by using $u_{n-2}, u_{n-3}, \ldots, u_{n-k-1}$, we can get the next symbol u_{n-k-2}, and so on until u_0. Thus, for information $(u_{n-1}, u_{n-2}, \ldots, u_{n-k})$ we obtain the check symbols step by step sequentially $(u_{n-k-1}, u_{n-k-2}, \ldots, u_0)$. A generalized encoder circuit using these difference equations is given in Fig. 3.8.

Initially, $c = 1$ for k cycles, during which period the register is loaded with the information $u_{n-1}, \ldots, u_{n-k}$, and these information symbols are also passed on to the channel. Then c is set to 0 and remains at 0 for $n - k$ cycles. Check symbols $u_{n-k-1}, u_{n-k-2}, \ldots, u_0$ are derived successively and are passed on to the channel. This encoder requires a k digit shift register, whereas the circuit

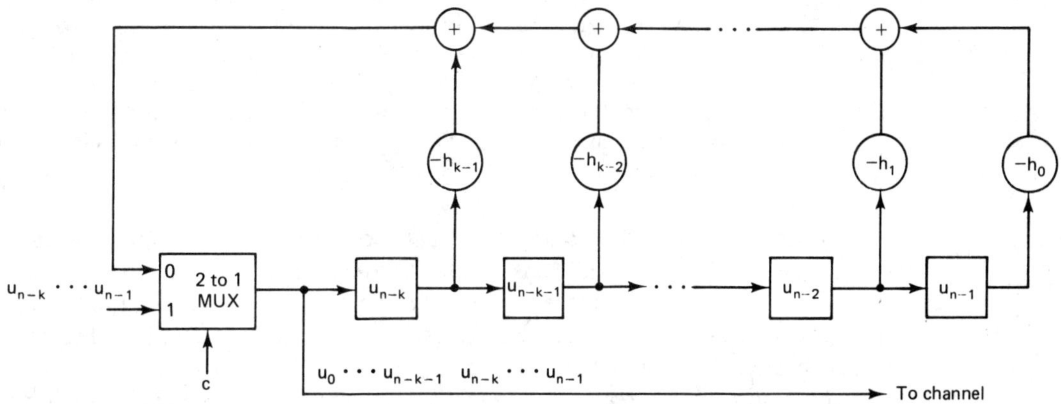

Figure 3.8 Systematic encoder using $\mathbf{h}(x)$.

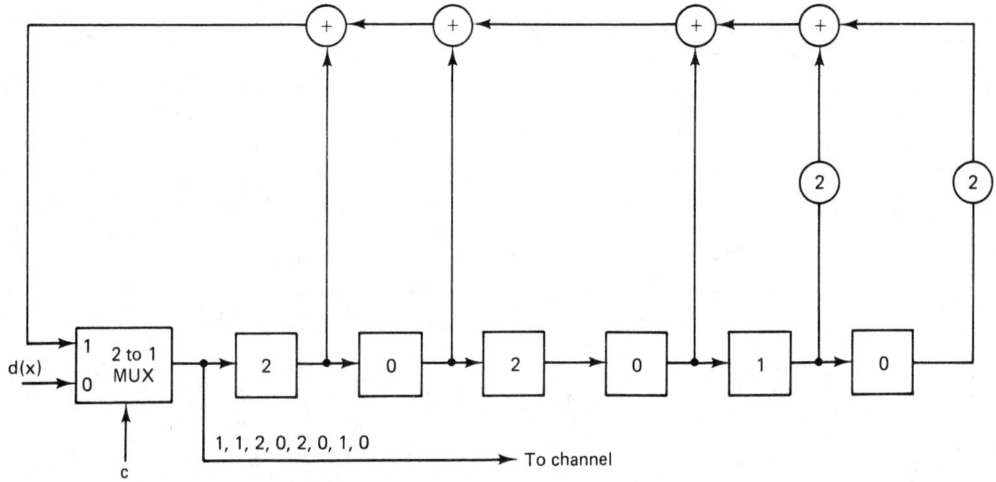

Figure 3.9 An encoder for the (8, 6) code over $GF(3)$ using $h(x) = x^6 + 2x^5 + 2x^4 + 2x^2 + x + 1$.

given by Fig. 3.6 requires an $n - k$ digit register. When $k < n - k$, the circuit of Fig. 3.8 is optimal; where $k > n - k$, the circuit of Fig. 3.6 is more appropriate. However, if the information can be loaded in parallel into the register of Fig. 3.8 as the initial step, then the codeword can be obtained in $n - k$ steps, which would be an advantage over the circuit of Fig. 3.6. To illustrate this encoding, we given an encoder for the same (8, 6) code over $GF(3)$ as follows. We have

$$x^8 - 1 = (x^2 + x + 2)(x^6 + 2x^5 + 2x^4 + 2x^2 + x + 1)$$

and therefore $\mathbf{h}(x) = x^6 + 2x^5 + 2x^4 + 2x^2 + x + 1$. The circuit connections based on the coefficients of $\mathbf{h}(x)$ are given in Fig. 3.9.

In the first six cycles (when $c = 0$), the information digits $0, 1, 0, 2, 0, 2$ corresponding to $\mathbf{d}(x) = x^4 + 2x^2 + 2$ are loaded into the shift register and also are transferred to the channel. The check digits coming out as feedback in the next two cycles are $1, 1$. Thus, the codeword $\mathbf{u} = (0, 1, 0, 2, 0, 2, 1, 1)$ corresponding to the code polynomial $x^6 + 2x^4 + 2x^2 + x + 1$ is obtained. This circuit can be implemented by parallel loading of $\mathbf{d}(x)$ and providing two more digit cells for the shift register at the right end to accommodate the eight-digit codeword. This implementation would require only two cycles (two shifts of the register) to obtain a codeword.

Syndrome generation and error detection/correction. In this section, we consider decoding logic that consists of syndrome generation, error computation, and error correction if the code is capable of correcting errors. As stated previously, if it is a distance-3 code, then single errors can be corrected. If it is a distance-4 code, then SEC-DED can be implemented.

The syndrome of a received polynomial can be obtained by a circuit similar to the encoder of Fig. 3.6. The received word $\mathbf{v}(x)$ is applied as input at the right end.

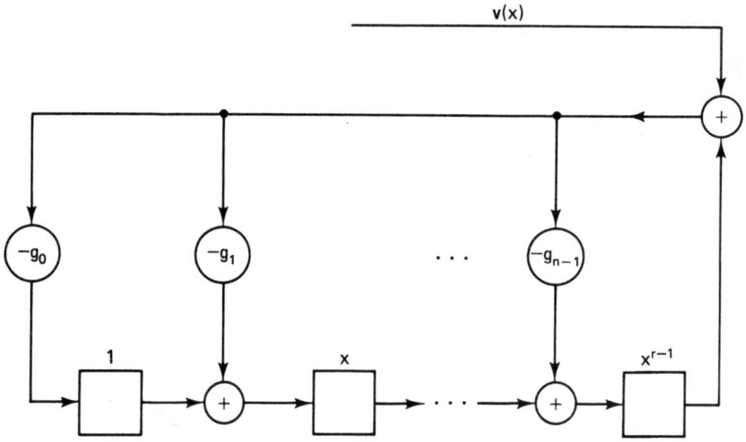

Figure 3.10 Syndrome generator circuit.

This application at the position of x^r amounts to premultiplying $\mathbf{v}(x)$ by x^r (Fig. 3.10).

At the end of n shifts, the syndrome of $x^r\mathbf{v}(x)$ is formed. Equation (3.40) represents this syndrome.

$$\mathbf{s}(x^r\mathbf{v}(x)) = x^r \cdot \mathbf{v}(x) \bmod \mathbf{g}(x) \tag{3.40}$$

If the input is applied at the left end, then the syndrome will be $\mathbf{v}(x) \bmod \mathbf{g}(x)$. The reason for getting the syndrome of $x^r \cdot \mathbf{v}(x)$, instead of the syndrome of $\mathbf{v}(x)$, is that the syndrome generation part will be similar to the encoder of Fig. 3.6 and also in some cases the error location will be simplified, as we will observe later. If the received polynomial $\mathbf{v}(x)$ is a code polynomial, then $x^r \cdot \mathbf{v}(x) \bmod \mathbf{g}(x) = 0$. On the other hand, if $\mathbf{e}(x)$ is an error polynomial for a transmitted code polynomial $\mathbf{u}(x)$, then the received polynomial is

$$\mathbf{v}(x) = \mathbf{u}(x) + \mathbf{e}(x) \tag{3.41}$$

Then the syndrome of $\mathbf{v}(x)$ is given by $\mathbf{e}(x) \bmod \mathbf{g}(x)$ as follows.

$$\begin{aligned} \mathbf{s}(\mathbf{v}(x)) &= \mathbf{s}(\mathbf{u}(x)) + \mathbf{s}(\mathbf{e}(x)) \\ &= \mathbf{u}(x) \bmod \mathbf{g}(x) + \mathbf{e}(x) \bmod \mathbf{g}(x) \\ &= \mathbf{0} + \mathbf{e}(x) \bmod \mathbf{g}(x) = \mathbf{s}(\mathbf{e}(x)) \end{aligned} \tag{3.42}$$

To illustrate the syndrome decoding, error location, and correction, we will use the same example of (7, 4) cyclic code over $GF(2)$ given in Example Set 3-8. It is to be noted that for this code the syndromes of single errors are distinct, and it is single-error correcting as can be seen from the following table.

$\mathbf{e}(x)$	$\mathbf{s}(\mathbf{e}(x))$	$\mathbf{s}(x^3\mathbf{e}(x))$
1	1	$x+1$
x	x	x^2+x
x^2	x^2	x^2+x+1
x^3	$x+1$	x^2+1
x^4	x^2+x	1
x^5	x^2+x+1	x
x^6	x^2+1	x^2

The decoder circuit for the (7, 4) SEC code is given as Fig. 3.11. The received polynomial $\mathbf{v}(x)$ is gated into the buffer register (BR) serially while it is applied as input to the syndrome generator. At the end of n cycles, the syndrome of $x^3 \cdot \mathbf{v}(x)$ is formed in the three-bit syndrome register (SR). If the single error is in position x^6 (i.e., $\mathbf{e}(x) = x^6$), then we have

$$\mathbf{s}(x^3\mathbf{v}(x)) = \mathbf{s}(x^3 \cdot \mathbf{e}(x)) = \mathbf{s}(x^3 \cdot x^6)$$
$$= \mathbf{s}(x^9) = x^9 \bmod x^3 + x + 1 = x^2$$

The syndrome decoder is designed to detect this value x^2 in SR. If this is detected,

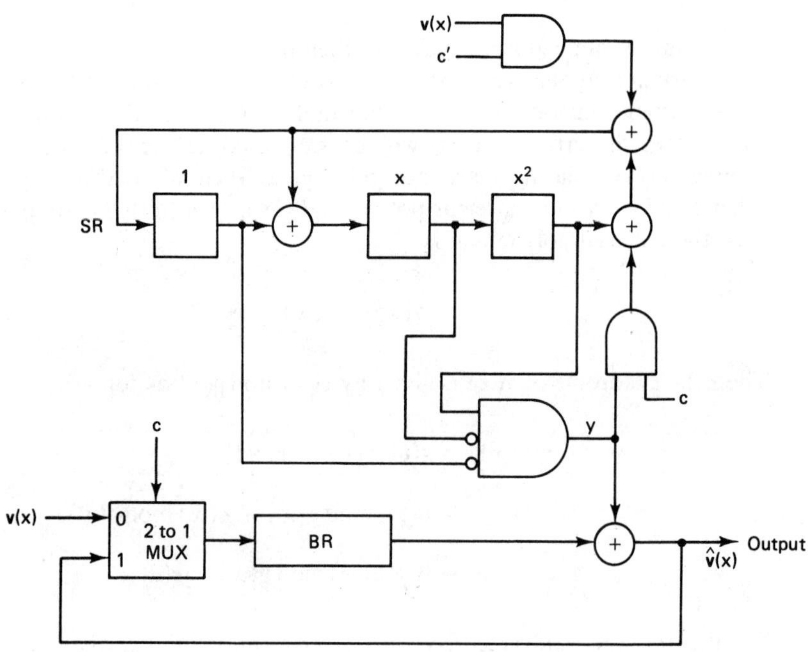

Figure 3.11 A (7, 4) cyclic code decoder with input applied at the right end.

the variable y in Fig. 3.11 will be a 1, which is applied to correct v_6 bit of the BR and obtain $\hat{v}_6$.

$$\hat{v}_6 = v_6 \oplus y \tag{3.43}$$

On the other hand, if the error position is not x^6 but elsewhere, then $y = 0$ and $\hat{v}_6 = v_6$ will be passed on as output. Suppose now that the error is in position x^5, then

$$\mathbf{s}(x^3 \cdot \mathbf{v}(x)) = \mathbf{s}(x^3 \cdot x^5) = x$$

By a cyclic shift of SR and BR, we advance the error to position x^6, the error is detected by y, and the correction can now be applied to position v_5. This process is continued for seven cycles, and at the end the corrected $\hat{\mathbf{v}}(x)$ is cycled back into BR.

Also to be noted is that when y turns to be 1, then SR is 001. By the next cycle, SR will be 000, and there will be no further correction required. The parts of the decoder—the syndrome generator, syndrome decoder, and error corrector—can be seen in Fig. 3.11 for the SEC code.

In Fig. 3.11, the control c will be 0 for the first seven syndrome generation cycles and will be 1 for the next seven error correction cycles. The foregoing circuit can also be implemented with input $\mathbf{v}(x)$ applied at the left end of the syndrome generator, in which case the syndrome decoder gate will be designed to detect $\mathbf{s}(x^6) = x^2 + 1$. That circuit is given in Fig. 3.12. Once y turns to 1, $z = y \cdot c$ will also be 1, and by the next cycle SR will be cleared to 0 as required. As can be seen, Fig. 3.12 is slightly more complicated compared with Fig. 3.11, and therefore the latter is often preferred.

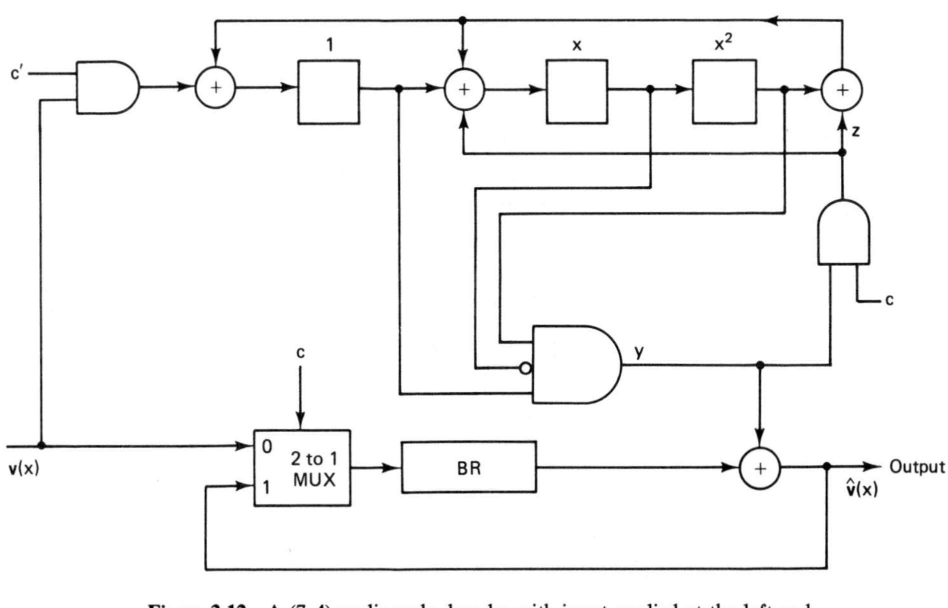

Figure 3.12 A (7, 4) cyclic code decoder with input applied at the left end.

3.2.4 Cyclic Hamming Codes

The binary (7, 4) cyclic code generated by $\mathbf{g}(x) = x^3 + x + 1$ (given in the previous example) is equivalent to the Hamming SEC code. Its $\mathbf{H}$ matrix can be given as

$$\mathbf{H} = \begin{bmatrix} | & | & | & | & | & | & | \\ 1 & \alpha & \alpha^2 & \alpha^3 & \alpha^4 & \alpha^5 & \alpha^6 \\ | & | & | & | & | & | & | \end{bmatrix}$$

$$= \begin{bmatrix} 0 & 0 & 1 & 0 & 1 & 1 & 1 \\ 0 & 1 & 0 & 1 & 1 & 1 & 0 \\ 1 & 0 & 0 & 1 & 0 & 1 & 1 \end{bmatrix}$$

where α^j is called the coefficient vector of $x^j \bmod \mathbf{g}(x)$ (for $j = 0, 1, \ldots, 6$). Alternately, α can be considered to be a zero of $\mathbf{g}(x)$, and the successive powers of α are all distinct 0 through $n - 1$. Then the columns of $\mathbf{H}$ are pairwise linearly independent and therefore the code has a distance of at least 3. The syndrome of $\mathbf{v}(x)$ is $\mathbf{v}(\boldsymbol{\alpha}) = \mathbf{v} \cdot \mathbf{H}^T$. Therefore, the class of cyclic Hamming SEC codes is described as follows.

$$\mathbf{g}(x) = \text{primitive polynomial of degree } r$$

$$n = \text{code length} = 2^r - 1$$

$$k = 2^r - 1 - r$$

$$\text{parity matrix } \mathbf{H} = \begin{bmatrix} | & | & | & & | \\ 1 & \alpha & \alpha^2 & \cdots & \alpha^{2^r-2} \\ | & | & | & & | \end{bmatrix}$$

$$\text{syndrome, } \mathbf{s} = \mathbf{v}(\alpha) \text{ for received polynomial } \mathbf{v}(x)$$

The encoder/decoder circuit for this class is a generalization of the (7, 4) code previously given. The syndrome generator of Fig. 3.12 can be considered as the generator of $\mathbf{v}(\alpha)$, and the generator in Fig. 3.11 corresponds to $\mathbf{v}(\alpha) \cdot \alpha^3$. The distance-4 Hamming (SEC–DED) code is described as follows.

$$\mathbf{g}(x) = (x + 1) \cdot \mathbf{p}(x), \qquad \mathbf{p}(x) \text{ a primitive polynomial of degree } r$$

$$n = 2^r - 1$$

$$k = 2^r - 2 - r$$

$$\text{parity matrix } \mathbf{H} = \begin{bmatrix} | & | & | & & | \\ 1 & \alpha & \alpha^2 & \cdots & \alpha^{2^r-2} \\ | & | & | & & | \\ 1 & 1 & 1 & & 1 \end{bmatrix}$$

$$\mathbf{s} = (\mathbf{v}(\alpha), \mathbf{v}(1))$$

An SEC–DED code can also be obtained by appending an overall parity bit to a cyclic SEC code. The code so constructed is not cyclic but it is called an *extended cyclic code*. Its parameters are given as follows.

$$n = 2^r \quad : \text{code length}$$
$$k = 2^r - r - 1 : \text{data length}$$
$$n - k = r + 1 \quad : \text{number of parities}$$

The decoder for an SEC–DED Hamming cyclic code is shown in Fig. 3.13.

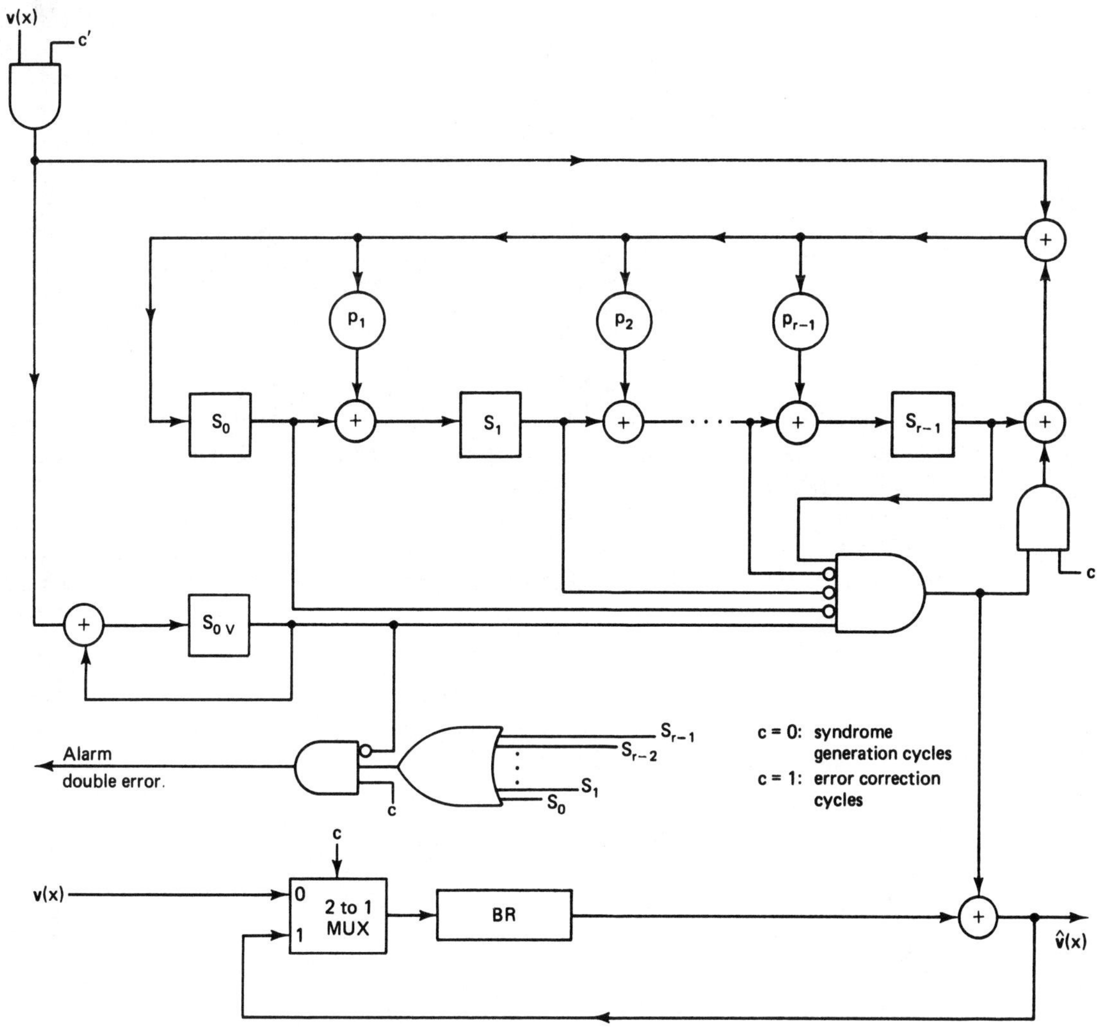

Figure 3.13 An SEC–DED Hamming cyclic code decoder.

3.2.5 Shortened Cyclic Codes

The information length k of the Hamming SEC code is $2^r - 1 - r$. These values are 4, 11, 26, 57, and 120 for $r = 3, 4, 5, 6$, and 7 respectively. If it is SEC–DED, then k will be one less. In computer systems, the data length is usually a multiple of 8. A half word for 16 bits, a word for 32 bits, double precision (word) for 64 bits, and extended precision (word) for 128 bits are common usage in computer systems. In order to have $k = 16, 32, 64, 128$, and so on, a cyclic code has to be *shortened* by l positions, illustrated as follows.

k	SEC Cyclic Code	Shortened Cyclic SEC Code	l
8	(15, 11)	(12, 8)	3
16	(31, 26)	(21, 16)	10
32	(63, 57)	(38, 32)	25
64	(127, 120)	(71, 64)	56

The shortening can be accomplished by assuming the higher order l terms of the data polynomial (as well as the code polynomial) to be 0's. The encoder of Fig. 3.6 can be used for shortened code without any change, actually ignoring the first l cycles of presumed 0's. For the decoder, however, the presumed leading l 0's cannot be ignored for reasons of speed and buffer space. Therefore, the decoder is considerably modified. First, consider the (15, 11) SEC code decoder given in Fig. 3.14.

In order to accommodate this code for data length $k = 8$, we shorten the (15, 11) code by three bits to obtain a (12, 8) code. This shortened code decoder is given in Fig. 3.15 and not only does it save the number of flipflops in BR by 3, it will also reduce the number of cycles for decoding by 6. Let $\mathbf{v} = (v_0, v_1, \ldots, v_{11})$ be the received vector (or polynomial). If $\mathbf{v}$ is gated into the syndrome register of Fig. 3.14, we would require three extra shifts of SR and BR for processing the three leading 0's. On the other hand, in Fig. 3.15, this is accomplished by premultiplying the input polynomial $\mathbf{v}(x)$ by $x^r \cdot x^l = x^{r+l} = x^{4+3} = x^7$. To obtain $x^7 \bmod \mathbf{g}(x)$, we actually divide as follows.

$$
\begin{array}{r|l}
 & x^3 + 1 \\
\hline
x^4 + x + 1 & x^7 \\
 & x^7 + x^4 + x^3 \\
\cline{2-2}
 & \quad x^4 + x^3 \\
 & \quad x^4 \qquad + x + 1 \\
\cline{2-2}
 & \qquad x^3 + x + 1
\end{array}
$$

Then the syndrome generated will be

$$
\begin{aligned}
\mathbf{s}\big(x^{r+l} \cdot \mathbf{v}(x)\big) &= x^7 \cdot \mathbf{v}(x) \bmod \mathbf{g}(x) \\
&= (x^3 + x + 1)\mathbf{v}(x) \bmod \mathbf{g}(x)
\end{aligned}
$$

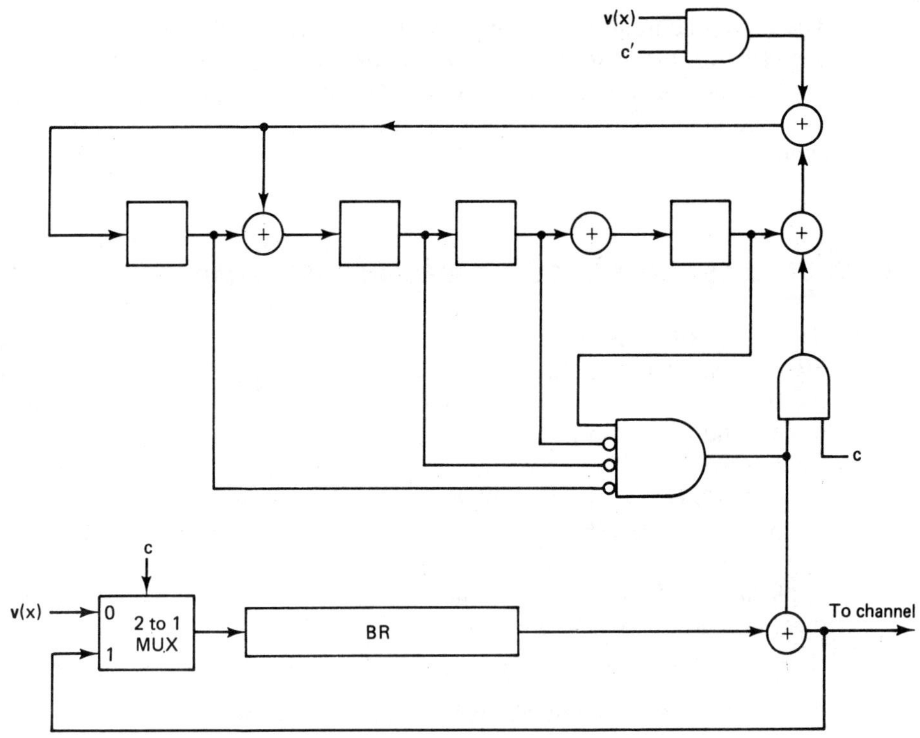

Figure 3.14 A (15, 11) SEC cyclic code decoder.

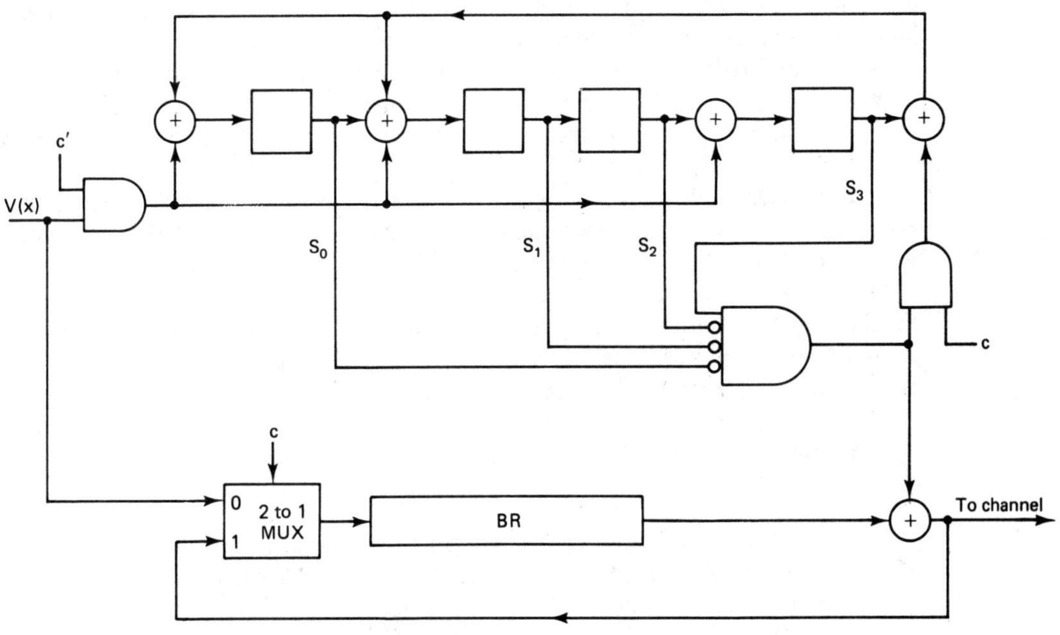

Figure 3.15 A (12, 8) shortened SEC cyclic code decoder.

Therefore, the input $\mathbf{v}(x)$ is applied at positions x^3, x, and 1 simultaneously. The decoder then processes the error correction part just as is done in Fig. 3.14.

A shortened cyclic SEC–DED code can be implemented in a similar fashion by combining the features of Figs. 3.13 and 3.15 (see Problem 3.10 at the end of the chapter). The principle of shortening a cyclic code can similarly be applied to larger distance codes as well.

3.3 OTHER CLASSES OF CYCLIC CODES AND ALGEBRAS

We have studied cyclic codes and their structure as ideals in the previous section. Here, we study these from the specification of the zeros of the generator polynomial. To see the structure from the point of view of the zeros, we need some further understanding of the polynomial algebras that are presented in the next section. This would lead to several important classes of cyclic codes: (1) Bose–Chaudhury–Hocquenghem (BCH) codes for random t-error correction (tEC) [BOSE 60, HOCQ 59]; (2) Reed–Solomon (RS) codes for random byte (or symbol) correction [REED 60]; and (3) burst error correcting codes [FIRE 59]. Several applications of these codes to high-speed memories and mass memories will be discussed in Chapters 4, 5, and 6.

3.3.1 Polynomial Algebras and Minimum Polynomials

We start with $\mathbf{g}(x) = x^3 + x + 1$ over $GF(2)$, which is used as the generator of the $(7, 4, 3)$ code in Section 3.2. As we stated in that section, if α is a zero of $\mathbf{g}(x)$, then α, α^2, α^3, α^4, α^5, α^6, and $\alpha^7 = 1$ are all distinct. Therefore, α is a primitive element, and $\mathbf{g}(x)$ is a primitive polynomial. A primitive polynomial over $GF(q)$ can be defined as an irreducible (or prime) polynomial, say degree r, such that the order of its zero α is $q^r - 1$. Alternately, $\mathbf{p}(x)$ is a primitive polynomial of degree r over $GF(q)$ if and only if the smallest positive n such that $\mathbf{p}(x)$ divides $x^n - 1$ is given by $q^r - 1$.

For the example $\mathbf{g}(x) = x^3 + x + 1$ over $GF(2)$ with α as a zero, we have that $\mathbf{g}(\alpha) = \alpha^3 + \alpha + 1 = 0$ and the smallest positive n such that $\alpha^n = 1$ is 7. Therefore, α is also a zero of $x^7 - 1$. Since $\mathbf{g}(\alpha^2) = \alpha^6 + \alpha^2 + 1 = (\alpha^3 + \alpha + 1)^2 = (\mathbf{g}(\alpha))^2 = 0$, α^2 is also a zero of $\mathbf{g}(x)$. Since α^2 is a zero, $(\alpha^2)^2 = \alpha^4$ must also be a zero. Further squaring of α^4 will give $(\alpha^4)^2 = \alpha^8 = \alpha$ the original zero. Thus, the degree-3 polynomial $\mathbf{g}(x)$ has three zeros α, α^2, and α^4. For a generalization over any $GF(q)$, we have the following.

Lemma 3-1. *For any $a \in GF(q)$, $a^q = a$. Also, for any $\mathbf{g}(x)$ over $GF(q)$, $(\mathbf{g}(x))^q = \mathbf{g}(x^q)$.*

Proof. All nonzero elements of $GF(q)$ form a multiplicative group of order $q - 1$. The order of $a \in GF(q)$, $a \neq 0$ is the smallest integer e such that $a^e = 1$. The order of a divides the order of the group, $q - 1$. Therefore, $a^{q-1} = 1$ and $a^q = a$, which proves the first part of the lemma.

Let $\mathbf{g}(x) = g_0 + g_1x + \cdots + g_rx^r$. Then, $\mathbf{g}(x)^q$ can be expanded by use of multinomial theorem. All those terms with a coefficient factor of q will drop out. Therefore we get

$$(\mathbf{g}(x))^q = (g_0)^q + (g_1x)^q + \cdots + (g_rx^r)^q$$

Since $g_i^q = g_i$, we get

$$(\mathbf{g}(x))^q = g_0 + g_1(x)^q + \cdots + g_r(x^r)^q = \mathbf{g}(x^q)$$

as to be proved.

Theorem 3-4. *Let $\mathbf{g}(x)$ be an irreducible polynomial of degree r over $GF(q)$. Then it has r zeros $\alpha, \alpha^q, \alpha^{q^2}, \ldots, \alpha^{q^{r-1}}$ in the extension $GF(q^r)$.*

Proof. Let α be a zero of $\mathbf{g}(x) = x^r + g_{r-1}x^{r-1} + \cdots + g_0$. Then, $GF(q^r)$ can be obtained as the set of all polynomials in α of degree less than r over $GF(q)$. Since $\mathbf{g}(\alpha) = 0$, by Lemma 3-1 we have

$$\mathbf{g}(\alpha^q) = (\mathbf{g}(\alpha))^q = 0$$

and α^q is also a zero of $\mathbf{g}(x)$. Since α^q is a zero, $(\alpha^q)^q = \alpha^{q^2}$ is also a zero. This process continues to $\alpha^{q^{r-1}}$. The next power $(\alpha^{q^{r-1}})^q = \alpha^{q^r} = \alpha$, because the order of α divides $q^r - 1$. Q.E.D.

As examples, consider $\mathbf{g}_1(x) = x^4 + x + 1$ and $\mathbf{g}_2(x) = x^4 + x^3 + x^2 + x + 1$ both over $GF(2)$. These can be verified easily to be irreducible polynomials. Let α be a zero of $\mathbf{g}_1(x)$ and β be a zero of $\mathbf{g}_2(x)$. The zeros of $\mathbf{g}_1(x)$ and $\mathbf{g}_2(x)$ are

$$\mathbf{g}_1(x) = x^4 + x + 1, \qquad \text{zeros are } \alpha, \alpha^2, \alpha^4, \alpha^8 \in GF(2^4)$$
$$\mathbf{g}_2(x) = x^4 + x^3 + x^2 + x + 1, \qquad \text{zeros are } \beta, \beta^2, \beta^4, \beta^8 \in GF(2^4)$$

Also, we can obtain all nonzero elements of $GF(2^4)$, as powers of α by using the equation $\alpha^4 = \alpha + 1$. We find α to be a primitive element in $GF(2^4)$, and its order is 15. On the other hand, β has an order of only 5, and it generates only a proper subgroup of the multiplicative group of $GF(16)$. To find β as a power of α, we proceed as follows.

Definition 3-5. Let β denote an element in $GF(q^m)$, the mth degree extension of $GF(q)$. Then the *minimum polynomial* (also called the *minimum function*) of β is a monic polynomial $\mathbf{m}(x)$ of the smallest degree with coefficients from $GF(q)$ such that $m(\beta) = 0$. That is, $\mathbf{m}(x)$ is the smallest degree polynomial with β as its zero.

It is fairly easy to show that $\mathbf{m}(x)$ is irreducible. If it has factors, $\mathbf{m}(x) = \mathbf{d}_1(x)\mathbf{d}_2(x)$, then $\mathbf{m}(\beta) = \mathbf{d}_1(\beta) \cdot \mathbf{d}_2(\beta) = 0$. That means either $d_1(\beta) = 0$ or $\mathbf{d}_2(\beta) = 0$, and β is a zero of a polynomial of smaller degree than $\mathbf{m}(x)$. That contradicts the definition. Therefore, $\mathbf{m}(x)$ must be irreducible.

TABLE 3.6 POWERS OF α AND β

	1	α	α^2	α^3		1	β	β^2	β^3
$\alpha =$	0	1	0	0	$\beta =$	0	0	1	0
$\alpha^2 =$	0	0	1	0	$\beta^2 =$	0	0	1	0
$\alpha^3 =$	0	0	0	1	$\beta^3 =$	0	0	0	1
$\alpha^4 =$	1	1	0	0	$\beta^4 =$	1	1	1	1
$\alpha^5 =$	0	1	1	0	$\beta^5 =$	1	0	0	0
$\alpha^6 =$	0	0	1	1					
$\alpha^7 =$	1	1	0	1					
$\alpha^8 =$	1	0	1	0					
$\alpha^9 =$	0	1	0	1					
$\alpha^{10} =$	1	1	1	0					
$\alpha^{11} =$	0	1	1	1					
$\alpha^{12} =$	1	1	1	1					
$\alpha^{13} =$	1	0	1	1					
$\alpha^{14} =$	1	0	0	1					
$\alpha^{15} =$	1	0	0	0					

The two polynomials $\mathbf{g}_1(x) = x^4 + x + 1$, and $\mathbf{g}_2(x) = x^4 + x^3 + x^2 + x + 1$ are also minimum polynomials of α and β, respectively. Also, the minimum polynomial of α^2 (α^4 and α^8) is $x^4 + x + 1$.

Now let us find the minimum polynomial of $\alpha^3 \in GF(2^4)$. From Table 3.6, we have $\alpha^{15} = 1$ and the order of α^3 is 5. Therefore, α^3 is a zero of $x^5 - 1$. However, $x^5 - 1 = (x-1)(x^4 + x^3 + x^2 + x + 1)$. From this we can see that α^3 is a zero of $\mathbf{g}_2(x) = x^4 + x^3 + x^2 + x + 1$ and $\mathbf{g}_2(x)$ is the minimum function of β. Therefore we can set $\beta = \alpha^3$. The zeros of $\mathbf{g}_2(x)$ are, therefore, $\beta = \alpha^3$, $\beta^2 = \alpha^6$, $\beta^4 = \alpha^{12}$, and $\beta^8 = \alpha^9$.

There are many formal methods to derive the minimum polynomial of a given element. We illustrate a few examples here.

Example 3-10

Let α be a zero of $\mathbf{g}_1(x) = x^4 + x + 1$ over $GF(2)$. Its powers $\alpha^j \in GF(2^4)$, $j = 1, 2, \ldots, 15$ are shown in Table 3.6. Let $\mathbf{m}_i(x)$ denote the minimum polynomial of α^i for all i. Then $\mathbf{m}_1(x) = \mathbf{m}_2(x) = \mathbf{m}_4(x) = \mathbf{m}_8(x) = \mathbf{g}_1(x)$. To obtain $\mathbf{m}_3(x)$, we list all its zeros. Since α^3 is a zero of $\mathbf{m}_3(x)$, $(\alpha^3)^2 = \alpha^6$, $(\alpha^6)^2 = \alpha^{12}$, and $(\alpha^{12})^2 = \alpha^9$ are also zeros of $\mathbf{m}_3(x)$. (Note that $(\alpha^9)^2 = \alpha^3$, and therefore the squaring stops here.) Therefore, we have

$$\begin{aligned}
\mathbf{m}_3(x) &= (x - \alpha^3)(x - \alpha^6)(x - \alpha^9)(x - \alpha^{12}) \\
&= x^4 + x^3(\alpha^3 + \alpha^6 + \alpha^9 + \alpha^{12}) \\
&\quad + x^2(\alpha^3 \cdot \alpha^6 + \alpha^3 \cdot \alpha^9 + \alpha^3 \cdot \alpha^{12} + \alpha^6 \cdot \alpha^9 + \alpha^6 \cdot \alpha^{12} + \alpha^9 \cdot \alpha^{12}) \\
&\quad + x(\alpha^3 \cdot \alpha^6 \cdot \alpha^9 + \alpha^3 \cdot \alpha^9 \cdot \alpha^{12} + \alpha^6 \cdot \alpha^9 \cdot \alpha^{12} + \alpha^3 \cdot \alpha^6 \cdot \alpha^{12}) \\
&\quad + \alpha^3 \cdot \alpha^6 \cdot \alpha^9 \cdot \alpha^{12}
\end{aligned}$$

By using Table 3.6, we obtain

$$\mathbf{m}_3(x) = x^4 + x^3 + x^2 + x + 1$$

To obtain $\mathbf{m}_5(x)$, we observe that its zeros are α^5 and $(\alpha^5)^2 = \alpha^{10}$. (Again, note that $(\alpha^{10})^2 = \alpha^5$.) Therefore,

$$\begin{aligned}\mathbf{m}_5(x) &= (x - \alpha^5)(x - \alpha^{10})\\ &= x^2 + (\alpha^5 + \alpha^{10})x + \alpha^5 \cdot \alpha^{10}\\ &= x^2 + x + 1\end{aligned}$$

$\mathbf{m}_7(x)$ has zeros α^7, α^{14}, α^{13}, and α^{11}. Therefore, its degree is 4. Let $\mathbf{m}_7(x) = x^4 + a_3x^3 + a_2x^2 + a_1x + a_0$. Clearly, a_0 must be equal to 1, otherwise $\mathbf{m}_7(x)$ will be reducible. To solve for a_3, a_2, and a_1, we have the following.

$$\begin{aligned}\mathbf{m}_7(\alpha^7) &= (\alpha^7)^4 + a_3(\alpha^7)^3 + a_2(\alpha^7)^2 + a_1(\alpha^7) + 1 = 0\\ &= \alpha^{13} + a_3 \cdot \alpha^6 + a_2 \cdot \alpha^{14} + a_1 \cdot \alpha^7 + 1 = 0\end{aligned}$$

From Table 3.6, we have

$$\mathbf{m}_7(\alpha^7) = \begin{bmatrix}1\\1\\0\\1\end{bmatrix} + a_3\begin{bmatrix}1\\1\\0\\0\end{bmatrix} + a_2\begin{bmatrix}1\\0\\0\\1\end{bmatrix} + a_1\begin{bmatrix}1\\0\\1\\1\end{bmatrix} + \begin{bmatrix}0\\0\\0\\1\end{bmatrix} = \begin{bmatrix}0\\0\\0\\0\end{bmatrix}$$

The above leads to the following equations.

$$\begin{aligned}1 + a_3 + a_2 + a_1 + 0 &= 0\\ 1 + a_3 + 0 + 0 + 0 &= 0\\ 0 + 0 + 0 + a_1 + 0 &= 0\\ 1 + 0 + a_2 + a_1 + 1 &= 0\end{aligned}$$

These are solved trivially, giving us $a_3 = 1$, $a_2 = a_1 = 0$. Therefore, $\mathbf{m}_7(x) = x^4 + x^3 + 1$. To summarize the minimum polynomials of α^j for all j, we give Table 3.7.

Table 3.7 will be used extensively in following sections and chapters of this book. Some further notes on this topic are appropriate. First, the minimum polynomial $\mathbf{m}_j(x)$ of α^j is of degree no greater than 4. Multiplying the polynomials of Table 3.7 we get

$$\begin{aligned}&\mathbf{m}_0(x) \cdot \mathbf{m}_1(x) \cdot \mathbf{m}_3(x) \cdot \mathbf{m}_5(x) \cdot \mathbf{m}_7(x)\\ &\quad= (x + 1)(x^4 + x + 1)(x^4 + x^3 + x^2 + x + 1)(x^2 + x + 1)(x^4 + x^3 + 1)\\ &\quad= x^{15} + 1 = x^{15} - 1 \qquad (3.44)\end{aligned}$$

Thus, the zeros of $x^{15} - 1$ are the nonzero elements of $GF(16)$, and the zeros of

TABLE 3.7 MINIMUM POLYNOMIALS FOR $\alpha^j \in GF(2^4)$

Minimum Polynomial	Zeros
$\mathbf{m}_0(x) = x + 1$	1
$\mathbf{m}_1(x) = x^4 + x + 1$	$\alpha, \alpha^2, \alpha^4, \alpha^8$
$\mathbf{m}_3(x) = x^4 + x^3 + x^2 + x + 1$	$\alpha^3, \alpha^6, \alpha^9, \alpha^{12}$
$\mathbf{m}_5(x) = x^2 + x + 1$	α^5, α^{10}
$\mathbf{m}_7(x) = x^4 + x^3 + 1$	$\alpha^7, \alpha^{11}, \alpha^{13}, \alpha^{14}$

$x^{16} - x$ are all the elements of $GF(16)$. A generalization of this result is given as a theorem without proof (see [PETE 72, ALBE 56]).

Theorem 3-5. *For α, a primitive element in $GF(q)$ we have*

$$x^q - x = x\prod_{j=0}^{q-2}(x - \alpha^j) \tag{3.45}$$

As a further illustration of the foregoing, we have, for $GF(3^2)$,

$$x^{3^2} - x = x(x-1)(x-\alpha)(x-\alpha^2)(x-\alpha^3)(x-\alpha^4)(x-\alpha^5)(x-\alpha^6)(x-\alpha^7)$$

where α is a primitive element in $GF(3^2)$. If α is a zero of the primitive polynomial $x^2 + x + 2$ over $GF(3)$, then we have

$$x^9 - x = x(x+2)(x^2+x+2)(x^2+1)(x+1)(x^2+2x+2)$$

Minimum polynomial	Zeros
x	0
$\mathbf{m}_0(x) = x + 2$	$\alpha^0 = 1 = \alpha^8$
$\mathbf{m}_1(x) = x^2 + x + 2$	α, α^3
$\mathbf{m}_2(x) = x^2 + 1$	α^2, α^6
$\mathbf{m}_4(x) = x + 1$	$\alpha^4 = 2$
$\mathbf{m}_5(x) = x^2 + 2x + 2$	α^5, α^7

3.3.2 Logic Circuits for Cyclic Codes

For implementing encoding and decoding logic of cyclic codes, we study here some switching circuits for polynomial algebras and Galois fields. We give a few examples to illustrate the implementations. For a more thorough understanding, the reader may refer to [PETE 72].

The basic elements of these switching circuits are given in Fig. 3.16: adder in $GF(q)$, multiplier by a scalar, and a storage device to store any element of $GF(q)$.

These three elements shown in Fig. 3.16 are extensively used in the logic circuits given here. If the field $GF(q)$ is such that $q = 2^b$, then a b-bit storage element (b flipflops) is assumed. In addition, some control gates, such as AND's

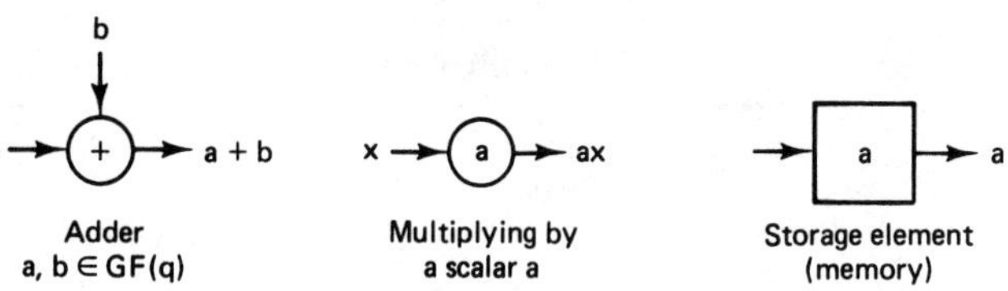

Figure 3.16 Basic elements of switching circuits for cyclic codes.

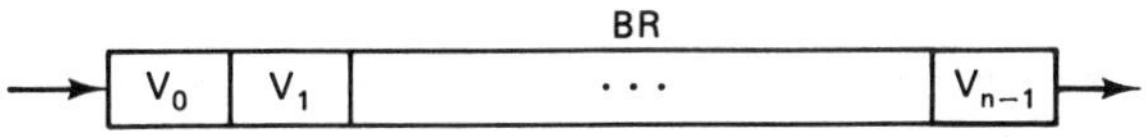

Figure 3.17 Register to store $\mathbf{v} = (v_0, \ldots, v_{n-1})$, $v_i \in GF(q)$.

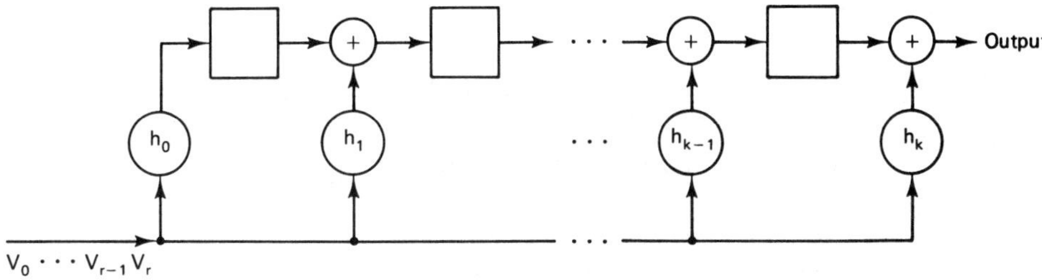

Figure 3.18 Multiply by $\mathbf{h}(x)$.

and 2 to 1 multiplexers, are also used in these circuits. A register named **BR** (for buffer register) is shown in Fig. 3.17, combining n storage elements. A polynomial $\mathbf{v}(x) = v_0 + v_1x + \cdots + v_{n-1}x^{n-1}$ can be gated into BR serially in n shift operations.

Multiplication circuit. To multiply a received polynomial $\mathbf{v}(x)$ by a fixed polynomial $\mathbf{h}(x) = h_0 + h_1x + \cdots + h_kx^k$, the following circuit can be used. The multiplicand $\mathbf{v}(x)$ is applied as input serially with the higher-order coefficients first. Product $\mathbf{h}(x)\mathbf{v}(x)$ is generated as the output with the higher-order coefficients first (see Fig. 3.18).

Initially the register contains all zeros. The first output term is h_kv_r, the coefficient of x^{k+r}. After one cycle, the register will contain values v_rh_0, $v_rh_1, \ldots, v_rh_{k-1}$. The second output term is $v_{r-1}h_k + v_rh_{k-1}$, which is the coefficient of x^{k+r-1}. Also, the register will contain values $v_{r-1}h_0, v_rh_0 + v_{r-1}h_1, \ldots, v_rh_{k-2} + v_{r-1}h_{k-1}$. The third output is $v_{r-2}h_k + v_{r-1}h_{k-1} + v_rh_{k-2}$, which is the coefficient of x^{k+r-2}, and so the operation continues until all terms are generated. It requires $k + r + 1$ cycles to output the product. Note that the input string will start with high order term v_r. It is followed by $v_{r-1}, \ldots, v_1, v_0, 0 \ldots 0$, a string of k zeros.

Division logic. A division circuit is very commonly employed to obtain a residue modulo a polynomial, say $\mathbf{g}(x)$. In polynomial algebras and Galois field algebras, the quotient is not often required, although it can be generated at the output. In Fig. 3.19 we consider a circuit for division by the monic polynomial $\mathbf{g}(x) = x^r + g_{r-1}x^{r-1} + \cdots + g_0$. The dividend $\mathbf{v}(x)$ is applied serially at the left with higher-order coefficients first. Initially the register is cleared.

The principle used in the division circuit is to obtain a remainder in the register when $\mathbf{v}(x)$ is divided by $\mathbf{g}(x)$. Note that

$$x^r = -g_{r-1}x^{r-1} - g_{r-2}x^{r-2} - \cdots - g_0 \textit{ modulo } \mathbf{g}(x)$$

and the output coming out at x^r term (highest stage) generates the feedbacks to lower stages.

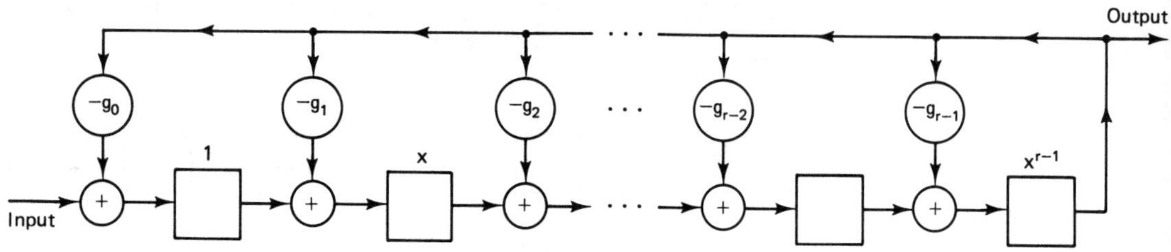

Figure 3.19 Division by $\mathbf{g}(x) = x^r + g_{r-1}x^{r-1} + \cdots + g_0$.

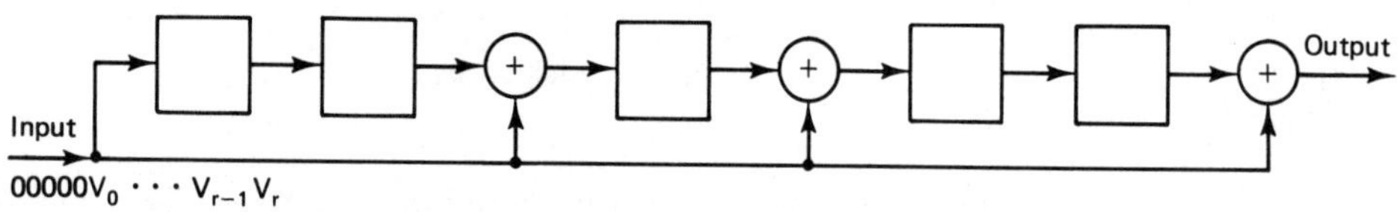

Figure 3.20 To multiply by $\mathbf{h}(x) = x^5 + x^3 + x^2 + 1$ over $GF(2)$.

Example Set 3-11

1. A circuit to multiply by $\mathbf{h}(x) = x^5 + x^3 + x^2 + 1$ over $GF(2)$ of an input polynomial $\mathbf{v}(x)$ is given in Fig. 3.20.
2. A circuit to divide by $\mathbf{g}(x) = x^4 + 2x^2 + x + 2$ over $GF(3)$ is given in Fig. 3.21.
3. A circuit to multiply by $\mathbf{h}(x) = x^3 + x^2 + 1$ and divide by $\mathbf{g}(x) = x^5 + x^2 + 1$ simultaneously of an input polynomial $\mathbf{v}(x)$ is given in Fig. 3.22. (All polynomials are over $GF(2)$.)

   After $r + 1$ cycles, the input v_0 enters into the circuit. By then, the residue of $\mathbf{v}(x)(x^3 + x^2 + 1)$ modulo $\mathbf{g}(x)$ is formed in the register.
4. A circuit for counting in $GF(2^b)$ can be obtained using a b-bit register with feedbacks connected based on a primitive polynomial of degree b over $GF(2)$. For example, to obtain a counter of $GF(2^4)$, we take $\mathbf{g}(x)$ as given in Fig. 3.23.

   The table of powers of α generated with that circuit is given in Table 3.8.
5. The circuit in Fig. 3.24 is a $GF(3^2)$ counter using the primitive polynomial $\mathbf{g}(x) = x^2 + x + 2$ over $GF(3)$.

   The table of powers of γ, where γ is a zero of $\mathbf{g}(x) = x^2 + x + 2$ over $GF(3)$ are given in Table 3.9.

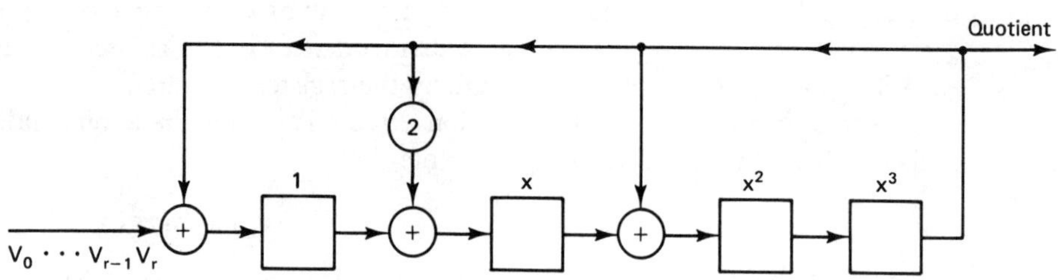

Figure 3.21 Division by $x^4 + 2x^2 + x + 2$ over $GF(3)$.

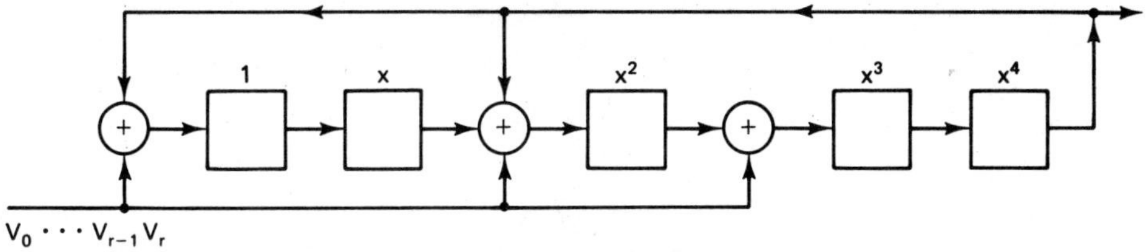

Figure 3.22 Simultaneous multiplication by $x^3 + x^2 + 1$ and division by $x^5 + x^2 + 1$ of an input polynomial $\mathbf{v}(x)$.

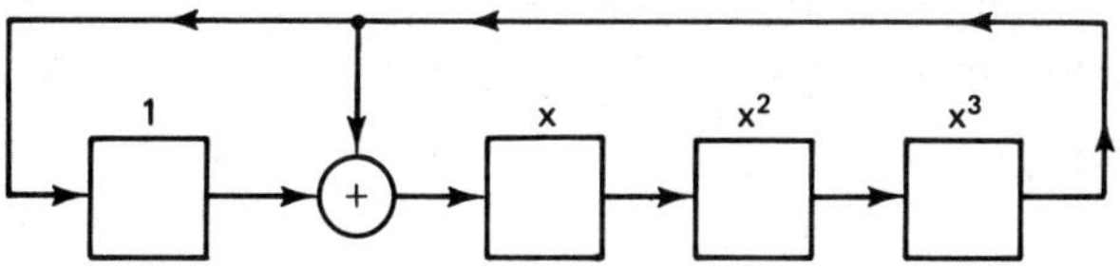

Figure 3.23 $GF(2^4)$ counter using $\mathbf{g}(x) = x^4 + x + 1$.

TABLE 3.8 COUNTER FOR $GF(16)$

Count	Register Values			
	1	α	α^2	α^3
1	1	0	0	0
α	0	1	0	0
α^2	0	0	1	0
α^3	0	0	0	1
α^4	1	1	0	0
⋮	⋮	⋮	⋮	⋮
α^{14}	1	0	0	1
$\alpha^{15} = 1$	1	0	0	0

TABLE 3.9 COUNTER FOR $GF(9)$

Count	Register Values	
	1	γ
1	1	0
γ	0	1
γ^2	1	2
γ^3	2	2
γ^4	2	0
γ^5	0	2
γ^6	2	1
γ^7	1	1
$\gamma^8 = 1$	1	0

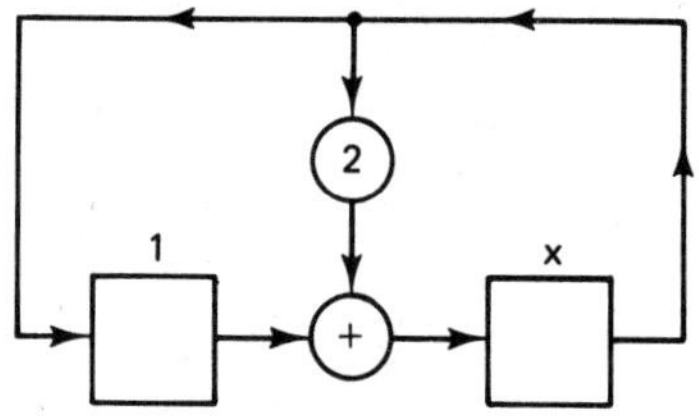

Figure 3.24 $GF(9)$ counter using $\mathbf{g}(x) = x^2 + x + 2$ over $GF(3)$.

***GF*(16) circuits.** In what follows, we assume α to be a zero of $x^4 + x + 1$ over $GF(2)$, and we use the table of powers of α given in Table 3.8 for deriving the circuits in this section.

The circuit of Fig. 3.23 multiplies the contents of the register by α for each shift. If the circuit is to multiply the contents by α^{-1}, we get a reverse counter. Since

$$\alpha^{14} = \alpha^{-1} = 1 + \alpha^3$$

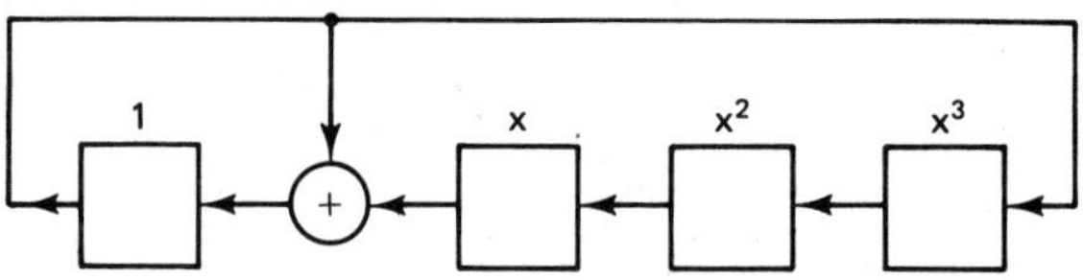

Figure 3.25 Reverse counter for $GF(2^4)$.

the feedback connections for the reverse counter are as follows. It is a simple exercise to verify this reverse counter (Fig. 3.25).

Let the initial contents of a register be $a(\alpha) = a_0 + a_1\alpha + a_2\alpha^2 + a_3\alpha^3$. A circuit to multiply the contents by α^6 is constructed using the following (see Fig. 3.26).

$$1 \cdot \alpha^6 = \alpha^2 + \alpha^3 = 0\ 0\ 1\ 1$$

$$\alpha \cdot \alpha^6 = 1 + \alpha + \alpha^3 = 1\ 1\ 0\ 1$$

$$\alpha^2 \cdot \alpha^6 = 1 + \alpha^2 = 1\ 0\ 1\ 0$$

$$\alpha^3 \cdot \alpha^6 = \alpha + \alpha^3 = 0\ 1\ 0\ 1$$

$$a(\alpha) \cdot \alpha^6 = \left(a_0 + a_1\alpha + a_2\alpha^2 + a_3\alpha^3\right)\alpha^6$$

$$= (a_1 + a_2) + (a_1 + a_3)\alpha + (a_0 + a_2)\alpha^2 + (a_0 + a_1 + a_3)\alpha^3$$

This circuit (Fig. 3.26) will multiply contents by α^6 for each shift.

Let $\mathbf{v}(x)$ be an input polynomial. To obtain $\mathbf{v}(\alpha)$, we use the division circuit of Fig. 3.23 slightly modified as follows. The register contents will equal $\mathbf{v}(\alpha)$ at the end of the shift operations (see Fig. 3.27).

To obtain $\mathbf{v}(\alpha) \cdot \alpha^4$, the input polynomial $\mathbf{v}(x)$ is applied on the right as shown in Fig. 3.28.

To form $\mathbf{v}(\alpha^3)$ of an input polynomial $\mathbf{v}(x)$, one may use the minimum polynomial of α^3, which is $m_3(x) = x^4 + x^3 + x^2 + x + 1$. The contents of the register after division logic is given by, say, $\mathbf{v}(\beta)$ where $\beta = \alpha^3$. Then we have

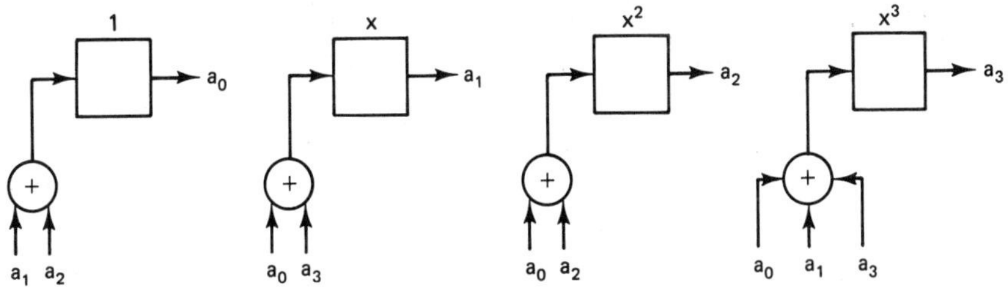

Figure 3.26 Multiplication of $a(\alpha)$ by α^6 in $GF(16)$.

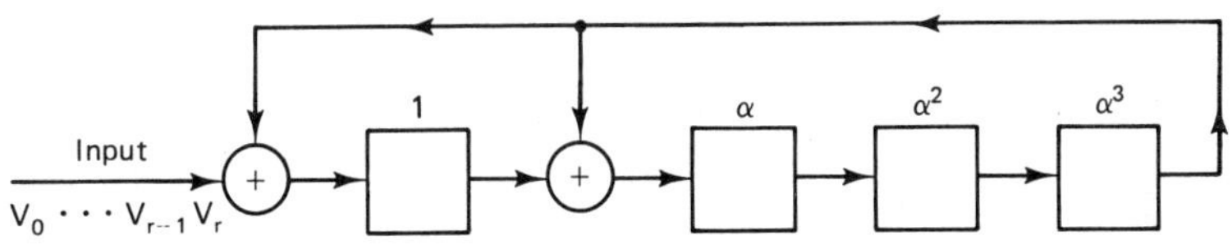

Figure 3.27 Circuit to obtain $\mathbf{v}(\alpha)$ of an input polynomial $\mathbf{v}(x)$ (α is a zero of $x^4 + x + 1$ over $GF(2)$).

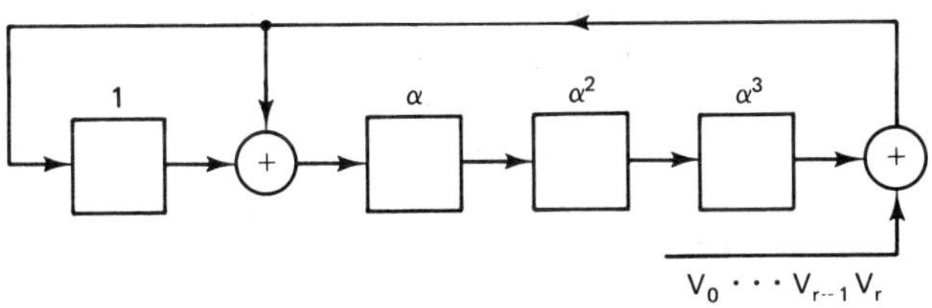

Figure 3.28 Circuit to obtain $\mathbf{v}(\alpha) \cdot \alpha^4$ for an input polynomial $\mathbf{v}(x)$.

$\mathbf{v}(\beta) = a_0 + a_1\beta + a_2\beta^2 + a_3\beta^3$. Substituting α^3 for β, and using Table 3.6, we get

$$\begin{aligned}\mathbf{v}(\alpha^3) &= a_0 + a_1\alpha^3 + a_2\alpha^6 + a_3\alpha^9 \\ &= a_0 + a_1\alpha^3 + a_2(\alpha^2 + \alpha^3) + a_3(\alpha + \alpha^3) \\ &= a_0 + a_3\alpha + a_2\alpha^2 + (a_1 + a_2 + a_3)\alpha^3\end{aligned}$$

Since the minimum polynomial of α^6 is $m_6(x) = m_3(x)$, the same generator can be used for $\mathbf{v}(\alpha^6)$. We get $\mathbf{v}(\alpha^6)$ by substituting α^6 for β.

$$\begin{aligned}\mathbf{v}(\alpha^6) &= a_0 + a_1\alpha^6 + a_2\alpha^{12} + a_3\alpha^{18} \\ &= a_0 + a_1(\alpha^2 + \alpha^3) + a_2(1 + \alpha + \alpha^2 + \alpha^3) + a_3\alpha^3 \\ &= (a_0 + a_2) + a_2\alpha + (a_1 + a_2)\alpha^2 + (a_1 + a_2 + a_3)\alpha^3\end{aligned}$$

Fig. 3.29 also shows the circuit connection for generating $\mathbf{v}(\alpha^6)$. For a more thorough understanding, the reader is advised to do Exercise 3.13 at the end of this chapter.

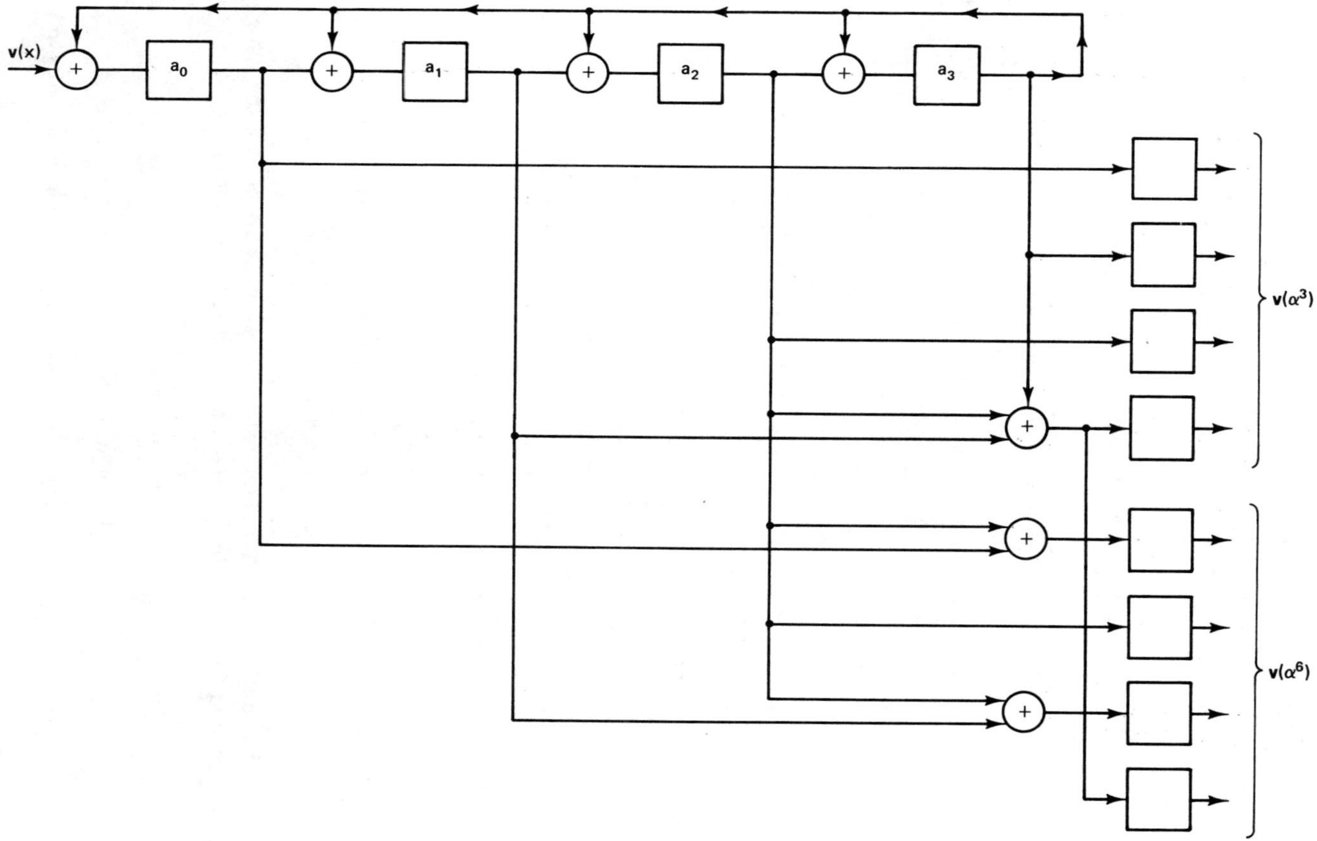

Figure 3.29 Circuit to obtain $\mathbf{v}(\alpha^3)$ and $\mathbf{v}(\alpha^6)$ of an input polynomial $\mathbf{v}(x)$.

Another method to obtain $\mathbf{v}(\alpha^6)$ for an input polynomial $\mathbf{v}(x)$ is to use the circuit of Fig. 3.26. By applying the input sequence ($\mathbf{v}$) to the leftmost EXOR gate (as an additional input) and shifting as required, $\mathbf{v}(\alpha^6)$ can be formed in the register. However, when $\mathbf{v}(\alpha^3)$ and $\mathbf{v}(\alpha^6)$ are both required, the circuit of Fig. 3.29 is more cost effective.

3.3.3 BCH Codes

Bose, Chaudhury [BOSE 60], and Hocquenghem [HOCQ 59] have independently found a class of multiple random error correcting codes called popularly *BCH codes*. These have been studied extensively by many researchers, and there is a large literature on this class and its extensions. We cover binary BCH codes as extensions to Hamming codes to correct small numbers of random errors.

BCH codes are cyclic codes generated by $\mathbf{g}(x)$, which has multiple factors. For a t-error correcting (tEC) binary BCH code, the generator is given by

$$\mathbf{g}(x) = \mathbf{m}_1(x)\mathbf{m}_3(x)\ldots\mathbf{m}_{2t-1}(x)$$

where $\mathbf{m}_i(x)$ is the minimum polynomial of α^i (for $i = 1, 3, 5, \ldots, 2t-1$), and α is an element of $GF(2^m)$ of order n. Typically, α is primitive and its order $n = 2^m - 1$. We can explain these codes by simple examples first. Let

$$\begin{aligned}\mathbf{g}(x) &= \mathbf{m}_1(x)\mathbf{m}_3(x)\\ &= (x^4 + x + 1)(x^4 + x^3 + x^2 + x + 1) \qquad \text{over } GF(2) \end{aligned} \tag{3.46}$$

where α is a zero of $\mathbf{m}_1(x) = x^4 + x + 1$, and the minimum polynomial of α^3 is $\mathbf{m}_3(x) = x^4 + x^3 + x^2 + x + 1$. Clearly, $\mathbf{g}(x)$ divides $(x^{15} - 1)$ and therefore generates a cyclic code of length 15. It is a (15, 7) code. Its $\mathbf{H}$ matrix is an (8×15) matrix and is of the form

$$\mathbf{H} = \begin{bmatrix}\mathbf{H}_1\\ \mathbf{H}_2\end{bmatrix} = \begin{bmatrix}1 & \alpha & \alpha^2 & \alpha^3 & \ldots & \alpha^{14}\\ 1 & \alpha^3 & \alpha^6 & \alpha^9 & \ldots & \alpha^{12}\end{bmatrix}$$

where $\mathbf{H}_1$ and $\mathbf{H}_2$ are the 4×15 submatrices given below.

$$\mathbf{H}_1 = [1, \alpha, \alpha^2, \alpha^3, \alpha^4, \ldots, \alpha^{14}] = \begin{bmatrix}1000 & 1001 & 1010 & 111\\ 0100 & 1101 & 0111 & 100\\ 0010 & 0110 & 1011 & 110\\ 0001 & 0011 & 0101 & 000\end{bmatrix}$$

$$\mathbf{H}_2 = [1, \alpha^3, \alpha^6, \alpha^9, \ldots, \alpha^{12}] = \begin{bmatrix}1000 & 1100 & 0110 & 001\\ 0001 & 1000 & 1100 & 011\\ 0010 & 1001 & 0100 & 101\\ 0111 & 1011 & 1101 & 111\end{bmatrix}$$

$\mathbf{H}_1$ is the parity matrix of the (15, 11) SEC cyclic code we studied before. $\mathbf{H}_1$ by itself cannot detect double errors when used as an SEC code. The submatrix $\mathbf{H}_2$ is to provide another independent estimate of the errors. Under the assumption that there are, at most, two errors, we can define the error polynomial as

$$\begin{aligned} \mathbf{e}(x) &= 0 & & & &\text{no error} \\ &= x^i, & & i \in \{0,1,\ldots,n-1\} & &\text{single error} \\ &= x^i + x^j, & i \neq j, \quad & i, j \in \{0,1,\ldots,n-1\} & &\text{double errors} \end{aligned} \tag{3.47}$$

Let $\mathbf{v}(x)$ be a received polynomial written as

$$\mathbf{v}(x) = \mathbf{u}(x) + \mathbf{e}(x)$$

for a codeword $\mathbf{u}(x)$ and $\mathbf{e}(x)$ as defined in (3.47). Then its syndrome $\mathbf{s}(\mathbf{v}) = (\mathbf{s}_1, \mathbf{s}_3)$ is given by

$$\begin{aligned} \mathbf{s}_1 &= \mathbf{v}(\alpha) = \mathbf{e}(\alpha) \\ \mathbf{s}_3 &= \mathbf{v}(\alpha^3) = \mathbf{e}(\alpha^3) \end{aligned} \tag{3.48}$$

For the case of no errors, $\mathbf{s}_1 = \mathbf{s}_3 = 0$, and for single errors $\mathbf{s}_1 = \alpha^i$, $\mathbf{s}_3 = \alpha^{3i} = \mathbf{s}_1^3$ will determine the index of the error position i. For double errors, we have

$$\begin{aligned} \mathbf{s}_1 &= \alpha^i + \alpha^j \\ \mathbf{s}_3 &= \alpha^{3i} + \alpha^{3j} \end{aligned} \tag{3.49}$$

There are just two equations in $GF(2^4)$ to solve for two unknowns, a and b:

$$\mathbf{s}_1 = a + b, \qquad \mathbf{s}_3 = a^3 + b^3$$

From the above, we write

$$\begin{aligned} \mathbf{s}_3 &= a^3 + b^3 = (a + b)(\mathbf{a}^2 + b^2 + ab) \\ &= \mathbf{s}_1(\mathbf{s}_1^2 + ab) \\ ab &= \frac{\mathbf{s}_3}{\mathbf{s}_1} + \mathbf{s}_1^2 \end{aligned}$$

To solve for a, b, we now have a quadratic with two roots:

$$\begin{aligned} \sigma(x) &= (1 + ax)(1 + bx) = 1 + (a + b)x + abx^2 \\ &= 1 + \mathbf{s}_1 x + \left(\frac{\mathbf{s}_3}{\mathbf{s}_1} + \mathbf{s}_1^2\right)x^2 = 0 \end{aligned} \tag{3.50}$$

$\sigma(x)$ is called the *error locator polynomial*, and its zeros (a^{-1} and b^{-1}) are the inverse of the error positions. Suppose that $\mathbf{s}_1 = \mathbf{0}$ and $\mathbf{s}_3 \neq \mathbf{0}$, then Equation (3.50) cannot be solved and there must be more than two errors. On the other hand, if $[(\mathbf{s}_3/\mathbf{s}_1) + \mathbf{s}_1^2] = ab = 0$, then (3.50) has only one root and the received vector has only one error. Thus, the roots of (3.50) give the error location uniquely up to two errors.

Example 3-12

Consider the (15, 7) DEC code with generator

$$\mathbf{g}(x) = (x^4 + x + 1)(x^4 + x^3 + x^2 + x + 1) = x^8 + x^7 + x^6 + x^4 + 1$$

Let $\mathbf{v}(x) = x^{10} + x^9 + x^8 + x^4 + x^2 = (000011100010100)$ be a received polynomial. Its syndrome $\mathbf{s} = (\mathbf{s}_1, \mathbf{s}_3)$ is computed using Table 3.6 as follows.

$$\begin{aligned}\mathbf{s}_1 &= \mathbf{v}(\alpha) = \alpha^{10} + \alpha^9 + \alpha^8 + \alpha^4 + \alpha^2 = \alpha^{12} = (1\ 1\ 1\ 1)\\ \mathbf{s}_3 &= \mathbf{v}(\alpha^3) = (\alpha^3)^{10} + (\alpha^3)^9 + (\alpha^3)^8 + (\alpha^3)^4 + (\alpha^3)^2\\ &= 1 + \alpha^{12} + \alpha^9 + \alpha^{12} + \alpha^6 = \alpha^{10} = (0\ 1\ 1\ 1)\end{aligned}$$

Setting $\mathbf{s}_1 = a + b$ and $\mathbf{s}_3 = a^3 + b^3$, we compute

$$\begin{aligned}ab &= (a^3 + b^3)/(a + b) + (a + b)^2 = (\mathbf{s}_3/\mathbf{s}_1) + \mathbf{s}_1^2\\ &= (\alpha^{10}/\alpha^{12}) + (\alpha^{12})^2 = (1\ 1\ 0\ 1) + (1\ 0\ 1\ 0)\\ &= (0\ 1\ 1\ 1) = \alpha^{10}\end{aligned}$$

The error locator polynomial is

$$\begin{aligned}\boldsymbol{\sigma}(x) &= 1 + \sigma_1 x + \sigma_2 x^2 = (1 + ax)(1 + bx)\\ &= 1 + (a + b)x + abx^2 = 1 + \alpha^{12}x + \alpha^{10}x^2 \qquad (3.51)\end{aligned}$$

The zeros of $\boldsymbol{\sigma}(x)$ are a^{-1} and b^{-1}, where a and b are the error positions. This quadratic cannot be solved by the traditional way because the characteristic of the field is 2 and $1 + 1 = 0$. It requires a search procedure [MACW 77, CHIE 64] or a base conversion procedure [RAO 81]. The search is to assume an error position, say $a = \alpha^{14}$ and check for $\boldsymbol{\sigma}(a^{-1}) = \boldsymbol{\sigma}(\alpha) = 0$. If this check succeeds, then one of the errors is α^{14} and the other zero is $(\mathbf{s}_1 - \alpha^{14})$. If the check fails, then the search proceeds for $\alpha^{13}, \alpha^{12}, \ldots,$ and so on. It requires a maximum of n cycles to find the errors. A detailed circuit to implement error correction using Chien's search [CHIE 64] is given in the next section.

For Equation (3.51), we obtain by search

$$\begin{aligned}\boldsymbol{\sigma}(\alpha^9) &= 1 + \alpha^{12}\alpha^9 + \alpha^{10}(\alpha^9)^2\\ &= 1 + \alpha^6 + \alpha^{13} = (0\ 0\ 0\ 1) + (1\ 1\ 0\ 0) + (1\ 1\ 0\ 1)\\ &= 0\end{aligned}$$

Therefore, one of the zeros is $a^{-1} = \alpha^9$. Correspondingly, one of the errors is $(\alpha^9)^{-1} = \alpha^6$. The other error is $\alpha^{12} - \alpha^6 = (1\ 1\ 1\ 1) + (1\ 1\ 0\ 0) = (0\ 0\ 1\ 1) = \alpha^4$. The other zero of (3.51) is $(\alpha^4)^{-1} = \alpha^{11}$. It is easily verified that $\sigma(\alpha^{11}) = 1 + \alpha^{12}\alpha^{11} + \alpha^{10}(\alpha^{11})^2 = 1 + \alpha^8 + \alpha^2 = 0$. The two error positions are α^6 and α^4. The received word is corrected to obtain

$$\begin{aligned}\hat{\mathbf{v}}(x) &= \mathbf{v}(x) + \mathbf{e}(x)\\ &= (x^{10} + x^9 + x^8 + x^4 + x^2) + (x^6 + x^4)\\ &= x^{10} + x^9 + x^8 + x^6 + x^2\end{aligned}$$

The corrected polynomial $\hat{\mathbf{v}}(x) = x^2 \cdot \mathbf{g}(x)$ and, therefore, it is a code polynomial.

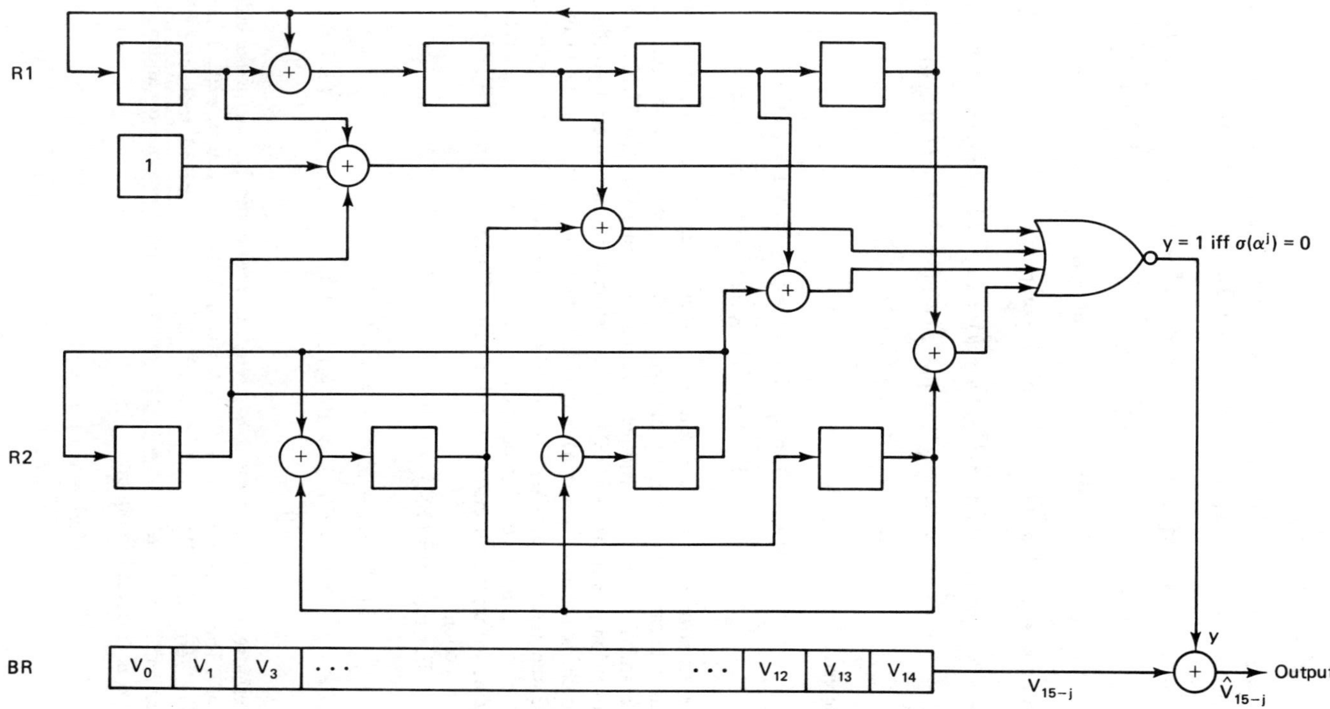

Figure 3.30 Double-error correcting code decoder (Chien's search).

Chien's search for DEC codes. The search procedure illustrated in the previous example is often called Chien's search [CHIE 64], and a circuit implementing this search is given in Fig. 3.30.

In Fig. 3.30, the top register (R1) multiplies its contents by α for each one shift. The bottom register (R2) multiplies its contents by α^2 for each shift. Initially, R1 is loaded with σ_1 and R2 is loaded with σ_2. Note that $\sigma_1 = a + b = \mathbf{s}_1$ and $\sigma_2 = ab = (\mathbf{s}_3/\mathbf{s}_1) + \mathbf{s}_1^2$. After one shift, the contents of R1 will be $(a + b)\alpha$ and the contents of R2 will be $a \cdot b \cdot \alpha^2$. The output value, y, of the logic circuit (between the two registers) is determined by an evaluation of

$$\sigma(\alpha) = 1 + (a + b)\alpha + ab\alpha^2 = 0 \tag{3.52}$$

If (3.52) holds, then α is a zero of $\sigma(x)$ and the output y is set (by the logic) to a 1. If $y = 1$, then α is a zero of $\sigma(x)$ and $\alpha^{-1} = \alpha^{14}$ is an error position. Consequently, the v_{14} of the buffer register is corrected to the value

$$\hat{v}_{14} = v_{14} + y = v_{14} + 1 = \bar{v}_{14} \ (\textit{complement of } v_{14})$$

If, on the other hand, α is not a zero of $\sigma(x)$, then $\hat{v}_{14} = v_{14} + 0 = v_{14}$ and no correction will be made. The search continues to the next cycle to see if α^2 is a zero of $\sigma(x)$. This is done by one shift of registers R1, R2, and BR. The search logic is to check if α^2 is a zero of $\sigma(x)$ and, if so, v_{13} needs to be complemented. Thus, the search continues for 15 cycles and the corrected word $\hat{v}$ is gated out.

Primitive binary BCH codes. We give here a general description of a class of binary t-error correcting (tEC) cyclic codes in its simplest form. The code is generated by

$$\mathbf{g}(x) = \mathbf{p}(x)\mathbf{m}_3(x)\mathbf{m}_5(x)\ldots\mathbf{m}_{2t-1}(x) \tag{3.53}$$

$\mathbf{p}(x)$ is a primitive polynomial of degree m over $GF(2)$ (i.e., its zero α is of order $2^m - 1$). $\mathbf{m}_j(x)$ (for $j = 3, 5, \ldots, 2t - 1$) is the minimum polynomial of α^j and is of degree $\leq m$. The degree of $\mathbf{g}(x)$, therefore, is less than or equal to mt. The code has the following parameters:

Block length:	$n = 2^m - 1$
Number of parities:	$r \leq tm$
Data length:	$k \geq 2^m - 1 - tm$

A general class of BCH codes can be given over any $GF(q)$ and $\mathbf{p}(x)$ may not necessarily be a primitive polynomial. However, for simplicity we give the primitive class of BCH codes. When $\mathbf{p}(x)$ is primitive, the codes are called primitive BCH codes.

The distance of the code generated by $\mathbf{g}(x)$ is given by the BCH theorem, which can be stated in its simplest form as follows.

Theorem 3-6. *The cyclic code generated by* $\mathbf{g}(x)$ *as given by* (3.53) *of length* $n = 2^m - 1$ *has a distance* $\geq 2t + 1$.

Proof. The first step is to observe the zeros of the factors of g(x) as follows.

$\mathbf{p(x)}$	$\alpha, \alpha^2, \alpha^4, \ldots$
$\mathbf{m}_3(x)$	$\alpha^3, \alpha^6, \ldots$
$\mathbf{m}_5(x)$	$\alpha^5, \alpha^{10}, \ldots$
	$\vdots$
$\mathbf{m}_{2t-1}(x)$	$\alpha^{2t-1}, \alpha^{4t-2}, \ldots$

The $2t$ successive powers of α, namely $\alpha, \alpha^2, \alpha^3, \ldots, \alpha^{2t-1}, \alpha^{2t}$ are zeros of $\mathbf{g(x)}$. A polynomial $\mathbf{u(x)}$ is a code polynomial if and only if $\mathbf{u}(\alpha^j) = 0$ for $j = 1, 2, \ldots, 2t$. This is equivalent to the statement $u \cdot \mathbf{H}^T = 0$, where $\mathbf{H}$ is the parity matrix of the code as follows.

$$\mathbf{H} = \begin{bmatrix} 1 & \alpha & \alpha^2 & \cdots & \alpha^{n-1} \\ 1 & (\alpha^2) & (\alpha^2)^2 & \cdots & (\alpha^2)^{n-1} \\ 1 & (\alpha^3) & (\alpha^3)^2 & \cdots & (\alpha^3)^{n-1} \\ \vdots & \vdots & \vdots & & \vdots \\ 1 & (\alpha^{2t}) & (\alpha^{2t})^2 & \cdots & (\alpha^{2t})^{n-1} \end{bmatrix} \tag{3.54}$$

To prove that the code has a distance of at least $2t + 1$, we need to show that every $2t$ columns of $\mathbf{H}$ are linearly independent (see Theorem 3-2). Therefore, we consider without loss of any generality the following $2t$ columns of $\mathbf{H}$, which form a $(2t \times 2t)$ square matrix $\mathbf{V}$ given below.

$$\mathbf{V} = \begin{bmatrix} \alpha^{j_1} & \alpha^{j_2} & \cdots & \alpha^{j_{2t}} \\ (\alpha^{j_1})^2 & (\alpha^{j_2})^2 & \cdots & (\alpha^{j_{2t}})^2 \\ (\alpha^{j_1})^3 & (\alpha^{j_2})^3 & \cdots & (\alpha^{j_{2t}})^3 \\ \vdots & \vdots & & \vdots \\ (\alpha^{j_1})^{2t} & (\alpha^{j_2})^{2t} & \cdots & (\alpha^{j_{2t}})^{2t} \end{bmatrix}$$

If the $2t$ columns of $\mathbf{V}$ are linearly dependent, then the determinant of $\mathbf{V}$ is 0. By taking out the factor α^{j_1} from the first column and α^{j_2} from the second column, and so on, we obtain a $(2t \times 2t)$ matrix $\mathbf{V}'$.

$$\mathbf{V}' = \begin{bmatrix} 1 & 1 & \cdots & 1 \\ \alpha^{j_1} & \alpha^{j_2} & \cdots & \alpha^{j_{2t}} \\ (\alpha^{j_1})^2 & (\alpha^{j_2})^2 & \cdots & (\alpha^{j_{2t}})^2 \\ (\alpha^{j_1})^3 & (\alpha^{j_2})^3 & \cdots & (\alpha^{j_{2t}})^3 \\ \vdots & \vdots & & \vdots \\ (\alpha^{j_1})^{2t-1} & (\alpha^{j_2})^{2t-1} & \cdots & (\alpha^{j_{2t}})^{2t-1} \end{bmatrix}$$

TABLE 3.10 PRIMITIVE BCH CODE EXAMPLES

$g(x)$	n	k	t	Zeros of $g(x)$ That Are Successive Powers of α
$(x^4+x+1)(x^4+x^3+x^2+x+1)$	15	7	2	$\alpha, \alpha^2, \alpha^3, \alpha^4$
$(x^4+x+1)(x^4+x^3+x^2+x+1)(x^2+x+1)$	15	5	3	$\alpha, \alpha^2, \alpha^3, \alpha^4, \alpha^5, \alpha^6$
$(x^5+x^2+1)(x^5+x^4+x^3+x^2+x+1)$	31	21	2	$\alpha, \alpha^2, \alpha^3, \alpha^4$
$(x^6+x^2+1)(x^6+x^4+x^2+x+1)$ $\cdot(x^6+x^5+x^2+x+1)$	63	45	3	$\alpha, \alpha^2, \alpha^3, \alpha^4, \alpha^5, \alpha^6$

$\mathbf{V}'$ is known as the Vandermonde matrix, and its *determinant* is nonzero [MACW 77]. Hence, the determinant of $\mathbf{V}$ is nonzero, and therefore every $2t$ columns of $\mathbf{H}$ are linearly independent. The code has $d_{\min} \geq 2t+1$. Q.E.D.

As mentioned before, it is not necessary for $\mathbf{p}(x)$ to be primitive, and its zero α can have order n, a divisor of $2^m - 1$. The proof is valid for any $\mathbf{g}(x)$ that has $2t$ successive powers of α as its zeros. Then, any polynomial $\mathbf{u}(x)$ is a code polynomial if and only if

$$\mathbf{u}(\alpha^j) = 0 \qquad \text{for} \qquad j = 1, 2, \ldots, 2t$$

The *designed* distance ($d_{\min}$) of the code is $2t+1$, but the *actual* distance can be greater in some cases. In Table 3.10, we can find some examples of primitive BCH codes. For each generator $\mathbf{g}(x)$, its zeros that are successive powers of a primitive element α are also given in that table. The (n, k, t) parameters of all BCH codes of length $2^m - 1$ for $m \leq 10$ and $t \geq 2$ are shown in Table 3.11. Some BCH code examples are further illustrated as follows.

Example Set 3-13

1. $\mathbf{g}(x) = (x^4+x^3+1)(x^4+x^3+x^2+x+1)(x^2+x+1)$
   $= x^{10}+x^9+x^8+x^6+x^5+x^2+1$

Polynomial	Zeros
x^4+x^3+1	$\alpha, \alpha^2, \alpha^4, \alpha^8$
$x^4+x^3+x^2+x+1$	$\alpha^3, \alpha^6, \alpha^9, \alpha^{12}$
x^2+x+1	α^5, α^{10}

   $\mathbf{g}(x)$ is of degree 10 and has ten zeros. Of these, only six—$\alpha, \alpha^2, \alpha^3, \alpha^4, \alpha^5, \alpha^6$—are successive powers of α; and by the BCH theorem the designed distance is at least 7. The weight of $\mathbf{g}(x)$ is 7, and therefore its actual distance is also 7, and hence it is a $(15, 5, 7)$ code.

2. $\mathbf{g}(x) = (x^6+x^2+1)(x^6+x^4+x^2+x+1)$ is the generator of a $(63, 51, 5)$ code, as can be verified easily.

TABLE 3.11 PARAMETERS OF PRIMITIVE BCH CODES OF LENGTH LESS THAN 2^{10} [LIN 83].

n	k	t	n	k	t	n	k	t
15	7	2	255	115	21	511	211	41
	5	3		107	22		202	42
31	21	2		99	23		193	43
	16	3		91	25		184	45
	11	5		87	26		175	46
	6	7		79	27		166	47
63	51	2		71	29		157	51
	45	3		63	30		148	53
	39	4		55	31		139	54
	36	5		47	42		130	55
	30	6		45	43		121	58
	24	7		37	45		112	59
	18	10		29	47		103	61
	16	11		21	55		94	62
	10	13		13	59		85	63
	7	15		9	63		76	85
127	113	2	511	493	2		67	87
	106	3		484	3		58	91
	99	4		475	4		49	93
	92	5		466	5		40	95
	85	6		457	6		31	109
	78	7		448	7		28	111
	71	9		439	8		19	119
	64	10		430	9		10	121
	57	11		421	10	1023	1003	2
	50	13		412	11		993	3
	43	14		403	12		983	4
	36	15		394	13		973	5
	29	21		385	14		963	6
	22	23		376	15		953	7
	15	27		376	16		943	8
	8	31		358	18		933	9
225	239	2		349	19		923	10
	231	3		340	20		913	11
	223	4		331	21		903	12
	215	5		322	22		893	13
	207	6		313	23		883	14
	199	7		304	25		873	15
	191	8		295	26		863	16
	187	9		286	27		858	17
	179	10		277	28		848	18
	171	11		268	29		858	19
	163	12		259	30		828	20
	155	13		250	31		818	21
	147	14		241	36		808	22
	139	15		238	37		798	23
255	131	18		229	38		788	24
	123	19		220	39		778	25

TABLE 3.11 Continued.

n	k	t	n	k	t	n	k	t
1023	768	26	1023	503	58	1023	238	109
	758	27		493	59		228	110
	748	28		483	60		218	111
	738	29		473	61		208	115
	728	30		463	62		203	117
	718	31		453	63		193	118
	708	34		443	73		183	119
	698	35		433	74		173	122
	688	36		423	75		163	123
	678	37		413	77		153	125
	668	38		403	78		143	126
	658	39		393	79		133	127
	648	41		383	82		123	170
	638	42		378	83		121	171
	628	43		368	85		111	173
	618	44		358	86		101	175
	608	45		348	87		91	181
	598	46		338	89		86	183
	588	47		328	90		76	187
	578	49		318	91		66	189
	573	50		308	93		56	191
	563	51		298	94		46	219
	553	52		288	95		36	223
	543	53		278	102		26	239
	533	54		268	103		16	147
	523	55		258	106		11	255
	513	57		248	107			

3. Let $\mathbf{m}_1(x) = x^6 + x^4 + x^2 + x + 1$ be the minimum polynomial of β of order 21. β can be equal to α^3, where α is a primitive element in $GF(2^6)$. Then the minimum polynomial of β^3 can be shown to be $\mathbf{m}_3(x) = x^3 + x^2 + 1$. Therefore, we can write $\mathbf{g}(x) = (x^6 + x^4 + x^2 + x + 1)(x^3 + x^2 + 1)$. This generates a cyclic code of length 21 and has a designed distance of 5. This is a (21, 12, 5) code. Since β is not primitive, this code is not a primitive BCH code.

Appendix C of [PETE 72] gives a very comprehensive table of primitive and irreducible polynomials of degree up to 34 over $GF(2)$. That table can be most useful in constructing BCH codes for any given n and t.

Decoding of BCH codes. The decoding of tEC BCH codes is a generalization of the 2EC BCH code decoding given before. Let $\mathbf{u}(x)$ denote a code polynomial in the tEC BCH code generated by (3.53), and let $\mathbf{v}(x)$ be a corresponding received polynomial such that

$$\mathbf{e}(x) = \mathbf{v}(x) - \mathbf{u}(x) = x^{j_1} + x^{j_2} + \cdots + x^{j_l}$$

is the error polynomial with l errors, $l \leq t$. The l error positions in $\mathbf{e}(x)$ are denoted $j_1, j_2, \ldots, j_l$. The values $\beta_1 = \alpha^{j_1}$, $\beta_2 = \alpha^{j_2}, \ldots, \beta_l = \alpha^{j_l}$ are called *error location numbers*.

The decoding consists of three steps as follows.

1. This step is to generate the syndrome $\mathbf{s}$ of $\mathbf{v}(x)$ given by

$$\mathbf{s} = (s_1, s_2, \ldots, s_{2t})$$

where $s_j = \mathbf{v}(\alpha^j) = \mathbf{e}(\alpha^j)$ for $j = 1, 2, \ldots, 2t$. The syndrome component s_j can be obtained by a division of $\mathbf{v}(x)$ by $m_j(x)$, the minimum polynomial of α^j. (For clarification, see Section 3.3.2 on Galois field circuits.)

2. From the syndrome components $s_1, s_2, \ldots, s_{2t}$, an *error locator polynomial*

$$\boldsymbol{\sigma}(x) = 1 + \sigma_1 x + \sigma_2 x^2 + \cdots + \sigma_l x^l$$

is to be generated by an appropriate algorithm. The algorithm we will study to derive $\boldsymbol{\sigma}(x)$ is known as Berlekamp's iterative algorithm.

3. The zeros of $\boldsymbol{\sigma}(x) = 1 + \sigma_1 x + \cdots + \sigma_l x^l = (1 - \beta_1 x)(1 - \beta_2 x) \cdots (1 - \beta_l x)$ are given by $\beta_1^{-1}, \beta_2^{-1}, \ldots, \beta_l^{-1}$, which are inverses of the error location numbers $\alpha^{j_1}, \alpha^{j_2}, \ldots, \alpha^{j_l}$, respectively (i.e., $\beta_i = \alpha^{j_i}$ for $i = 1, 2, \ldots, l$). By a search procedure, the zeros of $\boldsymbol{\sigma}(x)$ are determined and the correction is applied to $\mathbf{v}(x)$.

This decoding procedure is explained further as follows. We begin with the syndrome $\mathbf{s} = (s_1, s_2, \ldots, s_{2t})$ expressed as follows.

$$\begin{aligned}
s_1 &= \alpha^{j_1} + \alpha^{j_2} + \cdots + \alpha^{j_l} = \beta_1 + \beta_2 + \cdots + \beta_l \\
s_2 &= (\alpha^{j_1})^2 + (\alpha^{j_2})^2 + \cdots + (\alpha^{j_l})^2 = \beta_1^2 + \beta_2^2 + \cdots + \beta_l^2 \\
s_3 &= (\alpha^{j_1})^3 + (\alpha^{j_2})^3 + \cdots + (\alpha^{j_l})^3 = \beta_1^3 + \beta_2^3 + \cdots + \beta_l^3 \\
&\vdots \\
s_{2t} &= (\alpha^{j_1})^{2t} + (\alpha^{j_2})^{2t} + \cdots + (\alpha^{j_l})^{2t} = \beta_1^{2t} + \beta_2^{2t} + \cdots + \beta_l^{2t}
\end{aligned} \tag{3.55}$$

The error-locator polynomial $\boldsymbol{\sigma}(x)$ is given by

$$\begin{aligned}
\boldsymbol{\sigma}(x) &= 1 + \sigma_1 x + \sigma_2 x^2 + \cdots + \sigma_l x^l \\
&= (1 - \beta_1 x)(1 - \beta_2 x) \cdots (1 - \beta_l x)
\end{aligned} \tag{3.56}$$

Therefore, we obtain the following for σ_j $(j = 1, 2, \ldots, l)$:

$$\begin{aligned}
\sigma_1 &= -(\beta_1 + \beta_2 + \cdots + \beta_l) \\
\sigma_2 &= \beta_1\beta_2 + \beta_1\beta_3 + \beta_2\beta_3 \cdots + \beta_{l-1}\beta_l \\
\sigma_3 &= -(\beta_1\beta_2\beta_3 + \beta_1\beta_3\beta_4 + \cdots) \\
&\vdots \\
\sigma_l &= (-1)^l(\beta_1\beta_2 \ldots \beta_l)
\end{aligned} \tag{3.57}$$

The equations in (3.57) are known as *elementary symmetric equations*. What we need is a way to express the coefficients σ_j as functions of the syndrome components. This is accomplished in $2t + 1$ steps $(\mu = 0, 1, \ldots, 2t)$ by use of the following iterative algorithm due to Berlekamp [BERL 65], which is given here without proof.

TABLE 3.12 THE EVALUATION OF ERROR-LOCATOR POLYNOMIAL

μ	$\sigma^{(\mu)}(x)$	d_μ	l_μ	$\mu - l_\mu$	ρ
-1	1	1	0	-1	—
0	1	s_1	0	0	—
1	$\vdots$	$\vdots$			
2					
$\vdots$					
$2t$	$\sigma(x)$				

The first two steps (for iteration index $\mu = -1, 0$) are given as the first two rows of Table 3.12. The iterative steps follow by the following rules.

1. $$\begin{aligned} \sigma^{(\mu+1)}(x) &= \sigma^{(\mu)}(x) \ \text{ if } d_\mu = 0 \\ &= \sigma^{\mu}(x) - d_\mu d_p^{-1} x^{\mu-\rho} \sigma^{(\rho)}(x) \qquad \text{otherwise,} \end{aligned} \tag{3.58}$$

2. d_μ is the discrepancy at step μ and is given by

$$d_\mu = s_{\mu+1} + \sigma_{l_\mu}^{(\mu)} s_\mu + \sigma_2^{(\mu)} s_{\mu-1} + \cdots + \sigma_{l_\mu}^{(\mu)} s_{\mu+1-l_\mu} \tag{3.59}$$

and ρ is a step number prior to μ such that $d_\rho \neq 0$ and $\rho - l_p$ has the largest value (l_ρ is the degree of $\sigma^{(\rho)}(x)$ and $\sigma_j^{(\mu)}$ is the coefficient of the x^j term of $\sigma^{(\mu)}(x)$). This procedure terminates at step $2t$ with $\sigma(x) = \sigma^{(2t)}(x)$. If the errors are l in $\mathbf{e}(x)$, then $\sigma(x)$ will be of degree l.

The following example will illustrate the BCH decoding procedure.

Example 3-14

Consider the (15, 5, 7) BCH code generated by

$$\mathbf{g}(x) = (x^4 + x + 1)(x^4 + x^3 + x^2 + x + 1)(x^2 + x + 1)$$

Assume the transmitted

(a) code polynomial $\quad \mathbf{u}(x) = x^{10} + x^8 + x^5 + x^4 + x^2 + x + 1$
(b) received polynomial $\quad \mathbf{v}(x) = x^8 + x^4 + x^3 + x^2 + x + 1$
(c) error polynomial $\quad \mathbf{e}(x) = x^{10} + x^5 + x^3$

The syndrome $\mathbf{s} = (s_1, s_2, \ldots, s_6)$ is given by its components:

$$s_1 = \mathbf{v}(\alpha) = \alpha^3 + \alpha^5 + \alpha^{10} = \alpha^3 + 1 = \alpha^{14}$$

$$s_2 = \mathbf{v}(\alpha^2) = \alpha^6 + \alpha^{10} + \alpha^5 = \alpha^3 + \alpha^2 + 1 = \alpha^{13}$$

$$s_3 = \mathbf{v}(\alpha^3) = \alpha^9 + \alpha^{15} + \alpha^{15} = \alpha^9$$

$$s_4 = \mathbf{v}(\alpha^4) = \alpha^{12} + \alpha^5 + \alpha^{10} = \alpha + \alpha^2 + \alpha^3 = \alpha^{11}$$

$$s_5 = \mathbf{v}(\alpha^5) = \alpha^{15} + \alpha^{10} + \alpha^5 = 0$$

$$s_6 = \mathbf{v}(\alpha^6) = \left(\mathbf{v}(\alpha^3)\right)^2 = \alpha^{18} = \alpha^3$$

TABLE 3.13 TO FIND $\sigma(x)$

μ	$\sigma^{(\mu)}(x)$	d_μ	l_μ	$\mu - l_\mu$	ρ
-1	1	1	0	-1	—
0	1	α^{14}	0	0	—
1	$1 + \alpha^{14}x$	0	1	0	-1
2	$1 + \alpha^{14}x$	α^8	1	1	—
3	$1 + \alpha^{14}x + \alpha^9x^2$	0	2	1	0
4	$1 + \alpha^{14}x + \alpha^9x^2$	α^{12}	2	2	—
5	$1 + \alpha^{14}x + \alpha^{14}x^2 + \alpha^3x^3$	0	3	2	2
6	$1 + \alpha^{14}x + \alpha^{14}x^2 + \alpha^3x^3$	—	—	—	—

By iterations using rules (3.58) and (3.59), we obtain Table 3.13. The following computations explain the entries for $\sigma^{(\mu)}(x)$ and d_μ (for $\mu = 1, 2, \ldots, 6$) in Table 3.13 (for computation in powers of α, see Table 3.6).

$$\sigma^{(1)}(x) = \sigma^{(0)}(x) + \alpha^{14} \cdot 1 \cdot x = 1 + \alpha^{14}x$$

$$d_1 = s_2 + \sigma_1^{(1)}s_1 = \alpha^{13} + \alpha^{14} \cdot \alpha^{14} = 0$$

$$\sigma^{(2)}(x) = \sigma^{(1)}(x)$$

$$d_2 = s_3 + \sigma_1^{(2)}s_2 + \sigma_2^{(2)}s_1 = \alpha^9 + \alpha^{14} \cdot \alpha^{13} = \alpha^9 + \alpha^{12}$$

$$= 1 + \alpha^2 = \alpha^8$$

$$\sigma^{(3)}(x) = \sigma^{(2)}(x) + \alpha^8 \cdot (\alpha^{14})^{-1} \cdot x^2 \cdot \sigma^{(0)}(x) = 1 + \alpha^{14}x + \alpha^9x^2$$

$$d_3 = s_4 + \sigma_1^{(3)}s_3 + \sigma_2^{(3)}s_2 + \sigma_3^{(3)}s_1 = \alpha^{11} + \alpha^{14} \cdot \alpha^9 + \alpha^9 \cdot \alpha^{13}$$

$$= \alpha^{11} + \alpha^8 + \alpha^7 = 0$$

$$\sigma^{(4)}(x) = \sigma^{(3)}(x)$$

$$d_4 = s_5 + \alpha^{14} \cdot s_4 + \alpha^9 \cdot \alpha^9 = 0 + \alpha^{14} \cdot \alpha^{11} + \alpha^3 = \alpha^{10} + \alpha^3 = \alpha^{12}$$

$$\sigma^{(5)}(x) = \sigma^{(4)}(x) + \alpha^{12} \cdot (\alpha^8)^{-1} \cdot x^2 \cdot (1 + \alpha^{14} \cdot x)$$

$$= 1 + \alpha^{14}x + \alpha^9x^2 + \alpha^4x^2 + \alpha^3x^3$$

$$= 1 + \alpha^{14}x + \alpha^{14}x^2 + \alpha^3x^3$$

$$d_5 = s_6 + \sigma_1^{(5)}s_5 + \sigma_2^{(5)}s_4 + \sigma_3^{(5)}s_3 = s_6 + \alpha^{14}s_5 + \alpha^{14}s_4 + \alpha^3s_3$$

$$= \alpha^3 + \alpha^{14} \cdot 0 + \alpha^{14} \cdot \alpha^{11} + \alpha^3 \cdot \alpha^9 = \alpha^3 + 0 + \alpha^{10} + \alpha^{12} = 0$$

$$\sigma^{(6)}(x) = \sigma^{(5)}(x)$$

From Table 3.13, we get the error-locator polynomial

$$\sigma(x) = \sigma^{(6)}(x) = 1 + \alpha^{14}x + \alpha^{14}x^2 + \alpha^3x^3$$

As required for the search of zeros of $\sigma(x)$, we start substituting $\alpha, \alpha^2, \ldots$ in $\sigma(x)$. We get that

$$\sigma(\alpha^{12}) = \sigma(\alpha^{10}) = \sigma(\alpha^5) = 0$$

Therefore, the error locator numbers are α^3, α^5, and α^{10}, and the error vector is

$\mathbf{e}(x) = x^3 + x^5 + x^{10}$. The received polynomial $\mathbf{v}(x)$ is decoded into

$$\hat{\mathbf{v}}(x) = \mathbf{v}(x) + \mathbf{e}(x) = x^{10} + x^8 + x^5 + x^4 + x^2 + x + 1 = \mathbf{g}(x)$$

which is clearly a code polynomial.

Decoding implementation. BCH decoding requires three steps: (1) syndrome ($\mathbf{s}$) generation, (2) error-locator polynomial ($\boldsymbol{\sigma}(x)$) generation, and (3) finding zeros and error location numbers ($\beta_1, \beta_2, \ldots, \beta_l$) and applying correction. The first step is rather straightforward, and each component $s_j = \mathbf{v}(\alpha^j)$ can be determined in parallel by use of the circuits given in Section 3.3.2. Step 3 of finding zeros by Chien's search [CHIE 64] is a very practical hardwired approach. The more complex step is the determination of $\boldsymbol{\sigma}(x)$, which requires an iterative sequence of $2t$ steps. This implementation requires a complex set of computational and control circuits. It can be expensive but can be realized by Galois field logic circuits and hardwired control logic. The hardware and time complexities for BCH decoding can be shown to be of the order of $n \log_q n$ [PETE 72]. VLSI architectures for computing the multiplications and inverses in $GF(2^m)$ have been studied and can be found in [WANG 85]. For a more thorough understanding of BCH decoding algorithm and implementation, the reader is advised to refer to [FORN 65], [BERL 68], [MASS 69], [BURT 71b], [MAND 77], [WELC 79], [BLAH 83], and [WANG 85].

3.3.4 Reed–Solomon (RS) Codes

The RS codes are a subclass of BCH codes defined over $GF(q)$. Let α be an element in $GF(q)$ of order n. Then, n is a divisor of $q - 1$. We define

$$\mathbf{g}(x) = (x - \alpha)(x - \alpha^2) \cdots (x - \alpha^r)$$

as the generator of a cyclic code over $GF(q)$. First, it is easy to show that $\mathbf{g}(x)$ divides $x^n - 1$. We note that $\mathbf{g}(x)$ has r zeros that are successive powers of α and by BCH bound (Theorem 3-6) has $d_{\min} \geq r + 1$. Also, since the degree of $\mathbf{g}(x)$ is r, its weight cannot be greater than $r + 1$, therefore, its actual distance is $r + 1$. Furthermore, the degree of $\mathbf{g}(x)$ represents the number of parity symbols, the information length k equals $n - r$. Therefore, the code parameters are $(n, n - r, r + 1)$.

Any linear code with r parity checks can have at most distance $r + 1$, and RS codes meet this bound. Therefore, the RS code is a *maximal-separable distance* code. A few examples of RS codes are given in Table 3.14.

RS codes over $GF(2^m)$. RS codes over $GF(2^m)$ are very important for computer systems and are studied further in Chapter 5. Each symbol in $GF(2^m)$ is an m-bit byte (or symbol), and memory words can be composed a fixed number of m-bit bytes. For instance, if $m = 4$ and memory words are 32 bits long, one can consider each word to have 8 bytes (each byte has 4 bits). Normally in computer system terminology, a byte has 8 bits, but for this book and for coding applications, a byte simply represents a group of m bits. Typically, m is in the range [2, 8]. For

TABLE 3.14 EXAMPLES OF RS CODES

q	$\mathbf{g}(x)$	n	k	d	Zeros of $\mathbf{g}(x)$
11	$\prod_{i=1}^{4}(x-2^i)$	10	6	5	2, 4, 8, 5
17	$\prod_{i=1}^{3}(x-2^i)$	8	5	4	2, 4, 8
16	$\prod_{i=1}^{3}(x-\alpha^i)$	15	12	4	$\alpha, \alpha^2, \alpha^3$
8	$(x-\alpha)(x-\alpha^2)$	7	5	3	α, α^2

illustration, consider the third example of Table 3.14. It is a (15, 12, 4) code over $GF(2^4)$. When converted to binary form, this becomes a (60, 48) code capable of *single-byte error correction* and *double-byte error detection* (SbEC–DbED) for 4-bit bytes. Sometimes we also write this as the S4EC–D4ED code. This code is represented by its **H** matrix as follows.

$$\mathbf{H} = \begin{bmatrix} 1 & \alpha & \alpha^2 & \alpha^3 & \cdots & \alpha^{14} \\ 1 & \alpha^2 & \alpha^4 & \alpha^6 & \cdots & \alpha^{13} \\ 1 & \alpha^3 & \alpha^6 & \alpha^9 & \cdots & \alpha^{12} \end{bmatrix} \qquad \text{over } GF(16)$$

To obtain its binary form, each element $\alpha^j \in GF(16)$ in the **H** matrix is replaced by its corresponding binary *companion matrix* T_j defined as shown below.

$$\alpha^j \leftrightarrow T_j = \begin{bmatrix} | & | & \cdots & | \\ \alpha^j & \alpha^{j+1} & \cdots & \alpha^{j+m-1} \\ | & | & \cdots & | \end{bmatrix} \qquad \text{for } j = 0, 1, \ldots, 2^m - 1$$

The column $\begin{matrix}|\\ \alpha^i \\ |\end{matrix}$ (in T_j above) is also called the *coefficient vector* of x^i *mod* $\mathbf{g}(x)$. This is further illustrated by Example 3-15.

Example 3-15

The last row of Table 3.14 represents a (7, 5, 3) RS code over $GF(2^3)$. Its generator is

$$\mathbf{g}(x) = (x-\alpha)(x-\alpha^2)$$

where α is a primitive element of $GF(2^3)$. We can take α as a zero of the primitive polynomial $\mathbf{p}(x) = x^3 + x + 1$ and write its **H** matrix as follows.

$$\mathbf{H} = \begin{bmatrix} 1 & \alpha & \alpha^2 & \alpha^3 & \alpha^4 & \alpha^5 & \alpha^6 \\ 1 & \alpha^2 & \alpha^4 & \alpha^6 & \alpha & \alpha^3 & \alpha^5 \end{bmatrix} \qquad \text{over } GF(2^3) \tag{3.60}$$

The companion matrices for α^j (for $j = 0, 1, \ldots, 6$) are

$$1 \leftrightarrow T_0 = \begin{bmatrix} | & | & | \\ 1 & \alpha & \alpha^2 \\ | & | & | \end{bmatrix} = \begin{bmatrix} 1 & 0 & 0 \\ 0 & 1 & 0 \\ 0 & 0 & 1 \end{bmatrix}$$

$$\alpha \leftrightarrow T_1 = \begin{bmatrix} | & | & | \\ \alpha & \alpha^2 & \alpha^3 \\ | & | & | \end{bmatrix} = \begin{bmatrix} 0 & 0 & 1 \\ 1 & 0 & 1 \\ 0 & 1 & 0 \end{bmatrix}$$

$$\alpha^2 \leftrightarrow T_2 = \begin{bmatrix} | & | & | \\ \alpha^2 & \alpha^3 & \alpha^4 \\ | & | & | \end{bmatrix} = \begin{bmatrix} 0 & 1 & 0 \\ 0 & 1 & 1 \\ 1 & 0 & 1 \end{bmatrix}$$

$$\alpha^3 \leftrightarrow T_3 = \begin{bmatrix} | & | & | \\ \alpha^3 & \alpha^4 & \alpha^5 \\ | & | & | \end{bmatrix} = \begin{bmatrix} 1 & 0 & 1 \\ 1 & 1 & 1 \\ 0 & 1 & 1 \end{bmatrix}$$

$$\alpha^4 \leftrightarrow T_4 = \begin{bmatrix} | & | & | \\ \alpha^4 & \alpha^5 & \alpha^6 \\ | & | & | \end{bmatrix} = \begin{bmatrix} 0 & 1 & 1 \\ 1 & 1 & 0 \\ 1 & 1 & 1 \end{bmatrix}$$

$$\alpha^5 \leftrightarrow T_5 = \begin{bmatrix} | & | & | \\ \alpha^5 & \alpha^6 & 1 \\ | & | & | \end{bmatrix} = \begin{bmatrix} 1 & 1 & 1 \\ 1 & 0 & 0 \\ 1 & 1 & 0 \end{bmatrix}$$

$$\alpha^6 \leftrightarrow T_6 = \begin{bmatrix} | & | & | \\ \alpha^6 & 1 & \alpha \\ | & | & | \end{bmatrix} = \begin{bmatrix} 1 & 1 & 0 \\ 0 & 0 & 1 \\ 1 & 0 & 0 \end{bmatrix}$$

Also, the companion matrix of $\mathbf{0} \in GF(2^3)$ is the (3×3) zero matrix, and the set has the identical structure of $GF(2^3)$. Therefore, the translation of the **H** matrix over $GF(2^3)$ of (3.60) to binary form is the (6×21) binary matrix given as (3.61).

$$\mathbf{H} = \begin{bmatrix} 100 & 001 & 010 & 101 & 011 & 111 & 110 \\ 010 & 101 & 011 & 111 & 110 & 100 & 001 \\ 001 & 010 & 101 & 011 & 111 & 110 & 100 \\ - & - & - & - & - & - & - \\ 100 & 010 & 011 & 110 & 001 & 101 & 111 \\ 010 & 011 & 110 & 001 & 101 & 111 & 100 \\ 001 & 101 & 111 & 100 & 010 & 011 & 110 \end{bmatrix} \tag{3.61}$$

The $(21, 15)$ binary code represented by the **H** matrix of (3.61) is a single-byte error correcting (SbEC) code, and more specifically it is a S3EC code. Further discussion of SbEC, SbEC–DbED type of codes derived from RS codes are studied in Chapter 5 of this book.

A note on encoding and decoding RS codes. The cyclic code encoder circuit given in Fig. 3.6 can be appropriately used for RS code. The adder, multiplier, and storage elements are to be appropriately modified to $GF(q)$. If $q = 2^m$, then each adder in Fig. 3.6 is an m-bit adder (m EXOR's), and each multiplier is an m-bit $\times$ m-bit multiplier. Parallel computations for each multiplier can be used for fast encoding. Also, each storage cell for $GF(q)$ is an m-bit register. Bit-serial encoding for RS codes over $GF(2^m)$ can be found in [BERL 82, HSU 84]. RS code decoding is similar to the BCH decoding except for one additional step. The RS decoding steps are as follows.

Let $\mathbf{v}(x)$ and $\mathbf{e}(x)$ be the received and error polynomials, respectively. The error polynomial of weight l ($l \le t$) is denoted as

$$\mathbf{e}(x) = e_{j_1}x^{j_1} + e_{j_2}x^{j_2} + \cdots + e_{j_l}x^{j_l} \tag{3.62}$$

Equation (3.62) has the coefficients $e_{j_1}, e_{j_2}, \ldots, e_{j_l}$, which are error *magnitudes* corresponding to the positions $j_1, j_2, \ldots, j_l$. Also, $\beta_i = \alpha^{j_i}$ ($i = 1, 2, \ldots, l$) are error location numbers as defined previously.

Step 1: Determination of syndrome $\mathbf{s} = (s_1, s_2, \ldots, s_{2t})$, where

$$s_j = \mathbf{v}(\alpha^j) = \mathbf{e}(\alpha^j) \qquad \text{for } j = 1, 2, \ldots, 2t$$

We also obtain the *Syndrome Polynomial*

$$\mathbf{s}(x) = 1 + s_1x + s_2x^2 + \cdots + s_{2t}x^{2t}$$

Step 2: Determination of error-locator polynomial

$$\begin{aligned}\boldsymbol{\sigma}(x) &= 1 + \sigma_1x + \sigma_2x^2 + \cdots + \sigma_lx^l \\ &= (1 - \beta_1x)(1 - \beta_2x)\cdots(1 - \beta_lx)\end{aligned}$$

Step 3: Determination of zeros of $\boldsymbol{\sigma}(x)$.

The zeros are the inverses of error location numbers $\beta_1, \beta_2, \ldots, \beta_l$.

Step 4: Determination of error magnitudes.

We generate another degree l polynomial $\mathbf{z}(x)$, called the *evaluator polynomial,* which is given by

$$\begin{aligned}\mathbf{z}(x) = 1 &+ (s_1 + \sigma_1)x + (s_2 + \sigma_1s_1 + \sigma_2)x^2 \\ &+ (s_3 + \sigma_1s_2 + \sigma_2s_1 + \sigma_3)x^3 + \cdots \\ &+ (s_l + \sigma_1s_{l-1} + \sigma_2s_{l-2} + \cdots + \sigma_l)x^l\end{aligned} \tag{3.63}$$

Equation (3.63) consists of all terms of degree $\le l$ of the product $\boldsymbol{\sigma}(x)\mathbf{s}(x)$ (see [MACW 77]).

We compute the error magnitudes

$$e_{j_i} = \frac{\mathbf{z}(\beta_i^{-1})}{\prod_{v \ne i}(1 - \beta_v\beta_i^{-1})} \qquad \text{for } i = 1, 2, \ldots, l$$

Steps 3 and 4 give the error polynomial that is subtracted from the received polynomial $\mathbf{v}(x)$ as required for correction.

We illustrate the RS code decoding procedure by means of the following example.

Example 3-16

Here we take the (10, 6, 5) code over $GF(11)$ from Table 3.14. The generator is

$$\begin{aligned}\mathbf{g}(x) &= (x-2)(x-4)(x-8)(x-5)\\ &= x^4 + 3x^3 + 5x^2 + 8x + 1 \quad \text{over } GF(11)\end{aligned}$$

Let the received polynomial be

$$\mathbf{v}(x) = x^6 + 2x^5 + 6x^4 + 5x^3 + 6x^2 + 8x + 1$$

Step 1: Syndrome $\mathbf{s} = (s_1, s_2, s_3, s_4)$ is computed as follows.

$$s_1 = \mathbf{v}(2) = 8$$

$$s_2 = \mathbf{v}(2^2) = 0$$

$$s_3 = \mathbf{v}(2^3) = 9$$

$$s_4 = \mathbf{v}(2^4) = 8$$

Step 2: The error-locator polynomial $\sigma(x) = 1 + 4x + 3x^2$ is obtained by use of the Berlekamp algorithm given as follows.

μ	$\sigma^{(\mu)}(x)$	d_μ	l_μ	$\mu - l_\mu$	ρ
−1	1	1	0	−1	
0	1	8	0	0	
1	$1 + 3x$	2	1	0	−1
2	1	9	0	2	0
3	$1 + x + 3x^2$	6	2	1	1
4	$1 + 4x + 3x^2$	—	—	—	2

Step 3: Finding zeros of $\sigma(x)$ and determination of error location numbers through a search procedure. We have

$$\sigma(x) = 1 + 4x + 3x^2 = (1 - 8x)(1 - 10x) = (1 - 2^3x)(1 - 2^5x)$$

giving as the error location the numbers $\beta_1 = 2^3$ and $\beta_2 = 2^5$. (Note that $j_1 = 3$ and $j_2 = 5$.)

Step 4: Finding error magnitudes e_3 and e_5. The error-evaluator polynomial is obtained from (3.63) as follows.

$$\begin{aligned}\mathbf{z}(x) &= 1 + (s_1 + \sigma_1)x + (s_2 + \sigma_1 s_1 + \sigma_2)x^2\\ &= 1 + (8 + 4)x + (0 + 4 \cdot 8 + 3)x^2 = 1 + x + 2x^2\end{aligned}$$

Then

$$e_{j_1} = e_3 = \frac{\mathbf{z}(\beta_1^{-1})}{1 - \beta_2\beta_1^{-1}} = \frac{\mathbf{z}(7)}{1 - 10 \cdot 7} = \frac{7}{8} = 5$$

$$e_{j_2} = e_5 = \frac{\mathbf{z}(\beta_2^{-1})}{1 - \beta_1\beta_2^{-1}} = \frac{\mathbf{z}(10)}{1 - 8 \cdot 10} = \frac{2}{9} = 10$$

This gives us the error polynomial

$$\mathbf{e}(x) = e_3x^3 + e_5x^5 = 5x^3 + 10x^5$$

and the corrected polynomial

$$\begin{aligned}\hat{\mathbf{v}}(x) &= \mathbf{v}(x) - \mathbf{e}(x)\\ &= x^6 + 2x^5 + 6x^4 + 5x^3 + 6x^2 + 8x + 1 - (10x^5 + 5x^3)\\ &= x^6 + 3x^5 + 6x^4 + 6x^2 + 8x + 1 = (x^2 + 1)\mathbf{g}(x)\end{aligned}$$

which clearly is a code polynomial.

RS codes have found many applications for byte-error correction in high-speed memories to multiple byte errors and large burst errors in mass memories such as optical disk and digital audio tape systems. LSI implementation of RS encoding and decoding for these applications exist in [BERL 82], [HSU 84], [LIU 84], [SHAO 85], and [WANG 85].

3.3.5 Burst Error Codes

The codes studied so far are for random bit errors and random byte errors. The burst error channel defined in Chapter 1 gives rise to multiple bit errors confined over a b-bit position of the word. This was explained by examples in Chapter 1. For binary cyclic codes, we define a burst (a *cyclic burst* or cyclic burst error) of length b as follows. Bursts can also be defined over any $GF(q)$ [BLAH 83], but we restrict ourselves here to binary bursts.

Definition 3-6. A *cyclic burst* of length l is a binary vector whose 1's are among l (cyclically) successive bits of the vector, the first and last of which are 1's.

Here we are concerned with codes capable of correcting all (cyclic) burst of length l or less. As polynomials, a burst error $\mathbf{e}(x)$ of length l is given by

$$\mathbf{e}(x) = x^j\mathbf{b}(x) \bmod x^n - 1 \qquad \text{over } GF(2) \tag{3.64}$$

where $\mathbf{b}(x)$ is of degree $l - 1$ with $b_0 = 1$, and j defines the starting position for the burst. All bursts of length 3 in a cyclic code of (length n) are illustrated as

$$\left.\begin{aligned}\mathbf{e}(x) &= (x^2 + 1)x^j\\ &= (x^2 + x + 1)x^j\end{aligned}\right\} \qquad j = 0, 1, \ldots, n - 1$$

All bursts of length 3 or less are given by

$$\mathbf{e}(x) = \begin{Bmatrix} x^j \\ (x+1)x^j \\ (x^2+1)x^j \\ (x^2+x+1)x^j \end{Bmatrix} \qquad \text{for } j = 0, 1, \ldots, n-1$$

For example, 000001011000 and 100000000101 are bursts of length 4. Since there can be exactly 2^{l-2} bursts of length l from any given starting position, it is easy to show that there are exactly $n \cdot 2^{l-2}$ distinct cyclic bursts of length l (for $2 \leq l \leq n/2$) (see Problem 3.16).

For detecting bursts, we have the following.

Theorem 3-7. *A cyclic code generated by* $\mathbf{g}(x)$ *(of degree* r*) can detect any burst of length* r *or less.*

Proof. The syndrome of a burst $\mathbf{e}(x)$ is given by $\mathbf{e}(x) \bmod \mathbf{g}(x)$. Using (3.64), the syndrome is $\mathbf{e}(x) \bmod \mathbf{g}(x) = x^j \mathbf{b}(x) \bmod \mathbf{g}(x)$. Since $gcd\,(x^j, \mathbf{g}(x)) = 1$ and $\mathbf{b}(x)$ is of degree less than r, the syndrome must be nonzero, and therefore $\mathbf{e}(x)$ is detected. Q.E.D.

As an example, consider a burst-detecting code generated by $\mathbf{g}(x) = x^3 + 1$. This code detects all bursts of length 3 or less. Every burst of length 4 has a factor $\mathbf{b}(x)$ of the form

$$\mathbf{b}(x) = x^3 + a_2 x^2 + a_1 x + 1 \qquad \text{with } a_2, a_1 \in \{0, 1\}$$

Only one of four bursts (of length 4) escapes detection. For bursts of length > 4, only one out of eight bursts escapes detection (see Problem 3.17).

For correcting bursts, it is necessary and sufficient that all bursts of length b or less have distinct nonzero syndromes. It is easy to prove that a linear code must have at least $2b$ parities in order to correct bursts of length b. This is called Rieger bound and its proof is left as an exercise [RIEG 60] (see Problem 3.18).

A well-known class of cyclic codes for burst error correction is called *Fire Codes*. The following theorem for the binary case is given here.

Theorem 3-8 [FIRE 59]. *Let the generator of a cyclic code be*

$$\mathbf{g}(x) = (x^{2l-1} - 1)\mathbf{p}(x) \qquad \text{over } GF(2)$$

where $\mathbf{p}(x)$ *is an irreducible polynomial of degree* $m \geq l$ *and* $\mathbf{p}(x)$ *is not a divisor of* $x^{2l-1} - 1$. *Also let* e *be the smallest positive integer such that* $\mathbf{p}(x)$ *divides* $x^e - 1$. *Then the code has length* $n = \mathrm{LCM}(e, 2l-1)$ *and corrects all bursts of length* b *or less.*

Proof. Let $e_1(x) = x^i A(x)$ and $e_2(x) = x^j B(x)$ be two bursts of length $\leq l$ and $i, j < n$. Without any loss of generality, let $i \geq j$. Also, $A(x)$ and $B(x)$ are of the form

$$A(x) = x^{l_1-1} + a_{l_1-2} \cdot x^{l_1-2} + \cdots + a_1 x + 1, \qquad l_1 \le l \tag{3.65}$$

$$B(x) = x^{l_2-1} + b_{l_2-2} \cdot x^{l_2-2} + \cdots + b_1 x + 1, \qquad l_2 \le l \tag{3.66}$$

with all a_i's and b_i's in $GF(2)$. For the code to be a burst error correcting code for all bursts of length $\le l$, the syndromes of $e_1(x)$ and $e_2(x)$ must be distinct. That means

$$\begin{aligned} e_1(x) \bmod g(x) &\ne e_2(x) \bmod g(x) \\ \textit{or} \quad e_1(x) - e_2(x) &\bmod g(x) \ne 0 \end{aligned} \tag{3.67}$$

Assume that (3.67) does not hold. That is,

$$e_1(x) - e_2(x) \bmod g(x) = 0 \tag{3.68}$$

Setting $i - j = m < n$ and with some simple arithmetic, we get

$$x^m A(x) + B(x) \equiv 0 \,(\bmod\, g(x)) \tag{3.69}$$

The congruence (3.69) can be decomposed by use of the factors of $\mathbf{g}(x)$ to obtain

$$x^m A(x) + B(x) \equiv 0 \,(\bmod\, x^{2l-1} - 1) \tag{3.70}$$

$$x^m A(x) + B(x) \equiv 0 \,(\bmod\, p(x)) \tag{3.71}$$

Consider the term $x^m A(x) \bmod x^{2l-1} - 1$ in (3.70). Multiplying $A(x)$ by x^m modulo $x^{2l-1} - 1$ means a cyclic shift of the $(2l-1)$-tuple by m places. Considering $A(x)$ and $B(x)$ (given by (3.65) and (3.66)) as elements of the algebra of polynomials modulo $x^{2l-1} - 1$, (3.70) can hold only when $A(x) = B(x)$ and m is a multiple of $2l - 1$. Substituting this result in (3.71), we get

$$(x^m + 1) A(x) \equiv 0 \bmod p(x) \tag{3.72}$$

Since $A(x)$ and $p(x)$ are relatively prime, we get that $p(x)$ divides $x^m + 1$. This also means that m is a multiple of the order of $p(x)$ (the order of $p(x)$ is e). Thus we have that m, a multiple of $2l - 1$, is also a multiple of e. Therefore m is a multiple of $\text{LCM}(e, 2l-1) = n$. Since $m < n$, this is impossible. Therefore, our assumption of (3.68) is invalid and (3.67) holds. The code has distinct syndromes for each burst of length $\le l$. Q.E.D.

As an example of a binary Fire code, consider

$$g(x) = (x^5 - 1)(x^3 + x + 1) \qquad \text{over } GF(2)$$

In this example, $b = m = 3$ (the smallest integer e such that $x^3 + x + 1$ divides $x^e - 1$ is 7; e is also called the exponent of $x^3 + x + 1$). The length of the code is $n = \text{LCM}(7, 5) = 35$; the data length is $k = n - 8 = 27$. It is a $(35, 27)$ code capable of correcting any burst of length 3 or less.

TABLE 3.15 BINARY FIRE CODES

Generator, $\mathbf{g}(x)$	(n, k)	b
$(x^5 - 1)(x^3 + x + 1)$	(35, 27)	3
$(x^7 - 1)(x^4 + x + 1)$	(105, 94)	4
$(x^7 - 1)(x^5 + x^2 + 1)$	(217, 205)	4
$(x^9 - 1)(x^5 + x^2 + 1)$	(279, 265)	5

Fire codes require a minimum of $3b - 1$ parity bits to correct bursts of length b. More optimal codes for burst errors have been found by a computer search and are available in [BLAH 83], and [LIN 83]. Some binary Fire codes are given in Table 3.15.

Chapter 6 has further examples of Fire codes and their application to mass memories.

Error-trapping decoders for burst errors. The principle of error-trapping decoders, also called *Meggitt decoders* [MEGG 60], is to abstract or trap the error pattern $\mathbf{e}(x)$ into the syndrome register and use appropriate detection and correction logic. A simple example of the error-trapping principle is the (7, 4, 3) code decoder given in Fig. 3.11. For error $\mathbf{e}(x) = x^6$, we have seen that the syndrome of $x^3 \cdot \mathbf{e}(x)$ is given by

$$x^3\mathbf{e}(x) \bmod x^3 + x + 1 = x^9 \left(\bmod x^3 + x + 1\right) = x^2$$

In other words, the syndrome register has only one 1 among its contents.

The syndrome x^2 is recognized by the AND gate. For cyclic codes, if a pattern $\mathbf{e}(x)$ is correctable, then $x\mathbf{e}(x)$, $x^2\mathbf{e}(x)$, and so on are also correctable by cyclic shift operations. This is evident from the decoder of Fig. 3.11.

Another example to illustrate the error-trapping decoder concept is the (7, 3, 4) binary code generated by

$$\mathbf{g}(x) = (x + 1)(x^3 + x + 1) = x^4 + x^3 + x^2 + 1$$

This SEC–DED code can be used to correct bursts of length 2 or less. As a burst correcting code, consider the syndrome of the burst $\mathbf{e}(x) = x^6 + x^5$. If the received polynomial is applied as input at the right end as shown in Fig. 3.31, then the syndrome of $\mathbf{e}(x)$ is

$$\mathbf{e}(x)x^4 \bmod \mathbf{g}(x) = (x^6 + x^5)x^4 \bmod \mathbf{g}(x) = x^3 + x^2 \qquad (3.73)$$

Therefore, the syndrome register of Fig. 3.11 will detect the burst trapped at the right end.

In Fig. 3.31, the received polynomial $\mathbf{v}(x)$ is applied at the right end as shown, which amounts to a premultiplication by x^4. The LFSR feedbacks are connected for a division by $\mathbf{g}(x) = x^4 + x^3 + x^2 + 1$ and to obtain the syndrome in the four-bit register. Output $y = 1$ is produced when the two low-ordered bits of the syndrome

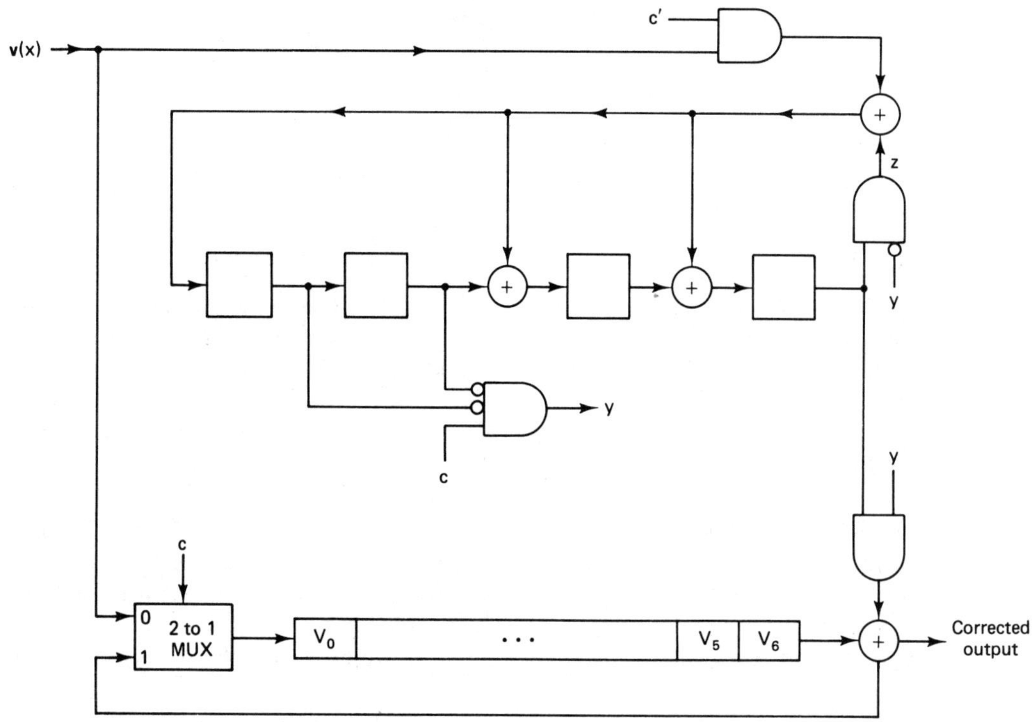

Figure 3.31 Error-trapping decoder for a $(7, 3)$ burst correcting code $b \leq 2$.

are zero and the error pattern is trapped in the other two bits. From (3.31), it is clear that the correction can proceed. Note that once y becomes 1, the feedbacks are disabled by the control gate (with output z). A general burst error decoder using the error-trapping principle is given in Fig. 3.32.

Let r denote the degree of $\mathbf{g}(x)$, then the leftmost (low-order) $r - b$ bits of syndrome register must be zeros for y to be a 1. As y becomes 1, a burst of length b or less gets trapped in the high-order part of the syndrome register, which then is applied for correction bit by bit.

Interleaved codes. Burst error codes can be constructed using simple random error codes by use of a technique called *interleaving* (or *interlacing*). As a simple example, we consider a three-way interlacing of the $(5, 4)$ even-parity code (of distance 2). This results in a $(15, 12)$ code capable of detecting single bursts of length ≤ 3. A codeword $\mathbf{U}$ in the interleaved code is of length 15 and can be arranged as an array as follows.

$$\mathbf{U} = \begin{bmatrix} u_0 & u_3 & u_6 & u_9 & u_{12} \\ u_1 & u_4 & u_7 & u_{10} & u_{13} \\ u_2 & u_5 & u_8 & u_{11} & u_{14} \end{bmatrix}$$

Each row of $\mathbf{U}$ is a codeword in the $(5, 4)$ code. A burst of length ≤ 3 can affect at

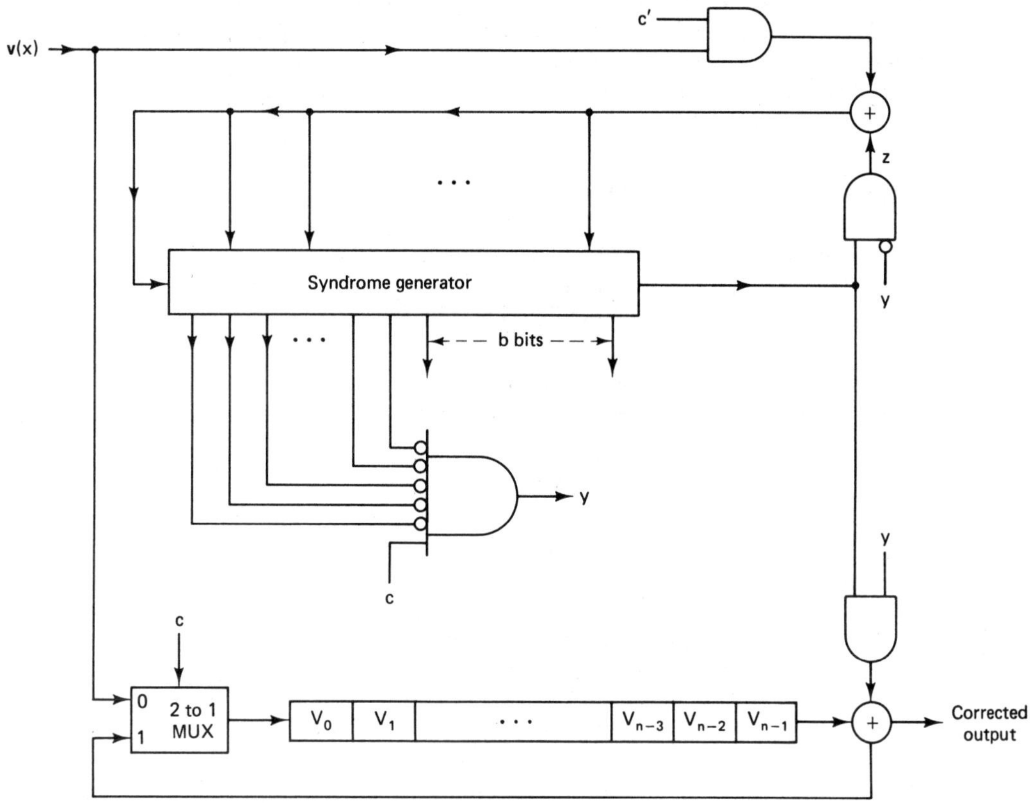

Figure 3.32 General burst error decoder using the error-trapping principle.

most one bit in each row, and hence it is detected. The parity matrix of the interleaved code can be given as

$$\mathbf{H} = \begin{bmatrix} 100 & 100 & 100 & 100 & 100 \\ 010 & 010 & 010 & 010 & 010 \\ 001 & 001 & 001 & 001 & 001 \end{bmatrix}$$

Let $\mathbf{g}_1(x) = x + 1$ be the generator of the (5, 4) code. Then $\mathbf{g}_2(x) = x^3 + 1 = \mathbf{g}_1(x^3)$ will be the generator of the (15, 12) code. An i-way interlacing of an (n, k) cyclic code with generator $\mathbf{g}(x)$ will give us an (ni, ki) cyclic code whose generator will be $\mathbf{g}(x^i)$.

As a further illustration of this technique, consider a (7, 4, 3) cyclic code generated by $\mathbf{g}_1(x) = x^3 + x + 1$ over $GF(2)$. By a three-way interleaving, we obtain a (21, 12) code, which can correct bursts of length 3 or less. A codeword $\mathbf{U}$ in the interleaved code can be written as an array.

$$\mathbf{U} = \begin{bmatrix} u_0 & u_3 & \cdots & u_{18} \\ u_1 & u_4 & \cdots & u_{19} \\ u_2 & u_5 & \cdots & u_{20} \end{bmatrix}$$

Each row of **U** is a codeword in a (7, 4, 3) code and so can correct single errors. Any burst of length 3 in **U** can be corrected by this technique. The generator of the interleaved code can be shown to be $\mathbf{g}_2(x) = \mathbf{g}_1(x^3) = x^9 + x^3 + 1$.

Interleaving can be an effective technique to design codes for correcting multiple bursts or long bursts. A b-way interleaving of tEC codes will enable correction of up to t bursts, each of length $\leq b$, or a single burst of length $\leq tb$. For burst correction, we can state the following.

Theorem 3-9. *If $\mathbf{g}(x)$ generates an (n, k) cyclic code capable of correcting single bursts of length $\leq l$, then $\mathbf{g}(x^i)$ generates an i-way interleaved (ni, ki) code capable of correcting single bursts of length $\leq il$.*

The proof is quite simple and is left as an exercise. For a more detailed treatment on this topic, the reader is advised to refer to [PETE 72].

3.4 ARITHMETIC CODES

Codes for arithmetic operations are a different class from the rest of the code classes studied so far. The codewords used for arithmetic operations are modeled as integers in some ring Z_M, with modulus M. The codewords are to be closed under addition of integers. Any integer N is expressed in *radix* r as a polynomial

$$N = a_n r^{n-1} + a_{n-2} r^{n-2} + \cdots + a_1 r + a_0 \tag{3.74}$$

for $a_i \in \{0, 1, \ldots, r-1\}$. The integer is written as the n-tu, $N = (a_{n-1}, a_{n-2}, \ldots, a_1, a_0)_r$.

Definition 3-7 [PETE 72]. We define the *arithmetic weight* of an integer N as $W_{ar}(N)$ given by the smallest number of nonzero terms in an expression for N of the form

$$N = \pm a_{n-1} r^{n-1} \pm a_{n-2} r^{n-2} \pm \cdots \pm a_0 \tag{3.75}$$

where $a_i \in \{0, 1, \ldots, r-1\}$ and r is the *radix* of the system. Equation (3.75) is also called a *minimal form* expression for N.

For example, the integer 29 in radix 2 is written as

$$29 = (11101)_2$$

and its arithmetic weight is obtained by an expression in its minimal form as

$$29 = 2^5 - 2^2 + 2^0$$

Therefore, $W_{ar}(29) = 3$. The arithmetic weight of an integer N is very much dependent on the radix r of the systems. It can be easily observed that $W_{ar}(29)$ in radix 3 is

$$W_{ar}(29) = W_{ar}(3^3 + 2) = 2$$

For this section we assume that the radix is 2 unless it is specifically stated otherwise.

Definition 3-8. The *arithmetic distance* between two integers N_1 and N_2, denoted $D_{ar}(N_1, N_2)$, is given by the arithmetic weight of $N_1 - N_2$.

For example, $D_{ar}(31, 39) = W_{ar}(31-39) = W_{ar}(-2^3) = 1$. The arithmetic distance so defined corresponds with the errors that occur in arithmetic units based on the error propagation. If an error of 8 has occurred in the result of an arithmetic operation, then it is a single error even though a number of bit positions are in error. To illustrate this, let R be the correct result of an arithmetic operation, and R' denote an erroneous result such that

$$R' = R + E$$

In binary forms let

$$R' = 011111 = 31$$

$$R = 100111 = 39$$

$$E = R' - R = -8$$

then $D_{ar}(R', R) = W_{ar}(R' - R) = W_{ar}(-8) = 1$. As an exercise, the reader is advised to prove that arithmetic distance is a metric satisfying the positive definiteness, symmetry, and triangular inequality defined in Section 1.2. Since it is a metric, it can be used to define the minimum distance of arithmetic codes and relate the minimum distance with error detection and correction properties of the code. It is interesting to note that if a code has a minimum arithmetic distance d, its Hamming distance is at least d. Therefore, an arithmetic code can also be used as a code for memories and communication channels.

The theory of arithmetic codes has many parallels with the linear (parity) codes studied in the previous sections. The code **C** with minimum arithmetic distance $d_{\min}$ provides the following properties that are analogous to the linear (parity) codes given in Chapter 1.

1. The code C can detect up to d arithmetic errors for $d < d_{\min}$.
2. The code C can correct t or fewer arithmetic errors if and only if $d_{\min} \geq 2t + 1$.
3. The code C can correct up to t errors and detect up to d errors with $d \geq t$ if and only if $d_{\min} \geq d + t + 1$.

There are many strikingly analogous results for arithmetic codes as given by [MASS 71] and [RAO 74]. We will study some of these results here.

3.4.1 Arithmetic Code Classes

We start with the concepts of *systematic* codes and *separate* codes. Systematicity and separateness denote the same concept in parity codes because there are no carry propagations in vector addition. For arithmetic codewords, there are carries between digits, and these carries between information digits and check digits may cause difficulties. Therefore, a distinction between systematic and separate codes is necessary, as follows [GARN 66, RAO 74].

Definition 3-9. An arithmetic code is said to be *systematic* if for each codeword (of n digits) there are specified k positions called information digits and the rest $n - k$ positions are check digits.

Definition 3-10. An arithmetic code is said to be a *separate* code if the code is systematic and the addition structure for the code has separate adders for information and check digits. That is, there are no carries between information digits and check digits during addition.

These definitions will be clear when we define code classes and illustrate them by examples. There are three distinct arithmetic code classes: (1) AN codes, which are nonsystematic; (2) residue codes, which are also called separate codes; and (3) systematic AN codes, derived from (nonsystematic) AN codes. The last class is systematic, but it is not separate in the sense that codewords are integers and there could be carry propagation between check and information parts. The examples in Table 3.16 illustrate these classes. For all the codes in Table 3.16, the range of information is $m = 8$, and the *check base* is 5. In the $5N$ code, the information N cannot be identified from the codewords. However, in the residue $[N, |N|_5]$ code, the information can be readily identified. In the systematic $5N$ code, each codeword is a multiple of 5 (as in $5N$ code), and the information bits can be found as the rightmost three bits. During addition of these codewords, a carry can move from information to check part. Therefore, an appropriate design method is required to

TABLE 3.16 ARITHMETIC CODE CLASSES

		Binary Arithmetic Codes Representing N		
Decimal N	Binary N	$5N$ Code	Residue Code	Systematic $5N$ Code
0	000	000000	(000, 000)	000000
1	001	000101	(001, 001)	011001
2	010	001010	(010, 010)	001010
3	011	001111	(011, 011)	100011
4	100	010100	(100, 100)	010100
5	101	011001	(101, 000)	000101
6	110	011110	(110, 001)	011110
7	111	100011	(111, 010)	001111

handle these carries and preserve codewords. These methods are not covered in this book, but the interested reader may refer to [RAO 74].

3.4.2 *AN* Codes

AN codes are somewhat analogous to the cyclic codes studied in Section 3.2. A is the generator of the code and N is the information represented. Every codeword is an integer of the form AN. For information $N \in Z_m = \{0, 1, \dots, m-1\}$, the codeword is $AN \in Z_M$ where $M = A \cdot m$. The integers m and M are called the *range* (of information) and *modulus* of the code, respectively. There are m codewords, namely $\{0, A, 2A, \dots, (m-1)A\}$. Each codeword is represented as a binary n-tuple, and therefore n satisfies

$$2^{n-1} < A(m-1) < 2^n \tag{3.76}$$

and n is called the *length* of the code.

It is easy to see that for two codewords AN_1 and AN_2, their sum

$$R = |AN_1 + AN_2|_M = A \cdot |N_1 + N_2|_m = AN_3 \tag{3.77}$$

is also a codeword. Thus, AN codes are also linear in the sense that the sum of two codewords is also a codeword. If an error e is introduced in the addition, then the erroneous result is given by

$$R' = |R + e|_M = |AN_3 + e|_M$$

To check for errors, we obtain the syndrome of R', denoted

$$\begin{aligned} S(R') &= |R'|_A \\ &= ||AN_3 + e|_M|_A = |e|_A \end{aligned} \tag{3.78}$$

Equation (3.78) is based on the fact that $||X|_M|_A = |X|_A$ if A divides M, which is easily proved.

Modular arithmetic weight and error sets. We need to further clarify errors in ring Z_M. Single errors correspond to integers whose arithmetic weight is 1 and are of the form

$$e = \pm 2^j \qquad \text{for } j = 0, 1, 2, \dots$$

However, when the arithmetic is carried out modulo M (i.e., Z_M), then $e = -2^j \equiv M - 2^j$ (modulo M). For instance, the set of single errors in Z_{32} are given by the set

$$E = \{1, 2, 4, 8, 16, 24, 28, 30, 31\}$$

In order to define error sets in Z_M, and for an appropriate consideration of the arithmetic weight (W_{ar}) of integers in Z_M, the following is introduced.

Definition 3-11 [RAO 71]. The *modular arithmetic weight* or *modular weight* of an integer N in Z_M, denoted $W_M(N)$, is given by

$$W_M(N) = \text{Min}\{W_{ar}(N), W_{ar}(M-N)\} \tag{3.79}$$

By this definition, we have that the arithmetic weight of 31 is 2, but its modular weight, $W_{32}(31) = 1$.

Definition 3-12. The *modular distance* between N_1 and N_2, denoted $D_M(N_1, N_2)$, is given by

$$D_M(N_1, N_2) = W_M(|N_1 - N_2|_M) \tag{3.80}$$

For convenience and simplicity, we write $N_1 - N_2$ to mean $|N_1 - N_2|_M$ and modulo M is to be understood by its context.

By use of these definitions, we can denote error sets in Z_M as follows. Let $E(M, d)$ denote the set of errors of modular weight d in Z_M, and $U(M, d)$ denote the set of errors of modular weight d or less. It is shown that for values, such as $M = 53$, the modular distance is not a metric [RAO 71]. However, it is a metric for $M = 2^n$ or $2^n - 1$, as proved by Massey and Garcia [MASS 71]. For greater detail and properties of modular distance, the reader may refer to [RAO 74].

Example 3-17

The following error sets can be easily verified.

$$E(64,1) = \{1,2,4,8,16,32,48,56,60,62,63\}$$

$$E(31,2) = \{3,5,6,7,9,10,11,12,13,14,17,18,19,20,21,22,24,25,26,28\}$$

$$U(31,2) = \{a \in Z_{31} \mid a \neq 0\}$$

Single-error detecting *AN* codes. We return to Equation (3.78), which gives the syndrome of error e as

$$S(e) = |e|_A \tag{3.81}$$

If e is a single error in Z_M, then $e \in E(M,1)$ and therefore

$$\begin{aligned} S(e) &= |2^j|_A \qquad \text{or} \qquad |M - 2^j|_A \\ &= |\pm 2^j|_A, \qquad \text{for} \qquad j = 0,1,2,\ldots,n-1 \end{aligned} \tag{3.82}$$

By (3.82), the syndrome is nonzero for any odd A, and the code can detect all single errors in Z_M. (Note here that A is also a divisor of M). Therefore, we have the following.

Theorem 3-10. *Any odd A that divides M is a generator of an AN code capable of detecting single errors in* Z_M.

TABLE 3.17 ERRORS AND SYNDROMES FOR 13N CODE OF DISTANCE 3

Error Position	$e \in E(65,1)$ 2^j	Syndrome $\|e\|_{13}$	$\bar{e} \in E(65,1)$ $M - 2^j$	Syndrome $\|\bar{e}\|_{13}$
0	1	1	64	12
1	2	2	63	11
2	4	4	61	9
3	8	8	57	5
4	16	3	49	10
5	32	6	33	7

Example 3-18

In Z_{63}, we can list the generators of single-error detecting AN codes as 3, 7, 9, and 21. The first three codes have an exact distance of 2, and 21 generates a distance-3 code. The codewords are given in the binary form for $7N$ and $21N$ codes as follows.

$$7N \text{ code} = \{000000, 000111, 001110, 010101, 011100, 100011, 101010, 110001, 111000\}$$
$$21N \text{ code} = \{000000, 010101, 101010\}$$

Single-error correcting (SEC) *AN* codes. The necessary and sufficient conditions for an SEC AN code is that $S(e)$ are nonzero and distinct for all $e \in E(M,1)$. Using (3.82) for syndromes, this condition translates to $S(e) = |\pm 2^j|_A \neq 0$, and the syndromes are distinct for all positions $j = 0, 1, 2, \ldots, n-1$, where n is the length of the code. To illustrate this condition we first give an example.

Example 3-19

Consider a $13N$ code in Z_{65}. Note that 13 divides 65. The codewords in binary form are:

$$\{000000, 001101, 011010, 100111, 110100\}$$

It is easy to verify that the $d_{\min}$ (modular distance) of the code is 3. Table 3.17 lists the single errors and their corresponding syndromes.

In order to find single-error correcting AN codes, we may start with an odd generator A of weight 3 or greater. Then we proceed to find the weights of $2A, 3A, 4A, \ldots,$ until for some smallest l $W_{ar}(lA) < 3$. Then the code $\{0, A, 2A, \ldots, (l-1)A\}$ has a $d_{\min} \geq 3$ and a range $m = l$. Since A is an odd integer and $mA = M$ cannot have weight 1, we therefore have that the modulus

$$M = mA = 2^k \pm 1$$

Therefore, we have the following theorem.

Theorem 3-11 [BROW 60]. *For a distance-3 AN code, the maximum range (of information) is given by the integer*

$$m_{\max} = (2^k \pm 1)/A \tag{3.83}$$

for the smallest positive integer k.

To construct distance-3 AN codes and to find m_{max}, one does not have to go through a weight search. The order of 2 in $GF(A)$, denoted $e(A)$, is the smallest positive integer j such that

$$2^j \equiv 1 \text{ modulo } A$$

If 2 is primitive in $GF(A)$, then $e(A) = A - 1$. Then, we can also show that the smallest positive power of 2 that equal $+1$ and -1 are given by

$$\begin{aligned} 2^{A-1} &\equiv 1 \bmod A \\ 2^{(A-1)/2} &\equiv -1 \bmod A \end{aligned} \tag{3.84}$$

If 2 is not primitive but -2 is primitive, then the corresponding powers are given by

$$\begin{aligned} (-2)^{(A-1)} = 2^{A-1} &\equiv 1 \pmod{A} \\ \text{and} \quad 2^{(A-1)/2} &\equiv 1 \pmod{A} \end{aligned} \tag{3.85}$$

For example, for $A = 11$, $e(11) = 10$ and $2^5 \equiv -1 \pmod{11}$ and $2^{10} \equiv 1 \pmod{11}$. For $A = 23$, -2 is primitive (but not 2), therefore $2^{11} \equiv 1 \pmod{23}$. By using these results and Theorem 3-11, we can obtain the following.

Theorem 3-12. *Let A be an odd prime and m_{max} denote the maximum range of distance-3 code generated by A. Then we have that 2 is primitive in $GF(A)$ if and only if*

$$m_{max} = (2^{(A-1)/2} + 1)/A \tag{3.86}$$

Also, -2 is primitive (but not 2) in $GF(A)$ if and only if

$$m_{max} = (2^{(A-1)/2} - 1)/A \tag{3.87}$$

The class of codes where A is a prime with 2, or -2 is prime in $GF(A)$, is called *Brown–Peterson* codes. These codes are single-error correcting codes, and some examples of them are given in Table 3.18.

3.4.3 Residue Codes

As defined earlier, the systematic codes that have separate adders for information and checks are called separate codes or residue codes. First, we discuss error detection using residue codes and then discuss error correction using *biresidue* codes. Only preliminary material on these codes is presented here, but for greater detail and more thorough treatment, the reader is advised to refer to [RAO 74].

TABLE 3.18 BROWN – PETERSON SEC CODES

A	$e(A)$	m_{max}	$M = A \cdot m_{max}$
11	10	3	$2^5 + 1$
13	12	5	$2^6 + 1$
19	18	27	$2^9 + 1$
*23	11	89	$2^{11} - 1$
29	28	565	$2^{14} + 1$
37	36	7,085	$2^{18} + 1$
*47	23	17,841	$2^{23} - 1$
53	52	1,266,205	$2^{26} + 1$
*61	30	17,602,325	$2^{30} - 1$
67	66	128,207,985	$2^{33} + 1$

*For these cases, -2 (not 2) is primitive in $GF(A)$.

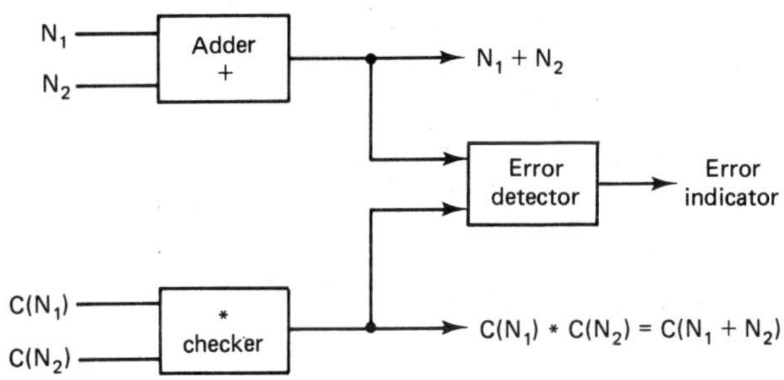

Figure 3.33 Separate adder and checker.

Error detection using residue codes. We consider here a separate adder and checker as shown in Fig. 3.33. The codewords applied here are of the form $[N, C(N)]$. Peterson showed [PETE 58] that the code is *closed* or *preserved* under the addition operation if and only if $C(N)$ is a residue check of N for some base b and the operation $*$ in the checker is addition modulo b. This is stated as a theorem as follows.

Theorem 3-13. *For the separate adder and checker of Fig. 3.33, assume that $C(N)$ requires fewer digits than required for the information N. Then the code is preserved under the operations, that is,*

$$C(N_1) * C(N_2) = C(N_1 + N_2) \tag{3.88}$$

if and only if $C(N)$ is $|N|_A$ for some base A and $*$ is addition modulo A.

That result is extended by Garner [GARN 66] as follows.

Theorem 3-14. *Let N_1 and N_2 be elements of Z_m and $+$ denote addition modulo m in Fig. 3.33, then the code is preserved, that is,* (3.88) *holds if and only if for* *some A*

(i) $C(N) = |N|_A$
(ii) * is addition modulo A, and (3.89)
(iii) A divides m.

For proofs of Theorems 3-13 and 3-14, see [RAO 74]. Theorem 3-14 establishes the conditions to construct $[N, |N|_A]$ (residue) codes in order to check for errors in addition. The function of the error detector circuit (in Fig. 3.33) is to verify whether the outputs of the adder and checker form a legitimate codeword in the $[N, |N|_A]$ code. This scheme operates under the assumptions that:

1. either adder or checker could be in error but not both,
2. the error detecting unit is error-free or is *self-checking* (see Chapter 8), and
3. errors occurring in the adder belong to a specified class, e.g., set of single errors.

The following residue code examples illustrate these concepts.

Example 3-20

Consider the adder in Fig. 3.33 to be a 1's complement 9-bit adder. Then it is shown that N_1 and N_2 can be modeled as elements of Z_m for $m = 2^9 - 1 = 511$ (see [RAO 74]). Then, to check for single errors, an $[N, |N|_A]$ code, where A is a proper divisor of 511, can be selected. Since $m = 511 = 7 \times 73$, the two choices for A are 7 and 73. Any single error in the adder is of the form $|\pm 2^j|_m$, which is detected by either check base. Therefore, $[N, |N|_7]$ and $[N, |N|_{73}]$ are the desired codes. If the check base is $A = m = 511$, then the checker is a duplicate of the adder and the error detector is a mere *match* circuit.

The $[N, |N|_{73}]$ code can be shown also to detect double errors, which are elements of $U(511, 2)$. The duplication ($[N, N]$) code detects all errors in the adder or checker.

As another example, let the adders be a 10-bit 2's complement adder. In this case, N_1 and N_2 are elements of Z_m, $m = 2^{10}$ (see [RAO 74]). It is easy to prove that there are no residue codes to check errors for this adder, except the trivial duplication code.

Low-cost residue codes. For binary adders, the check bases of the form $A = 2^c - 1$ are known to be very cost effective from the implementation point of view. Generation of residues $|N|_{2^c-1}$ and addition of residues modulo $2^c - 1$ are known to be very simple compared with the other types of check bases, and therefore this type of residue code is called a *low-cost residue* code. This is illustrated as follows.

The low-cost residue codes have a check base $A = 3, 7, 15, 31$, and so on. Consider that $N = (10111010011)_2$ and its check $|N|_7$ is to be generated. Then N is divided into bytes of length 3 starting from the right, and these bytes are added modulo 7 (i.e., with an end-around-carry as in 1's complement number). This is due

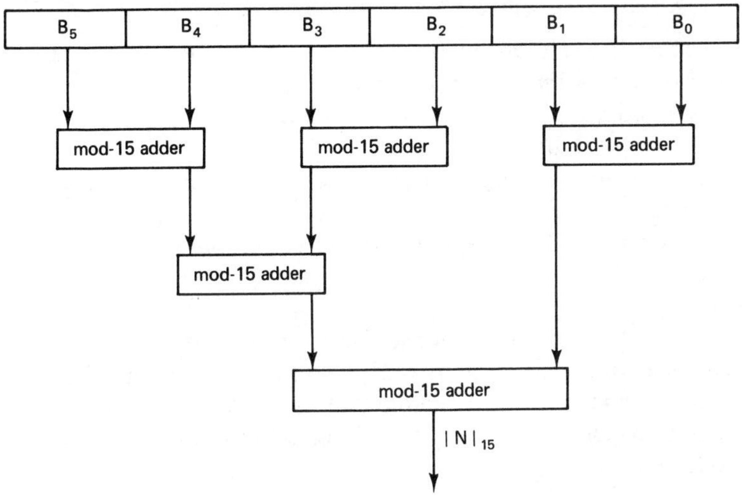

Figure 3.34 Parallel residue generator modulo 15.

to the fact that $|2^{3t}|_7 = 1$ for all $t = 0, 1, 2, \ldots$. Let $N = 110|111|010|011 = 3539$. The 3-bit bytes are added as follows.

$$
\begin{array}{r}
0\ 1\ 1 \\
0\ 1\ 0 \\
\hline
1\ 0\ 1 \\
1\ 1\ 1 \\
\hline
\textcircled{1}\,1\ 0\ 0 \\
\rightarrow 1 \\
\hline
1\ 0\ 1 \\
1\ 1\ 0 \\
\hline
\textcircled{1}\,0\ 1\ 1 \\
\rightarrow 1 \\
\hline
1\ 0\ 0
\end{array}
$$

$$|n|_7 = 100_2 = 4$$

A parallel residue generator circuit for a 24-bit N modulo 15 is given in Fig. 3.34. Residue generation for check bases A of a more general form (not of the form $2^c - 1$) is not as simple. Serial and parallel generator circuits for $A = 29$ can be found in [RAO 74].

Error correction using biresidue codes. A separate code with two or more residue checks is called a *multiresidue* code. Here we study $[N, |N|_{A_1}, |N|_{A_2}]$ codes called *biresidue* codes. A_1 and A_2 are called the check bases, and $N \in Z_m$. As an extension of Theorem 3-14, we can show that this code is closed under addition if and only if $A_i|m$ for $i = 1$ and 2. If $m = 2^k - 1$, then the information is a k-bit block and addition in Z_m has 1's complement structure. We can choose A_i to be low-cost check bases (i.e., $A_1 = 2^c - 1$, $A_2 = 2^d - 1$ for positive integers c and d). Then selection of integers c and d is based on the following.

Lemma 3-2. *For positive integers c, k, and $r \geq 2$, $r^c - 1$ divides $r^k - 1$ if and only if c divides k.*

The proof is left out as an exercise for the reader. Based on the foregoing lemma, the biresidue code with $m = 2^k - 1$, $A_1 = 2^c - 1$ and $A_2 = 2^d - 1$ must satisfy that $c|k$ and $d|k$, and therefore that the LCM(c, d) divides k. This leads us to an important theorem for single error correction using biresidue codes that is given as follows.

Theorem 3-15 [RAO 70, RAO 74]. *Consider a biresidue code with $m = 2^k - 1$, $A_1 = 2^c - 1$, and $A_2 = 2^d - 1$ for $c \neq d$. This code can correct any single error in the adder or any error in one of the checkers if and only if $k =$ LCM(c, d).*

A detailed proof can be found in [RAO 70] or [RAO 74]. An outline of the proof is given after the following discussion and example.

The syndrome of a 3-tuple (x, y, z) is given by

$$\mathbf{s}(x, y, z) = (s_1, s_2) = \left(|x - y|_{A_1}, |x - z|_{A_2}\right) \tag{3.90}$$

It is assumed here that the three components of the code are processed in separate units, called the adder (sometimes also called the processor), checker 1, and checker 2, respectively, and therefore at most one of the components of the result will be erroneous at any given time.

A triple (x, y, z) is a codeword if and only if $\mathbf{s}(x, y, z) = (0, 0)$. For a codeword (x, y, z), consider the three separate cases of errors.

1. Error in the adder unit.
   Let (x', y, z) denote the erroneous word due to an error in the adder, such that $x' = |x + e|_m$. Then the syndrome

$$\begin{aligned}\mathbf{s}(x', y, z) = \mathbf{s}(e, 0, 0) &= \left(|x' - y|_{A_1}, |x' - z|_{A_2}\right)\\ &= \left(|e|_{A_1}, |e|_{A_2}\right)\end{aligned} \tag{3.91}$$

2. Error in checker 1.
   The erroneous word is of the form (x, y', z) where $y' = |y + e|_{A_1}$. Its syndrome

$$\begin{aligned}\mathbf{s}(x, y', z) &= \left(|x - y'|_{A_1}, |x - z|_{A_2}\right)\\ &= \left(|-e|_{A_1}, 0\right)\end{aligned} \tag{3.92}$$

3. Error in checker 2.

The erroneous word is of the form (x, y, z') where $z' = |z + e|_{A_2}$. Its syndrome

$$\begin{aligned} \mathbf{s}(x, y, z') &= \left(|x - y|_{A_1}, |x - z'|_{A_2}\right) \\ &= \left(0, |-e|_{A_2}\right) \end{aligned} \tag{3.93}$$

From the above, we have the following for syndrome $\mathbf{s} = (s_1, s_2)$.

$s_1 = 0, s_2 = 0$: no error

$s_1 \neq 0, s_2 \neq 0$: error in the adder

$s_1 \neq 0, s_2 = 0$: error in checker 1

$s_1 = 0, s_2 \neq 0$: error in checker 2

For the cases when there is an error in one of the checkers, it can be easily corrected by computing the check value from x. When the error is in the adder unit, the syndromes corresponding to the set of single errors must be distinct. To illustrate this correspondence we give the following example.

Example 3-21

To satisfy the conditions of Theorem 3-15, we select $m = 2^{12} - 1$ and $A_1 = 2^3 - 1$ and $A_2 = 2^4 - 1$. The syndromes corresponding to single errors in the adder are listed in Table 3.19. These syndromes are all clearly distinct for $i = 0, 1, \ldots, 11$. However, for $i = 12$, the syndrome of $s(2^{12}, 0, 0) = (1, 1) = s(2^0, 0, 0)$. Thus, the code can correct single errors in the adder for $k = 12$.

TABLE 3.19 SYNDROMES OF SINGLE ERRORS FOR THE BIRESIDUE CODE WITH $k = 12$, $c = 3$ AND $d = 4$

i	Syndrome $\mathbf{s}(2^i, 0, 0) = (\|2^i\|_7, \|2^i\|_{15})$	Syndrome $\mathbf{s}(m_0 - 2^i, 0, 0) = (\|-2^i\|_7, \|-2^i\|_{15})$
0	(1, 1)	(6, 14)
1	(2, 2)	(5, 13)
2	(4, 4)	(3, 11)
3	(1, 8)	(6, 7)
4	(2, 1)	(5, 14)
5	(4, 2)	(3, 13)
6	(1, 4)	(6, 11)
7	(2, 8)	(5, 7)
8	(4, 1)	(3, 14)
9	(1, 2)	(6, 13)
10	(2, 4)	(5, 11)
11	(4, 8)	(3, 7)
12	(1, 1)	(6, 14)

Outline of Proof of Theorem 3-15. From the previous discussion, we know that k must be a multiple of LCM(c, d). Therefore, there are two cases to consider: (1) $k = \text{LCM}(c, d)$, (2) $k = a \cdot \text{LCM}(c, d)$ for some integer $a \geq 2$. The proof consists of showing that for case 1 (i.e., $k = \text{LCM}(c, d)$), the syndromes of all single errors in the adder are distinct, and for case (2) the syndromes are not distinct.

Let $k = \text{LCM}(c, d)$, and we consider single errors in the adder that are of the form

$$\mathbf{e} = \pm 2^j \qquad \text{for } j = 0, 1, \ldots, k-1$$

Using (3.91), the corresponding syndromes are $\mathbf{s}(e, 0, 0) = (| \pm 2^j|_{A_1}, | \pm 2^j|_{A_2})$. Assume that $s(2^i, 0, 0) = \mathbf{s}(2^j, 0, 0)$ for $i \neq j$, $i, j < k$. Then we get $|2^i|_{A_l} = |2^j|_{A_l}$ for $l = 1, 2$. From Lemma 3-2, this means that c and d both divide $i - j$. That is, $k = \text{LCM}(c, d)$ divides $i - j$, which is impossible. Therefore, our assumption $\mathbf{s}(2^i, 0, 0) = \mathbf{s}(2^j, 0, 0)$ is invalid. Next, assume that $\mathbf{s}(2^i, 0, 0) = \mathbf{s}(-2^j, 0, 0)$. Then we get $2^{i-j} \equiv -1 \pmod{A_l}$ for $l = 1, 2$. This can hold only if $A_1 = A_2 = 3$, which is a contradiction. Therefore, we conclude that the syndromes of all single errors are distinct. If errors are in one of the checkers, then one component of the syndrome is zero and the other nonzero. It is easy to detect and correct these errors. Q.E.D.

Separate codes, particularly the biresidue codes, are quite attractive from the point of view of application. The adder or checker unit error can be corrected by the biresidue code. Its implementation, however, has to consider the problem of errors in the residue generator and error corrector units. These units are considered to be relatively small compared with the adder unit and, therefore, can be assumed to operate free of errors. On the other hand, one may like to implement these units using *self-checking logic*, which we will study in Chapters 8 and 9.

There are many classes of arithmetic codes for multiple error detection and correction. Some of these are derived as duals of Brown–Peterson (BP) codes, and these have large distances ($d \geq 4$). Cyclic AN codes are also defined as ideals in ring Z_m, when $m = 2^n - 1$. These advanced topics can be found in [RAO 74], [BARR 66], [MAND 67], and [CHIE 71].

EXERCISES

3.1. Consider a systematic (8, 4) code over $GF(2)$, whose parity equations are given below.

$$P_5 = M_1 + M_2 + M_4$$
$$P_6 = M_1 + M_3 + M_4$$
$$P_7 = M_1 + M_2 + M_3$$
$$P_8 = M_2 + M_3 + M_4$$

where M_i are message bits. Find the parity and generator matrix for this code. Determine its $d_{\min}$.

3.2. Given the parity matrix **H** of a linear code **C**,

$$\mathbf{H} = \begin{bmatrix} 0 & 1 & 1 & 2 \\ 1 & 0 & 2 & 2 \end{bmatrix} \qquad \text{over } GF(3)$$

(a) determine its $d_{\min}$.
(b) obtain its generator matrix and list all code words.
(c) for the standard array decoding table, obtain all coset leaders of smallest possible weights and their corresponding syndromes.

3.3. Let **H** be the parity matrix for an (n, k) binary linear code **C** that has odd minimum distance d. A new code $\mathbf{C}_1$ is constructed with the following parity matrix.

$$\mathbf{H}_1 = \left[\begin{array}{ccccccc|c} & & & \mathbf{H} & & & & \begin{matrix} 0 \\ 0 \\ \cdot \\ 0 \end{matrix} \\ \hline 1 & 1 & 1 & \cdot\ \cdot\ \cdot & 1 & 1 & & 1 \end{array}\right] \qquad \text{over } GF(2)$$

(a) Prove that every code vector in $\mathbf{C}_1$ has even weight.
(b) Prove that the minimum distance of $\mathbf{C}_1$ is $d + 1$.

3.4. Obtain all cyclic codes in the algebra of polynomials modulo $x^6 - 1$ over $GF(2)$. For each code, give its generator and the information rate and also determine its $d_{\min}$.

3.5. For the cyclic code generated by $x^4 + x^3 + 1$, obtain its encoding logic circuit. If $x^6 + x^2$ is the information polynomial, show the encoding steps and obtain its code polynomial.

3.6. Given a linear code, **V**, whose parity matrix is

$$\mathbf{H} = \begin{bmatrix} a & b & 1 & 1 \\ b & a & 0 & 1 \end{bmatrix} \qquad \text{over } GF(4),$$

(a) obtain its generator matrix in canonical form.
(b) encode a given message $(a, 1)$.
(c) decode a received word $(b, 0, 1, b)$.

3.7. Obtain generator polynomials of all cyclic codes of length
(a) $n = 3,\ q = 4$.
(b) $n = 4,\ q = 3$.

3.8. **(a)** If $\mathbf{g(x)} = (x^3 + x^2 + 1)$ over $GF(2)$ is the generator of a shortened cyclic code of length 6, draw the diagram of an encoder and decoder.
(b) If the message polynomial is $x^2 + x + 1$, determine the code polynomial by using the encoder. Give the contents of the shift register and its output for each cycle of operation.
(c) If $\mathbf{v}(x) = x^3 + x$ is received, show at each step the contents of the syndrome register and the formation of corrected output using the decoder.

3.9. Obtain the minimum polynomials of
(a) α^2, where α is a zero of $x^2 + x + 2$ over $GF(3)$.
(b) α^3, where α is a zero of $x^5 + x^2 + 1$ over $GF(2)$.

3.10. Obtain a decoder logic circuit for a (13, 8, 4) SEC–DED code. If the received polynomial $\mathbf{v}(x) = x^{10} + x^3 + x^2$, show how it is decoded by the circuit.

3.11. $\mathbf{h}^*(x)$ is the reciprocal polynomial of $\mathbf{h}(x)$ as given by (3.33). Prove the validity of (3.34).

3.12. For the double-error correcting BCH code generated by $\mathbf{g}(x) = (x^4 + x + 1)(x^4 + x^3 + x^2 + x + 1)$, decode the received polynomials
(a) $\mathbf{v}_1(x) = x^9 + x^8 + x^3 + x^2$.
(b) $\mathbf{v}_2(x) = x^{13} + x^{12} + x^9 + x^5 + 1$.

3.13. Devise circuits to obtain $\mathbf{s} = (s_1 \ldots s_6)$, where $s_j = \mathbf{v}(\alpha^j)$ for $j = 1, 2, \ldots, 6$ and α is a primitive element in $GF(16)$. If $\mathbf{v}(x) = x^{10} + x^7 + 1$, show the syndromes obtained by the circuits.

3.14. What is the dual code of the (10, 6, 5) RS code over $GF(11)$ given in Table 3.14? Prove that the dual code is a *RS* code.

3.15. For the (10, 6, 5) *RS* code over $GF(11)$ given in Table 3.14, if $\mathbf{v}(x) = 3x^8 + 7x^2$ is a received word, decode it.

3.16. **(a)** Obtain all cyclic bursts of length 4 or less among 8-tuples (i.e., $n = 8$).
(b) How many cyclic bursts are there of length l or less among n-tuples?

3.17. Let $\mathbf{g}(x)$ of degree r generate a binary cyclic code used for burst error detection. Show that only one out of 2^r of the bursts of length $b > r + 1$ are missed from being detected by the code.

3.18. Show that a linear code must have at least $2b$ parities to be able to correct all single bursts of length b or less. (Hint: First show that any burst of length $2b$ or less cannot be a codeword.)

3.19. Obtain a decoder for the (35, 27) burst correcting code.

3.20. Prove Theorem 3-9.

3.21. Show that D_{ar} (the arithmetic distance) is a metric.

3.22. Show that $||X|_M|_A = |X|_A$ for any X, if and only if $A|M$.

3.23. Show that for positive integers c, k, and $r > 2$, r^c divides r^k if and only if c divides k.

3.24. **(a)** Obtain all codewords of the AN code generated by $A = 73$ in Z_{511}.
(b) Find its $d_{\min}$.
(c) Give the set of all errors correctable by the code and the corresponding syndromes.

3.25. Let l denote the smallest positive power such that $2^l \equiv \pm 1 \bmod A$. Show that
(a) if 2 is primitive in $GF(A)$, then $l = (A - 1)/2$ and $2^l \equiv \pm 1 \bmod A$.
(b) if 2 is not primitive in $GF(A)$ but -2 is, then $l = (A - 1)/2$ and that $2^l \equiv \pm 1 \bmod A$.

3.26. Find the range m and modulus M of AN codes of distance 3 for
(a) $A = 29$.
(b) $A = 45$.

REFERENCES

[ALBE 56] A. A. Albert. *Fundamental Concepts of Higher Algebra*. Chicago: University of Chicago Press, 1956.

[BARR 66] J. T. Barrows, Jr. *A New Method for Constructing Multiple Error Correcting Linear Residue Codes*. Coordinated Sci. Lab. Report R-277. Champaign: University of Illinois Press, 1966.

[BERL 65] E. R. Berlekamp. "On Decoding Binary BCH Codes." *IEEE Transactions on Information Theory* IT-11 (October 1965): 577–79.

[BERL 68] E. R. Berlekamp. *Algebraic Coding Theory*. New York: McGraw-Hill, 1968.

[BERL 82] E. R. Berlekamp. "Bit-serial Reed-Solomon Encoders." *IEEE Transactions on Information Theory* IT-28 (November 1982): 869–74.

[BLAH 83] R. E. Blahut. *Theory and Practice of Error Control Codes*. Cambridge: Addison-Wesley, 1983.

[BOSE 60] R. C. Bose and D. K. Ray-Chaudhuri. "On a Class of Error Correcting Binary Group Codes." *Information and Control 3* (1960): 68–79.

[BROW 60] D. T. Brown. "Error Detecting and Correcting Binary Codes for Arithmetic Operations." *IEEE Transactions on Elec. Comput*. EC-9 (September 1960): 333–37.

[BURT 65] H. O. Burton and E. J. Weldon, Jr. "Cyclic Product Codes." *IEEE Transactions on Information Theory* IT-11 (July 1965): 433–39.

[BURT 71a] H. O. Burton. "Some Asymptotically Optimal Burst-Correcting Codes and Their Relation to Single-Error-Correcting Reed-Solomon Codes." *IEEE Transactions on Information Theory* IT-17 (January 1971): 92–95.

[BURT 71b] H. O. Burton. "Inversionless Decoding of Binary BCH Codes." *IEEE Transactions on Information Theory* IT-17 (January 1971): 464–66.

[CHIE 64] R. T. Chien. "Cyclic Decoding Procedures for BCH Codes." *IEEE Transactions on Information Theory* IT-10 (October 1964): 357–63.

[CHIE 71] R. T. Chien, S. J. Hong and F. P. Preparata. "Some Results in the Theory of Arithmetic Codes." *Information and Control* 19 (1971): 246–64.

[FIRE 59] P. Fire. *A Class of Multiple-Error-Correcting Binary Codes for Non-Independent Errors*. Sylvania Report no. RSL-E-2. Mountain View, Calif.: Sylvania Electronic Defense Laboratory, Reconnaissance, Systems Division, 1959.

[FORN 65] G. D. Forney, Jr. "On Decoding BCH Codes." *IEEE Transactions on Information Theory* IT-11 (October 1965): 549–57.

[GARN 66] H. L. Garner. "Error Codes for Arithmetic Operations." *IEEE Transactions on Elec. Comput.*, EC-15 (October 1966): 763–70.

[HOCQ 59] A. Hocquenghem. "Codes Correcteurs D'erreurs." *Chiffres* 2 (1959): 147–56.

[HSIA 70a] M. Y. Hsiao. "A Class of Optimal Minimum Odd-Weight-Column SEC-DED Codes." *IBM Journal of Research Development* (July 1970): 395–401.

[HSU 84] I. S. Hsu, I. S. Reed, T. K. Truong, K. Wang, C. S. Yeh and L. J. Deutsch. "The VLSI Implementation of a Reed-Solomon Encoder Using Berlekamp's Bit-Serial Multiplier Algorithm." *IEEE Transactions on Computers* C-33 (October 1984): 906–11.

[LIN 83] S. Lin and D. J. Costello, Jr. *Error Control Coding: Fundamentals and Applications*. Englewood Cliffs, N.J.: Prentice Hall, 1983.

[LIU 84] K. Y. Liu. "Architecture for VLSI Design of Reed-Solomon Decoders." *IEEE Transactions on Computers* C-33 (February 1984): 178–89.

[MACW 77] F. J. McWilliams and N. J. A. Sloane. *The Theory of Error-Correcting Codes*. New York: North-Holland Publishing, 1977.

[MAND 67] D. Mandelbaum. "Arithmetic Codes with Large Distance." *IEEE Transactions on Information Theory* IT-13 (April 1967): 237–657.

[MAND 77] D. M. Mandelbaum. "Decoding Beyond the Designed Distance for Certain Algebraic Codes." *Information and Control* 25(1977): 209–88.

[MASS 69] J. L. Massey. "Shift-Register Synthesis and BCH Decoding." *IEEE Transactions on Information Theory* IT-15 (January 1969): 122–27.

[MASS 71] J. L. Massey and O. N. Garcia. "Error Correcting Codes in Computer Arithmetic." In *Advances in Information System Sciences*, ed. J. L. Tow, vol. 4, 273–326. New York: Plenum Press, 1971.

[MEGG 60] J. E. Meggitt. "Error Correcting Codes for Correcting Bursts of Errors." *IBM Journal of Research and Development* 4 (1960): 329–34.

[PETE 58] W. W. Peterson. "On Checking Adder." *IBM Journal of Research and Development* 2(April 1958): 166–68.

[PETE 72] W. W. Peterson and E. J. Weldon, Jr. *Error Correcting Codes*, 2d. ed. Cambridge: MIT Press, 1972.

[RAO 70] T. R. N. Rao. "Biresidue Error-Correcting Codes for Computer Arithmetic." *IEEE Transactions on Computers* C-19 (May 1970): 398–402.

[RAO 71] T. R. N. Rao and O. N. Garcia. "Cyclic and Multiresidue Codes for Arithmetic Operations." *IEEE Transactions on Information Theory* IT-17 (January 1971): 85–91.

[RAO 74] T. R. N. Rao. *Error Coding for Arithmetic Processors*. New York: Academic Press, 1974.

[RAO 81] T. R. N. Rao, L. M. L. Delcambre and A. Iskender. "Cyclic Codes and Finite Field Arithmetic Proc." *First Conference Foundation of Software Technology and Theoretical Computer Science, Tata Institute of Fundamental Research, Bombay, India* (1981).

[REED 60] I. S. Reed and G. Solomon. "Polynomial Codes over Certain Finite Fields." *Journal Soc. Ind. Appl. Math.* 8 (June 1960): 300–304.

[RIEG 60] S. H. Rieger. "Codes for the Correction of 'Clustered' Errors." *IRE Transactions on Information Theory* IT-6 (March 1960): 16–21.

[SHAO 85] H. M. Shao, T. K. Truong, L. J. Duetsch, J. H. Yuen and I. S. Reed. "A VLSI Design of a Pipelined R-S Decoder." *IEEE Transactions on Computers* C-34 (May 1985): 393–403.

[WANG 85] C. C. Wang, T. K. Truong, H. M. Shao, L. J. Deutsch, J. K. Omura and I. S. Reed. "VLSI Architectures for Computing Multiplications and Inverse in $GF(2^m)$." *IEEE Transactions on Computers* C-34 (August 1985): 709–17.

[WELC 79] L. R. Welch and R. A. Scholtz. "Continued Fractions and Berlekamp's Algorithm." *IEEE Transactions on Information Theory* IT-25 (January 1979): 19–27.

4

Codes for High-Speed Memories I: Bit Error Correcting/Detecting Codes

Several types of error correcting codes have been applied successfully to memory systems. One can say that every memory designer has adopted some form of error detecting or correcting code in order to enhance reliability [RAO 68a, HSIA 69, TANG 69, FUJI 82, CHEN 84, BOSE 86b, FUJI 88a]. In Chapters 4 and 5, we discuss error correcting codes for high-speed memories (i.e., for control memories, cache memories, main memories, or sometimes for disk cache memories). These memories all employ Random Access Memory (RAM) semiconductor chips. Therefore, we may call these applications *codes for semiconductor memories*. Chapter 4 covers bit error correcting code applications, whereas Chapter 5 covers the byte error corrections.

One of the notable features of the codes for high-speed memories is that *parallel encoding and decoding* is required to maintain high rates of throughput. Therefore, encoding and decoding circuits are implemented by combinational logic instead of linear feedback shift register (LFSR) logic [SRIN 67, 71a, 71b, HSIA 69, FUJI 75].

In high-speed memories, single-bit error correcting and double-bit error detecting codes (SED–DED codes) are most commonly used. This is because many semiconductor RAM chips are organized for one bit of data output at a time, and therefore any failure in one chip manifests itself as one bit in error. Moreover, for the purpose of improving reliability and of correcting *soft errors* induced by *α particles*, some new techniques and some advanced error correcting codes may be required in large-capacity, high-speed memories [HSIA 70b, SRIN 71a, 71b, SZYG 71, 73, IMAI 77b, BOSS 80]. Following these considerations, this chapter deals with codes, such as modified Hamming SEC–DED codes, and double-bit error correcting codes (DEC codes). This chapter also deals with enhancement techniques based on using the error correction and detection capability of these codes in an efficient and adaptive manner (e.g., *erasure correction*, *addressing-skewing*, *rotational code design*, and so on).

4.1 MODIFIED HAMMING SEC – DED CODES

A Hamming distance-4 code [HAMM 50] can correct single-bit errors and also detect double-bit errors (SEC–DED). This code can be formed by extending a distance-3 Hamming code with an overall parity check, that is, a check on all the symbols in the code (see Section 3.1).

This section shows that this Hamming SEC–DED code can be modified and optimized from the practical point of view. The resulting code is called a *modified Hamming SEC–DED code*. This code can also be used to solve multiple soft error problems.

Another important application of this code is in recovery from multiple errors. This is done with an *automatic reconfiguration* technique that uses the concept of address skewing to disperse such multiple errors into correctable errors. These applications are discussed in the following sections.

4.1.1 Hsiao Code

The minimum distance of an SEC–DED code is at least 4. Since an n-tuple of weight 3 or less is not a codeword, any set of three columns of the **H** matrix should be linearly independent. Note that *the sum of two odd-weight r-tuples is an even-weight r-tuple* (*i.e.*, *odd* + *odd* = *even*, *even* + *odd* = *odd*, *even* + *even* = *even*). Because of this property, an SEC–DED code with r check bits can be constructed with its **H** matrix consisting of distinct nonzero r-tuples of column vectors having odd weight [HSIA 70a]. This code is different from the original Hamming SEC–DED code whose **H** matrix has an all 1-row vector in addition to the SEC code **H** matrix. Therefore, this code is called a modified Hamming code or, more specifically, an *odd-weight-column SEC–DED code*, because every **H** matrix column vector is odd weight.

This code has the minimum number of 1's in the **H** matrix, which makes the hardware and the speed of the encoding/decoding circuit optimal. That is, it satisfies the condition of the *minimum-equal-weight code* (see Section 4.4.1), and hence this code is called optimal from the practical point of view.

Following these considerations, the **H** matrix of this code is constructed as follows:

1. All $\binom{r}{1}$ weight-1 columns are used for the r check-bit positions.

2. Next, if $\binom{r}{3} \geq k$, where k is information-bit length, select k weight-3 columns out of all possible $\binom{r}{3}$ combinations. If $\binom{r}{3} < k$, all $\binom{r}{3}$ columns should

TABLE 4.1 SAMPLE EXAMPLES ON THE CODE PARAMETER RELATIONS

n	k	r	Structure of **H***: $\binom{r}{1}$	$\binom{r}{3}$	$\binom{r}{5}$	Total Number of 1's in **H**	Average Number of 1's in **H** for Rows	I_S
8	4	4	$\binom{4}{1}$ +	$\binom{4}{3}$		16	4	$\lceil \log_2 4 \rceil^{\dagger} = 2$
22	16	6	$\binom{6}{1}$ +	$16/\binom{6}{3}$		54	9	$\lceil \log_2 9 \rceil = 4$
30	24	6	$\binom{6}{1}$ +	$\binom{6}{3}$	+ $4/\binom{6}{5}$	86	14.3	$\lceil \log_2 15 \rceil = 4$
39	32	7	$\binom{7}{1}$ +	$32/\binom{7}{3}$		103	14.7	$\lceil \log_2 15 \rceil = 4$
55	48	7	$\binom{7}{1}$ +	$\binom{7}{3}$	+ $13/\binom{7}{5}$	177	25.3	$\lceil \log_2 26 \rceil = 5$
72	64	8	$\binom{8}{1}$ +	$\binom{8}{3}$	+ $8/\binom{8}{5}$	216	27	$\lceil \log_2 27 \rceil = 5$
137	128	9	$\binom{9}{1}$ +	$\binom{9}{3}$	+ $44/\binom{9}{5}$	481	53.4	$\lceil \log_2 54 \rceil = 6$

*The notation $j/\binom{r}{i}$ means that j out of all possible $\binom{r}{i}$ combinations is used.

$^{\dagger}\lceil x \rceil$ is the smallest integer greater than or equal to x, called the ceiling of x. $\lfloor x \rfloor$ is the largest integer less than or equal to x, called the floor of x.

be selected. The leftover columns are then first selected from among all $\binom{r}{5}$ weight-5 columns, and so on. The process is continued until all k columns (corresponding to information positions) have been specified.

If the code length $n = k + r$ is exactly equal to

$$\sum_{\substack{i=1 \\ i=odd}}^{i \le r} \binom{r}{i} = 2^{r-1} \tag{4.1}$$

then each row of the **H** matrix will have the following number of 1's.

$$\frac{1}{r} \sum_{\substack{i=1 \\ i=odd}}^{i \le r} i \cdot \binom{r}{i} \tag{4.2}$$

If n does not exactly satisfy Equation (4.1), then a proper selection of the $\binom{r}{i}$ cases should make the number of 1's in each row close to the average number, as shown in Table 4.1. In this table I_S represents the number of *gate levels* required to generate syndrome S, assuming 2-input modulo-2 adders (exclusive-or gates) only are used. Here, gate level is defined as the time required for the signal to pass through one gate.

A simple example of the odd-weight-column SEC–DED code and its decoding circuit is illustrated in Example 4-1.

Example 4-1

Memory readout word: $D = [d_0, d_1, d_2, d_3, c_0, c_1, c_2, c_3]$.

$$\begin{array}{cccc|cccc} \multicolumn{4}{c}{\textit{Information bits}} & \multicolumn{4}{c}{\textit{Check bits}} \\ d_0 & d_1 & d_2 & d_3 & c_0 & c_1 & c_2 & c_3 \end{array}$$

$$\mathbf{H} = \left[\begin{array}{cccc|cccc} 1 & 1 & 1 & 0 & 1 & 0 & 0 & 0 \\ 1 & 1 & 0 & 1 & 0 & 1 & 0 & 0 \\ 1 & 0 & 1 & 1 & 0 & 0 & 1 & 0 \\ 0 & 1 & 1 & 1 & 0 & 0 & 0 & 1 \end{array}\right]$$

Syndrome: $S = D \cdot \mathbf{H}^T = [s_0, s_1, s_2, s_3]$

$$\begin{aligned} s_0 &= d_0 \oplus d_1 \oplus d_2 \oplus c_0 \\ s_1 &= d_0 \oplus d_1 \oplus d_3 \oplus c_1 \qquad \oplus: \textit{modulo}-2 \textit{ addition} \\ s_2 &= d_0 \oplus d_2 \oplus d_3 \oplus c_2 \\ s_4 &= d_1 \oplus d_2 \oplus d_3 \oplus c_3 \end{aligned}$$

Parallel decoding circuit (Fig. 4.1):

An algorithm for correcting single errors and detecting multiple errors by using the syndrome $S = (s_0, s_1, \ldots, s_{r-1})$ is as follows:

1. Test whether S is **0**. If S is **0**, the word is assumed to be error free.
2. If $S \neq \mathbf{0}$, try to find a perfect match between S and a column of the **H** matrix. The match can be implemented in r-input AND gates.
3. If S is the same as the ith column of **H** from step 2, the ith bit of the word is in error and hence inverted.
4. If $S \neq \mathbf{0}$ and overall parity (i.e., the EX-OR sum) of all syndrome bits is equal to zero, a double error (or even number of errors) is detected. This condition is expressed in logical form as

$$\left(\bigcup_{i=0}^{r-1} s_i\right) \cdot \left(\overline{\sum_{i=0}^{r-1}{}^{\oplus} s_i}\right) = 1 \tag{4.3}$$

$\bigcup$: *OR operation*, $\Sigma^{\oplus}$: *mod 2 sum*, $\bar{x}$: *complement value of x*

5. If a nonzero S is equal to none of the columns of **H**, and the overall parity of all syndrome bits is equal to 1, then three or more odd number of errors are detected.

An example of the **H** matrix for the (72, 64) code is shown on p. 142 (4.4).*

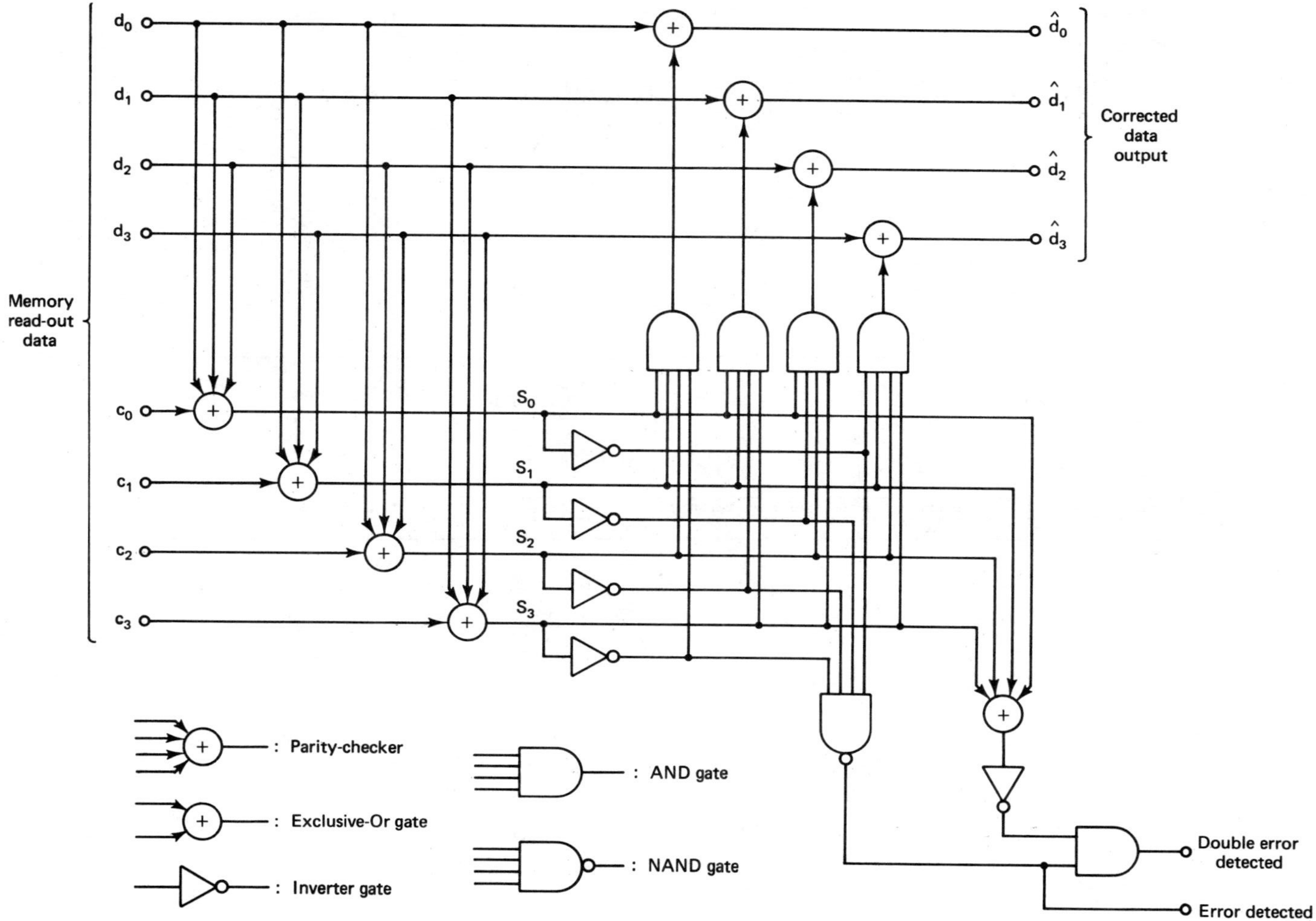

Figure 4.1 Parallel decoding circuit.

Byte	1								2								3								4							
Bit	0	1	2	3	4	5	6	7	8	9	10	11	12	13	14	15	16	17	18	19	20	21	22	23	24	25	26	27	28	29	30	31
S_0	1	1	1	1	1	1	1	1			1			1	1			1			1			1	1			1				
S_1	1	1	1						1	1	1	1	1	1	1	1			1			1	1			1			1			1
S_2				1	1	1			1	1	1						1	1	1	1	1	1	1	1			1			1	1	
S_3				1			1	1				1	1	1			1	1	1						1	1	1	1	1	1	1	1
S_4				1								1			1	1				1	1	1			1	1	1					
S_5	1			1								1								1			1	1				1	1	1		
S_6		1			1			1	1			1								1								1			1	1
S_7			1			1	1			1			1			1	1			1								1				

Byte	5								6								7								8								Check							
Bit	32	33	34	35	36	37	38	39	40	41	42	43	44	45	46	47	48	49	50	51	52	53	54	55	56	57	58	59	60	61	62	63	C_0	C_1	C_2	C_3	C_4	C_5	C_6	C_7
S_0				1								1			1	1				1	1	1			1	1	1						1							
S_1	1			1								1								1			1	1				1	1	1				1						
S_2		1			1			1	1			1								1								1			1	1			1					
S_3			1			1	1			1			1			1	1			1								1								1				
S_4	1	1	1	1	1	1	1	1			1			1	1			1			1			1	1			1									1			
S_5	1	1	1						1	1	1	1	1	1	1	1			1			1	1			1			1			1						1		
S_6				1	1	1			1	1	1						1	1	1	1	1	1	1	1			1			1	1								1	
S_7				1			1	1				1	1	1			1	1	1						1	1	1	1	1	1	1	1								1

(4.4)

TABLE 4.2 PROBABILITY OF ERROR DETECTION FOR (72, 64) CODES

Code Type	Probability of Triple-Error Detection (%); P_3	Probability of Quadruple-Error Detection (%); P_4
Odd-weight-column code shown in (4.4)	43.72	99.19
Hamming distance-4 code (non-odd-weight-column code)	24.0 ~ 43.5	98.90 ~ 99.18

Under the code condition that is not minimum weight, a (72, 64) SEC–DED code with $P_3 = 45.17\%$, and $P_4 = 99.21\%$ has been obtained [AZUM 75].

From the practical point of view, it is important for the SEC–DED code to minimize the probability of *miscorrection* when triple or more errors occur. A *miscorrection* here refers to an erroneous decoding that results in an actual increase in the number of errors in the decoded word. Now consider the (72, 64) codes further. Since these codes are *shortened codes* and are used for single-error correction and double-error detection, there are several cases in which triple errors generate syndrome patterns outside the columns of the code's **H** matrix. In these cases, the triple errors will be correctly detected. If the syndrome pattern coincides with some column of **H**, then the decoder mistakes it for a single error and applies a miscorrection. Table 4.2 shows the probability of detected triple errors and quadruple errors of the (72, 64) SEC–DED codes. From this table, we see that the code shown in (4.4) gives better protection.

In general, the undetectable error probabilities of triple errors and quadruple errors (P_{UD_3} and P_{UD_4}, respectively) for SEC–DED codes depend on the number of codewords with minimum weight 4, A_4, as follows.

$$P_{UD_3} = 4 \cdot A_4 \Big/ \binom{n}{3}, \quad P_{UD_4} = A_4 \Big/ \binom{n}{4}$$

A method of constructing codes with a reduced number of codewords of weight 4 is proposed in [MATS 87].

From these analyses, we find odd-weight-column SEC–DED codes to have practical advantages and also a lower probability of erroneous decoding. These codes are therefore widely implemented in such computer systems as IBM 370/168, 303X, 308X, 4300 series, Cray 1, Tandem, and so on [CHEN 84]. We can get parallel error detection and correction circuit ICs based on the Hsiao codes, e.g., 48 pin, 16-bit ICs, 65 ns for error correction, expandable to 64-bit [ADVA 81], 52 pin, 32-bit ICs using advanced low power Schottky TTL technologies [TEXA 83], and 68 pin, 16-bit ICs, 67 ns for error correction, expandable to 80-bit, using HMOS technologies [INTE 82].

4.1.2 Erasure Correction for Soft Error Problems

High-density memory chips create new reliability problems: one good example is the α-particle problem in high-density RAM (Random Access Memory) chips

[NOOR 80, SAIH 82, SAVA 86]. These *soft errors* may line up with existing hard errors, giving rise to multiple errors that are not correctable with SEC–DED codes.

In order to solve these problems, extended reliability design techniques have been proposed for large-capacity memory systems that already have SEC–DED facilities [KANE 84b, AICH 84]. Some designs use the *read–retry technique*, in which the soft errors disappear during the repeated read cycles, the *sparing technique*, which replaces a defective component with a spare without requiring manual intervention, and the *mask error correction technique*, which requires some additional operations for detection and correction of hard errors. The mask error correction technique is illustrated in the following example.

Example 4-2

The following sequence of operations allows for mask error correction of hard-plus-soft errors using the SEC–DED code:

1 0 0 1 1 1 0 1 1	Correct data
h α	Faults (h: hard error position, α: soft error position)
↓ ↓	
1 0 ① 1 ⓪ 1 0 1 1	Read from storage: Uncorrectable error (○)
0 1 0 0 1 0 1 0 0	Complement, written
0 1 1 0 1 0 1 0 0	Read from storage
1 0 0 1 [0] 1 0 1 1	Recomplement: Correctable error (□)
1 0 0 1 1 1 0 1 1	Correct data rewritten
1 0 [1] 1 1 1 0 1 1	Read on refetch: Correctable error (□)

From the foregoing Read-Invert-Write-Read-Invert procedure, we can correct double errors using only the SEC–DED code.

Another effective method for correcting multiple errors is to apply an error location technique to distance-4 codes (i.e., *erasure correction technique*). Thereby we can correct soft errors as well as hard errors [BOSS 80, DEZA 82]. In this subsection we will concentrate on erasure correction. Error location capability enables a distance-4 code (SEC–DED code) to correct up to three errors. Here, we have a method for correcting one hard and one soft error [BOSS 80]. In the algorithm used here, the hard error is dynamically located during the correction process, and an algorithmic modification of the original syndrome allows correction of the soft error. The corrected information is then rewritten into memory. Since the soft error induced by the α particle is transient, subsequent read operations are expected to have only the single solid error to correct. In this way, no extra auxiliary storage will be required.

Let h be the hard-error position and α be the soft-error bit position; then the resultant syndrome S_u is the exclusive-or of the syndromes due to erroneous bits α and h (i.e., $S_u = S_\alpha \oplus S_h$).

The decoding algorithm is as follows.

1. *Detect the uncorrectable error, represented by S_u, a double error syndrome. Save the codeword with errors as well as the syndrome.*
2. *Using the exerciser diagnostic patterns, locate position h of the solid error. Knowing the index h, generate S_h.*
3. *Determine $S_\alpha = S_u \oplus S_h$.*
4. *Decode S_α to correct bit α in the data. Invert bit h (determined in step 2) to correct the hard error.*

This algorithm can be implemented by hardware, as shown in Fig. 4.2. This is an example for use of the (72, 64) SEC–DED code. In step 2 of the foregoing algorithm, three diagnostic test patterns at most are required to locate the hard error

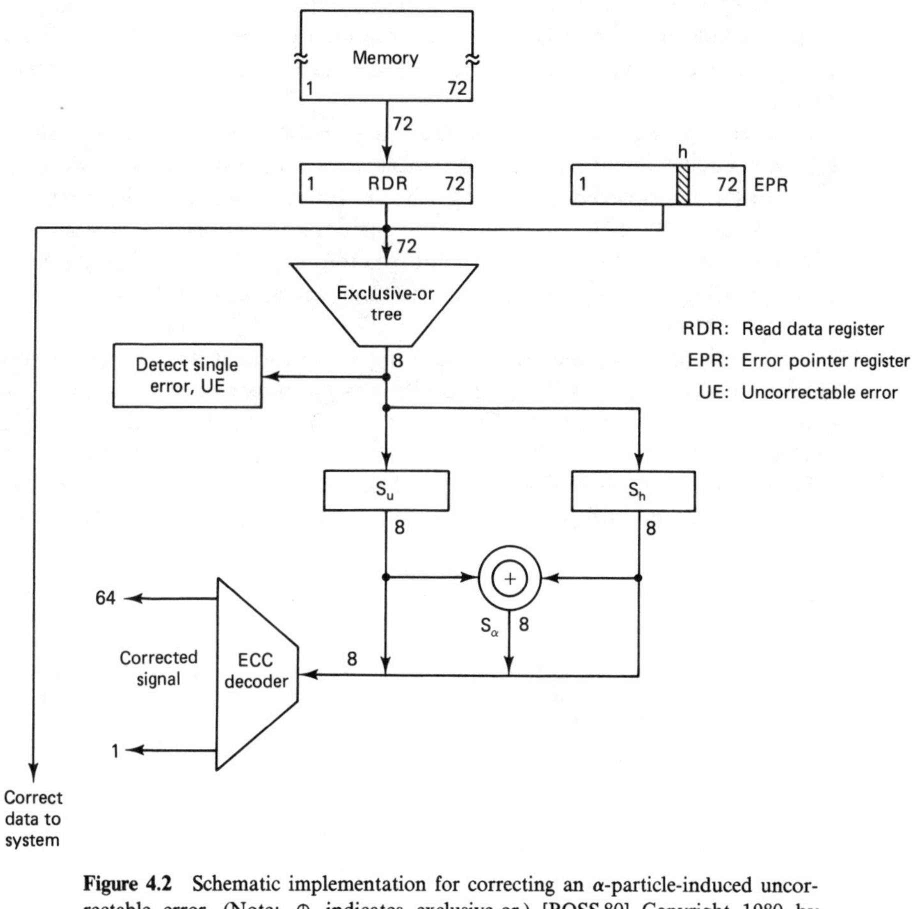

Figure 4.2 Schematic implementation for correcting an α-particle-induced uncorrectable error. (Note: $\oplus$ indicates exclusive-or.) [BOSS 80] Copyright 1980 by International Business Machines Corporation; reprinted with permission.

position. However, if an *even-weight-row SEC–DED code* is used, only two patterns are required, because of the fact that a bit-wise complement of the codeword is also a codeword (see Section 4.4.3).

The reliability improvement achieved by applying the above technique is analyzed as follows. Consider a 9.2-megabyte capacity memory module consisting of 72 cards, one bit per card, for a (72, 64) SEC–DED codeword organization. Assume using 16K-bit chips, each of which has an average of 0.005% hard failure rate per 1,000 power-on hours and 1% soft failure rate per 1,000 hours; the improvement in the uncorrectable error rate is 100 times that obtained using the code with only single-error correction capability. For complete details, see [BOSS 80].

In general, how we get the *error pointers* is an important problem for this technique. In the foregoing method, the pointers are obtained by applying the test patterns to the memories. Another method is to generate them through the Read-Invert-Write-Read-Invert procedure (see Example 4-2). However, these error pointers are good only for hard errors.

Error pointers may also be obtained from the parity checking output of each chip in which parity checking facilities are incorporated [DEZA 82, RENN 86]. By using these error pointers, double or triple errors (including soft errors) can be corrected.

Memory cell arrays are constructed in a two-dimensional way, as shown in Fig. 4.3. Each cell can be accessed by fixing both row and column addresses.

In the multiplexed addressing scheme, row address is applied first at the RAS (Row Address Strobe) timing point and then column address is applied at the CAS (Column Address Strobe) timing point. Therefore, at the RAS timing point, all cells corresponding to the row address are first accessed and then their read/write operations started.

In this method, the parity checking is performed at a specified row of the memory cell arrays, and then the resultant is given as one of the chip outputs. This helps to locate the position of the error chip without the need for the diagnostic patterns in the former method. An important benefit is that this also points out the soft error chip position. Considering all 0-error or all 1-error in a row, two parity bits (i.e., even and odd parity bits) are prepared in every row in RAM chips, shown

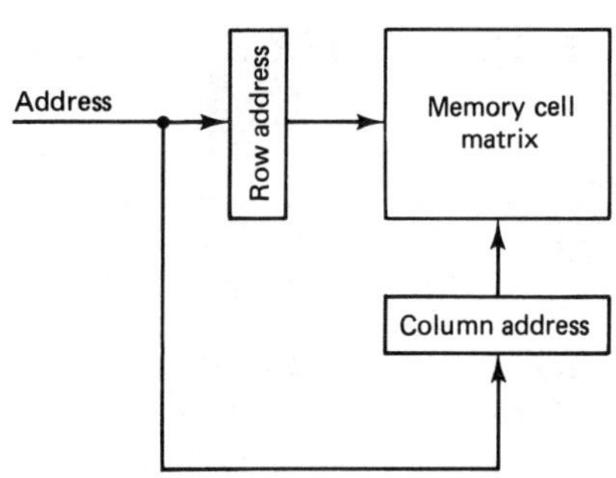

Figure 4.3 Memory cell array.

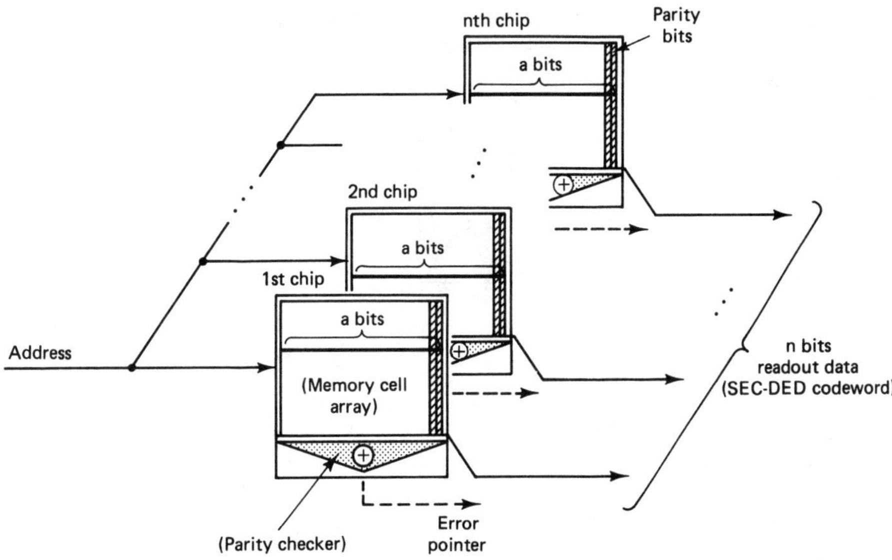

Figure 4.4 Memory chips having parity-checking facilities.

as follows.

$$\begin{array}{ll} \underbrace{000\ldots0}_{\text{data}} & \underbrace{01}_{\text{parity}} \rightarrow \text{normal} \\ 000\ldots0 & 00 \rightarrow \text{errors} \end{array}$$

For the 64K-bit RAM chip example, 512 bits are redundant, which means only a 0.8% redundancy ratio. Let the SEC–DED code have code length n, and let each memory chip have one data output. Let each row in the cell array have a bits. Then, a bits of a particular row in all n chips are accessed at the RAS timing point simultaneously, and then their parities are checked. The parity failure of a chip is indicated by the error pointer. Once we have detected these failures, error indication will be preserved. Fig. 4.4 shows this scheme of the memory chips having parity-checking facilities. This $(a \times n)$ memory block is regarded as one subblock and is shown in Fig. 4.5.

Here, we have to refer to the write operation. In this operation, we have to pay attention to the one write data bit in the particular row of this chip. The parity bit should be changed only when the new write data bit is different from that already written. Therefore, a new parity bit can be determined in the following operation.

$$\text{new parity bit} = \text{old written data bit} \oplus \text{new write data bit} \oplus \text{old parity bit}$$

We need one read and compare operation before a new data bit is written.

Let's consider the failure cases in this memory subblock. Fig. 4.6(a), (b), and (c) show the subblocks, each of which has just two chip failure indicators. Part (c) shows the subblock that has an all one-row failure and a one-bit failure.

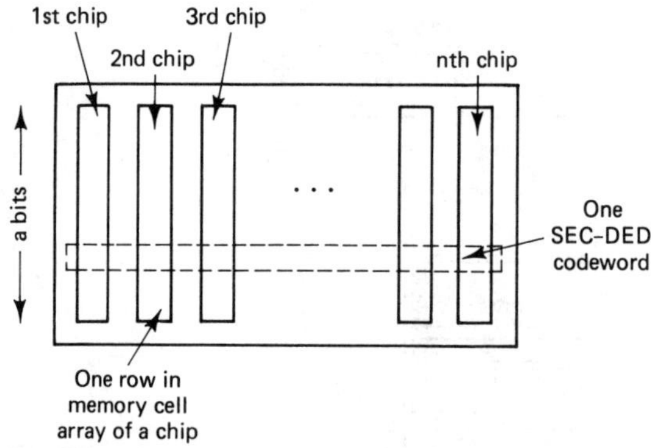

Figure 4.5 Structure of a subblock [DEZA 82]. © 1982 IECE Japan.

In Fig. 4.6, P shows the parity-error indicator whose 1 shows the position of the failed chip, while SE shows the single-bit error and DE the double-bit error in a codeword. In these cases, the data readout contains either no error, single error, or double error. Therefore, the decoding algorithm is as follows:

If syndrome = 0, *then the word is regarded as error free*;
If single error is detected, *then*
  do;
    Investigate the chips that give parity error.
    If the number of parity errors ≤ 2, *then perform single error correction*; *else only error detection.*
  end;
If double error is detected, *then*
  do;
    Investigate the chips that give parity error.
    If the number of parity error = 2, *then perform corresponding two bits inversion*; *else only error detection.*
  end;
If triple error is detected, *then regard as errors detected.*

This algorithm can be extended to triple-error correction. For example, in Fig. 4.6(d), there are three failed chips, denoted ith, jth, and kth chips. In this case, double errors (e.g., ith and jth errors) can be corrected as follows:

Invert ith, *jth*, *and kth bits.*
Then, *ith and jth bits are now corrected*,
  but the previously correct kth bit now becomes an error.
Next, *SEC–DED code can be used to correct this single error bit*
  and obtain error-free data.

Fig. 4.6(e) also shows an example of triple errors in a word. For a (72, 64) SEC–DED code, the probability of a miscorrection due to triple errors is more than 50% (see Table 4.2). The decoding algorithm which uses the parity checking result in

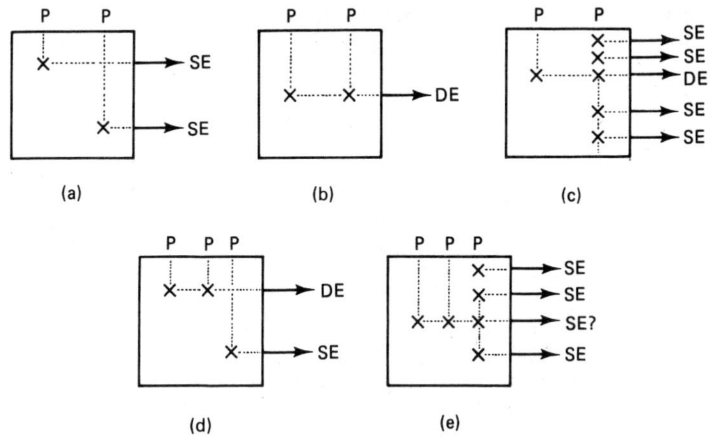

Figure 4.6 Examples of failures in a subblock [DEZA 82]. © 1982 IECE Japan.

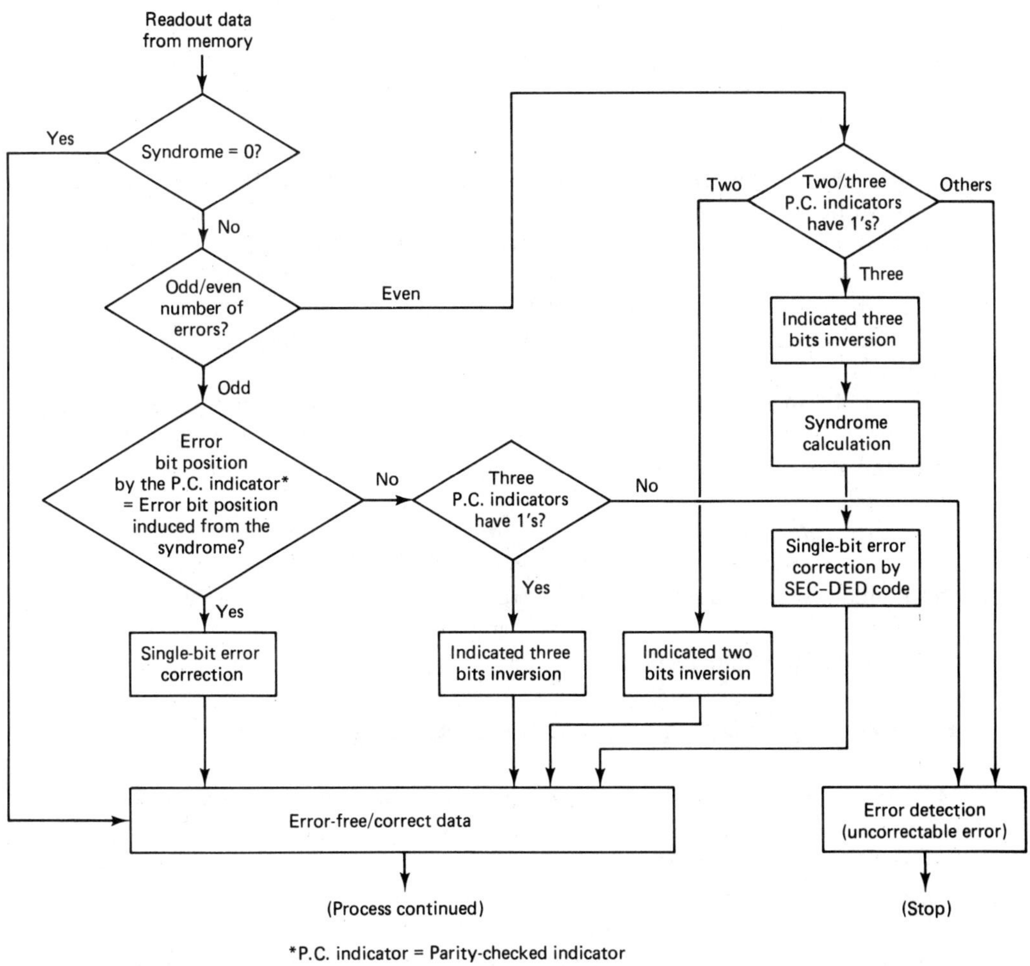

Figure 4.7 Decoding algorithm.

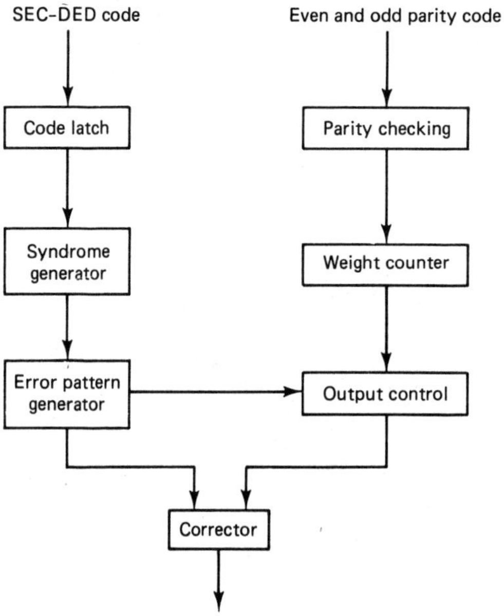

Figure 4.8 Block diagram of the decoder [DEZA 82]. © 1982 IECE Japan.

a chip as well as the syndrome by the SEC–DED code, however, can correct triple errors without miscorrection. This is done only by inverting these three bits indicated by the parity-error indicators. This is because single errors can be corrected only when parity error indication P coincides with the error position pointed by the syndrome of the SEC–DED code.

Fig. 4.7 shows the decoding algorithm for correcting these double and triple errors.

Fig. 4.8 shows the block diagram of the decoder. High-speed parallel decoding can be performed because parity checking is started at the RAS timing point in the chip, and therefore this parity-checked output and the syndrome can be processed in parallel.

There are other schemes for the correction of multiple erasures [KAMB 76, KUZN 78, CHEN 85]. These schemes involve the design of codes with additional check bits, which are used to make the erasures in decoding. For example, a (76, 64) code can be designed to correct double erasures and single random errors, and to detect double random errors [KUZN 78].

4.1.3 Multiple-Error Recovery by Address Skewing

Most large- and medium-sized semiconductor memories are byte-per-card organizations. In this chapter, we concern ourselves with bit-error correction and assume that at most one bit per chip or card is retrieved and assembled into words. The various bit positions have separate address circuitry on the array cards. This organization, therefore, provides us an effective *address skewing scheme* to allow an appropriate realignment of errors and enable correction of errors that are otherwise uncorrectable [HSIA 75, BOSS 84].

Hard-wired address skewing. Let us assume a bit-per-card organization with each card containing 16 chips. A 4-bit address will be used to select the chip in each card. These four address bits are sent in parallel to each of the cards from the memory address register (MAR). If address 0101 is sent to each card, then chip 5 on each card gets selected. Fig. 4.9 illustrates a hard-wired address skewing technique. While the 4-bit address applied to this system is $ABCD$, the actual addresses to the individual cards are $ABCD$, $ABC\overline{D}$, $AB\overline{C}D$, $AB\overline{C}\,\overline{D}$, and so on.

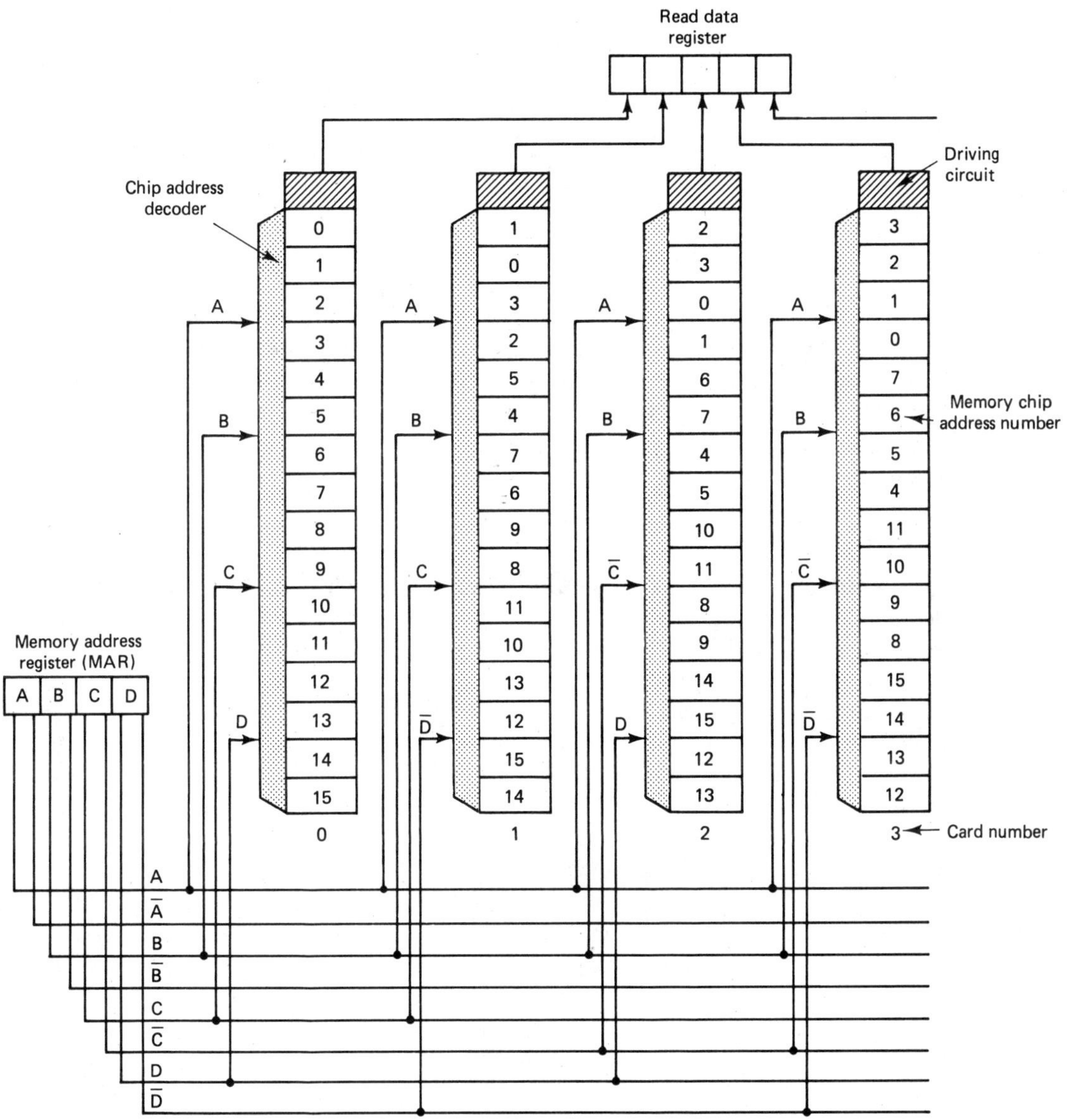

Figure 4.9 Skewed address pattern using hard-wired inversions [BOSS 84]. Copyright 1984 by International Business Machines Corporation; reprinted with permission.

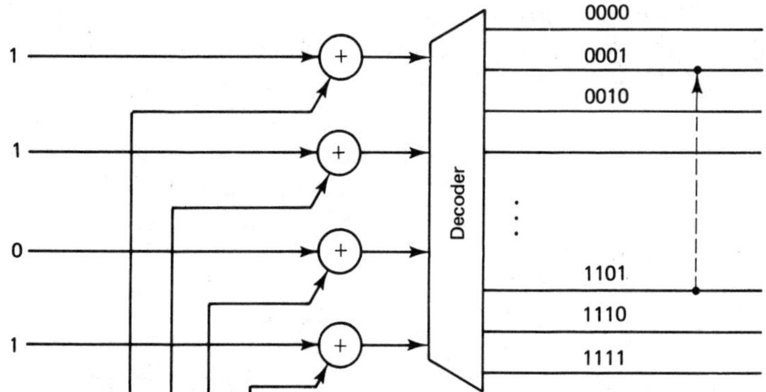

$$\begin{pmatrix}1\\1\\0\\1\end{pmatrix} \oplus \begin{pmatrix}1\\1\\0\\0\end{pmatrix} \rightarrow \begin{pmatrix}0\\0\\0\\1\end{pmatrix}$$

Figure 4.10 Writable EX-OR address skewing.

With such an arrangement, a skewed pattern of selected chips occurs, as shown in Fig. 4.9. For example, for MAR address 0000, card 0 selects chip 0000, card 1 selects chip 0001, card 2 selects chip 0010, and so on. Now suppose that chip 0000 on card 0 and chip 0001 on card 1 are bad, causing an uncorrectable error. All that needs to be done to avoid this uncorrectable error is to swap card 0 and, for example, card 2. Now the bad chips will never be selected with the same MAR address.

Address skewing using writable exclusive-or circuits. Fig. 4.10 shows a method of fault realignment for the purpose of avoiding uncorrectable errors using exclusive-or (EX-OR) circuits and storage elements in conjunction with address lines.

For a card-organized memory, as in the previous discussion, each of the four address lines feeds an EX-OR circuit whose other input is the content of a storage element, or latch. Depending on the binary value stored in each latch, each address bit is either inverted or not before it goes to the address decoder. The latches are writable. The effect in this case is to provide 2^4 possible permutations of the chip addresses on each card of the memory. The set of latches on each card is called a *control register* (*CR*), and the contents of the control registers for the entire memory is called the *permutation vector*. Fig. 4.11 illustrates this scheme. Shown in this example are the actual chips addressed in response to the system address 0011 when the various cards have CR values as shown.

An immediate problem to be solved is the following. Given a set of faults in the memory, some of which may line up within a given codeword, how can a permutation vector be found that will enable the memory to function without any uncorrectable errors? An algorithmic approach takes advantage of the algebraic property of the EX-OR function to solve for a permutation vector. The algorithm

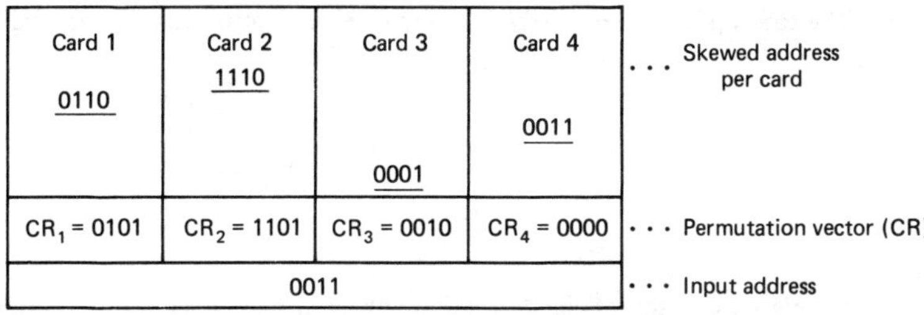

Figure 4.11 Four card memory skewing addressed chips.

requires as its input the fault map, which gives the fault status of every chip on every array card [BOSS 84].

Latin square skewing. A considerable problem in practical system implementations of address permutations is how to efficiently obtain the diagnostic fault map required to execute algorithms. In order to avoid having to diagnose the memory, a scheme for determining permutation vectors with fairly powerful error dispersion capability is proposed by using the theory of orthogonal Latin squares [HSIA 75].

Definition 4-1. A *Latin square of order m* is an $(m \times m)$ square array of digits $0, 1, \ldots, m-1$, with each row and column a permutation of the digits $0, 1, \ldots, m-1$. Two Latin squares are *orthogonal* if, when one Latin square is superimposed on the other, every ordered pair of elements appears only once.

We illustrate by means of an example how an orthogonal Latin square structure can be built into a memory organization.

Example 4-3*

The simplest example to consider is a memory having four 1-bit-organized memory cards, each card having four address positions. Let us consider the three (4×4) Latin squares T_1, T_2, and T_3 as follows.

address position ↑ (rows); card position → (columns)

$$T_1 = \begin{array}{cccc} 0 & 1 & 2 & 3 \\ 1 & 0 & 3 & 2 \\ 2 & 3 & 0 & 1 \\ 3 & 2 & 1 & 0 \end{array} \qquad T_2 = \begin{array}{cccc} 0 & 2 & 3 & 1 \\ 1 & 3 & 2 & 0 \\ 2 & 0 & 1 & 3 \\ 3 & 1 & 0 & 2 \end{array} \qquad T_3 = \begin{array}{cccc} 0 & 3 & 1 & 2 \\ 1 & 2 & 0 & 3 \\ 2 & 1 & 3 & 0 \\ 3 & 0 & 2 & 1 \end{array}$$

*[HSIA 75]. Copyright 1975 by International Business Machines Corporation; reprinted with permission.

The result of a *superimposition* of the first two Latin squares, for example, is as follows.

$$\begin{bmatrix} 0,0 & 1,2 & 2,3 & 3,1 \\ 1,1 & 0,3 & 3,2 & 2,0 \\ 2,2 & 3,0 & 0,1 & 1,3 \\ 3,3 & 2,1 & 1,0 & 0,2 \end{bmatrix}$$

In this array, each of the 4^2 possible ordered pairs occurs exactly once. This holds for all other examples as well, and hence these Latin squares are orthogonal.

The vertical coordinate is used as the address position and the horizontal position is used as the card position. Inside each card, the word address number is not coded in the conventional binary form, but rather in the form of a Galois field element, as shown below.

Conventional Form	Galois Field Element Representation
0 = 00	$0 = \phi = 00$
1 = 01	$1 = \alpha^0 = 10$
2 = 10	$2 = \alpha^1 = 01$
3 = 11	$3 = \alpha^2 = 11$

α: The root of a polynomial $x^2 + x + 1$.

This new representation requires no change on the input address line. The three copies of the orthogonal Latin square actually are orthogonal to the following original address square T_0, that is,

$$\begin{matrix} 0 & 0 & 0 & 0 \\ 1 & 1 & 1 & 1 \\ 2 & 2 & 2 & 2 \\ 3 & 3 & 3 & 3 \end{matrix}$$

T_0

Here, T_0 (which obviously is not a Latin square) represents the original address distribution condition. T_1, T_2, and T_3 describe possible address skewing patterns after a double error has occurred. The binary representation of the address in terms of Galois field elements enables the generation of T_1, T_2, and T_3 by a linear feedback shift register, as shown in Fig. 4.12.

This can be seen from the simple four-card memory with four chips per card of Fig. 4.13, where the $2^2 - 1 = 3$ orthogonal Latin square skewed address patterns are shown along with the original unskewed address pattern.

In operation, the initial state of each register is set to $00\ldots0$. When the first double error occurs, each card is set to a different initial state, corresponding to 1, x, $x^2, \ldots, x^k \bmod g(x)$, the generator polynomial for the linear feedback shift register. Following each occurrence of a double error, all registers are simultaneously given by a single shift pulse. Let's examine this in more detail. The generation of T_0, T_1, T_2, and T_3 follows directly from the state transition condition Q_0, Q_1, Q_2, Q_3 of each card. Notice that all memory cards are of the same structure.

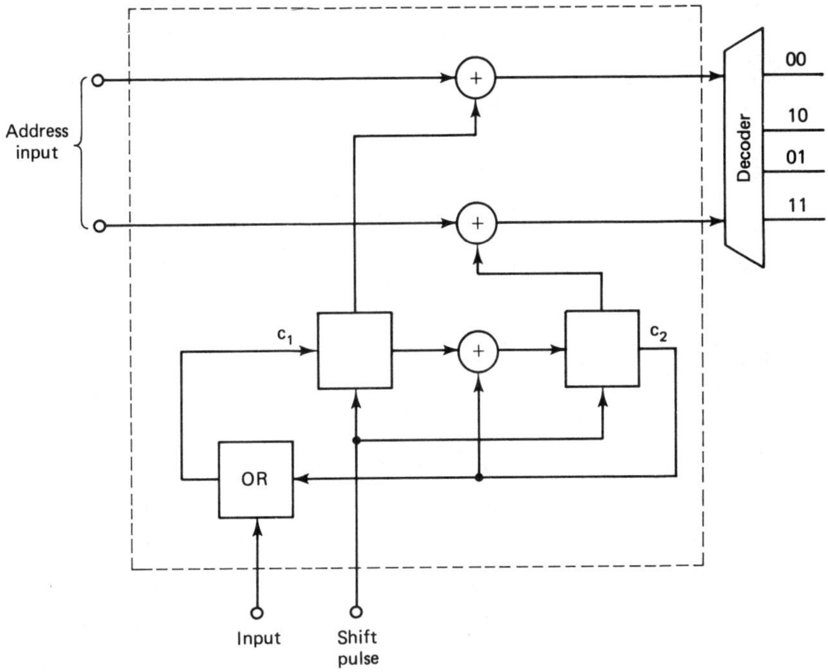

Figure 4.12 Control register (linear feedback shift register) with $g(x) = x^2 + x + 1$ feedback connection [BOSS 84]. Copyright 1984 by International Business Machines Corporation; reprinted with permission.

The different address skew pattern T_1, T_2, and T_3 can be achieved by setting the different Q_1 on cards 2, 3, and 4 only once. For example, if the $Q_1 = 10$ is gated into the two shift-register cells, and it then becomes its initial state on card 2, it will be added (as modulo-2 operation) to any incoming address. As shown in Fig. 4.13, the address $00 + 10 = 10$ becomes address $1 = 10$ at time T_1 on card 2; similarly for other addresses. Q_2 and Q_3 can be obtained by merely shifting the contents of the shift register on cards 2, 3, and 4. Fig. 4.14 shows an example of how to reconfigure the bit-sliced SEC–DED code memory shown in Fig. 4.13.

In general, a large-size orthogonal Latin square set can correct many errors and has a high probability of success in a few tries. For a memory of 2^s addresses, there exists $(2^s - 1)$ distinct orthogonal Latin squares, which is more than necessary for practical applications. The generation of these $(2^s - 1)$ orthogonal Latin squares can always be achieved by an s-stage linear feedback shift register characterized by a primitive polynomial of degree s. If a memory has 2^s words, each having n bits where $2^s \geq n$, then any multiple error of t bits in a single word where $1 \leq t \leq n$ can be dispersed into t single-bit errors occurring at t different words using orthogonal Latin squares of order 2^s [HSIA 75].

Simulation results under common large memory organizations and reasonable intrinsic failure rate assumptions have shown the decrease in the frequency of card

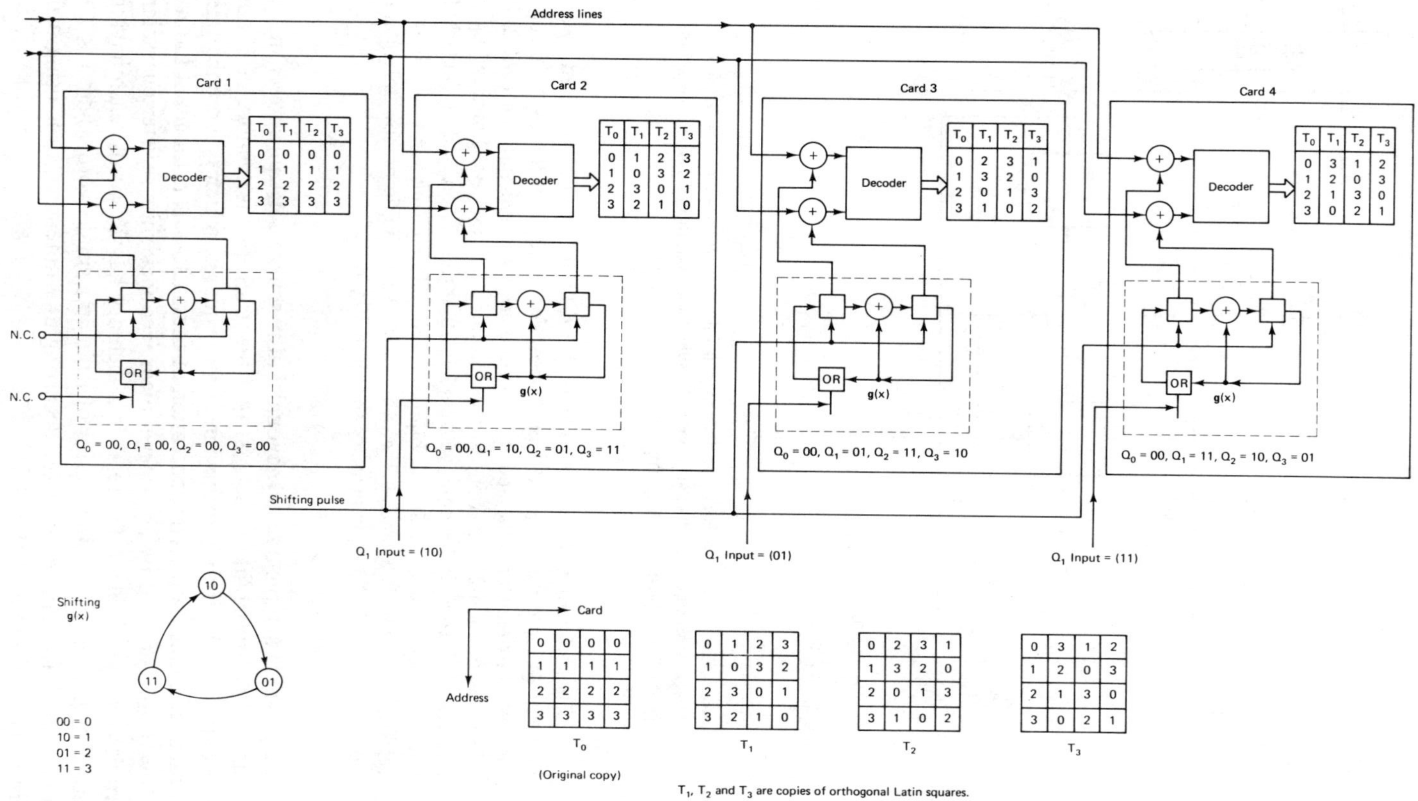

Figure 4.13 Memory organization showing Latin square configuration [HSIA 75]. Copyright 1975 by International Business Machines Corporation; reprinted with permission.

	Cards				
Address	1	2	3	4	
0	0	0	0	[0]	T_0 configuration: single-bit errors (boxes) and a third error (circle) causes a double (uncorrectable) error
1	1	1	1	1	
2	2	2	(2)	[2]	
3	3	3	3	3	
0	0	1	[2]	3	T_1 configuration: with three tolerable single-bit errors, a fourth, uncorrectable error occurs (circle)
1	1	0	3	[2]	
2	2	3	0	1	
3	3	(2)	1	[0]	
0	0	(2)	3	1	T_2 configuration: the fourth error is no longer aligned with any other error; however, another configuration is needed because two previous errors are aligned
1	1	3	[2]	[0]	
2	2	0	1	3	
3	3	1	0	[2]	
0	0	3	1	[2]	T_3 configuration: no double errors exist, but any additional error is unrecoverable
1	1	[2]	0	3	
2	2	1	3	[0]	
3	3	0	[2]	1	

Figure 4.14 Address skewing used to reconfigure the bit-sliced SEC–DED code memory shown in Fig. 4.13.

replacement by a factor of 10, compared to the frequency that would be tolerated without address permutation [BOSS 84, RYAN 83].

4.2 RANDOM DOUBLE-ERROR CORRECTING CODES

System reliability generally tends to decrease as the capacity of a memory system increases. To maintain the same high level of reliability, or to improve reliability, a double-bit error correcting (DEC) code, a double-bit error correcting and triple-bit error detecting (DEC–TED) code (both of them are based on the well-known BCH code [see Chapter 3]), or a multiple-error correcting *majority-logic decodable code* [PETE 72] can be applied to large-scale memory systems. However, use of these codes generally makes the decoding slower and increases the code redundancy.

With these problems in mind, some new extended codes based on the BCH code [PATE 72a, IMAI 77b, 79a] and new majority-logic decodable codes [HSIA 70b, SRIN 71a, CHEN 73, HORI 75a, MATS 77, 78] have been studied. Furthermore, some double-error correction schemes using the BCH code in an adaptive manner are also proposed in [PATE 72b, FUJI 76b, IMAI 77a, HOWE 77, YAMA 80, GOLA 83, OKAN 87].

TABLE 4.3 CHECK-BIT LENGTH OF THE DEC CODES

Code \ Information-Bit Length k	32	64	128
BCH code	12	14	16
Imai-Kamiyanagi code [IMAI 77b]	14 ~ 16	15 ~ 19	19 ~ 23
Horiguchi-Morita code* [HORI 75a]	16 ~ 19	22 ~ 26	31 ~ 37
MA code* [MATS 77]	23	31	40
Orthogonal Latin square code* [HSIA 70b]	24	32	48

*Majority-logic decodable code.

Table 4.3 shows the check-bit length of the foregoing new codes for double error correction. These two types of codes have the following general features:

1. BCH-based codes have a minimum or smaller number of check bits but have complex decoding hardware and a longer decoding time.
2. Majority-logic decodable codes have a high decoding speed and simple decoding hardware but a large number of check bits (i.e., nearly one-half of the information-bit length).

4.2.1 BCH-Based Code

We will study a new code based on the DEC–BCH code. Next, we will have some new parallel algebraic decoding methods for the DEC–BCH code.

Imai–Kamiyanagi code [IMAI 77b]. The basic structure of the BCH code is as follows (see Section 3.3.3):

Let α be a primitive element in $GF(2^m)$ and α^i be a coefficient binary column vector corresponding to $x^i \bmod \mathbf{g}(x)$, where $\mathbf{g}(x)$ is a primitive polynomial having degree m. By using these elements, the following matrix can be obtained.

$$\left.\begin{aligned}\mathbf{H}_1 &= \left[\alpha^0, \alpha^1, \ldots, \alpha^{n_1-1}\right] \\ \mathbf{H}_3 &= \left[\alpha^0, \alpha^3, \ldots, \alpha^{3(n_1-1)}\right]\end{aligned}\right\} \tag{4.5}$$

In this case, $n_1 = 2^m - 1$. The BCH codes can be expressed as

$$\begin{bmatrix}\mathbf{H}_1 \\ \mathbf{H}_3\end{bmatrix}_{2m \times n_1}$$

Imai and Kamiyanagi [IMAI 77b] gave a modified structure of the BCH codes such that some all 0 row vectors and all 1 row vectors are added to the original structure of the BCH codes. The resultant code has the following characteristics:

1. The decoding hardware has nearly the same complexity as that of the majority-logic decodable code but much simpler than that of the original DEC–BCH code.
2. The decoding can be made faster than that of the DEC–BCH code.
3. The check-bit number is only slightly larger than that of the DEC–BCH code.

The following notations are defined.

1_n: all 1 n-tuple row vector
0_n: all 0 n-tuple row vector
$\mathbf{I}_n$: $(n \times n)$ unit matrix
$\mathbf{0}_{k \times l}$: $(k \times l)$ zero matrix

The following two matrices **A** and **B** have an important role in this code construction.

A: $(r_0 \times n_0)$ matrix over $GF(2)$. The rightmost r_0 column vectors are linearly independent. The ith (for $i = 1, 2, \ldots, n_0$) column vector is denoted as $\mathbf{a}_i$.
B: $(r_1 \times n_0)$ matrix over $GF(2)$. This has r_1 linearly independent column vectors. The ith column vector is denoted as $\mathbf{b}_i$.

By using these matrices, the following three matrices can be constructed.

$$\tilde{\mathbf{H}}_1 = \left[\mathbf{A} \otimes \mathbf{H}_1, \mathbf{0}_{mr_0 \times r_1}\right]$$

$$\tilde{\mathbf{H}}_2 = \left[\mathbf{B} \otimes 1_{n_1}, \mathbf{I}_{r_1}\right]$$

$$\tilde{\mathbf{H}}_3 = \left[1_{n_0} \otimes \mathbf{H}_3, \mathbf{0}_{m \times r_1}\right]$$

Here, $\otimes$ shows the kronecker product (see Example 4-4). Then,

$$\mathbf{H} = \begin{bmatrix} \tilde{\mathbf{H}}_1 \\ \tilde{\mathbf{H}}_2 \\ \tilde{\mathbf{H}}_3 \end{bmatrix}$$

shows the **H** matrix of this new code. The codeword in this code can be expressed as $(n_0 + 1)$ blocks (i.e., n_0 blocks each of length n_1 and one block of length r_1). The code parameter of this code is as follows.

code length: $n = n_0 n_1 + r_1$
information-bit length: $k = n_0 n_1 - (r_0 + 1)m$
check-bit length: $n - k = (r_0 + 1)m + r_1$

Example 4-4*

Let $n_0 = 3$, $\mathbf{A} = \begin{bmatrix} 1 & 1 & 0 \\ 1 & 0 & 1 \end{bmatrix}$, and $\mathbf{B} = \begin{bmatrix} 0 & 1 & 0 \\ 0 & 0 & 1 \end{bmatrix}$. In this case, $r_0 = 2$, and $r_1 = 2$. Hence, $\tilde{\mathbf{H}}_1 = \begin{bmatrix} \mathbf{H}_1 & \mathbf{H}_1 & \mathbf{0}_{m\times n_1} & \mathbf{0}_{m\times 2} \\ \mathbf{H}_1 & \mathbf{0}_{m\times n_1} & \mathbf{H}_1 & \mathbf{0}_{m\times 2} \end{bmatrix}$, $\tilde{\mathbf{H}}_2 = \begin{bmatrix} 0_{n_1} & 1_{n_1} & 0_{n_1} & 10 \\ 0_{n_1} & 0_{n_1} & 1_{n_1} & 01 \end{bmatrix}$ and $\tilde{\mathbf{H}}_3 = [\mathbf{H}_3 \;\; \mathbf{H}_3 \;\; \mathbf{H}_3 \;\; \mathbf{0}_{m\times 2}]$. Then,

$$\mathbf{H} = \begin{bmatrix} \mathbf{H}_1 & \mathbf{H}_1 & \mathbf{0}_{m\times n_1} & \mathbf{0}_{m\times 2} \\ \mathbf{H}_1 & \mathbf{0}_{m\times n_1} & \mathbf{H}_1 & \mathbf{0}_{m\times 2} \\ 0_{n_1} & 1_{n_1} & 0_{n_1} & 10 \\ 0_{n_1} & 0_{n_1} & 1_{n_1} & 01 \\ \mathbf{H}_3 & \mathbf{H}_3 & \mathbf{H}_3 & \mathbf{0}_{m\times 2} \end{bmatrix}$$

If $m = 5$, we can get $n_1 = 31$, and therefore an $(n, k) = (95, 78)$ linear code can be obtained.

The principle for correcting a double-bit error is such that a double-bit error in one block can be corrected by the matrix $\begin{bmatrix} \mathbf{H}_1 \\ \mathbf{H}_3 \end{bmatrix}$ (i.e., DEC–BCH code) included in each block, and errors over two blocks can also be corrected by the structure of both matrix **A** and matrix **B**.

For further discussion on this code, refer to [IMAI 77b].

Parallel algebraic decoding method. We present here an algebraic, parallel decoding method for the DEC–BCH code [PATE 72b, HOWE 77, TAKE 77, GOLA 83]. From Equation (4.5), the DEC–BCH code can be written in the form:

$$\mathbf{H} = \begin{bmatrix} \mathbf{H}_1 \\ \mathbf{H}_3 \end{bmatrix} = \begin{bmatrix} H_{1,0} & H_{1,1} & \cdots & H_{1,n-1} \\ H_{3,0} & H_{3,1} & \cdots & H_{3,n-1} \end{bmatrix}$$

where $H_{1,i}$, $H_{3,i}$, $i \in \{0, 1, \ldots, n-1\}$ are elements of $GF(2^m)$ and are expressed as column vectors (m-tuples) over $GF(2)$. The syndromes S_1 and S_3 are defined by

$$S_1 = U \cdot \mathbf{H}_1^T, \qquad S_3 = U \cdot \mathbf{H}_3^T$$

Here, U is a received word from the memory that is to be decoded. In this decoder, the locator x of the single-bit and the double-bit errors can be found as a solution of the Equation (4.6). (See also Equation (3.50).)

$$\left(\frac{x}{S_1}\right)^2 \oplus \frac{x}{S_1} = 1 \oplus \frac{S_3}{S_1^3} \tag{4.6}$$

To implement the parallel decoder, two types of circuits have been proposed: the

*[IMAI 77b]. © 1977 IECE Japan.

first type employs only combinational circuits such as square, invert, and multiply circuits [IMAI 77a], the second type employs ROMs that store the table that can obtain the solution x from the input $(1 \oplus S_3/S_1^3)$ from Equation (4.6) [HOWE 77, YAMA 80, OKAN 87].

We also have a different method of parallel decoding [TAKE 77, GOLA 83]. This method is based on finding all nonzero solutions of the key equation

$$f(S_1 \oplus X) = S_3 \oplus f(X) \tag{4.7}$$

where $X \in \{H_{1,0}, H_{1,1}, \ldots, H_{1,n-1}\}$, and the function f is defined by

$$f(y) = \begin{cases} H_{3,i} & \text{if } y = H_{1,i} \in \mathbf{H}_1, 0 \le i \le n-1 \\ 0 & \text{if } y = 0 \end{cases}$$

This guarantees that for a nonzero syndrome the column vector $X \in \{H_{1,i}\}$ can be a solution of the key equation (4.7) only if it is a locator of single or double-bit errors. For the DEC–BCH code, it is clear that the function f is as follows.

$$f(y) = y^3$$

Although Equation (4.7) is equivalent to Equation (4.6) in the DEC–BCH code, the correction mechanism gives a different decoder construction (i.e., bit-sliced decoder). The correction algorithm follows.

1. *Find syndromes S_1 and S_3.*
2. *If $S_1 = S_3 = 0$, no correction, end.*
3. *To decompose the syndrome S_1 and S_3, add S_1 to all $H_{1,i}$'s and S_3 to all $H_{3,i}$'s:*

$$\begin{aligned} S_{1,i} &= S_1 \oplus H_{1,i} \\ S_{3,i} &= S_3 \oplus H_{3,i} \end{aligned} \qquad 0 \le i \le n-1 \tag{4.8}$$

4. *For $i = 0, 1, \ldots, n-1$, find the values of $f(S_{1,i})$ by Equation* (4.8).
5. *Find if there are any i's for which the key equation in the form*

$$f(S_{1,i}) = S_{3,i} \tag{4.9}$$

   is satisfied, and if it does for any i, then invert the ith bit of the word.
6. *If there is no i satisfying Equation* (4.9), *then an uncorrectable error is signaled. End.*

The decoder can be bit sliced as can be seen in Fig. 4.15.

Another high-speed algebraic method is called the *syndrome trapping technique* [PATE 72b]. The decoding of the DEC–BCH code having codeword length n requires establishing a one-to-one correspondence between the $n(n+1)/2$ distinct error patterns and the corresponding syndromes. However, in this technique, the $n(n+1)/2$ distinct syndromes are mapped into $(n+1)/2$ fixed syndromes by an arithmetic operation. The principle is given on p. 163 and explained through a simple example (Example 4-5).

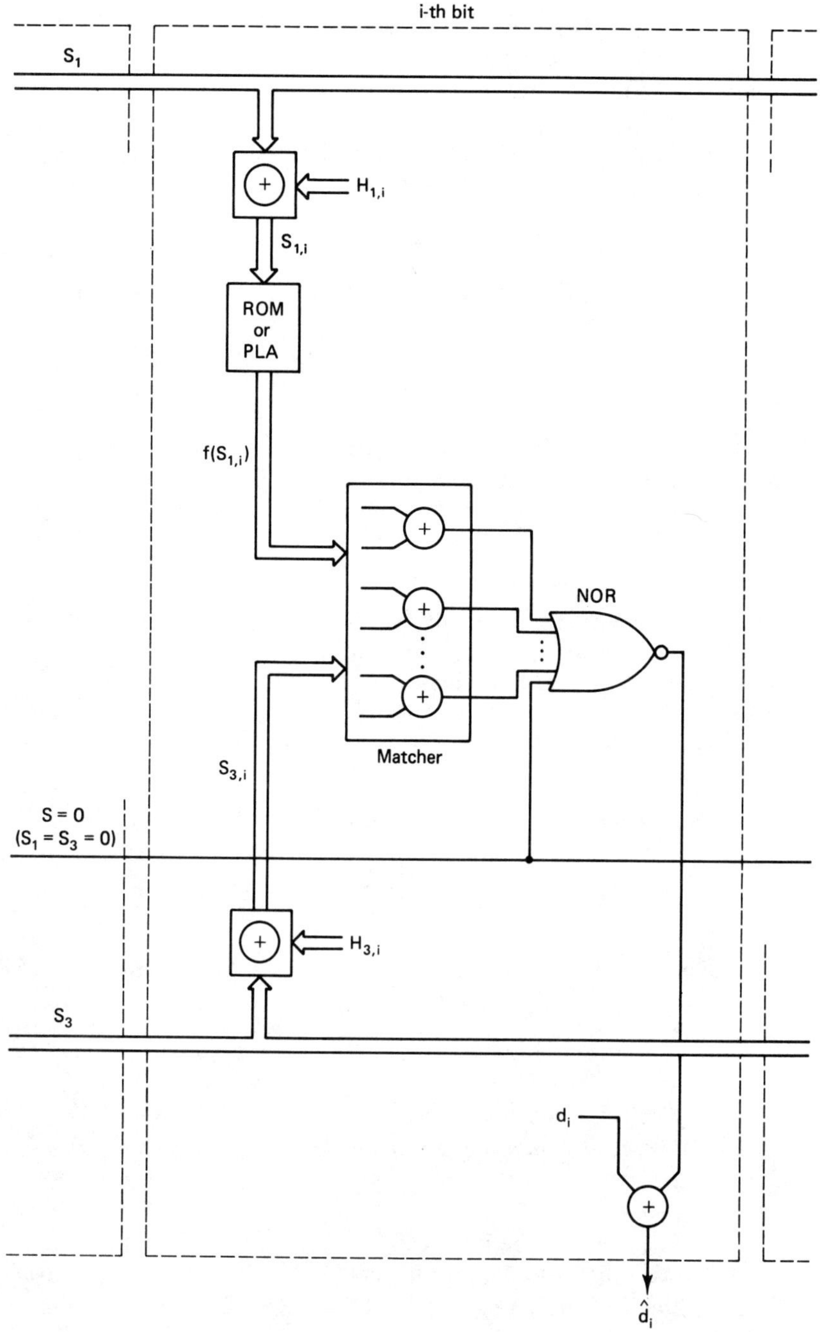

Figure 4.15 Bit-sliced decoder.

The syndrome for errors in positions i and j is given by

$$S = \begin{bmatrix} S_1 \\ S_3 \end{bmatrix} = \begin{bmatrix} \alpha^i \oplus \alpha^j \\ \alpha^{3i} \oplus \alpha^{3j} \end{bmatrix} = \begin{bmatrix} \alpha^p \\ \alpha^q \end{bmatrix}$$

where α is a primitive element of $GF(2^m)$ represented by a binary column vector, and n is given by $2^m - 1$. The foregoing syndrome is normalized to a form

$$S' = \begin{bmatrix} S_1' \\ S_3' \end{bmatrix} = \begin{bmatrix} \alpha^0 \\ \alpha^{q-3p} \end{bmatrix} = \begin{bmatrix} \alpha^{i-p} \oplus \alpha^{j-p} \\ \alpha^{3(i-p)} \oplus \alpha^{3(j-p)} \end{bmatrix} = \begin{bmatrix} \alpha^{i'} \oplus \alpha^{j'} \\ \alpha^{3i'} \oplus \alpha^{3j'} \end{bmatrix}$$

where $i' = (i - p) \bmod n$ and $j' = (j - p) \bmod n$. The above relation characterizes the syndrome for an error in each position i' and j'. Conversely, each double-error syndrome, in which $S_1 = \alpha^0$, characterizes n different double-error syndromes with $S_1 = \alpha^p$, where $p \in \{1, 2, \ldots, n\}$. Hence, in view of the uniqueness of the double-error syndromes, there are $n(n+1)/2$ distinct double-error syndromes and $(n+1)/2$ distinct values of S_3'. Hence, there are only $(n+1)/2$ distinct values of S' to cover all possible single and double errors. The strategy is to map the double-error syndromes S into a subclass of double-error syndromes S' in which $S_1' = \alpha^0$. Error positions corresponding to the resulting S' are then mapped into error locations i and j.

With this technique, the decoder can be implemented with simpler hardware, for example, by using ROMs that store the table of mapping from $k = q - 3p$ to (i', j'). The decoder will also have a higher decoding speed than that of the original BCH code.

The actual decoding algorithm can be summarized as follows.

1. *From the received information, obtain the syndrome S in the form*

$$S = \begin{bmatrix} S_1 \\ S_3 \end{bmatrix} = \begin{bmatrix} \alpha^p \\ \alpha^q \end{bmatrix}$$

2. *Identify p and q.*
3. *Obtain $k = q + (-3p) \bmod n$.*
4. *From the table, find i' and j' corresponding to k.*
5. *Obtain $i = p + i'$ and $j = p + j'$.*
6. *Decode i and j into error pointers.*

Example 4-5

Let m equal 4 and α be a primitive element of $GF(2^4)$ generated from the polynomial $g(x) = x^4 + x + 1$. Then, n is given by $2^4 - 1 = 15$. In this case, the table in step 4 of the above algorithm takes the form given in Table 4.4.

TABLE 4.4 MAPPING TABLE FROM k TO (i', j') FOR $n = 15$ [PATE 72b]

k	i'	j'
10	1	4
5	2	8
8	3	14
0	5	10
1	6	13
4	7	9
2	11	12
15	15	15
Others	0	0

Sequential erasure correction [FUJI 76b]. If double errors, ith-bit and jth-bit errors, are detected, the resultant syndrome S can be expressed as

$$S = S_i \oplus S_j \qquad 0 \le i < j \le n - 1$$

where S_i is the syndrome of the ith bit and S_j the syndrome of the jth bit. Assume that the ith error bit position is found out by some method. Then, its partner (jth bit error) position can be easily found out by adding the syndrome S_i to the original syndrome S,

$$S_j = S \oplus S_i$$

Since the syndrome based on the single error is a unique pattern equal to the column vector of the **H** matrix, this jth-bit error position can be uniquely determined. Based on the foregoing ideas, if we add the patterns equal to the column vectors of the **H** matrix bit by bit sequentially to the original syndrome S, then, at the ith addition point, the syndrome can be separated correctly to the syndrome of the ith-bit error and that of the jth-bit error. Since at this point the generated pattern S_j is equal to the jth-column vector of the **H** matrix, then we can correct both the ith-bit and jth-bit errors. This is the principle of the sequential erasure correction method.

This decoding method can sometimes be very slow, depending on the error positions. However, the method is based on the assumption that the occurrence of the double error is very rare in practice. Therefore, on the average, the decoding time is about the same as single-error decoding time.

If the ith bit is not in error, then the syndrome $S_j = S \oplus S_i$ corresponds to the syndrome of a triple error. Since the $d_{\min}$ is 5 for the code, S_j cannot be a syndrome of a single error. Theoretically, we can apply the distance-5 code as an SEC–TED (single-error correcting and triple-error detecting) code instead of as a DEC code. An SEC–TED code, however, is unable to distinguish between double errors and triple errors from the obtained syndrome. For this reason, we may apply a DEC–TED (double-error correcting and triple-error detecting) code (i.e., distance-6 code) to this decoding method.

The syndrome pattern S_i, which is equal to the column vector of the **H** matrix of the DEC–TED BCH code, is generated automatically by using LFSR and then added to the obtained syndrome S. This operation is performed for each S_i sequentially. The generator polynomial $\mathbf{G}(x)$ of the DEC–TED BCH code having Hamming distance-6 is given by the irreducible polynomials $\mathbf{m}_0(x), \mathbf{m}_1(x), \mathbf{m}_3(x)$, having elements $\alpha^0, \alpha^1, \alpha^3$ on $GF(2^m)$ as roots, respectively.

$$\mathbf{G}(x) = \mathbf{m}_0(x) \cdot \mathbf{m}_1(x) \cdot \mathbf{m}_3(x)$$

This code has the following relation between the check-bit length r, the information-bit length k, and the codeword length n.

$$\begin{aligned} r &= n - k = 2m + 1 \\ n &\leq 2^m - 1 \end{aligned} \tag{4.10}$$

Example 4-6

Let $m = 7$. Then, from Equation (4.10), $r = 15$. The irreducible polynomials $\mathbf{m}_0(x), \mathbf{m}_1(x), \mathbf{m}_3(x)$ based on the elements $\alpha^0, \alpha^1, \alpha^3$ on $GF(2^7)$ as roots, respectively, can be expressed as follows.

$$\begin{aligned} \mathbf{m}_0(x) &= x + 1 \\ \mathbf{m}_1(x) &= x^7 + x^3 + 1 \\ \mathbf{m}_3(x) &= x^7 + x^3 + x^2 + x + 1 \end{aligned}$$

From this, the generator polynomial $\mathbf{G}(x)$ is as follows.

$$\begin{aligned} \mathbf{G}(x) &= \mathbf{m}_0(x) \cdot \mathbf{m}_1(x) \cdot \mathbf{m}_3(x) \\ &= x^{15} + x^{14} + x^{10} + x^8 + x^7 + x^4 + x^3 + 1 \end{aligned} \tag{4.11}$$

This polynomial gives the **H** matrix of the shortened (79, 64) DEC–TED code, shown in Fig. 4.16, whose column vectors are all odd weight. That is, the ith column vector is equal to the coefficient vector of $x^i \; mod \; \mathbf{G}(x)$. The syndrome pattern S_i can be generated by using the LFSR based on this generator polynomial $\mathbf{G}(x)$ (shown in Fig. 4.17). This LFSR can generate patterns (equal to the column vectors of the **H** matrix shown in Fig. 4.16) sequentially by advancing the clock.

The double-error correction algorithm based on this method is shown in Fig. 4.18.

4.2.2 Majority-Logic Decodable Codes

Other types of double-error correcting codes are majority-logic decodable codes. One of them is a code derived from the concept of *t-design* [HALL 67], called the *MA code* [MATS 77], which is an extended *self-orthogonal code*. Here, we study the codes derived from the Latin squares [HSIA 70b] and also some efficient one-step majority-logic decodable codes with shorter check-bit lengths [HORI 75a].

Orthogonal Latin square code [HSIA 70b]. This code belongs to the class of one-step majority-logic decodable codes [MASS 63, PETE 72] derived from a set

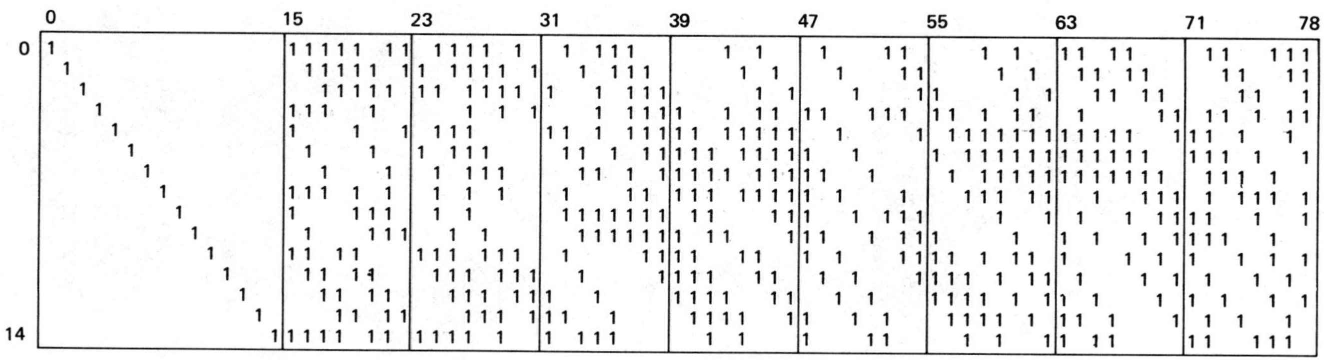

Figure 4.16 Shortened (79, 64) DEC–TED code [FUJI 76b]. © 1976 IECE Japan.

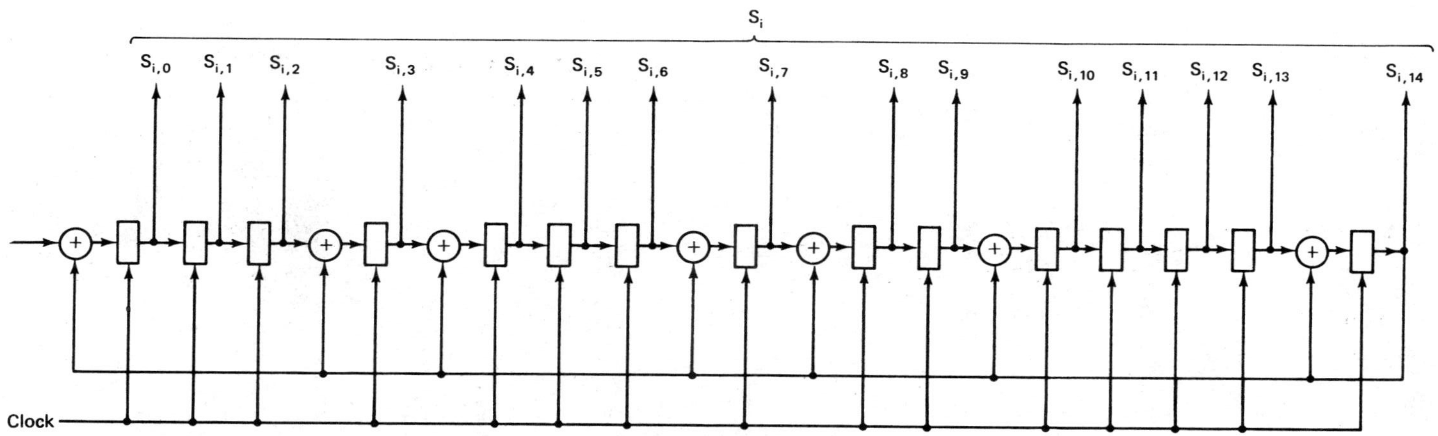

Figure 4.17 An example of LFSR for S_i pattern generation [FUJI 76b]. © 1976 IECE Japan.

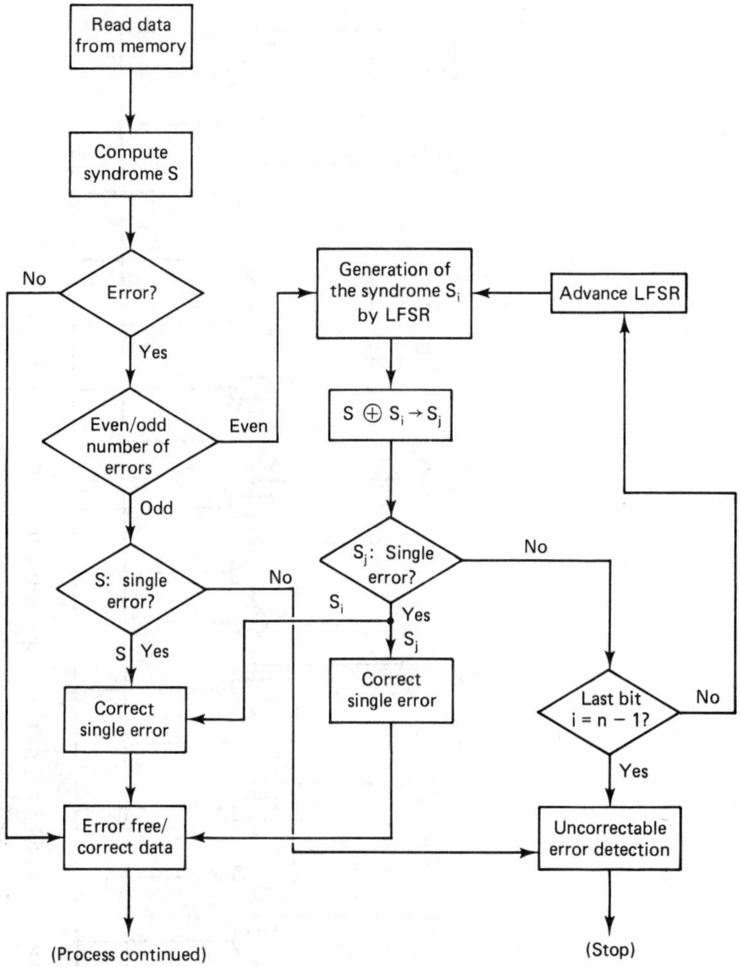

Figure 4.18 Algorithm for sequential erasure correction [FUJI 76b]. © 1976 IECE Japan.

of orthogonal Latin squares (see Section 4.1.3). This mutually orthogonal property provides a class of codes having a unique feature of "modularity." The **H** matrix possesses a uniform pattern and results in a small number of inputs to modulo 2 adders.

Let's study how the properties of a set of orthogonal Latin squares can be used to construct the **H** matrix of a *t*-error correcting majority-logic decodable code. The method of constructing orthogonal Latin squares is included in [MANN 49], and existing orthogonal squares are found in the table of [FISH 57].

Definition 4-2 [HSIA 70b]. A set of parity equations defined by the **H** matrix is said to be *orthogonal* on the digit d_i if, for any two parity equations p_1 and p_2 that contain d_i, d_i is the only common variable involved in p_1 and p_2.

If there is a set of $(2t + 1)$ parity equations orthogonal on d_i, then d_i can be decoded correctly by majority decoding in the presence of t errors [PETE 72]. The number of 1's in each column of the information bit positions of the **H** matrix should be at least $2t$ for a t-error correction. In the codes, the number of 1's in each column is exactly $2t$ (i.e., a constant-weight column). This t-error correcting code can be derived from the existing orthogonal Latin squares as follows.

Let the m^2 information bits be denoted by a vector

$$D = [d_0, d_1, \ldots, d_{m^2-1}].$$

Then, the $2tm$ check-bit equations for t-error corrections are obtained from the following **H** matrix.

$$\mathbf{H} = \left[\begin{array}{c|c} \mathbf{M}_1 & \\ \mathbf{M}_2 & \\ \mathbf{M}_3 & \mathbf{I}_{2tm} \\ \vdots & \\ \mathbf{M}_{2t} & \end{array}\right]$$

$\mathbf{I}_{2tm}$ is an identity matrix of rank $2tm$, and $\mathbf{M}_1, \mathbf{M}_2, \ldots, \mathbf{M}_{2t}$ are submatrices of size $(m \times m^2)$. The matrices $\mathbf{M}_1$ and $\mathbf{M}_2$ have the following form.

$$\mathbf{M}_1 = \begin{bmatrix} \overbrace{11\ldots1}^{m} & & & \\ & \overbrace{11\ldots1}^{m} & & \\ & & \ddots & \\ & & & \overbrace{11\ldots1}^{m} \end{bmatrix}_{m\times m^2}$$

$$\mathbf{M}_2 = \begin{bmatrix} \mathbf{I}_m & \mathbf{I}_m & \cdots & \mathbf{I}_m \end{bmatrix}_{m\times m^2}$$

The matrices $\mathbf{M}_3, \ldots, \mathbf{M}_{2t}$ are derived from the existing set of orthogonal Latin squares $\mathbf{L}_1, \mathbf{L}_2, \ldots, \mathbf{L}_{2t-2}$ of size $(m \times m)$, as given by Definition 4-1. Denote the set of Latin squares as

$$\mathbf{L}_1 = \left[l_{ij}^1\right]_{m\times m}$$

$$\mathbf{L}_2 = \left[l_{ij}^2\right]_{m\times m}$$

$$\vdots$$

$$\mathbf{L}_{2t-2} = \left[l_{ij}^{2t-2}\right]_{m\times m}$$

where

$$l_{ij} \in \{1, 2, \ldots, m\}$$

For any given Latin square having m elements, one can associate an incidence matrix defined on one of its elements as follows.

Definition 4-3*. Let $\mathbf{L} = [l_{ij}]_{m\times m}$ be a Latin square; then an *incidence matrix* defined with respect to the element δ ($1 \le \delta \le m$, integer), denoted by $\mathbf{Q}_\delta = [q_{ij}^\delta]$, is defined by the rules

$$q_{ij}^\delta = \begin{cases} 1 & \text{if } l_{ij} = \delta \\ 0 & \text{if } l_{ij} \neq \delta \end{cases}$$

For each Latin square of m elements, there exist m incidence matrices $\mathbf{Q}_1, \mathbf{Q}_2, \ldots, \mathbf{Q}_m$. Each incidence matrix is concatenated into a vector form,

$$V_\delta = \begin{bmatrix} q_{11}^\delta & \cdots & q_{1m}^\delta & q_{21}^\delta & \cdots & q_{2m}^\delta & \cdots & q_{m1}^\delta & \cdots & q_{mm}^\delta \end{bmatrix}$$

If submatrix $\mathbf{M}_i$ is derived from a unique Latin square $\mathbf{L}_j$, then

$$\mathbf{M}_i = \begin{bmatrix} V_1 \\ V_2 \\ \vdots \\ V_m \end{bmatrix}$$

where $V_1, V_2, \ldots, V_m$ are derived from $\mathbf{L}_j$.

The foregoing procedure leads to the following theorem.

Theorem 4-1*. *For an existing set of λ_m $(m \times m)$ orthogonal Latin squares $(\lambda_m \le m - 1)$, there exists a t-error correcting code, where*

$$t = \left\lfloor \frac{\lambda_m}{2} \right\rfloor + 1$$

under the previously described procedure of constructing the **H** *matrix.*

Proof. It is necessary that the entire set of parity check equations specified by the **H** matrix is pairwise orthogonal. This is clearly true for the equations in $\mathbf{M}_1$ and $\mathbf{M}_2$. For $\mathbf{M}_3, \ldots, \mathbf{M}_{2t}$, no two elements of an $\mathbf{M}_i$ have any intersections. Suppose now that an element of $\mathbf{M}_i$ and an element of $\mathbf{M}_j$, for $i, j \in \{3, 4, \ldots, 2t\}$ and $i \neq j$, have more than one intersection. This implies that the superposition of Latin squares $\mathbf{L}_i$ and $\mathbf{L}_j$ has an ordered pair occurring more than once, contrary to their orthogonality. Suppose that some element of $\mathbf{M}_i$ for $i \neq 1, 2$ has more than one intersection with either $\mathbf{M}_1$ or $\mathbf{M}_2$. This means that $\mathbf{M}_i$ is not a Latin square.

Q.E.D.

*[HSIA 70b]. Copyright 1970 by International Business Machines Corporation; reprinted with permission.

Example 4-7*

Given $k = 25$, design a system derived from an orthogonal Latin square code of class (n, k). Fig. 4.19 shows the (35, 25) single-error correcting code, the (45, 25) double-error correcting code, and the (55, 25) triple-error correcting code. It also shows the decoder circuit for data bit d_0. For the single-error correcting code, only $\mathbf{M}_1$ and $\mathbf{M}_2$ are used. For double- and triple-error correcting codes, the following four orthogonal squares of order 5 are used.

$$\mathbf{L}_1 = \begin{bmatrix} 0 & 1 & 2 & 3 & 4 \\ 1 & 2 & 3 & 4 & 0 \\ 2 & 3 & 4 & 0 & 1 \\ 3 & 4 & 0 & 1 & 2 \\ 4 & 0 & 1 & 2 & 3 \end{bmatrix} \qquad \mathbf{L}_2 = \begin{bmatrix} 0 & 1 & 2 & 3 & 4 \\ 2 & 3 & 4 & 0 & 1 \\ 4 & 0 & 1 & 2 & 3 \\ 1 & 2 & 3 & 4 & 0 \\ 3 & 4 & 0 & 1 & 2 \end{bmatrix}$$

$$\mathbf{L}_3 = \begin{bmatrix} 0 & 1 & 2 & 3 & 4 \\ 3 & 4 & 0 & 1 & 2 \\ 1 & 2 & 3 & 4 & 0 \\ 4 & 0 & 1 & 2 & 3 \\ 2 & 3 & 4 & 0 & 1 \end{bmatrix} \qquad \mathbf{L}_4 = \begin{bmatrix} 0 & 1 & 2 & 3 & 4 \\ 4 & 0 & 1 & 2 & 3 \\ 3 & 4 & 0 & 1 & 2 \\ 2 & 3 & 4 & 0 & 1 \\ 1 & 2 & 3 & 4 & 0 \end{bmatrix}$$

For double-error correction, the code uses Latin squares $\mathbf{L}_1$ and $\mathbf{L}_2$. For triple-error correction, the code uses all squares $\mathbf{L}_1$, $\mathbf{L}_2$, $\mathbf{L}_3$, and $\mathbf{L}_4$.

The circuit necessary for correcting additional errors can be added to the existing error correcting circuit as a modular arrangement, as in Section II and Section III in Fig. 4.19. This arrangement allows for considerable flexibility in circuits that can be built in modular form and easily packaged.

The **H** matrix of this code is of low density, and therefore results in high redundancy. The decoder, however, shows simplicity and regularity because only mod 2 adders and $(2t + 1)$-way voting gates are required.

The code parameters of this code are as follows:

$$\begin{cases} \text{codeword length: } n \le m^2 + 2mt \\ \text{check-bit length: } r = 2mt \end{cases}$$

$$t \le \left\lfloor \frac{m}{2} \right\rfloor + 1$$

Horiguchi–Morita code [HORI 75a]. We will now study a new class of one-step majority-logic decodable codes. From Table 4.3 we see that these codes can be realized with fewer check bits than the other majority-logic decodable codes.

In order to illustrate this, we start with a simple example. Let m be any odd integer, such as 5, and let 5^2 information bits, $d_0, d_1, \ldots, d_{24}$, be arranged as in Fig. 4.20.

*[HSIA 70b]. Copyright 1970 by International Business Machines Corporation; reprinted with permission.

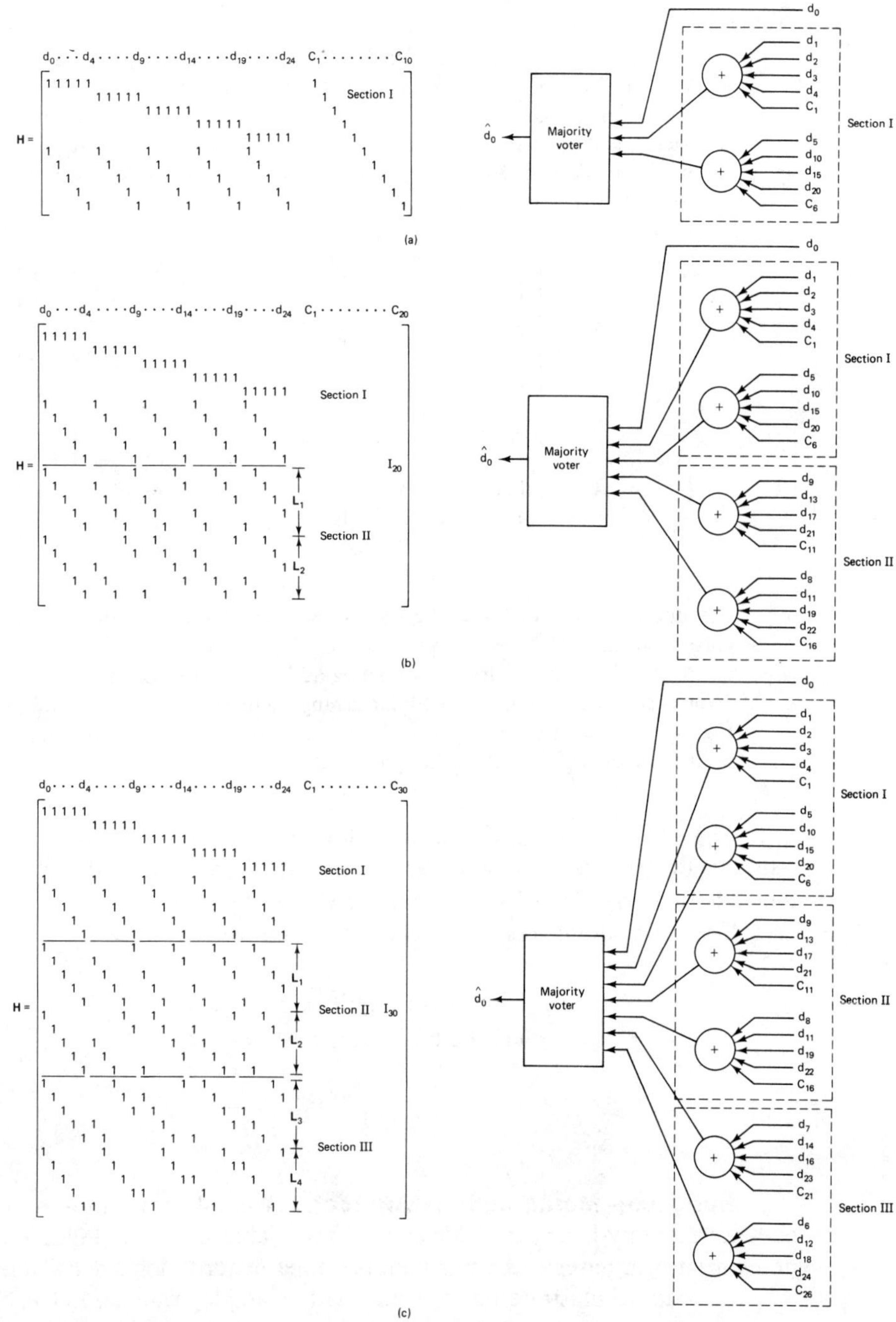

Figure 4.19 **H** matrices and decoder circuits for data-bit d_0. (a) Single-error correcting code (35, 25); (b) double-error correcting code (45, 25); and (c) triple-error correcting code (55, 25) [HSIA 70b]. Copyright 1970 by International Business Machines Corporation; reprinted with permission.

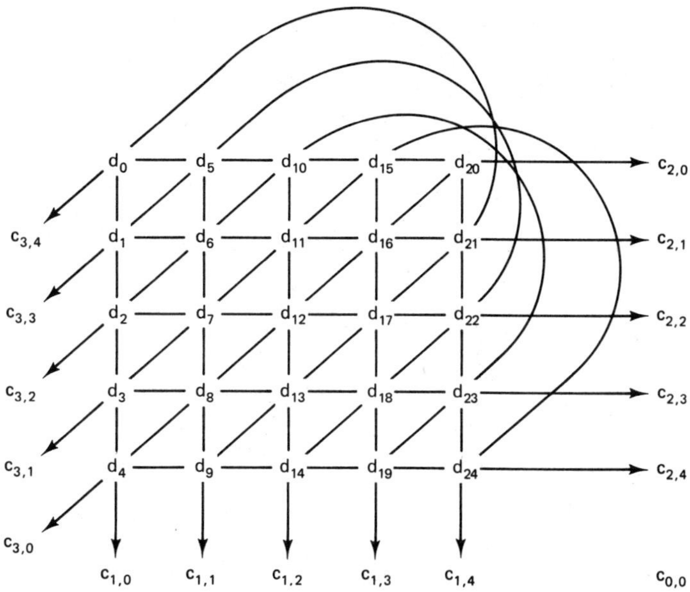

Figure 4.20 Square data arrangement and check-bit generation. [HORI 75a]. © 1975 IECE Japan.

As shown in Fig. 4.20, check bit $c_{1,i}$ $(i = 0, 1, 2, 3, 4)$ can be obtained by modulo 2 addition of the column data bits arranged in vertical direction, check bit $c_{2,i}$ also by modulo 2 addition of the row data bits arranged in horizontal direction, check bit $c_{3,i}$ by modulo 2 addition of the diagonal data bits arranged in oblique direction, and check bit $c_{0,0}$ by modulo 2 addition of the whole data bits. Therefore, we can obtain the **H** matrix of this code shown as follows.

$$
\begin{array}{c|ccccc|ccccc|ccccc|ccccc|ccccc|c}
 & 0&1&2&3&4 & & & & &9 & & & & &14 & & & & &19 & & & & &24 & 40 \\
\hline
C_{10} & 1&1&1&1&1 & & & & & & & & & & & & & & & & & & & & & \\
C_{11} & & & & & & 1&1&1&1&1 & & & & & & & & & & & & & & & & \\
C_{12} & & & & & & & & & & & 1&1&1&1&1 & & & & & & & & & & & \\
C_{13} & & & & & & & & & & & & & & & & 1&1&1&1&1 & & & & & & \\
C_{14} & & & & & & & & & & & & & & & & & & & & & 1&1&1&1&1 & \\
\hline
C_{20} & 1& & & & & 1& & & & & 1& & & & & 1& & & & & 1& & & & & \\
C_{21} & &1& & & & &1& & & & &1& & & & &1& & & & &1& & & & \\
C_{22} & & &1& & & & &1& & & & &1& & & & &1& & & & &1& & & \mathbf{I}_{16} \\
C_{23} & & & &1& & & & &1& & & & &1& & & & &1& & & & &1& & \\
C_{24} & & & & &1 & & & & &1 & & & & &1 & & & & &1 & & & & &1 & \\
\hline
C_{30} & & & & &1 & & & &1& & & &1& & & &1& & & & 1& & & & & \\
C_{31} & & & &1& & & &1& & & &1& & & & 1& & & & & & & & &1 & \\
C_{32} & & &1& & & &1& & & & 1& & & & & & & & &1 & & & &1& & \\
C_{33} & &1& & & & 1& & & & & & & & &1 & & & &1& & & &1& & & \\
C_{34} & 1& & & & & & & & &1 & & & &1& & & &1& & & &1& & & & \\
\hline
C_{00} & 1&1&1&1&1 & 1&1&1&1&1 & 1&1&1&1&1 & 1&1&1&1&1 & 1&1&1&1&1 &
\end{array}
\qquad (4.12)
$$

This code has parameters $k = m^2$, $r = 3m + 1$, where $m = 5$.

Next, it will be shown that this code is really a double-error correcting majority-logic decodable code. Let e_i denote an ith data bit error and $E_{i,j}$ denote a check bit $c_{i,j}$ error. Then the syndrome can be obtained by the parity equations given as follows.

$$S_{0,0} = \sum_{i=0}^{24} e_i + E_{00}$$

$$S_{1,0} = e_0 + e_1 + e_2 + e_3 + e_4 + E_{1,0}$$

$$S_{1,1} = e_5 + e_6 + e_7 + e_8 + e_9 + E_{1,1}$$

$$S_{1,2} = e_{10} + e_{11} + e_{12} + e_{13} + e_{14} + E_{1,2}$$

$$S_{1,3} = e_{15} + e_{16} + e_{17} + e_{18} + e_{19} + E_{1,3}$$

$$S_{1,4} = e_{20} + e_{21} + e_{22} + e_{23} + e_{24} + E_{1,4}$$

$$S_{2,0} = e_0 + e_5 + e_{10} + e_{15} + e_{20} + E_{2,0}$$

$$S_{2,1} = e_1 + e_6 + e_{11} + e_{16} + e_{21} + E_{2,1}$$

$$S_{2,2} = e_2 + e_7 + e_{12} + e_{17} + e_{22} + E_{2,2}$$

$$S_{2,3} = e_3 + e_8 + e_{13} + e_{18} + e_{23} + E_{2,3}$$

$$S_{2,4} = e_4 + e_9 + e_{14} + e_{19} + e_{24} + E_{2,4}$$

$$S_{3,4} = e_0 + e_9 + e_{13} + e_{17} + e_{21} + E_{3,4}$$

$$S_{3,3} = e_1 + e_5 + e_{14} + e_{18} + e_{22} + E_{3,3}$$

$$S_{3,2} = e_2 + e_6 + e_{10} + e_{19} + e_{23} + E_{3,2}$$

$$S_{3,1} = e_3 + e_7 + e_{11} + e_{15} + e_{24} + E_{3,1}$$

$$S_{3,0} = e_4 + e_8 + e_{12} + e_{16} + e_{20} + E_{3,0}$$

In the above equations there are syndrome components, $S_{1,0}$, $S_{2,0}$, and $S_{3,4}$, that include e_0 and do not include any other e_i's commonly. Therefore, $(S_{1,0}, S_{2,0}, S_{3,4})$ is orthogonal on e_0 from Definition 4-2. The syndrome $S_{0,0}$ also includes e_0 but is not orthogonal to $(S_{1,0}, S_{2,0}, S_{3,4})$. The following syndrome sum, however, is orthogonal to $(S_{1,0}, S_{2,0}, S_{3,4})$ on e_0.

$$\begin{aligned} S_{0,0} &+ S_{1,2} + S_{1,4} + S_{2,2} + S_{2,4} + S_{3,1} + S_{3,3} \\ &= e_0 + e_6 + e_7 + e_8 + e_{11} + e_{12} + e_{16} \\ &\quad + E_{0,0} + E_{1,2} + E_{1,4} + E_{2,2} + E_{2,4} + E_{3,1} + E_{3,3} \end{aligned}$$

Therefore, e_0 can be obtained by the following majority function having threshold-

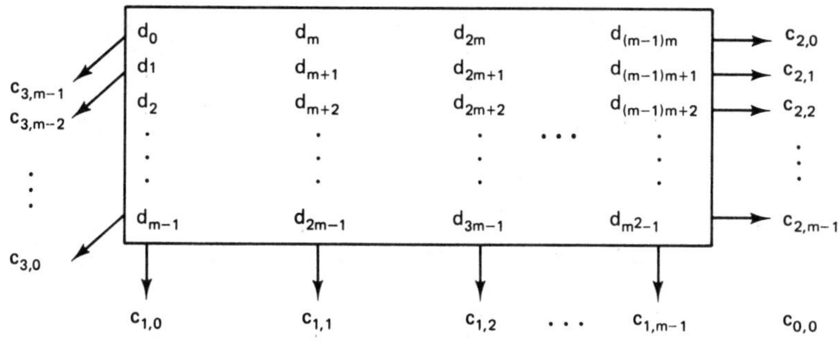

Figure 4.21 Square arrangement of the m^2 data.

level 3 (i.e., Maj (3)).

$$e_0 = \text{Maj}\,(3)\left[S_{0,0} + S_{1,2} + S_{1,4} + S_{2,2} + S_{2,4} + S_{3,1} + S_{3,3},\ S_{1,0},\ S_{2,0},\ S_{3,4}\right]$$

Hence, we have four check sums orthogonal on e_0. Similarly, for other positions, there are also at least four check sums orthogonal on each bit. Then, this code has a minimum distance of at least five and can correct any double errors [PETE 72]. We can generalize this example and have the following theorem.

Theorem 4-2. *Let* $(m \times m)$, $m =$ *odd integer, data be arranged in square form as shown in Fig.* 4.21. *And let the following* $r = 3m + 1$ *check bits be given by modulo* 2 *addition of the data bits; check bit* $c_{0,0}$ *is obtained from the whole data,* $c_{1,0}, c_{1,1}, \ldots, c_{1,m-1}$ *are obtained from the vertical direction of the data in the square,* $c_{2,0}, c_{2,1}, \ldots, c_{2,m-1}$ *are obtained from the horizontal direction of the data, and* $c_{3,0}, c_{3,1}, \ldots, c_{3,m-1}$ *are obtained from the oblique direction of the data as in Figure* 4.21. *Then, this code is a double-error correcting majority-logic decodable code with* $k = m^2$ *and* $r = 3m + 1$.

The decoder logic for this code can be seen in Fig. 4.22. The whole decoding circuit necessitates m^2 such circuits, as shown in this figure.

By adding any other DEC one-step majority-logic decodable code to an existing ($k = m^2$, $r = 3m + 1$) code, a new extended DEC code can be obtained. In Fig. 4.23, (a) expresses the existing ($k = m^2$, $r = 2m + 1$) code: $\mathbf{M}_1(m)$ shows the parity check matrix for the vertical direction of check-sums in Fig. 4.21; $\mathbf{M}_2(m)$ shows the parity check matrix for the horizontal direction of check sums; and $\mathbf{M}_3(m)$ shows the parity check matrix for the oblique direction of check sums. Part (b) shows the $\mathbf{H}$ matrix of an arbitrary ($k = k_1$, $r = m + 1$) double-error correcting, one-step majority-logic decodable code. Using matrices (a) and (b), we can obtain the new code shown in (c). The resulting code is a ($k = m^2 + 3k_1$, $r = 3m + 1$) code. The code shown in (4.13) is an example of the (86, 64) code. For more details refer to [HORI 75a].

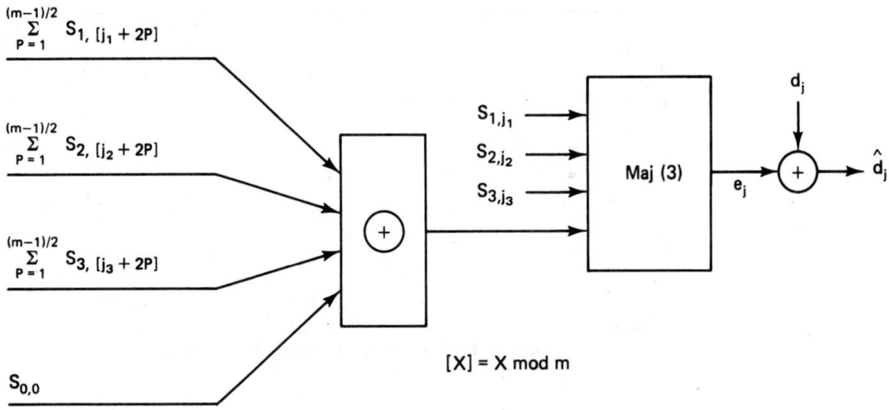

Figure 4.22 Decoder for the jth bit. [HORI 75a]. © 1975 IECE Japan.

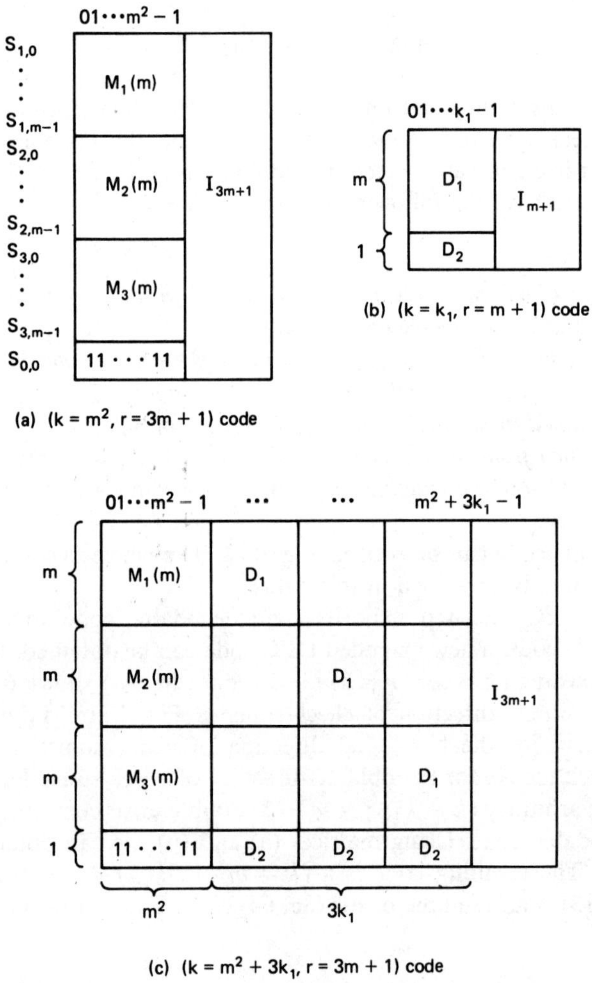

Figure 4.23 ($k = m^2 + 3k_1$, $r = 3m + 1$) code [HORI 75a]. © 1975 IECE Japan.

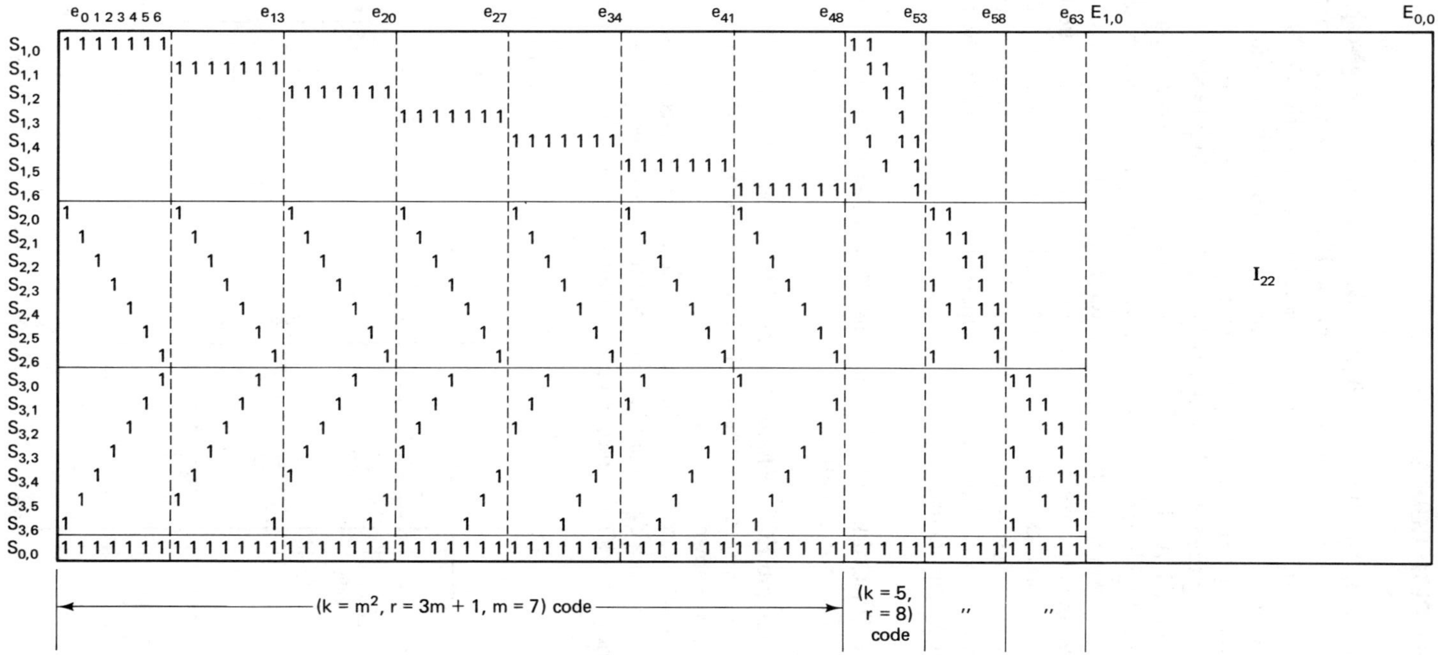
e0 1 2 3 4 5 6
e13
e20
e27
e34
e41
e48
e53
e58
e63
E1,0
E0,0
S1,0
S1,1
S1,2
S1,3
S1,4
S1,5
S1,6
S2,0
S2,1
S2,2
S2,3
S2,4
S2,5
S2,6
S3,0
S3,1
S3,2
S3,3
S3,4
S3,5
S3,6
S0,0
I22
(k = m2, r = 3m + 1, m = 7) code
(k = 5, r = 8) code
"
"

$$(4.13)$$

4.3 MEMORY-CHIP CODES

In working with the recent high-packing-density and large-capacity RAM or ROM chips, we have to overcome several problems. Among these are soft errors induced by α particles emitted from packaging material [MAY 79, SAIH 82] and yield degradation problems caused by increased defects in the enlarged chip [WOOD 86]. An on-chip error checking/correcting (*on-chip ECC*) technique is a good method for solving these problems [CLIF 74, 80, NOOR 80, MANO 83, GHAF 84, DAVI 85, FUJA 85, HAN 87, YAMA 88]. By using an error-correcting code on the chip we can get highly reliable, cost-effective, large-capacity memory chips. With this technique, however, we have to pay careful attention to the circuit increase due to error checking and correcting circuit and extra memory cells for check bits. Because these circuit increases require an enlarged chip, they produce more defects, or more α particles. This is the real problem. Therefore, the type of code we use with the on-chip ECC technique is very important for minimizing the difficulties that result from circuit increases.

4.3.1 On-Chip, Two-Dimensional, Cross-Parity Codes for Soft Error Problems

The on-chip ECC technique is one of the essential techniques for protection of data from soft errors in megabit MOS RAMs. A block diagram of a RAM with ECC circuit is shown in Fig. 4.24.

Each word line in this organization is connected to the regular memory cells that contain a data word and also to the extra memory cells required for check bits. Extra bit lines and sense circuits are included in order to transmit the check bits to

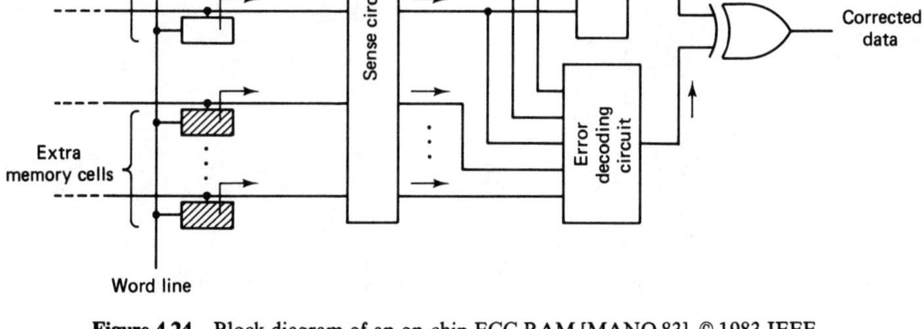

Figure 4.24 Block diagram of an on-chip ECC RAM [MANO 83]. © 1983 IEEE.

an error decoding circuit, where the decoding is carried out according to the code adopted. If a bit error is detected, the output data of the multiplexer is corrected through an exclusive-or circuit. This ECC operation is performed during *read/write* memory cycles. Furthermore, in order to prevent bit-error accumulation, this operation should also be carried out during *refresh* memory cycles.

The soft error containment by use of the on-chip ECC technique depends on the capability of the code used on a RAM. Although there are many kinds of codes, consideration here is limited to those codes having single-bit error correction capability.

The occurrence rate of soft errors in a conventional dynamic MOS RAM without an ECC code is determined by the probability that one α particle hits a single memory cell [SAIH 82]. On the other hand, the error rate in a dynamic MOS RAM with an ECC code is dependent on the probability that data stored in two or more memory cells are damaged by α particles within an error correction period t_0.

Assuming that the probability of an α particle striking incidence is given by a Poisson distribution—and, moreover, one incident α particle always generates a single-bit error—the soft error rate of a RAM with an ECC code is obtained as follows [MANO 83]:

$$R_{\text{ECC}} = MN^2S_0 - (N/t_0)\{\ln(1 + MNS_0t_0)\}$$

where M is the α-flux density, N^2 is the number of memory cells on a chip, and S_0 is the effective area of a memory cell. On the other hand, the error rate of a RAM (without an ECC code) is as follows.

$$R_0 = MN^2S_0$$

The soft error rate characteristic of a RAM with an ECC code, as compared to one without ECC code, is shown in Fig. 4.25.

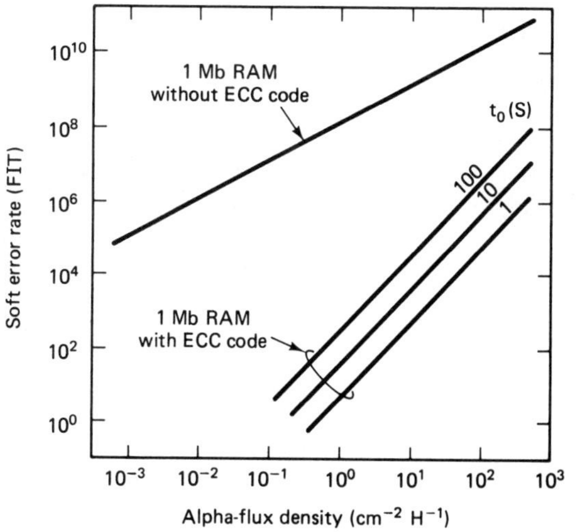

Figure 4.25 Soft error rate characteristic of the on-chip ECC RAM and the conventional RAM (Effective storage area in a single transistor cell is assumed to be 10 μm^2.) [MANO 83]. © 1983 IEEE.

The improvement becomes greater in the region where the α-flux density is smaller. The improvement factor is more than 10^6 at an α-flux density of 1 cm^{-2} h^{-1}. Therefore, high α-particle immunity will be achieved by an on-chip, single-bit, error correcting code.

In order to implement an on-chip ECC circuit, it is necessary to reduce the silicon area used for logic and the decoding (or correcting) logic delay. As mentioned before, an on-chip ECC circuit is composed mainly of extra memory cells and the error decoding circuit.

Here we consider the two-dimensional cross-parity code (a distance-4 code) and the Hamming (distance-3) code as illustrations [MANO 83]. In a two-dimensional cross-parity code, horizontal and vertical parity bits are appended to a two-dimensional matrix of information bits. This is shown in Fig. 4.26 (depicted according to the block diagram of a RAM shown in Fig. 4.24). In this case, if a single-bit error in the information bits occurs, it can simply be decoded by using the horizontal and vertical parity checked syndromes.

Another type of block diagram requires two ways of parity—row parity and block parity—where the memory array consists of some blocks. Row parity can be

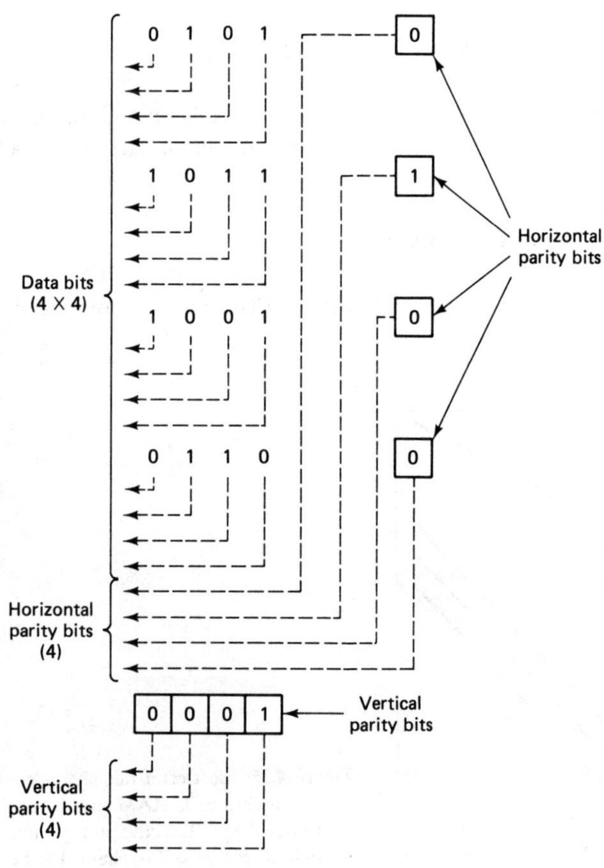

Figure 4.26 Principle of cross-parity decoding [MANO 83].

implemented by adding row bits in each block and block parity; although an extra block is needed for this parity, it can be implemented by adding the corresponding bits of the same address positions of all blocks [OSMA 82].

Here we will concentrate on the type of diagram shown in Fig. 4.24 and Fig. 4.26. By transferring the information bits and check bits along the dotted-line arrows in Fig. 4.26, the two-dimensional matrix can be transformed into a codeword vector that corresponds to the memory cells connected with each word line. This readout word is entered into the decoding circuit, and then vertical and horizontal parities are checked. Each information bit is checked uniquely by two checks, called *cross-parity checks*. For example, bit-3 in the second row belongs to parity-2 of horizontal group (**H** group) and parity-3 of vertical group (**V** group); therefore, that bit is corrected only when its cross-parity checks are 1's. The decoding circuit of this code is shown in Fig. 4.27. Fig. 4.28 shows, more specifically, a logic diagram of a RAM with a two-dimensional cross-parity code.

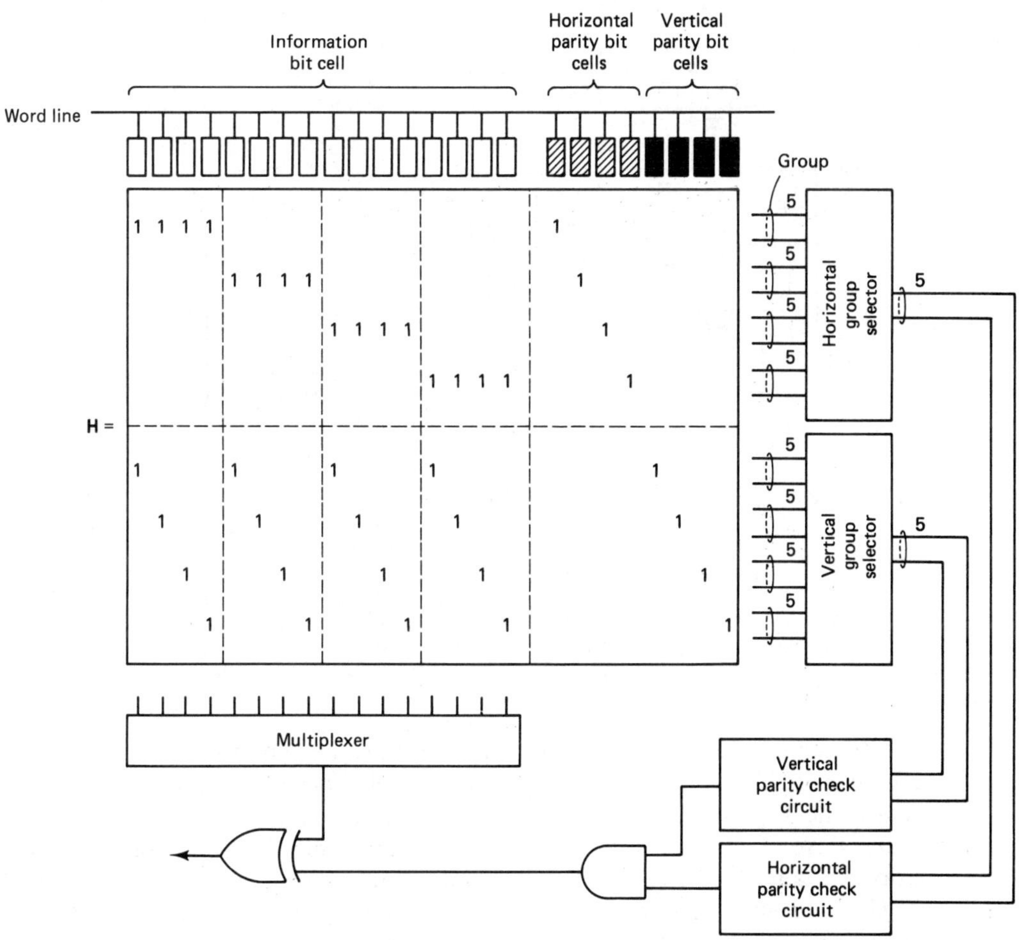

Figure 4.27 On-chip error decoding circuit for a two-dimensional cross-parity code.

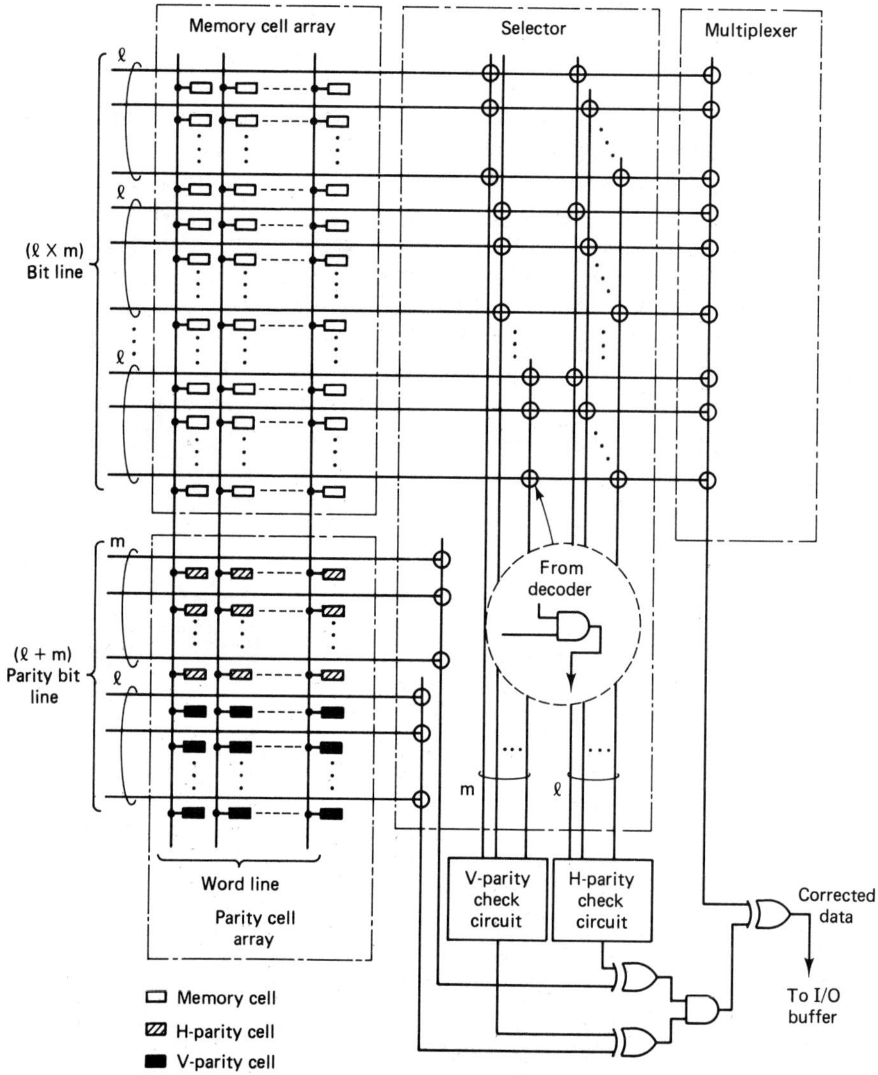

Figure 4.28 Logic diagram of the on-chip ECC RAM using a two-dimensional cross-parity code [MANO 83]. © 1983 IEEE.

In addition to $(l \times m)$ regular memory cells, $(l + m)$ parity cells are included in each word line. As we said before, each regular memory cell belongs to two groups, the **V** group and the **H** group. For error correction, two kinds of parity checking are carried out using m-bit **V**-group data, l-bit **H**-group data, and 2-bit parity cell data. In the case of this two-dimensional cross-parity code, the column decoder for a multiplexer can also be used for a selector. Therefore, there is no need for an additional decoder for memory cell selection. Hence, the error decoding

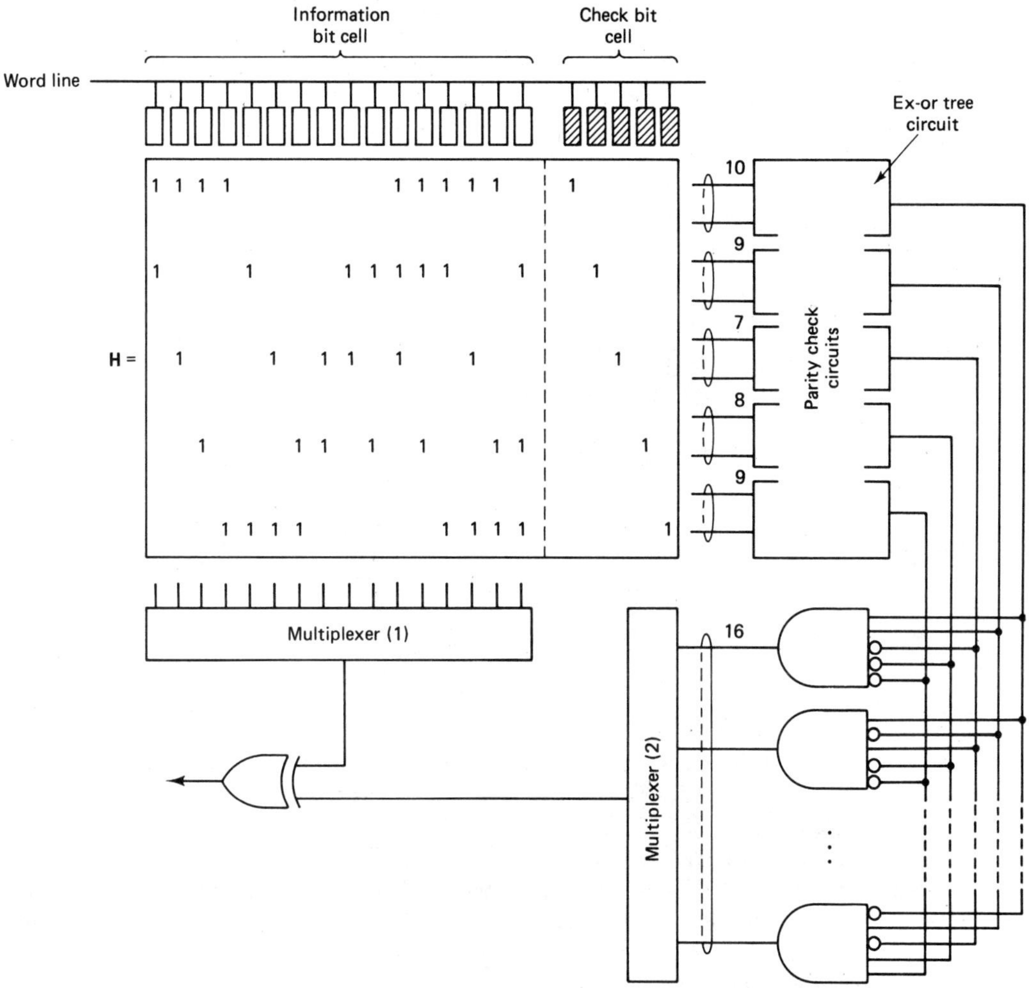

Figure 4.29 On-chip error decoding circuit for a Hamming SEC code.

circuit shown in Fig. 4.28 (or Fig. 4.27) has a simple structure and provides high-speed decoding.

On the other hand, if we use a Hamming code, the number of extra memory cells can be minimized, whereas the size of the error decoding circuit becomes larger than that of the two-dimensional cross-parity code. An example of this decoding circuit is shown in Fig. 4.29, which has the same information-bit length and the check-bit length in a word line as in Fig. 4.27. From this consideration, it is clear that the on-chip ECC technique using a two-dimensional cross-parity code is a better way to reduce the soft error rate. As a single-bit error per word line is correctable with this ECC technique, the soft error rate of a high-packing density RAM can be drastically improved.

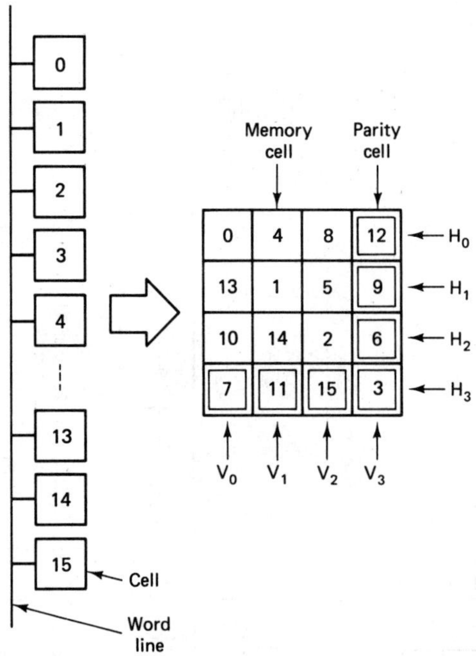

Figure 4.30 An example of the efficient logical cell alignment for two-dimensional cross-parity codes [MANO 87]. © 1987 IEEE.

Fig. 4.30 shows an example of an efficient cell alignment for the two-dimensional cross-parity codes [YAMA 87b]. The adjacent cell failures on a word line can be detected in an efficient way.

The on-chip ECC technique using a two-dimensional cross-parity code has been applied to 256K-bit RAM design [MANO 83]. In addition to 256K regular memory cells, the RAM has 24K parity cells for two-dimensional parity checking. In this RAM, 512 (= 16 × 32) memory cells and 48 (= 16 + 32) parity cells are connected with each word line.

This on-chip ECC technique is extended to decode 4-bit byte errors by performing double-precision horizontal and vertical parity checking [YAMA 84]. This is shown in Fig. 4.31. The technique is applied to a 1 megabit dynamic RAM. The result is that the ECC circuit occupies about 12% of the 52 mm^2 (= 6.4 mm × 8.2 mm) entire chip area, and the error correction time is 20 ns, with a 140 ns chip access time. A further improved design method of the on-chip ECC circuit is proposed for 16 megabit dynamic RAM in [MANO 87, YAMA 87b] such that selector circuits and parity checkers are placed so as not to have long bus lines. This gives below 5 ns penalty in access time of 80 ns and occupies about 10% of the 8.9 mm × 16.6 mm entire chip area. This chip has been designed and fabricated using a 0.7 μm CMOS process.

Further extension of an on-chip error correction technique is proposed using a two-dimensional code of two SEC codes, two SEC–DED codes, and an SEC–DED code and a simple parity check code [FUJA 85] (see Problem 4.14). Another is proposed using double-error correcting and triple-error detecting majority-logic

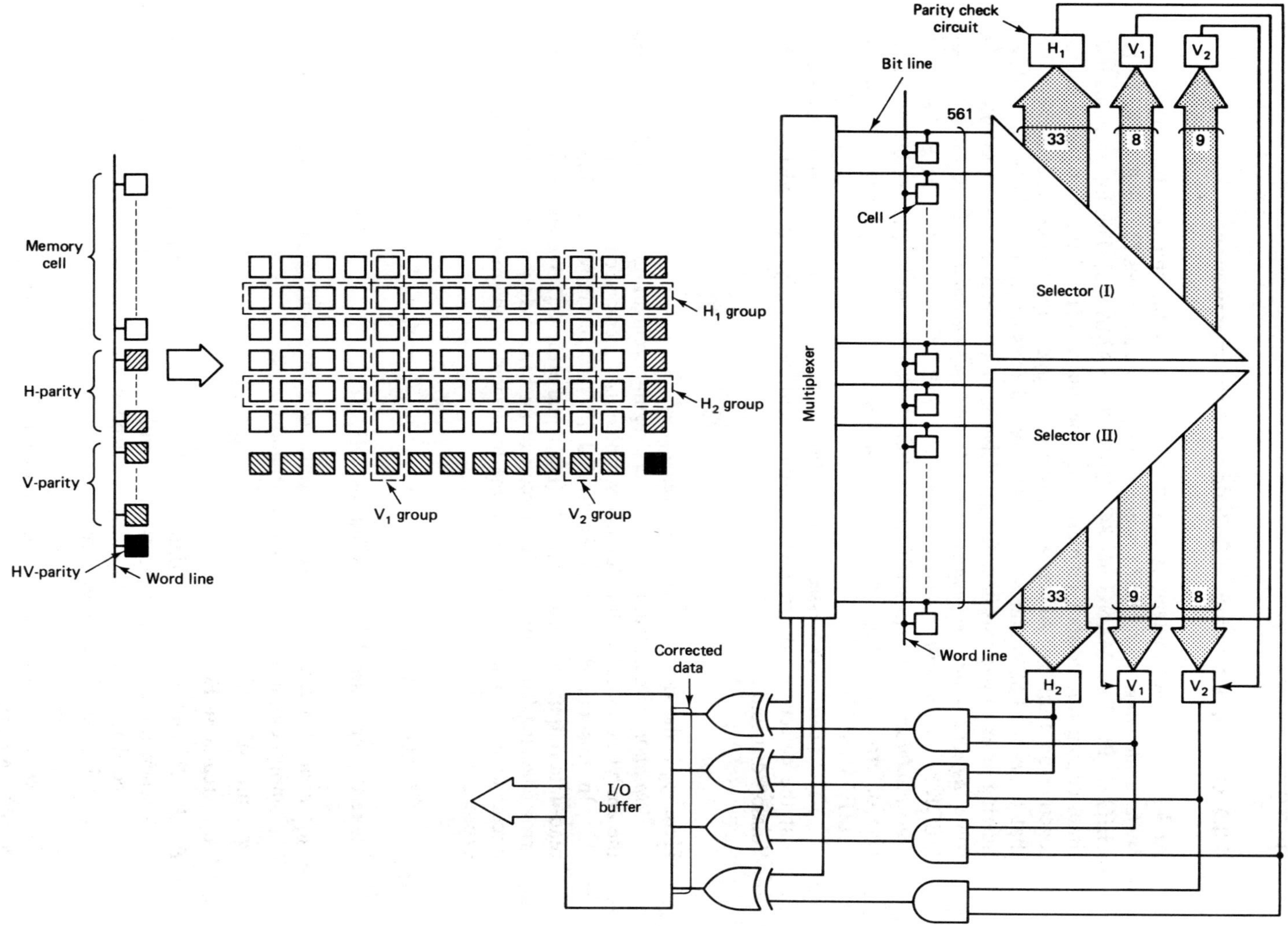

Figure 4.31 Schematic diagram and the logic diagram of a 4-bit byte ECC circuit [YAMA 84].

decodable codes [TANN 84] derived from a class known as *projective geometry codes* [PETE 72].

4.3.2 On-Chip Hamming SEC Code for Yield Improvement

As VLSI technology advances to very high densities, the chip also becomes larger. *Wafer scale integration* (*WSI*) is one of the recent advances in this field [KITA 80, LEIG 82, PELT 83, MANG 84a, 84b, CARL 86, YAMA 87a]. This integration sometimes contains processors, memories, and peripheral control functions all mounted together on a full-size silicon wafer, one very large chip. Therefore, it is inevitable that large-size LSI contains process-induced defects, such as pinholes in oxide or missing or extra patterns in diffusion, polysilicon, or metal [STAP 80, 83]. Recently, some *defect-tolerant techniques* (e.g., *N-modular redundancy* (*NMR*) [KITA 80, UEOK 84], *m-out-of-n modular redundancy* [SMIT 81, MANO 82, MOOR 86], *address reallocation techniques* [BEAU 73, EGAW 80], and so forth, have been studied. Use of error correcting codes is also a good candidate for yield improvement [CLIF 74, MATS 88].

Yield can be expressed as a function of circuit area, a (i.e., $y(a)$) assuming that the defects are distributed randomly, and hence they are modeled using the Poisson distribution.*

$$y(a) = y_0^{a/a_0}$$

Here, y_0 is the yield for a specific area a_0.

Memory circuit features are of very regular configuration. Fig. 4.32 illustrates the analytical model with redundancy, which uses memory circuit features.

In this model, memory is divided into $l \times n$ units, each having one-bit read-data output and equal capacity (i.e., equal area, a_m). We also assume that the error checking/correcting (ECC) circuit of an SEC code is implemented by some circuit area, a_t. Under this model, the total yield of this memory module can be expressed as

$$Y = y(a_t)\left\{n(y(a_m))^{n-1}(1 - y(a_c)) + (P_0 + P_x + P_y + P_{xy})(y(a_c))^n\right\}^l$$

where the terms are defined as follows [OHNI 81].

a_c: area of a circuit that is commonly used in a unit, such as address buffer, input–output data control circuit, and the like.

a_m: area of a unit.

a_t: area of an ECC circuit.

P_0, P_x, P_y, and P_{xy}: probabilities of tolerable defects in every memory cell array when no defect exists in both X and Y decoders, when defects exist in X decoder, when defects exist in Y decoder, and when defects exist in both X and Y decoders, respectively.

*Negative binomial statistics are proposed to be better suited for large chips or wafers [STAP 83, 84, 85, 86].

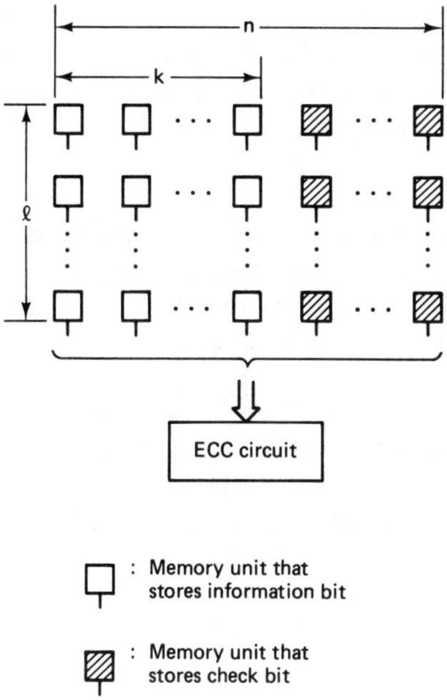

Figure 4.32 Memory models using an (n, k) code.

In this memory model, we have to give careful attention to the percentage in chip area of the ECC portion of the circuit. This is especially so if the area of the ECC circuit is a large portion; then it has a rather negative effect on yield improvement. This is because defects in this area are not tolerated at all.

One good example is an application of the Hamming SEC code to the 1 megabit ROM chip [SHIN 83, DAVI 85]. This ROM has a 128K-word × 8-bit organization [SHIN 83]. Fig. 4.33 shows an ECC circuit of the (38, 32) Hamming SEC code.

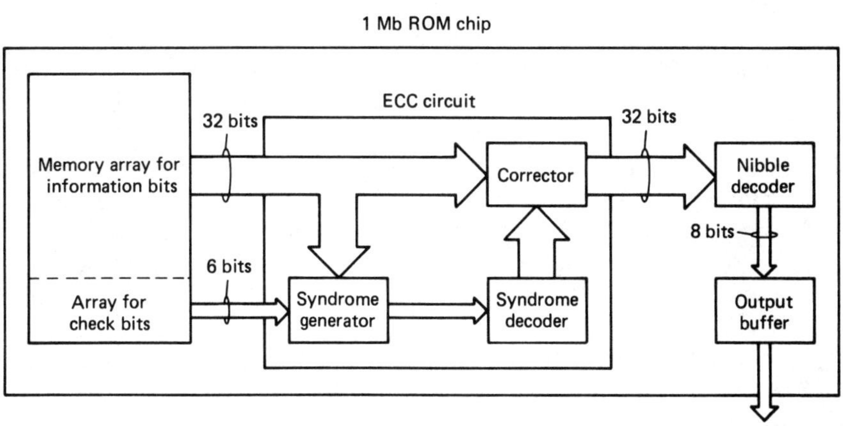

Figure 4.33 An on-chip ECC circuit.

The total 38-bit word, consisting of 32 information bits and 6 check bits, is simultaneously read out from the ROM and is entered into the ECC circuit. The corrected 32 information bits are transferred to a nibble decoder and divided into four blocks. The output buffer drives 8 bits. The ECC circuit consumes less than 20% of the total chip area. Even though it increases chip area, the theoretical yield can be enhanced by a factor of 3 at about 2.5 particles/cm^2 defect density.

As the number of data bits read out in one cycle increases, the area for the ECC circuit also increases, whereas the ratio of the number of check bits to the total word length decreases. In order to minimize chip area, an information length of 32 bits is required according to [SHIN 83]. The rate of the access time increased by the ECC circuit is less than 15%.

Another example is also an application of the Hamming SEC code to a 64K-bit CMOS *Electrically Erasable Read Only Memory* (*EEROM*) [MEHR 84]. In this 8K-word × 8-bit EEROM, a (12, 8) Hamming SEC code is implemented. It corrects all single-bit errors in the data readout from the memory cells. In this example, the ECC circuit increases the propagation delay by 15 ns in a typical 100 ns access time of the chip and occupies approximately 20% of the chip area.

4.4 CODE DESIGN TECHNIQUES FOR HIGH-SPEED MEMORIES

Most of the codes for high-speed memories are *shortened codes*, in that the code length is less than the maximum for a given number of check bits. This is because the information-bit length (k) for most high-speed memories is less than 150 bits, and these lengths are rather short compared to the codes for mass memories. There are various ways of shortening a maximum-length memory code. Usually a code designer constructs a shortened code to meet certain objectives for a particular application. These objectives may include the minimization of a number of factors —the number of circuits, the decoding circuit delay, or the probability of miscorrecting multiple errors—or the modular construction of an encoding/decoding circuit suitable for LSI implementation.

In this section, some practical code-design techniques are discussed using these concepts. It is important that these techniques can be adopted to any memory codes, such as SEC–DED codes, SEC–DED–SbED codes, SbEC–DbED codes, and so on.

Some of the code design techniques have already been mentioned, such as the minimum-equal-weight code and the odd-weight-column code (e.g., the Hsiao code in Section 4.1.1). These techniques can sometimes be combined; for example, the condition for an odd-weight-column code can be combined with that for a rotational code, and the resultant code will be called a rotational odd-weight-column code.

Here, we summarize and generalize those techniques already mentioned, and we introduce new design techniques, such as the even/odd-weight-row code and the rotational code.

4.4.1 Minimum-Equal-Weight Code

From some decoding circuit examples (e.g., Fig. 4.1 in Example 4.1), it can be easily understood that fewer 1's in the **H** matrix means fewer modulo-2 additions (i.e., faster encoding/decoding). Fewer gates also means lower cost and more reliable hardware. Therefore, the selection of the **H** matrix for a given (n, k) code is based on the following constraints [HSIA 70a].

1. The total number of 1's in the **H** matrix should be minimum.
2. The number of 1's in each row of the **H** matrix should be made equal, or as close as possible, to the average number (i.e., the total number of 1's in **H** divided by the number of rows).

Definition 4-4. A *minimum-equal-weight code* is a code that has the minimum-weight in the **H** matrix and in which the number of 1's in each row of **H** is equal, or as close as possible, to the average number.

4.4.2 Generalized Odd-Weight-Column Code

Let **H** be the **H** matrix of an (n, k) code over $GF(2^b)$. **H** is an $(r \times n)$ matrix over $GF(2^b)$. A generalization of the previously given binary odd-weight-column code is as follows [FUJI 78, 81a].

Definition 4-5. If the **H** matrix of code **C** over $GF(2^b)$ satisfies the condition (4.14) for every column in the **H** matrix, then **C** is called a *generalized odd-weight-column code.*

$$\sum_{i=0}^{r-1} h_{i,j} = I, \qquad \text{for columns } j = 0, 1, \ldots, n-1 \tag{4.14}$$

where

$h_{i,j}$: ith element in the jth column vector $\in GF(2^b)$

I: Identity element in $GF(2^b)$

$\sum$: Summation in $GF(2^b)$

To convert the (n, k) code over $GF(2^b)$ to binary form, we replace each element of $GF(2^b)$ in **H** to a corresponding $(b \times b)$ matrix over $GF(2)$. Then this binary **H** matrix is $(R \times N)$, where $R = b \cdot r$ and $N = b \cdot n$.

Theorem 4-3. *If the* **H** *matrix of a code over* $GF(2^b)$ *satisfies Equation* (4.14), *then its corresponding binary converted form of matrix is an odd-weight-column matrix over the binary field.*

In other words, if **H** *is a* $(r \times n)$ *generalized-odd-weight-column matrix over* $GF(2^b)$, *then the binary conversion of* **H** *will yield a* $(R \times N)$ *binary odd-weight-column matrix.*

Proof. Let $h_{i,j}$ be the ith row and the jth column element of the $(r \times n)$ **H** matrix over $GF(2^b)$, where $0 \le i \le r-1$, $0 \le j \le n-1$. Every element of $GF(2^b)$ can be expressed by a $(b \times b)$ binary matrix, called its *companion matrix*, as further explained in Chapter 5. In particular, identity element **I** of $GF(2^b)$ is equivalent to the $(b \times b)$ identity matrix. Now let $\mathbf{h}_{i,j}$ be shown as the following $(b \times b)$ matrix.

$$\mathbf{h}_{i,j} = \begin{bmatrix} (a_{0,0})_i & \cdots & (a_{0,l})_i & \cdots & (a_{0,b-1})_i \\ & & (a_{1,l})_i & & \\ \vdots & & \vdots & & \vdots \\ & \cdots & (a_{l,l})_i & \cdots & \\ \vdots & & \vdots & & \\ (a_{b-1,0})_i & \cdots & (a_{b-1,l})_i & \cdots & (a_{b-1,b-1})_i \end{bmatrix}_{b \times b}$$

$$\{(a_{0,l})_i, (a_{1,l})_i, \ldots, (a_{l,l})_i, \ldots, (a_{b-1,l})_i\} \in GF(2)$$
$$0 \le l \le b-1, 0 \le i \le r-1$$

From Equation (4.14), the following relation can be obtained for $0 \le l \le b-1$.

$$\sum_{i=0}^{r-1}{}^{\oplus} (a_{l,l})_i = 1, \qquad \sum{}^{\oplus} : \textit{mod 2 sum}$$

This shows that the modulo-2 sum of the corresponding diagonal elements in the binary square matrices $\mathbf{h}_{i,j}$'s is equal to 1 of the corresponding element in the identity matrix **I**. Thus, the binary represented set $\{(a_{l,l})_0, (a_{l,l})_1, \ldots, (a_{l,l})_{r-1}\}$ has an odd number of 1's (i.e., it is odd weight).

On the other hand, the following relation holds for $0 \le m \ne l \le b-1$.

$$\sum_{i=0}^{r-1}{}^{\oplus} (a_{m,l})_i = 0$$

This shows that the modulo-2 sum of the corresponding nondiagonal elements in the binary square matrices $\mathbf{h}_{i,j}$'s is equal to 0 of the corresponding element in the identity matrix **I**. Thus, the binary represented set $\{(a_{m,l})_0, (a_{m,l})_1, \ldots, (a_{m,l})_{r-1}\}$, where $m \ne l$, has an even number of 1's (i.e., it is even weight). As a result, the foregoing equations give the following relation.

$$\sum_{i=0}^{r-1}{}^{\oplus} \sum_{m=0}^{b-1}{}^{\oplus} (a_{m,l})_i = 1$$

This shows that the lth column vector of the binary **H** matrix is of odd weight.

These relations hold for any integer l and j. Hence, every column vector of the binary **H** matrix that satisfies Equation (4.14) is of odd weight. Q.E.D.

The odd-weight-column code gives good discrimination of even number and odd number of errors. Therefore, it gives better multiple-error detection capability than the non-odd-weight-column code, as shown in Table 4.2 and Table 5.1 [HSIA 70a, FUJI 78].

4.4.3 Even / Odd-Weight-Row Code

The **H** matrix can also be expressed as r row vectors as follows.

$$\mathbf{H} = \begin{bmatrix} P_0 \\ P_1 \\ \vdots \\ P_{r-1} \end{bmatrix}$$

Definition 4-6. If each row vector $P_i = (h_{i,0}, \ldots, h_{i,n-1})$ of the **H** matrix of code **C** satisfies Equation (4.15), then **C** is called an *even-weight-row code*.

$$\sum_{j=0}^{n-1} h_{i,j} = 0, \qquad \text{for rows } i = 0, 1, \ldots, r-1 \tag{4.15}$$

Here, notations express the following.

$h_{i,j}$: jth element in the ith row vector $\in GF(2^b)$
0: Zero element in $GF(2^b)$
$\sum$: Summation in $GF(2^b)$

Similarly to Theorem 4-3, it can be easily proved that the code satisfying Equation (4.15) has all even-weight rows in the binary form of **H**. This code has an important characteristic, given as follows.

Definition 4-7. For every codeword W of code **C**, if its bitwise complement $\overline{W}$ is also in **C**, then **C** is called a *self-complementing code*.

Theorem 4-4. *Every even-weight-row code* **C** *is a self-complementing code.*

Proof. Let the codeword W of code **C** be expressed as

$$W = [D, P] = [d_0, d_1, \ldots, d_{k-1}, p_0, p_1, \ldots, p_{r-1}]$$

where $D = (d_0, d_1, \ldots, d_{k-1})$ is an information part, and $P = (p_0, p_1, \ldots, p_{r-1})$ is a check part. In addition, let the **H** matrix be expressed as $\mathbf{H} = [\mathbf{H}', \ \mathbf{I}]$, where $\mathbf{H}'$ is an $(r \times k)$ information part of **H**, and **I** is an $(r \times r)$ binary identity matrix for the check part of **H**. Clearly, **H**′ has odd-weight row vectors, $h'_0, h'_1, \ldots, h'_{r-1}$. Therefore, each check bit can be obtained by the following relation:

$$p_i = (d_0, d_1, \ldots, d_{k-1}) \cdot (h'_i)^T, \qquad 0 \le i \le r-1$$

Let the bitwise complement of W be $\overline{W} = [\overline{d_0}, \overline{d_1}, \ldots, \overline{d_{k-1}}, \overline{c_0}, \ldots, \overline{c_{r-1}}] = [\overline{D}, \overline{P}]$. For $\overline{D} = (\overline{d_0}, \overline{d_1}, \ldots, \overline{d_{k-1}})$, the following relation always holds because every row vector h'_i is of odd weight.

$$\left(\overline{d_0}, \overline{d_1}, \ldots, \overline{d_{k-1}}\right) \cdot (h'_i)^T = \overline{p_i} \qquad 0 \le i \le r-1$$

This means that $\overline{D} \cdot H'^T = \overline{P}$, and hence the code is self-complementing. Q.E.D.

By making use of the above characteristic of the even-weight-row code, an SEC–DED code satisfying the even-weight-row condition can be useful for *mask error correction* of double errors in memory words [SUND 78, 79, WALK 79, AICH 84 (see Example 4.2)]. This can also be applied to memory testing because it allows use of small test-access numbers to the memory unit being tested (see Section 4.5). Another application is a mask error correction in logic circuits, which is called *alternate data retry* [YAMA 70, SHED 78].

Several well-known codes, such as m-out-of-$2m$ codes, complemented duplication codes, residue codes with checkbase $2^a - 1$ (low-cost residue codes), and self-complementing $AN + B$ codes (e.g., $3N + 2$ code [BROW 60, RAO 74]) also satisfy the condition that the bitwise complement of the codeword is also a codeword.

Corollary 4-1. *If the* **H** *matrix of a code* **C** *satisfies both odd-weight-column and even-weight-row conditions, then the code length of* **C** *is even.*

Also, we consider codes whose rows (of **H** matrix) are of odd weight. These codes satisfy the following.

Theorem 4-5. *For a codeword* $W = [D, P]$ *of an odd-weight-row code* **C**, *where D is the information part and P is the check part as before,* $W' = [\overline{D}, P]$ *is also a codeword of* **C**.

The proof is similar to the previous one, and hence it is omitted.

An odd-weight-column and odd-weight-row SEC–DED code, called a *Maintenance code* (*M code*), is shown to be useful for mask error correction in memory units [CART 76].

Example 4-8

As for an even-weight-row code whose **H** matrix row vector is of even weight, let's consider the following simple code example.

$$\mathbf{H} = \begin{bmatrix} 1\,0\,1\,1 & 1\,0\,0\,0 \\ 1\,1\,0\,1 & 0\,1\,0\,0 \\ 1\,1\,1\,0 & 0\,0\,1\,0 \\ 0\,1\,1\,1 & 0\,0\,0\,1 \end{bmatrix}$$

All row vectors have even-weight 4. The codeword $W = [D, P]$ is shown as follows. There exist 16 codewords.

$$W = [D, P]$$

$$= \left[\begin{array}{cc}
0\,0\,0\,0 & 0\,0\,0\,0 \\
1\,0\,0\,0 & 1\,1\,1\,0 \\
0\,1\,0\,0 & 0\,1\,1\,1 \\
1\,1\,0\,0 & 1\,0\,0\,1 \\
0\,0\,1\,0 & 1\,0\,1\,1 \\
1\,0\,1\,0 & 0\,1\,0\,1 \\
0\,1\,1\,0 & 1\,1\,0\,0 \\
1\,1\,1\,0 & 0\,0\,1\,0 \\
\hdashline
0\,0\,0\,1 & 1\,1\,0\,1 \\
1\,0\,0\,1 & 0\,0\,1\,1 \\
0\,1\,0\,1 & 1\,0\,1\,0 \\
1\,1\,0\,1 & 0\,1\,0\,0 \\
0\,0\,1\,1 & 0\,1\,1\,0 \\
1\,0\,1\,1 & 1\,0\,0\,0 \\
0\,1\,1\,1 & 0\,0\,0\,1 \\
1\,1\,1\,1 & 1\,1\,1\,1
\end{array}\right] \begin{array}{c} \uparrow \\ \cdots \\ \downarrow \end{array}$$

These codewords are self-complementary, as can be seen.

As for an odd-weight-row code, let's consider the code with its **H** matrix as follows.

$$\mathbf{H} = \left[\begin{array}{cc}
1\,0\,0\,1\,1\,1 & 1\,0\,0\,0\,0 \\
1\,0\,1\,0\,1\,1 & 0\,1\,0\,0\,0 \\
1\,1\,0\,1\,0\,1 & 0\,0\,1\,0\,0 \\
0\,1\,1\,0\,1\,1 & 0\,0\,0\,1\,0 \\
0\,1\,1\,1\,0\,1 & 0\,0\,0\,0\,1
\end{array}\right]$$

$$\begin{array}{c}\text{Codewords}\\
\left[\begin{array}{cc}
0\,0\,0\,0\,0\,0 & 0\,0\,0\,0\,0 \\
1\,0\,0\,0\,0\,0 & 1\,1\,1\,0\,0 \\
0\,1\,0\,0\,0\,0 & 0\,0\,1\,1\,1 \\
1\,1\,0\,0\,0\,0 & 1\,1\,0\,1\,1 \\
0\,0\,1\,0\,0\,0 & 0\,1\,0\,1\,1 \\
1\,0\,1\,0\,0\,0 & 1\,0\,1\,1\,1 \\
0\,1\,1\,0\,0\,0 & 0\,1\,1\,0\,0 \\
1\,1\,1\,0\,0\,0 & 1\,0\,0\,0\,0 \\
0\,0\,0\,1\,0\,0 & 1\,0\,1\,0\,0 \\
1\,0\,0\,1\,0\,0 & 0\,1\,0\,0\,1 \\
\vdots & \vdots
\end{array}\right]\\
D \qquad\qquad P
\end{array}
\Longleftrightarrow
\begin{array}{c}\text{Codewords}\\
\left[\begin{array}{cc}
1\,1\,1\,1\,1\,1 & 0\,0\,0\,0\,0 \\
0\,1\,1\,1\,1\,1 & 1\,1\,1\,0\,0 \\
1\,0\,1\,1\,1\,1 & 0\,0\,1\,1\,1 \\
0\,0\,1\,1\,1\,1 & 1\,1\,0\,1\,1 \\
1\,1\,0\,1\,1\,1 & 0\,1\,0\,1\,1 \\
0\,1\,0\,1\,1\,1 & 1\,0\,1\,1\,1 \\
1\,0\,0\,1\,1\,1 & 0\,1\,1\,0\,0 \\
0\,0\,0\,1\,1\,1 & 1\,0\,0\,0\,0 \\
1\,1\,1\,0\,1\,1 & 1\,0\,1\,0\,0 \\
0\,1\,1\,0\,1\,1 & 0\,1\,0\,0\,1 \\
\vdots & \vdots
\end{array}\right]\\
\bar{D} \qquad\qquad P
\end{array}$$

For these codewords, check bits remain the same if the information part is bitwise complemented.

4.4.4 Rotational Code [CART 73, BOSS 74, FUJI 77a]

Definition 4-8. A code whose **H** matrix has the following d submatrices is called a *rotational code*. In this case, d is a divisor of r and of n.

$$\mathbf{H} = \left[\mathbf{H}_0|\mathbf{H}_1| \cdots |\mathbf{H}_j| \cdots |\mathbf{H}_{d-1}\right]_{r\times n}$$
$$\mathbf{H}_j = \mathbf{R}^j \cdot \mathbf{H}_0, \qquad j = 1,2,\ldots, d-1 \tag{4.16}$$

$\mathbf{R} =$

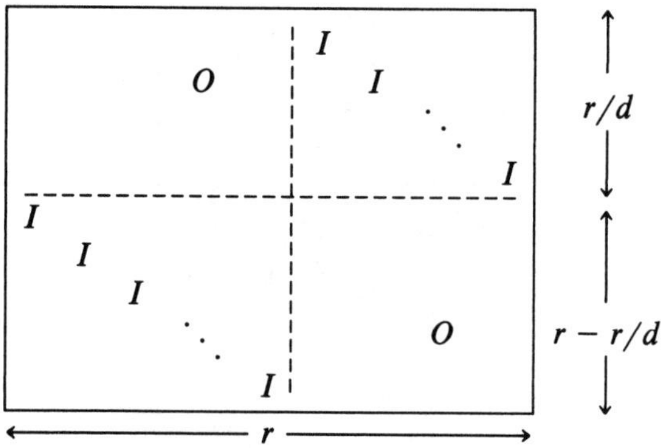

$\{O, I\} \in GF(2^b)$

In this definition, $\mathbf{H}_0$ and **R** are called the *generating submatrix* and *rotational operating matrix*, respectively. The **H** matrix design of rotational codes is such as to give r/d cyclic shifts of rows in a vertical direction between adjacent submatrices.

The unique feature of the rotational code is that its encoding/decoding circuit can be implemented with d identical subcircuits specified by the generating submatrix $\mathbf{H}_0$, each by simply altering the input/output connections [CART 73, BOSS 74, FUJI 77a]. Therefore, the rotational code gives a modularized encoding/decoding circuit, suitable for LSI implementation [FUJI 80b].

In order to understand the concept of rotational code, a simple example is presented here.

Example 4-9

The code with an **H** matrix given in Example 4-1 can be made rotational by permuting its column vectors, as shown below. In this case, d is equal to r. Fig. 4.34 shows the modularized decoding circuit defined by $\mathbf{H}'$.

$$\mathbf{H}' = \begin{array}{c} \begin{array}{cccccccc} d_0 & c_0 & d_3 & c_1 & d_2 & c_2 & d_1 & c_3 \end{array} \\ \left[\begin{array}{cccccccc} 1 & 1 & 0 & 0 & 1 & 0 & 1 & 0 \\ 1 & 0 & 1 & 1 & 0 & 0 & 1 & 0 \\ 1 & 0 & 1 & 0 & 1 & 1 & 0 & 0 \\ 0 & 0 & 1 & 0 & 1 & 0 & 1 & 1 \end{array}\right] \\ \begin{array}{cccc} \mathbf{H}_0 & \mathbf{H}_1 & \mathbf{H}_2 & \mathbf{H}_3 \end{array} \end{array} \qquad \mathbf{H}_0 = \begin{bmatrix} 1 & 1 \\ 1 & 0 \\ 1 & 0 \\ 0 & 0 \end{bmatrix}$$

$$\{0,1\} \in GF(2)$$

$$\mathbf{H}_j = \mathbf{R}^j \cdot \mathbf{H}_0, \qquad j = 1, 2, 3, \qquad \mathbf{R} = \begin{bmatrix} 0 & 0 & 0 & 1 \\ 1 & 0 & 0 & 0 \\ 0 & 1 & 0 & 0 \\ 0 & 0 & 1 & 0 \end{bmatrix}$$

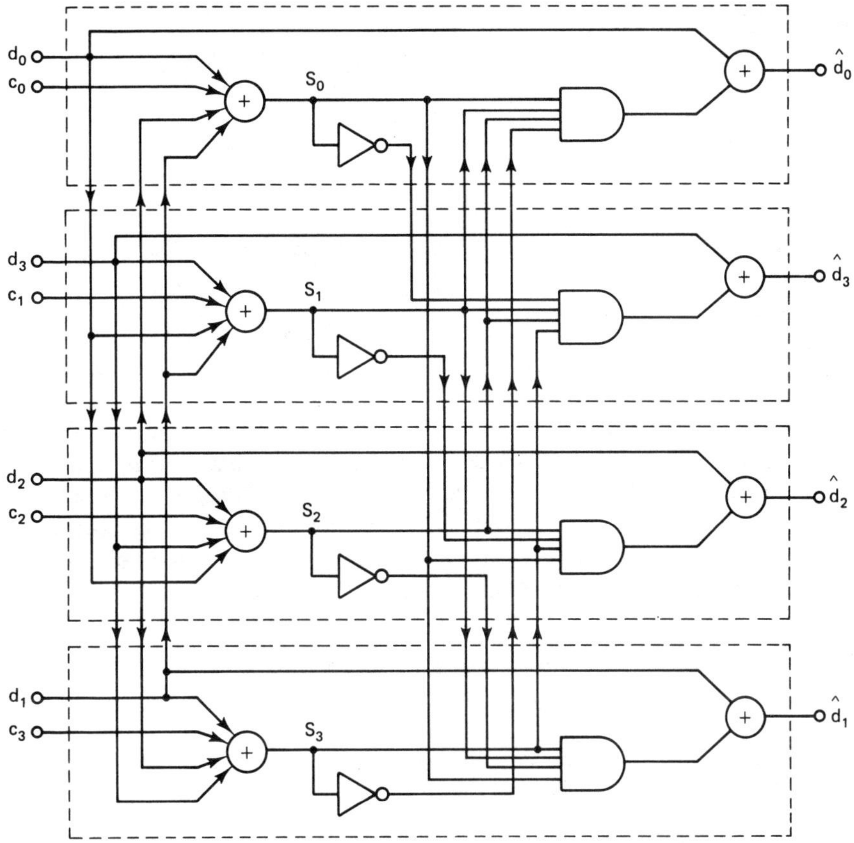

Figure 4.34 Modularized decoding circuit for rotational code **H′**.

In Fig. 4.34, four identical subcircuits, each having seven inputs and four outputs including signals communicating with other subcircuits, and also having a four-input parity checker, an inverter, a four-input AND gate, and an exclusive-or gate, give the whole decoding circuit specified by the rotational (8, 4) SEC–DED code. The modularity is the main feature of this decoder.

Now let's consider the maximal code length of a rotational code. As a simple example, we deal with a rotational single-bit error correcting (SEC) code. Other rotational memory codes (e.g., rotational SbEC codes, rotational SbEC–DbED codes, and so on) are given in Chapter 5.

Definition 4-9. Let the ith cyclic shift of a vector $H = (h_0, h_1, \ldots, h_{r-1})$ be denoted by

$$H^{(i)} = (h_i, h_{i+1}, \ldots, h_{r-1}, h_0, \ldots, h_{i-1})$$

A set of all distinct vectors obtained by cyclic shifts of a vector is called a *cyclic equivalence class*.

Example 4-10

The cyclic equivalence classes of binary 4-tuples sequences are as follows.

$$E_1 = \{0000\}$$
$$E_2 = \{1111\}$$
$$E_3 = \{1010, 0101\}$$
$$E_4 = \{0001, 0010, 0100, 1000\}$$
$$E_5 = \{0011, 0110, 1100, 1001\}$$
$$E_6 = \{0111, 1110, 1101, 1011\}$$

Each cyclic equivalence class (of r-tuples) will have m vectors, where m is a divisor of r. If $m \neq r$ for any class, then it is called a *degenerate equivalence class*. In the above example, E_1, E_2, and E_3 are degenerate cyclic equivalence classes, whereas E_4, E_5, and E_6 are *nondegenerate cyclic equivalence classes*.

In general, for r and q-ary sequence, the number of nondegenerate cyclic equivalence classes, $N_q(r)$, is given as follows [GOLO 58].

$$N_q(r) = \frac{1}{r} \sum_{m|r} \mu(m) \cdot q^{r/m} \tag{4.17}$$

Here, $\Sigma_{m|r}$ expresses the summation over all m that divide r, and $\mu(m)$ is the *Möbius function* [PETE 72] defined as

$$\begin{aligned} \mu(m) &= 1; \quad m = 1 \\ &= 0; \quad m \text{ has any square factor} \\ &= (-1)^l; \quad m = p_1 p_2 \dots p_l, \text{ where the } p_i\text{'s are distinct primes.} \end{aligned}$$

The values of $\mu(m)$ for $m = 1$ to 15 is shown in Table 4.5.

Table 4.6 shows $N_2(r)$, (i.e., the number of nondegenerate cyclic equivalence classes for binary r-tuples).

TABLE 4.5 MÖBIUS FUNCTION

m	1	2	3	4	5	6	7	8	9	10	11	12	13	14	15
$\mu(m)$	1	−1	−1	0	−1	1	−1	0	0	1	−1	0	−1	1	1

TABLE 4.6 NUMBER OF NONDEGENERATE CYCLIC EQUIVALENCE CLASSES, $N_2(r)$

r	3	4	5	6	7	8	9	10	11	12	13	14	15	16
$N_2(r)$	2	3	6	9	18	30	56	99	186	335	630	1161	2182	4096

For Example 4-10, $N_2(4) = 3$. The **H** matrix of a rotational SEC code can be constructed by using the nondegenerate cyclic equivalence classes, as follows.

$$\mathbf{H} = \begin{array}{cccccccccccc} c_0 & d_0 & d_1 & c_1 & d_2 & d_3 & c_2 & d_4 & d_5 & c_3 & d_6 & d_7 \end{array}$$
$$\mathbf{H} = \left[\begin{array}{ccc|ccc|ccc|ccc} 1 & 1 & 1 & 0 & 0 & 0 & 0 & 0 & 1 & 0 & 1 & 1 \\ 0 & 1 & 1 & 1 & 1 & 1 & 0 & 0 & 0 & 0 & 0 & 1 \\ 0 & 0 & 1 & 0 & 1 & 1 & 1 & 1 & 1 & 0 & 0 & 0 \\ 0 & 0 & 0 & 0 & 0 & 1 & 0 & 1 & 1 & 1 & 1 & 1 \end{array}\right]$$
$$\qquad \mathbf{H}_0 \qquad\qquad \mathbf{H}_1 \qquad\qquad \mathbf{H}_2 \qquad\qquad \mathbf{H}_3$$

Here, we consider the code length of a rotational SEC code. Let the number of cyclic equivalence classes for a binary sequence having length m be $N_2(m)$, where m is a divisor of r.

In Example 4-10, we have $N_2(1) = 2$, $N_2(2) = 1$, and $N_2(4) = 3$. Therefore, the following relation is satisfied for the cyclic equivalence classes of binary 4-tuples.

$$1 \cdot N_2(1) + 2 \cdot N_2(2) + 4 \cdot N_2(4) = 2^4$$

In general, for binary r-tuples, the following relation holds.

$$2^r = \sum_{m|r} m \cdot N_2(m) \tag{4.18}$$

In order to obtain the code length of a rotational SEC code, we have to obtain the number of nondegenerate cyclic equivalence class, $N_2(r)$.

For functions f and g over integers m and r, we have the following.

Definition 4-10. If the following relation holds for an arbitrary positive integer r

$$f(r) = \sum_{m|r} g(m)$$

then $g(r)$ can be expressed by $f(r)$ as

$$g(r) = \sum_{m|r} \mu(m) \cdot f\left(\frac{r}{m}\right)$$

This inversion formula is called the *Möbius inversion formula*.

We can apply a Möbius inversion formula to Equation (4.18) and obtain the following equation.

$$N_2(r) = \frac{1}{r} \sum_{m|r} \mu(m) \cdot 2^{r/m}$$

This is equal to Equation (4.17) for $q = 2$. Therefore, the code length n of a

TABLE 4.7 CODE LENGTHS OF AN SEC CODE

r	$n_{\text{rotational}}$	$n_{\text{nonrotational}}$
3	6	7
4	12	15
5	30	31
6	54	63
7	126	127
8	240	255
9	504	511
10	990	1023
11	2046	2047
12	4020	4095

$$n_{\text{rotational}} = \sum_{m|r} \mu(m) \cdot 2^{r/m}$$

$$n_{\text{nonrotational}} = 2^r - 1$$

rotational SEC code can be expressed as

$$n = r \cdot N_2(r) = \sum_{m|r} \mu(m) \cdot 2^{r/m}$$

Table 4.7 shows the code length of this code as well as that of the ordinary nonrotational SEC code.

Since high-speed memory codes are shortened, a rotational code suits as well as a nonrotational code. Rotational code offers modularity in decoding and, hence, will be most practical for LSI/VLSI implementations [FUJI 80b].

4.5 TEST PATTERNS FOR SEMICONDUCTOR MEMORIES

Introduction. With the advent of megabit class, high-density RAMs, the time required for testing these RAMs or memory modules has become a crucial problem. For example, if we test 64K-bit, 256K-bit, and 1M-bit RAM chips using a test pattern generator based on, for example, N^2*-patterns* with 100 ns cycle time, testing time for these chips will be about 40 minutes, 11 hours, and 8 days, respectively.

Functional testing of memories comprises primarily read/write testing and address decoding testing. The data read/write test is a basic memory test used to check whether data 0 and 1 can be written in and read out from every memory cell. The address decoding test is also a basic test to check whether the data stored in a designated cell can be read or whether the data can be written in a designated cell by correct decoding of the address information. This address decoding test is important because it can check for decoder faults that sometimes activate multiple word lines (and hence access multiple cells simultaneously) or no word line (and hence access no cell). Such faults are caused not only by stuck faults but also by noise or electrical coupling of the lines in the decoder circuit. This test can also check for faults resulting from cell interference that causes the stored data to be changed by the data in the adjacent memory cell (called *data interference*) or by the access action to the other memory cells (called *access interference*). The faults based on the interference are sometimes caused by the electrical coupling between the word lines or the leakage current due to the PN junction fatigue of the MOS transistors. Thus these faults occur under some critical conditions, and so access sequence—that is, how cells are accessed by changing address sequence—is an important problem in this address decoding test. There have been many address decoding test patterns that are named after the address sequence. For example, the *walking pattern* and the *galloping pattern*, which are called *N^2-patterns*, whose testing time is proportional to the square of the memory capacity N, give precise access sequence and hence have an excellent fault detection capability. There are also the *N-patterns*, whose testing time is proportional to the memory capacity N, such as the *marching pattern* and the *checkerboard pattern*, which have a short testing time but do not always give a precise address sequencing test. Hence, there has been a requirement for such test patterns (for high-density and large-capacity memory chips) to have both the high-speed testing of N-pattern testing and the high-quality and a precise access sequence of N^2-pattern testing.

Various functional testing schemes have been proposed and used in industry [BREU 76]. Recently, built-in, compact testing schemes or test procedures for a class of pattern-sensitive faults have been presented in [HAYE 75, 80, THAT 77, SRIN 78, NAIR 78, SUK 80, 81, SETH 81, SUN 84, NICO 85b, SALU 85, KINO 86, MIUR 86, JAIN 86, and FUJI 88b].

Here, we introduce interesting test patterns based on the new concept that the *physical distance* between the designated tested cells and the other untested cells that can generate interference with the tested cells is related to the code distance between the tested cell address and the untested cell address [KISH 77, KNAI 77, ISHI 81]. And all memory cells are partitioned into some sets in which the distance between cell addresses is guaranteed to be greater than or equal to some fixed value. Then the cell included in one set is tested by storing a different data to that of adjacent cells included in the other sets. This testing concept gives the possibility for both high-speed testing and precise access sequence testing.

Fault classes and test patterns. Faults in a memory can be classified into the following three types:

1. *Cell-stuck faults.* With this type of fault, readout data from the specified cell is always stuck to whatever data is written in this cell. This type of fault includes sensing amplifier faults.

2. *Decoding faults.* Address information is always decoded, and hence only one word line is activated. The following three cases will be considered as due to faults in the decoding circuit: (a) nonselection faults, (b) erroneous selection faults, and (c) multiple selection faults.

3. *Interference between memory cells.* This memory fault occurs when stored data is changed by data interference or by access interference, as mentioned above. The influence of interference from near memory cells, and especially from adjacent memory cells, is considered to be strong.

Among these fault types, nonselection faults give the same results as the cell-stuck faults, that is, in these faults, the data cannot be written or read out. In the multiple selection faults, the readout data is equal to the logical-OR of the data from the correctly selected cell and the data from the erroneously selected cell, and hence the test pattern capable of detecting the multiple selection faults can also detect erroneous selection faults.

From this consideration, we will obtain the test patterns capable of detecting cell-stuck faults (Fc), multiple selection faults (Fs), and faults caused by data interference and access interference (called Fd and Fa, respectively).

Here, we define the *specified cells*, called SC, which are those being tested, and the *background cells*, called BG, which are cells other than those being tested. Furthermore, we define the following properties in the test patterns.

Property 1. There exists both write and read operations having data both 0 and 1 for every memory cell, and, further, there exists the sequence both from 0 to 1 and from 1 to 0 for write operations.

Property 2. The stored data in SC is opposite to that in BG.

Property 3. There exists a sequence of "write to SC → write to or read from BG → read from SC."

Property 4. In properties 2 and 3, all memory cells act as SC sequentially.

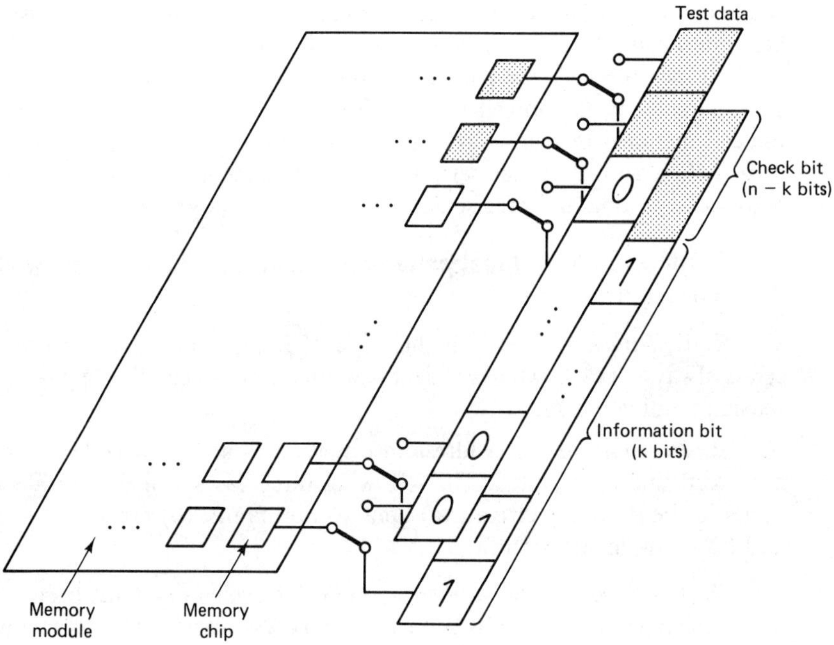

Figure 4.35 Memory module and test data.

Theorem 4-6 [ISHI 81]. *The test patterns having properties* 1, 2, 3, *and* 4 *can detect the faults Fc, Fs, Fd, and Fa.*

This theorem can be easily proved because property 1 can detect Fc; property 2, Fs and Fd; property 3, Fa; and property 4, Fs, Fd, and Fa for every memory cell.

Here, we have to refer to the test data that can test the memory modules using some error correcting/detecting code. Let the memory module use an (n, k) code, shown in Fig. 4.35. In general, a memory module is organized such that each bit position of the codeword is fed from a different chip and is quite often from a different array card. To test this memory module, we have to give such reciprocal two-test data as n-bit all 0's and n-bit all 1's. In this case, we have to pay attention to the check-bit patterns in the test data, that is, even if information bits in these two-test data are reciprocal, check bits are not always reciprocal. Therefore, we need to prepare one more test data, that is, a third test data, in order to test chips in which check bits are stored. According to Theorem 4-4, use of the even-weight-row code allows a complete test of the memory module using two-test data (see Section 4.4.3).

Example 4-11

Let the memory module use the following simple (12, 8) SEC code.

$$\begin{array}{cccccccccccccc} & d_0 & d_1 & d_2 & d_3 & d_4 & d_5 & d_6 & d_7 & & c_0 & c_1 & c_2 & c_3 \end{array}$$

$$\mathbf{H} = \begin{bmatrix} 1 & 1 & 0 & 1 & 1 & 1 & 0 & 0 & & 1 & 0 & 0 & 0 \\ 1 & 0 & 1 & 1 & 0 & 1 & 1 & 1 & & 0 & 1 & 0 & 0 \\ 0 & 1 & 1 & 1 & 1 & 0 & 0 & 1 & & 0 & 0 & 1 & 0 \\ 1 & 1 & 1 & 0 & 0 & 0 & 1 & 0 & & 0 & 0 & 0 & 1 \end{bmatrix}$$

$$W_0 = [0 \quad 0 \quad 0 \quad 0 \quad 0 \quad 0 \quad 0 \quad 0 \qquad 0 \quad 0 \quad 0 \quad 0]$$

$$W_1 = [1 \quad 1 \quad 1 \quad 1 \quad 1 \quad 1 \quad 1 \quad 1 \qquad 1 \quad 0 \quad 1 \quad 0]$$

For information parts of all 0 and all 1 data, the check parts are [0 0 0 0] and [1 0 1 0], respectively. Therefore, we do not have reciprocal data in c_1 and c_3, and hence we cannot test memory chips corresponding to c_1 and c_3. In order to solve this problem, we have to add one more test data, for example, W_2 to W_0 and W_1 as follows.

$$W_2 = [1 \quad 1 \quad 1 \quad 1 \quad 1 \quad 0 \quad 0 \quad 0 \qquad 0 \quad 1 \quad 0 \quad 1]$$

If we use the following even-weight-row (12, 8) SEC code, only two test data W_0' and W_1' will be sufficient.

$$\mathbf{H}' = \begin{bmatrix} 1 & 1 & 0 & 1 & 1 & 1 & 0 & 0 & & 1 & 0 & 0 & 0 \\ 1 & 0 & 1 & 1 & 0 & 1 & 1 & 0 & & 0 & 1 & 0 & 0 \\ 0 & 1 & 1 & 1 & 1 & 0 & 0 & 1 & & 0 & 0 & 1 & 0 \\ 1 & 1 & 1 & 0 & 0 & 0 & 1 & 1 & & 0 & 0 & 0 & 1 \end{bmatrix}$$

$$W_0' = [0 \quad 0 \quad 0 \quad 0 \quad 0 \quad 0 \quad 0 \quad 0 \qquad 0 \quad 0 \quad 0 \quad 0]$$

$$W_1' = [1 \quad 1 \quad 1 \quad 1 \quad 1 \quad 1 \quad 1 \quad 1 \qquad 1 \quad 1 \quad 1 \quad 1]$$

Next we consider the address test patterns in relation to the code distance of the address information.

4.5.1 Test Patterns Based on Hamming Distance [ISHI 81]

Definition 4-11. If the memory address subset M_i, $i = 0, 1, \ldots, t-1$, included in the whole memory address set M satisfies the following relation, each subset is called an *HD-d set*.

$$(1)\ M_0 \cup M_1 \cup M_2 \cup \ldots \cup M_{t-1} = M, \qquad M_i \cap M_j = \emptyset, \qquad 0 \le i \ne j \le t-1$$

$$(2)\ d_H(\mathbf{a}_l, \mathbf{a}_m) \ge d, \qquad \mathbf{a}_l, \mathbf{a}_m \in M_i\ (l \ne m, 0 \le i \le t-1)$$

Here, $d_H(\mathbf{a}_l, \mathbf{a}_m)$ means the Hamming distance between the addresses $\mathbf{a}_l$ and $\mathbf{a}_m$ included in a certain address subset.

Definition 4-12. Let $\mathbf{a}', \mathbf{a}'', \ldots,$ be multiple selected addresses caused by a multiple selection faults under the original address $\mathbf{a}$. If the maximum Hamming distance between the original address and the multiple selected addresses is equal to p, then these faults are called *distance-p multiple selection faults* (*distance-p Fs*).

Similarly, distance-p Fd, and distance-p Fa can be defined.

Theorem 4-7. *Let HD-d set act as SC. Then, the test pattern having properties* 2, 3, *and* 4 *can detect distance-*$(d-1)$ *multiple selection faults.*

Proof. Assume that the memory is accessed with an address $\mathbf{a}$ included in an HD-d set M_i. And assume that distance-l Fs exists, and hence there is an address $\mathbf{a}'$, which has Hamming distance between $\mathbf{a}'$ and $\mathbf{a}$ is l (i.e., $d_H(\mathbf{a}, \mathbf{a}') = l$). For the address $\mathbf{a}''$ included in M_i, $d_H(\mathbf{a}, \mathbf{a}'') \ge d$. Therefore, if $l \le d-1$, the cell having address $\mathbf{a}'$ is not included in M_i. The other cells that are also erroneously selected are not included in M_i. If M_i acts as SC, then the same data as that in SC are written in the erroneously selected cells that are included in BG. Then these faults can be detected. Q.E.D.

Corollary 4-2. *If the addresses included in an HD-d set are all odd weight or all even weight, the test pattern having properties* 2, 3, *and* 4 *can detect faults in the cells whose addresses have a distance-odd number between those included in an HD-d set and the erroneous ones.*

Proof. The weight of the erroneously selected address $\mathbf{a}'$ is different from that of the original address $\mathbf{a}$ such that if the former has even weight, the latter has odd weight, and vice versa. Therefore, $\mathbf{a}$ and $\mathbf{a}'$ are not included in the same HD-d set, and hence we can detect the erroneously selected address $\mathbf{a}'$. Q.E.D.

Next, we consider how to construct HD-d sets.

	Coset leaders							
M_0	000 000	001 011	010 110	011 101	100 101	101 110	110 011	111 000
M_1	000 001	001 010	010 111	011 100	100 100	101 111	110 010	111 001
M_2	000 010	001 001	010 100	011 111	100 111	101 100	110 001	111 010
M_3	000 011	001 000	010 101	011 110	100 110	101 101	110 000	111 011
M_4	000 100	001 111	010 010	011 001	100 001	101 010	110 111	111 100
M_5	000 101	001 110	010 011	011 000	100 000	101 011	110 110	111 101
M_6	000 110	001 101	010 000	011 011	100 011	101 000	110 101	111 110
M_7	000 111	001 100	010 001	011 010	100 010	101 001	110 100	111 111

Figure 4.36 HD-3 sets M_0 to M_7 based on the Hamming (6, 3) SEC code.

Theorem 4-8. *In the* $(2^{n-k} \times 2^k)$ *standard array (see Chapter 3) made from the* (n, k) *linear code having minimum distance d, each coset having* 2^k *vectors is an HD-d set. Each coset is called a coset code (see Section 3.1).*

This theorem can be easily proved, in that every coset of an (n, k, d) code is a coset code of distance d, and therefore each coset of the standard array is an HD-d set.

Example 4-12

Let's construct the HD-3 sets by using the (6, 3) Hamming SEC code (distance-3 code) defined by the following **H** matrix:

$$\mathbf{H} = \begin{bmatrix} 1 & 1 & 0 & 1 & 0 & 0 \\ 0 & 1 & 1 & 0 & 1 & 0 \\ 1 & 0 & 1 & 0 & 0 & 1 \end{bmatrix}$$

Fig. 4.36 shows the HD-3 sets based on the Theorem 4-8. In this standard array, those coset leaders are selected whose first 3 bits are all 0's and whose lower 3 bits are distinct patterns.

By using the HD-d set, we present the new test sequence shown in Fig. 4.37. In this test, access sequence in M_i is arbitrary. These test sequences are called the *HD-d test pattern*.

Theorem 4-9. *The HD-d test pattern can detect faults of Fc, Fs, Fd, and Fa.*

Proof. These test patterns can be shown to satisfy properties 1 to 4. Hence, from Theorems 4-6 and 4-7, these can detect Fc, distance-$(d-1)$ Fs, Fd, and Fa.

Q.E.D.

Fig. 4.38 shows a test sequence based on the HD-3 sets in Fig. 4.36. Here, 0w and 1w represent 0 and 1 write operations to all cells in the set, respectively. Also, 0R and 1R represent 0 and 1 read and check operations, respectively, and 1R/0w represents 0w after 1R. The test is performed from the top of the leftmost column to the bottom of the rightmost column, that is, from sequence 1 to sequence 10 in Figure 4.38.

Fig. 4.39 shows the HD-d test pattern generator based on Theorem 4-8.

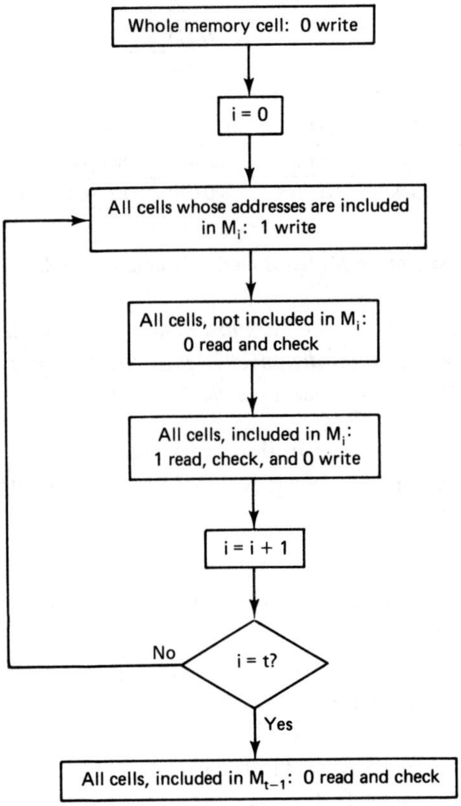

Figure 4.37 Test sequences.

Set \ Sequence	1	2	3	4	5	6	7	8	9	10
M_0	0_W	1_W	$1_R/0_W$	0_R	0_R	0_R	0_R	0_R	0_R	0_R
M_1	0_W	0_R	1_W	$1_R/0_W$	0_R	0_R	0_R	0_R	0_R	0_R
M_2	0_W	0_R	0_R	1_W	$1_R/0_W$	0_R	0_R	0_R	0_R	0_R
M_3	0_W	0_R	0_R	0_R	1_W	$1_R/0_W$	0_R	0_R	0_R	0_R
M_4	0_W	0_R	0_R	0_R	0_R	1_W	$1_R/0_W$	0_R	0_R	0_R
M_5	0_W	0_R	0_R	0_R	0_R	0_R	1_W	$1_R/0_W$	0_R	0_R
M_6	0_W	0_R	0_R	0_R	0_R	0_R	0_R	1_W	$1_R/0_W$	0_R
M_7	0_W	0_R	0_R	0_R	0_R	0_R	0_R	0_R	1_W	$1_R/0_W/0_R$

Figure 4.38 Test sequence of the HD-3 pattern [ISHI 81]. © 1981 IECE Japan.

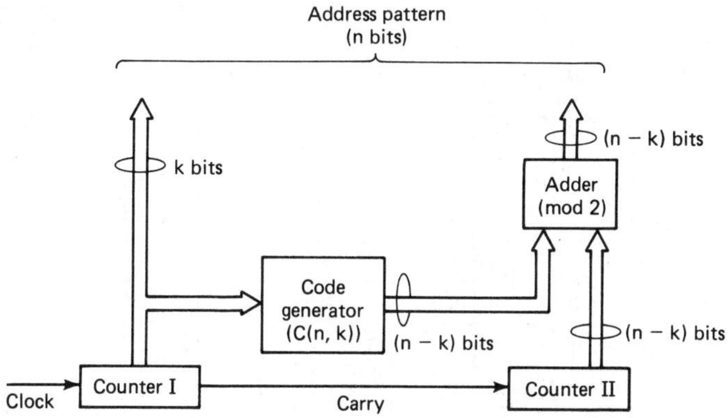

Figure 4.39 HD-*d* pattern generator [ISHI 81]. © 1981 IEEE Japan.

Definition 4-13. The *physical distance* d_p between the memory cell $m_{i,j}$ (ith row, jth column cell) and the memory cell $m_{i',j'}$ (i'th row, j'th column cell) is defined as $d_p = |i - i'| + |j - j'|$.

Theorem 4-10. *Let the Hamming-distance d_H between addresses of the adjacent rows and also between addresses of the adjacent columns always be* 1. *In such a memory, the physical distance between the memory cells included in HD-d set is greater than or equal to d.*

Proof. Let the lth row address be $\mathbf{a}_l$, and let $\mathbf{e}_i$ denote the vector that has only one 1 in the ith bit. Then, we have the following.

$$\begin{aligned} d_H(\mathbf{a}_l, \mathbf{a}_{l+1}) &= d_H(\mathbf{a}_l, \mathbf{a}_l + \mathbf{e}_i) \\ &= d_H(0, \mathbf{e}_i) = 1 \\ d_H(\mathbf{a}_l, \mathbf{a}_{l+2}) &= d_H(\mathbf{a}_l, \mathbf{a}_l + \mathbf{e}_i + \mathbf{e}_j) \qquad i \neq j \\ &= d_H(0, \mathbf{e}_i + \mathbf{e}_j) = 2 \\ d_H(\mathbf{a}_l, \mathbf{a}_{l+3}) &= d_H(\mathbf{a}_l, \mathbf{a}_l + \mathbf{e}_i + \mathbf{e}_j + \mathbf{e}_k) \qquad j \neq k \\ &= \begin{cases} 3 & i \neq k \\ 1 & i = k \end{cases} \end{aligned}$$

In general, $d_H(\mathbf{a}_l, \mathbf{a}_{l+m}) \leq m$. This relation also holds for column addresses. Therefore, $d_H \leq d_p$. On the other hand, since the Hamming distance between the addresses in an HD-*d* set is greater than or equal to *d*, the physical distance d_p is greater than or equal to *d* in the HD-*d* set. Q.E.D.

An address assignment that satisfies Theorem 4-10 can be realized by using the Gray code [SCOT 60]. Fig. 4.40(a) shows an example of this address assignment. In

Column address

Row address	000	001	011	010	110	111	101	100
000	0	1	3	2	6	7	5	4
001	3	2	0	1	5	4	6	7
011	5	4	6	7	3	2	0	1
010	6	7	5	4	0	1	3	2
110	3	2	0	1	5	4	6	7
111	0	1	3	2	6	7	5	4
101	6	7	5	4	0	1	3	2
100	5	4	6	7	3	2	0	1

(a) Address assignment by Gray code

	000	001	010	011	100	101	110	111
000	0	1	2	3	4	5	6	7
001	3	2	1	0	7	6	5	4
010	6	7	4	5	2	3	0	1
011	5	4	7	6	1	0	3	2
100	5	4	7	6	1	0	3	2
101	6	7	4	5	2	3	0	1
110	3	2	1	0	7	6	5	4
111	0	1	2	3	4	5	6	7

(b) Address assignment with the ordinary address decoder

$\boxed{k} \in M_k$

Figure 4.40 Physical position of HD-3 sets [ISHI 81]. © 1981 IECE Japan.

the memory that has this type of address assignment, the HD-d test pattern can detect distance-($d-1$) Fd, distance-($d-1$) Fa as well as Fc, and distance-($d-1$) Fs. However, in the usual memory that has the address assignment shown in Fig. 4.40(b), there exist some two cells even included in an HD-d set that have a distance less than d between them.

The number of access to memory cells in this test pattern can be expressed as

$$A_N = \left(t \cdot N + 3N + \frac{N}{t}\right) \times 2$$

where N is the memory capacity, and t is the number of HD-d sets. In this case, t is dependent on the code adopted. In general, t is satisfied by using the Hamming bound and the Varsharmov–Gilbert bound [PETE 72], as follows.

$$d;\ \text{odd:} \quad \sum_{i=0}^{(d-1)/2} \binom{n}{i} \le t \le \sum_{i=0}^{d-2} \binom{n-1}{i}$$

$$d;\ \text{even:} \quad 2 \cdot \sum_{i=0}^{(d/2)-1} \binom{n-1}{i} \le t \le 2 \cdot \sum_{i=0}^{d-3} \binom{n-2}{i}$$

$$n = \log_2 N$$

Table 4.8 shows t for linear code having $d = 2$, 3, and 4. From this, order of t is $(\log_2 N)^m$ where m is $(d-1)/2 \sim d-2$ for odd d, and m is $(d/2) - 1 \sim d - 3$ for even d. That is, this new test pattern is equal to the *N-pattern* for $d = 2$, *$N \log_2 N$-pattern* for $d = 3, 4$, and *$N(\log_2 N)^2$*- or *$N(\log_2 N)^3$-pattern* for $d = 5$, 6,

TABLE 4.8 NUMBER OF HD-d SETS

<table>
<tr><td colspan="2">Memory Capacity
(Bit)
(Address Length)</td><td>8

(3)</td><td>16

(4)</td><td>64

(6)</td><td>256

(8)</td><td>1K

(10)</td><td>4K

(12)</td><td>16K

(14)</td><td>64K

(16)</td><td>256K

(18)</td><td>1M

(20)</td></tr>
<tr><td rowspan="3">t</td><td>HD-2</td><td colspan="10">2</td></tr>
<tr><td>HD-3</td><td>4</td><td colspan="2">8</td><td colspan="4">16</td><td colspan="3">32</td></tr>
<tr><td>HD-4</td><td colspan="2">8</td><td colspan="2">16</td><td colspan="4">32</td><td colspan="2">64</td></tr>
</table>

Source: [ISHI 81]. © 1981, IECE Japan.

and so on. Testing time for N = 64K-bit, and 1M-bit chip is about 0.5 s and 14 s, respectively under HD-4 test pattern and chip cycle time of 100 ns.

4.5.2 Test Patterns Based on Residue Classes [KISH 77, KNAI 77]

The HD-d pattern has the problem that some two cells included in an HD-d set are adjacent with each other using the ordinary address decoder shown in Fig. 4.40(b).

Here, we consider the test pattern that is efficient even in the address decoder shown in Fig. 4.40(b), based on the following idea. The difference l between the n-bit addresses of the adjacent cells ($d_p = 1$) that are expressed by decimal number is the following.

$$l = \pm 1, \pm 2^i,$$
$$1 \leq i \leq n$$

Here, i expresses the number of bits for row or column address. Hence, if the residue of l divided by some value A is not equal to zero, we can have residue classes in which any two cells have $d_p \geq 2$. The smallest value of A for l is 3, that is,

$$|l|_{A=3} = \begin{cases} |1|_3 = 1 \\ |2^i|_3 = \begin{cases} 1 & i\text{: even} \\ 2 & i\text{: odd,} \end{cases} \end{cases}$$

where $|x|_y$ is the residue of x modulo y.

Hence, we have the following three residue classes for all addresses.

$$\Gamma_0 = \{0\}$$
$$\Gamma_1 = \{1\}$$
$$\Gamma_2 = \{2\}$$

Then, the test sequence similar to the HD-d pattern is shown in Fig. 4.41.

Fig. 4.41 shows the test sequence only for test data D, and hence it is necessary to have another test sequence for data $\overline{D}$. The total number of accesses to

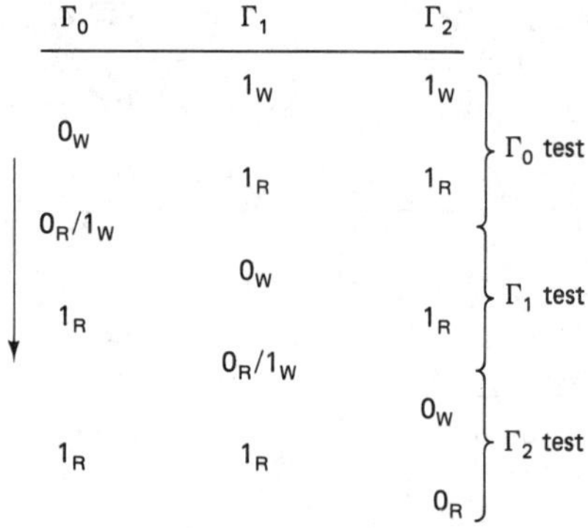

Figure 4.41 Test sequence based on residue classes.

memory cells can be expressed as follows.

$$\left.\begin{array}{ll}\text{write access:} & \dfrac{13}{3}N \\ \text{read access:} & 6N\end{array}\right\} \dfrac{31}{3}N \qquad N\text{: memory capacity}$$

Therefore, this test pattern is an N-pattern. We call this test pattern *residue class-2* (*RC*-2) *pattern*, since it is guaranteed to check the cells having physical distance-2. This RC-2 pattern is also called a *Waltzing pattern* [KISH 77].

Let's further extend this test pattern for $d_p > 2$. We can obtain the residue classes in which cells have physical distance $d_p \geq 3$. In this case, difference l can be expressed as follows.

$$l = \pm 1, \pm 2, \pm 2^i, \pm 2^i \pm 1, \pm 2^{i+1}$$

We have to obtain the minimum number A that satisfies all the following conditions for any value of i.

$$\begin{aligned} |1|_A &\neq 0, \\ |2|_A &\neq 0, \\ |2^i|_A &\neq 0, \\ |2^i \pm 1|_A &\neq 0, \\ |2^{i+1}|_A &\neq 0, \qquad 1 \leq i \leq n \end{aligned}$$

In this case, $A_{\min} = 6$. The total number of test accesses for the *residue class*-3 (*RC*-3) *pattern* is as follows.

$$\left.\begin{array}{ll}\text{write access:} & \dfrac{31}{6}N \\ \text{read access:} & 12N\end{array}\right\} \dfrac{103}{6}N$$

This type of test is summarized in Fig. 4.42. Fig. 4.43 shows the number of test accesses of this test pattern as compared to existing test patterns.

Pattern	Physical cell distance	SC-BG*	Condition	A_{min}	Access number
RC − 2	$d_p \geq 2$		$\lvert 1 \rvert_A \neq 0$ $\lvert 2^i \rvert_A \neq 0$	3	$\frac{31}{3}N$
RC − 3	$d_p \geq 3$	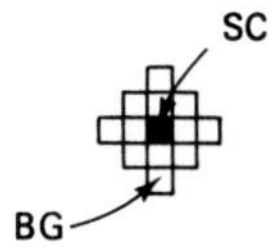	$\lvert 1 \rvert_A \neq 0$ $\lvert 2 \rvert_A \neq 0$ $\lvert 2^i \rvert_A \neq 0$ $\lvert 2^{i+1} \rvert_A \neq 0$ $\lvert 2^i \pm 1 \rvert_A \neq 0$	6	$\frac{103}{6}N$
RC − 4	$d_p \geq 4$	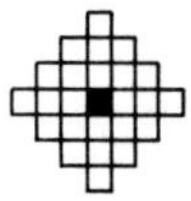	$\lvert 1 \rvert_A \neq 0$ $\lvert 2 \rvert_A \neq 0$ $\lvert 3 \rvert_A \neq 0$ $\lvert 2^i \rvert_A \neq 0$ $\lvert 2^{i+1} \rvert_A \neq 0$ $\lvert 2^{i+2} \rvert_A \neq 0$ $\lvert 2^i \pm 1 \rvert_A \neq 0$ $\lvert 2^i \pm 2 \rvert_A \neq 0$ $\lvert 2^{i+1} \pm 1 \rvert_A \neq 0$	12	$\frac{355}{12}N$

*Specified Cell – Back Ground cells

Figure 4.42 Residue class test pattern.

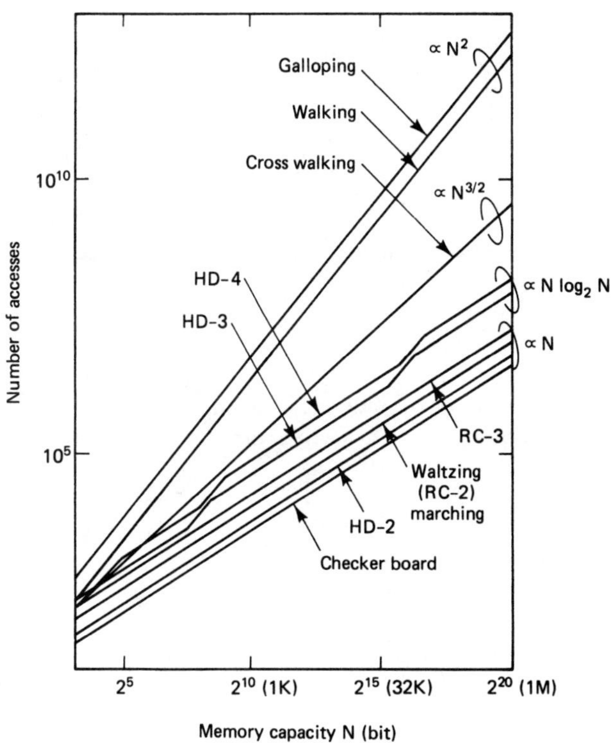

Figure 4.43 Number of accesses [KISH 77, ISHI 81]. © 1981 IECE Japan.

EXERCISES

4.1. Given the following **H** matrix, do the following.

(a) Encode the data $(d_0, d_1, \ldots, d_9) = (1\ 0\ 1\ 1\ 0\ 1\ 1\ 0\ 1\ 0)$.

(b) The received data $(d_0, d_1, \ldots, d_9, c_0, \ldots, c_4) = (1\ 0\ 1\ 0\ 1\ 0\ 0\ 1\ 0\ 1\ 1\ 0\ 0\ 0\ 1)$ has a single-bit error. Which bit is in error?

(c) In the received data, d_1 and d_9 are in error. Write the syndrome pattern.

(d) In this code, we can detect some three or more odd number of bit errors. Write the syndrome pattern of this case.

(e) There are some cases in which we cannot detect 4-bit errors. Find some undetectable 4-bit errors.

(f) Assume that we have already had three error pointers on d_3, d_7, and c_2 bit positions, and now we get a syndrome of $S = (0\ 0\ 1\ 1\ 0)$. Explain how to correct the errors.

H =

d_0	d_1	d_2	d_3	d_4	d_5	d_6	d_7	d_8	d_9	c_0	c_1	c_2	c_3	c_4
1	0	0	1	1	1	0	1	1	0	1	0	0	0	0
1	1	0	0	1	0	1	0	1	1	0	1	0	0	0
1	1	1	0	0	1	0	1	0	1	0	0	1	0	0
0	1	1	1	0	1	1	0	1	0	0	0	0	1	0
0	0	1	1	1	0	1	1	0	1	0	0	0	0	1

4.2. Obtain the odd-weight-column (32, 26) SEC–DED code and design its parallel decoding circuit.

4.3. Prove that the codeword of an odd-weight-column SEC–DED code is of even weight.

4.4. Discuss error control using coding techniques for both memory address information and memory read/write data.

4.5. Consider the operation sequence of the partial store of the memory with an ECC code. Partial store is such a special write operation that the specified part of the codeword (i.e., not all the codeword) is changed by the new data, but the other part is unchanged. Further, consider the fast operation sequence of the partial store, and indicate the ECC circuit block diagram.

4.6. Suppose that the memory having codeword $(d_0, d_1, d_2, d_3, c_0, c_1, c_2, c_3)$ defined by the following **H** matrix has a single soft error in position d_2 in addition to the already existing single hard error in position c_2. Explain how to correct these double errors using the mask error correction technique.

$$\begin{array}{cccccccc} d_0 & d_1 & d_2 & d_3 & c_0 & c_1 & c_2 & c_3 \end{array}$$

$$\mathbf{H} = \begin{bmatrix} 1 & 0 & 1 & 1 & 1 & 0 & 0 & 0 \\ 1 & 1 & 0 & 1 & 0 & 1 & 0 & 0 \\ 1 & 1 & 1 & 0 & 0 & 0 & 1 & 0 \\ 0 & 1 & 1 & 1 & 0 & 0 & 0 & 1 \end{bmatrix}$$

4.7. Show that the code defined by the following **H** matrix (*Melas code* [MELA 60]) is a DEC code.

$$\mathbf{H} = \begin{bmatrix} 1 & \alpha & \alpha^2 & \cdots & \alpha^i & \cdots & \alpha^{n-1} \\ 1 & \alpha^{-1} & \alpha^{-2} & \cdots & \alpha^{-i} & \cdots & \alpha^{-(n-1)} \end{bmatrix}$$

$\alpha^i \in GF(2^m), 0 \le i \le n-1, n = 2^m - 1, r = 2m$ and m is an odd number

Next, obtain the parallel decoding procedure of this code [HORI 76].

4.8. In a syndrome trapping technique, show that there are only $(n+1)/2$ distinct values of the normalized syndrome S' to cover all possible single and double errors.

4.9. Design the decoding circuit of the sequential erasure correction according to the algorithm shown in Fig. 4-18.

4.10. Obtain the 2-bit error correction algorithm of the sequential erasure correction method using the SEC–DED code with $k = 64$. Design the decoding circuit. Find the miscorrection probability.

4.11. Obtain the (32, 16) orthogonal Latin square code with the parameters, $m = 4$, $t = 2$.

4.12. Obtain the Horiguchi–Morita code with $k = 32$.

4.13. Prove that the code shown in Equation (4-13) is a one-level decodable code.

4.14. Assume that the two-dimensional code, which includes an (n_1, k_1) row code with minimum distance d_1 and an (n_2, k_2) column code with minimum distance d_2, is expressed as an (n_1, k_1, n_2, k_2) code with minimum distance d, as shown below, and has the constraints on the decoding such that the estimate of any symbol in the information array be a function of only the row and column to which that symbol belongs, rather than the whole codeword.

Then, the code has the error correcting capability of the sum of the minimum distances (i.e., $d \ge d_1 + d_2 - 1$) of the constituent codes rather than their product [FUJA 85].

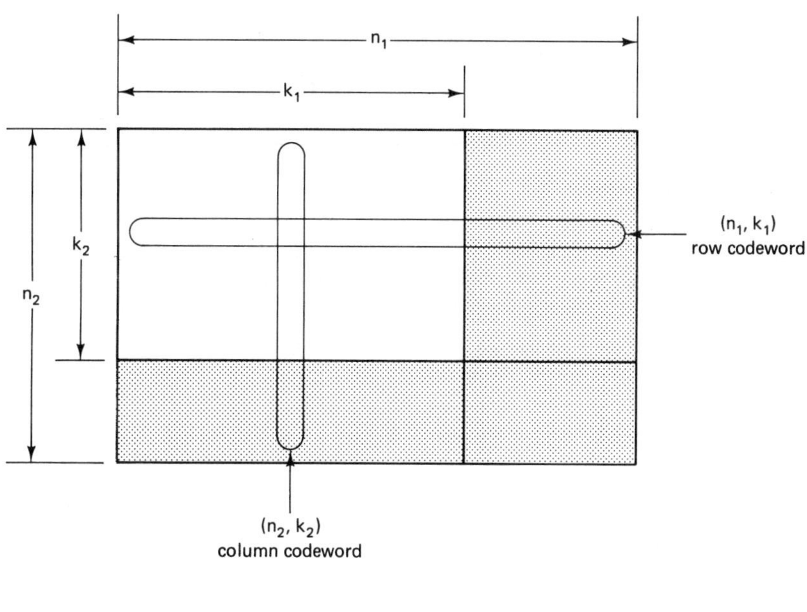

Prove this conclusion. Obtain the error correcting capability and the decoding procedure of the SED/SED code (SED: Single bit error detecting), the SEC/SEC code, and the SED/SEC–DED code, where the A/B code shows the A code for row code and the B code for column code, or vice versa, in a two-dimensional code.

4.15. Prove Corollary 4-1.

4.16. Prove Theorem 4-5.

4.17. Obtain the **H** matrix of a rotational odd-weight-column (30, 24) SEC–DED code and design its modularized decoding circuit.

4.18. Obtain the generating submatrix $\mathbf{H}_0$ of a rotational odd-weight-column (63, 56) SEC–DED code.

4.19. Let α_i be the number of 0's between the ith 1 and the $(i + 1)$th 1 ($i + 1$: mod r) in the vector having r elements. And also let w be the weight of the vector. Obtain the relation between α_i, r, and w.

Show that a distinct cyclic shift of the vector $(\alpha_1, \alpha_2, \ldots, \alpha_w)$ gives column vectors of the generating submatrix of a rotational SEC code.

4.20. Obtain the code length n of a rotational SEC–DED code by using the Möbius function.

4.21. Suppose that the encoding–decoding procedure for an (n, k) SEC–DED code is as follows: (1) input k-bits data are encoded, (2) δ bits $(1 \leq \delta < n)$ in the n bits encoded data are inverted, (3) these n-bit data are stored, (4) the corresponding δ bits in the readout data are inverted, and (5) these resulting n bits are decoded.

Find the conditions under which this encoding–decoding scheme can detect all 0 and all 1 readout data errors (i.e., unidirectional errors).

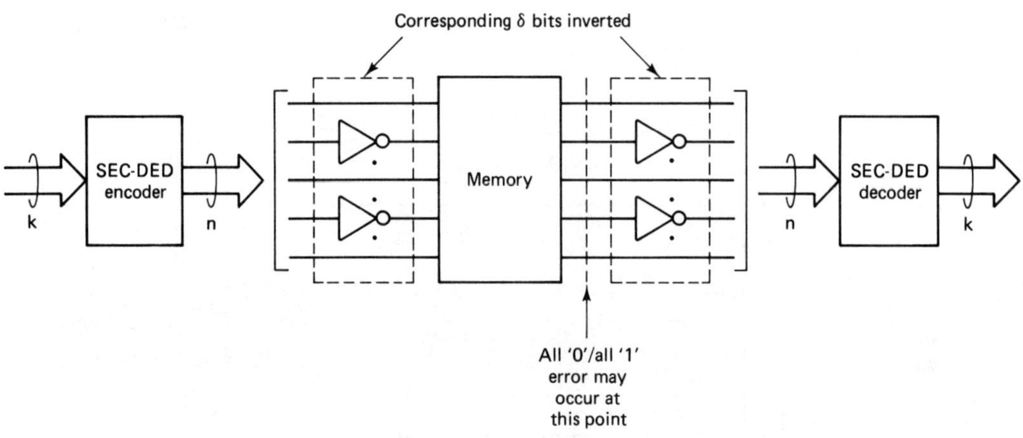

4.22. Obtain $A_{\min}$ and the number of test accesses under physical distance $d_p \geq 5$ for RC-5 test patterns.

REFERENCES

[ADVA 81] Advanced Micro Devices. "Am 2960 EDC. Cascadable 16-bit Error Detection and Correction Unit." *Bipolar Microprocessor Logic and Interface Data Book* (1981): 7.2–7.40.

[AICH 84] F. J. Aichelmann, Jr. "Fault-Tolerant Design Techniques for Semiconductor Memory Applications." *IBM Journal of Research and Development* 28 (March 1984): 177–183.

[AZUM 75] S. Azumi and T. Kasami. "On the Optimal Modified Hamming Codes" (in Japanese). *Transactions of the IECE Japan* 58-A (June 1975): 325–30.

[BEAU 73] W. F. Beausolail. "Monolithic Memory Utilizing Defective Storage Cells." U.S. Patent 3781826 (December 25, 1973).

[BOSE 86b] B. Bose and J. Metzner. "Coding Theory for Fault-Tolerant Systems." Chap. 4 in *Fault-Tolerant Computing, Theory and Techniques*, ed. D. K. Pradhan. Englewood Cliffs, N.J.: Prentice Hall, 1986.

[BOSS 74] D. C. Bossen, S. J. Hong, M. Y. Hsiao, and A. M. Patel. "Modular Distributed Error Detection and Correction Apparatus and Method." U.S. Patent 3825893 (July 23, 1974).

[BOSS 80] D. C. Bossen and M. Y. Hsiao. "A System Solution to the Memory Soft Error Problem." *IBM Journal of Research and Development* 24 (May 1980): 390–97.

[BOSS 84] D. C. Bossen, C. L. Chen, and M. Y. Hsiao. "Fault Alignment Execution for Memory Using Address Permutation." *IBM Journal of Research and Development* 28 (March 1984): 170–76.

[BREU 76] M. A. Breuer and A. D. Friedman. *Diagnosis & Reliable Design of Digital Systems*, 156–160. Rockville, Md.: Computer Science Press, 1976.

[BROW 60] D. T. Brown. "Error Detecting and Correcting Binary Codes for Arithmetic Operations." *IEEE Transactions on Elec. Comput.* EC-9 (September 1960): 333–37.

[CARL 86] R. O. Carlson and C. A. Neugebauer. "Future Trends in Wafer Scale Integration." *Proceedings of the IEEE* 74 (December 1986): 1741–52.

[CART 73] W. C. Carter, K. A. Duke, and D. C. Jessep, Jr. "Lookaside Techniques for Minimum Circuit Memory Translators." *IEEE Transactions on Computers* C-22 (March 1973): 283–89.

[CART 76] W. C. Carter and C. E. McCarthy. "Implementation of an Experimental Fault-Tolerant Memory System." *IEEE Transactions on Computers* C-25 (June 1976): 557–68.

[CHEN 73] C. L. Chen and W. T. Warren. "A Note on One-Step Majority-Logic Decodable Codes." *IEEE Transactions on Information Theory* IT-19 (January 1973): 135–37.

[CHEN 84] C. L. Chen and M. Y. Hsiao, "Error-Correcting Codes for Semiconductor Memory Applications: A State of the Art Review." *IBM Journal of Research and Development* 28 (March 1984): 124–34.

[CHEN 85] C. L. Chen. "Linear Codes for Masking Memory Defects." *IEEE Transactions on Information Theory* IT-31 (January 1985): 105–6.

[CLIF 74] R. A. Cliff and T. R. N. Rao. "Improving the Yield of LSI Memory Chips by the Application of Coding." *Proceedings of 8th Annual Princeton Conference Information Sci. Syst.* (1974): 386–90.

[CLIF 80] R. A. Cliff. "Acceptable Testing of VLSI Components Which Contain Error Correctors." *IEEE Journal of Solid-State Circuits* SC-15 (February 1980): 61–70.

[DAVI 85] H. L. Davis. "A Word-Wide 1 *Mb* ROM with Error Correction." *Dig., 1985 IEEE Int. Solid-State Circuits Conference*, WAM3.2 (February 1985): 40–41.

[DEZA 82] K. Dezaki and H. Imai. "Error Control for Main Memories Using Parity Checkers in Memory Chips" (in Japanese). *Transactions of the IECE Japan* J65-D (August 1982): 1034–1040.

[EGAW 80] Y. Egawa, T. Wada, Y. Ohmori, N. Tsuda, and K. Masuda. "A 1-Mbit Full-Wafer MOS RAM." *IEEE Journal of Solid-State Circuits* SC-15 (August 1980): 677–86.

[FISH 57] R. A. Fisher and F. Yates. *Statistical Tables for Biological Agricultural and Medical Research*. Hafner Publishing, 1957.

[FUJA 85] T. Fuja, C. Heegard, and R. Goodman. "Some Linear Sum Codes for Random Access Memories." *Proceedings of the IEEE Int. Symposium Information Theory* (June 1985).

[FUJI 75] E. Fujiwara and K. Aoki. "Reliability of Main Memories" (in Japanese). *Journal of Information Processing Society of Japan* 16 (April 1975): 295–304.

[FUJI 76b] E. Fujiwara and T. Kawakami. "*A Memory Having Double Error Correction Capability—Sequential Correction for BCH Code*." (in Japanese). *Paper of Technical Group* EC 76-20. *IECE Japan*, June 1976.

[FUJI 77a] E. Fujiwara. "A Modularized *b*-Adjacent Error Correction Memory Unit." *Transactions of the IECE Japan* E60 (February 1977): 69–76.

[FUJI 78] E. Fujiwara. "Odd-Weight-Column *b*-Adjacent Error Correcting Codes." *Transactions of the IECE Japan* E61 (October 1978): 781–87.

[FUJI 80b] E. Fujiwara and K. Haruta. "Design of Main Storage Error Checking and Correcting Circuit for LSI Implementation" (in Japanese). *Transactions of the IECE Japan* 63-D (February 1980): 129–36.

[FUJI 81a] E. Fujiwara. "Error Correcting Code and its Application to Digital Systems" (in Japanese). Ph.D. diss., Tokyo Institute of Technology, Tokyo, April 1981.

[FUJI 82] E. Fujiwara and S. Kaneda. "Application of Error Correcting Codes for Increasing Computer System Reliability" (in Japanese). *Journal of Information Processing Society (IPS) of Japan* 23 (April 1982): 292–98.

[FUJI 88a] E. Fujiwara. Chapter 4 in *Essentials of Error-Correcting Coding Techniques*, ed. H. Imai. New York: Academic Press, 1988.

[FUJI 88b] E. Fujiwara. "Referenceless Signature Testing Using Bi-Directional LFSR." *Transactions of the IECE Japan* E71 (October 1988).

[GHAF 84] K. A. Ghaffar and R. J. McEliece., "Soft Error Correction for Increased Densities in VLSI Memories." *Proceedings of the Eleventh Annual Int. Symposium Computer Architecture* (1984): 248–50.

[GOLA 83] P. Golan and J. Hlavika. "A Method for Parallel Decoding of Double-Error Correcting Group Codes." *Dig., 13th Annual Int. Symposium Fault-Tolerant Comput.* (June 1983): 338–41.

[GOLO 58] S. W. Golomb, B. Gordon, and L. R. Welch. "Comma-Free Codes." *Canadian Journal of Mathematics* 10 (1958): 202–4.

[HALL 67] M. Hall. *Combinatorial Theory*. Waltham, Mass.: Blaisdell Publishing Co., 1967.

[HAMM 50] R. W. Hamming. "Error Detecting and Error Correcting Codes." *Bell System Technical Journal* 26 (April 1950): 147–60.

[HAN 87] S. H. Han and M. Molek. "A New Technique for Error Detection and Correction in Semiconductor Memories." *Proceedings of IEEE International Test Conference* (1987): 864–70.

[HAYE 75] J. P. Hayes. "Detection of Pattern-Sensitive Faults in Random-Access Memories." *IEEE Transactions on Computers* C-24 (October 1975): 150–57.

[HAYE 80] J. P. Hayes, "Testing Memories for Single-Cell Pattern-Sensitive Faults." *IEEE Transactions on Computers* C-29 (March 1980): 249–54.

[HORI 75a] T. Horiguchi and K. Morita. "A Parallel Memory with Double Error Correction Capability—A Class of One-Step Majority-Logic Decodable Error Correction Codes." (in Japanese). *Paper of Technical Group* EC 75-42. *IECE Japan*, November 1975.

[HORI 76] T. Horiguchi. "A Double Error Correcting Code in Main Memory—On Parallel Decoding of DEC-Melas Codes and BCH Codes" (in Japanese). *Paper of Technical Group*. EC 76-61. *IECE Japan*, November 1976.

[HOWE 77] T. H. Howell, G. E. Cregg, and L. Rabins. "Table Lookup Direct Decoder for Double-Error Correcting DEC BCH Codes Using a Pair of Syndromes." U.S. Patent 4030067 (June 14, 1977).

[HSIA 69] M. Y. Hsiao and J. T. Tou. "Application of Error-Correcting Codes in Computer Reliability Studies." *IEEE Transactions on Reliability* R-18 (August 1969): 108–18.

[HSIA 70a] M. Y. Hsiao. "A Class of Optimal Minimum Odd-Weight-Column SEC–DED Codes." *IBM Journal of Research Development* 14 (July 1970): 395–401.

[HSIA 70b] M. Y. Hsiao, D. C. Bossen, and R. T. Chen. "Orthogonal Latin Square Codes." *IBM Journal of Research and Development* 14 (July 1970): 390–94.

[HSIA 75] M. Y. Hsiao and D. C. Bossen. "Orthogonal Latin Square Configuration for LSI Memory Yield and Reliability Enhancement." *IEEE Transactions on Computers* C-24 (May 1975): 512–16.

[HSIA 77] M. Y. Hsiao, A. M. Patel, and D. K. Pradhan. "Store Address Generator with On-Line Fault-Detection Capability." *IEEE Transactions on Computers* C-26 (November 1977): 1144–47.

[IMAI 77a] H. Imai and Y. Kamiyanagi. "On Parallel Decoders for Double-Error-Correcting BCH Codes" (in Japanese). *Transactions of the IECE Japan*, J60-D (September 1977): 761–62.

[IMAI 77b] H. Imai and Y. Kamiyanagi. "A Construction Method for Double-Error Correcting Codes for Application to Main Memories" (in Japanese). *Transactions of the IECE Japan*, J60-D (October 1977): 861–68.

[IMAI 79a] H. Imai and H. Fujiya. "A Construction Method for Simply-Decodable Error-Correcting Codes" (in Japanese). *Transactions of the IECE Japan* J62-A (May 1979): 271–77.

[INTE 82] Intel. "8206 Error Detection and Correction Unit." *Intel Component Data Catalog* (1982): 9–98, 116.

[ISHI 81] T. Ishikawa and K. Matsuzawa. "Memory Test-Pattern Considering Hamming Distance between Addresses" (in Japanese). *Transactions of the IECE Japan* J64-D (September 1981): 807–14.

[JAIN 86] S. K. Jain and C. E. Stroud. "Built-In Self Testing of Embedded Memories." *IEEE Design & Test* (October 1986): 27–37.

[KAMB 76] Y. Kambayashi, K. Inagaki, and S. Yajima. "Multiple-error Correction Scheme for LSI Memory Systems by the Utilization of the Property of Permanent Faults" (in Japanese). *Paper of Technical Group* EC76-66. *IECE Japan*, December 1976.

[KANE 84b] S. Kaneda and H. Fukuda. "Reliability Design of Memory Systems Considering Soft-Error" (in Japanese). *Transactions of the IECE Japan* J67-D (September 1984): 1036–43.

[KINO 86] K. Kinoshita and K. K. Saluja. "Built-In Testing of Memory Using On-Chip Compact Testing Scheme." *IEEE Transactions on Computers* C-35 (October 1986): 863–70.

[KISH 77] M. Kishi. "Testing Method Using the Waltzing Pattern for IC Memory Devices" (in Japanese). *Transactions of the IECE Japan* J60-D (December 1977): 1031–38.

[KITA 80] Y. Kitano, S. Kohda, H. Kikuchi, and S. Sakai. "A 4-Mbit Full-Wafer ROM." *IEEE Journal of Solid-State Circuits* SC-15 (August 1980): 686–93.

[KNAI 77] J. Knaizuk, Jr. and C. R. P. Hartmann. "An Optimal Algorithm for Testing Stuck-at Faults in Random Access Memories." *IEEE Transactions on Computers* C-26 (November 1977): 1141–44.

[KUZN 78] A. V. Kuznetsov, T. Kasami, and S. Yamamura. "An Error Correcting Scheme for Defective Memory." *IEEE Transactions on Information Theory* IT-24 (November 1978): 712–18.

[LEIG 82] F. T. Leighton and C. E. Leiserson. "Wafer Scale Integration of Systolic Arrays." *Proceedings of the Twenty-Third Annual Symposium on Foundation of Computer Science, Chicago* (1982): 297–311.

[MANG 84a] T. E. Mangir. "Sources of Failures and Yield Improvement for VLSI and Restructurable Interconnects for RVLSI and WSI: Part I—Sources of Failures and Yield Improvement for VLSI." *Proceedings of the IEEE* 72 (June 1984): 690–708.

[MANG 84b] T. E. Mangir. "Sources of Failures and Yield Improvement for VLSI and Restructurable Interconnects for RVLSI and WSI: Part II—Restructurable Interconnects for RVLSI and WSI." *Proceedings of the IEEE* 72 (December 1984): 1687–94.

[MANN 49] H. S. Mann. *Analysis and Design of Experiments*. New York: Dover, 1949.

[MANO 82] T. Mano, M. Wada, N. Ieda, and M. Tanimoto. "A Redundancy Circuit for a Fault-Tolerant 256K MOS RAM." *IEEE Journal of Solid-State Circuits* SC-17 (August 1982): 726–31.

[MANO 83] T. Mano, J. Yamada, J. Inoue, and S. Nakajima. "Circuit Techniques for a VLSI Memory." *IEEE Journal of Solid-State Circuits* SC-18 (October 1983): 463–70.

[MANO 87] T. Mano, T. Matsumura, J. Yamada, J. Inoue, S. Nakajima, K. Minegishi, K. Miura, T. Matsuda, C. Hashimoto, and H. Namatsu. "Circuit Technologies for 16 *Mb* DRAMs." *Dig., 1987 IEEE Int. Solid-State Circuit Conference*. (February 1987): 22–23.

[MASS 63] J. L. Massey. *Threshhold Decoding*. Cambridge: MIT Press, 1963.

[MATS 77] K. Matsuzawa and Y. Tohma. "A Way of Multiple Error Correction for Computer Main Memory" (in Japanese). *Transactions of the IECE Japan* J60-D (October 1977): 869–76.

[MATS 78] K. Matsuzawa and Y. Tohma. "An Adjacent-Error-Correcting Code Based on the Threshold Decoding." *Dig., 8th Annual Int. Symposium Fault-Tolerant Comput.* (1978): 225.

[MATS 87] H. Matsuda and M. Kasahara. "A New Method of Constructing SEC–DED Codes with Reduced Number of Codewords of Weight 4." *Transactions of the IECE Japan* J70-A (August 1987): 1036–45.

[MATS 88] K. Matsuzawa and E. Fujiwara. "Masking Asymmetric Line Faults Using Semi-Distance Codes." *Dig., 18th Annual Int. Symposium Fault-Tolerant Comput.* (June 1988).

[MAY 79] T. C. May. "Soft Errors in VLSI: Present and Future." *IEEE Transactions on Components, Hybrids and Manufacturing Technology* CHMT-2 (December 1979): 377–87.

[MEHR 84] S. Mehrotra, T. C. Wu, T. L. Chiu, and G. Perlegos. "A 64Kb CMOS EEROM with On-Chip ECC." *Dig., 1984 IEEE Int. Solid-State Circuits Conference* (February 1984): THAM 10.4; 142–43.

[MELA 60] C. M. Melas. "A Cyclic Code for Double Error Correction." *IBM Journal* (July 1960): 364–66.

[MIUR 86] Y. Miura, H. Tomamoto, and Y. Narita. "A Built-In Testing for Functional Testing in Semiconductor Random Access Memories" (in Japanese). *Transactions of the IECE Japan* J69-D (October 1986): 1416–23.

[MOOR 86] W. R. Moore. "A Review of Fault-Tolerant Techniques for the Enhancement of Integrated Circuit Yield." *Proceedings of the IEEE* 74 (May 1986): 684–98.

[NAIR 78] R. Nair, S. M. Thatte, and J. A. Abraham. "Efficient Algorithms for Testing Semiconductor Random-Access Memories." *IEEE Transactions on Computers* C-27 (June 1978): 572–76.

[NICO 85b] M. Nicolaidis. "An Efficient Built-In Self-Test Scheme for Functional Test of Embedded RAMs." *Dig., 15th Annual Int. Symposium Fault-Tolerant Comput.* (June 1985): 118–23.

[NOOR 80] D. J. W. Noorlag, L. M. Terman and A. G. Konhein. "The Effect of Alpha-Particle-Induced Soft Error on Memory Systems with Error Correction." *IEEE Journal of Solid-State Circuits* SC-15 (June 1980): 319–25.

[OHNI 81] N. Ohnishi, T. Ishikawa, and N. Mutoh. "System Configuration on Full Wafer LSI." *Proc. of the Int. Symposium Mini and Microcomputers* (January 1981): 7–11.

[OKAN 87] H. Okano and H. Imai. "A Construction Method of High-Speed Decoders Using ROMs for Bose-Chaudhuri-Hocquenghem and Reed-Solomon Codes." *IEEE Transactions on Computers* C-36 (October 1987): 1165–71.

[OSMA 82] F. I. Osman. "Error Correction Technique for Random-Access Memories." *IEEE Journal of Solid-State Circuits* SC-17 (October 1982): 877–81.

[PATE 72a] A. M. Patel and M. Y. Hsiao. "An Adaptive Error Correction Scheme for Computer Memory System." *Proceedings of Fall Joint Computer Conference* AFIPS (1972): 83–87.

[PATE 72b] A. M. Patel and S. J. Hong. "Syndrome Trapping Technique for Fast Double-Error Correction." *Proceedings of the IEEE International Symposium on Information Theory* (1972). (See also U.S. Patent 3714629, January 1973.)

[PELT 83] D. L. Peltzer. "Wafer-Scale Integration: The Limits of VLSI?" *VLSI Design* (September 1983): 43–47.

[PETE 72] W. W. Peterson and E. J. Weldon, Jr. *Error Correcting Codes*, 2d. ed. Cambridge: MIT Press, 1972.

[RAO 68a] T. R. N. Rao. "Use of Error Correcting Codes on Memory Words for Improved Reliability." *IEEE Transactions on Reliability* R-17 (June 1968): 91–96.

[RAO 74] T. R. N. Rao. *Error Coding for Arithmetic Processors*. New York: Academic Press, 1974.

[RENN 86] D. A. Rennels and S. Chau. "A Self-Exercising Self-Checking Memory Design." *Dig., 16th Annual Int. Symposium Fault-Tolerant Comput.* (June 1986): 358–63.

[RYAN 83] P. M. Ryan. "Large System Fault Tolerant Memory Techniques." *Dig. 13th Annual Int. Symposium Fault-Tolerant Comput.* (June 1983): 342–45.

[SAIH 82] G. A. Sai-Halasz, M. R. Wordeman and R. H. Dennard. "Alpha-Particle-Induced Soft Error Rate in VLSI Circuits." *IEEE Journal of Solid-State Circuits* SC-17 (April 1982): 355–61.

[SALU 85] K. K. Saluja and K. Kinoshita. "Test Pattern Generation for API Faults in RAM." *IEEE Transactions on Computers* C-34 (March 1985): 284–87.

[SAVA 86] Y. Savaria, N. C. Rumin, J. F. Hayes, and V. K. Agrawal. "Soft-Error Filtering: A Solution to the Reliability Problem of Future VLSI Digital Circuits." *Proceedings of the IEEE* 74 (May 1986): 669–87.

[SCOT 60] N. R. Scot. *Analog and Digital Computer Technique*. New York: McGraw-Hill, 1960.

[SETH 81] S. C. Seth and K. Narayanaswamy. "A Graph Model for Pattern-Sensitive Faults in Random Access Memories." *IEEE Transactions on Computers* C-30 (December 1981): 973–77.

[SHED 78] J. J. Shedletsky. "Error Correction by Alternate-Data Retry." *IEEE Transactions on Computers* C-27 (February 1978): 106–12.

[SHIN 83] T. Shinoda, Y. Ohnishi, H. Kawamoto, K. Takizawa, and K. Narita. "A 1 Mb ROM with On-Chip ECC for Yield Enhancement." *Dig., 1983 IEEE Int. Solid-State Circuits Conference* (February 1983): 158–59.

[SMIT 81] R. T. Smith, J. D. Chlipala, J. F. M. Bindels, R. G. Nelson, F. H. Fischer, and T. F. Mantz. "Laser Programmable Redundancy and Yield Improvement in a 64K DRAM." *IEEE Journal of Solid-State Circuits* SC-16 (October 1981): 506–14.

[SRIN 67] C. V. Srinivasan. "Codes for Error Correction in Memory Systems." *Proceedings of the First IEEE Computer Conference* (September 1967): 42–45.

[SRIN 71a] C. V. Srinivasan. "Codes for Error Correction in High-Speed Memory Systems—Part I: Correction of Cell Defects in Integrated Memories." *IEEE Transactions on Computers* C-20 (August 1971): 882–88.

[SRIN 71b] C. V. Srinivasan. "Codes for Error Correction in High-Speed Memory Systems—Part II: Correction of Temporary and Catastrophic Errors." *IEEE Transactions on Computers* C-20 (December 1971): 1514–20.

[SRIN 78] V. P. Srini. "Fault Location in a Semiconductor Random-Access Memory Unit." *IEEE Transactions on Computers* C-27 (April 1978): 349–58.

[STAP 80] C. H. Stapper, A. N. Mclaren, and M. Dreckmann. "Yield Model for Productivity Optimization of VLSI Memory Chips with Redundancy and Partially Good Product." *IBM Journal of Research and Development* 24 (May 1980): 398–409.

[STAP 83] C. H. Stapper. "Modelling of Integrated Circuit Defect Sensitivities." *IBM Journal of Research and Development* 27 (November 1983): 549–57.

[STAP 84] C. H. Stapper. "Yield Model for Fault Clusters Within Integrated Circuits." *IBM Journal of Research and Development* 28 (September 1984): 636–90.

[STAP 85] C. H. Stapper. "The Effects of Wafer to Wafer Perfect Density Variations on Integrated Circuit Defect and Fault Distributions." *IBM Journal of Research and Development* 29 (January 1985): 87–97.

[STAP 86] C. H. Stapper. "On Yield, Fault Distributions and Clustering of Particles." *IBM Journal of Research and Development* 30 (May 1986): 326–38.

[SUK 80] D. S. Suk and S. M. Reddy. "Test Procedures for a Class of Pattern-Sensitive Faults in Semiconductor Random-Access Memories." *IEEE Transactions on Computers* C-29 (June 1980): 419–29.

[SUK 81] D. S. Suk and S. M. Reddy. "A March Test for Functional Faults in Semiconductor Random Access Memories." *IEEE Transactions on Computers* C-30 (December 1981): 982–85.

[SUN 84] Z. Sun and L. T. Wang. "Self-Testing of Embedded RAMs." *Proceedings of IEEE International Test Conference* (1984): 148–56.

[SUND 78] C-E, W. Sundberg. "Erasure and Error Decoding for Semiconductor Memories." *IEEE Transactions on Computers* C-27 (August 1978): 696–705.

[SUND 79] C-E, W. Sundberg. "Properties of Transparent Shortened Codes for Memories With Stuck-at Faults." *IEEE Transactions on Computers* C-28 (September 1979): 686–90.

[SZYG 71] S. A. Szygenda and M. J. Flynn. "Failure Analysis of Memory Organization for Utilization in a Self-Repair Memory System." *IEEE Transactions on Reliability* R-20 (May 1971): 64–70.

[SZYG 73] S. A. Szygenda and M. J. Flynn. "Self-Diagnosis and Self-Repair in Memory: An Integrated System Approach." *IEEE Transactions on Reliability* R-22 (April 1973): 2–12.

[TAKE 77] T. Takezono and H. Ando. "Error Correcting Circuit Arrangement Using Cube Circuits." U.S. Patent 4064483 (December 1977).

[TANG 69] D. T. Tang and R. T. Chien. "Coding for Error Control." *IBM System Journal* 8, (1969): 48–86.

[TANN 84] R. M. Tanner. "Fault-Tolerant 256K Memory Designs." *IEEE Transactions on Computers* C-33 (April 1984): 314–22.

[TEXA 83] Texas Instruments. "SN54ALS632—SN54ALS635, 32-Bit Parallel Error Detection and Correction Circuits." in *ALS/AS Logic Circuits Data Book*, 2-313-2-326. Texas Instruments, 1983.

[THAT 77] S. M. Thatte and J. A. Abraham. "Testing of Semiconductor Random Access Memories." *Dig., 7th Annual Int. Symposium Fault-Tolerant Comput.* (1977): 81–87.

[UEOK 84] Y. Ueoka, C. Minagawa, M. Oka, and A. Ishimoto. "A Defect-Tolerant Design for Full-Wafer Memory LSI." *IEEE Journal of Solid-State Circuits* SC-19 (June 1984): 319–24.

[WALK 79] W. K. S. Walker, C-E. W. Sundberg, and C. J. Black. "A Reliable Spaceborne Memory with a Single Error and Erasure Correction Scheme." *IEEE Transactions on Computers* C-28 (July 1979): 493–500.

[WOOD 86] M. H. Wood. "MOS VLSI Reliability and Yield Trends." *Proceedings of the IEEE* 74 (December 1986): 1715–29.

[YAMA 70] H. Yamamoto, T. Watanabe, and Y. Urano. "Alternating Logic and Its Application to Fault Detection." *Proceedings 1970 IEEE Int. Comput. Group Conference* (June 1970): 220–28.

[YAMA 80] A. Yamagishi and H. Imai. "A Construction Method for Decoders of BCH Codes Using ROM's" (in Japanese). *Transactions of the IECE Japan* 63-D (December 1980): 1034–41.

[YAMA 84] J. Yamada, T. Mano, J. Inoue, S. Nakajima, and T. Matsuda. "A Submicron VLSI Memory with a 4 Bit-at-a-Time Built-in ECC Circuit." *Dig., 1984 IEEE Int. Solid-State Circuits Conference* (February 1984): 104–105.

[YAMA 87a] K. Yamashita, A. Kanasugi, S. Hijiya, G. Goto, N. Matsumura, and T. Shirato. "A Wafer-Scale 170,000-Gate FFT Processor with Built-In Test Circuits." *Proceedings of IEEE 1987 Custom Integrated Circuits Conference* (May 1987): 207–10.

[YAMA 87b] J. Yamada. "Selector-Line Merged Built-In ECC Technique for DRAMs." *IEEE Journal of Solid-State Circuits* SC-22 (October 1987): 868–73.

[YAMA 88] T. Yamada, H. Kotani, J. Matsushima and M. Inoue. "A 4-M Bit DRAM with 16-Bit Concurrent ECC." *IEEE Journal of Solid-State Circuits* SC-23 (February 1988): 20–26.

5

Codes for High-Speed Memories II: Byte Error Correcting/Detecting Codes

In the application of error correcting codes to digital computer systems, there are a number of situations for which an error correcting code capable of correcting clusters of adjacent bits in error is uniquely suited. An example would be the errors due to a failure in a b-bit organized memory card or a b-bit organized semiconductor memory chip. These are called *byte-organized memories*. With the advent of high-density semiconductor memory chips, these b-bit organized RAM chips (e.g., 64K-word × 4-bit, 256K-word × 4-bit, or 128K-word × 8-bit RAM chips) have been fabricated and are now marketed. If a failure occurs in such a chip or a card, the resulting information read out from the memory is likely to have a b-bit block in error. Here, we refer to this block of b bits, $b \geq 2$, as a *byte*. In this kind of application, it may be desirable to have an error correcting code capable of correcting/detecting byte errors as well as bit errors [FUJI 82, HORI 83, CHEN 83, DENG 87, FUJI 88].

This chapter deals with the codes for high-speed memories, especially from the standpoint of byte error correcting/detecting codes. These code classes are abbreviated and designated as follows:

1. SbEC codes: *S*ingle b-bit byte *e*rror *c*orrecting codes.
2. SbEC–DbED codes: *S*ingle b-bit byte *e*rror *c*orrecting and *d*ouble b-bit byte *e*rror *d*etecting codes.
3. SEC–DED–SbED codes: *S*ingle b-bit byte *e*rror *d*etecting *SEC–DED* codes.

The SbEC–DbED codes have found applications in such recent large commercial computer systems as the Fujitsu M-380/382 systems and the NEC ACOS 1500, 2000 systems, and the SEC–DED–SbED codes have been applied in Fujitsu M-780 systems, all with byte size $b = 4$ bits.

5.1 SINGLE-BYTE ERROR CORRECTING (SbEC) CODES

In this section, we discuss a class of single-symbol error correcting codes over $GF(2^b)$. Each symbol is a b-bit byte, and therefore these are SbEC codes.

5.1.1 Hamming-Type Codes

It is well known that a Hamming single-error correcting code can be constructed with symbols from any finite field [HAMM 50]. If F is such a field, then the $\mathbf{H}$ matrix for a single-error correcting code with elements from F is constructed as follows: Choose as columns of the $\mathbf{H}$ matrix all the nonzero r-tuples of elements from F such that no column of $\mathbf{H}$ is a multiple of another column. By that, since every pair of columns is linearly independent, we have $d_{\min} = 3$ for the code, and it is capable of correcting single (symbol) errors.

If F, in particular, is $GF(2^b)$, these Hamming codes are an SbEC class of codes. In order to implement the Hamming-type SbEC codes, it is necessary to transform the $\mathbf{H}$ matrix over $GF(2^b)$ to a binary form as follows [BOSS 70a, HONG 72].

Definition 5-1. Given a binary primitive polynomial $\mathbf{g}(x)$ of degree b, the *companion matrix* $\mathbf{T}$ corresponding to $\mathbf{g}(x)$ is defined as follows.

$$\mathbf{g}(x) = \sum_{i=0}^{b} g_i x^i, \qquad g_0 = g_b = 1$$

$$\mathbf{T} = \begin{bmatrix} 0 \; 0 \; \cdots \; 0 & g_0 \\ \begin{array}{|c|}\hline \\ \mathbf{I}_{b-1} \\ \\ \hline \end{array} & \begin{matrix} g_1 \\ \vdots \\ g_{b-1} \end{matrix} \end{bmatrix}_{b \times b} \tag{5.1}$$

$$\mathbf{I}_{b-1}\text{: } (b-1) \times (b-1) \text{ identity matrix}$$

Let α be a primitive element in $GF(2^b)$ and a root of $\mathbf{g}(x)$. Its companion matrix $\mathbf{T}$ has as its columns $\underset{|}{\overset{|}{\alpha^i}}$ for $i = 1, 2, \ldots, b$, where $\underset{|}{\overset{|}{\alpha^i}}$ is the coefficient vector of $x^i \; mod \; \mathbf{g}(x)$. The companion matrix of α^j is $\mathbf{T}^j$, and its column vectors are shown in

(5.2). (Also see Example 5-1.)

$$\mathbf{T} = \begin{bmatrix} | & | & | & & | \\ \alpha & \alpha^2 & \alpha^3 & \cdots & \alpha^b \\ | & | & | & & | \end{bmatrix}_{b\times b}$$
$$\mathbf{T}^j = \begin{bmatrix} | & | & & | \\ \alpha^j & \alpha^{j+1} & \cdots & \alpha^{j+b-1} \\ | & | & & | \end{bmatrix}_{b\times b} \tag{5.2}$$

Some of the properties of the companion matrix are as follows [HONG 72].

Property 1. Let e be the exponent of $\mathbf{g}(x)$ (i.e., $y = e$ is the least positive solution of $x^y \equiv 1 \, mod \, \mathbf{g}(x)$).

(a) $\mathbf{T}$ is nonsingular.
(b) $\mathbf{T}^0 = \mathbf{T}^e = \mathbf{I}_b$.
(c) $\mathbf{T}^i = \mathbf{T}^j$ if and only if $i \equiv j \, mod \, e$.

Property 2. The ith column of the $\mathbf{T}^j$ is the same as the coefficient vector of the $(b-1)$th degree polynomial $x^{i+j-1} \, mod \, \mathbf{g}(x)$.

Property 3. Let V be the coefficient column vector of $\mathbf{v}(x) = \sum_{i=0}^{b-1} v_i x^i$ and V' for $\mathbf{v}'(x) = \sum_{i=0}^{b-1} v_i' x^i$. Then, $\mathbf{T}^i \cdot V = V'$ if and only if $x^i \mathbf{v}(x) = \mathbf{v}'(x) \, mod \, \mathbf{g}(x)$.

The set of companion matrices and the zero matrix included has the same structure as $GF(2^b)$ and is field isomorphic to $GF(2^b)$. Therefore, we state

$$\left\{\mathbf{0}, \mathbf{T}, \mathbf{T}^2, \mathbf{T}^3, \ldots, \mathbf{T}^{2^b-2}, \mathbf{T}^{2^b-1} = \mathbf{I}\right\} = GF(2^b)$$

where $\mathbf{I}$ is the $(b \times b)$ identity matrix, and $\mathbf{0}$ is the $(b \times b)$ zero matrix. In the following we use the $\mathbf{T}$ matrices to represent $GF(2^b)$ as well as the vectors (b-tuples over binary) as required.

Example 5-1

The companion matrix $\mathbf{T}$ in $GF(2^4)$ defined by the primitive polynomial $\mathbf{g}(x) = x^4 + x + 1$ is given as follows.

$$\mathbf{T} = \begin{bmatrix} 0 & 0 & 0 & 1 \\ 1 & 0 & 0 & 1 \\ 0 & 1 & 0 & 0 \\ 0 & 0 & 1 & 0 \end{bmatrix}$$

By using this matrix, all elements included in $GF(2^4)$ can be expressed in binary form as follows.

$$\mathbf{0} = \begin{bmatrix} & & & \\ & & & \\ & & & \\ & & & \end{bmatrix} \quad \mathbf{I} = \begin{bmatrix} 1 & & & \\ & 1 & & \\ & & 1 & \\ & & & 1 \end{bmatrix} \quad \mathbf{T} = \begin{bmatrix} & & & 1 \\ 1 & & & 1 \\ & 1 & & \\ & & 1 & \end{bmatrix} \quad \mathbf{T}^2 = \begin{bmatrix} & & 1 & \\ & & 1 & 1 \\ 1 & & & 1 \\ & 1 & & \end{bmatrix}$$

$$\mathbf{T}^3 = \begin{bmatrix} & 1 & & \\ & 1 & 1 & \\ & & 1 & 1 \\ 1 & & & 1 \end{bmatrix} \quad \mathbf{T}^4 = \begin{bmatrix} 1 & & & 1 \\ 1 & 1 & & 1 \\ & 1 & 1 & \\ & & 1 & 1 \end{bmatrix} \quad \mathbf{T}^5 = \begin{bmatrix} & & 1 & 1 \\ 1 & & 1 & \\ 1 & 1 & & 1 \\ & 1 & 1 & \end{bmatrix} \quad \mathbf{T}^6 = \begin{bmatrix} & 1 & 1 & \\ & 1 & & 1 \\ 1 & & 1 & \\ 1 & 1 & & 1 \end{bmatrix}$$

$$\mathbf{T}^7 = \begin{bmatrix} 1 & 1 & & 1 \\ 1 & & 1 & 1 \\ & 1 & & 1 \\ 1 & & 1 & \end{bmatrix} \quad \mathbf{T}^8 = \begin{bmatrix} 1 & & 1 & \\ & 1 & 1 & 1 \\ 1 & & 1 & 1 \\ & 1 & & 1 \end{bmatrix} \quad \mathbf{T}^9 = \begin{bmatrix} & 1 & & 1 \\ 1 & 1 & 1 & 1 \\ & 1 & 1 & 1 \\ 1 & & 1 & 1 \end{bmatrix} \quad \mathbf{T}^{10} = \begin{bmatrix} 1 & & 1 & 1 \\ 1 & 1 & 1 & \\ 1 & 1 & 1 & 1 \\ & 1 & 1 & 1 \end{bmatrix}$$

$$\mathbf{T}^{11} = \begin{bmatrix} & 1 & 1 & 1 \\ 1 & 1 & & \\ 1 & 1 & 1 & \\ 1 & 1 & 1 & 1 \end{bmatrix} \quad \mathbf{T}^{12} = \begin{bmatrix} 1 & 1 & 1 & 1 \\ 1 & & & \\ 1 & 1 & & \\ 1 & 1 & 1 & \end{bmatrix} \quad \mathbf{T}^{13} = \begin{bmatrix} 1 & 1 & 1 & \\ & & & 1 \\ 1 & & & \\ 1 & 1 & & \end{bmatrix} \quad \mathbf{T}^{14} = \begin{bmatrix} 1 & 1 & & \\ & & 1 & \\ & & & 1 \\ 1 & & & \end{bmatrix}$$

The addition and multiplication rules in $GF(2^4)$ are determined as follows.

+	0	I	T^{1}	T^{2}	T^{3}	T^{4}	T^{5}	T^{6}	T^{7}	T^{8}	T^{9}	T^{10}	T^{11}	T^{12}	T^{13}	T^{14}
0	0	I	T^{1}	T^{2}	T^{3}	T^{4}	T^{5}	T^{6}	T^{7}	T^{8}	T^{9}	T^{10}	T^{11}	T^{12}	T^{13}	T^{14}
I	I	0	T^{4}	T^{8}	T^{14}	T^{1}	T^{10}	T^{13}	T^{9}	T^{2}	T^{7}	T^{5}	T^{12}	T^{11}	T^{6}	T^{3}
T^{1}	T^{1}	T^{4}	0	T^{5}	T^{9}	I	T^{2}	T^{11}	T^{14}	T^{10}	T^{3}	T^{8}	T^{6}	T^{13}	T^{12}	T^{7}
T^{2}	T^{2}	T^{8}	T^{5}	0	T^{6}	T^{10}	T^{1}	T^{3}	T^{12}	I	T^{11}	T^{4}	T^{9}	T^{7}	T^{14}	T^{13}
T^{3}	T^{3}	T^{14}	T^{9}	T^{6}	0	T^{7}	T^{11}	T^{2}	T^{4}	T^{13}	T^{1}	T^{12}	T^{5}	T^{10}	T^{8}	I
T^{4}	T^{4}	T^{1}	I	T^{10}	T^{7}	0	T^{8}	T^{12}	T^{3}	T^{5}	T^{14}	T^{2}	T^{13}	T^{6}	T^{11}	T^{9}
T^{5}	T^{5}	T^{10}	T^{2}	T^{1}	T^{11}	T^{8}	0	T^{9}	T^{13}	T^{4}	T^{6}	I	T^{3}	T^{14}	T^{7}	T^{12}
T^{6}	T^{6}	T^{13}	T^{11}	T^{3}	T^{2}	T^{12}	T^{9}	0	T^{10}	T^{14}	T^{5}	T^{7}	T^{1}	T^{4}	I	T^{8}
T^{7}	T^{7}	T^{9}	T^{14}	T^{12}	T^{4}	T^{3}	T^{13}	T^{10}	0	T^{11}	I	T^{6}	T^{8}	T^{2}	T^{5}	T^{1}
T^{8}	T^{8}	T^{2}	T^{10}	I	T^{13}	T^{5}	T^{4}	T^{14}	T^{11}	0	T^{12}	T^{1}	T^{7}	T^{9}	T^{3}	T^{6}
T^{9}	T^{9}	T^{7}	T^{3}	T^{11}	T^{1}	T^{14}	T^{6}	T^{5}	I	T^{12}	0	T^{13}	T^{2}	T^{8}	T^{10}	T^{4}
T^{10}	T^{10}	T^{5}	T^{8}	T^{4}	T^{12}	T^{2}	I	T^{7}	T^{6}	T^{1}	T^{13}	0	T^{14}	T^{3}	T^{9}	T^{11}
T^{11}	T^{11}	T^{12}	T^{6}	T^{9}	T^{5}	T^{13}	T^{3}	T^{1}	T^{8}	T^{7}	T^{2}	T^{14}	0	I	T^{4}	T^{10}
T^{12}	T^{12}	T^{11}	T^{13}	T^{7}	T^{10}	T^{6}	T^{14}	T^{4}	T^{2}	T^{9}	T^{8}	T^{3}	I	0	T^{1}	T^{5}
T^{13}	T^{13}	T^{6}	T^{12}	T^{14}	T^{8}	T^{11}	T^{7}	I	T^{5}	T^{3}	T^{10}	T^{9}	T^{4}	T^{1}	0	T^{2}
T^{14}	T^{14}	T^{3}	T^{7}	T^{13}	I	T^{9}	T^{12}	T^{8}	T^{1}	T^{6}	T^{4}	T^{11}	T^{10}	T^{5}	T^{2}	0

×	0	I	T^{1}	T^{2}	T^{3}	T^{4}	T^{5}	T^{6}	T^{7}	T^{8}	T^{9}	T^{10}	T^{11}	T^{12}	T^{13}	T^{14}
0	0	0	0	0	0	0	0	0	0	0	0	0	0	0	0	0
I	0	I	T^{1}	T^{2}	T^{3}	T^{4}	T^{5}	T^{6}	T^{7}	T^{8}	T^{9}	T^{10}	T^{11}	T^{12}	T^{13}	T^{14}
T^{1}	0	T^{1}	T^{2}	T^{3}	T^{4}	T^{5}	T^{6}	T^{7}	T^{8}	T^{9}	T^{10}	T^{11}	T^{12}	T^{13}	T^{14}	I
T^{2}	0	T^{2}	T^{3}	T^{4}	T^{5}	T^{6}	T^{7}	T^{8}	T^{9}	T^{10}	T^{11}	T^{12}	T^{13}	T^{14}	I	T^{1}
T^{3}	0	T^{3}	T^{4}	T^{5}	T^{6}	T^{7}	T^{8}	T^{9}	T^{10}	T^{11}	T^{12}	T^{13}	T^{14}	I	T^{1}	T^{2}
T^{4}	0	T^{4}	T^{5}	T^{6}	T^{7}	T^{8}	T^{9}	T^{10}	T^{11}	T^{12}	T^{13}	T^{14}	I	T^{1}	T^{2}	T^{3}
T^{5}	0	T^{5}	T^{6}	T^{7}	T^{8}	T^{9}	T^{10}	T^{11}	T^{12}	T^{13}	T^{14}	I	T^{1}	T^{2}	T^{3}	T^{4}
T^{6}	0	T^{6}	T^{7}	T^{8}	T^{9}	T^{10}	T^{11}	T^{12}	T^{13}	T^{14}	I	T^{1}	T^{2}	T^{3}	T^{4}	T^{5}
T^{7}	0	T^{7}	T^{8}	T^{9}	T^{10}	T^{11}	T^{12}	T^{13}	T^{14}	I	T^{1}	T^{2}	T^{3}	T^{4}	T^{5}	T^{6}
T^{8}	0	T^{8}	T^{9}	T^{10}	T^{11}	T^{12}	T^{13}	T^{14}	I	T^{1}	T^{2}	T^{3}	T^{4}	T^{5}	T^{6}	T^{7}
T^{9}	0	T^{9}	T^{10}	T^{11}	T^{12}	T^{13}	T^{14}	I	T^{1}	T^{2}	T^{3}	T^{4}	T^{5}	T^{6}	T^{7}	T^{8}
T^{10}	0	T^{10}	T^{11}	T^{12}	T^{13}	T^{14}	I	T^{1}	T^{2}	T^{3}	T^{4}	T^{5}	T^{6}	T^{7}	T^{8}	T^{9}
T^{11}	0	T^{11}	T^{12}	T^{13}	T^{14}	I	T^{1}	T^{2}	T^{3}	T^{4}	T^{5}	T^{6}	T^{7}	T^{8}	T^{9}	T^{10}
T^{12}	0	T^{12}	T^{13}	T^{14}	I	T^{1}	T^{2}	T^{3}	T^{4}	T^{5}	T^{6}	T^{7}	T^{8}	T^{9}	T^{10}	T^{11}
T^{13}	0	T^{13}	T^{14}	I	T^{1}	T^{2}	T^{3}	T^{4}	T^{5}	T^{6}	T^{7}	T^{8}	T^{9}	T^{10}	T^{11}	T^{12}
T^{14}	0	T^{14}	I	T^{1}	T^{2}	T^{3}	T^{4}	T^{5}	T^{6}	T^{7}	T^{8}	T^{9}	T^{10}	T^{11}	T^{12}	T^{13}

By using these elements expressed in binary form, Hamming codes over $GF(2^b)$ are transformed as Hamming-type SbEC codes. This is illustrated by Example 5-2.

Example 5-2

We can obtain a (72, 64) S2EC code from a (36, 32) code over $GF(2^2)$. The companion matrix **T** is derived using the primitive polynomial $g(x) = x^2 + x + 1$. The following **H** matrix shows an example of the (72, 64) S2EC code whose weight (i.e., total number of 1's in the **H** matrix) is near minimal [BOSS 70a]. Note that every column here has at least one identity element **I**, as can be seen.

H =

I	I	I	T^2	T	I	I	I	T^2	T	O	O	I	I	I	I	I	I	I	O	O	O	O	O	O	O	O	O	O	T^2	T	I	I	O	O	O
T^2	T	I	O	O	O	I	I	I	I	T^2	T	O	O	I	I	I	I	O	I	O	O	O	T^2	T	I	I	I	I	O	O	O	O	I	O	O
O	O	O	I	I	I	T	T^2	I	I	I	I	T^2	T	O	O	O	I	I	I	I	I	I	O	O	O	T^2	T	I	O	O	O	O	O	I	O
O	O	O	O	O	O	T^2	T	O	O	I	I	I	I	T^2	T	I	O	I	I	T^2	T	I	I	I	I	O	O	O	I	I	I	O	O	O	I

$O = \begin{bmatrix} 0 & 0 \\ 0 & 0 \end{bmatrix}$ $I = \begin{bmatrix} 1 & 0 \\ 0 & 1 \end{bmatrix}$ $T = \begin{bmatrix} 0 & 1 \\ 1 & 1 \end{bmatrix}$ $T^2 = \begin{bmatrix} 1 & 1 \\ 1 & 0 \end{bmatrix}$

(5.3)*

The symbols n and k denote the block length and information length of the Hamming-type code over $GF(2^b)$. Then the SbEC code derived from that will be an (N, K) code in binary form, where $N = n \cdot b$ and $K = k \cdot b$. Also, the number of check bits is $R = r \cdot b = (n - k) \cdot b$.

The maximum length (in bits) of this class of SbEC codes is given by

$$N_H = b \cdot n = b(2^{br} - 1)/(2^b - 1). \tag{5.4}$$

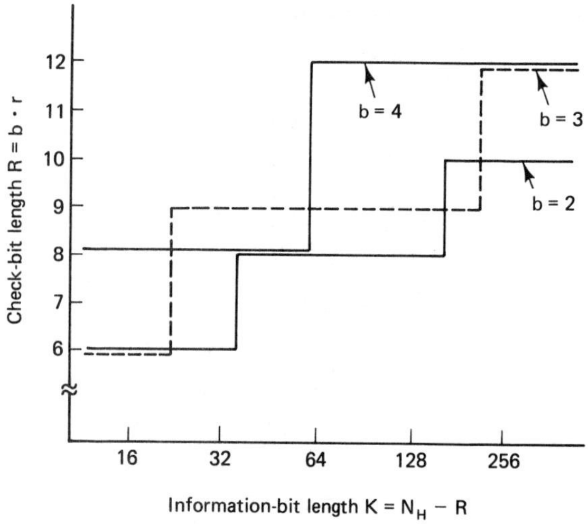

Figure 5.1 Check-bit length of the Hamming-type SbEC code [FUJI 81a].

Fig. 5.1 shows the relation between the information-bit length K and the check-bit length R of this code for $b = 2$, 3, and 4.

Next, a possible method of implementing single-error correction with Hamming-type codes is shown. Let syndrome be equal to $S = (S_0, S_1, \ldots, S_{r-1})$ and the ith column vector of the $\mathbf{H}$ matrix be $(h_{0,i}, h_{1,i}, \ldots, h_{r-1,i})^T$. Then, an error of value E ($E \in GF(2^b)$) in symbol i yields a syndrome that is equal to

$$S = \left(E \cdot h_{0,i}, E \cdot h_{1,i}, \ldots, E \cdot h_{r-1,i}\right).$$

Since every column of $\mathbf{H}$ contains at least one identity element $\mathbf{I}$, then the original syndrome contains the error magnitude in one of the positions $S_0, S_1, \ldots, S_{r-1}$. Without loss of generality, assume that $h_{j,i}$ is equal to $\mathbf{I}$. Then

$$S_j = E \cdot h_{j,i} = E \cdot \mathbf{I} = E.$$

That is, the error pattern E equals S_j. Under this condition, the error byte pointer g_i is a scalar that indicates the location of the ith byte error and is given by the Boolean expression

$$g_i = \bigcap_{\substack{m=0 \\ m \neq j}}^{r-1} \left[S_m = S_j \cdot h_{m,i}\right]. \qquad \bigcap: \text{AND}$$

This means that g_i equals 1 only if every relation of $S_m = S_j \cdot h_{m,i}$ is satisfied for $m = 0, 1, 2, \ldots, r-1$, $m \neq j$.

From the above, the corrected ith byte data $\hat{D}_i$ can be obtained as

$$\hat{D}_i = D_i + g_i \cdot E \qquad \text{for } i = 0, 1, \ldots, k-1.$$

In this equation, + expresses addition in $GF(2^b)$.

5.1.2 Burton Codes and Generalized Burton Codes

There is an interesting subclass of Hamming codes over $GF(2^b)$ that have only two check symbols and are capable of single-error correction in $GF(2^b)$. These codes are known as *2-redundant code* for this reason [BOSS 70a]. The **H** matrix of the Hamming-type 2-redundant code can have the following form.

$$\mathbf{H} = \begin{bmatrix} \mathbf{I} & \mathbf{I} & \mathbf{I} & \cdots & \mathbf{I} & \mathbf{I} & \mathbf{0} \\ \mathbf{I} & \mathbf{T} & \mathbf{T}^2 & \cdots & \mathbf{T}^{2^b-2} & \mathbf{0} & \mathbf{I} \end{bmatrix}$$

It is clear that no two columns of **H** are linearly dependent, so the code has distance 3 and is, therefore, a single-error correcting code over $GF(2^b)$.

Burton code [BURT 71a] is also a 2-redundant SbEC code. This code is a class of phased-burst error correcting cyclic code. The generator polynomial of the code is the following:

$$\mathbf{g}(x) = (x^b + 1) \cdot \mathbf{p}(x) \tag{5.5}$$

Here, $\mathbf{p}(x)$ is an irreducible polynomial of degree b. The maximal code length N of this code is given by:

$$N = LCM\,(e, b)$$

where LCM denotes the Least Common Multiple and e the exponent of $\mathbf{p}(x)$. The code defined by Equation (5.5) can be expressed as the following **H** matrix.

$$\mathbf{H} = \left[\begin{array}{ccccc} \mathbf{I}_b & \mathbf{I}_b & \mathbf{I}_b & \mathbf{I}_b & \cdots \mathbf{I}_b \\ \hline & \mathbf{H}' & \mathbf{H}' & \cdots \mathbf{H}' & \end{array}\right] \tag{5.6}$$

Here, $\mathbf{I}_b$ is the $(b \times b)$ identity matrix and the $\mathbf{H}'$ is the **H** matrix of the binary Hamming code generated by polynomial $\mathbf{p}(x)$. $\mathbf{H}'$ is given by

$$\mathbf{H}' = \begin{bmatrix} | & | & | & & | \\ 1 & \alpha & \alpha^2 & \cdots & \alpha^{e-1} \\ | & | & | & & | \end{bmatrix}$$

where $\begin{matrix} | \\ \alpha^i \\ | \end{matrix}$ is the coefficient vector of $x^i \; mod \; \mathbf{p}(x)$. If $\mathbf{p}(x)$ is primitive, then $e = 2^b - 1$.

On the other hand, the companion matrix **T**, defined by the primitive polynomial $\mathbf{p}(x)$ of degree b, and $\mathbf{T}^i$ (for $i = 0, 1, \ldots, 2^b - 2$) are expressed as in Equation (5.2). Therefore, the **H** matrix shown in (5.6) can be rewritten by using these **T** and $\mathbf{T}^i$ as

$$\mathbf{H} = \begin{bmatrix} \mathbf{I}_b & \mathbf{I}_b & \mathbf{I}_b & \cdots & \mathbf{I}_b & \cdots & \mathbf{I}_b \\ \mathbf{I}_b & \mathbf{T}^b & \mathbf{T}^{2b} & \cdots & \mathbf{T}^{ib} & \cdots & \mathbf{T}^{(e-1)b} \end{bmatrix}$$

This matrix can be reduced to echelon canonical form as:

$$\mathbf{H} = \begin{bmatrix} \mathbf{I}_b & \mathbf{0} & \mathbf{h}_{0,2} & \mathbf{h}_{0,3} & \cdots & \mathbf{h}_{0,i} & \cdots & \mathbf{h}_{0,e-1} \\ \mathbf{0} & \mathbf{I}_b & \mathbf{h}_{1,2} & \mathbf{h}_{1,3} & \cdots & \mathbf{h}_{1,i} & \cdots & \mathbf{h}_{1,e-1} \end{bmatrix}$$

where $\mathbf{0}, \mathbf{I}_b, \mathbf{h}_{0,2}, \ldots, \mathbf{h}_{0,i}, \mathbf{h}_{1,i}, \ldots, \mathbf{h}_{1,e-1}$ are all elements in $GF(2^b)$.

This matrix can have the following properties for $j = 0, 1, 2, \ldots, e - 1$ [FUJI 76a]:

Property 1. $$\mathbf{h}_{0,j} + \mathbf{h}_{1,j} = \mathbf{I}_b \tag{5.7}$$

Property 2. $$\mathbf{H}_j = \begin{bmatrix} \mathbf{h}_{0,j} \\ \mathbf{h}_{1,j} \end{bmatrix} = \mathbf{H}_{j-1} + \begin{bmatrix} \mathbf{T}^{(j-1)b} \\ \mathbf{T}^{(j-1)b} \end{bmatrix} \tag{5.8}$$

Property 3. $$\mathbf{h}_{0,2} = \mathbf{T}^b \tag{5.9}$$

where + expresses addition in $GF(2^b)$.

Example 5-3 [FUJI 76a]

The (21, 15) Burton code is defined by the generator polynomial $\mathbf{g}(x) = (x^3 + 1) \cdot \mathbf{p}(x)$, where $\mathbf{p}(x) = x^3 + x + 1$ is primitive with exponent $e = 7$. Its $\mathbf{H}$ matrix in canonical form is given below.

$$\mathbf{H} = \begin{bmatrix} | & | & | & | & & | \\ \beta^0 & \beta^1 & \beta^2 & \beta^3 & \ldots & \beta^{20} \\ | & | & | & | & & | \end{bmatrix} = \begin{array}{cccccc|ccccccccccccccc} 0 & 1 & 2 & 3 & 4 & 5 & 6 & 7 & 8 & 9 & 10 & 11 & 12 & 13 & 14 & 15 & 16 & 17 & 18 & 19 & 20 \\ \hline 1 & & & & & & 1 & & 1 & & 1 & 1 & & & 1 & 1 & 1 & & 1 & 1 & 1 \\ & 1 & & & & & 1 & 1 & 1 & 1 & 1 & & 1 & & 1 & & & 1 & 1 & & \\ & & 1 & & & & & 1 & 1 & 1 & 1 & 1 & & 1 & & 1 & & & 1 & 1 & \\ & & & 1 & & & & & 1 & 1 & 1 & 1 & 1 & & 1 & & 1 & & & 1 & 1 \\ & & & & 1 & & 1 & & 1 & 1 & & & 1 & 1 & 1 & & 1 & 1 & 1 & 1 & \\ & & & & & 1 & & 1 & & 1 & 1 & & & 1 & 1 & 1 & & 1 & 1 & 1 & 1 \end{array}$$

As before, β^i is the coefficient vector of $x^i \; mod \; \mathbf{g}(x)$. Next, let's divide this $\mathbf{H}$ matrix by (3×3) square matrix as follows:

$$\mathbf{H} = \left[\begin{array}{ccc|ccc|ccc|ccc|ccc|ccc|ccc} 1 & & & & & & 1 & & 1 & & 1 & 1 & & & 1 & 1 & 1 & & 1 & 1 & 1 \\ & 1 & & & & & 1 & 1 & 1 & 1 & 1 & & 1 & & 1 & & & 1 & 1 & & \\ & & 1 & & & & & 1 & 1 & 1 & 1 & 1 & & 1 & & 1 & & & 1 & 1 & \\ \hline & & & 1 & & & & & 1 & 1 & 1 & 1 & 1 & & 1 & & 1 & & & 1 & 1 \\ & & & & 1 & & 1 & & 1 & 1 & & & 1 & 1 & 1 & & 1 & 1 & 1 & 1 & \\ & & & & & 1 & & 1 & & 1 & 1 & & & 1 & 1 & 1 & & 1 & 1 & 1 & 1 \end{array}\right] \tag{5.10}$$

On the other hand, $\mathbf{H}'$ can be given by

$$\mathbf{H}' = \begin{bmatrix} | & | & | & | & | & | & | \\ 1 & \alpha & \alpha^2 & \alpha^3 & \alpha^4 & \alpha^5 & \alpha^6 \\ | & | & | & | & | & | & | \end{bmatrix}$$

where α is a root of $\mathbf{p}(x)$. From the polynomial $\mathbf{p}(x)$, the following companion matrices and the addition table on $GF(2^3)$ can be derived.

$$\mathbf{T} = \begin{bmatrix} 0 & 0 & 1 \\ 1 & 0 & 1 \\ 0 & 1 & 0 \end{bmatrix}$$

+	**0**	**I**	**T**	$\mathbf{T}^2$	$\mathbf{T}^3$	$\mathbf{T}^4$	$\mathbf{T}^5$	$\mathbf{T}^6$
0	**0**	**I**	**T**	$\mathbf{T}^2$	$\mathbf{T}^3$	$\mathbf{T}^4$	$\mathbf{T}^5$	$\mathbf{T}^6$
I	**I**	**0**	$\mathbf{T}^3$	$\mathbf{T}^6$	**T**	$\mathbf{T}^5$	$\mathbf{T}^4$	$\mathbf{T}^2$
T	**T**	$\mathbf{T}^3$	**0**	$\mathbf{T}^4$	**I**	$\mathbf{T}^2$	$\mathbf{T}^6$	$\mathbf{T}^5$
$\mathbf{T}^2$	$\mathbf{T}^2$	$\mathbf{T}^6$	$\mathbf{T}^4$	**0**	$\mathbf{T}^5$	**T**	$\mathbf{T}^3$	**I**
$\mathbf{T}^3$	$\mathbf{T}^3$	**T**	**I**	$\mathbf{T}^5$	**0**	$\mathbf{T}^6$	$\mathbf{T}^2$	$\mathbf{T}^4$
$\mathbf{T}^4$	$\mathbf{T}^4$	$\mathbf{T}^5$	$\mathbf{T}^2$	**T**	$\mathbf{T}^6$	**0**	**I**	$\mathbf{T}^3$
$\mathbf{T}^5$	$\mathbf{T}^5$	$\mathbf{T}^4$	$\mathbf{T}^6$	$\mathbf{T}^3$	$\mathbf{T}^2$	**I**	**0**	**T**
$\mathbf{T}^6$	$\mathbf{T}^6$	$\mathbf{T}^2$	$\mathbf{T}^5$	**I**	$\mathbf{T}^4$	$\mathbf{T}^3$	**T**	**0**

Hence, the **H** matrix of this code can be expressed as:

$$\mathbf{H} = \left[\begin{array}{ccccccc} \mathbf{I}_3 & \mathbf{I}_3 & \mathbf{I}_3 & \mathbf{I}_3 & \mathbf{I}_3 & \mathbf{I}_3 & \mathbf{I}_3 \\ \hline & \mathbf{H}' & & \mathbf{H}' & & \mathbf{H}' & \end{array}\right]$$

$$= \left[\begin{array}{ccc|ccc|ccc|ccc|ccc|ccc|ccc} 1 & 0 & 0 & 1 & 0 & 0 & 1 & 0 & 0 & 1 & 0 & 0 & 1 & 0 & 0 & 1 & 0 & 0 & 1 & 0 & 0 \\ 0 & 1 & 0 & 0 & 1 & 0 & 0 & 1 & 0 & 0 & 1 & 0 & 0 & 1 & 0 & 0 & 1 & 0 & 0 & 1 & 0 \\ 0 & 0 & 1 & 0 & 0 & 1 & 0 & 0 & 1 & 0 & 0 & 1 & 0 & 0 & 1 & 0 & 0 & 1 & 0 & 0 & 1 \\ \hline \multicolumn{7}{c|}{1 \;\; \alpha \;\; \alpha^2 \;\; \alpha^3 \;\; \alpha^4 \;\; \alpha^5 \;\; \alpha^6} & \multicolumn{7}{c|}{1 \;\; \alpha \;\; \alpha^2 \;\; \alpha^3 \;\; \alpha^4 \;\; \alpha^5 \;\; \alpha^6} & \multicolumn{7}{c}{1 \;\; \alpha \;\; \alpha^2 \;\; \alpha^3 \;\; \alpha^4 \;\; \alpha^5 \;\; \alpha^6} \end{array}\right]$$

$$= \left[\begin{array}{ccccccc} \mathbf{I}_3 & \mathbf{I}_3 & \mathbf{I}_3 & \mathbf{I}_3 & \mathbf{I}_3 & \mathbf{I}_3 & \mathbf{I}_3 \\ \hline \mathbf{I}_3 & \mathbf{T}^3 & \mathbf{T}^6 & \mathbf{T}^2 & \mathbf{T}^5 & \mathbf{T} & \mathbf{T}^4 \end{array}\right]$$

$$= \left[\begin{array}{ccccccc} \mathbf{I}_3 & \mathbf{0} & \mathbf{T}^3 & \mathbf{T}^4 & \mathbf{T} & \mathbf{T}^6 & \mathbf{T}^5 \\ \hline \mathbf{0} & \mathbf{I}_3 & \mathbf{T} & \mathbf{T}^5 & \mathbf{T}^3 & \mathbf{T}^2 & \mathbf{T}^4 \end{array}\right]$$

This resulting **H** matrix having echelon-canonical form is equivalent to the matrix shown in (5.10). It is clear that this matrix satisfies the properties shown in (5.7), (5.8), and (5.9).

The interesting properties of the Burton code, especially property 1 in (5.7), can make this an odd-weight-column SbEC code. Actually, every column vector of the **H** matrix shown in (5.10) is of odd weight, and property 1 in (5.7) satisfies Definition 4-5 of the odd-weight-column code (see Section 4.4.2).

On the other hand, property 2 in (5.8) and property 3 in (5.9) express the cyclic structure of this code. These are not important when parallel decoding is employed as required for high-speed memories.

Next, we consider the double-byte error detection capability of these 2-redundant SbEC codes.

Theorem 5-1 [FUJI 77b]. *The double-byte error detection capability, P_d, of the 2-redundant $((k + 2) \cdot b, k \cdot b)$ SbEC code is given by*

$$P_d = 1 - \frac{k}{2^b - 1}$$

Proof. P_d is the fraction of double-byte errors that are detected by this code. Double-byte errors, say E_1 and E_2, may generate a syndrome that may equal the syndrome corresponding to a single-byte error such as E_3. This will result in a miscorrection as stated before. We analyze these following cases.

Case 1: E_1, E_2, and E_3 are in information-bit part.
Case 2: E_1 and E_2 are in information-bit part and E_3 is in check-bit part.
Case 3: E_1 is in information-bit part, and E_2 and E_3 are in check-bit part.
Case 4: E_1, E_2, and E_3 are all in check-bit part. (Miscorrection will be harmless if it occurs.)

For each case, the number of miscorrections can be counted as follows.

Case 1: $3(2^b - 1)\binom{k}{3}$

Case 2: $2 \times 3(2^b - 1)\binom{k}{2}$

Case 3: $3(2^b - 1)\binom{k}{1}$

Case 4: 0

Therefore, the detection ability, P_d, is as follows.

$$P_d = 1 - \frac{3(2^b - 1)\left\{\binom{k}{3} + 2\binom{k}{2} + \binom{k}{1}\right\}}{\binom{k+2}{2} \sum_{i,j=1}^{b} \binom{b}{i} \cdot \binom{b}{j}}$$

By simple algebra, this expression reduces to $1 - [k/(2^b - 1)]$ to complete the proof. Q.E.D.

Example 5-4

The 2-redundant (80, 64) S8EC code has the following double-byte error detection probability: $P_d = 1 - 8/(2^8 - 1) = 0.9686$. That is, 96.86% of all double-byte errors are detected, and it is "very nearly" an S8EC–D8ED code.

Theorem 5-1 gives us the important result that for a large value of b (e.g., $b = 8, 12, 16$), the 2-redundant SbEC code is very nearly an SbEC–DbED code. Also, it is practical and suitable to high-speed memories because the information-bit length for these memories is rather short [ARLA 84]. Thus, the class of SbEC–DbED codes discussed later may not be all that necessary for the case when b is large.

Here, we consider a generalized class of Burton codes that can be constructed by using a generator polynomial $\mathbf{g}(x) = (x^b + 1)\mathbf{p}(x)$, where the degree of $\mathbf{p}(x)$ is l.

It is important that if l is equal to b, the codes defined by the polynomial $\mathbf{g}(x)$ are equal to Burton codes. If l is greater than b, the codes can also correct all single-byte errors [VARA 83]. If $\mathbf{p}(x)$ is a primitive polynomial of degree l, then the code-bit length N and the check-bit length R can be expressed as

$$N = b(2^l - 1)$$

$$R = l + b.$$

If l is less than b, the codes can correct single-bit errors and detect double-bit errors and single b-bit burst errors [VARA 83]. This will be shown in Section 5.3.1.

Since the generalized codes are cyclic, they can be implemented efficiently by LFSR logic when high-speed logic is not mandatory.

5.1.3 Fujiwara Codes

From the property of the Burton code, Fujiwara derives a new class of SbEC codes that has an odd-weight-column characteristic [FUJI 77b, FUJI 78].

In an odd-weight-column-matrix code over $GF(2^b)$ (see Definition 4-5 in Section 4.4.2), no two columns are identical and no column is all zero or a multiple of another column. The last is true because if a column vector H_i is a multiple of H_j (i.e., $H_i = \beta \cdot H_j$ where $\beta \in GF(2^b)$, and $\beta \neq 0$, $\beta \neq 1$), then the sum of the elements of H_i equals β, contradicting the odd-weight-column property. Therefore, columns H_i and H_j are a linearly independent pair and the code is of distance 3 or higher. Therefore, we have proved the following.

Theorem 5-2. *An odd-weight-column-matrix code over $GF(2^b)$ is an SbEC code.*

Lemma 5-1. *There exists exactly $2^{b(r-1)}$ odd-weight-column vectors, each having r elements over $GF(2^b)$.*

Proof. Let H be an odd-weight-column vector over $GF(2^b)$. Also let the sum of the first $(r - 1)$ elements of this vector be γ. Then, the remaining one element can only be $(\gamma + 1)$, that is, the last element of this column vector is uniquely determined from the other previous $(r - 1)$ elements, which are arbitrary. Since each element can have any one of 2^b values, there are exactly $2^{b(r-1)}$ such column vectors. Q.E.D.

This gives the maximal code-bit length N_F of the Fujiwara code to be

$$N_F = b \cdot n = b \cdot 2^{b(r-1)}. \tag{5.11}$$

Compared to the Hamming-type SbEC code, this code has to be shorter in block

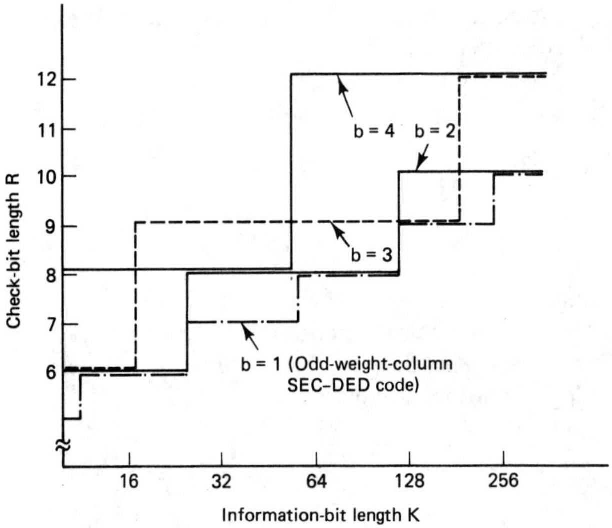

Figure 5.2 Check-bit length of the Fujiwara SbEC code [FUJI 81a].

length. From Equations (5.4) and (5.11), the ratio N_F/N_H is shown as follows.

$$N_F/N_H = 1 - \frac{2^{b(r-1)} - 1}{2^{br} - 1}$$

$$\approx 1 - \frac{1}{2^b} \qquad \text{for } r \cdot b \gg 1$$

This code is equivalent to the popular odd-weight-column SEC–DED code (see Section 4.1.1), especially for $b = 1$. Therefore, this code can be said to include the odd-weight-column SEC–DED code as a special case of $b = 1$. Fig. 5.2 shows the relation between the information-bit length K and the check-bit length R of this code for $b = 1$, 2, 3, and 4.

Example 5-5

Consider a (72, 64) S2EC code having parameters $b = 2$ and $r = 4$. The companion matrix $\mathbf{T}$ is determined by the polynomial $\mathbf{g}(x) = x^2 + x + 1$. Its $\mathbf{H}$ matrix is given as follows.

$$\mathbf{H} = \left[\begin{array}{cccccccccccccccccccccccccccccccccccc}
I & I & I & T & T & I & T^2 & T^2 & T & T^2 & O & O & O & O & O & O & T^2 & T & T & T & I & T^2 & T^2 & I & I & I & T & I & T & T^2 & I & T^2 & I & O & O & O \\
I & I & T & I & T & T^2 & I & T^2 & I & I & I & T & T & I & T^2 & T^2 & T & T^2 & O & O & O & O & O & O & T^2 & T & T & T & I & T^2 & T^2 & I & O & I & O & O \\
T^2 & T & T & T & I & T^2 & T^2 & I & I & I & T & I & T & T^2 & I & T^2 & I & I & I & T & T & I & T^2 & T^2 & T & T^2 & O & O & O & O & O & O & O & O & I & O \\
T & T^2 & O & O & O & O & O & O & T^2 & T & T & T & I & T^2 & T^2 & I & I & I & T & I & T & I & T & T^2 & I & T^2 & I & I & I & T & T & I & T^2 & T^2 & O & O & O & I
\end{array}\right]$$

$$O = \begin{bmatrix} 0 & 0 \\ 0 & 0 \end{bmatrix} \quad I = \begin{bmatrix} 1 & 0 \\ 0 & 1 \end{bmatrix} \quad T = \begin{bmatrix} 0 & 1 \\ 1 & 1 \end{bmatrix} \quad T^2 = \begin{bmatrix} 1 & 1 \\ 1 & 0 \end{bmatrix} \qquad (5.12)$$

The decoding procedure of this code can be as follows. Let the ith column vector in the $\mathbf{H}$ matrix be $(h_{0,i}, h_{1,i}, \ldots, h_{r-1,i})^T$, where $h_{m,i} \in GF(2^b)$, $m = 0, 1, \ldots, r-1$, and the syndrome due to error in the ith position is $(S_0, S_1, \ldots, S_{r-1})$. Then, an error E in symbol i yields a syndrome that is equal to

$$S_m = E \cdot h_{m,i}, \qquad \text{for } m = 0, 1, \ldots, r-1$$

Clearly for odd-weight-column codes, the sum of syndrome components must equal E, that is,

$$E = \sum_{i=0}^{r-1} S_i, \qquad \sum : \text{addition in } GF(2^b)$$

The error byte pointer g_i is given, for example, by substituting E by $S_0 \cdot h_{0,i}^{-1}$,

$$g_i = \bigcap_{m=1}^{r-1} \left[S_m = S_0 \cdot h_{0,i}^{-1} \cdot h_{m,i} \right]$$

From these, the corrected ith byte data $\hat{D}_i$ can be obtained as

$$\hat{D}_i = D_i + g_i \cdot E \qquad \text{for } i = 0, 1, \ldots, k-1$$

In this equation, + expresses addition in $GF(2^b)$. Fig. 5.3 shows the decoding circuit of the odd-weight-column SbEC code.

Another important feature of this odd-weight-column SbEC code exists in its error detection capability for certain double-byte errors.

Theorem 5-3. *Odd-weight-column SbEC codes can detect two byte errors in positions i and j provided their error values E_i and E_j are equal.*

Proof. The condition for detecting double-byte errors is given by

$$E_i \cdot H_i + E_j \cdot H_j \neq E_k \cdot H_k \tag{5.13}$$

for all nonzero E_i, E_j, and E_k values in three distinct positions i, j, and k. The corresponding column vectors of the $\mathbf{H}$ matrix are H_i, H_j and H_k.

Since it is an SbEC code, $E_i \cdot H_i + E_j \cdot H_j \neq 0$. If $E_i = E_j$, the sum of all elements of the vector $E_i \cdot H_i + E_j \cdot H_j$ is equal to the error value $E_i + E_j$ and hence equals zero. However, the sum of the elements of the vector $E_k \cdot H_k$ is equal

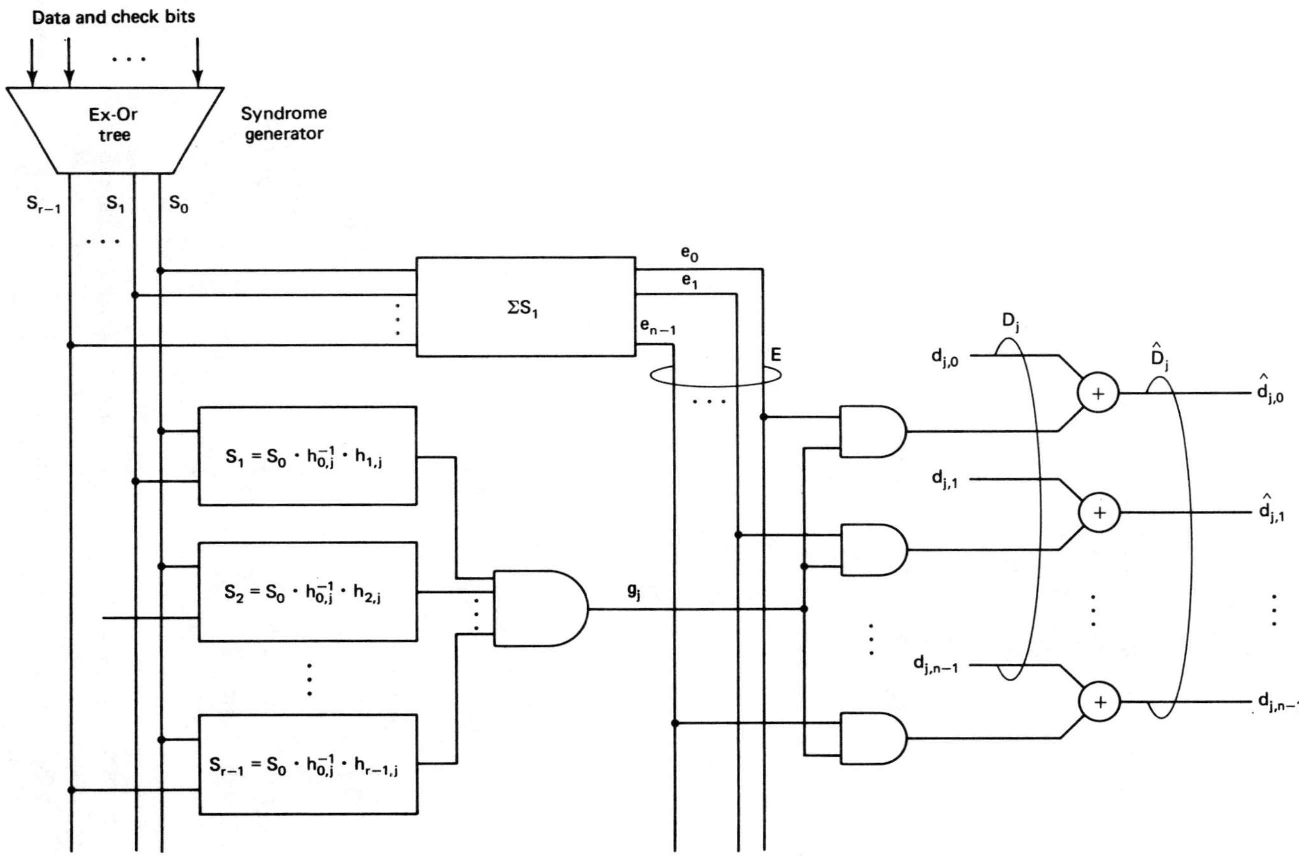

$\oplus$: Exclusive-or

$D_j = (d_{j,0} \sim d_{j,n-1})$: Read-out data

$\hat{D}_j = (\hat{d}_{j,0} \sim \hat{d}_{j,n-1})$: Corrected data

E: Error pattern

g_j: Error byte pointer

$S_0 \sim S_{r-1}$: Syndrome

Figure 5.3 Error correction scheme for byte j [FUJI 81a].

TABLE 5.1 MISCORRECTION PROBABILITIES OF THE (72, 64) S2EC CODES

Codes	Probability of Miscorrected Double 2-Bit-Byte Errors (percent)	Probability of Miscorrected 2-Bit Errors over Double Bytes (percent)
Hamming-type (72, 64) S2EC code shown in (5.3)	45.9	48.3
Odd-weight-column (72, 64) S2EC code shown in (5.12)	33.6	25.2

Source: [FUJI 77b]. © 1977 IEEE.

to the error value E_k and does not equal zero. Therefore, Equation (5.13) holds for $E_i = E_j$ and the theorem is proved. Q.E.D.

Theorem 5-3 guarantees the partial double-byte error detection of these codes. Especially, all bit errors in two bytes (i.e., $2b$-bit errors over any two bytes) can be detected.

In addition, from the odd-weight-column characteristic of this code, the following relations are also valid:

1. The even number of bit errors over two bytes cannot be miscorrected to the odd number of bit errors over single bytes.
2. The odd number of bit errors over two bytes cannot be miscorrected to the even number of bit errors over single bytes.

It is important for SbEC codes to minimize the probability of miscorrection of double-byte errors. Table 5.1 compares the miscorrection probability of the typical (72, 64) S2EC codes. From these results, odd-weight-column S2EC codes have better error detection capability for double-byte errors than the non-odd-weight-column S2EC codes. For more details, refer to [FUJI 78].

Rotational Fujiwara codes. We can also derive another class called rotational odd-weight-column SbEC codes [FUJI 77b, FUJI 78]. Before obtaining the code length of this code, we need the following *modified Möbius inversion formula.*

Theorem 5-4 [FUJI 78]. *If the following relation is valid between two functions, $f(r)$ and $g(r)$, for any positive integer r,*

$$f(r) = \sum_{(r/m):\ odd} g(m) \tag{5.14}$$

then, $g(r)$ can be expressed by $f(r)$ as

$$g(r) = \sum_{\substack{m|r \\ m;\ odd}} \mu(m) \cdot f\left(\frac{r}{m}\right) \tag{5.15}$$

Here $\mu(m)$ is called the Möbius function and $\sum_{\substack{m|r \\ m:\ odd}}$ means the summation over all odd m that divides r.

Proof. As Equation (5.14) is valid for any positive integer, the following relation should hold for any divisor m of r.

$$f\left(\frac{r}{m}\right) = \sum_{(r/m)/c;\ odd} g(c)$$

This is substituted to the right-hand side of Equation (5.14). The group of all combinations of m and c that satisfies $\substack{m|r \\ m;\ odd}$ and $(r/m)/c;\ odd$ is equivalent to the group of all combinations of m and c that satisfies $c|r$ and $\substack{m|(r/c) \\ (r/c);\ odd}$. Then, the following equation is valid.

$$\begin{aligned} \sum_{\substack{m|r \\ m;\ odd}} \mu(m) \cdot f\left(\frac{r}{m}\right) &= \sum_{\substack{m|r \\ m;\ odd}} \mu(m) \cdot \sum_{(r/m)/c;\ odd} g(c) \\ &= \sum_{c|r} g(c) \cdot \sum_{\substack{m|(r/c) \\ (r/c);\ odd}} \mu(m) \end{aligned} \tag{5.16}$$

The property of a Möbius function says that

$$\sum_{m|n} \mu(m) = \begin{cases} 1; & n = 1 \\ 0; & n > 1 \end{cases}$$

As a result, the right-hand side of Equation (5.16) equals $g(r)$. Hence, the relation in (5.15) is proved. Q.E.D.

The discussion that follows is similar to the rotational-bit error correcting codes (see Section 4.4.4).

The **H** matrix of the rotational odd-weight-column codes has r rows and n columns. The column vector that has r elements is assumed to have some nondegenerate cyclic equivalence classes, each of which has m elements of $GF(2^b)$. The summation of m elements of the class is equal to **I**. Moreover, the whole summation of r elements of the column vector should be equal to **I**. Thus, r divided by m should be an odd integer.

Let $n(r, b)$ be a total number of nondegenerate cyclic equivalence classes that have m elements of $GF(2^b)$. Then, the following equation is valid.

$$2^{b(r-1)} = \sum_{(r/m);\ odd} m \cdot n(m, b)$$

From the modified Möbius inversion formula of Theorem 5-4, $n(r, b)$ can be easily obtained as follows.

$$n(r, b) = \frac{1}{r} \sum_{\substack{m|r \\ m;\ odd}} \mu(m) \cdot 2^{b(r/m-1)}$$

TABLE 5.2 CODE BYTE-LENGTH n OF THE ROTATIONAL FUJIWARA SbEC CODES COMPARED TO THE NONROTATIONAL CODES

r \ b	1*	2	3	4	6	8
2	$\frac{2^{**}}{2}$	$\frac{4}{4}$	$\frac{8}{8}$	$\frac{16}{16}$	$\frac{64}{64}$	$\frac{256}{256}$
3	$\frac{3}{4}$	$\frac{15}{16}$	$\frac{63}{64}$	$\frac{255}{256}$	$\frac{4095}{4096}$	$\frac{65535}{65536}$
4	$\frac{8}{8}$	$\frac{64}{64}$	$\frac{512}{512}$	$\frac{4096}{4096}$	—	—
5	$\frac{15}{16}$	$\frac{255}{256}$	$\frac{4095}{4096}$	$\frac{65535}{65536}$	—	—
6	$\frac{30}{32}$	$\frac{1020}{1024}$	$\frac{32760}{32768}$	—	—	—
7	$\frac{63}{64}$	$\frac{4095}{4096}$	—	—	—	—
8	$\frac{128}{128}$	$\frac{16384}{16384}$	—	—	—	—

*Rotational odd-weight-column SEC–DED code, $n = \sum_{\substack{m|r \\ m;\ odd}} \mu(m) \cdot 2^{(r/m-1)}$

** 2 → *rotational*
$\overline{2}$ → *nonrotational*

$$H_0 = \begin{bmatrix} T & T^2 & I & T & I & T & T^2 & T & I \\ T & T^2 & T & I & T^2 & T^2 & T & O & O \\ T & T^2 & T & T & T^2 & O & O & T^2 & O \\ T^2 & T & O & O & O & O & O & O & O \end{bmatrix} \qquad H_0 = \begin{bmatrix} I & I & I & T & T & I & T^2 & T^2 & I \\ I & I & T & I & T & T^2 & I & T^2 & O \\ T^2 & T & T & T & I & T^2 & T^2 & I & O \\ T & T^2 & O & O & O & O & O & O & O \end{bmatrix}$$

(a) (b)

$$T = \begin{bmatrix} 0 & 1 \\ 1 & 1 \end{bmatrix} \quad T^2 = \begin{bmatrix} 1 & 1 \\ 1 & 0 \end{bmatrix} \quad I = \begin{bmatrix} 1 & 0 \\ 0 & 1 \end{bmatrix} \quad O = \begin{bmatrix} 0 & 0 \\ 0 & 0 \end{bmatrix} \qquad R = \begin{bmatrix} O & O & O & I \\ I & O & O & O \\ O & I & O & O \\ O & O & I & O \end{bmatrix}$$

$$H = [H_0 \mid R \cdot H_0 \mid R^2 \cdot H_0 \mid R^3 \cdot H_0]$$

Figure 5.4 Two examples of the rotational Fujiwara (72, 64) S2EC codes [FUJI 78]. © 1978 IECE Japan.

Here, $n(r, b)$ means the length of each H_i of the rotational **H** matrix. Thus, the code length of the rotational odd-weight-column SbEC code is expressed as

$$n = r \cdot n(r, b) = \sum_{\substack{m \mid r \\ m;\ odd}} \mu(m) \cdot 2^{b(r/m-1)}.$$

Table 5.2 shows the code length n of this code. Note that there is no significant difference between the code lengths of the rotational and nonrotational codes. And for $b = 1$, this is equal to the code length of the rotational odd-weight-column SEC–DED codes.

Fig. 5.4 shows two examples of the rotational Fujiwara (72, 64) S2EC codes.

5.1.4 Maximal SbEC Codes—Hong–Patel Codes

We study here a class of SbEC codes over $GF(2^b)$ called Hong–Patel codes [HONG 72]. A byte is not equated to a symbol from $GF(2^b)$, but instead is treated as a convenient cluster of b individual bits. The number of check bits may or may not be a multiple of b, and sometimes it may be arbitrary. Hong–Patel codes contain subclasses that are equivalent to all single-symbol error correcting codes over $GF(2^b)$, including the binary Hamming codes. Furthermore, these codes are easily implementable and expandable, and are either *perfect* or *maximal*: hence, they are called the *general class of maximal codes* [HONG 72]. Here, a *maximal code* is defined such that no longer code with the same error-correcting capability for a given check-bit length exists.

Given a check-bit length R and a byte-length b, consider the matrix on page 239 $\mathbf{H}_{R,b}$, where $R \geq 2b$:

$$
\mathbf{H}_{R,b} = \left[\begin{array}{cccc|cccc|c|cccc|c|cccc}
1 & & & & 1 & & & & & 1 & & & & & 1 & & & \\
& 1 & & & & 1 & & & & & 1 & & & & & 1 & & \\
& & \ddots & & & & \ddots & & & & & \ddots & & & & & \ddots & \\
& & & 1 & & & & 1 & \cdots & & & & 1 & \cdots & & & & 1 \\
\hline
| & | & & | & | & | & & | & & | & | & & | & & | & | & & | \\
\alpha^0 & \alpha^1 & \cdots & \alpha^{b-1} & \alpha^1 & \alpha^2 & \cdots & \alpha^b & & \alpha^i & \alpha^{i+1} & \cdots & \alpha^{i+b-1} & & \alpha^{2^{R-b}-2} & \alpha^0 & \cdots & \alpha^{b-2} \\
| & | & & | & | & | & & | & & | & | & & | & & | & | & & |
\end{array}\right]
\begin{array}{c} \uparrow \\ b \\ \downarrow \\ \uparrow \\ R-b \\ \downarrow \end{array}
$$

$$
= \left[\begin{array}{c|c|c|c|c|c|c}
\mathbf{I}_b & \mathbf{I}_b & \cdots & \mathbf{I}_b & \cdots & \mathbf{I}_b \\
\hline
\mathbf{I}_b & \mathbf{T} & & \mathbf{T}^i & & \mathbf{T}^{2^{R-b}-2}
\end{array}\right]
$$

$$
\mathbf{I}_b = \begin{bmatrix} 1 & & & \\ & 1 & & \\ & & 1 & \\ & & & \ddots & \\ & & & & 1 \end{bmatrix}_{b \times b}
\qquad
\mathbf{T}^i = \begin{bmatrix} | & | & & | \\ \alpha^i & \alpha^{i+1} & \cdots & \alpha^{i+b-1} \\ | & | & & | \end{bmatrix}_{(R-b) \times b}
\qquad
i = 0, 1, \ldots, 2^{R-b} - 2
$$

where α is a primitive element in $GF(2^{R-b})$, that is, it is a root of a primitive polynomial $\mathbf{g}(x)$ of degree $(R - b)$, and hence $\left|\alpha^i\right|$ is the coefficient vector of $x^i \bmod \mathbf{g}(x)$.

Lemma 5-2. *The code given by the following* **H** *matrix corrects all single-byte errors*:

$$\mathbf{H} = \left[\mathbf{H}_{R,b} \quad | \quad \mathbf{I}_R\right]$$

The information bits can be grouped as $(2^{R-b} - 1)$ bytes, $D_0, D_1, \ldots, D_{2^{R-b}-2}$. The check bits are similarly grouped as check bytes $C_0, C_1, \ldots, C_{r-1}$, where $r = \left\lceil \frac{R}{b} \right\rceil$, and C_{r-1} is the last check byte and may be of a length less than b. For the codeword $W = [D_0, D_1, \ldots, D_{2^{R-b}-2}, C_0, C_1, \ldots, C_{r-1}]$, we have $W \cdot \mathbf{H}^T = 0$. The erroneous word W' then produces a syndrome S given by

$$S = W' \cdot \mathbf{H}^T = [S_0, S_1, \ldots, S_{r-1}]$$

The syndrome consists of r bytes called syndrome bytes. With the above considerations, we can now proceed to prove Lemma 5-2.

First, any error byte in the information portion, say, error pattern $E_i \neq 0$ in the ith byte, gives the following syndrome

$$S_0 = E_i$$

and

$$[S_1, S_2, \ldots, S_{r-1}] = E_i \cdot \mathbf{T}^i$$

From these, $S_0 = E_i \neq 0$ and $[S_1, S_2, \ldots, S_{r-1}] \neq 0$. The error byte in the check portion, however, gives the following syndromes. Let $E_j \neq 0$ in the jth check byte.

$$S_\lambda = 0, \qquad \lambda \neq j$$

$$S_j = E_j \neq 0$$

Hence, an error in the information portion must give at least two bytes of nonzero syndromes, and an error in the check portion gives only one nonzero syndrome byte. Distinct errors in the check portion obviously yield distinct syndromes. Now, suppose byte errors $E_i \neq 0$ and $E_j \neq 0$ in the ith and the jth $(i \neq j)$ information bytes generate identical syndromes. Then, we have

$$E_i = E_j \qquad \text{and} \qquad E_i \cdot \mathbf{T}^i = E_j \cdot \mathbf{T}^j$$

Since $\mathbf{T}^i \neq \mathbf{T}^j$ for $i \neq j$, this cannot occur. Therefore, errors in information bytes have distinct syndromes and hence are correctable.

Lemma 5-3. *The code described by the following* **H** *matrix corrects all single-byte errors:*

$$\mathbf{H} = \left[\mathbf{H}_{R,b} \left| \begin{array}{c} \mathbf{0}_b \ \ \mathbf{0}_b \cdots \mathbf{0}_b \\ \hline \mathbf{H}_{R-b,b} \end{array} \right| \mathbf{I}_R \right], \qquad R \geq 3b \tag{5.17}$$

where $\mathbf{0}_b$ *is a* $(b \times b)$ *zero matrix.*

Proof. Let the information portions corresponding to $\mathbf{H}_{R,b}$ and $\mathbf{H}_{R-b,b}$ be called the first and the second partition of information bytes. An error byte in the first partition yields $S_0 \neq 0$ and at least one more nonzero syndrome byte. An error byte in the second partition yields $S_0 = 0$, $S_1 \neq 0$, and at least one more nonzero syndrome byte. This is because $\mathbf{H}_{R-b,b}$ itself is a single-byte error correcting code having $(R - b)$ check bits. An error byte in the check portion yields one and only one nonzero syndrome byte. Distinct byte errors in the same partition yield distinct syndromes due to Lemma 5-2. Q.E.D.

Lemma 5-3 suggests an iterative concatenation of partitions as defined in (5.17), maintaining the single-byte error correcting capability. From these lemmas, a new class of code can be defined as the code given by the following **H** matrix.

$$\mathbf{H} = \left[\begin{array}{c|c|c|c|c|c} & \mathbf{0}_b \ \mathbf{0}_b \cdots \mathbf{0}_b & \mathbf{0}_b \ \mathbf{0}_b \cdots \mathbf{0}_b & & \mathbf{0}_b \ \mathbf{0}_b \cdots \mathbf{0}_b & \\ \cline{2-2} & & \mathbf{0}_b \ \mathbf{0}_b \cdots \mathbf{0}_b & & \mathbf{0}_b \ \mathbf{0}_b \cdots \mathbf{0}_b & \\ \cline{3-3}\cline{5-5} \mathbf{H}_{R,b} & & & \cdots & \vdots & \mathbf{I}_R \\ & \mathbf{H}_{(R-b),b} & & & & \\ \cline{5-5} & & \mathbf{H}_{(R-2b),b} & & & \\ & & & & \mathbf{H}_{(2b+c),b} & \end{array} \right] \tag{5.18}$$

$$= [\mathbf{P}_0 \mid \mathbf{P}_1 \mid \mathbf{P}_2 \mid \cdots \mid \mathbf{P}_{r-2} \mid \mathbf{I}_R]$$

The second form shown above is to define $(r - 1)$ partitions for the information portion. Each partition $\mathbf{P}_j$ contains $b \cdot (2^{(r-j-1)b+c} - 1)$ columns.

Theorem 5-5. *The code defined by the* **H** *matrix of* (5.18) *corrects all single-byte errors.*

Proof. Any two distinct errors within a partition or within the check portion yield distinct syndromes due to Lemma 5-3. A single error $E \neq 0$ in the ith byte of partition $\mathbf{P}_j$ yields the syndrome

$$S_0 = S_1 = \cdots = S_{j-1} = 0$$

$$S_j = E$$

$$\left[S_{j+1}, \ldots, S_{r-1}\right] = E \cdot \mathbf{T}^i \neq 0$$

which is distinct from the syndrome of any single-byte error in another partition or in the check portion. Q.E.D.

A few remarks about the structure of this code follow.

1. When $b = 1$, the code length n becomes

$$n = \sum_{j=1}^{r-1} (2^{(r-j)} - 1) + r = \sum_{i=1}^{r-1} 2^i + 1 \qquad (5.19)$$
$$= 2^r - 1$$

   which is the code length of the Hamming code. Therefore, this new code defines an alternative structure for a single-error correcting Hamming code.
2. The structure of each partition $\mathbf{H}_{(R-jb),b}$ resembles very closely that of a Fire code [FIRE 59]. In fact, when b and $(2^{R-b} - 1)$ are relatively prime, the Fire code given by the following $\mathbf{H}$ matrix, $\mathbf{H}'_{R,b}$, has the same properties as $\mathbf{H}_{R,b}$:

$$\mathbf{H}'_{R,b} = \left[\begin{array}{c} \mathbf{I}_b \;\; \mathbf{I}_b \cdots \mathbf{I}_b \\ \hline \mathbf{H}' \;\; \mathbf{H}' \cdots \mathbf{H}' \end{array}\right]$$

   where $\mathbf{H}'$ denotes the binary Hamming code generated by a primitive polynomial $\mathbf{g}(x)$ of degree $(R - b)$. There are b repetitions of the $\mathbf{H}'$ in $\mathbf{H}'_{R,b}$.
3. The code construction reveals a systematic and regular method of code concatenation whereby the code length is increased in an iterative fashion.

Next, let's consider the code length of this code. We have already shown in Equation (5.19) that this code is a perfect code when $b = 1$. A code is called *perfect* if all possible 2^R syndromes are used to correct 2^R different error patterns. A code is called *maximal* if a longer code with the same error correcting capability for a given R does not exist.

In this code, how the check bits are divided into bytes (in case b does not divide R exactly) gives rise to the following two classes of codes called MC_1 and

MC_2, respectively.

$$\mathbf{I}_R = \begin{bmatrix} \mathbf{I}_b & & & & \\ & \mathbf{I}_b & & & \\ & & \ddots & & \\ & & & \mathbf{I}_b & \\ & & & & \mathbf{I}_{b+c} \end{bmatrix} \begin{matrix} \left.\vphantom{\begin{matrix}a\\a\\a\\a\end{matrix}}\right\} (r-1)\ \mathbf{I}_b \text{ matrices} \\ \} \ 1\ \mathbf{I}_{b+c} \text{ matrix} \end{matrix} \tag{5.20}$$

$$\mathbf{I}_R = \begin{bmatrix} \mathbf{I}_b & & & & \\ & \mathbf{I}_b & & & \\ & & \ddots & & \\ & & & \mathbf{I}_b & \\ & & & & \mathbf{I}_c \end{bmatrix} \begin{matrix} \left.\vphantom{\begin{matrix}a\\a\\a\\a\end{matrix}}\right\} r\ \mathbf{I}_b \text{ matrices} \\ \} \ 1\ \mathbf{I}_c \text{ matrix} \end{matrix} \tag{5.21}$$

In general, the check-bit length $R = r \cdot b + c$, where $0 \le c < b$. The leftover c check bits, if any, may form a special check byte. Another way is to form $(r-1)$ regular size check bytes and allow a special check byte of length $(b+c)$.

Here, MC_1 is defined as the code given by the $\mathbf{H}$ matrix of (5.18), where the check portion $\mathbf{I}_R$ is divided into bytes according to (5.20). MC_2 is given by the same matrix except that the check portion is divided into bytes according to (5.21).

Theorem 5-6. *MC_1 is a perfect code.*

Proof. Given R, define M_1 to be the number of distinct error patterns that MC_1 can correct. From (5.18) and (5.20), we see that for $R = r \cdot b + c \ge 2b$,

$$\begin{aligned} M_1 &= \sum_{j=1}^{r-1} (2^b - 1)(2^{(r-j)b+c} - 1) + (r-1)(2^b - 1) + (2^{b+c} - 1) + 1 \\ &= (2^b - 1) \sum_{i=1}^{r-1} 2^{ib+c} + 2^{b+c} \\ &= 2^{b+c}(2^b - 1)\frac{2^{(r-1)b} - 1}{2^b - 1} + 2^{b+c} \\ &= 2^{rb+c} = 2^R \end{aligned}$$

Q.E.D.

As for MC_2, it is perfect only when $c = 0$ and is maximal whenever $c = 1$ for $R = r \cdot b + c$. For the special case of $c = 0$ and 1, the code-bit length of the MC_2 can be expressed as follows [HONG 72].

$$N = b\frac{2^R - 1 - 2^b(2^c - 1)}{2^b - 1}$$

Note that whenever b divides the given number of check bits R, MC_1 and MC_2 are exactly the same, $M_1 = M_2 = 2^R$ (M_2: number of distinct error patterns that MC_2 can correct), and the code length becomes equal to that of the Hamming-type code, expressed as Equation (5.4).

The number of information bits, K, is the same in both MC_1 and MC_2.

$$K = b \cdot \left(\sum_{j=1}^{r-1} (2^{(r-j)b+c} - 1) \right)$$

$$= b \cdot \left(\frac{2^R - 2^{b+c}}{2^b - 1} - (r-1) \right)$$

$$= b \frac{2^R - 1 - 2^b(2^c - 1)}{2^b - 1} - R + c$$

Example 5-6

Consider a Hong–Patel code with $b = 2$ and $K = 64$. This can have check-bit length $R = 7$. First, for $R - b = 5$, obtain the primitive element α_0 of the primitive polynomial $\mathbf{g}(x) = 1 + x^2 + x^5$ in $GF(2^{R-b}) = GF(2^5)$. From this, we can construct $\mathbf{H}_{7,2}$ as the following.

$$\mathbf{H}_{7,2} = \left[\frac{\mathbf{I}_2 \quad \mathbf{I}_2 \quad \mathbf{I}_2 \cdots \mathbf{I}_2}{\mathbf{A}_{0,0} \quad \mathbf{A}_{0,1} \quad \mathbf{A}_{0,2} \cdots \mathbf{A}_{0,30}} \right]$$

where

$$\mathbf{A}_{0,0} = [I, \alpha_0]$$
$$\mathbf{A}_{0,1} = [\alpha_0, \alpha_0^2]$$
$$\mathbf{A}_{0,2} = [\alpha_0^2, \alpha_0^3]$$
$$\vdots$$
$$\mathbf{A}_{0,30} = [\alpha_0^{30}, I]$$

$$I = \begin{bmatrix} 1 \\ 0 \\ 0 \\ 0 \\ 0 \end{bmatrix}, \quad \alpha_0 = \begin{bmatrix} 0 \\ 1 \\ 0 \\ 0 \\ 0 \end{bmatrix}, \quad \alpha_0^2 = \begin{bmatrix} 0 \\ 0 \\ 1 \\ 0 \\ 0 \end{bmatrix}, \ldots, \quad \alpha_0^{30} = \begin{bmatrix} 0 \\ 1 \\ 0 \\ 0 \\ 1 \end{bmatrix}$$

Next, for R-$2b = 3$, obtain the primitive element α_1 of the primitive polynomial $\mathbf{g}(x) = 1 + x + x^3$ in $GF(2^{R-2b}) = GF(2^3)$. Similarly, we can obtain

$$\mathbf{H}_{5,2} = \left[\frac{\mathbf{I}_2 \quad \mathbf{I}_2 \quad \mathbf{I}_2 \cdots \mathbf{I}_2}{\mathbf{A}_{1,0} \quad \mathbf{A}_{1,1} \quad \mathbf{A}_{1,2} \cdots \mathbf{A}_{1,6}} \right]$$

where

$$\mathbf{A}_{1,0} = [I, \alpha_1]$$
$$\mathbf{A}_{1,1} = [\alpha_1, \alpha_1^2]$$
$$\mathbf{A}_{1,2} = [\alpha_1^2, \alpha_1^3]$$
$$\vdots$$
$$\mathbf{A}_{1,6} = [\alpha_1^6, I]$$

$$I = \begin{bmatrix} 1 \\ 0 \\ 0 \end{bmatrix}, \quad \alpha_1 = \begin{bmatrix} 0 \\ 1 \\ 0 \end{bmatrix}, \quad \alpha_1^2 = \begin{bmatrix} 0 \\ 0 \\ 1 \end{bmatrix}, \ldots, \quad \alpha_1^6 = \begin{bmatrix} 1 \\ 0 \\ 1 \end{bmatrix}$$

As a result, the (71, 64) S2EC code on p. 245 can be obtained.

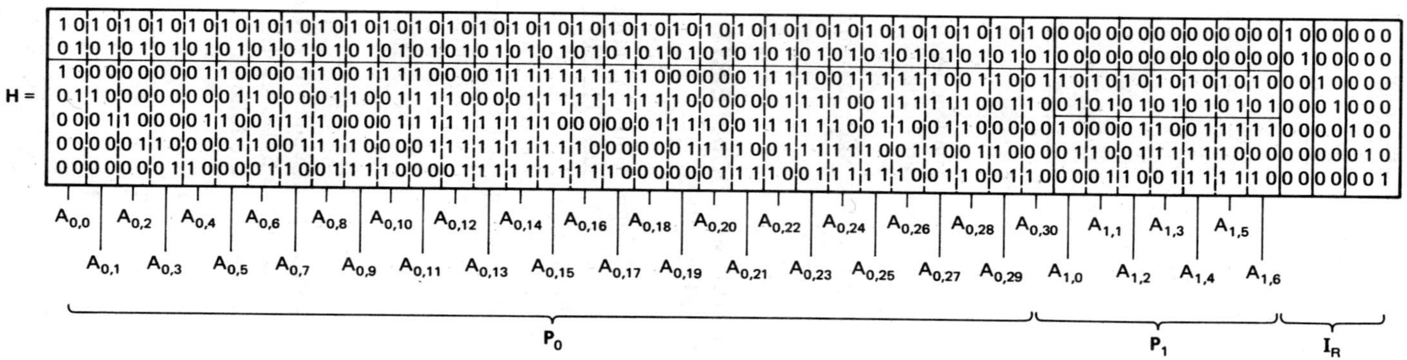

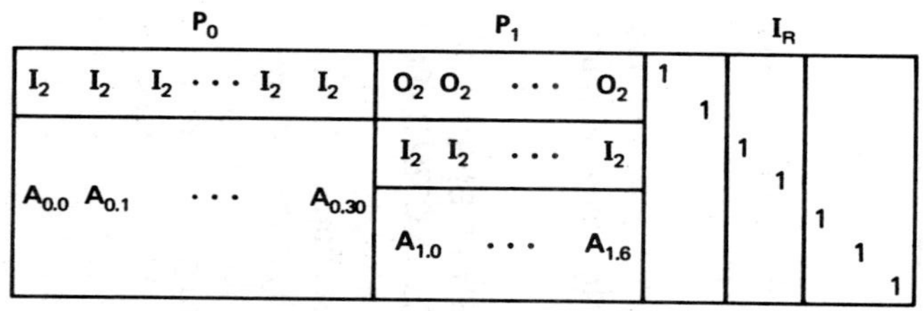

TABLE 5.3 MAXIMAL CODE-LENGTH COMPARISON

Check Bits	SEC Length	Maximal S2EC Length	SEC–DED Length
R	$N = 2^R - 1$	$N = 2\dfrac{2^R - 1 - 4(2^c - 1)}{3} + c$	$N = 2^{R-1}$
2	3	2	2
3	7	3	4
4	15	10	8
5	31	19	16
6	63	42	32
7	127	83	64
8	255	170	128
9	511	339	256
10	1023	782	512

Source: [HONG 72]. © 1972 IEEE.

In this example, the maximal code with byte length $b = 2$ and information bit length $K = 64$ has one less check bit, compared to the equivalent Hamming-type code.

Table 5.3 gives the maximal lengths of the SEC, maximal S2EC, and SEC–DED codes for given R ranging from 2 to 10.

5.2 SINGLE-BYTE ERROR CORRECTING AND DOUBLE-BYTE ERROR DETECTING (SbEC – DbED) CODES

This section deals with the class of single b-bit byte error correcting and double b-bit byte error detecting (SbEC–DbED) codes. The SbEC codes have a problem from the practical point of view in that detection of random double-bit errors spanning over double bytes is not guaranteed. Due to this consideration, SbEC–DbED codes have already been applied to commercial computer systems with byte length $b = 4$. This is because 4-bit-byte organized RAM chips are used in high-speed memory systems.

5.2.1 Reed – Solomon Codes

Reed–Solomon codes are a general class of codes of any distance d over $GF(q)$ [REED 60]. As a special case, we can derive SbEC–DbED codes having distance-4 over $GF(2^b)$. This code can be expressed as the following $\mathbf{H}$ matrix:

$$\mathbf{H} = \begin{bmatrix} \mathbf{I} & \mathbf{I} & & \mathbf{I} & & \mathbf{I} \\ \mathbf{I} & \mathbf{T} & \cdots & \mathbf{T}^i & \cdots & \mathbf{T}^{2^b-2} \\ \mathbf{I} & \mathbf{T}^2 & & \mathbf{T}^{2i} & & \mathbf{T}^{2(2^b-2)} \end{bmatrix} \tag{5.22}$$

where $\{\mathbf{0}, \mathbf{T}, \mathbf{T}^2, \ldots, \mathbf{T}^{2^b-2}, \mathbf{T}^{2^b-1} = \mathbf{I}\} \in GF(2^b)$ and $\mathbf{T}$ is the companion matrix defined in Equation (5.1).

TABLE 5.4 CODE PARAMETERS FOR R – S CODES

b	N	K
2	12	6
3	30	21
4	72	60

Wolf [WOLF 69] proposed the lengthened Reed–Solomon codes by appending three columns to the **H** matrix without weakening the error control capability of these codes. The appended columns are the (3 × 3) identity matrix shown in the following.

$$\mathbf{H} = \left[\begin{array}{ccccc|ccc} \mathbf{I} & \mathbf{I} & & \mathbf{I} & \mathbf{I} & \mathbf{I} & \mathbf{0} & \mathbf{0} \\ \mathbf{I} & \mathbf{T} & \cdots & \mathbf{T}^{i} \cdots & \mathbf{T}^{2^b-2} & \mathbf{0} & \mathbf{I} & \mathbf{0} \\ \mathbf{I} & \mathbf{T}^{2} & & \mathbf{T}^{2i} & \mathbf{T}^{2(2^i-2)} & \mathbf{0} & \mathbf{0} & \mathbf{I} \end{array}\right] \tag{5.23}$$

The code-bit length N of this modified code is equal to

$$N = b \cdot (2^b + 2) \tag{5.24}$$

An implementation of the high-speed parallel encoder/decoder of the extended Reed–Solomon code is given in [BHAT 78].

In large-scale general purpose computer systems, information-bit length $K = 64$, 128 bits are very common. The above conventional Reed–Solomon SbEC–DbED codes, hereafter abbreviated as R–S SbEC–DbED codes, however, cannot be applied to memory systems with byte length $b = 2$, 3, and 4 bits. This is because the maximal information-bit lengths of these codes are 6, 21 and 60 bits, for $b = 2$, 3, and 4 bits, respectively. This is shown in Table 5.4 according to Equation (5.24). For this reason, some modified R–S SbEC–DbED codes have been proposed to fit any byte size and code length [CART 74, 80, KANE 82, ITOH 83a, CHEN 86a, 86b].

5.2.2 Kaneda – Fujiwara Codes

The R–S SbEC–DbED codes always have three check bytes and hence do not have the flexibility to extend the code length. Here, a new class of SbEC–DbED codes is shown for an arbitrary code and byte length [KANE 82].

The **H** matrix shown in (5.23) can be converted to the form of an **H** matrix whose first row is an all **I**'s vector. This can be accompanied by the following algorithm.

1. *The second row of* (5.23) *is multiplied by a suitable nonzero element* $\mathbf{T}^a$, *where* $0 \le a \le 2^b - 2$.

2. *The multiplied result and the third row vector are added to the first row vector in* (5.23).
3. *If an element of the resultant (first) row vector is then not equal to* **I**, *then it can be made equal to* **I** *by multiplying the column by a nonzero scalar. Note that multiplying a column of* **H** *by a nonzero scalar does not change the distance of the code.*

As an example, let **H** be the following (12, 6) S2EC–D2ED codes.

$$\mathbf{H} = \begin{bmatrix} \mathbf{I} & \mathbf{I} & \mathbf{I} & \mathbf{I} & \mathbf{0} & \mathbf{0} \\ \mathbf{I} & \mathbf{T}^2 & \mathbf{T} & \mathbf{0} & \mathbf{I} & \mathbf{0} \\ \mathbf{I} & \mathbf{T} & \mathbf{T}^2 & \mathbf{0} & \mathbf{0} & \mathbf{I} \end{bmatrix} \tag{5.25}$$

Here, **T** is the companion matrix defined by the primitive polynomial $g(x) = x^2 + x + 1$, **I** is a (2×2) identity matrix, and **0** is a (2×2) zero matrix. According to the algorithm mentioned above, the **H** matrix can be converted to the form by following two steps.

1. Multiply the second row by **T** and add the second and third rows to the first. We then get **H′**.

$$\mathbf{H}' = \begin{bmatrix} \mathbf{T} & \mathbf{T} & \mathbf{I} & \mathbf{I} & \mathbf{T} & \mathbf{I} \\ \mathbf{T} & \mathbf{I} & \mathbf{T}^2 & \mathbf{0} & \mathbf{T} & \mathbf{0} \\ \mathbf{I} & \mathbf{T} & \mathbf{T}^2 & \mathbf{0} & \mathbf{0} & \mathbf{I} \end{bmatrix}$$

2. To obtain all **I**'s in the first row we need to multiply columns 1, 2, and 5 by $\mathbf{T}^2$. We then get **H″**, which is the following derived form.

$$\mathbf{H}'' = \begin{bmatrix} \mathbf{I} & \mathbf{I} & \mathbf{I} & \mathbf{I} & \mathbf{I} & \mathbf{I} \\ \mathbf{I} & \mathbf{T}^2 & \mathbf{T}^2 & \mathbf{0} & \mathbf{I} & \mathbf{0} \\ \mathbf{T}^2 & \mathbf{I} & \mathbf{T}^2 & \mathbf{0} & \mathbf{0} & \mathbf{I} \end{bmatrix} \tag{5.26}$$

In general, we can find at least one a ($a \leq 2^b - 2$) to multiply the second row by $\mathbf{T}^a$ to get **H** to the form given in (5.26). This is easy to prove.

Here, we can also write the converted matrix of (5.26) as

$$\mathbf{H}_1 = \begin{bmatrix} \mathbf{I} & \mathbf{I} & \mathbf{I} & \cdots & \mathbf{I} \\ \mathbf{h}_0 & \mathbf{h}_1 & \mathbf{h}_2 & \cdots & \mathbf{h}_{n-1} \end{bmatrix}, \qquad n = 2^b + 2 \tag{5.27}$$

where $\mathbf{h}_0, \mathbf{h}_1, \ldots, \mathbf{h}_{n-1}$ are column vectors with two elements each.

For the examples in (5.26), we set

$$\mathbf{h}_0 = \begin{pmatrix} \mathbf{I} \\ \mathbf{T}^2 \end{pmatrix} \quad \mathbf{h}_1 = \begin{pmatrix} \mathbf{T}^2 \\ \mathbf{I} \end{pmatrix} \quad \mathbf{h}_2 = \begin{pmatrix} \mathbf{T}^2 \\ \mathbf{T}^2 \end{pmatrix} \quad \mathbf{h}_3 = \begin{pmatrix} \mathbf{0} \\ \mathbf{0} \end{pmatrix} \quad \mathbf{h}_4 = \begin{pmatrix} \mathbf{I} \\ \mathbf{0} \end{pmatrix} \quad \mathbf{h}_5 = \begin{pmatrix} \mathbf{0} \\ \mathbf{I} \end{pmatrix}$$

Using the above approach and notation, a new class of SbEC–DbED codes is obtained by means of the following theorem.

Theorem 5-7. *Let $\mathbf{H}_1$ be the converted* **H** *matrix of an $(N_1, N_1 - R_1)$ SbEC–DbED code whose first row is an all-***I***'s vector of the form of* (5.27),

$$\mathbf{H}_1 = \begin{bmatrix} \mathbf{I} & \mathbf{I} & \mathbf{I} & \cdots & \mathbf{I} \\ \mathbf{h}_0 & \mathbf{h}_1 & \mathbf{h}_2 & \cdots & \mathbf{h}_{n_1-1} \end{bmatrix}$$

where $N_1 = n_1 \cdot b$, $R_1 = r_1 \cdot b$. Let $\mathbf{H}_2$ be the nonconverted **H** *matrix of an $(N_2, N_2 - R_2)$ SbEC–DbED code, where $N_2 = n_2 \cdot b$, $R_2 = r_2 \cdot b$. The linear code defined by the* **H** *matrix*

$$\mathbf{H} = \left[\begin{array}{cccc|ccc|c|ccc} & \mathbf{H}_2 & & & & \mathbf{H}_2 & & \cdots & & \mathbf{H}_2 & \\ \mathbf{h}_0 & \mathbf{h}_0 \cdots & \mathbf{h}_0 & \mathbf{h}_0 & \mathbf{h}_1 & \mathbf{h}_1 \cdots & \mathbf{h}_1 & & \mathbf{h}_{m-1} & \mathbf{h}_{m-1} & \cdots \mathbf{h}_{m-1} \end{array}\right] \qquad (5.28)$$

is an SbEC–DbED code of length $n_1 \cdot n_2$ bytes with $r_1 + r_2 - 1$ check bytes.

This theorem can be easily proved so that every combination of three or fewer columns in the **H** matrix shown in (5.28) is linearly independent. The detailed proof is left to the reader.

Theorem 5-8. *Let $\mathbf{H}_0$ be the* **H** *matrix of an $(N, N - R)$ SbEC–DbED code, where $N = n \cdot b$, $R = r \cdot b$. The code defined by the following* **H** *matrix is a $(2N, 2N - R - b)$ SbEC–DbED code.*

$$\mathbf{H} = \left[\begin{array}{c|c} \mathbf{H}_0 & \mathbf{H}_0 \\ \hline \mathbf{0}\ \mathbf{0}\ \mathbf{0} \cdots \mathbf{0} & \mathbf{I}\ \mathbf{I}\ \mathbf{I} \cdots \mathbf{I} \end{array}\right] \qquad \{\mathbf{0} \cdot \mathbf{I}\} \in GF(2^b) \qquad (5.29)$$

Proof. It is fairly simple to show that the **H** matrix defined by (5.29) has an SbEC property. If there are double-byte errors, E_1 and E_2, in the received word such that one byte error E_1 is in the first portion in **H** that has all **0** in the bottom row, and the other byte error E_2 is in the second portion that has all **I** in the bottom row, the resultant syndrome can be expressed as

$$E_1 \cdot \begin{bmatrix} \mathbf{h}_{0,i} \\ \mathbf{h}_{1,i} \\ \vdots \\ \mathbf{h}_{r-1,i} \\ \mathbf{0} \end{bmatrix} + E_2 \cdot \begin{bmatrix} \mathbf{h}_{0,j} \\ \mathbf{h}_{1,j} \\ \vdots \\ \mathbf{h}_{r-1,j} \\ \mathbf{I} \end{bmatrix} = \begin{bmatrix} E_1 \cdot \mathbf{h}_{0,i} + E_2 \cdot \mathbf{h}_{0,j} \\ E_1 \cdot \mathbf{h}_{1,i} + E_2 \cdot \mathbf{h}_{1,j} \\ \vdots \\ E_1 \cdot \mathbf{h}_{r-1,i} + E_2 \cdot \mathbf{h}_{r-1,j} \\ E_2 \end{bmatrix}$$

where $[\mathbf{h}_{0,i}, \mathbf{h}_{1,i}, \ldots, \mathbf{h}_{r-1,i}, \mathbf{0}]^{\mathrm{T}}$ is the ith column vector included in the first portion in $\mathbf{H}$, and $[\mathbf{h}_{0,j}, \mathbf{h}_{1,j}, \ldots, \mathbf{h}_{r-1,j}, \mathbf{I}]^{\mathrm{T}}$ is the jth column vector included in the second portion. It can be easily seen that this syndrome is nonzero and not equal to that of the single-byte errors. Therefore, the code defined by (5.29) is an SbEC–DbED code. Q.E.D.

Example 5-7

Let $\mathbf{H}_2$ be the following (12, 6) S2EC–D2ED code.

$$\mathbf{H}_2 = \begin{bmatrix} \mathbf{I} & \mathbf{I} & \mathbf{I} & \mathbf{I} & \mathbf{0} & \mathbf{0} \\ \mathbf{I} & \mathbf{T}^1 & \mathbf{T}^2 & \mathbf{0} & \mathbf{I} & \mathbf{0} \\ \mathbf{I} & \mathbf{T}^2 & \mathbf{T}^1 & \mathbf{0} & \mathbf{0} & \mathbf{I} \end{bmatrix} \tag{5.30}$$

As mentioned before, the $\mathbf{H}$ matrix (5.30) can be converted to the form of (5.31) by choosing $\mathbf{T}^a = \mathbf{T}$ as follows.

$$\mathbf{H}_1 = \begin{bmatrix} \mathbf{I} & \mathbf{I} & \mathbf{I} & \mathbf{I} & \mathbf{I} & \mathbf{I} \\ \mathbf{I} & \mathbf{T}^2 & \mathbf{T}^2 & \mathbf{0} & \mathbf{I} & \mathbf{0} \\ \mathbf{T}^2 & \mathbf{I} & \mathbf{T}^2 & \mathbf{0} & \mathbf{0} & \mathbf{I} \end{bmatrix} \tag{5.31}$$

By using $\mathbf{H}_1$ defined in (5.31) and $\mathbf{H}_2$ in (5.30), the following (72, 62) S2EC–D2ED code can be constructed [KANE 82].

$$\mathbf{H} = \left[\begin{array}{cccccc|cccccc|cccccc|cccccc|cccccc|cccccc}
I & I & I & I & & & I & I & I & I & & & I & I & I & I & & & I & I & I & I & & & I & I & I & I & & & I & I & I & I & & \\
I & T^1 & T^2 & & I & & I & T^1 & T^2 & & I & & I & T^1 & T^2 & & I & & I & T^1 & T^2 & & I & & I & T^1 & T^2 & & I & & I & T^1 & T^2 & & I & \\
I & T^2 & T^1 & & & I & I & T^2 & T^1 & & & I & I & T^2 & T^1 & & & I & I & T^2 & T^1 & & & I & I & T^2 & T^1 & & & I & I & T^2 & T^1 & & & I \\
\hline
I & I & I & I & I & I & T^2 & T^2 & T^2 & T^2 & T^2 & T^2 & T^2 & T^2 & T^2 & T^2 & T^2 & T^2 & & & & & & & I & I & I & I & I & I & & & & & & \\
T^2 & T^2 & T^2 & T^2 & T^2 & T^2 & I & I & I & I & I & I & T^2 & T^2 & T^2 & T^2 & T^2 & T^2 & & & & & & & & & & & & & I & I & I & I & I & I
\end{array}\right]$$

In the same manner, the S2EC–D2ED codes whose $\mathbf{H}$ matrices have seven rows are obtained from two S2EC–D2ED codes—one having five rows and the other having three rows. In general, the SbEC–DbED codes, whose $\mathbf{H}$ matrices have an odd number of rows, can be obtained according to this method.

If an even number of rows, for example six rows, is required, Theorem 5-8 gives an $\mathbf{H}$ matrix as shown in 5.32 on p. 251 [KANE 82].

H = 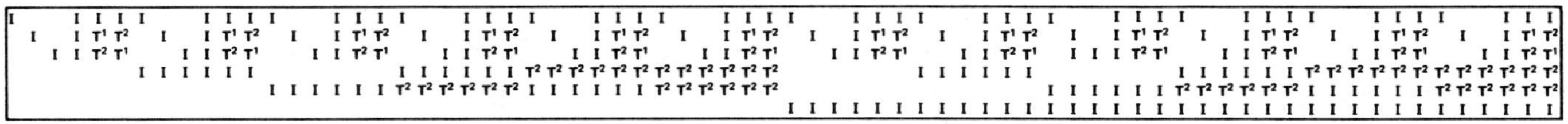 (5.32)

H = 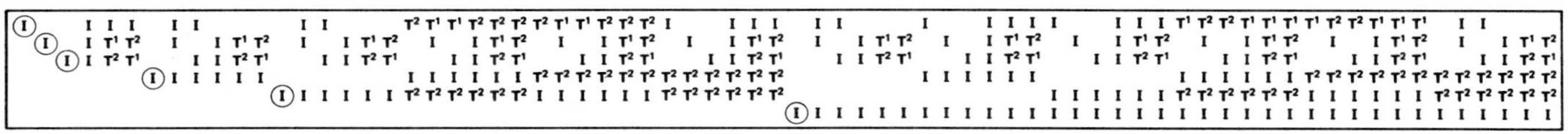 (5.32)′

TABLE 5.5 CODE-BIT LENGTH N OF THE KANEDA – FUJIWARA SbEC – DbED CODE

r: Number of row*	b: Byte Length (bit)				
	1†	2	3	4	5
3	4	12	30	72	170
4	8	24	60	144	340
5	16	72	300	1,296	5,780
6	32	144	600	2,592	11,560
7	64	432	3,000	23,328	196,520

*Number of check bit = $b \times r$.
†SEC–DED codes.
Source: [KANE 82]. © 1982 IEEE.

The **H** matrix shown in (5.32) does not give the check byte positions clearly. The fourth, fifth, and sixth rows in this matrix are added to the first row. From this, we can obtain the check bytes whose columns have exactly one **I** element and then zeros in other positions. The check byte positions can be seen by the circled Ⓘ's. The resultant matrix is shown in (5.32)′ on p. 251 [KANE 82].

The code length N of this code is given as follows.

$$N = \begin{cases} b \cdot (2^b + 2)^{(r-1)/2} & r\text{: odd } (\geq 3) \\ 2b \cdot (2^b + 2)^{(r-2)/2} & r\text{: even } (\geq 4) \end{cases}$$

Table 5.5 shows the code-bit length N for byte length b and the number of rows r. For byte length $b = 1$ bit, the code reduces to the SEC–DED code.

Fig. 5.5 shows the check-bit length of this SbEC–DbED code for byte length $b = 2$, 3, and 4 bits.

The decoding procedure of this code is simple. A single-byte error is corrected by using the same procedure as that of SbEC codes. A double-byte error is detected when the syndrome is nonzero and none of the error byte pointers indicate an error.

Rotational / modularized SbEC – DbED codes. Theoretical derivation of the rotational SbEC–DbED codes is rather difficult and as of now not obtainable for arbitrary values of b and r. However, for some practical code parameters such as byte length $b = 4$ and information length $K = 64$, or 128 bits, some excellent codes have been obtained by a computer search using the approach of minimum-equal-weight code construction [KANE 82]. Some *modularized codes* that are not equal to rotational codes, but give modular organizations for encoding/decoding circuits, are given, and they have been applied to commercial computer systems. First, we provide some concepts of modularization and give some examples of codes.

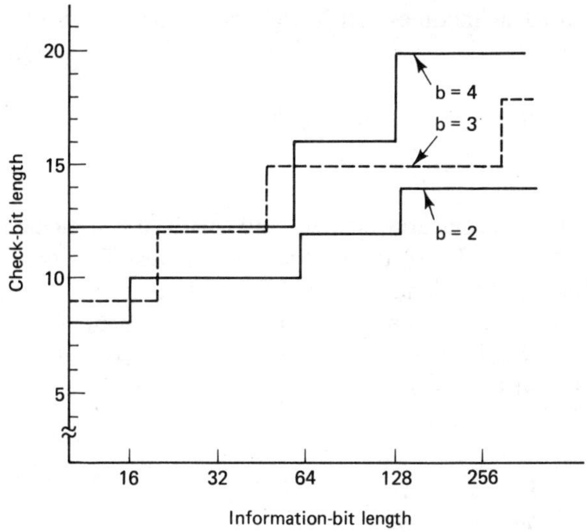

Figure 5.5 Check-bit length of the Kaneda–Fujiwara SbEC–DbED code [FUJI 81a].

Definition 5-2. The SbEC–DbED codes, whose encoding/decoding circuits can be organized using p identical circuit modules, are called *p-modularized SbEC–DbED codes*.

Theorem 5-9. *The code shown in* (5.33) *presents* 2-*modularized SbEC–DbED codes*.

$$\mathbf{H} = \left[\begin{array}{ccccc|ccccc|ccc} \mathbf{I} & \mathbf{I} & \mathbf{I} & \cdots & \mathbf{I} & \mathbf{I} & \mathbf{I} & \mathbf{I} & \cdots & \mathbf{I} & \mathbf{I} & & \\ \mathbf{T}^1 & \mathbf{T}^2 & \mathbf{T}^3 & \cdots & \mathbf{T}^p & \mathbf{T}^{-p} & \mathbf{T}^{-p+1} & \mathbf{T}^{-p+2} & \cdots & \mathbf{T}^{-1} & & \mathbf{I} & \\ \mathbf{T}^{-1} & \mathbf{T}^{-2} & \mathbf{T}^{-3} & \cdots & \mathbf{T}^{-p} & \mathbf{T}^p & \mathbf{T}^{p-1} & \mathbf{T}^{p-2} & \cdots & \mathbf{T}^1 & & & \mathbf{I} \end{array}\right]$$

$$\longleftarrow \text{module } 0 \longrightarrow\longleftarrow \text{module } 1 \longrightarrow \qquad (5.33)$$

where **0** *and* **I** *are zero element and identity element in* $GF(2^b)$, *respectively*, *and*

$$\{\mathbf{0}, \mathbf{I}, \mathbf{T}^1, \mathbf{T}^2, \mathbf{T}^3, \ldots, \mathbf{T}^p, \mathbf{T}^{-1}, \mathbf{T}^{-2}, \mathbf{T}^{-3}, \ldots, \mathbf{T}^{-p}\} \in GF(2^b), \text{ for } p = 2^{b-1} - 1$$

Proof. In the original Reed–Solomon SbEC–DbED code shown in (5.22), the second column vector in its **H** matrix is divided by **T**, and the third column vector is divided by $\mathbf{T}^2$. In the same manner, the ith column vector is divided by $\mathbf{T}^{i-1}$. In this case, the first column vector (all **I** vector) is removed. Next, each row of the obtained matrix is cyclically shifted upward by one place. Finally, the (3×3) identity matrix is appended to the resultant matrix to derive the **H** matrix of (5.33). Therefore, this code satisfies SbEC–DbED conditions. The module 0 and the module 1 shown in (5.33) have the same circuits for encoding/decoding because the same three row vectors are used in modules. Thus, the code shown in (5.33) is a 2-modularized SbEC–DbED code. Q.E.D.

The code length of this 2-modularized code is given by

$$N = b \cdot (2^b + 1)$$

In (5.33), the product value of the second row element and the third row element in each column gives a constant value, **I**, except for the check bytes. This constant value can be selected as any nonzero element over $GF(2^b)$. If there is a column vector whose second row element is the same as the third row element, then that column must be removed. The **H** matrix shown in (5.34) shows an example of this type of 2-modularized (68, 56) S4ED–D4ED code, whose constant product value is $\mathbf{T}^{14}$.

$$\mathbf{H} = \left[\begin{array}{ccccc:cccc:ccc} \mathbf{I} & \mathbf{I} & \mathbf{I} & \cdots & \mathbf{I} & \mathbf{I} & \mathbf{I} & \cdots & \mathbf{I} & \mathbf{I} & & \\ \mathbf{I} & \mathbf{T}^1 & \mathbf{T}^2 & \cdots & \mathbf{T}^6 & \mathbf{T}^{14} & \mathbf{T}^{13} & \cdots & \mathbf{T}^8 & & \mathbf{I} & \\ \mathbf{T}^{14} & \mathbf{T}^{13} & \mathbf{T}^{12} & \cdots & \mathbf{T}^8 & \mathbf{I} & \mathbf{T}^1 & \cdots & \mathbf{T}^6 & & & \mathbf{I} \end{array}\right] \qquad (5.34)$$

In this case, the companion matrix **T** is derived from the primitive polynomial $g(x) = x^4 + x + 1$.

Another interesting type of modularized code is introduced in [NARA 80]. The following code is an example of modularized (80, 64) S4ED–D4ED code.

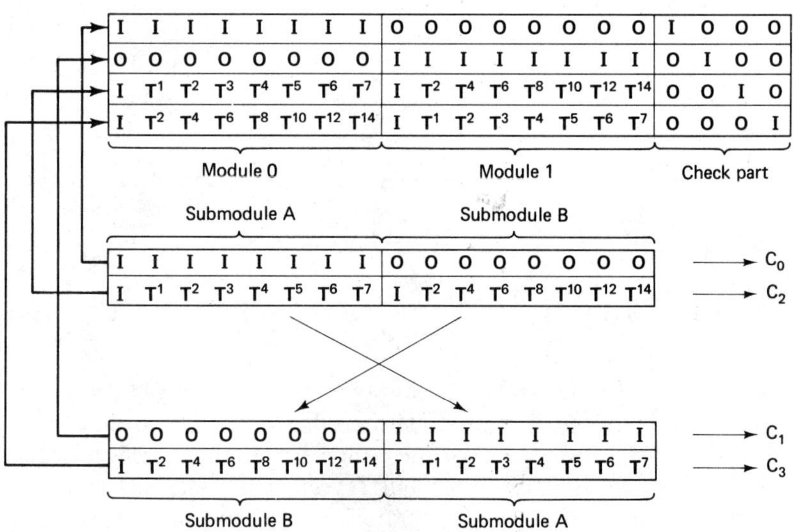

(5.35)

This matrix also has two identical modules, module 0 and module 1 in (5.35). In addition to this, each module can be comprised of two types of submodules, submodule A and submodule B in (5.35). Hence, this organization gives easy implementation of the encoding/decoding circuitry. Obviously, this type of modularized code can be extended by increasing the number of check bytes.

We introduce rotational SbEC–DbED codes next. These codes are sometimes derived from computer (exhaustive) search and hence are optimized from the point of minimum-equal-weight code. In order to increase the modularity of organization, the 2-modularized technique shown in Theorem 5-9 is introduced into the rotational SbEC–DbED code. That is, this technique is applied to the basic submatrix $\mathbf{H}_0$ in the $\mathbf{H}$ matrix of the rotational code. Let submatrix $\mathbf{H}_0$ have an all $\mathbf{I}$ vector in the first row. The product of the second row element and the third row element gives a constant in each column of $\mathbf{H}_0$, except for the check byte. Thus, submatrix $\mathbf{H}_0$ has a 2-modularized organization.

Using an easy example, this property is shown as follows. In this example, companion matrix $\mathbf{T}$ is derived from the polynomial $\mathbf{g}(x) = x^4 + x + 1$.

Eight column vectors and one check column vector are selected from (5.34), as shown in (5.36). In order to have four submatrices in the $\mathbf{H}$ matrix of the rotational code, one all $\mathbf{0}$ row vector is added.

$$\mathbf{H}_0 = \left[\begin{array}{cccc:cccc:c} \mathbf{I} & \mathbf{I} & \mathbf{I} & \mathbf{I} & \mathbf{I} & \mathbf{I} & \mathbf{I} & \mathbf{I} & \mathbf{I} \\ \mathbf{T}^{14} & \mathbf{T}^{13} & \mathbf{T}^{12} & \mathbf{T}^{11} & \mathbf{I} & \mathbf{T}^{1} & \mathbf{T}^{2} & \mathbf{T}^{3} & \mathbf{0} \\ \mathbf{I} & \mathbf{T}^{1} & \mathbf{T}^{2} & \mathbf{T}^{3} & \mathbf{T}^{14} & \mathbf{T}^{13} & \mathbf{T}^{12} & \mathbf{T}^{11} & \mathbf{0} \\ \mathbf{0} & \mathbf{0} & \mathbf{0} & \mathbf{0} & \mathbf{0} & \mathbf{0} & \mathbf{0} & \mathbf{0} & \mathbf{0} \end{array}\right] \tag{5.36}$$

The rotational code produced from submatrix (5.36) does not always have D4ED property. This should be verified through a computer program. Thirty-five $\left(= \binom{7}{4}\right)$ submatrices and 15 product values are selected. Table 5.6 shows the number of rotational (144, 128) S4EC–D4ED codes for each product value. In these rotational (144, 128) S4EC–D4ED codes, (5.37) shows a minimum-equal-weight code. The weight of this matrix is equal to 592.

TABLE 5.6 NUMBER OF ROTATIONAL (144, 128) S4EC – D4ED CODES

Product Value	$\mathbf{I}$	$\mathbf{T}$	$\mathbf{T}^2$	$\mathbf{T}^3$	$\mathbf{T}^4$	$\mathbf{T}^5$	$\mathbf{T}^6$	$\mathbf{T}^7$	$\mathbf{T}^8$	$\mathbf{T}^9$	$\mathbf{T}^{10}$	$\mathbf{T}^{11}$	$\mathbf{T}^{12}$	$\mathbf{T}^{13}$	$\mathbf{T}^{14}$
Number of Codes	0	4	4	11	4	0	11	11	4	11	0	11	11	11	11

Source: [KANE 82]. © 1982 IEEE.

$$
H = \left[\begin{array}{cccc:cccc:c|cccc:cccc:c|cccc:cccc:c|cccc:cccc:c}
I & I & I & I & I & I & I & I & I & & & & & & & & & & T^3 & T^2 & T^1 & I & T^{14} & T^{13} & T^{12} & T^{11} & & T^{11} & T^{12} & T^{13} & T^{14} & I & T^1 & T^2 & T^3 & \\
T^{11} & T^{12} & T^{13} & T^{14} & I & T^1 & T^2 & T^3 & & I & I & I & I & I & I & I & I & I & & & & & & & & & & T^3 & T^2 & T^1 & I & T^{14} & T^{13} & T^{12} & T^{11} & \\
T^3 & T^2 & T^1 & I & T^{14} & T^{13} & T^{12} & T^{11} & & T^{11} & T^{12} & T^{13} & T^{14} & I & T^1 & T^2 & T^3 & & I & I & I & I & I & I & I & I & I & & & & & & & & & \\
 & & & & & & & & & T^3 & T^2 & T^1 & I & T^{14} & T^{13} & T^{12} & T^{11} & & T^{11} & T^{12} & T^{13} & T^{14} & I & T^1 & T^2 & T^3 & & I & I & I & I & I & I & I & I & I
\end{array}\right] \tag{5.37}
$$

$$
\underbrace{\qquad\qquad}_{H_0}\quad \underbrace{\qquad\qquad}_{H_1}\quad \underbrace{\qquad\qquad}_{H_2}\quad \underbrace{\qquad\qquad}_{H_3}\quad (b = 4)
$$

$$\left[\begin{array}{cccc|cccc|c}
I & I & I & I & I & I & I & I & I \\
I & T^1 & T^3 & T^{14} & T^2 & T^{13} & T^4 & T^7 & O \\
T^2 & T^{13} & T^4 & T^7 & I & T^1 & T^3 & T^{14} & O \\
O & O & O & O & O & O & O & O & O
\end{array}\right]
\qquad
\left[\begin{array}{cccc|cccc|c}
I & I & I & I & I & I & I & I & I \\
I & T^1 & T^2 & T^{14} & T^4 & T^{13} & T^3 & T^{12} & O \\
T^4 & T^{13} & T^3 & T^{12} & I & T^1 & T^2 & T^{14} & O \\
O & O & O & O & O & O & O & O & O
\end{array}\right]$$

$$\left[\begin{array}{cccc|cccc|c}
I & I & I & I & I & I & I & I & I \\
I & T^1 & T^2 & T^{14} & T^6 & T^{13} & T^3 & T^{12} & O \\
T^6 & T^{13} & T^3 & T^{12} & I & T^1 & T^2 & T^{14} & O \\
O & O & O & O & O & O & O & O & O
\end{array}\right]
\qquad
\left[\begin{array}{cccc|cccc|c}
I & I & I & I & I & I & I & I & I \\
I & T^1 & T^2 & T^5 & T^{12} & T^3 & T^{13} & T^{14} & O \\
T^{12} & T^3 & T^{13} & T^{14} & I & T^1 & T^2 & T^5 & O \\
O & O & O & O & O & O & O & O & O
\end{array}\right]$$

[b = 4]

$$H = \left[\begin{array}{c|c|c|c} H_0 & & & \end{array}\right]$$

Figure 5.6 Basic submatrices for rotational (144, 128) S4EC–D4ED code [KANE 82]. © 1982 IEEE.

Fig. 5.6 shows four $\mathbf{H}_0$ submatrices satisfying minimum-equal-weight rotational (144, 128) S4EC–D4ED codes and not having the constant product value in each column. The weight of each $\mathbf{H}$ matrix is equal to 568. These codes, including (5.37), give an 8-modularized organization of their encoding/decoding circuitries.

As another practical example, a minimum-equal-weight (80, 64) S4EC–D4ED code is shown as follows.

$$H = \left[\begin{array}{ccccc|ccccc|ccccc|ccccc}
I & I & I & I & I & & & & & & T^2 & T^1 & I & T^{14} & & T^{14} & I & T^1 & T^2 & \\
T^{14} & I & T^1 & T^2 & & I & I & I & I & I & & & & & & T^2 & T^1 & I & T^{14} & \\
T^2 & T^1 & I & T^{14} & & T^{14} & I & T^1 & T^2 & & I & I & I & I & I & & & & & \\
 & & & & & T^2 & T^1 & I & T^{14} & & T^{14} & I & T^1 & T^2 & & I & I & I & I & I
\end{array}\right] \tag{5.38}$$

$\underbrace{\qquad}_{H_0}$ $\underbrace{\qquad}_{H_1}$ $\underbrace{\qquad}_{H_2}$ $\underbrace{\qquad}_{H_3}$

(b = 4)

Fig. 5.7 shows an example of the syndrome decoder for $\mathbf{H}_0$ of the (5.38) code. The gate complexity and the propagation delay for SbEC–DbED codes of $K = 64$ and 128 bits represent a 20 to 30% increase, as compared with the conventional SEC–DED codes [KANE 82].

5.2.3 Chen Codes

We now introduce a new class of SbEC–DbED codes that is more efficient than the Kaneda–Fujiwara codes [CHEN 86a, 86b]. The code construction method is, however, based on Theorems 5-7 and 5-8, as shown in the Kaneda–Fujiwara codes. In this new code, $\mathbf{H}_1$ and $\mathbf{H}_2$ in Theorem 5-7 can be given by the codes based on the theory of a *generalized BCH bound* [HART 72].

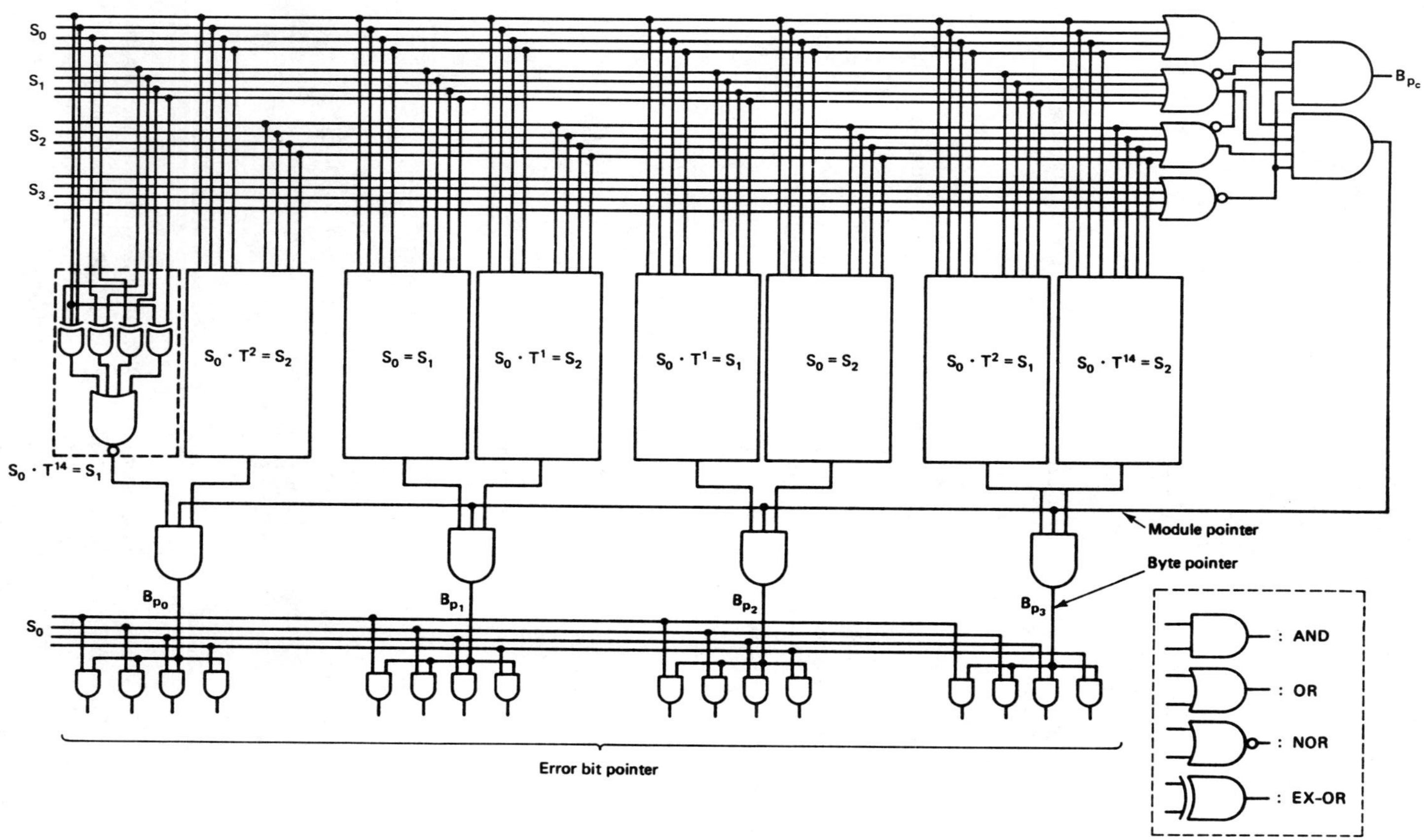

Figure 5.7 Syndrome decoder LSI for $\mathbf{H}_0$ module of the (5.38) code [KANE 82]. © 1982 IEEE.

The following theorem is a special case of the generalized BCH bound:

Theorem 5-10 [HART 72]. *Let β be a primitive root of $x^n - 1$, and let*

$$\{\beta^{a_0}, \beta^{a_0+a_1}, \beta^{a_0+a_2}, \beta^{a_0+a_1+a_2}\}$$

be a subset of the zeros of the generator polynomial of a cyclic code of length n over $GF(q)$, where $q = 2^b$. If a_1 and a_2 are relatively prime to n, then the minimum distance of the code is equal to or greater than 4.

Theorem 5-11 [CHEN 86a]. *Let* **C** *be a cyclic code over $GF(q)$ of length $n = q^m + 1$, generated by the minimum polynomial of β, where $q = 2^b$, m is even, and β is a primitive root of $x^n - 1$. Then* **C** *is an SbEC–DbED code with $2m$ check bytes.*

Proof. Since the generator polynomial $\mathbf{g}(x)$ of the cyclic code over $GF(q)$ is the minimum polynomial of β, the roots of $\mathbf{g}(x)$ can be expressed as β^i, where

$$i = 1, q, q^2, \ldots, q^m, q^{m+1}, \ldots, q^{2m-1}$$

Since $\beta^n = 1$, then $\beta^{q^m} = \beta^{-1}$, and $\beta^{q^{m+1}} = \beta^{-q}$. Thus, $\mathbf{g}(x)$ contains a subset of the roots $\beta, \beta^q, \beta^{-q}, \beta^{-1}$. Let $a_0 = 1$, $a_1 = q - 1$, and $a_2 = -(q + 1)$. Since m is even, a_1 and a_2 are relatively prime to n. According to Theorem 5-10, the code is an SbEC–DbED code. Since the degree of $\mathbf{g}(x)$ is $2m$, the number of check bytes of the code is $2m$. Q.E.D.

Example 5-8

Let $b = 2$, $q = 2^2$, and $m = 2$, then $n = 17$. There exists a cyclic SbEC–DbED code over $GF(2^2)$ of byte-length 17. The code contains 13 information bytes in a codeword.

Theorem 5-12 [CHEN 86a]. *A cyclic code over $GF(q)$ of length $n = q^{2m} - 1$ generated by the product of the minimum polynomials of 1, β, and β^{q^m+1}, where $q = 2^b$ and β is a primitive root of $x^n - 1$, is an SbEC–DbED code with $(3m + 1)$ check bytes.*

Proof. The generator polynomial is the product of $(x - 1)$ and the minimum polynomials of β and β^{q^m+1}. The degrees of the minimum polynomials of β and β^{q^m+1} are $2m$ and m, respectively. Thus, the number of check bytes is $3m + 1$. The generator polynomial contains as roots the elements 1, β, β^{q^m} and β^{q^m+1}. Let $a_0 = 0$, $a_1 = 1$, $a_2 = q^m$. Since a_1 and a_2 are relatively prime to n, the cyclic code is an SbEC–DbED code according to Theorem 5-10. Q.E.D.

Example 5-9

Let $b = 3$, $q = 2^3 = 8$, $m = 2$, then $n = 4095$. A cyclic SbEC–DbED code over $GF(2^3)$ of length 4095 with seven check bytes can be constructed. The generator

TABLE 5.7 THE CODE LENGTH n OF THE CHEN CODES

Class	H_1^*	H_2^*	n	r
1	Extended R–S code	Code of Theorem 5-11	$(q+2)(q^m+1)$	$2m+2$ m:even
2	Extended R–S code	Code of Theorem 5-13	$(q+2)q^{2m}$	$3m+3$
3	Code of Theorem 5-12	Code of Theorem 5-11	$(q^{2m_1}-1)(q^{m_2}+1)$	$3m_1+2m_2$ m_2:even
4	Code of Theorem 5-12	Code of Theorem 5-13	$(q^{2m_1}-1)q^{2m_2}$	$3m_1+3m_2+1$

*$\mathbf{H}_1$ and $\mathbf{H}_2$ are defined in Theorem 5-7.
Source: [CHEN 86a]. © 1986 IEEE.

polynomial can be taken as the product of the minimum polynomials of 1, β, and β^{65}, where β is a primitive root of $x^{4095}-1$.

Since the generator polynomial of a code in Theorem 5-12 contains 1 as the root, the **H** matrix of the code can be arranged so that the first row is an all one's vector. Using this form of the **H** matrix, the code can be extended by one byte by adding to the matrix a column vector of one followed by $3m$ zeros. It can be shown that the extended code is also an SbEC–DbED code. We state this result as the next theorem.

Theorem 5-13 [CHEN 86a]. *An SbEC–DbED code of byte length* $n = q^{2m}$ *with* $3m+1$ *check bytes, where* $q = 2^b$, *can be obtained by extending the code of Theorem* 5-12.

The codes obtained by Theorems 5-11, 5-12, and 5-13 can be used as $\mathbf{H}_1$ in Theorem 5-7. Theorem 5-8 can also be applied to the codes just presented to double the lengths of the codes. The code length can be obtained as in Table 5.7.

Table 5.8 shows the code bit length $N = n \cdot b$ of the Chen code.

TABLE 5.8 CODE LENGTH N OF THE CHEN CODES

r^* \ b	2	3	4	5	
3	12	30	72	170	R–S code
4	34	195	1028	5,125	Theorem 5-11
5	68†	390†	2,056	10,250	Theorem 5-8
6	204	1,950	18,504	174,250	Class 1
7	876	12,672	264,192	5,253,120	Construction 4 in [CHEN 86b]

*Check-bit length $R = r \cdot b$.
†(82, 72) S2EC–D2ED code and (399, 384) S3EC–D3ED code were obtained by computer experiments in [ITOH 83a] and [CHEN 86b], respectively.
Sources: [CHEN 86a, 86b].

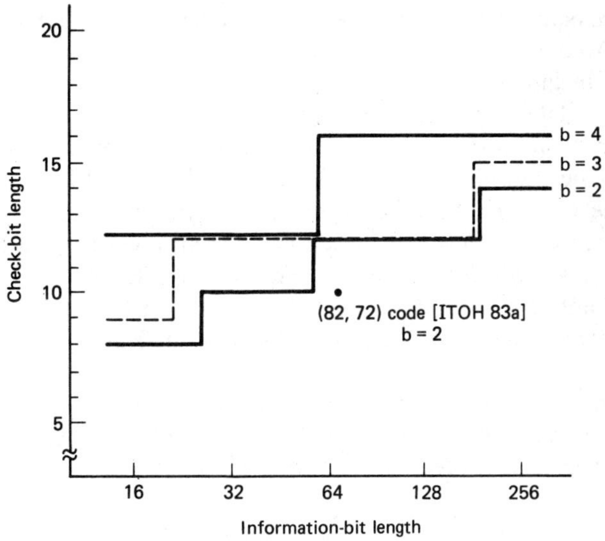

Figure 5.8 Check-bit length of the Chen SbEC–DbED code [ITOH 83a].

Fig. 5.8 shows the check-bit length of this SbEC–DbED code for byte length $b = 2$, 3, and 4 bits.

5.3 BYTE / BURST ERROR DETECTING SEC – DED CODES

We recall here the definitions of *byte* and *burst errors* given in Chapter 1. A word is divided into bytes of length b; a single-byte error is meant to be any number of errors confined to one byte. On the other hand, a burst (or burst error) of length b is any number of errors confined to b adjacent positions. A burst of length b may begin on any bit position of the word and can spread over portions of two adjacent bytes. Also, a code capable of detecting (or correcting) bursts of length b implies that it is capable of detecting (or correcting) all bursts of smaller length also. For the purpose of this book, a byte always refers to a byte of length b; and a burst refers to a burst of length b or less. Since we do not cover multiple burst error codes, burst here will mean single burst only.

The SEC–DED codes are not capable of correcting or detecting byte errors. On the other hand SbEC codes and SbEC–DbED codes can correct byte errors but require higher redundancy. From this consideration, codes to detect single-byte errors as well as to correct single-bit errors and to detect double-bit errors are required. This class of codes is practical from the standpoint of requiring small additional redundancy to the existing SEC–DED codes and hence has become very popular in commercial applications.

5.3.1 Burst Error Detecting SEC – DED Codes (SEC – DED – BED Codes)

Some types of codes that meet the requirements mentioned above have been proposed in [BOSS 78, REDD 78, FUJI 80a, VARA 83]. It turns out, however, that all these proposed codes are equivalent to the same type of codes (i.e., single-burst, error detecting SEC–DED codes [KANE 83]). Generally, the single-burst, error detecting SEC–DED codes include single-byte, error detecting SEC–DED codes as a special case. Therefore, in later sections, more efficient codes (i.e., codes with smaller check-bit length) are proposed as a class of single-byte, error detecting SEC–DED codes. They will be studied in Section 5.3.2 as SEC–DED–SbED codes.

Here, we consider the first type of codes as the single-byte, error detecting SEC–DED codes. And then, we will show that these codes can also be single-burst, error detecting SEC–DED codes, which will be called SEC–DED–BED codes. The reader should be careful to note and distinguish the abbreviations BED and SbED. The BED stands for burst error detection, and SbED stands for single-byte (of length b) error detection.

Now, we consider two sets of errors, $\mathbf{E}_1$ and $\mathbf{E}_2$, where $\mathbf{E}_1$ is the error set consisting of all single-bit errors and $\mathbf{E}_2$ is the error set consisting of all byte errors, excluding single-bit errors. Hence, $\mathbf{E}_1 \cap \mathbf{E}_2 = \emptyset$. ($\emptyset$ is the empty set.)

Theorem 5-14. *Let $\mathbf{E}_1$ and $\mathbf{E}_2$ be two error sets with $\mathbf{E}_1 \cap \mathbf{E}_2 = \emptyset$. A linear code, described by the matrix $\mathbf{H}$, corrects all errors in $\mathbf{E}_1$ and detects all errors in $\mathbf{E}_2$, if and only if*

(a) *for all $E \in \{\mathbf{E}_1 \cup \mathbf{E}_2\}$, $E \cdot \mathbf{H}^T \neq 0$*

(b) *for every E_i, $E_j \in \mathbf{E}_1$, $E_i \cdot \mathbf{H}^T + E_j \cdot \mathbf{H}^T \neq 0$, and*

(c) *for every $E_j \in \mathbf{E}_2$, there does not exist an $E_i \in \mathbf{E}_1$ such that $E_j \cdot \mathbf{H}^T + E_i \cdot \mathbf{H}^T = 0$.*

This theorem can be easily proved so that the conditions (a) and (b) are those for satisfying the single-error correction, and the conditions (a) and (c) are for the single-byte error detection. The codes satisfying all these conditions will be referred to as SEC–SbED codes.

Theorem 5-15 [BOSS 78]. *Let $\mathbf{H}$ be the $(r \times Jb)$ matrix.*

$$\mathbf{H} = \begin{bmatrix} \mathbf{M}_1 & \mathbf{M}_2 & \cdots & \mathbf{M}_J \\ \mathbf{Q} & \mathbf{Q} & \cdots & \mathbf{Q} \end{bmatrix} = \begin{bmatrix} \mathbf{H}_1 & \mathbf{H}_2 & \cdots & \mathbf{H}_J \end{bmatrix}$$

where

$$\mathbf{H}_i = \begin{bmatrix} \mathbf{M}_i \\ \mathbf{Q} \end{bmatrix}, \qquad 1 \leq i \leq J, \qquad J = 2^{r-b+1} - 1$$

$$\mathbf{Q} = \begin{bmatrix} 0 & \\ 0 & \\ \cdot & \mathbf{I}_{b-1} \\ \cdot & \\ 0 & \end{bmatrix}_{(b-1)\times b}$$

Q *is a* $(b-1)\times b$ *matrix consisting of an all-0's column and the identity matrix of dimension* $b-1$, *and* $\mathbf{M}_i$ *is an* $(r-b+1)\times b$ *matrix whose columns are b copies of the binary representation of integer i. The code expressed as the foregoing* **H** *matrix is a single b-bit byte error detecting SEC code (SEC–SbED code) having code-bit length* $N = b\cdot(2^{r-b+1}-1)$.

For this chapter, the code-bit length N is a multiple of b, whereas the check-bit length R is not always a multiple of b. The reader should be cautious not to confuse these with the notations of a previous section.

This theorem can be easily proved so that this code satisfies the conditions (a), (b), and (c) in the previous theorem.

Example 5-10

For $r = 6$, $b = 4$, we have a (28, 22) SEC–S4ED code with an **H** matrix:

$$\mathbf{H} = \begin{bmatrix} 0000 & 0000 & 0000 & 1111 & 1111 & 1111 & 1111 \\ 0000 & 1111 & 1111 & 0000 & 0000 & 1111 & 1111 \\ 1111 & 0000 & 1111 & 0000 & 1111 & 0000 & 1111 \\ 0100 & 0100 & 0100 & 0100 & 0100 & 0100 & 0100 \\ 0010 & 0010 & 0010 & 0010 & 0010 & 0010 & 0010 \\ 0001 & 0001 & 0001 & 0001 & 0001 & 0001 & 0001 \end{bmatrix}$$

The foregoing can be made an SEC–DED–S4ED code by adding an all-1's row to the matrix. The following matrix expresses a simple example of this type of SED–DED–S4ED code.

$$\mathbf{H} = \begin{bmatrix} 1111 & 1111 & 1111 & 1111 \\ 0000 & 0000 & 1111 & 1111 \\ 0000 & 1111 & 0000 & 1111 \\ 0100 & 0100 & 0100 & 0100 \\ 0010 & 0010 & 0010 & 0010 \\ 0001 & 0001 & 0001 & 0001 \end{bmatrix}$$

In general, for SEC–DED–SbED codes, the following stronger condition is necessary in addition to the conditions (a), (b), and (c) in Theorem 5-14:

(d) for every $E_i, E_j, E_k \in \mathbf{E}_1$, with distinct i, j, k, $E_i\cdot\mathbf{H}^T + E_j\cdot\mathbf{H}^T \neq E_k\cdot\mathbf{H}^T$.

Theorem 5-16 [REDD 78]. *The codes given by the* **H** *matrix at top of p.* 264 *are SEC–SbED codes when* $b = 2$, 3, *or* 4. *When* $b \geq 5$, *the codes are SEC–DED–SbED. The code-bit length of the codes is* $N = b\cdot(2^{r-b+1}-1)$.

Proof. The possible patterns of syndromes corresponding to the single-bit errors and single-byte errors are given in Fig. 5.9 (a) to (c). These patterns indicate whether the top $(r-b+1)$ positions of the syndrome are zero or nonzero and also

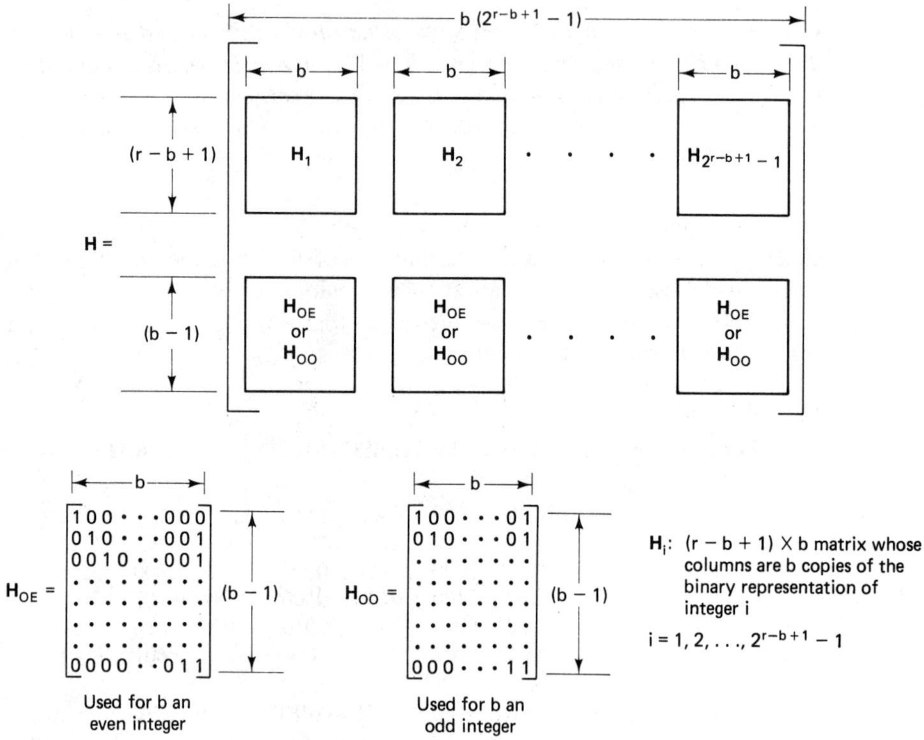

the number of ones or the actual bit pattern in the last $(b - 1)$ positions of the syndrome. From Fig. 5.9 (a) to (c), we note that the syndromes for the byte errors are nonzero and are different from the syndromes for single-bit errors. Hence, for $2 \le b \le 4$, the codes simultaneously correct all single-bit errors and detect all single-byte errors. Similarly, for $b \ge 5$, the possible pattern of syndromes corresponding to single-bit errors, double-bit errors, and single-byte errors are given in Fig. 5.10 (a) and (b). From this, it is apparent that the syndromes for the single-byte errors and double-bit errors are nonzero and are different from the syndromes for single-bit errors. Hence, for $b \ge 5$, the codes simultaneously correct all single-bit errors and detect all double-bit errors and all single-byte errors. Q.E.D.

Example 5-11

For $r = 6$ and $b = 3$, we have a (45, 39) SEC–S3ED code with the following **H** matrix.

$$\mathbf{H} = \begin{bmatrix} 000 & 000 & 000 & 000 & 000 & 000 & 000 & 111 & 111 & 111 & 111 & 111 & 111 & 111 & 111 \\ 000 & 000 & 000 & 111 & 111 & 111 & 111 & 000 & 000 & 000 & 000 & 111 & 111 & 111 & 111 \\ 000 & 111 & 111 & 000 & 000 & 111 & 111 & 000 & 000 & 111 & 111 & 000 & 000 & 111 & 111 \\ 111 & 000 & 111 & 000 & 111 & 000 & 111 & 000 & 111 & 000 & 111 & 000 & 111 & 000 & 111 \\ 101 & 101 & 101 & 101 & 101 & 101 & 101 & 101 & 101 & 101 & 101 & 101 & 101 & 101 & 101 \\ 011 & 011 & 011 & 011 & 011 & 011 & 011 & 011 & 011 & 011 & 011 & 011 & 011 & 011 & 011 \end{bmatrix}$$

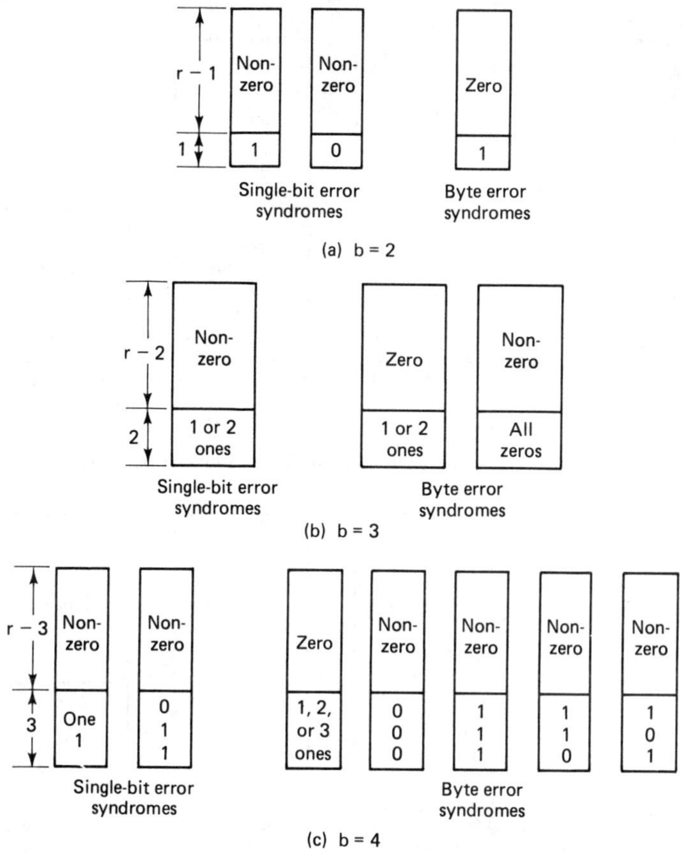

Figure 5.9 Syndromes for $b = 2, 3$, and 4 [REDD 78]. © 1978 IEEE.

If one desires to detect double-bit errors for $2 \leq b \leq 4$, an extra overall parity bit is added. From the above **H** matrix, we can also have the following (24, 18) SEC–DED–S3ED code.

$$\mathbf{H} = \begin{bmatrix} 111 & 111 & 111 & 111 & 111 & 111 & 111 & 111 \\ 000 & 000 & 000 & 000 & 111 & 111 & 111 & 111 \\ 000 & 000 & 111 & 111 & 000 & 000 & 111 & 111 \\ 000 & 111 & 000 & 111 & 000 & 111 & 000 & 111 \\ 101 & 101 & 101 & 101 & 101 & 101 & 101 & 101 \\ 011 & 011 & 011 & 011 & 011 & 011 & 011 & 011 \end{bmatrix}$$

Theorem 5-17(a) [FUJI 80a]. *The codes given by the* **H** *matrix on p. 267 are SEC–SbED codes. The code-bit length is* $N = b \cdot (2^{r-b+1} - 1)$.

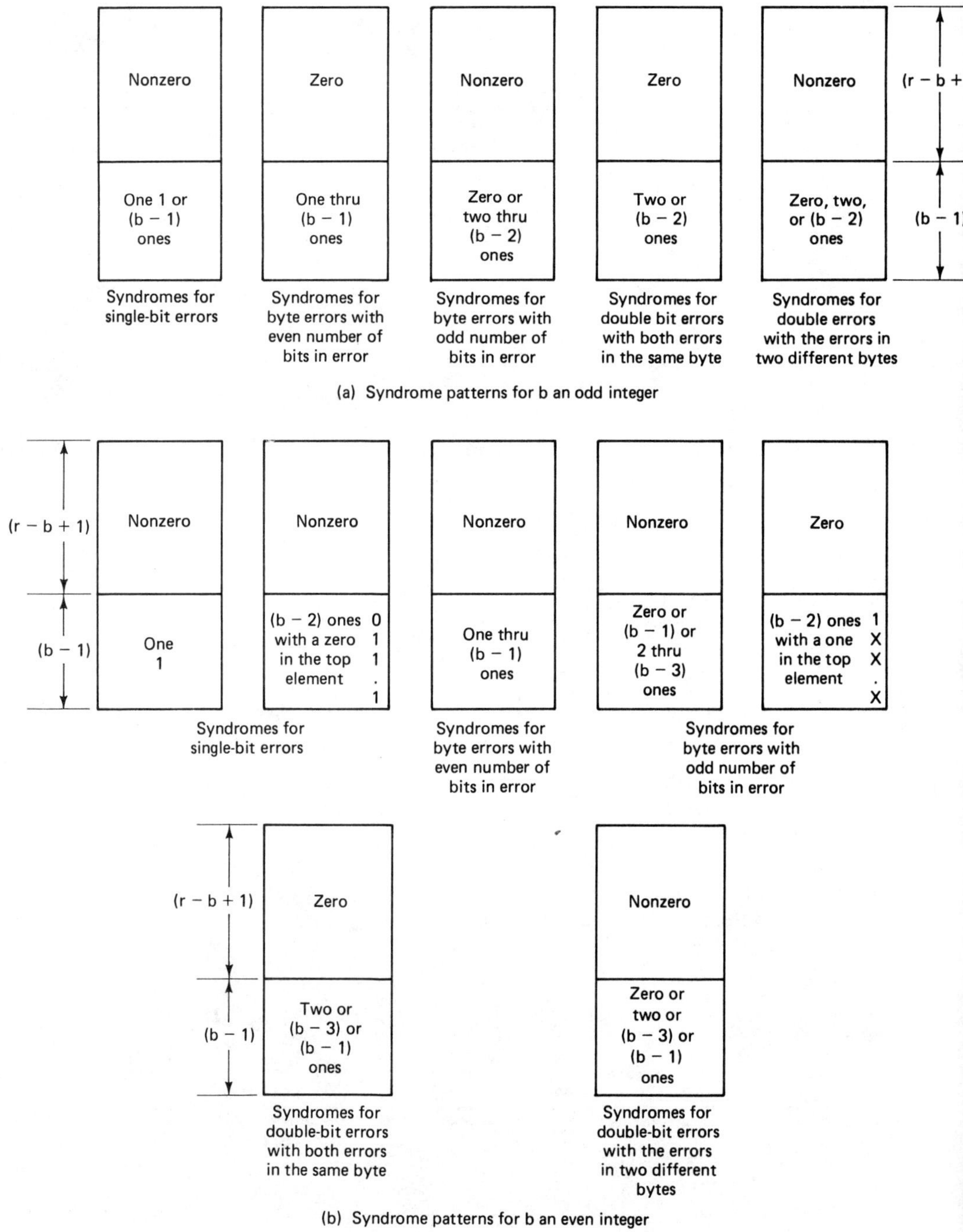

Figure 5.10 Syndromes for $b \geq 5$ [REDD 78]. © 1978 IEEE.

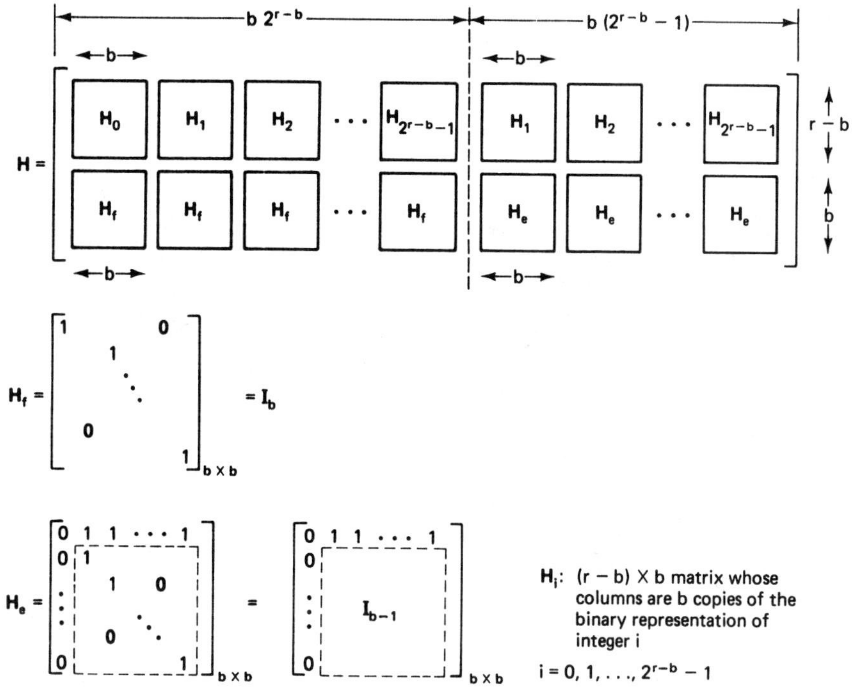

Proof. Let the syndrome pattern from the **H** matrix in this theorem be as follows.

$$S = \begin{bmatrix} S_0 \\ \vdots \\ S_{r-b-1} \\ \hline S_{r-b} \\ \vdots \\ S_{r-1} \end{bmatrix} = \begin{bmatrix} S_{\mathrm{I}} \\ \hline S_{\mathrm{II}} \end{bmatrix}$$

The weights of the syndrome parts are defined as follows.

$$W_{\mathrm{I}} = W(S_{\mathrm{I}}) = \text{weight of } S_{\mathrm{I}}$$
$$W_{\mathrm{II}} = W(S_{\mathrm{II}}) = \text{weight of } \mathrm{S}_{\mathrm{II}}$$

Then, for error sets $\mathbf{E}_1$ and $\mathbf{E}_2$, Table 5.9 shows the weight of the syndromes. From this, the syndromes corresponding to byte errors are nonzero and are different from those corresponding to single-bit errors. Q.E.D.

Example 5-12

The **H** matrix at top of p. 268 shows the (60, 53) SEC–S4ED code.

H =

c3	c4	c5	c6	d0	d1	d2	d3	d4	d5	d6	d7	d8	d9	d10	d11	d12	d13	d14	d15	d16	d17	d18	d19	d20	d21	d22	d23	d24	d25	d26	d27	c2	d28	d29	d30	c1	d31	d32	d33	d34	d35	d36	d37	c0	d38	d39	d40	d41	d42	d43	d44	d45	d46	d47	d48	d49	d50	d51	d52
																1	1	1	1	1	1	1	1	1	1	1	1	1	1	1	1													1	1	1	1	1	1	1	1	1	1	1	1	1	1	1	1
								1	1	1	1	1	1	1	1									1	1	1	1	1	1	1	1					1	1	1	1	1	1	1	1									1	1	1	1	1	1	1	1
				1	1	1	1					1	1	1	1					1	1	1	1					1	1	1	1	1	1	1	1					1	1	1	1					1	1	1	1					1	1	1	1
1				1				1				1				1				1				1				1					1	1	1		1	1	1		1	1	1		1	1	1		1	1	1		1	1	1		1	1	1
	1				1				1				1				1				1				1				1				1				1				1				1				1				1				1		
		1				1				1				1				1				1				1				1				1				1				1				1				1				1				1	
			1				1				1				1				1				1				1				1				1				1				1				1				1				1				1

$d_0 \sim d_{52}$: information bits

$c_0 \sim c_6$: check bits

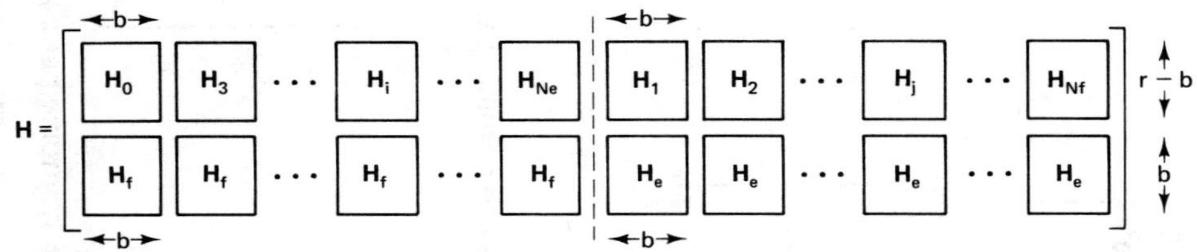

$\mathbf{H}_0, \mathbf{H}_1, \mathbf{H}_2, \ldots, \mathbf{H}_f, \mathbf{H}_e$ are the same matrices shown in Theorem 5-17(a)

i: integer whose binary representation has even weight

N_e: maximal integer i no greater than $(2^{r-b} - 1)$

j: integer whose binary representation has odd weight

N_f: maximal integer j no greater than $(2^{r-b} - 1)$

TABLE 5.9 WEIGHT OF THE SYNDROMES FOR ERRORS $\mathbf{E}_1$ AND $\mathbf{E}_2$

Error Location \ Error	$\mathbf{E}_1$: Errors in the Information-Bit Part	$\mathbf{E}_1$: Errors in the Check-Bit Part	$\mathbf{E}_2$	
Errors in the former data part having $b \cdot 2^{r-b}$ bit length	$W_{\mathrm{I}} \neq 0$ $W_{\mathrm{II}} = 1$	$W_{\mathrm{I}} = 0$ $W_{\mathrm{II}} = 1$	$W(\mathbf{E}_2)$ = even (≥ 2)	$W_{\mathrm{I}} = 0$ $W_{\mathrm{II}} = W(\mathbf{E}_2)$ = even (≥ 2)
			$W(\mathbf{E}_2)$ = odd (≥ 3)	$W_{\mathrm{I}} \neq 0$ $W_{\mathrm{II}} = W(\mathbf{E}_2)$ = odd (≥ 3)
Errors in the latter data part having $b \cdot (2^{r-b} - 1)$ bit length	$W_{\mathrm{I}} \neq 0$ $W_{\mathrm{II}} = \begin{cases} 0 \\ 2^* \end{cases}$	$W_{\mathrm{I}} = 1$ $W_{\mathrm{II}} = 0$	$W(\mathbf{E}_2)$ = even (≥ 2)	$W_{\mathrm{I}} = 0$ $W_{\mathrm{II}} = W(\mathbf{E}_2)$ = even (≥ 2)
			$W(\mathbf{E}_2)$ = odd (≥ 3)	$W_{\mathrm{I}} \neq 0$ $W_{\mathrm{II}} = \begin{Bmatrix} W(\mathbf{E}_2)^* - 1 \\ W(\mathbf{E}_2) + 1 \end{Bmatrix}$ = even (≥ 2)

*As for $W(\mathbf{E}_2) = 3$, $S_{r-b} = 1$ for $\mathbf{E}_1$ and $S_{r-b} = 0$ for $\mathbf{E}_2$.

Theorem 5-17(b) [FUJI 80a]. *The codes given by the* **H** *matrix at bottom of p. 268 are SEC–DED–SbED codes. The code-bit length is* $N = b \cdot 2^{r-b}$.

Proof. The **H** matrix shown in Theorem 5-17(b) is clearly a part of the **H** matrix of the SEC–SbED codes shown in Theorem 5-17(a). Also, since every column vector in this matrix is odd weight, it has DED property. Therefore, it is an SEC–DED–SbED code. Q.E.D.

Example 5-13

For $b = 4$, $r = 7$, the following **H** matrix shows the (32, 25) SEC–DED–S4ED code.

	c_3	c_4	c_5	c_6	d_0	d_1	d_2	d_3	d_4	d_5	d_6	d_7	d_8	d_9	d_{10}	d_{11}	c_2	d_{12}	d_{13}	d_{14}	c_1	d_{15}	d_{16}	d_{17}	c_0	d_{18}	d_{19}	d_{20}	d_{21}	d_{22}	d_{23}	d_{24}
									1	1	1	1	1	1	1	1									1	1	1	1	1	1	1	1
					1	1	1	1					1	1	1	1					1	1	1	1					1	1	1	1
					1	1	1	1	1	1	1	1					1	1	1	1									1	1	1	1
H =	1				1				1				1					1	1	1		1	1	1		1	1	1		1	1	1
		1				1				1				1				1				1				1				1		
			1				1				1				1				1				1				1				1	
				1				1				1				1				1				1				1				1

$c_0 \sim c_6$: check bits

$d_0 \sim d_{24}$: information bits

The **H** matrices of the codes defined in Theorem 5.17(a) and (b) have the nice characteristic that the check-bit position can be directly determined without requiring any row operations.

Theorem 5-18 [VARA 83]. *Let* $\mathbf{p}(x)$ *be a polynomial of degree* $l < b$ *and of exponent* e *such that* $e > b$ *and* $GCD\ (e, b) = 1$, *where* $GCD\ (e, b)$ *expresses the greatest common divisor of* e *and* b. *Then the* $(N, N - b - l)$ *cyclic code generated by* $\mathbf{g}(x) = (x^b - 1)\mathbf{p}(x)$ *with* $N = e \cdot b$ *is SEC–DED–SbED code.*

Proof. Let α be a primitive root of $\mathbf{p}(x)$, $\mathbf{I}_b$ be the identity matrix of size b, and $\mathbf{E}(x)$ be the error pattern. Then, the **H** matrix can be constructed as

$$\mathbf{H} = \left[\begin{array}{c} 1\,\alpha\,\alpha^2 \cdots \alpha^{e-1} \quad 1\,\alpha\,\alpha^2 \cdots \alpha^{e-1} \cdots 1\,\alpha\,\alpha^2 \cdots \alpha^{e-1} \\ \hdashline \mathbf{I}_b \quad \mathbf{I}_b \cdots \mathbf{I}_b \cdots \mathbf{I}_b \quad \mathbf{I}_b \end{array}\right]$$

and the syndrome $\mathbf{S}(x)$ can be generated as two parts, $\mathbf{S}_1(x)$ and $\mathbf{S}_2(x)$, due to the factors $\mathbf{p}(x)$ and $(x^b - 1)$, respectively.

$$\mathbf{S}(x) = (\mathbf{S}_1(x), \mathbf{S}_2(x))$$

$$\mathbf{S}_1(x) \equiv \mathbf{E}(x) \mod \mathbf{p}(x)$$

$$\mathbf{S}_2(x) \equiv \mathbf{E}(x) \mod (x^b - 1)$$

Since $GCD\ (e, b) = 1$, that is, e and b are relatively prime, there are no two identical columns in the matrix **H**, and hence the single errors are correctable. Also, $\mathbf{S}_2(x)$ provides the byte error pattern, and it is not equal to that of single-bit errors. Next, we prove that the two components $\mathbf{S}_1(x)$ and $\mathbf{S}_2(x)$ together detect random double-bit errors as follows: If two random bit errors occur, we need to consider the possibility that the erroneous bits may be in the same byte or in different bytes. In the first case, it is a byte error and it is detectable by $\mathbf{S}_2(x)$. In the latter case, the assumption $GCD\ (e, b) = 1$ guarantees two bit errors having different values at least for $\mathbf{S}_1$ or $\mathbf{S}_2$. Therefore, two bit errors have either (1) different values for $\mathbf{S}_1$ and also $\mathbf{S}_2$, (2) different values for $\mathbf{S}_1$ and the same values for $\mathbf{S}_2$, or (3) the same values for $\mathbf{S}_1$ and different values for $\mathbf{S}_2$. Therefore, random double-bit errors are detectable. Thus the code is SEC–DED–SbED code. Q.E.D.

If we use the primitive polynomial of degree $l = r - b$ as $\mathbf{p}(x)$, the code-bit length of this code can be expressed as

$$N = b \cdot (2^{r-b} - 1)$$

Example 5-14

Let the primitive polynomial of degree 3 be $\mathbf{p}(x) = x^3 + x + 1$ and $b = 4$, $l = 3$. Then, $GCD\ (e, b) = GCD\ (2^3 - 1, 4) = 1$, and the following (28, 21) cyclic SEC–DED–S4ED code can be obtained.

$$
\mathbf{H} = \left[\begin{array}{cccc|cccc|cccc|cccc|cccc|cccc|cccc}
1 & & & 1 & & 1 & 1 & 1 & & & 1 & & 1 & 1 & 1 & & & 1 & & 1 & 1 & 1 & & & 1 & & 1 & 1 \\
& 1 & & 1 & 1 & 1 & & & 1 & & 1 & 1 & 1 & & & 1 & & 1 & 1 & 1 & & & 1 & & 1 & 1 & 1 & \\
& & 1 & & 1 & 1 & 1 & & & 1 & & 1 & 1 & 1 & & & 1 & & 1 & 1 & 1 & & & 1 & & 1 & 1 & 1 \\
\hline
1 & & & & 1 & & & & 1 & & & & 1 & & & & 1 & & & & 1 & & & & 1 & & & \\
& 1 & & & & 1 & & & & 1 & & & & 1 & & & & 1 & & & & 1 & & & & 1 & & \\
& & 1 & & & & 1 & & & & 1 & & & & 1 & & & & 1 & & & & 1 & & & & 1 & \\
& & & 1 & & & & 1 & & & & 1 & & & & 1 & & & & 1 & & & & 1 & & & & 1
\end{array}\right]
\begin{array}{l} \ell = 3 \\ \\ b = 4 \end{array}
$$

Generalized burst-error detecting SEC–DED codes [KANE 83]. We consider a class of generalized burst error detecting SEC–DED codes (i.e., generalized SEC–DED–BED codes), which include the codes just mentioned. Here, it will be shown that the foregoing codes are equivalent to single-burst, error detecting SEC–DED codes.

Definition 5-3. A code of length N, where N is an integer multiple of b, is said to be *b-grouped parity checkable* if it can be divided equally into b groups in interlaced form and the mod 2 sum of the data included in each group has constant value regardless of the input codewords.

The concept of this b-grouped parity checking is shown in Fig. 5.11.

Definition 5-4. Let b be the byte length and r be the check-bit length of the code defined by the matrix **H**. A $(b \times r)$ binary matrix **A** of rank b is referred to as a *grouping matrix* that groups the r row vectors of the **H** matrix into b groups in which vectors are added.

Let the **H** matrix of a code be denoted by its r row vectors $H_0, H_1, \ldots, H_{r-1}$. The product $\mathbf{A} \cdot \mathbf{H}$ is a matrix **F** and its row vectors are denoted $F_0, F_1, \ldots, F_{b-1}$.

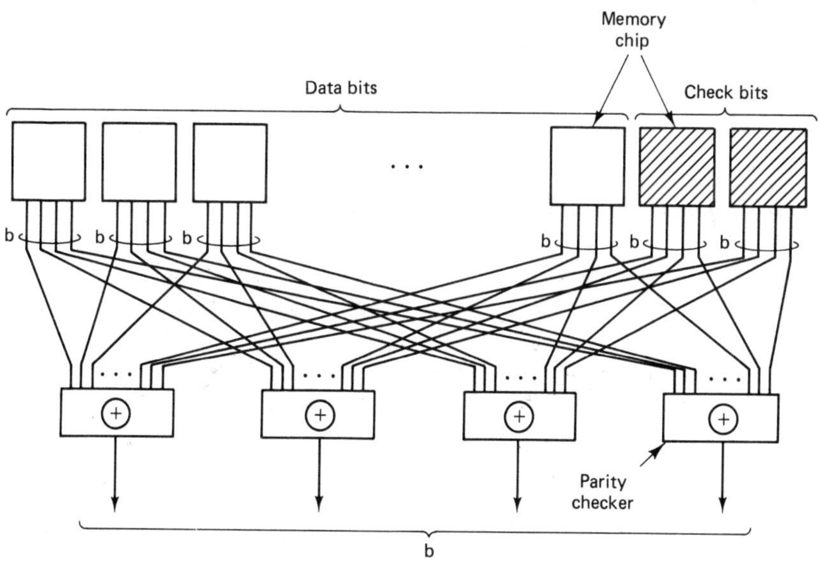

Figure 5.11 *b*-Grouped parity checking [KANE 83]. © 1983 IECE Japan.

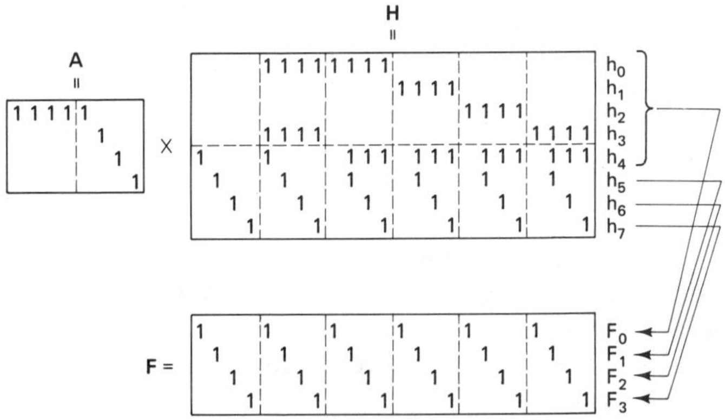

Figure 5.12 An example of the grouping matrix **A** [KANE 83]. © 1983 IECE Japan.

Then F_i is the result of a bit-by-bit (mod 2) sum of all H_j's for which $a_{ij} = 1$. Here, $a_{i,j} \in \{0, 1\}$ is the element of **A**.

$$\begin{bmatrix} F_0 \\ F_1 \\ \vdots \\ F_{b-1} \end{bmatrix} = [\mathbf{A}] \cdot \begin{bmatrix} H_0 \\ H_1 \\ \vdots \\ H_{r-1} \end{bmatrix}$$

Fig. 5.12 shows an example of the multiplication of **A** to **H**. In this example, for byte length $b = 4$ and check-bit length $r = 8$, the **H** matrix defines the type of code stated in Example 5-13. The first five rows of **H** are added to obtain F_0. The sixth, seventh, and eighth rows of **H** are the same as F_1, F_2, and F_3, respectively.

The following theorem is relevant to the design of b-grouped parity checkable codes using the grouping matrix **A**.

Theorem 5-19. *The code is b-grouped parity checkable, if and only if there exists a matrix* **A** *such that the product of* **A** *and* **H** *is identical to the concatenation of the* $(b \times b)$ *identity matrices.*

Proof. Let $H_0, H_1, \ldots, H_{r-1}$ be the row vectors of the **H** matrix. For a given codeword W and an arbitrary value of j,

$$W \cdot H_j^T = 0 \qquad 0 \le j \le r - 1$$

Let $D_0, D_1, \ldots, D_{p-1}$ represent some of the row vectors in **H** that are included in F_i (i.e., p is the number of 1's in the ith row of **A**). Then, F_i can be expressed as follows:

$$F_i = a_{i,0} \cdot H_0 + a_{i,1} \cdot H_1 + \cdots + a_{i,r-1} \cdot H_{r-1} = D_0 + D_1 + \cdots + D_{p-1}$$

where + is the vector sum. The product of the codeword W and the vector F_i yields

$$W \cdot F_i^T = W \cdot \left(D_0^T + D_1^T + \cdots + D_{p-1}^T \right)$$

$$= W \cdot D_0^T + W \cdot D_1^T + \cdots + W \cdot D_{p-1}^T$$

$$= 0$$

This says that the mod 2 sum of the data included in the ith group has a constant value (zero) regardless of the codeword W. Since each column vector of **F** has weight 1, and each row vector of **F** also has equal constant weight, the code derived from the **H** matrix is b-grouped parity checkable. That proves the necessity of the condition and its sufficiency can also be proven in a similar manner. Q.E.D.

Fig. 5.13 shows the b-grouped parity checking of the arbitrary codewords, W_1 and W_2.

Theorem 5-19 states that if the addition of subsets of row vectors of **H** as prescribed by **A** yields a concatenation of $(b \times b)$ identity matrices, then the code represented by **H** is b-grouped parity checkable.

Theorem 5-20. *Assume that the* **H** *matrix of a code* **C** *has distinct columns, and the code is b-grouped parity checkable. Then* **C** *is an SEC–DED–BED code with length*

$$N = b \cdot 2^{r-b}$$

Proof. Let $H_0, H_1, \ldots, H_{r-1}$ be row vectors of **H**. Since the vector sum of some H_i's yields F_i, $0 \le i \le b-1$, there cannot be an all-0 column vector in **H**. And also from the assumption these column vectors in **H** are distinct. Thus, the code can correct all single-bit errors.

According to Theorem 5-19, the mod 2 sum of $F_0, \ldots, F_{b-1}$ yields an all-1 row vector. Therefore, this code can also detect all double-bit errors.

Next, let us examine a vector obtained by multiplying the syndrome to the grouping matrix **A**. It is fairly simple to observe that the result is identical to the single-byte error pattern. This pattern can indicate whether the error is a correctable single-bit error or an uncorrectable byte error. On the other hand, since the product of **A** and **H** yields the concatenation of $(b \times b)$ identity matrices, this byte error pattern can always indicate any b-adjacent errors, that is, burst errors. This means the code can detect single b-bit burst errors.

Let's consider the bit length of this code. Since the product of **A** and **H** (i.e., **F**) is the concatenation of identity matrices, the bit having 1 in the vector F_i shows that the corresponding **H** matrix column vectors are included uniquely in the ith group. Let $(x_0, x_1, \ldots, x_{r-1})$ represent the **H** matrix column vector included in the ith group. These column vectors should satisfy the following relation. Note that only

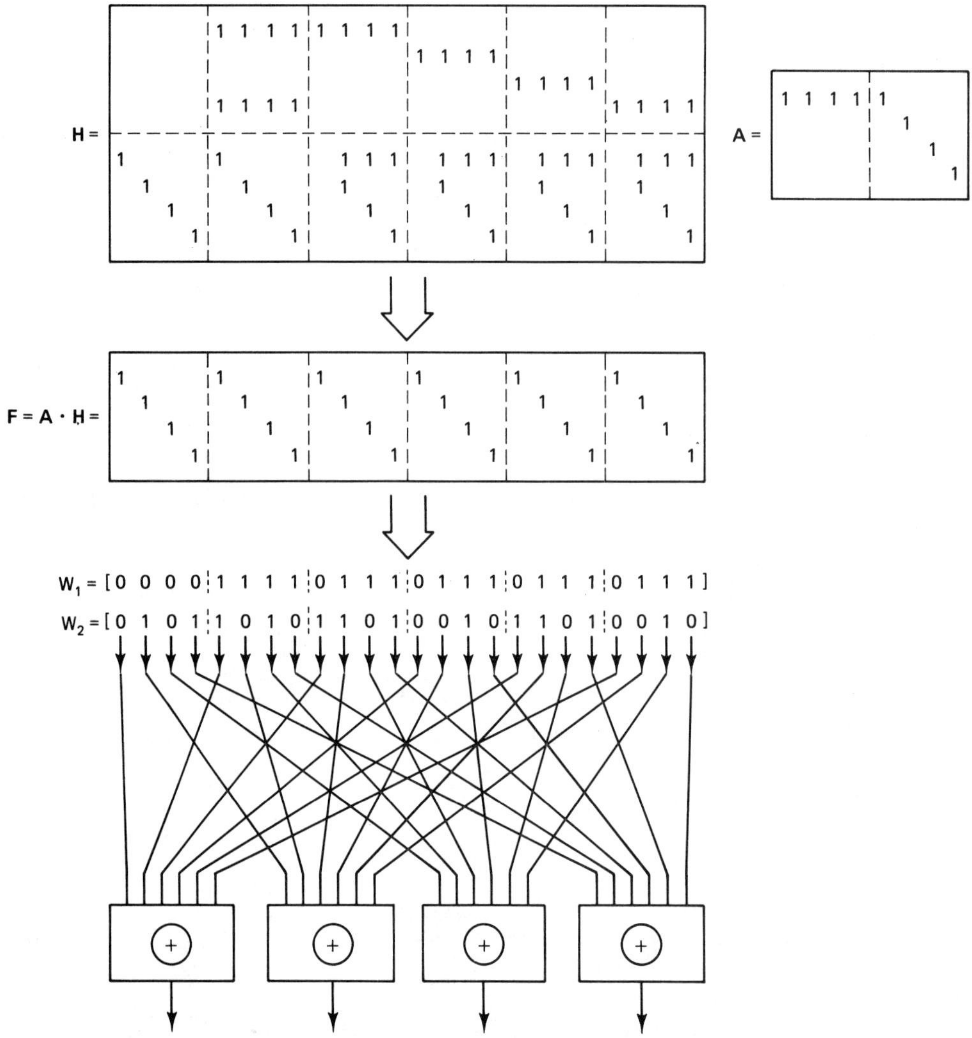

Figure 5.13 *b*-Grouped parity checking of the codewords W_1 and W_2 [KANE 83]. © 1983 IECE Japan.

the ith element F_i of the vector on the left-hand side is 1, and the other elements are all 0's.

$$i)\ \begin{bmatrix} 0 \\ \vdots \\ 0 \\ 1 \\ 0 \\ \vdots \\ 0 \end{bmatrix}_b = [\mathbf{A}]_{b \times r} \cdot \begin{bmatrix} x_0 \\ x_1 \\ \vdots \\ x_{r-1} \end{bmatrix} \tag{5.39}$$

According to Definition 5-4, the rank of **A** is b. Using linear algebra, the first order equation of (5.39) has 2^{r-b} solutions of $(x_0, x_1, \ldots, x_{r-1})$. Therefore, the bit length N of this code is $b \cdot 2^{r-b}$. Q.E.D.

Fig. 5.14 shows some grouping matrices for SEC–DED–BED codes of Theorems 5-15 through 18.

In Fig. 5.14 we can prove that the codes of Theorems 5-15, 16 (for $b \leq 4$), and 17(b) are equivalent to each other. The codes of Theorem 5-18 have a cyclic structure and have smaller code length than the other codes. However, those are also b-grouped parity checkable codes.

The grouping matrix **A** has the following properties.

Property 1. If every column in **A** has odd weight, then every column in **H** of the SEC–DED–BED code also has odd weight. (As examples, see Fig. 5.12 and Equation (5.40).)

Property 2. If each column in **A** has weight 1, then some r columns in **H** of the single SEC–DED–BED code generated by **A** has weight 1, and hence these r columns can be designated as check-bit columns of **H**. (As an example, see Fig. 5.12.)

Property 3. If every column in **A** has weight 1 and every row in **A** has constant weight, then the check-bit columns in **H** of the SEC–DED–BED code correspond exactly to check byte (see, for example (5.40)).

Here, let's consider another b-grouped parity checkable code (shown in Equation (5.40)) whose matrix **A** is different from those shown in Fig. 5.14. The matrix **A** of this code satisfies properties 1, 2, and 3. The **H** matrix has all odd-weight columns and satisfies the condition for minimum-equal-weight code (see Section 4.4.2).

$$
\mathbf{H} = \left[\begin{array}{cccc|cccc|cccc|cccc|cccc|cccc|cccc|cccc|cccc|cccc}
1&&& & 1&&& & 1&1&1&1 & 1&1&1& & 1&&& & &&& & &&& & &1&1&1 & &1&1& & &&& \\
&1&& & &1&1&1 & 1&1&& & 1&&&1 & &1&& & &&& & &&1&1 & 1&&& & 1&1&&1 & &&& \\
&&1&1 & 1&1&1& & &&1& & 1&&&1 & &&1& & &&&1 & 1&1&& & &&& & 1&&1&1 & &&& \\
1&1&1&1 & &&&1 & &&&1 & &1&1& & &&&1 & 1&1&1& & &&& & &&& & &1&1&1 & &&& \\
\hline
&&& & &&& & &1&1&1 & &1&1& & &&& & 1&&& & 1&&& & 1&1&1&1 & 1&1&1& & 1&&& \\
&&& & &&1&1 & 1&&& & 1&1&&1 & &&& & &1&& & &1&1&1 & 1&1&& & 1&&&1 & &1&& \\
&&&1 & 1&1&& & &&& & 1&&1&1 & &&& & &&1&1 & 1&1&1& & &&1& & 1&&&1 & &&1& \\
1&1&1& & &&& & &&& & &1&1&1 & &&& & 1&1&1&1 & &&&1 & &&&1 & &1&1& & &&&1
\end{array}\right] \tag{5.40}
$$

$$
\mathbf{A} = \left[\begin{array}{cccc|cccc}
1&&& & 1&&& \\
&1&& & &1&& \\
&&1& & &&1& \\
&&&1 & &&&1
\end{array}\right]
$$

The error detection circuit of the b-grouped parity checkable codes can be systematically obtained by multiplying the syndrome to matrix **A**. Fig. 5.15 shows this circuit of the code in (5.40).

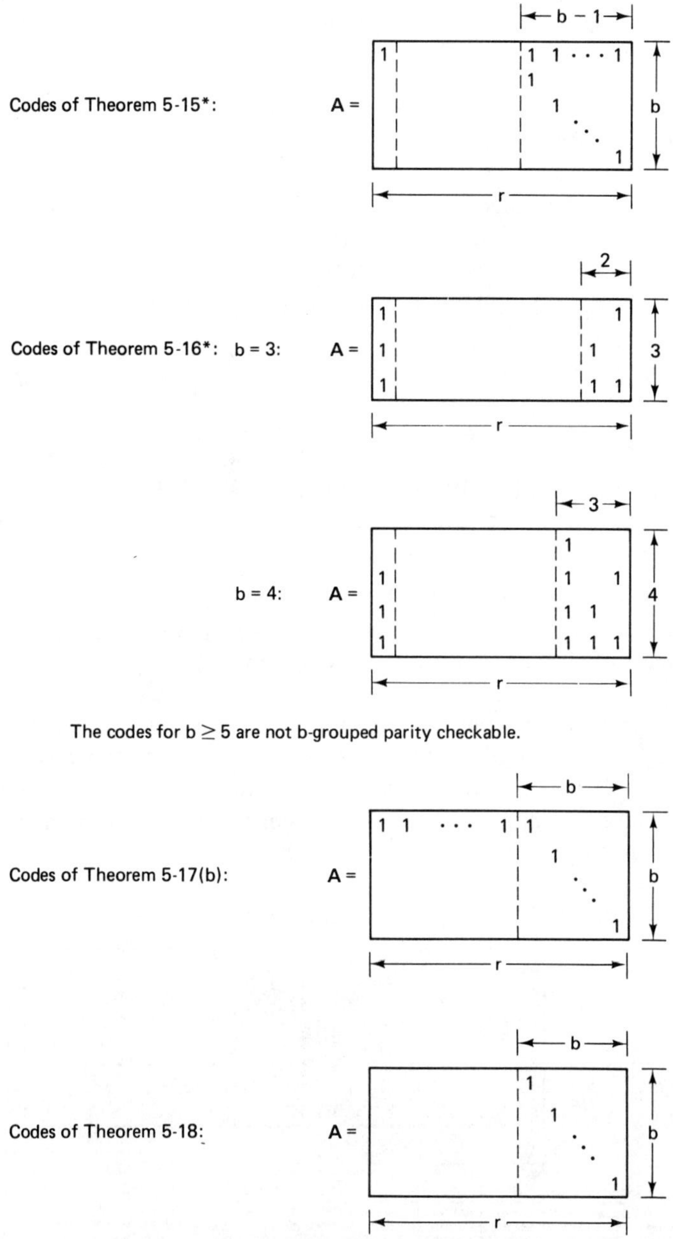

*In order to have double-bit error detection ability, an all 1's row vector is added to **H**.

Figure 5.14 Grouping matrices for the existing SEC–DED–BED codes [KANE 83].

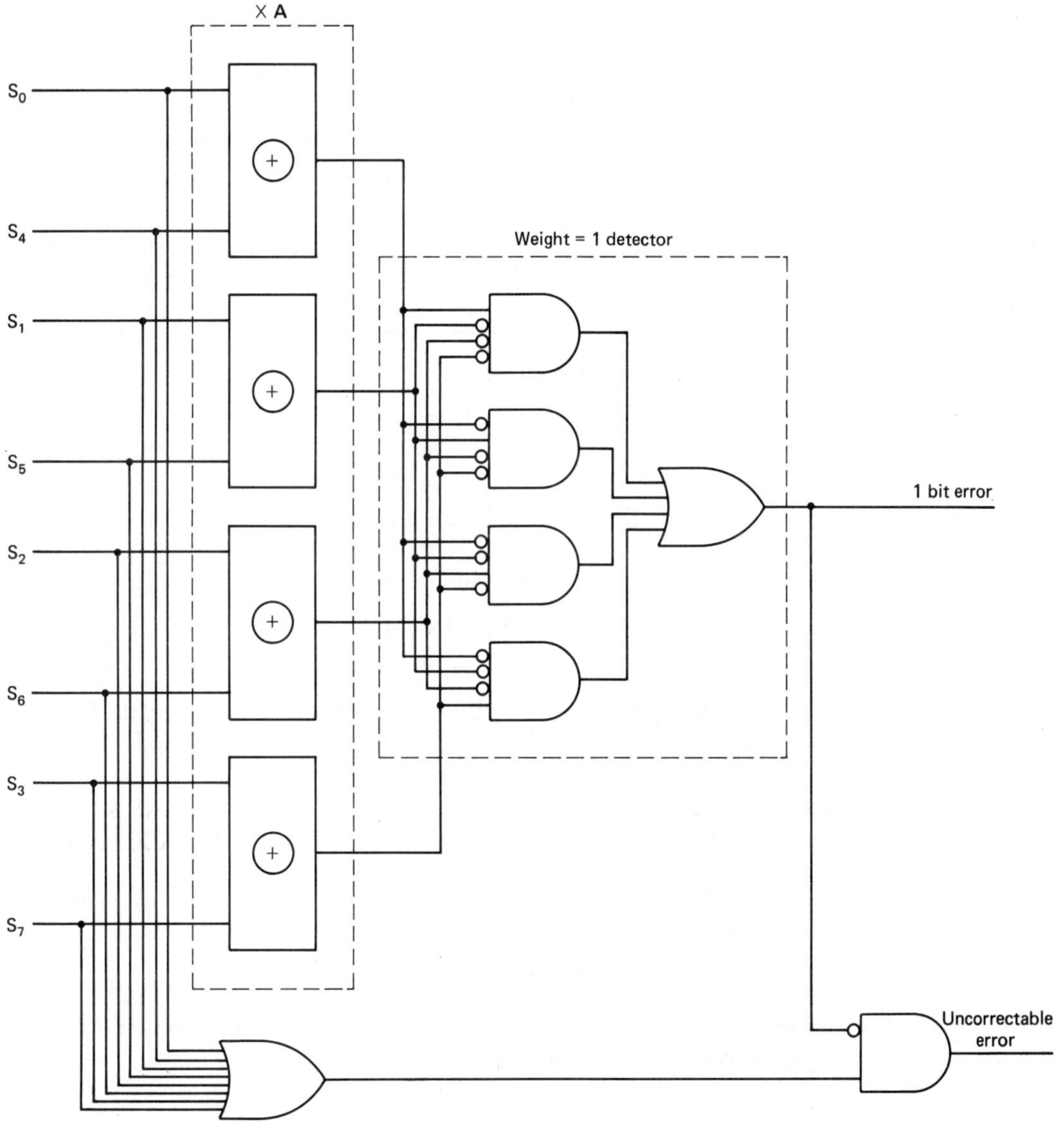

Figure 5.15 Error detection circuit for the (40, 32) SEC–DED–BED code shown in (5.40) [KANE 83]. © 1983 IECE Japan.

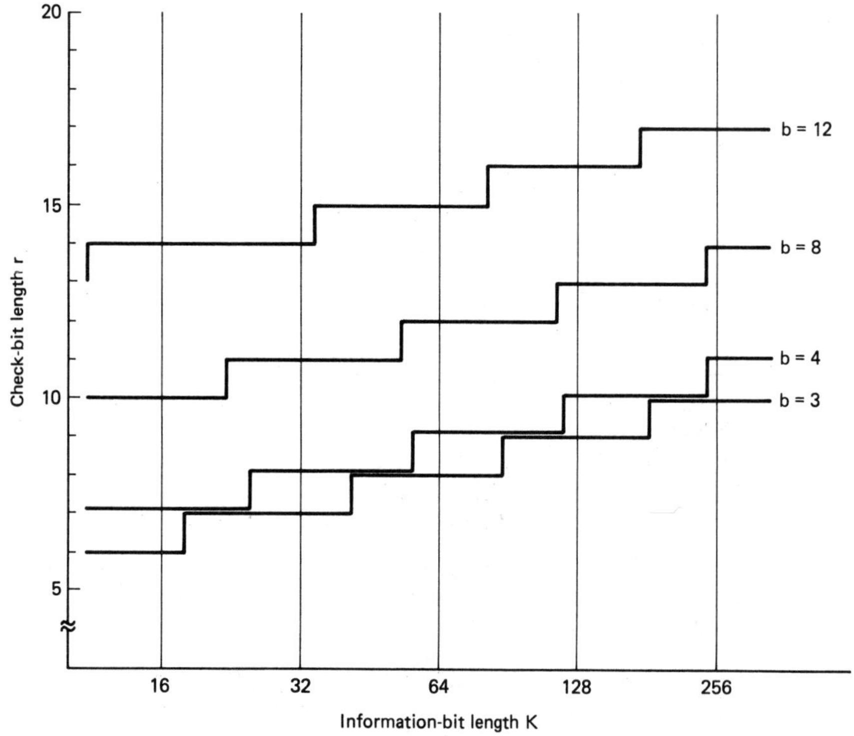

Figure 5.16 Check-bit length of the SEC–DED–BED code.

Fig. 5.16 shows the relation between the information-bit length K and the check-bit length r of the SEC–DED–BED codes for $b = 3$, 4, 8, and 12 bits.

Rotational burst error detecting SEC–DED codes [KANE 83]. Based on the generalized codes, we consider the rotational SEC–DED–BED codes next.

Theorem 5-21. *If the grouping matrix* **A** *is given as a concatenation of* r/b b*th degree identity matrices* $\mathbf{I}_b$,

$$\mathbf{A} = [\mathbf{I}_b \quad \mathbf{I}_b \quad \cdots \quad \mathbf{I}_b]_{r/b}$$

then the code generated by **A** *is a rotational SEC–DED–BED code whose* **H** *matrix has* r/b *submatrices. The code-bit length of this code is given as follows.*

$$N = b \cdot \sum_{\substack{m|(r/b) \\ m;\ odd}} \mu(m) \cdot 2^{[(r/m)-b]}$$

Here, summation is performed over the odd divisors of r/b.

This theorem can be proved by using the definitions of the grouping matrix **A**, the b-grouped parity checkable code, and the rotational code. The code length can be deduced by using the modified Möbius inversion formula given in Section 5.1.3.

TABLE 5.10 CODE-BIT LENGTH OF THE ROTATIONAL SEC – DED – BED CODE

r/b \ b	1*	2	3	4	5	6
2	$\frac{2^\dagger}{2}$	$\frac{8}{8}$	$\frac{24}{24}$	$\frac{64}{64}$	$\frac{160}{160}$	$\frac{384}{384}$
3	$\frac{3}{4}$	$\frac{30}{32}$	$\frac{189}{192}$	$\frac{1{,}020}{1{,}024}$	$\frac{5{,}115}{5{,}120}$	$\frac{24{,}570}{24{,}576}$
4	$\frac{8}{8}$	$\frac{128}{128}$	$\frac{1{,}536}{1{,}536}$	$\frac{16{,}384}{16{,}384}$	$\frac{163{,}840}{163{,}840}$	$\frac{1{,}572{,}864}{1{,}572{,}864}$
5	$\frac{15}{16}$	$\frac{510}{512}$	$\frac{12{,}285}{12{,}288}$	—	—	—

*Rotational odd-weight-column SEC–DED code.

† $\frac{2}{2}$ ← *rotational* (numerator) / ← *nonrotational* (denominator)

Source: [KANE 83]. © 1983 IECE Japan.

From Property 1 of the grouping matrix **A**, this code is an odd-weight-column code. The code-bit length N of this code is shown in Table 5.10.

An example of the rotational (45, 36) SEC–DED–BED code (with $b = 3$) is given as follows.

$$\mathbf{H} = \left[\begin{array}{ccc|ccc|ccc|ccc|ccc|ccc|ccc|ccc|ccc|ccc|ccc|ccc|ccc|ccc|ccc}
1&& & &1& & 1&&1 & 1&1&1 & 1&& & && & && & && & &&1 & && & && & 1&1& & &&1 & &1& & && \\
1&1&1 & 1&1&1 & && & && & &1& & && & && & && & &1& & && & 1&&1 & 1&&1 & &1& & && & && \\
&1&1 & && & 1&1&1 & && & &&1 & && & && & && & 1&& & && & &1& & &&1 & 1&1& & 1&&1 & && \\
\hline
&& & 1&1& & &&1 & &1& & && & 1&& & &1& & 1&&1 & 1&1&1 & 1&& & && & && & && & &&1 & && \\
1&&1 & 1&&1 & &1& & && & && & 1&1&1 & 1&1&1 & && & && & &1& & && & && & && & &1& & && \\
&1& & &&1 & 1&1& & 1&&1 & && & &1&1 & && & 1&1&1 & && & &&1 & && & && & && & 1&& & && \\
\hline
&& & && & && & &&1 & && & && & 1&1& & &&1 & &1& & && & 1&& & &1& & 1&&1 & 1&1&1 & 1&& \\
&& & && & && & &1& & && & 1&&1 & 1&&1 & &1& & && & && & 1&1&1 & 1&1&1 & && & && & &1& \\
&& & && & && & 1&& & && & &1& & &&1 & 1&1& & 1&&1 & && & &1&1 & && & 1&1&1 & && & &&1
\end{array}\right]$$

$$\mathbf{A} = \left[\begin{array}{ccc|ccc|ccc}
1&& & 1&& & 1&& \\
&1& & &1& & &1& \\
&&1 & &&1 & &&1
\end{array}\right]$$

Another example has already been presented in (5.40). This is a rotational (40, 32) SEC–DED–BED code with $b = 4$.

5.3.2 Byte Error Detecting SEC – DED codes (SEC – DED – SbED Codes)

We can say that the SEC–DED–SbED code is a special case of the SEC–DED–BED code in the sense that the burst is confined to the bounds of one byte. A BED code is also an SbED code, but not necessarily the other way around. The SbED codes have the possibility to have fewer check bits than BED codes. For one of the practical code parameters of information-bit length $K = 64$ and byte length $b = 4$, especially, an SbED code may have the check-bit length $r = 8$ (i.e., the same check-bit length of the SEC–DED code having $K = 64$). On the other hand, from Fig. 5.16, the SEC–DED–BED code requires a check-bit length $r = 9$ for $K = 64$.

The SEC–DED–SbED codes are interesting from the practical point of view, and they are actively researched. Some excellent codes have been proposed in [CHEN 83, KANE 84a, 85, and DUNN 83, 85]. Chen [CHEN 83] proposed the design method for the codes constructed from the structure of *orthogonal flats* in finite Euclidean geometry. The codes with $b = 3$ especially meets the upper bound. As for $b = 4$, Kaneda [KANE 84a] proposed the optimal one of this type. Dunning [DUNN 85] proposed an excellent code for $r = b + 2$. The "best" code that meets the upper bound on code length for an arbitrary byte length b has not been found as yet. Here, codes for $b = 4$ and $r = b + 2$, and rotational SEC–DED–SbED codes are introduced.

Codes for $b = 4$ [KANE 84a]. We will now examine the SEC–DED–SbED codes with a 4-bit byte (i.e., $b = 4$). This code is rather important from the practical point of view because 4-bit byte organized RAM chips have become popular in high-speed memories. Compared to the SEC–DED–BED code, the check-bit length can be decreased by one bit for information-bit length $K = 64$. This is the same check-bit length as for the SEC–DED code of $K = 64$. We can design the (72, 64) SEC–DED–S4ED code according to the following construction method.

CONSTRUCTION 1

Step 1: Let r be an arbitrary but positive even integer ($r > 3$). Let G denote a column vector having $r/2$ binary elements. Vector G is arbitrary, but $G =$ all 1's vector is advisable to reduce the **H** matrix weight.

Step 2: Let F_q denote a column vector having $r/2$ binary elements. The weight of F_q must be even for an odd weight of G and must be odd for an even weight of G. The number of F_q's is $2^{(r/2-1)}$ ($q = 0, 1, \ldots, 2^{(r/2-1)} - 1$).

Step 3: Two column vectors F_i and F_j are selected arbitrarily from the F_q's where $0 \le i \le 2^{(r/2-1)} - 1$, $0 \le j \le 2^{(r/2-1)} - 1$, and $i \ne j$. Using F_i and F_j, the following $(r \times 4)$ matrix, $\mathbf{H}_{i,j}$, is defined.

$$\mathbf{H}_{i,j} = \begin{bmatrix} G + F_i + F_j & G + F_i + F_j & F_i & F_j \\ F_i & F_j & G + F_i + F_j & G + F_i + F_j \end{bmatrix}$$

Here, + represents the mod 2 sum of the column vectors.

Step 4: The **H** matrix can be constructed as follows.

$$\mathbf{H} = \left[\mathbf{H}_{0,1}, \mathbf{H}_{0,2}, \mathbf{H}_{0,3}, \ldots, \mathbf{H}_{i,j}, \ldots, \mathbf{H}_{p-1,p}\right], \qquad p \le 2^{r/2-1} - 1 \quad (5.41)$$

CONSTRUCTION 2

Let W be a row vector of N 0's followed by N 1's and $N = n \cdot b$. Define

$$\mathbf{H}_{r+1} = \left[\begin{array}{cc} \multicolumn{2}{c}{W} \\ \hline \mathbf{H}_r & \mathbf{H}_r \end{array}\right]$$

Then the code $\mathbf{C}(r + 1, b)$ with $\mathbf{H}_{r+1}$ as its check matrix is an SEC–DED–SbED code with a length of $2n$ b-bit bytes. Here, $\mathbf{C}(r, b)$ denotes an SEC–DED–SbED code with r check bytes and b bits in a byte. In addition, let $\mathbf{H}_r$ be the check matrix of $\mathbf{C}(r, b)$. This is the same code extension method as that shown in Theorem 5-8.

Theorem 5-22. *The code constructed by Construction* 1 *is an odd-weight-column SEC–DED–S4ED code with an even number of check bits larger than* 3 *and a code length of* $n = 2^{r-3} - 2^{(r/2-2)}$ *bytes.*

Proof. Obviously, the column vectors in (5.41) are odd weight. Now let's assume that F_i is odd weight. In this case, G must be even weight. When F_i is even weight, the proof is the same, as will be shown.

1. Proof of single-error correcting capability: The weight of F_i is odd and the weight of $G + F_i + F_j$ is even. Thus, the following equations should be satisfied to show the nonuniqueness of the column vectors.

$$F_i = F_i'$$

$$G + F_i + F_j = G + F_i' + F_j'$$

where if $F_i = F_i'$, then F_j must not be equal to F_i' from the definition in Construction 1. However, we can derive $F_i = F_i'$ and $F_j = F_j'$ from these equations, which is absurd. Thus, the column vectors in (5.41) are distinct. Consequently, the codes of (5.41) are SEC–DED codes.

2. Proof of single 4-bit byte error detecting capability: Double-bit errors within each byte can be detected through the DED capability. Let's verify this error detection capability for triple-bit errors and quadruple-bit errors within a byte.

(a) Triple-bit errors: For each byte of (5.41), let's choose arbitrary three-column vectors from the byte and sum them. The resultant column vector pattern is then a syndrome for a triple-bit error. It can easily be shown that either the lower-half $r/2$ bits or the upper-half $r/2$ bits in the syndrome are equal to G. From the definition in Construction 1, F_i is not equal to F_j. Therefore, $G + F_i + F_j$ cannot be equal to G. As a consequence, triple-bit errors within a byte can be detected.

(b) Quadruple-bit errors: For each byte in (5.41), sum four column vectors. Obviously, the resultant column vector is even weight and is not equal to the all-0's vector. Thus, quadruple-bit errors within a byte can be detected.

Note that the number of F_q's is $2^{(r/2-1)}$. In addition, the number of $\mathbf{H}_{ij}$'s is the combination number with selection of two elements from $2^{(r/2-1)}$ elements. Hence, the code length is equal to $n = 2^{(r/2-1)}(2^{(r/2-1)} - 1)/2 = 2^{r-3} - 2^{(r/2-2)}$ bytes. Q.E.D.

If an odd number of check bits is required, Construction 2 can be applied to the code in Theorem 5-22. The codes obtained have a code length of $(2^{r-3} - 2^{(r-3)/2})$ bytes with r (= odd) check bytes.

Example 5-15 [KANE 84a]

For $b = 4$ and $r = 8$, let G be an all-1's vector.

$$G = \begin{bmatrix} 1 \\ 1 \\ 1 \\ 1 \end{bmatrix}$$

This G is even weight; therefore, F_q must be odd weight. There are eight F_q's, as follows.

$$\begin{matrix} 0 & 0 & 0 & 1 & 1 & 1 & 1 & 0 \\ 0 & 0 & 1 & 0 & 1 & 1 & 0 & 1 \\ 0 & 1 & 0 & 0 & 1 & 0 & 1 & 1 \\ 1 & 0 & 0 & 0 & 0 & 1 & 1 & 1 \end{matrix}$$

Among these F_q's, two columns are chosen, and the $\mathbf{H}_{ij}$ can be constructed. There are $\binom{8}{2} = 28$ $\mathbf{H}_{ij}$'s. As examples, $\mathbf{H}_{01}$ and $\mathbf{H}_{02}$ are as follows.

$$\mathbf{H}_{01} = \begin{bmatrix} 1 & 1 & 0 & 0 \\ 1 & 1 & 0 & 0 \\ 0 & 0 & 0 & 1 \\ 0 & 0 & 1 & 0 \\ \hdashline 0 & 0 & 1 & 1 \\ 0 & 0 & 1 & 1 \\ 0 & 1 & 0 & 0 \\ 1 & 0 & 0 & 0 \end{bmatrix} \qquad \mathbf{H}_{02} = \begin{bmatrix} 1 & 1 & 0 & 0 \\ 0 & 0 & 0 & 1 \\ 1 & 1 & 0 & 0 \\ 0 & 0 & 1 & 0 \\ \hdashline 0 & 0 & 1 & 1 \\ 0 & 1 & 0 & 0 \\ 0 & 0 & 1 & 1 \\ 1 & 0 & 0 & 0 \end{bmatrix}$$

The complete $\mathbf{H}$ matrix for $b = 4$ and $r = 8$ is given in (5.42). This is a (112, 104) code.

The code shown in (5.43) is an odd-weight-column (72, 64) SEC–DED–S4ED code shortened and converted from the code of (5.42). Check columns are concentrated into two bytes using a row vector operation (i.e., successive addition of one row vector to another).

As a consequence, we can realize an SEC–DED–S4ED code having the same check-bit length of $r = 8$ for information-bit length $K = 64$ as that of the SEC–DED code for the same information-bit length. Furthermore, the parallel encoding/de-

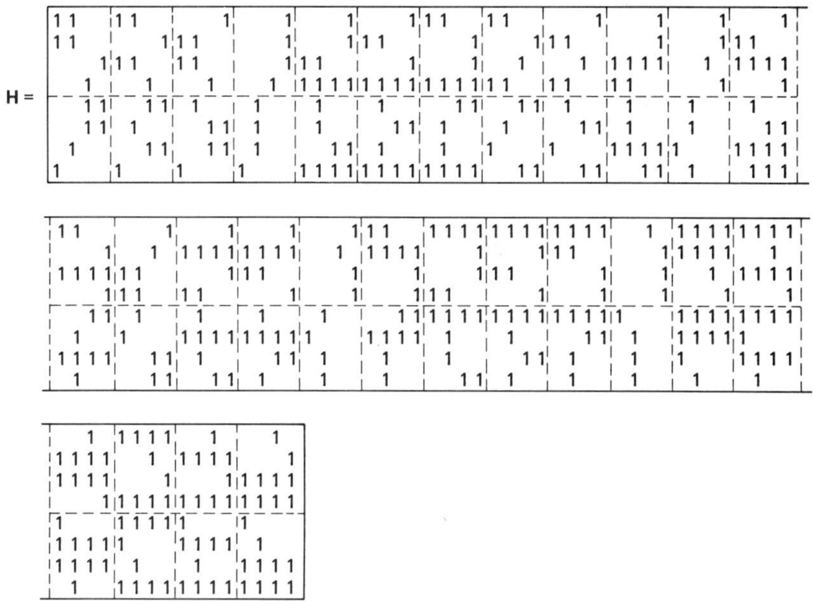

$$(5.42)$$

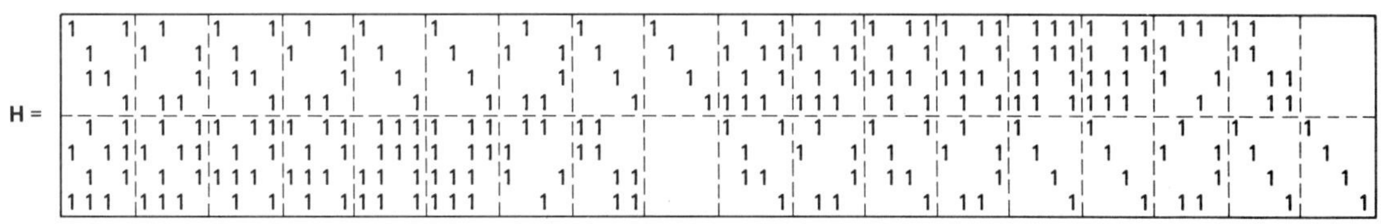

$$(5.43)$$

coding circuit of this (72, 64) SEC–DED–S4ED code has almost the same hardware gate amount as that of the (72, 64) SEC–DED codes. Fig. 5.17 shows the error detection circuit for the code of (5.43).

Codes for $b = 4$ are important from a practical point of view. This type of code has already been practically applied to the commercial computers of the Fujitsu M-780 system [TSUC 86]. In this system, 64K-word × 4-bit byte ($b = 4$ bits) organized high-speed static RAMs are employed in the main storage units, and therefore the following code* has been adopted for $K = 64$, and $r = 8$.

$$\mathbf{H} = \begin{bmatrix}
1000 & 0010 & 1000 & 1111 & 0100 & 0000 & 0001 & 0010 & 1000 & 0010 & 1000 & 1111 & 1111 & 0001 & 0100 & 0001 & 1001 & 0100 \\
0110 & 0100 & 1111 & 1100 & 0100 & 0010 & 1000 & 0001 & 1100 & 1000 & 0011 & 0100 & 1000 & 0010 & 1101 & 1000 & 0010 & 1000 \\
1001 & 1101 & 1010 & 0001 & 0001 & 0011 & 1100 & 0001 & 0001 & 0000 & 1000 & 0011 & 0100 & 1100 & 1000 & 1000 & 1101 & 0010 \\
0001 & 1000 & 0010 & 1000 & 1100 & 1000 & 0101 & 0010 & 0100 & 1111 & 0010 & 0101 & 0001 & 0110 & 0010 & 0100 & 1011 & 0001 \\
0010 & 1000 & 0100 & 1000 & 0010 & 0100 & 0001 & 0101 & 1001 & 0100 & 1111 & 0010 & 0010 & 0011 & 1010 & 1001 & 0100 & 0011 \\
1100 & 0100 & 0100 & 0010 & 0010 & 0001 & 0100 & 1000 & 0010 & 0011 & 1100 & 0100 & 1000 & 1001 & 0001 & 1100 & 1111 & 0101 \\
0011 & 0001 & 0001 & 1011 & 1010 & 0010 & 0010 & 0100 & 0110 & 0001 & 0010 & 1100 & 0011 & 1000 & 1111 & 0000 & 1000 & 0010 \\
0100 & 0001 & 0001 & 0100 & 1000 & 0001 & 1000 & 0110 & 0011 & 1100 & 1111 & 1000 & 0100 & 0100 & 1000 & 1111 & 0001 & 0100
\end{bmatrix} \qquad (5.44)$$

*[tSUC 86] Copyright 1986 by Nikkei-McGraw-Hill, Inc. Reprinted with permission.

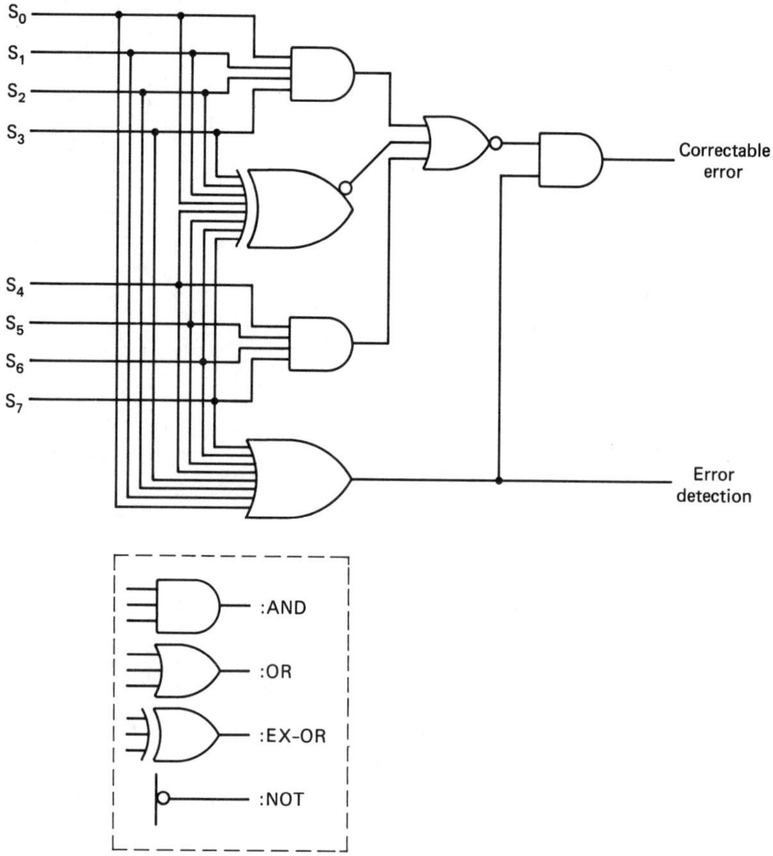

Figure 5.17 Error detection circuit for the code of (5.43) [KANE 84a]. © 1984 IEEE.

This code has the following properties:

1. Odd-weight-column code (see Section 4.4.2).
2. Minimum-equal-weight code (see Section 4.4.1).
3. Eight bits error detection over any two bytes.

Codes for $r = b + 2$ and others [DUNN 85]. Dunning [DUNN 85] has proposed an excellent design method for a rotational SEC–DED–SbED code for $r = b + 2$. Here, we deal with the codes for other code parameters b and r as well as this code for $r = b + 2$.

Theorem 5-23 [DUNN 85]. *Let $b > 2$ be given and define a $(b - 1) \times (b - 2)$ matrix $\mathbf{T} = [T_{ij}]$ by $T_{ij} = 1$ if $i = j$ or $i = j + 1$ and $T_{ij} = 0$ otherwise. The basic* **H** *matrix for an SEC–DED–SbED code with byte length b, check-bit length $r = b + 2$,* *and code length of $(b+2)$ bytes is given by*

$$\mathbf{H}_0 = \begin{bmatrix} 0 & 1 & 0_{b-2} \\ 1 & 1 & 1_{b-2} \\ 0 & 1 & 0_{b-2} \\ \mathbf{0}_{b-1,2} & & \mathbf{T} \end{bmatrix}_{r \times b}$$

*Here, 0_{b-2} means a row vector of $(b-2)$ copies of 0, 1_{b-2} means a row vector of $(b-2)$ copies of 1, and $\mathbf{0}_{b-1,2}$ means $(b-1) \times 2$ all-0 matrix. The resulting **H** matrix is given by a concatenation of r $\mathbf{H}_i$'s whose row vectors are cyclically rotated by one row compared to adjacent $\mathbf{H}_i$'s (see Section 4.4.4).*

$$\mathbf{H} = [\mathbf{H}_0 | \mathbf{H}_1 | \cdots | \mathbf{H}_i | \cdots | \mathbf{H}_{r-1}]$$

$$\mathbf{H}_i = \mathbf{R}^i \cdot \mathbf{H}_0, \qquad \mathbf{R} = \begin{bmatrix} 0 & 0 & & 0 & 1 \\ 1 & 0 & & 0 & 0 \\ 0 & 1 & & 0 & 0 \\ \vdots & \vdots & \ddots & \vdots & \vdots \\ 0 & 0 & & 1 & 0 \end{bmatrix}_{r \times r}$$

Example 5-16

For $b = 3$, the (15, 10) SEC–DED–S3ED code can be given by

$$\mathbf{H} = \begin{bmatrix} 010 & 001 & 001 & 010 & 111 \\ 111 & 010 & 001 & 001 & 010 \\ 010 & 111 & 010 & 001 & 001 \\ 001 & 010 & 111 & 010 & 001 \\ 001 & 001 & 010 & 111 & 010 \end{bmatrix}$$

For $b = 4$, the (24, 18) SEC–DED–S4ED code can be given by

$$\mathbf{H} = \begin{bmatrix} 0100 & 0001 & 0011 & 0010 & 0100 & 1111 \\ 1111 & 0100 & 0001 & 0011 & 0010 & 0100 \\ 0100 & 1111 & 0100 & 0001 & 0011 & 0010 \\ 0010 & 0100 & 1111 & 0100 & 0001 & 0011 \\ 0010 & 0010 & 0100 & 1111 & 0100 & 0001 \\ 0001 & 0011 & 0010 & 0100 & 1111 & 0100 \end{bmatrix}$$

The codes defined in Theorem 5-23 are optimal because the codes are odd-weight-column rotational codes and also minimum-weight codes; that is, the number of 1's in **H** is minimum, which is just equal to the minimum number of 1's in **H** of the corresponding SEC–DED codes.

Here, we consider the SEC–DED–SbED codes having other code parameters [GILS 86]. In [DUNN 85], the codes defined in Theorem 5-16 are shown to be best for $b = 5$, and $r = b + 1$ for $b \geq 5$. Table 5.11 shows the best codes so far obtained for byte length b and check-bit length r.

TABLE 5-11 CODE-BYTE LENGTH *n* OF THE SEC – DED – SbED CODES

Check bit length r \ Byte length b	3	4	5	6	7	8	9	b > 9
b + 1	2 (a)	2 (b)	(d) 3	3	3	3	3	3
b + 2	5	6	7	8 (c)	9	10	11	b + 2
b + 3	10	12	15	18 (e)	24	27 (g)	33	3(b + 2) (h)
b + 4	21	28	31	36	56	63	77	7(b + 2)
b + 5	42	56	63	75 (f)	120	135	165	15(b + 2)
b > 5	$\lfloor(2^{r-1}-1)/3\rfloor$	$2^{r-3}-2^{\lceil r/2-2\rceil}$	$2^{r-b+1}-1$	$5(2^{r-7}-1)$	$8(2^{r-8}-1)$	$9(2^{r-9}-1)$	$11(2^{r-10}-1)$	$(2^{r-b-1}-1)(b+2)$

$\lfloor x \rfloor$: the largest integer smaller than or equal to x

$\lceil x \rceil$: the smallest integer greater than or equal to x

▢ : the same type of code

(a): [CHEN 83]

(b): [KANE 84a]

(c): [DUNN 85]

(d): [REDD 78]

(e): [CHEN 83]

(f), (g), (h): [DUNN 85]

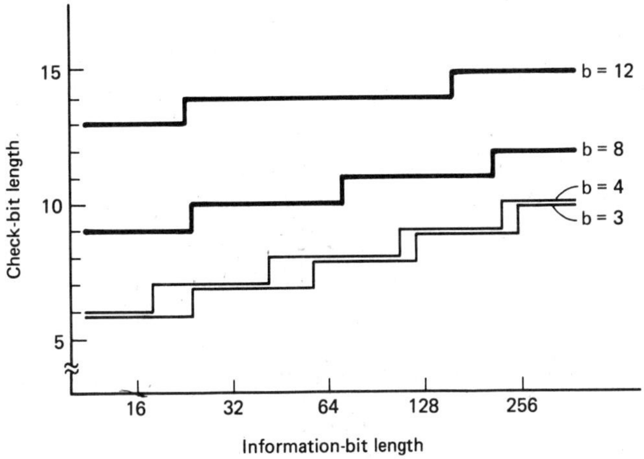

Figure 5.18 Check-bit length of the SEC–DED–SbED code.

Fig. 5.18 shows the relation between the information-bit length K and the check-bit length r of the already obtained excellent SEC–DED–SbED codes for $b = 3, 4, 8$, and 12 bits.

Rotational SEC – DED – SbED codes. We will now examine a class of rotational SEC–DED–SbED codes. An excellent rotational SEC–DED–SbED code for $r = b + 2$ has already been given, as mentioned in Theorem 5-23. Another excellent rotational code satisfying the minimum weight condition has been proposed [KANE 84a]. This code has code bit length $b(b + 2)$, regardless of the value of r. Here, a new type of rotational SEC–DED–SbED code will be introduced [FUJI 81b]. This code design method gives rotational codes for all values of b.

First, we define the following two square matrices.

Definition 5-5. A $(b \times b)$ binary *nonsingular matrix* **P** is defined as

$$\mathbf{P} = \begin{bmatrix} | & | & & | & & | \\ \alpha_0 & \alpha_1 & \cdots & \alpha_i & \cdots & \alpha_{b-1} \\ | & | & & | & & | \end{bmatrix}_{b \times b}$$

where $\overset{|}{\underset{|}{\alpha_i}}$'s, $i = 0, 1, \ldots, b-1$, are column vectors having b binary elements and are linearly independent over the binary field $GF(2)$. The matrix obtained from a cyclic q (mod b) column shift in the foregoing matrix is defined as follows.

$$\mathbf{P}_q = \begin{bmatrix} | & | & & | & & | \\ \alpha_{b-q} & \alpha_{b-q+1} & \cdots & \alpha_{b-q+i} & \cdots & \alpha_{b-q-1} \\ | & | & & | & & | \end{bmatrix}_{b \times b}$$

$$b - q + i;\ mod\, b, \qquad 0 \le i \le b - 1$$

Definition 5-6. Let $U = (a_{b-1}, a_{b-2}, \ldots, a_1, a_0)^T$ be a b-bit binary column vector representating integer U, $0 \leq U \leq 2^b - 1$. Using this vector, the $(b \times b)$ *square matrix* $\mathbf{M}_u$ is defined as

$$\mathbf{M}_u = [U, U, \ldots, U]_{b \times b}$$

where $U \notin \left\{ \begin{matrix} | & | & & | \\ \alpha_0, & \alpha_1, & \ldots, & \alpha_{b-1} \\ | & | & & | \end{matrix} \right\}$

Corollary 5-1. *The minimum-weight nonsingular matrix is an identity matrix* **I**.

The cyclic q $(mod\, b)$ column shift of the identity matrix is expressed as $\mathbf{I}_q$. From the definitions, there exist b $\mathbf{I}_q$'s and $(2^b - b)$ $\mathbf{M}_u$'s.

Example 5-17

For $b = 3$, $\mathbf{I}_q$'s and $\mathbf{M}_u$'s are as follows.

$$\mathbf{I}_0 = \begin{bmatrix} 1 & 0 & 0 \\ 0 & 1 & 0 \\ 0 & 0 & 1 \end{bmatrix} \quad \mathbf{I}_1 = \begin{bmatrix} 0 & 1 & 0 \\ 0 & 0 & 1 \\ 1 & 0 & 0 \end{bmatrix} \quad \mathbf{I}_2 = \begin{bmatrix} 0 & 0 & 1 \\ 1 & 0 & 0 \\ 0 & 1 & 0 \end{bmatrix}$$

$$\mathbf{M}_0 = \begin{bmatrix} 0 & 0 & 0 \\ 0 & 0 & 0 \\ 0 & 0 & 0 \end{bmatrix} \quad \mathbf{M}_3 = \begin{bmatrix} 0 & 0 & 0 \\ 1 & 1 & 1 \\ 1 & 1 & 1 \end{bmatrix} \quad \mathbf{M}_5 = \begin{bmatrix} 1 & 1 & 1 \\ 0 & 0 & 0 \\ 1 & 1 & 1 \end{bmatrix}$$

$$\mathbf{M}_6 = \begin{bmatrix} 1 & 1 & 1 \\ 1 & 1 & 1 \\ 0 & 0 & 0 \end{bmatrix} \quad \mathbf{M}_7 = \begin{bmatrix} 1 & 1 & 1 \\ 1 & 1 & 1 \\ 1 & 1 & 1 \end{bmatrix}$$

By using these elements ($\mathbf{I}_q$'s and $\mathbf{M}_u$'s), a new class of SEC–SbED codes can be constructed as shown in the following theorem.

Theorem 5-24. *Let* **H**-*matrix column vectors be constructed from r elements of* $\mathbf{M}_u$ *and* $\mathbf{I}_q$. *In this case, there should be at least one* $\mathbf{I}_q$ *in each column vector. An* **H** *matrix that has these distinct column vectors shows SEC–SbED codes.*

Proof. It is evident that the SEC function is satisfied, because every nonzero binary column vector is distinct. Next, we consider the SbED function. Let E_j be an error in byte j, $j = 0, 1, \ldots, n-1$. The syndrome for this byte error is given as follows:

$$[S_0, S_1, \ldots, S_i, \ldots, S_{r-1}]^T = E_j \cdot \left[\mathbf{h}_{0,j}, \mathbf{h}_{1,j}, \ldots, \mathbf{h}_{i,j}, \ldots, \mathbf{h}_{r-1,j}\right]^T$$

where $[\mathbf{h}_{0,j}, \mathbf{h}_{1,j}, \ldots, \mathbf{h}_{r-1,j}]^T$ is the jth column vector of the **H** matrix that has at least one $\mathbf{I}_q$ element, and $[S_0, S_1, \ldots, S_{r-1}]^T$ is the obtained syndrome. Let $\mathbf{h}_{i,j}$ be $\mathbf{I}_q$. The relation between the jth error pattern E_i, $j = 0, 1, \ldots, n-1$, and the syndrome is shown in Table 5.12. In this case, $W(E_j)$ means the weight of error pattern E_j. From this table, the syndrome of the single-byte errors is not equal to that of the single-bit errors. Hence, single-byte errors can be detected. Q.E.D.

TABLE 5.12 RELATION BETWEEN THE ERROR PATTERN E_J IN THE JTH BYTE AND THE SYNDROME

Syndrome \ Error	$W(E_j) = 1$ (single-bit error)	$W(E_j) \geq 2$ (byte error)
The ith syndrome S_i for $\mathbf{h}_{i,j} = \mathbf{I}_q$	$S_i \in \{\alpha_0, \alpha_1, \cdots, \alpha_{b-1}\}$ $\neq 0$	$S_i \notin \{\alpha_0, \alpha_1, \cdots, \alpha_{b-1}\}$ $\neq 0$
The kth syndrome S_k $(k \neq i)$ for $\mathbf{h}_{k,j} = \mathbf{M}_u$	$S_k = U \notin \{\alpha_0, \alpha_1, \cdots, \alpha_{b-1}\}$	$S_k = 0$ or $= U \notin \{\alpha_0, \alpha_1, \cdots, \alpha_{b-1}\}$

0: Column vector that has b binary zero elements.
Source: [FUJI 81b]. © 1981 IECE Japan.

If we append the odd-weight-column characteristic to the SEC–SbED code, then the resultant code would be an SEC–DED–SbED code. In order to satisfy both Theorem 5-24 of the SEC–SbED code and the odd-weight-column characteristic, there should be included at least one element of $\mathbf{I}_q$ and, as a result, there should be an odd number of odd-weight elements of $\mathbf{I}_q$ and $\mathbf{M}_u$ in each $\mathbf{H}$-matrix column vector. The number of cases to satisfy this is such that

$$\sum_{\substack{l=1 \\ l:\, odd}}^{m} \binom{r}{l}$$

where $m = 2\left\lfloor \dfrac{r+1}{2} \right\rfloor - 1$, and $\lfloor x \rfloor$ means the largest integer no greater than x.

For example, there are the following four cases for $r = 3$. In this case, *odd* means the odd-weight element and *even* means the even-weight element.

$$\begin{bmatrix} odd \\ odd \\ odd \end{bmatrix} \quad \begin{bmatrix} odd \\ even \\ even \end{bmatrix} \quad \begin{bmatrix} even \\ odd \\ even \end{bmatrix} \quad \begin{bmatrix} even \\ even \\ odd \end{bmatrix}$$

There are 2^{b-1} $\mathbf{M}_u$'s that have even-weight columns, and $(2^{b-1} - b)$ $\mathbf{M}_u$'s that have odd-weight columns. The number of column vectors that have l $(1 \leq l \leq r)$ odd-weight elements and have p $(1 \leq p \leq l)$ $\mathbf{I}_q$'s within these odd-weight elements is shown as follows.

$$\delta_l = (2^{b-1})^{r-l} \sum_{p=1} \binom{p}{l} \cdot b^{p-1} \cdot (2^{b-1} - b)^{l-p}$$

$$= \frac{1}{b}\left\{(2^{b-1})^{r} - (2^{b-1})^{r-l} \cdot (2^{b-1} - b)^{l}\right\}$$

From this, the total number of column vectors is given as follows.

$$n = \sum_{\substack{l=1 \\ l:\,odd}}^{m} \binom{r}{l} \cdot \delta_l$$

$$= \frac{1}{2b}\left[2^{br} - \left\{(2^b - b)^r - b^r\right\}\right]$$

In the right-hand side of the equation, the first term $2^{br}/2$ means the number of odd-weight column vectors constructed from all α_i's and U's. Also, the second term $[(2^b - b)^r - b^r]/2$ means the number of odd-weight-column vectors constructed from r U's. From the above, we can obtain the SEC–DED–SbED code having the code-bit length

$$N = b \cdot n = \left\{2^{br} + b^r - (2^b - b)^r\right\}/2$$

The (207, 198) SEC–DED–S3ED code for $b = 3$ and $r = 3$ is shown in (5.45).

$$\mathbf{H} = \left[\begin{array}{ccccccccccccccccccccccccccccccccccc}
I_0 & I_0 & I_0 & I_0 & I_0 & I_0 & I_0 & I_0 & I_0 & I_0 & I_0 & I_0 & I_0 & I_0 & I_0 & M_0 & M_0 & M_0 & M_3 & M_5 & M_6 & M_3 & M_5 & M_6 & M_3 & M_5 & M_6 & M_3 & M_5 & M_6 & M_3 & M_5 & M_6 & M_0 & M_0 \\
M_3 & M_5 & M_6 & M_0 & M_0 & M_0 & M_3 & M_3 & M_3 & M_5 & M_5 & M_5 & M_6 & M_6 & M_6 & I_0 & I_0 & I_0 & I_0 & I_0 & I_0 & I_0 & I_0 & I_0 & I_0 & I_0 & I_0 & I_0 & I_0 & I_0 & M_0 & M_0 & M_0 & M_3 & M_5 \\
M_0 & M_0 & M_0 & M_3 & M_5 & M_6 & M_3 & M_5 & M_6 & M_3 & M_5 & M_6 & M_3 & M_5 & M_6 & M_3 & M_5 & M_6 & M_0 & M_0 & M_0 & M_3 & M_3 & M_3 & M_5 & M_5 & M_5 & M_6 & M_6 & M_6 & I_0 & I_0 & I_0 & I_0 & I_0
\end{array}\right.$$

$$\begin{array}{cccccccccccccccccccccccccccccccccc}
 & & & & & & & & & & & & & & & & & & & & & & \ast & & & & & & & \ast & \ast & & & \\
M_0 & M_3 & M_3 & M_3 & M_5 & M_5 & M_5 & M_6 & M_6 & M_6 & I_0 & M_7 & M_7 & I_0 & I_0 & I_0 & I_0 & I_1 & I_2 & M_7 & M_7 & M_7 & I_0 & I_0 & I_1 & I_0 & I_0 & I_2 & I_0 & I_0 & I_0 & I_0 & M_0 & M_0 \\
M_6 & M_3 & M_5 & M_6 & M_3 & M_5 & M_6 & M_3 & M_5 & M_6 & M_7 & I_0 & M_7 & I_0 & I_1 & I_2 & M_7 & M_7 & M_7 & I_0 & I_0 & I_0 & I_0 & I_0 & I_0 & I_1 & I_0 & I_0 & I_2 & I_1 & I_2 & M_0 & I_0 & M_0 \\
I_0 & I_0 & I_0 & I_0 & I_0 & I_0 & I_0 & I_0 & I_0 & I_0 & M_7 & M_7 & I_0 & M_7 & M_7 & M_7 & I_0 & I_0 & I_0 & I_0 & I_1 & I_2 & I_0 & I_1 & I_0 & I_0 & I_2 & I_0 & I_0 & I_2 & I_1 & M_0 & M_0 & I_0
\end{array}\left.\vphantom{\begin{array}{c}a\\a\\a\\a\end{array}}\right]$$

(5.45)

Rotational SEC–DED–SbED codes can be constructed from the original SEC–DED–SbED codes by selecting the **H**-matrix column vectors that satisfy the rotational characteristic. For example, from the (207, 198) SEC–DED–S3ED code, we can construct a rotational (198, 189) SEC–DED–S3ED code by deleting the column vectors marked with $*$ in (5.45).

$$\mathbf{H} = \underbrace{\left[\begin{array}{cccccccccccccccccccccc}
I_0 & I_0 \\
M_3 & M_5 & M_6 & M_0 & M_0 & M_0 & M_3 & M_3 & M_3 & M_5 & M_5 & M_5 & M_6 & M_6 & M_6 & M_7 & I_0 & I_1 & I_2 & I_0 & I_0 & M_0 \\
M_0 & M_0 & M_0 & M_3 & M_5 & M_6 & M_3 & M_5 & M_6 & M_3 & M_5 & M_6 & M_3 & M_5 & M_6 & M_7 & M_7 & M_7 & M_7 & I_1 & I_2 & M_0
\end{array}\right.}_{\mathbf{H}_0}$$

$$\underbrace{\begin{array}{cccccccccccccccccccccc}
M_0 & M_0 & M_0 & M_3 & M_5 & M_6 & M_3 & M_5 & M_6 & M_3 & M_5 & M_6 & M_3 & M_5 & M_6 & M_7 & M_7 & M_7 & M_7 & I_1 & I_2 & M_0 \\
I_0 & I_0 \\
M_3 & M_5 & M_6 & M_0 & M_0 & M_0 & M_3 & M_3 & M_3 & M_5 & M_5 & M_5 & M_6 & M_6 & M_6 & M_7 & I_0 & I_1 & I_2 & I_0 & I_0 & M_0
\end{array}}_{\mathbf{H}_1}$$

$$\underbrace{\left.\begin{array}{cccccccccccccccccccccc}
M_3 & M_5 & M_6 & M_0 & M_0 & M_0 & M_3 & M_3 & M_3 & M_5 & M_5 & M_5 & M_6 & M_6 & M_6 & M_7 & I_0 & I_1 & I_2 & I_0 & I_0 & M_0 \\
M_0 & M_0 & M_0 & M_3 & M_5 & M_6 & M_3 & M_5 & M_6 & M_3 & M_5 & M_6 & M_3 & M_5 & M_6 & M_7 & M_7 & M_7 & M_7 & I_1 & I_2 & M_0 \\
I_0 & I_0
\end{array}\right]}_{\mathbf{H}_2}$$

$$I_0 = \begin{bmatrix} 1&0&0 \\ 0&1&0 \\ 0&0&1 \end{bmatrix} \quad M_3 = \begin{bmatrix} 0&0&0 \\ 1&1&1 \\ 1&1&1 \end{bmatrix}$$

$$I_1 = \begin{bmatrix} 0&1&0 \\ 0&0&1 \\ 1&0&0 \end{bmatrix} \quad M_5 = \begin{bmatrix} 1&1&1 \\ 0&0&0 \\ 1&1&1 \end{bmatrix}$$

$$I_2 = \begin{bmatrix} 0&0&1 \\ 1&0&0 \\ 0&1&0 \end{bmatrix} \quad M_6 = \begin{bmatrix} 1&1&1 \\ 1&1&1 \\ 0&0&0 \end{bmatrix}$$

$$M_7 = \begin{bmatrix} 1&1&1 \\ 1&1&1 \\ 1&1&1 \end{bmatrix}$$

$$M_0 = \begin{bmatrix} 0&0&0 \\ 0&0&0 \\ 0&0&0 \end{bmatrix}$$

$$\mathbf{H} = \left[\,\mathbf{H}_0 \;\vdots\; \mathbf{H}_1 \;\vdots\; \mathbf{H}_2\,\right]$$

H =

	d 0	d 1	d 2	d 3	d 4	d 5	d 6	d 7	d 8	d 9	d 10	d 11	d 12	d 13	d 14	d 15	c 0	c 1	c 2	c 3
S_0	1				1				1				1				1			
S_1		1				1				1				1				1		
S_2			1				1				1				1				1	
S_3				1				1				1				1				1
S_4	1	1	1	1	1	1	1	1												
S_5									1	1	1	1	1	1	1	1				
S_6	1	1	1	1					1	1	1	1								
S_7					1	1	1	1					1	1	1	1				

H_0

	d 16	d 17	d 18	d 19	d 20	d 21	d 22	d 23	d 24	d 25	d 26	d 27	d 28	d 29	d 30	d 31	c 4	c 5	c 6	c 7
S_0	1	1	1	1	1	1	1	1												
S_1									1	1	1	1	1	1	1	1				
S_2	1	1	1	1					1	1	1	1								
S_3					1	1	1	1					1	1	1	1				
S_4	1				1				1				1				1			
S_5		1				1				1				1				1		
S_6			1				1				1				1				1	
S_7				1				1				1				1				1

H_1

Rotational (40, 32) SEC-DED-S4ED code

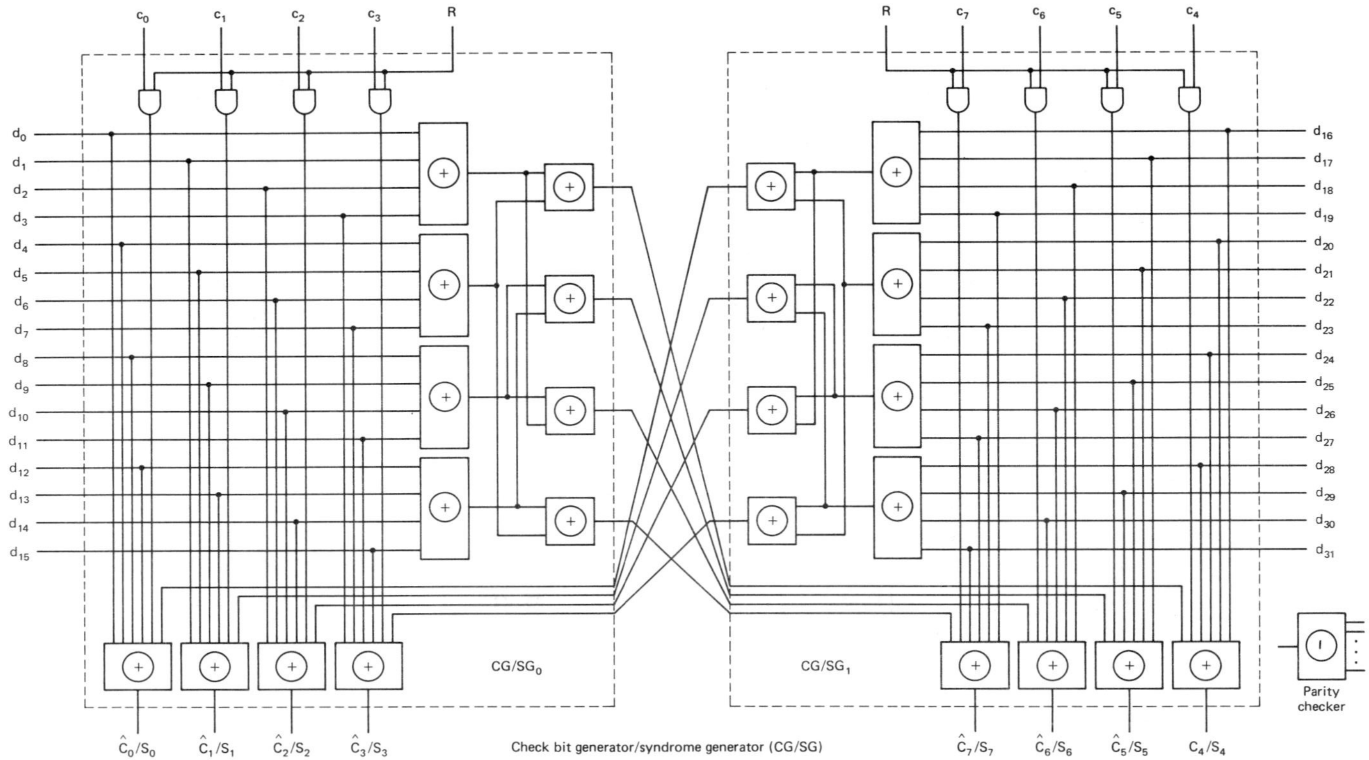

Figure 5.19 Rotational (40, 32) SEC–DED–S4ED code and its modularized encoding/decoding circuit [FUJI 81b]. © 1981 IECE Japan.

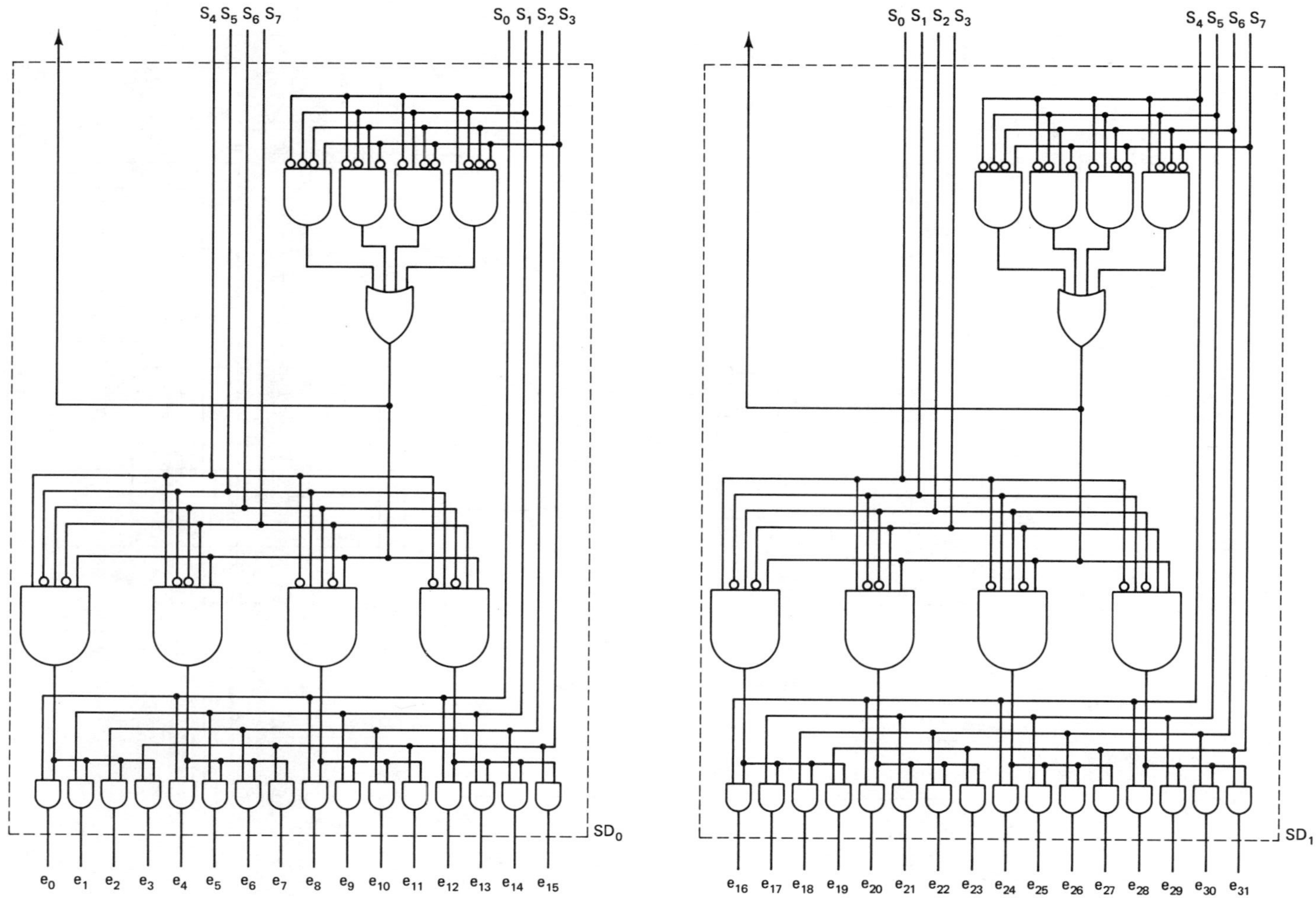

Syndrome decoder (SD)

Figure 5.19 Continued.

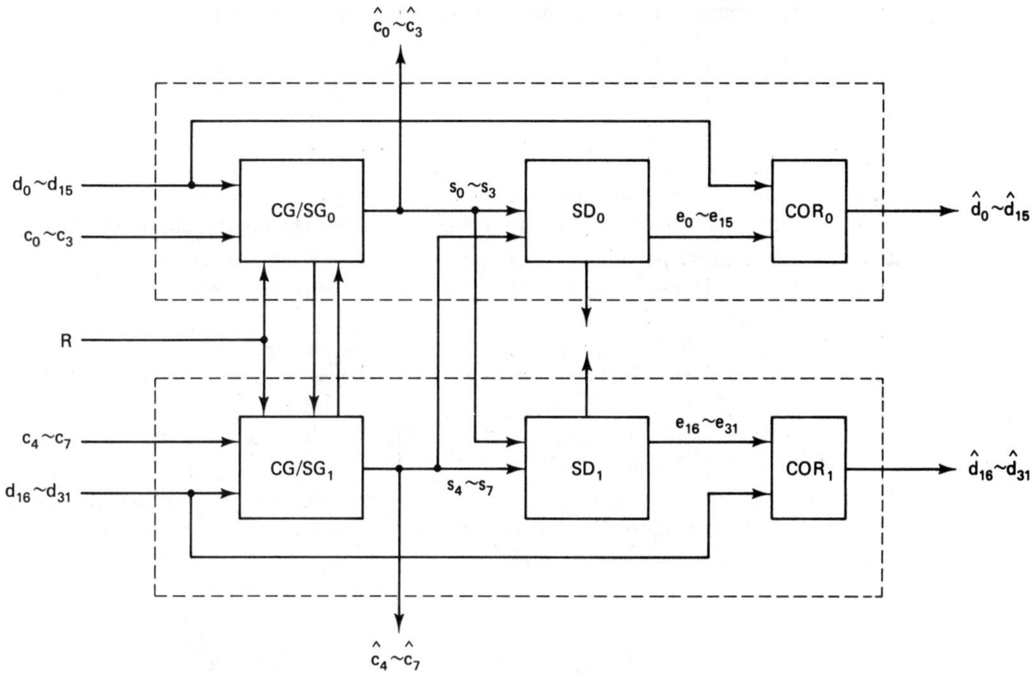

Figure 5.19 Continued.

The code-bit length of this rotational SEC–DED–SbED code is given as follows.

$$N = \frac{1}{2} \sum_{\substack{m|r \\ m;\ odd}} \mu(m)\left\{(2^b)^{r/m} + b^{r/m} - (2^b - b)^{r/m}\right\} GCD\,(m, b) \quad (5.46)$$

Here, $GCD\,(m, b)$ means Greatest Common Divisor of m and b, and $\sum_{\substack{m|r \\ m;\ odd}}$ means the summation for an odd number of m that divides r.

Fig. 5.19 shows an example of a rotational (40, 32) SEC–DED–S4ED code and its modularized encoding/decoding circuit.

EXERCISES

5.1. Using the following (18, 12) S2EC code, perform the following operations.

$$\mathbf{H} = \begin{bmatrix} \mathbf{T}^2 & \mathbf{0} & \mathbf{T} & \mathbf{I} & \mathbf{T}^2 & \mathbf{T}^2 & \mathbf{I} & \mathbf{0} & \mathbf{0} \\ \mathbf{T} & \mathbf{T}^2 & \mathbf{0} & \mathbf{T}^2 & \mathbf{T}^2 & \mathbf{I} & \mathbf{0} & \mathbf{I} & \mathbf{0} \\ \mathbf{0} & \mathbf{T} & \mathbf{T}^2 & \mathbf{T}^2 & \mathbf{I} & \mathbf{T}^2 & \mathbf{0} & \mathbf{0} & \mathbf{I} \end{bmatrix}$$

T: companion matrix defined by the polynomial of $\mathbf{g}(x) = x^2 + x + 1$.
Received Data: $[D|C] = [D_0, D_1, D_2, D_3, D_4, D_5|C_0, C_1, C_2]$

$$D_i = (d_{i,0}, d_{i,1}) \quad C_j = (c_{j,0}, c_{j,1})$$

(a) Encode the data $[D_0, D_1, D_2, D_3, D_4, D_5] = [1\ 0\ 1\ 1\ 0\ 1\ 0\ 0\ 1\ 1\ 0\ 1]$.
(b) The received data $[D|C] = [1\ 1\ 0\ 1\ 1\ 0\ 1\ 1\ 0\ 0\ 1\ 0|1\ 0\ 1\ 1\ 1\ 1]$ has a single-byte error. Obtain the correct data.
(c) Let $[D|C]$ be a codeword. Obtain the codeword for $\overline{D}$, complement of D.

5.2. Using the primitive polynomial of $\mathbf{g}(x) = x^2 + x + 1$, do the following.
(a) Obtain the **H** matrix of a single-symbol error correcting code over $GF(2^2)$ with $k = 18$ (i.e., $K = 36$).
(b) By choosing the column vectors in the **H** matrix obtained in (a), construct the **H** matrix of the minimum-weight single-symbol error correcting code over $GF(2^2)$ with $n = 12$, $k = 9$.
(c) Design the parallel decoding circuit of the (12, 9) code obtained in (b) by using only AND, OR, NOT, and EX-OR gates.

5.3. Under the following **H** matrix, assume that the obtained nonzero syndrome does not point to any one byte error, and two error pointers have already been given in the byte positions 1 and 5, shown by ↓ in **H**.

$$\begin{array}{c} \qquad\ \downarrow \qquad\qquad\qquad\qquad \downarrow \\ \mathbf{H} = \begin{bmatrix} \mathbf{I} & \mathbf{I} & \mathbf{I} & \mathbf{I} & \mathbf{I} & \mathbf{I} & \mathbf{I} & \mathbf{0} \\ \mathbf{I} & \mathbf{T} & \mathbf{T}^2 & \mathbf{T}^3 & \mathbf{T}^4 & \mathbf{T}^5 & \mathbf{0} & \mathbf{I} \end{bmatrix} \begin{matrix} \to S_0 \\ \to S_1 \end{matrix} \end{array}$$

T: companion matrix defined by the primitive polynomial $\mathbf{g}(x) = x^4 + x + 1$.

Show that we can correct these double-byte errors, and express the error patterns E_1 and E_5 by using the syndromes S_0 and S_1.

5.4. Prove properties 1 to 3 of the companion matrix **T**.

5.5. Show that the rotational Hamming-type SbEC code has the code length

$$N = \frac{b}{2^b - 1} \sum_{d|r} \mu(d) \left\{ (2^b)^{r/d} - 1 \right\} GCD\,(d, 2^b - 1)$$

where $\sum_{d|r}$ means the summation of d that divides r, $\mu(d)$ is a Möbius function $GCD\ (x, y)$ means the greatest common divisor of x and y [IMAI 79b].

5.6. Prove that the Burton code has properties 1 to 3 of Equations (5.7) to (5.9).

5.7. Obtain the **H** matrix of the Fujiwara S4EC code with $K = 56$. Next, by using this **H** matrix, obtain the rotational Fujiwara S4EC code with $K = 56$. In this case, let the companion matrix **T** be defined by the primitive polynomial $\mathbf{g}(x) = x^4 + x + 1$.

5.8. Obtain the generating submatrix $\mathbf{H}_0$ of the rotational Fujiwara S3EC code with $K = 180$.

5.9. Obtain the Hong–Patel S2EC code with $K = 32$.

5.10. Prove Theorem 5-7.

5.11. Obtain the Kaneda–Fujiwara S4EC–D4EC code with $K = 128$.

5.12. Design the modularized decoding circuit of the code shown in Equation (5.35).

5.13. Assume that the code expressed by matrix $\mathbf{H}'$, which includes submatrix $\mathbf{H}_0$ having an all-$\mathbf{I}$ (identity element $\in GF(2^b)$) row, is a $((k + r)b, kb)$ SbEC–DbED code. Prove that the following code expressed by $\mathbf{H}$ is a 2-modularized $((2k + r + 1)b, 2kb)$ SbEC–DbED code.

$$\mathbf{H}' = \left[\ \overbrace{\begin{bmatrix} (\mathbf{I}\ \ \mathbf{I}\ \ \cdots\ \ \mathbf{I}) \\ \\ \mathbf{H}_0 \\ \\ \end{bmatrix}}^{kb} \ \vdots\ \overbrace{\begin{matrix} \mathbf{I} & & & \\ & \mathbf{I} & & \\ & & \ddots & \\ & & & \mathbf{I} \end{matrix}}^{rb}\ \right]$$

$$\mathbf{H} = \left[\ \underbrace{\begin{matrix} \begin{bmatrix} \\ \mathbf{H}_0 \\ \\ \end{bmatrix} \\ \mathbf{0}\ \ \mathbf{0}\ \ \cdots\ \ \mathbf{0} \end{matrix} \ \vdots\ \begin{matrix} \mathbf{0}\ \ \mathbf{0}\ \ \cdots\ \ \mathbf{0} \\ \begin{bmatrix} \\ {}^{0}\mathbf{H} \\ \\ \end{bmatrix} \end{matrix}}_{2kb} \ \vdots\ \underbrace{\begin{matrix} \mathbf{I} & & & \\ & \mathbf{I} & & \\ & & \ddots & \\ & & & \mathbf{I} \end{matrix}}_{(r+1)b}\ \right]$$

Here, ${}^{0}\mathbf{H}$ is a matrix whose order of row vectors in $\mathbf{H}_0$ is changed upside down.

According to this code construction method, obtain the 2-modularized S2EC–D2ED code with $N = 76$ and $K = 64$.

5.14. Obtain the $\mathbf{H}$ matrix of the Chen S3EC–D3ED code with $K = 183$.

5.15. Obtain the SEC–DED–BED codes with $b = 4$ and $K = 56$ by using the methods of Theorems 5-15, 5-16, 5-17(b) and 5-18.

5.16. Prove properties 1 to 3 of grouping matrix $\mathbf{A}$.

5.17. Obtain the basic submatrix $\mathbf{H}_0$ of the rotational SEC–DED–BED code with $b = 3$, $N = 189$.

5.18. Obtain the SEC–DED–S4ED code with information-bit length $K = 41$ and check-bit length $r = 7$.

5.19. The following $\mathbf{H}$ matrix shows a (40, 32) SEC–DED–S4ED code [LUI 78]. Explain how this code satisfies SEC–DED–S4ED function.

$$\mathrm{H} = \left[\begin{array}{cccc:cccc:cccc:cccc:cccc:cccc:cccc:cccc:cccc:cccc}
1&1&1&1 & 1&1&1&1 & &&& & 1&&& & 1&&& & 1&&& & 1&&& & &&& & 1&&& & &&& \\
1&&& & 1&&& & 1&1&1&1 & 1&1&1&1 & &&& & &1&& & &&& & 1&&& & &1&& & &&& \\
&1&& & &&& & 1&&& & &&& & 1&1&1&1 & 1&1&1&1 & &1&& & &1&& & &&1& & &&& \\
&&1& & &1&& & &1&& & &1&& & &&& & &&& & 1&1&1&1 & 1&1&1&1 & &&&1 & &&& \\
&&& & 1&1&1&1 & &&1& & &&1& & &1&& & 1&1&1&1 & &&1& & &&& & &&& & 1&&& \\
&&&1 & &&1& & &&&1 & &&&1 & 1&1&1&1 & &&& & &&& & 1&1&1&1 & &&& & &1&& \\
1&1&1&1 & &&& & 1&1&1&1 & &&& & &&1& & &&1& & &&&1 & &&1& & &&& & &&1& \\
&&& & &&&1 & &&& & 1&1&1&1 & &&&1 & &&&1 & 1&1&1&1 & &&&1 & &&& & &&&1
\end{array}\right]$$

5.20. Prove that the SEC–DED–SbED code corrects a single-byte error in the presence of a single-byte error pointer (i.e., erases a single-byte error).

5.21. Verify that the code shown in Equation (5.44) has the property of eight bits error detection over two bytes.

REFERENCES

[ARLA 84] J. Arlat and W. C. Carter. "Implementation and Evaluation of a (b, k)-Adjacent Error Correcting/Detecting Scheme for Supercomputer Systems." *IBM Journal of Research and Development* 28 (March 1984): 159–68.

[BHAT 78] A. K. Bhatt and L. L. Kinney. "A High Speed Parallel Encoder/Decoder for b-Adjacent Error-Checking Codes." *Proceedings of the Third USA-Japan Comput. Conference* (1978): 203–7.

[BOSS 70a] D. C. Bossen. "b-Adjacent Error Correction." *IBM Journal of Research and Development* 14 (July 1970): 402–8.

[BOSS 78] D. C. Bossen, L. C. Chang, and C. L. Chen. "Measurement and Generation of Error Correcting Codes for Package Failures." *IEEE Transactions on Computers* C-27 (March 1978): 201–4.

[BURT 71a] H. O. Burton. "Some Asymptotically Optimal Burst-Correcting Codes and Their Relation to Single-Error-Correcting Reed-Solomon Codes." *IEEE Transactions on Information Theory* IT-17 (January 1971): 92–95.

[CART 74] W. C. Carter, G. B. Leeman, Jr., and A. B. Wadia. "Practical Length Single-Bit Error Correction/Double-Bit Error Detection Codes for Small Values of b." *IBM Tech. Disclosure Bulletin* 17 (December 1974): 2174–76.

[CART 80] W. C. Carter and A. B. Wadia. "Design and Analysis of Codes and Their Self-Checking Circuit Implementations for Correction and Detection of Multiple-b-Adjacent Errors." *Dig., 10th Annual Int. Symposium Fault-Tolerant Comput.* (October 1980): 35–40.

[CHEN 83] C. L. Chen. "Error-Correcting Codes with Byte Error-Detection Capability." *IEEE Transactions on Computers* C-32 (July 1983): 615–21.

[CHEN 86a] C. L. Chen. "Byte-Oriented Error-Correcting Codes for Semiconductor Memory Systems." *IEEE Transactions on Computers* C-35 (July 1986): 646–48.

[CHEN 86b] C. L. Chen. "Error-Correcting Codes for Byte-Organized Memory Systems." *IEEE Transactions on Information Theory* IT-32 (March 1986): 181–85.

[DENG 87] R. H. Deng and D. J. Costello, Jr. "Decoding of DBEC–TBED Reed-Solomon Codes." *IEEE Transactions on Computers* C-36 (November 1987): 1359–63.

[DUNN 83] L. A. Dunning and M. R. Varanasi. "Code Constructions for Error Control in Byte Organized Memory Systems." *IEEE Transactions on Computers* C-32 (June 1983): 535–42.

[DUNN 85] L. A. Dunning. "SEC–BED–DED Codes for Error Control in Byte-Organized Memory Systems." *IEEE Transactions on Computers* C-34 (June 1985): 557–62.

[FIRE 59] P. Fire. *A Class of Multiple-Error-Correcting Binary Codes for Non-Independent Errors*. Sylvania Report no. RSL-E-2. Mountain View, Calif.: Sylvania Electronic Defense Laboratory, Reconnaissance, Systems Division, 1959.

[FUJI 76a] E. Fujiwara. "Modularized b-Adjacent Error Correction" (in Japanese). *Paper of Technical Group* EC76-19. *IECE Japan*, 1976.

[FUJI 77a] E. Fujiwara. "A Modularized b-Adjacent Error Correction Memory Unit." *Transactions of the IECE Japan*. E60 (February 1977): 69–76.

[FUJI 77b] E. Fujiwara and T. Kawakami. "Modularized b-Adjacent Error Correction." *Dig., 7th Annual Int. Symposium Fault-Tolerant Comput.* (June 1977): 199.

[FUJI 78] E. Fujiwara. "Odd-Weight-Column *b*-Adjacent Error Correcting Codes." *Transactions of the IECE Japan* E61 (October 1978): 781–87.

[FUJI 80a] E. Fujiwara. "Error Control for Byte-per-Package Organized Memory Systems." *Transactions of the IECE Japan* E-63 (February 1980): 98–103.

[FUJI 81a] E. Fujiwara. "Error Correcting Code and its Application to Digital Systems" (in Japanese). *Ph.D. Diss., Tokyo Institute of Technology, Tokyo* (April 1981).

[FUJI 81b] E. Fujiwara and S. Kaneda. "Rotational Byte Error Detecting Codes for Memory Systems." *Transactions of the IECE Japan* E-64 (May 1981): 342–49.

[FUJI 82] E. Fujiwara and S. Kaneda. "Application of Error Correcting Codes for Increasing Computer System Reliability" (in Japanese). *Journal of Information Processing Society (IPS) of Japan* 23 (April 1982): 292–8.

[FUJI 88] E. Fujiwara, Chapter 4 in *Essentials of Error-Correcting Coding Techniques*, ed. H. Imai. New York: Academic Press, 1988.

[GILS 86] W. J. van Gils. "An Error-Control Coding System for Storage of 16-bit Words in Memory Arrays Composed of Three 9-bit Wide Units." *Philips Journal Res.* 41, no. 4 (1986): 391–99.

[HAMM 50] R. W. Hamming. "Error Detecting and Error Correcting Codes." *Bell Sys. Tech. Journal* 26 (April 1950): 147–60.

[HART 72] C. R. P. Hartman and K. K. Tzeng. "Generalization of the BCH Bound." *Information and Control* 18 (1972): 489–98.

[HONG 72] S. J. Hong and A. M. Patel. "A General Class of Maximal Codes for Computer Applications." *IEEE Transactions on Computers* C-21 (December 1972): 1322–31.

[HORI 83] T. Horiguchi and Y. Sato. "A Decoding Method for Reed-Solomon Codes over $GF(2^m)$" (in Japanese). *Transactions of the IECE Japan* J66-A (January 1983): 97–98.

[IMAI 79b] H. Imai and Y. Kamiyanagi. "On Burst-Error-Correcting Codes for Application to Main Memories" (in Japanese). *Transactions of the IECE Japan* J62-D (October 1979): 633–40.

[ITOH 83a] H. Itoh and M. Nakamichi. "SbEC–DbED Codes Derived from Experiments on a Computer for Semiconductor Memory Systems" (in Japanese). *Transactions of the IECE Japan* J66-A (August 1983): 741–48.

[KANE 82] S. Kaneda and E. Fujiwara. "Single Byte Error Correcting–Double Byte Error Detecting Codes for Memory Systems". *IEEE Transactions on Computers* C-31 (July 1982): 596–602. (Also shown in *Dig., 10th Annual Int. Symposium Fault-Tolerant Comput.* (October 1980): 41–46).

[KANE 83] S. Kaneda. "A Class of SEC–DED–SbED Codes Detecting Byte Error through *b*-Grouped Parity-Checking" (in Japanese). *Transactions of the IECE Japan* J66-D (June 1983): 699–706.

[KANE 84] S. Kaneda. "A Class of Odd-Weight-Column SEC–DED–SbED Codes for Memory System Applications." *IEEE Transactions on Computers* C-33 (August 1984): 737–39. (Also shown in *Dig. 14th Annual Int. Symposium Fault-Tolerant Comput.* (June 1984): 88–93.)

[KANE 85] S. Kaneda. "A Class of SEC–DED–SbED Codes for Semiconductor Memory Systems" (in Japanese). *Transactions of the IECE Japan* J68-D (January 1985): 17–24.

[LUI 78] A. S. Lui and M. Arbab. "Error Checking and Correcting Device." U.S. Patent 4077028 (February 28, 1978).

[NARA 80] Y. Nara, Y. Sohma, and A. Hattori. "Error-Correcting and Error-Detecting System." U.S. Patent 4214228 (July 22, 1980).

[REDD 78] S. M. Reddy. "A Class of Linear Codes for Error Control in Byte-per-Card Organized Digital Systems." *IEEE Transactions on Computers* C-27 (May 1978): 455–59.

[REED 60] I. S. Reed and G. Solomon. "Polynomial Codes over Certain Finite Fields." *Journal Soc. Ind. Appl. Math.* 8 (June 1960): 300–304.

[TSUC 86] T. Tsuchimoto, K. Shimizu, M. Takamura, M. Shinohara, T. Miyazawa, and H. Tone. "A Large Computer System M-780" (in Japanese). *Nikkei Electronics* 396 (June 2, 1986): 179–209.

[VARA 83] M. R. Varanasi, T. R. N. Rao, and S. Pham. "Memory Package Error Detection and Correction." *IEEE Transactions on Computers* C-32 (September 1983): 872–74.

[WOLF 69] J. K. Wolf. "Adding Two Information Symbols to Certain Nonbinary BCH Codes and Some Applications." *Bell Syst. Tech. Journal* (September 1969): 2405–24.

6

Codes for Mass Memories

This chapter deals with the codes for mass memories such as magnetic tapes, magnetic disks, optical disks, and bubble memories. Characteristic problems with these memories include burst errors, caused by defects and dust particles on the recording surfaces, and random errors caused by noise in the read/write heads. Burst error correcting codes, such as *Fire codes* [FIRE 59], have been developed for use with these memories and, recently Reed–Solomon byte error correcting/detecting codes [REED 60], combined with interleaving methods or erasure correction methods, have been applied in order to extend their error correction capabilities [BOUR 73, HORI 75b, PATE 74, 80, DOI 79, HODG 80, BERL 80, PATE 86]. Also, high-speed, efficient decoding can be implemented using LSI circuits for these codes [BERL 82, HSU 84, YEH 84, BREN 84, WANG 85, KIMU 86, OHNI 86, YAMA 86, OKAN 87, DENG 87, IWAM 88].

6.1 TAPE MEMORY CODES

Magnetic tapes are widely used in computer systems. The half-inch, 9-track tape system is especially prevalent, having evolved through the extensive use of tapes over many years. The 8-bit byte of information and a parity check bit are accommodated vertically in these 9 tracks. The ninth parity track is usually called the *vertical redundancy check* (*VRC*) track. In addition to this vertical direction, the parity of the bits are appended horizontally in each track at the end of the record. This check byte is often called a *longitudinal redundancy check* (*LRC*). In low-density recording tape, the VRC and LRC were sufficient. As the bit density increased, another technique, called the *cyclic redundancy check* (*CRC*), was added to provide a single-track error correction system that can correct a total track failure within a block of data in the nine-parallel-track system [BROW 70].

Because of increased bit densities and/or tape speeds, the new tape systems require more sophisticated error correction codes. The new coding schemes presented here are an *optimal rectangular code* (*ORC*) for the 6250 bits-per-inch (bpi) 9-track tape units [PATE 74] and an *adaptive cross parity* (*AXP*) *code* for the higher density, 18-track tape units [PATE 85].

While progress has been made in developing correction codes for half-inch tape systems, a *mass storage system* (*MSS*), which combines even greater data storage with extremely low-cost, has also been developed. For example, the IBM 3850 MSS uses a cartridge and a rotating head, and a new data encoding method is adopted [PATE 80]. The cartridge concept provides a different data format than the conventional parallel-track system, thus abandoning the track correction scheme. Instead, it uses an interleaved byte error correction code to correct single burst error sections. This new coding scheme is also presented here.

Errors in magnetic tape recording are primarily caused by *defects* on the magnetic media or variations in head–media separation in the presence of *dust particles*. These errors often affect as many as 100 bits at a time, depending on the density of recording. Furthermore, long errors can occur through loss of synchronization of the read clock, which renders subsequent data unreadable. As recording density is increased, another type of error plays a more important role: the *bit-shift phenomenon*, in which magnetic flux transition is shifted from its normal position because of interference from neighboring flux transitions. The bit shift usually results in a two-bit error, where *01* is read in place of *10* or *vice versa*.

Thus, the data in magnetic tape systems are organized to facilitate recovery from mixed-mode errors in magnetic recording read-write processes involving one-bit errors caused by *random noise*, multiple two-bit errors caused by *bit shifts*, and clusters of errors caused by *defects* and *dust particles* [PATE 80].

As for other tape recording systems, powerful error correcting codes, such as a *product code* using two Reed–Solomon codes, *cross-interleaved codes*, and a combination of the Reed–Solomon code and *cyclic redundancy check* (*CRC*) *code*, have been extensively applied to recent digital audio and video systems, such as the PCM tape recording system with multitrack, DAT (digital audio tape) units, and 8 mm video units [INOU 78, TANA 80, IMAI 88].

6.1.1 Optimal Rectangular Code (ORC)

The optimal rectangular code (ORC) [PATE 74] is designed to correct any single track or, given erasure pointers, any double-track errors in the tape. Codewords of the ORC have a rectangular format, and check bits are located on two orthogonal sides of the rectangle. The data format for the ORC of 9-track tapes is illustrated in Fig. 6.1. B_1 through B_7 denote the seven bytes of information in standard 8-bit bytes. C denotes the check byte computed from the information bits. This format shows how the information bits are written as B_i.

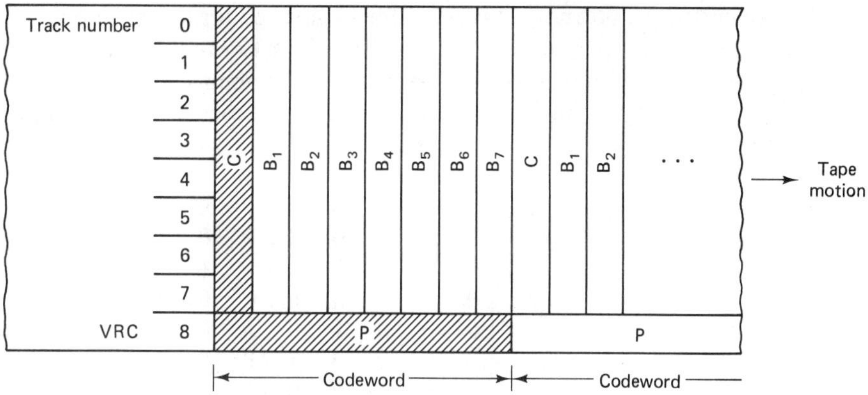

Figure 6.1 The data format for ORC showing the information bytes as vertical columns [PATE 74]. © 1974 by International Business Machines Corporation; reprinted with permission.

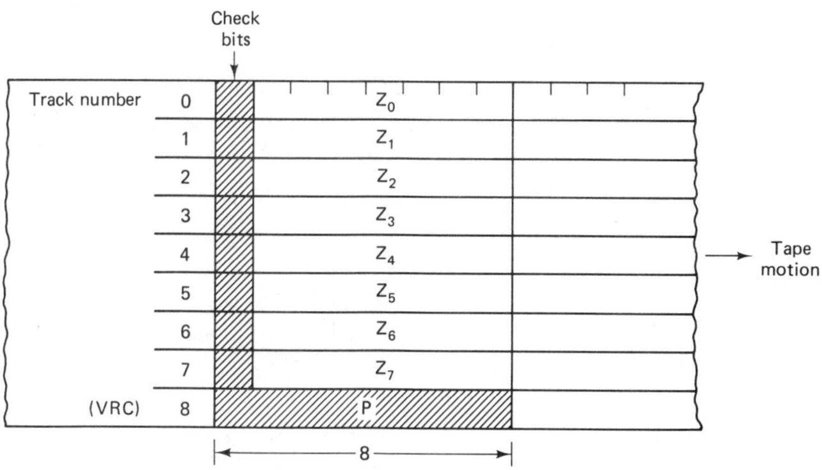

Figure 6.2 The horizontal track bytes in ORC [PATE 74]. © 1974 by International Business Machines Corporation; reprinted with permission.

The code corrects track errors as errors in clusters of b bits along tracks. For a natural description of the code, the track vectors of the codeword will be used as track bytes, denoted by Z_i's in Fig. 6.2.

First, the error correcting capability of the code is established in this Z_i notation of Fig. 6.2. Later, a novel feature of the orthogonal symmetry of the ORC gives the conversion of this Z_i notation to the B_i notation of Fig. 6.1.

The ORC can be generated using the companion matrix **T** (see Section 5.1.1) of the irreducible polynomial $\mathbf{g}(x)$ of degree 8 with binary coefficients g_i (i.e., $\mathbf{g}(x) = \sum_{i=0}^{8} g_i \cdot x^i$). Here, $\mathbf{g}(x)$ is selected to obtain some specific advantages: (1)

exponent of the polynomial is small for high-speed error correction, and (2) $\mathbf{g}(x)$ is a *self-reciprocal polynomial* (i.e., $\mathbf{g}(x) = x^8 \cdot \mathbf{g}(1/x)$) for read backward facility [PATE 74]. Therefore, the self-reciprocal polynomial $\mathbf{g}(x) = 1 + x^3 + x^4 + x^5 + x^8$ having a minimum exponent $e = 17$ is chosen for ORC application. The corresponding companion matrix $\mathbf{T}$ is, then,

$$\mathbf{T} = \begin{bmatrix} 0 & 0 & 0 & 0 & 0 & 0 & 0 & 1 \\ 1 & 0 & 0 & 0 & 0 & 0 & 0 & 0 \\ 0 & 1 & 0 & 0 & 0 & 0 & 0 & 0 \\ 0 & 0 & 1 & 0 & 0 & 0 & 0 & 1 \\ 0 & 0 & 0 & 1 & 0 & 0 & 0 & 1 \\ 0 & 0 & 0 & 0 & 1 & 0 & 0 & 1 \\ 0 & 0 & 0 & 0 & 0 & 1 & 0 & 0 \\ 0 & 0 & 0 & 0 & 0 & 0 & 1 & 0 \end{bmatrix}$$

The parity-check matrix $\mathbf{H}$ of the ORC is expressed as

$$\mathbf{H} = \begin{bmatrix} \mathbf{I} & \mathbf{I} & \mathbf{I} & \mathbf{I} & \mathbf{I} & \mathbf{I} & \mathbf{I} & \mathbf{I} & \mathbf{I} \\ \mathbf{I} & \mathbf{T} & \mathbf{T}^2 & \mathbf{T}^3 & \mathbf{T}^4 & \mathbf{T}^5 & \mathbf{T}^6 & \mathbf{T}^7 & \mathbf{0} \end{bmatrix} \tag{6.1}$$

that is, this is equivalent to the (72, 56) 2-redundant S8EC code (see Section 5.1.2). In this case, the codeword is expressed as $W = [Z_0, Z_1, Z_2, Z_3, Z_4, Z_5, Z_6, Z_7, P]$, and $\mathbf{I}$ is an (8×8) identity matrix and $\mathbf{0}$ is an (8×8) matrix with all zero elements. Therefore, any correct codeword W should satisfy the parity check rules $\mathbf{H} \cdot W^T = 0$, that is, it should satisfy the parity check equations given by

$$\left[\sum_{i=0}^{7}{}^{\oplus} Z_i\right] \oplus P = 0 \tag{6.2}$$

and

$$\left[\sum_{i=0}^{7}{}^{\oplus} \mathbf{T}^i \cdot Z_i\right] = 0 \tag{6.3}$$

where 0 is the null vector with all zero elements.

When the codeword is corrupted by either a single- or double-track error, the erroneous received word is denoted by $W' = [Z_0', Z_1', Z_2', Z_3', Z_4', Z_5', Z_6', Z_7', P']$. From the received word W', the syndromes S_1 and S_2 of error are computed as

$$S_1 = \left[\sum_{i=0}^{7}{}^{\oplus} Z_i'\right] \oplus P' \tag{6.4}$$

$$S_2 = \sum_{i=0}^{7}{}^{\oplus} \mathbf{T}^i \cdot Z_i' \tag{6.5}$$

Obviously, if there is no error, $S_1 = S_2 = 0$. Suppose that only the ith track $(0 \le i \le 8)$ has errors and the error pattern is denoted by an eight-digit vector E

(i.e., $E = Z_i \oplus Z_i'$). In this case, Equations (6.4) and (6.5) can be expressed as

$$S_1 = E \tag{6.6}$$

$$S_2 = \begin{cases} \mathbf{T}^i \cdot E & \cdots \quad 0 \le i \le 7 \\ 0 & \cdots \quad i = 8 \end{cases} \tag{6.7}$$

If $S_2 \neq 0$, then the track position i is uniquely determined from the following fact.

$$\mathbf{T}^{-i} \cdot S_2 = S_1 = E \tag{6.8}$$

The erroneous tracks are often identified by the external pointers that are obtained externally by detecting, for example, loss of signal in the read amplifiers, excessive phase shift in clock, inadmissible recording patterns, and so on. We will show that if the erroneous two tracks are identified by some external pointers, any two track bytes in error in the ORC are correctable.

Let E_i and E_j denote the two error-pattern vectors representing errors in the tracks i and j, respectively ($i < j$). That is, the received bytes are error free except in tracks i and j, where $Z_i' = Z_i \oplus E_i$, and $Z_j' = Z_j \oplus E_j$, or $P' = P \oplus E_j$ if $j = 8$. Then, syndromes S_1 and S_2 of Equations (6.4) and (6.5) can be represented in the following way.

$$S_1 = E_i \oplus E_j$$

$$S_2 = \begin{cases} \mathbf{T}^i \cdot E_i \oplus \mathbf{T}^j \cdot E_j & \cdots \quad 0 \le i \neq j \le 7 \\ \mathbf{T}^i \cdot E_i & \cdots \quad j = 8 \text{ or } j = i \end{cases}$$

These equations uniquely determine the error patterns E_i and E_j as

$$E_i = S_1 \oplus E_j$$

and

$$E_j = \begin{cases} [\mathbf{I} \oplus \mathbf{T}^{j-i}]^{-1} \cdot (S_1 \oplus \mathbf{T}^{-i} \cdot S_2) & \cdots \quad 0 \le i \neq j \le 7 \\ [S_1 \oplus \mathbf{T}^{-i} \cdot S_2] & \cdots \quad j = 8 \text{ or } j = i \end{cases}$$

Here, an interesting conversion of the parity check matrix into the information-byte format is presented. This alternate form allows direct computation of the check byte and syndromes. In addition, the new format allows a fast implementation of ORC requiring *no buffer* for encoding.

Fig. 6.3 shows the binary representation of the **H** matrix shown in (6.1), where α^i is an element of $GF(2^8)$ expressed as an 8-digit column vector α^i of the binary coefficients of the polynomial x^i modulo $\mathbf{g}(x)$. First, consider the column of the **H** matrix corresponding to the bit $Z_i(j)$ of the track byte Z_i for all i and j such that $0 \le i \le 7$ and $0 \le j \le 7$. The lower half of this column is α^k, where $k = i + j$, which is the same for the column corresponding to $Z_j(i)$.

This property is called the *orthogonal symmetry* of the code. To complete the symmetry, let B_0 denote the check byte C. Then,

$$Z_j(i) \equiv B_i(j) \qquad \text{for } 0 \le i \le 7, \text{ and } 0 \le j \le 7$$

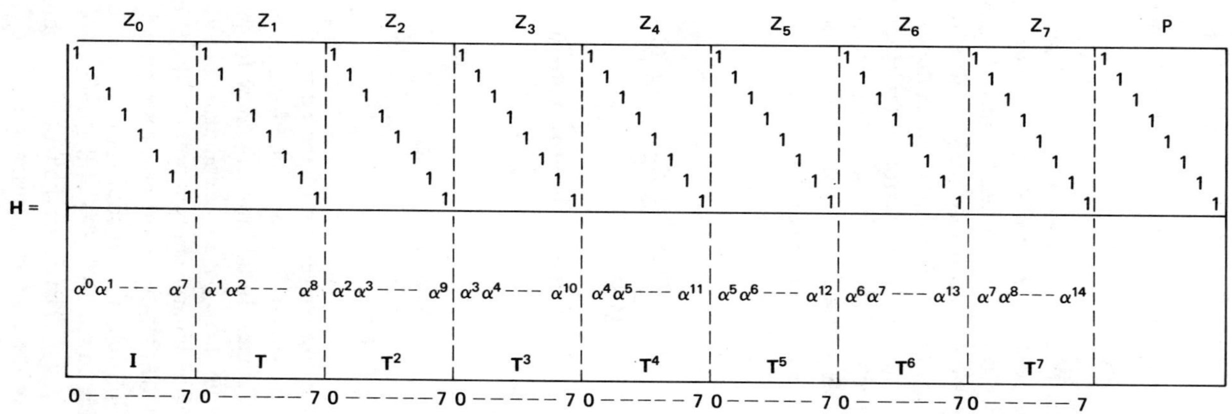

Figure 6.3 The **H** matrix for syndrome decoding [PATE 74]. © 1974 by International Business Machines Corporation; reprinted with permission.

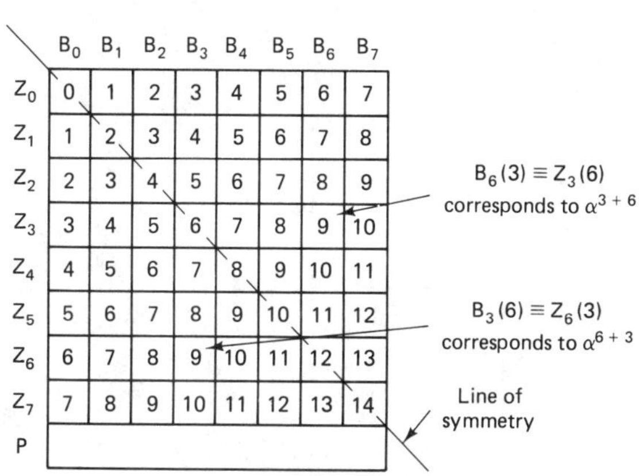

Figure 6.4 The orthogonal symmetry and powers of α in **H** matrix [PATE 74]. © 1974 by International Business Machines Corporation; reprinted with permission.

Fig. 6.4 shows the orthogonal symmetry and the powers of α that appear in the lower half columns of the **H** matrix. Now, proceed to rearrange the columns of the **H** matrix of Fig. 6.3 to obtain another **H** matrix, **H′** in Fig. 6.5, corresponding to a codeword W' in terms of the information bytes written as $W' = [B_0, B_1, B_2, B_3, B_4, B_5, B_6, B_7, P]$.

Note that this rearrangement does not alter the parity checking rules. The orthogonal symmetry of the code has produced $\mathbf{T}^i$ in the recorded lower half of the matrix **H′**, corresponding to the information byte B_i, which is the same as that corresponding to the track byte Z_i. The upper half of **H′** is the conventional VRC and can be represented by a matrix $\mathbf{G}_i$, where $\mathbf{G}_i$ is an (8×8) all-zero matrix, except the row i, which is all ones. Thus, the new parity check matrix **H′** appears as follows:

$$\mathbf{H}' = \begin{bmatrix} \mathbf{G}_0 & \mathbf{G}_1 & \mathbf{G}_2 & \mathbf{G}_3 & \mathbf{G}_4 & \mathbf{G}_5 & \mathbf{G}_6 & \mathbf{G}_7 & \mathbf{I} \\ \mathbf{I} & \mathbf{T} & \mathbf{T}^2 & \mathbf{T}^3 & \mathbf{T}^4 & \mathbf{T}^5 & \mathbf{T}^6 & \mathbf{T}^7 & 0 \end{bmatrix} \tag{6.9}$$

for the codeword $W' = [B_0, B_1, B_2, B_3, B_4, B_5, B_6, B_7, P]$. The parity checking equation is

$$\mathbf{H}' \cdot (W')^T = 0$$

Alternatively, the parity check can be computed from the information bytes as

$$C \equiv B_0 = \sum_{i=1}^{7}{}^{\oplus}\, \mathbf{T}^i \cdot B_i \tag{6.10}$$

and

$$P(i) = \sum_{j=0}^{7}{}^{\oplus}\, B_i(j), \qquad 0 \le i \le 7 \tag{6.11}$$

Equation (6.11) represents the conventional parity computation, which can be implemented by the usual exclusive-or network. Equation (6.10) can be imple-

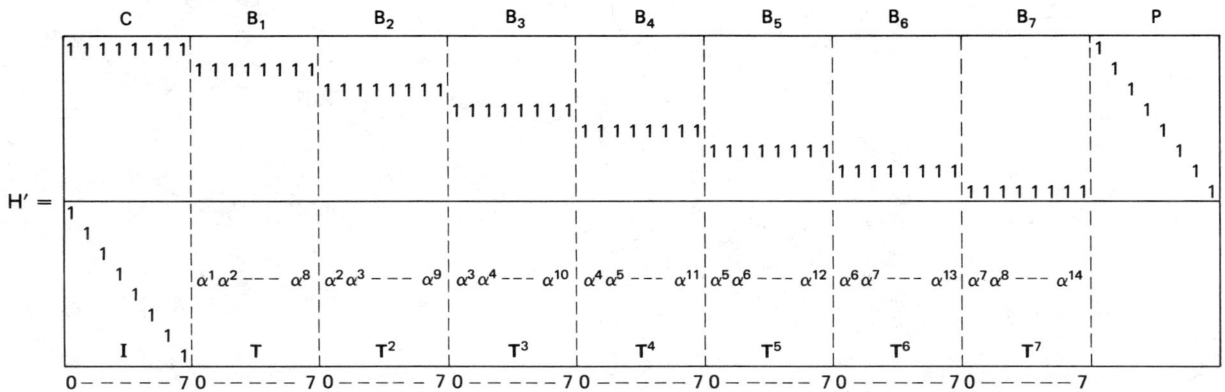

Figure 6.5 The **H** matrix for encoding and syndrome generation [PATE74]. © 1974 by International Business Machines Corporation; reprinted with permission.

mented by means of a linear feedback shift register (LFSR) connected for modulo $\mathbf{g}(x)$ operation (shown in Fig. 6.6).

The shifting operation in this LFSR corresponds to multiplying the content polynomial by x modulo $\mathbf{g}(x)$, which is equivalent to multiplying the content vector by the companion matrix **T**. Input connections are such that the entering information bytes are premultiplied by **T**. Initially, this LFSR contains all zeros. The information bytes $B_7, B_6, B_5, \ldots, B_2, B_1$ are successively shifted in parallel into the LFSR, in that order. Thus, at the end of seven shifts, the LFSR contains the vector $\mathbf{T} \cdot B_1 \oplus \mathbf{T}^2 \cdot B_2 \oplus \cdots \oplus \mathbf{T}^7 \cdot B_7$, which equals the check byte C.

Syndrome generation, especially generation of S_2, can be implemented using a LFSR similar to the one used in encoding. This can be accomplished by satisfying the equation

$$S_2 = C' \oplus \sum_{i=1}^{7}{}^{\oplus} \mathbf{T}^i \cdot B_i'$$

where B_i' and C' denote the received vectors that may be corrupted by error. The erroneous track can be uniquely pointed out only when Equation (6.8) is satisfied. If we use a *backward shifting register* [PATE 74], its contents after i shifts should match $S_1 = E$. Thus, when a match occurs, the number of shifts determines the track position. Alternatively, a forward shifting register, such as the LFSR shown in Fig. 6.6, can be used for determination of error track position i. Because $\mathbf{T}^{-i} = \mathbf{T}^{n-j}$, this requires a maximum of n shifts to determine the index i. In this case, the polynomial $\mathbf{g}(x)$ with the lowest exponent n saves correction time.

When tracks have erasures (instead of errors), double-track erasures can be corrected. (See [PATE 74] or [LIN 83].) The ORC is extended to become a code that can correct a track error together with a track erasure, or three track erasures. This can also be generalized to a $B(n, m)$ code of $(n + 1) \times n$ array code in an $(n + 1)$-track tape, where there are check columns $B_0, B_1, \ldots, B_m$, $0 \leq m \leq n - 1$, that can correct s track errors and t track erasures, whenever $2s + t \leq m + 2$ [BLAU 85]. So, the ORC code is a particular case of this family, $B(8, 0)$.

6.1.2 Adaptive Cross-Parity (AXP) Code

This new code was developed for a new high-density, 18-track tape storage subsystem [PATE 85]. In this coding scheme, the 18 tracks are divided into two sets of 9 tracks, with each set consisting of 7 data tracks and 2 check tracks. The proportion of check tracks is thus the same as in the 9-track scheme. However, through adaptive use of the checks in the two sets, the new scheme corrects up to 3 erased tracks in any one set of 9 tracks and up to 4 erased tracks in the two sets together. The coding structure, however, is simple, for it avoids the complex computations of Galois fields. It is based on vertical and cross-parity checks.

Figure 6.7 shows the data format for 18 tracks grouped into two sets. The set A consists of any 9 parallel tracks, and the set B consists of the remaining 9 parallel

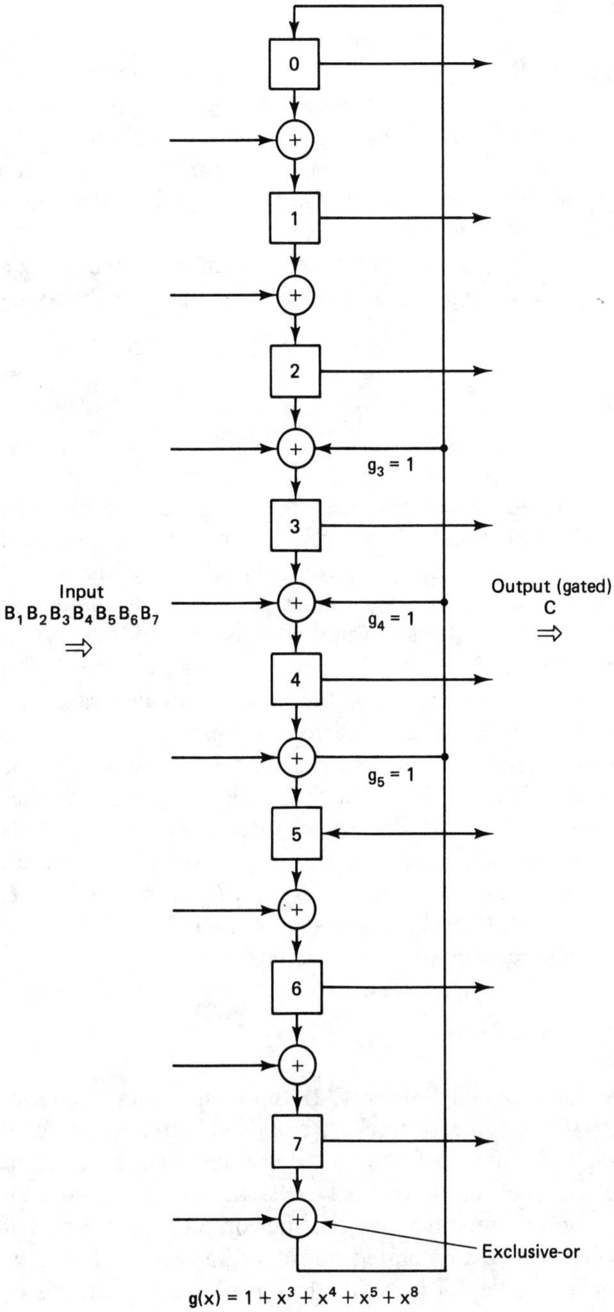

Figure 6.6 LFSR encoder (information bytes arrive from $B_7, B_6, \ldots, B_1$ in parallel to the shift register) [PATE 74]. © 1974 by International Business Machines Corporation; reprinted with permission.

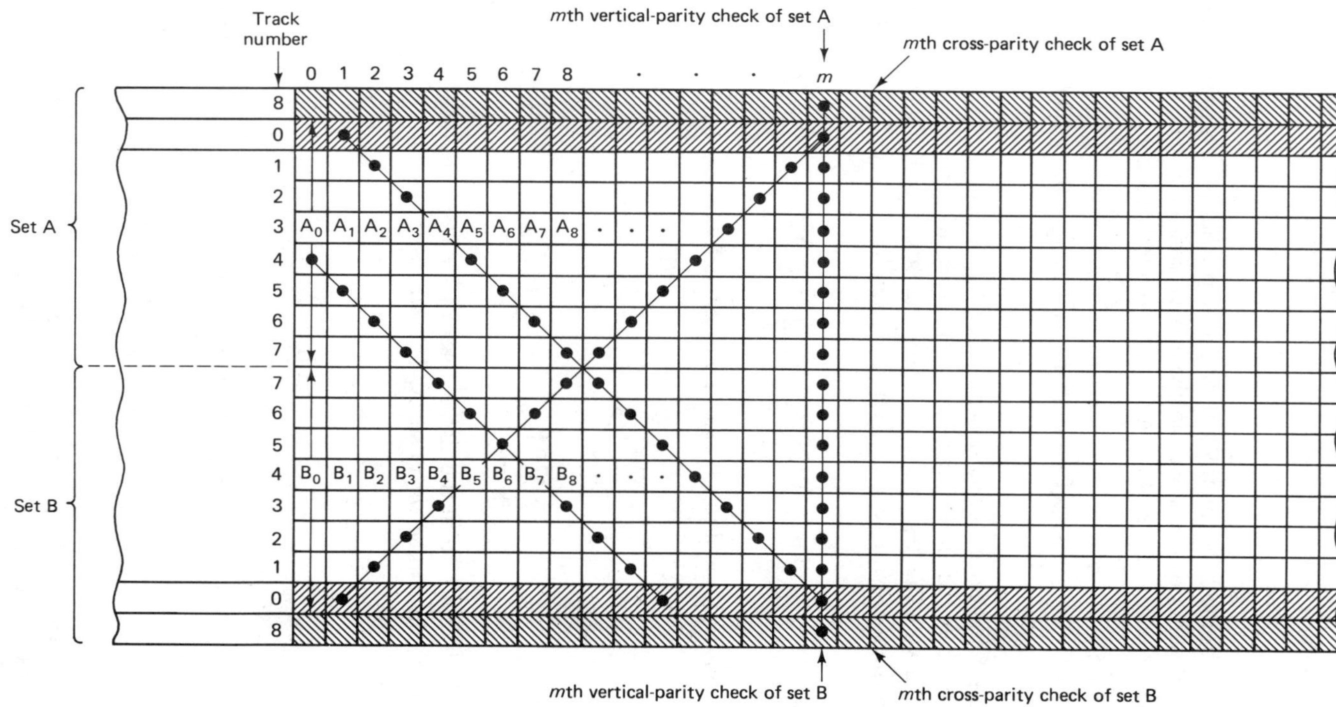

Figure 6.7 Data format: 18 tracks grouped into two sets [PATE 85]. © 1985 by International Business Machines Corporation; reprinted with permission.

tracks. In Fig. 6.7 the two sets are shown side by side with a symmetrically ordered arrangement of the tracks.

Let $A_m(t)$ and $B_m(t)$ denote the mth bit in the track t of sets A and B, respectively. The track number t takes on values from 0 to 8 in each set. The bit position m takes on values from 0 to M. Tracks labeled 0 and 8 in each set are check tracks.

Each check bit in track 0 of set A provides a *cross-parity check* along the diagonal with positive slope, involving bits from both sets, as seen in Fig. 6.7. The mth cross-parity check of set A is given by the encoding equation

$$A_m(0) = \sum_{t=1}^{7}{}^{\oplus} A_{m-t}(t) \oplus \sum_{t=0}^{7}{}^{\oplus} B_{m+t-15}(t) \tag{6.12}$$

where $\Sigma^{\oplus}$ indicates modulo-2 sum.

Each check bit in track 0 of set B provides a cross-parity check along the diagonal with the negative slope, involving bits from both sets, as seen in Fig. 6.7. The mth cross-parity check of set B is given by the encoding equation

$$B_m(0) = \sum_{t=1}^{7}{}^{\oplus} B_{m-t}(t) \oplus \sum_{t=0}^{7}{}^{\oplus} A_{m+t-15}(t) \tag{6.13}$$

Equations (6.12) and (6.13) can be written as follows.

$$\sum_{t=0}^{7}{}^{\oplus} \left[A_{m-t}(t) \oplus B_{m+t-15}(t)\right] = 0 \tag{6.14}$$

$$\sum_{t=0}^{7}{}^{\oplus} \left[B_{m-t}(t) \oplus A_{m+t-15}(t)\right] = 0 \tag{6.15}$$

Each check bit in the eighth track of set A is a vertical parity over the bits of same position number m in set A. The mth vertical-parity bit of set A is given by the equation

$$A_m(8) = \sum_{t=0}^{7}{}^{\oplus} A_m(t) \tag{6.16}$$

Similarly, the mth vertical-parity bit of set B is given by the equation

$$B_m(8) = \sum_{t=0}^{7}{}^{\oplus} B_m(t) \tag{6.17}$$

The encoding equations (6.12), (6.13), (6.16), and (6.17) are simple parity equations. These can be implemented by means of exclusive-or circuits receiving inputs of appropriate data bit values.

Let $A'_m(t)$ and $B'_m(t)$ denote the bit values corresponding to $A_m(t)$ and $B_m(t)$, respectively, as they are read from the tape. These bits may be corrupted by errors. A nonzero syndrome shows an indication of the presence of an error.

From Equations (6.14) through (6.17), the syndrome can be computed as follows.

$$Sd_m^a = \sum_{t=0}^{7}{}^{\oplus} [A'_{m-t}(t) \oplus B'_{m+t-15}(t)]$$

$$Sd_m^b = \sum_{t=0}^{7}{}^{\oplus} [B'_{m-t}(t) \oplus A'_{m+t-15}(t)]$$

$$Sv_m^a = \sum_{t=0}^{8}{}^{\oplus} A'_m(t)$$

$$Sv_m^b = \sum_{t=0}^{8}{}^{\oplus} B'_m(t)$$

Here, Sd_m^a is the mth cross-parity syndrome of set A; Sd_m^b is the mth cross-parity syndrome of set B; Sv_m^a is the mth vertical syndrome for set A; and Sv_m^b is the mth vertical syndrome for set B.

The modulo-2 difference between the read $A'_m(t)$ and the written $A_m(t)$ is called the error pattern $E_m^a(t)$ in the mth position of track t in set A. So for set A we have

$$E_m^a(t) = A'_m(t) \oplus A_m(t)$$

Similarly, for set B,

$$E_m^b(t) = B'_m(t) \oplus B_m(t)$$

From the above relations we have the following syndromes expressed by the error patterns

$$Sd_m^a = \sum_{t=0}^{7}{}^{\oplus} [E_{m-t}^a(t) \oplus E_{m+t-15}^b(t)]$$

$$Sd_m^b = \sum_{t=0}^{7}{}^{\oplus} [E_{m-t}^b(t) \oplus E_{m+t-15}^a(t)]$$

$$Sv_m^a = \sum_{t=0}^{8}{}^{\oplus} E_m^a(t)$$

$$Sv_m^b = \sum_{t=0}^{8}{}^{\oplus} E_m^b(t)$$

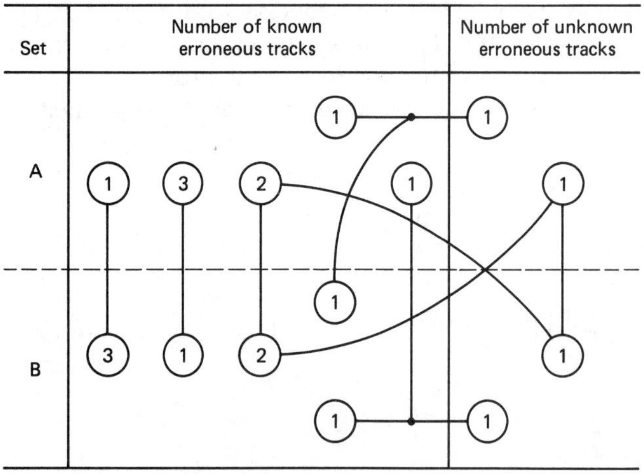

Figure 6.8 Correctable error cases by the AXP code. (The numbers within the circles show the maximum number of correctable tracks.)

The erroneous track may be identified by the external pointers mentioned before. In the absence of the pointers, the erroneous track can be identified by processing the syndromes. According to [PATE 85], any one of the following combinations of track errors can be corrected using the AXP code.

1. Up to three known erroneous tracks in one set and up to one known erroneous track in the other set.
2. Up to one unknown or two known erroneous tracks in each of the two sets.
3. Up to one known and one unknown erroneous track in one set and up to one known erroneous track in the other set.

Fig. 6.8 shows the combinations of track errors correctable by the AXP code.

Error correction for just a few basic cases will be mentioned here. For error correction of other cases and detailed implementation methods, the reader is referred to the original paper [PATE 85].

First, we consider error correction for three known erroneous tracks in set A which are correctable if set B is error free or has only one known erroneous track. The erroneous tracks are indicated by track-error pointers i, j, and k in set A and l in set B. For convenience, assume that $i < j < k$.

Since set B has only one known erroneous track, the vertical parity-check syndromes Sv_m^b yield the error patterns for this track.

$$Sv_m^b = E_m^b(l) \tag{6.18}$$

Assume that all errors have been corrected up to byte $(m - 1)$ and that the syndrome equations have been adjusted for all corrected error patterns. Then, as shown in Fig. 6.9, the error patterns for the mth position of tracks i, j, and k of set A can be determined from the syndromes Sd^a_{m+i}, Sd^b_{m+15-k}, and Sv^a_m, as follows.

$$Sd^a_{m+i} = E^a_m(i) \tag{6.19}$$

$$Sd^b_{m+15-k} = \begin{cases} E^a_m(k) \oplus E^b_{m+15-l-k}(l) & \cdots \quad \text{if } l < 8 \\ E^a_m(k) & \cdots \quad \text{if } l = 8 \text{ or set B is error free} \end{cases} \tag{6.20}$$

$$Sv^a_m = E^a_m(i) \oplus E^a_m(j) \oplus E^a_m(k) \tag{6.21}$$

From Equation (6.18) we have

$$Sv^b_{m+15-l-k} = E^b_{m+15-l-k}(l) \tag{6.22}$$

Equations (6.19) through (6.22) yield the following error pattern.

$$E^a_m(i) = Sd^a_{m+i}$$

$$E^a_m(k) = \begin{cases} Sd^b_{m+15-k} \oplus Sv^b_{m+15-l-k} & \cdots \quad \text{if } l < 8 \\ Sd^b_{m+15-k} & \cdots \quad \text{if } l = 8 \text{ or set B is error free} \end{cases}$$

$$E^a_m(j) = Sv^a_m \oplus E^a_m(i) \oplus E^a_m(k)$$

The mth bits in tracks i, j, and k are corrected, using these error patterns as follows.

$$A_m(i) = A'_m(i) \oplus E^a_m(i)$$
$$A_m(j) = A'_m(j) \oplus E^a_m(j)$$
$$A_m(k) = A'_m(k) \oplus E^a_m(k)$$

Before proceeding to the correction of the next position, we must modify the syndromes affected by these corrections. The modification is shown by an arrow pointing from the previous value of a syndrome to its new value.

$$Sd^a_{m+i} \leftarrow Sd^a_{m+i} \oplus E^a_m(i)$$
$$Sd^a_{m+j} \leftarrow Sd^a_{m+j} \oplus E^a_m(j) \qquad \text{if } j < 8$$
$$Sd^a_{m+k} \leftarrow Sd^a_{m+k} \oplus E^a_m(k)$$
$$Sd^b_{m+15-i} \leftarrow Sd^b_{m+15-i} \oplus E^a_m(i)$$
$$Sd^b_{m+15-j} \leftarrow Sd^b_{m+15-j} \oplus E^a_m(j) \qquad \text{if } j < 8$$
$$Sd^b_{m+15-k} \leftarrow Sd^b_{m+15-k} \oplus E^a_m(k)$$

Now the decoding procedure can be applied to the next bit position by changing the value of m by 1.

Next, we consider determination of the track error pointers. Errors confined to only one unknown track in set A can be detected and corrected if set B has at most

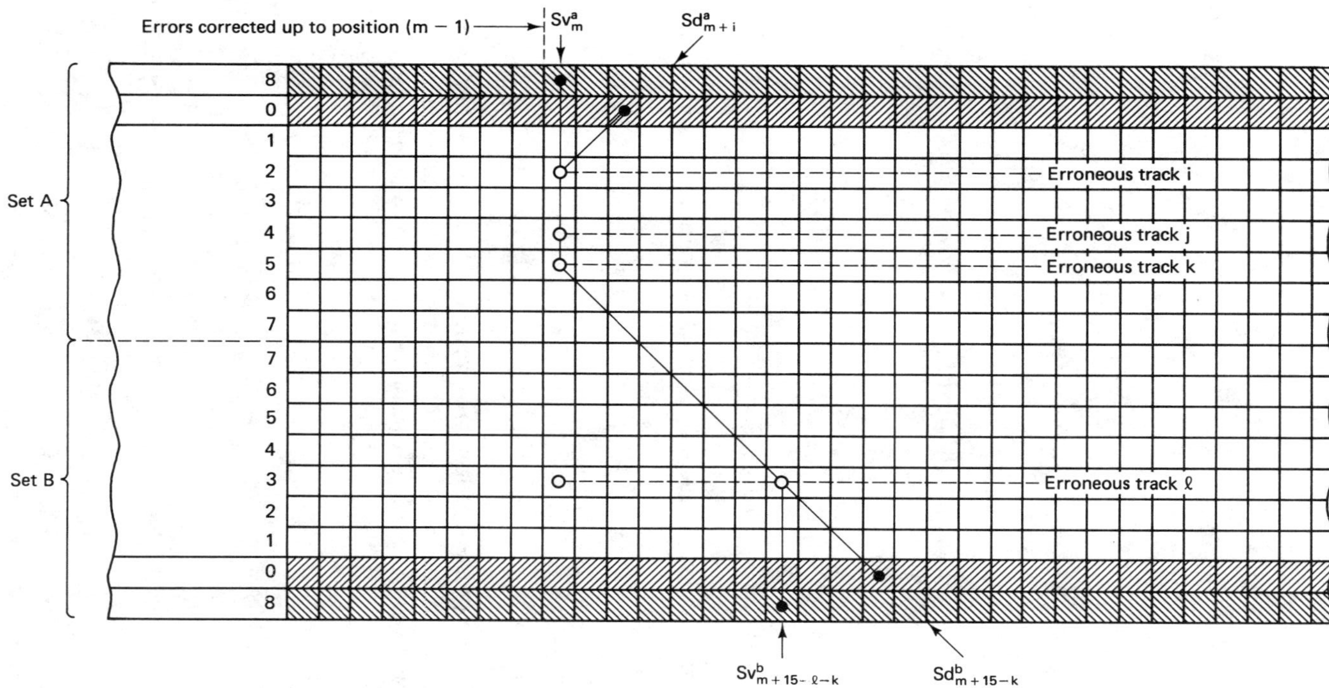

Figure 6.9 Example of a three-track error correction in set A [PATE 85]. © 1985 by International Business Machines Corporation; reprinted with permission.

one unknown or two known erroneous tracks. It is assumed that errors in all tracks of set B have been corrected up to bit position $(m - 1)$ and that the syndrome values have been adjusted for all corrected error patterns. When all tracks in set A are error free, the parity-check syndromes Sv_m^a and Sd_m^a are equal to zero for $0 < i < 7$. When any of these syndromes are found to be nonzero, it is indicated that an error is present in at least one of the tracks in the neighborhood. Assuming that only one erroneous track is affecting the syndromes, the index of the erroneous track can be determined by examining syndromes Sd_{m+7}^a and Sv_m^a as the bit position value m progresses.

Let m_1 and m_2 denote the lowest values of bit positions such that

$$\begin{aligned} Sd_{m+i}^a &\neq 0 \qquad \text{for } m = m_1 \text{ and } i = 7 \\ Sv_m^a &\neq 0 \qquad \text{for } m = m_2 \end{aligned}$$

Then, track q is in error at bit position m_2 and the track index q is given by

$$q = \begin{cases} 7 - (m_2 - m_1) & \text{if } m_2 \geq m_1 \\ 8 & \text{otherwise} \end{cases}$$

Fig. 6.10 shows the case in which m_2 is greater than or equal to m_1. Note that if the resulting value q in this case is smaller than zero, then the syndromes are affected by two or more unknown erroneous tracks and the errors are uncorrectable. The error can be easily corrected by using the syndrome Sv_m^a as follows.

$$\begin{aligned} E_{m_2}(q) &= Sv_{m_2}^a \\ A_{m_2}(q) &= A'_{m_2}(q) \oplus E_{m_2}(q) \end{aligned}$$

Also, syndromes should be adjusted as

$$\begin{aligned} Sv_{m_2}^a &\leftarrow Sv_{m_2}^a \oplus E_{m_2}(q) \\ Sd_{m_1+7}^a &\leftarrow Sd_{m_1+7}^a \oplus E_{m_2}(q) \end{aligned}$$

Next, we consider the case in which set A is being corrected for errors in a known erroneous track, and another, unknown track in set A begins to be affected by errors. These erroneous tracks of set A can be corrected provided that set B has at most one known erroneous track. It is recommended that the reader demonstrate the correction procedure for this case.

Since the coding rules possess a built-in mirror-image symmetry around set A and set B, the encoding and decoding equations for set B obviously can be obtained from those of set A by substitution of the corresponding variables.

6.1.3 Interleaved R – S SbEC Code for Mass Storage System (MSS)

The mass storage system (MSS), as for example, in the IBM 3850, stores digital data on flexible magnetic tape media; however, it is different in many respects from the conventional multitrack tape machines. The IBM system consists of an array of data

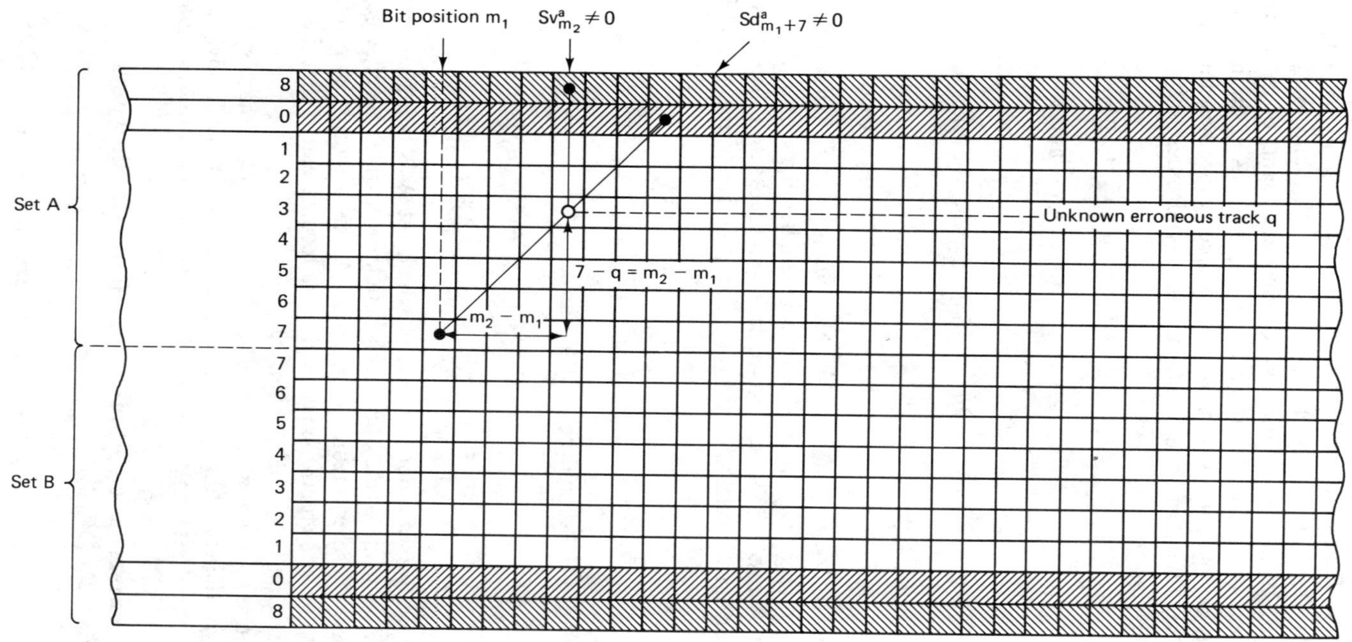

Figure 6.10 Generation of a pointer to the first erroneous track when $q \neq 8$ [PATE 85]. © 1985 by International Business Machines Corporation; reprinted with permission.

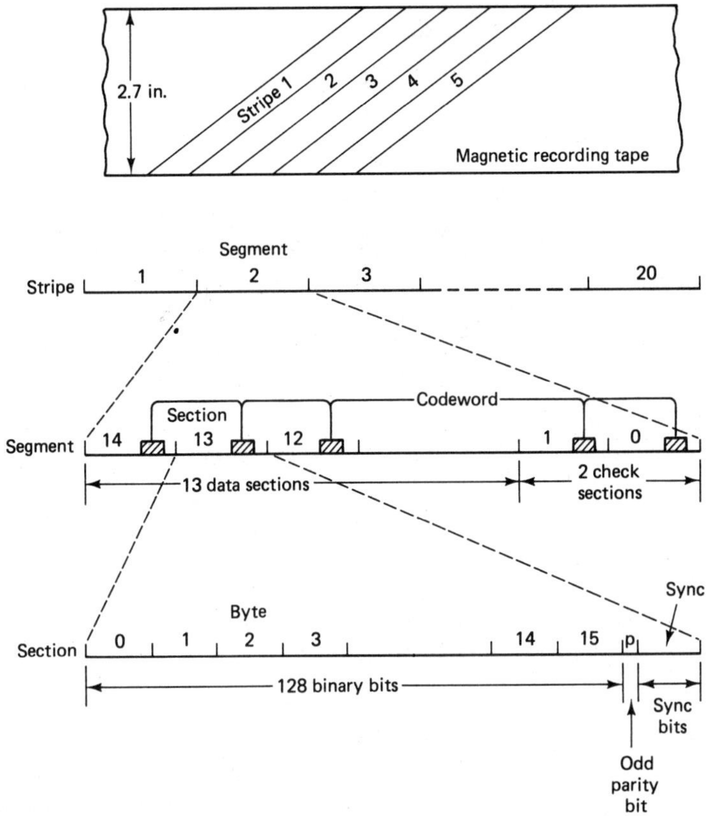

Figure 6.11 Stripe data format [PATE 80]. © 1980 by International Business Machines Corporation; reprinted with permission.

cartridges about 1.9 in (4.8 cm) in diameter and 3.5 in (8.9 cm) long, each with a capacity of 50.4 million bytes (byte = 8-bit) of data. Each cartridge contains a spool of magnetic tape of 2.7 in (6.9 cm) wide and 64 ft (195 meters) long. Up to 4,720 cartridges are stored in hexagonal compartments in a honeycomblike apparatus that includes mechanisms for fetching cartridges from the compartments, for reading and writing of data on them, and for the replacement of cartridges in the compartments. Unlike the conventional fixed head of the multitrack tape machines, this system uses a rotary read–write head.

Data are recorded in short slanted stripes across the tape. The tape follows a helical path around a read–write mandrel and is stepped in position from one slanted stripe to the next over a circular slit. The rotary read–write heads revolve with the mandrel. The stripe is divided into 20 segments, each of which consists of 13 data sections followed by 2 check sections. Each section consists of 16 bytes (a total of 128 bits). This arrangement is shown in Fig. 6.11. Fig. 6.12 shows the rectangular array of each segment, in which 15 bytes in each column form a codeword from a (15, 13) single-symbol error correcting code with symbols from the

Section	0	1	2 (Codeword)	3	4	---	k	---	14	15	Odd parity	
14	$B_{14\text{-}0}$	$B_{14\text{-}1}$	$B_{14\text{-}2}$	$B_{14\text{-}3}$	$B_{14\text{-}4}$	---	$B_{14\text{-}k}$	---	$B_{14\text{-}14}$	$B_{14\text{-}15}$	P Sync	13 data sections
13	$B_{13\text{-}0}$	$B_{13\text{-}1}$	$B_{13\text{-}2}$	$B_{13\text{-}3}$	$B_{13\text{-}4}$	---	$B_{13\text{-}k}$	---	$B_{13\text{-}14}$	$B_{13\text{-}15}$	P Sync	
12	$B_{12\text{-}0}$	$B_{12\text{-}1}$	$B_{12\text{-}2}$	$B_{12\text{-}3}$	$B_{12\text{-}4}$	---	$B_{12\text{-}k}$	---	$B_{12\text{-}14}$	$B_{12\text{-}15}$	P Sync	
11	$B_{11\text{-}0}$	$B_{11\text{-}1}$	$B_{11\text{-}2}$	$B_{11\text{-}3}$	$B_{11\text{-}4}$	---	$B_{11\text{-}k}$	---	$B_{11\text{-}14}$	$B_{11\text{-}15}$	P Sync	
⋮							⋮					
j	$B_{j\text{-}0}$	$B_{j\text{-}1}$	$B_{j\text{-}2}$	$B_{j\text{-}3}$	$B_{j\text{-}4}$	---	$B_{j\text{-}k}$	---	$B_{j\text{-}14}$	$B_{j\text{-}15}$	P Sync	
⋮							⋮					
2	$B_{2\text{-}0}$	$B_{2\text{-}1}$	$B_{2\text{-}2}$	$B_{2\text{-}3}$	$B_{2\text{-}4}$	---	$B_{2\text{-}k}$	---	$B_{2\text{-}14}$	$B_{2\text{-}15}$	P Sync	
1	$B_{1\text{-}0}$	$B_{1\text{-}1}$	$B_{1\text{-}2}$	$B_{1\text{-}3}$	$B_{1\text{-}4}$	---	$B_{1\text{-}k}$	---	$B_{1\text{-}14}$	$B_{1\text{-}15}$	P Sync	2 check sections
0	$B_{0\text{-}0}$	$B_{0\text{-}1}$	$B_{0\text{-}2}$	$B_{0\text{-}3}$	$B_{0\text{-}4}$	---	$B_{0\text{-}k}$	---	$B_{0\text{-}14}$	$B_{0\text{-}15}$	P Sync	

Figure 6.12 A segment: 15 sections formed with 16 interleaved codewords [PATE 80]. © 1980 by International Business Machines Corporation; reprinted with permission.

Galois field $GF(2^8)$ (i.e., each 8-bit byte represents an element in $GF(2^8)$). The codewords are interleaved in the data format of 15 sections in a segment.

All detected errors, such as errors in a ZM (zero modulation) decoding algorithm, which checks for errors through stringent runlength and d.c. charge constraints, and odd parity checked errors at the end of each section are reported to the decoder of the error correction code for error recovery.

When a defect or dust particle affects up to two full sections (i.e., 32 data bytes), the resultant error is recoverable by correcting the corresponding two bytes in each of the 16 codewords.

The basic structure of the codeword W is designated as

$$W = [B_0, B_1, B_2, \ldots, B_{14}]$$

In this codeword, B_0 and B_1 are the check bytes, and the remaining 13 bytes are the data bytes. Consider the Galois field $GF(2^8)$, which is constructed based on the primitive polynomial

$$\mathbf{p}(x) = 1 + x + x^3 + x^5 + x^8 \tag{6.23}$$

Let α be a primitive element in $GF(2^8)$ such that

$$\mathbf{p}(\alpha) = 1 + \alpha + \alpha^3 + \alpha^5 + \alpha^8 = 0$$

Let $\beta = \alpha^\lambda$ represent a primitive element of the 16 element subfield of $GF(2^8)$, where λ is a multiple of 17 and prime to 15. The choice of $\lambda = 68$ was made simply because it provided a minimum number of hardware connections in the implementation of multiplication by β [PATE 80]. Therefore, we can easily check that

$$0, 1, \beta, \beta^2, \ldots, \beta^{14}$$

from the field $GF(2^4)$, which is a subfield of $GF(2^8)$. Then the code is generated by

$$\begin{aligned} \mathbf{g}(x) &= (x + 1)(x + \beta) \\ &= \beta + (1 + \beta)x + x^2 \end{aligned} \tag{6.24}$$

This code can also be expressed as the binary form by using the companion matrix **T**, an (8×8) matrix obtained from the primitive polynomial of Equation (6.23), given as follows.

$$\mathbf{T} = \begin{bmatrix} 0 & 0 & 0 & 0 & 0 & 0 & 0 & 1 \\ 1 & 0 & 0 & 0 & 0 & 0 & 0 & 1 \\ 0 & 1 & 0 & 0 & 0 & 0 & 0 & 0 \\ 0 & 0 & 1 & 0 & 0 & 0 & 0 & 1 \\ 0 & 0 & 0 & 1 & 0 & 0 & 0 & 0 \\ 0 & 0 & 0 & 0 & 1 & 0 & 0 & 1 \\ 0 & 0 & 0 & 0 & 0 & 1 & 0 & 0 \\ 0 & 0 & 0 & 0 & 0 & 0 & 1 & 0 \end{bmatrix}$$

The **H** matrix of this code is shown as

$$\mathbf{H} = \begin{bmatrix} \mathbf{I} & \mathbf{I} & \mathbf{I} & \cdots & \mathbf{I} \\ \mathbf{I} & \mathbf{T}^{\lambda} & \mathbf{T}^{2\lambda} & \cdots & \mathbf{T}^{14\lambda} \end{bmatrix} \tag{6.25}$$

where **I** is an (8×8) identity matrix, and λ is 68. This code has minimum distance 3 and, therefore, can correct any single byte errors. The coding rules are given in the form of the following matrix (modulo-2) equations.

$$B_0 \oplus B_1 \oplus B_2 \oplus \cdots \oplus B_{14} = 0$$

$$B_0 \oplus \mathbf{T}^{\lambda} \cdot B_1 \oplus \mathbf{T}^{2\lambda} \cdot B_2 \oplus \cdots \oplus \mathbf{T}^{14\lambda} \cdot B_{14} = 0$$

The encoding circuit for this code is presented in Fig. 6.13. This block diagram of the shift register can be derived from Equation (6.24). As soon as the 13 data symbols have been shifted into the register, the parity-check symbols B_0 and B_1 are in the low- and high-order stages.

Suppose that the ith byte B_i is in error. Let E_i denote the error pattern.

Then,

$$B_i' = B_i \oplus E_i$$

The syndrome can be obtained such that

$$\left.\begin{aligned} S_0 &= E_i \\ S_1 &= \mathbf{T}^{i\lambda} \cdot E_i \end{aligned}\right\} \tag{6.26}$$

Thus the error pattern E_i is determined by the syndrome S_0. Also, from these

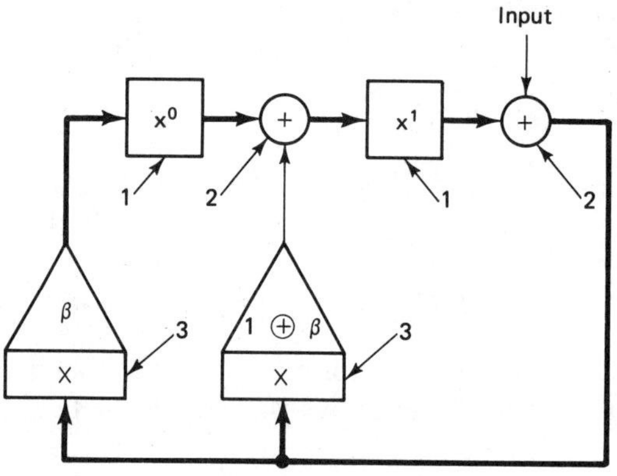

Figure 6.13 Block diagram of encoding network. 1: Storage of field element. 2: Addition of field elements. 3: Multiplication by a field element. [PATE 80]. © 1980 by International Business Machines Corporation; reprinted with permission.

equations, we have

$$\mathbf{T}^{-i\lambda} \cdot S_1 = S_0 = E_i \tag{6.27}$$

that is,

$$\mathbf{T}^{(15-i)\lambda} \cdot S_1 = S_0 = E_i \tag{6.28}$$

(since $T^{15\lambda} = I$). Therefore, the error byte position i is uniquely determined from the fact that Equation (6.27) or (6.28) is satisfied. Error correction is then accomplished by adding $S_0 = E_i$ to B_i.

When the erroneous sections are indicated by external pointers, this information is passed on to the decoder in the form of error pointers. Let i and j denote the position values of two erroneous bytes in a codeword, where $i < j$. The error patterns E_i and E_j are errors in bytes B_i and B_j, respectively, so that

$$B_i' = B_i \oplus E_i \qquad \text{and} \qquad B_j' = B_j \oplus E_j$$

The syndrome can be obtained such that

$$S_0 = E_i \oplus E_j$$

$$S_1 = \mathbf{T}^{i\lambda} \cdot E_i \oplus \mathbf{T}^{j\lambda} \cdot E_j$$

Since i and j are known, the two simultaneous equations may be solved for the two unknown variables E_i and E_j, to obtain

$$E_j = [\mathbf{I} \oplus \mathbf{T}^{(j-i)\lambda}]^{-1} \cdot [S_0 \oplus \mathbf{T}^{-i\lambda} \cdot S_1]$$

and

$$E_i = S_0 \oplus E_j$$

Let $[\mathbf{I} \oplus \mathbf{T}^{(j-i)\lambda}]^{-1} = \mathbf{T}^{q\lambda}$ and $\mathbf{T}^{-i\lambda} = \mathbf{T}^{p\lambda}$. Then, we obtain the following.

$$E_i = S_0 \oplus E_j$$

$$E_j = \mathbf{T}^{q\lambda} \cdot [S_0 \oplus \mathbf{T}^{p\lambda} \cdot S_1]$$

TABLE 6.1 PARAMETER p AS A FUNCTION OF i

i	0	1	2	3	4	5	6	7	8	9	10	11	12	13	14
p	15	14	13	12	11	10	9	8	7	6	5	4	3	2	1

Source: [PATE 80]. © 1980 by International Business Machines Corporation; reprinted with permission.

TABLE 6.2 PARAMETER q AS A FUNCTION OF $(j - i)$

$j - i$	1	2	3	4	5	6	7	8	9	10	11	12	13	14
q	3	6	11	12	5	7	2	9	13	10	1	14	8	4

Source: [PATE 80]. © 1980 by International Business Machines Corporation; reprinted with permission.

The parameters p and q for all possible values of i and j are listed in Table 6.1 and Table 6.2, respectively.

The decoder then consists of the following four single steps.

Step 1. Multiply S_1 by the matrix $\mathbf{T}^{p\lambda}$.
Step 2. Add S_0 to the result of step 1.
Step 3. Multiply the result of step 2 by $\mathbf{T}^{q\lambda}$. This gives the error pattern E_j.
Step 4. Add S_0 to the result of step 3. This results in the error pattern E_i.
Step 5. Add E_i to byte B_i' and E_j to byte B_j'.

For a more detailed description of the decoding circuit and the system, the reader is referred to [PATE 80].

6.2 DISK MEMORY CODES

Magnetic disk memory has played an important role in high-speed, large-capacity file memory in computer systems over many years. Since the 1960s, disk technology has greatly improved in terms of density, storage capacity, data rate, cost, and reliability. In terms of areal density, for example, there has been an improvement of about four orders of magnitude (i.e., from 10^3 to 10^7 bits per square inch (bpsi) [HSIA 81]).

The disk has a higher data rate than tape, due to its higher rotation speed. Hence its sensing circuit design has to allow for greater tolerance. In the early stage of magnetic disk memories, only *simple parity checks* were used for checking data integrity. In the next stage, the *burst error detecting 16-bit polynomial code* was used for improved error detection capability. In the 1970s, a high-density and high-data-rate disk (e.g., IBM 3330) established a new basic disk technology. This disk memory used a *Fire code* to have a burst error correction and detection capability.

In recent disk design, an *interleaved Reed–Solomon code* is used in place of the Fire code for error correction. Besides error correction/detection codes, other important recovery techniques used to enhance reliability and data integrity are: *defect skip*, *alternate data block*, and *reread* [HSIA 81].

As with magnetic tape systems, burst errors predominate in magnetic disk systems. Most errors are related to imperfections on disk surfaces, or surface irregularities, such as defects. The remaining errors are mostly due to heads, which are susceptible to random noise-induced errors [HOWE 84].

Digital optical disks are a relatively new technology for storing data. Each disk is coated with special reflective materials. Reading and writing are performed using a laser. More specifically, reading involves determining the reflectivity of a given position on the disk, while writing usually consists of melting holes into the coating (at a high power setting of the laser).* The bit density on digital optical disks can be much higher, as optical recording permits a much finer "grain" than magnetic recording. Therefore, this medium can be expected to play an increasingly important role in memory systems—document file, image file, digital data file for large computers systems, and so forth [LEIS 84].

Errors are primarily due to the optical disk medium itself, since fabrication of a stable disk utilizing high-performance and high-reliability coatings has not yet been established at a reasonable price. Almost all errors are related to imperfections in the disk, and the remaining errors result from focusing shift in recording or random noise in reading. Therefore, both burst error correcting and random error correcting facilities are needed for optical disk memories [SAIT 86, ITAO 87]. Presently, powerful error correction techniques, such as a *doubly encoded Reed–Solomon code* or a combination of a cyclic code and the Reed–Solomon code, are applied to attain the same level of reliability as that had with the magnetic media.

Here, an adaptive method using Fire codes and interleaved Reed–Solomon codes is introduced for magnetic disk memories, and more powerful *cross interleaved Reed–Solomon codes* (*CIRC*) are shown to be required for optical disk memories.

6.2.1 Fire Code for Magnetic Disk Memory

The Fire code [FIRE 59], which is capable of correcting any burst of length l or less, and of simultaneously detecting any burst of length $d \geq l$, is generated by the following generator polynomial.

$$\mathbf{g}(x) = (x^c + 1)\mathbf{p}(x)$$

Here $\mathbf{p}(x)$ is an irreducible polynomial of degree m with exponent e and $l \leq m$, $c \geq l + d - 1$. The length n of this code is equal to the least common multiple

*In erasable disks, however, magneto-optical recording has a different reading/writing principle, one based on the Faraday-effect and Curie-point reorientation.

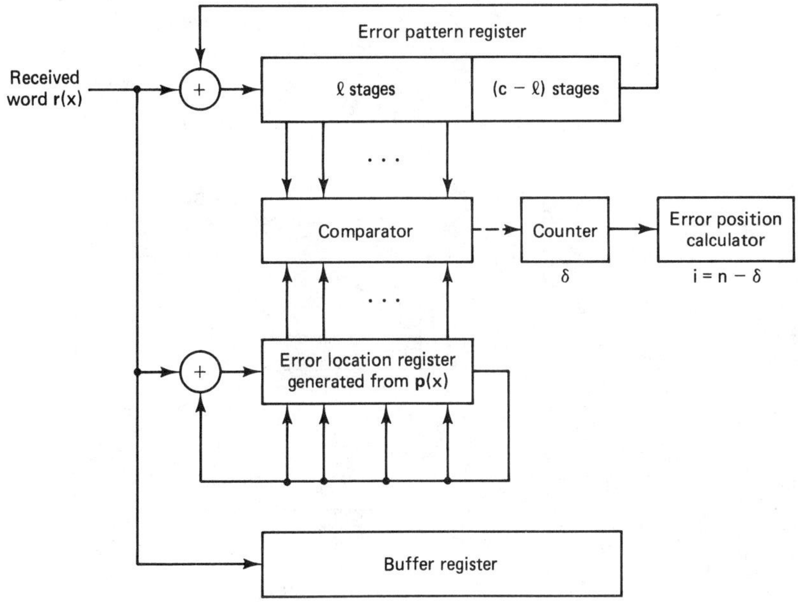

Figure 6.14 Fire code decoder.

(LCM) of e and c,

$$n = \text{LCM}(e, c)$$

The number of check digits of this code is $(c + m)$.

Let's consider the decoding scheme of this code. Fig. 6.14 shows the decoding circuit for this code. The received word $\mathbf{r}(x)$ is stored in the buffer register and, at the same time, is entered into the two shift registers, called the error pattern register and the error location register, to store residue polynomials divided by $(x^c + 1)$ and $\mathbf{p}(x)$, respectively. Let the transmitted codeword be $\mathbf{v}(x)$, and let the burst error polynomial be $\mathbf{b}(x)$ whose degree is less than or equal to $l - 1$. Then $\mathbf{r}(x)$ can be expressed as

$$\mathbf{r}(x) = \mathbf{v}(x) + \mathbf{x}^i \cdot \mathbf{b}(x)$$

where i shows the position that the burst error starts. If $\mathbf{b}(x) = 0$, then $\mathbf{r}(x)$ can be divided by both $(x^c + 1)$ and $\mathbf{p}(x)$, and hence the residue is equal to zero. If $\mathbf{b}(x) \neq 0$, the shift registers have the following residues.

$$x^i \cdot \mathbf{b}(x) = \mathbf{s}_1(x) \qquad \text{mod}\,(x^c + 1) \tag{6.29}$$

$$x^i \cdot \mathbf{b}(x) = \mathbf{s}_2(x) \qquad \text{mod}\,\mathbf{p}(x) \tag{6.30}$$

By using these residues, $\mathbf{s}_1(x)$ and $\mathbf{s}_2(x)$, we have to obtain $\mathbf{b}(x)$ and the value i.

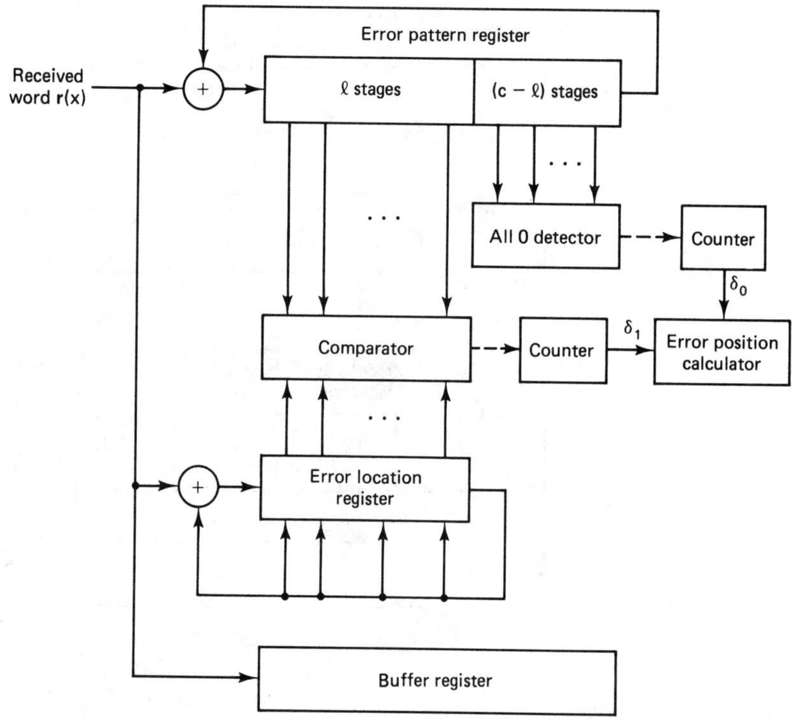

Figure 6.15 High-speed decoder for Fire codes.

After $(n - i)$ shifts of these shift registers, these yield the following residues.

$$\begin{aligned} \mathbf{s}_1(x) \cdot x^{n-i} &= x^n \cdot \mathbf{b}(x) \\ &= \mathbf{b}(x) \qquad \text{mod}\,(x^c + 1) \\ \mathbf{s}_2(x) \cdot x^{n-i} &= x^n \cdot \mathbf{b}(x) \\ &= \mathbf{b}(x) \qquad \text{mod}\,\mathbf{p}(x) \end{aligned}$$

In other words, when the contents of the lower part of the l registers of the error pattern are equal to those of the error location register after δ shifts of these registers, the burst error pattern, expressed as polynomial $\mathbf{b}(x)$, can be set in these registers. In addition to this $\mathbf{b}(x)$, error position i can be calculated from the number of shifts $\delta(= n - i)$, and hence $i = n - \delta$.

The foregoing decoding method necessitates greater decoding time when i is small compared to n. Therefore, we consider the high-speed decoding method [CHIE 69]. Assume that c and e are relatively prime. Fig. 6.15 shows a high-speed decoding circuit.

In this decoding method, the received word $\mathbf{r}(x)$ is simultaneously entered into the buffer register, the error pattern register, and the error location register. Then residues expressed by Equations (6.29) and (6.30) are obtained in the error pattern register and the error location register, respectively. At this stage, from these obtained residues, we can decode the received word as follows.

$$\mathbf{s}_1(x) = \mathbf{s}_2(x) = 0 \to \mathbf{r}(x)\text{: error free}$$

$$\left.\begin{array}{l}\mathbf{s}_1(x) \neq 0 \text{ and } \mathbf{s}_2(x) = 0\\ \mathbf{s}_1(x) = 0 \text{ and } \mathbf{s}_2(x) \neq 0\end{array}\right\} \to \mathbf{r}(x)\text{: uncorrectable}$$

If $\mathbf{s}_1(x) \neq 0$ and $\mathbf{s}_2(x) \neq 0$, the decoding can be processed by the following algorithm:

1. *Shift the error pattern register until the contents of the higher $(c - l)$ registers are all 0's, and store the required number of shifts δ_0. If the contents of the error pattern register are not equal to all 0's after $(c - l)$ shifts, an uncorrectable error is assumed to have occurred; therefore, stop the decoding process.*
2. *Shift the error location register until its contents are equal to those of the lower l bits of the error pattern register, and store the number of shifts δ_1. If the contents of the lower part of the error pattern register are not equal to those of the error location register after $(e - 1)$ shifts, an uncorrectable error is assumed to have occurred; therefore, stop the decoding process.*
3. *The error position i can be calculated from the values δ_0 and δ_1, and hence the errors can be corrected by using the error pattern $\mathbf{b}(x)$. That is, the contents of the lower l bits of the error pattern register denote $\mathbf{b}(x)$.*

In the above algorithm, the error position can be calculated by using the Chinese Remainder Theorem (see Section 2.4), such that

$$\begin{aligned}\delta_0 &= c - i\\ &= -i \bmod c\\ \delta_1 &= e - i\\ &= -i \bmod e\end{aligned}$$

then, $-i = \delta_0 \cdot A_0 \cdot e + \delta_1 \cdot A_1 \cdot c \bmod n$, where A_0 and A_1 are such integers that satisfy

$$A_0 \cdot e + A_1 \cdot c = 1 \bmod n$$

The computation of A_0 and A_1 can be done easily off line with the numbers $A_0 \cdot e$ and $A_1 \cdot c$ stored in the error position calculator shown in Fig. 6.15. In this decoding, the maximum number of shifts is $(e + c - 2)$, whereas in the former decoding, it is $(e \cdot c - 1)$, and hence this decoding is much faster than the former.

Next we consider a new class of codes that is a *generalization of the Fire codes* [CHIE 69]. They are generated by a polynomial of the form

$$\mathbf{g}(x) = (x^c - 1)\prod_{i=1}^{h} \mathbf{p}_i(x) \tag{6.31}$$

where $\mathbf{p}_i(x)$ is a distinct irreducible polynomial having exponent e_i and degree r_i. It is further assumed that the e_i's ($i = 1, 2, \ldots, h$) do not divide c. The code length is

$$n = \mathrm{LCM}\,(c, e_1, e_2, \ldots, e_h)$$

Theorem 6-1 [CHIE 69]. *The code generated by* $\mathbf{g}(x)$ *given by Equation* (6.31) *detects all error bursts of length* $\leq d$; *it corrects all bursts* $\mathbf{b}(x)$ *of length* $\leq l$ *that are relatively prime to* $\prod_{i=1}^{h} \mathbf{p}_i(x)$, *provided* $c \geq l + d - 1$ *and* $l \leq \sum_{i=1}^{h} r_i$.

Equations that determine the error position i can be written as

$$-i = \delta_0 \cdot A_0 \cdot \prod_{j=1}^{h} e_j + c \cdot \sum_{j=1}^{h} \delta_j \cdot A_j \cdot \prod_{\substack{k=1 \\ k \neq j}}^{h} e_k \tag{6.32}$$

$$A_0 \cdot \prod_{j=1}^{h} e_j + c \cdot \sum_{j=1}^{h} A_j \cdot \prod_{\substack{k=1 \\ k \neq j}}^{h} e_k = 1 \tag{6.33}$$

The IBM 3330-compatible disk systems use the *generalized Fire code* generated by the following polynomial:

$$\mathbf{g}(x) = (x^{22} + 1) \prod_{i=1}^{3} \mathbf{p}_i(x)$$

where

$$\mathbf{p}_1(x) = 1 + x + x^6 + x^7 + x^{11}$$

$$\mathbf{p}_2(x) = 1 + x + x^2 + x^3 + x^4 + x^5 + x^6 + x^7 + x^8 + x^9 + x^{10} + x^{11} + x^{12}$$

$$\mathbf{p}_3(x) = 1 + x + x^5 + x^6 + x^7 + x^9 + x^{11}$$

are distinct irreducible polynomials. The exponents of $\mathbf{p}_1(x)$, $\mathbf{p}_2(x)$, and $\mathbf{p}_3(x)$ are 89, 13, and 23, respectively. Therefore, the code length is

$$n = \mathrm{LCM}\,(22, 89, 13, 23) = 585{,}442$$

It has $22 + 11 + 12 + 11 = 56$ check bits and is capable of correcting any single burst of length 11 or less.

From Equations (6.32) and (6.33), equations that determine the error position can be written as follows.

$$i = \delta_0 A_0 e_1 e_2 e_3 + \delta_1 A_1 c e_2 e_3 + \delta_2 A_2 c e_1 e_3 + \delta_3 A_3 c e_1 e_2 \bmod n \tag{6.34}$$

where A_0, A_1, A_2, and A_3 satisfy the following.

$$A_0 e_1 e_2 e_3 + A_1 c e_2 e_3 + A_2 c e_1 e_3 + A_3 c e_1 e_2 = -1 \bmod n \tag{6.35}$$

For this code, we can find that

$$\begin{aligned} A_0e_1e_2e_3 &= -1 \bmod c \\ A_1ce_2e_3 &= -1 \bmod e_1 \\ A_2ce_1e_3 &= -1 \bmod e_2 \\ A_3ce_1e_2 &= -1 \bmod e_3 \end{aligned} \tag{6.36}$$

The minimum integers that satisfy Equations (6.35) and (6.36) are $A_0 = 5$, $A_1 = 78$, $A_2 = 6$, and $A_3 = 10$. These integers are substituted into Equation (6.34), and then we have the following equation that can determine the error position.

$$i = 133{,}055\delta_0 + 513{,}084\delta_1 + 270{,}204\delta_2 + 254{,}540\delta_3 \bmod 585{,}442$$

The decoding circuit for this code is shown in Fig. 6.16.

Shift operations of the error pattern register are performed until the contents of the upper 10 stages of the register are all 0's. Shift operations of the error location registers are also performed until all contents of the three error location registers are equal to those of the lower 11 stages of the error pattern register. Given that these numbers of shifts are δ_0, δ_1, δ_2, and δ_3, then $K_0 = 133{,}055\delta_0$, $K_1 = 513{,}084\delta_1$, $K_2 = 270{,}204\delta_2$, and $K_3 = 254{,}540\delta_3$ are calculated, and hence i can be obtained by $i = K_0 + K_1 + K_2 + K_3 \bmod n$.

Another faster error correction scheme using the ordinary Fire code has been proposed in [ADI 84]. This is a hybrid technique combining sequential error trapping and table lookup techniques. The decoder needs at most $(c + m - 1)$ shift cycles to find both the burst error pattern and its location. The decoder can be implemented by making use of programmable read only memories (PROMs) and field programmable logic arrays (FPLAs) suitable for LSI implementation.

6.2.2 Interleaved R–S SbEC–DbED Code for Magnetic Disk Memory

A high-performance burst error correction scheme using a byte-error correcting code is given in [HORI 75b]. The recently developed magnetic disk system (such as that found in the IBM 3370 and 3380 systems) adopts an interleaved Reed–Solomon (R–S) distance-4 code, and this is discussed in [HODG 80]. This system uses a fixed-block data format. Each data block consists of 512 bytes. For error control, nine check bytes are appended to it. The code used in this system is a shortened Reed–Solomon distance-4 code with symbols from the field $GF(2^8)$. The generator polynomial of the code is

$$\mathbf{g}(x) = (x + 1)(x + \alpha)(x + \alpha^{-1})$$

where α is the primitive element of $GF(2^8)$ and is a root of $\mathbf{p}(x) = 1 + x^2 + x^3 + x^4 + x^8$. This code is capable of correcting any single symbol (one-byte) error and simultaneously detecting any combination of double-symbol (two-byte) errors. The code is a (174, 171) code over $GF(2^8)$.

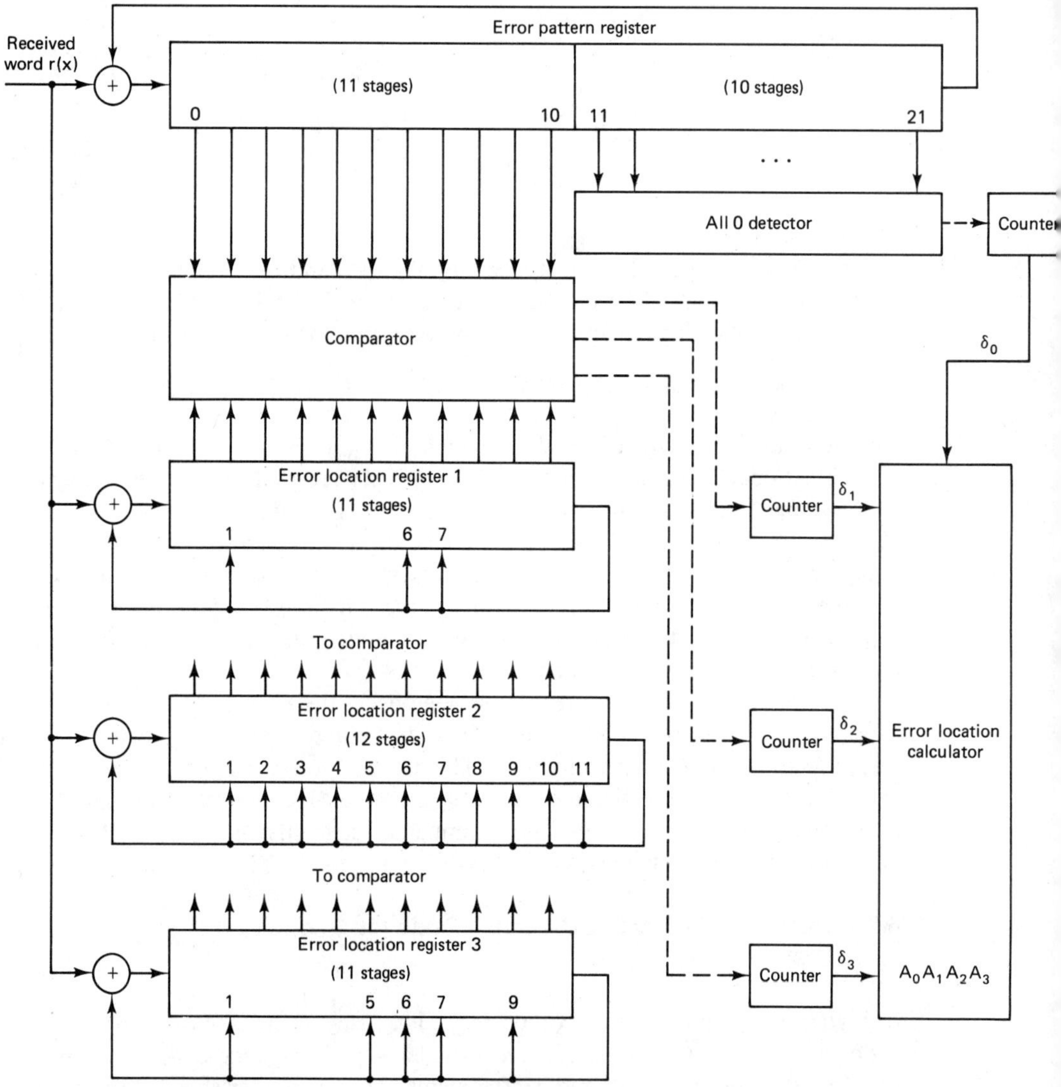

Figure 6.16 Decoding circuit for the generalized Fire code used in IBM 3330-compatible disk systems.

For encoding, a data block is divided into three subblocks, $\mathbf{D}_{-1}$, $\mathbf{D}_0$, and $\mathbf{D}_1$, each consisting of 171 bytes. We represent these three subblocks in polynomial form as follows.

$$\mathbf{D}_i(x) = D_{i,170}x^{170} + D_{i,169}x^{169} + \cdots + D_{i,1}x + D_{i,0}$$
$$i = -1, 0, 1$$

where each byte $D_{i,k}$, $(i = -1, 0, 1,\ k = 0, 1, \ldots, 170)$, is regarded as a symbol in

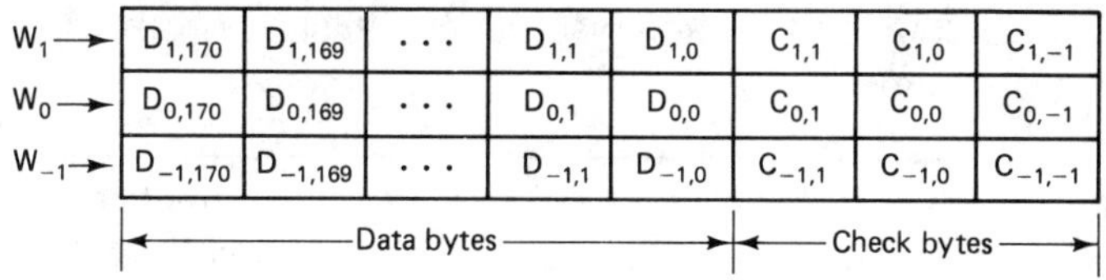

Figure 6.17 Codewords, $\mathbf{W}_1, \mathbf{W}_0$, and $\mathbf{W}_{-1}$.

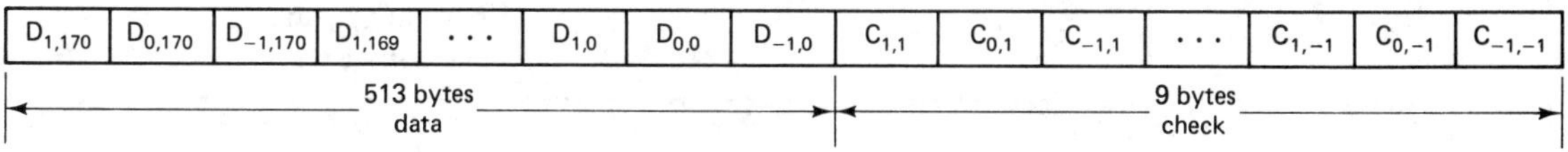

Figure 6.18 Overall interleaved codeword.

$GF(2^8)$. The three check bytes for $\mathbf{D}_i$, denoted $C_{i,-1}$, $C_{i,0}$, and $C_{i,1}$, $i = -1, 0, 1$, are obtained as follows.

$$C_{i,j} = x \cdot \mathbf{D}_i(x) \bmod (x + \alpha^j)$$

$$i = -1, 0\ 1, \qquad j = -1, 0, 1$$

Note the difference between this encoding method and the method used for encoding cyclic codes, where all three check bytes are computed by dividing $x^3 \cdot \mathbf{D}_i(x)$ by $\mathbf{g}(x)$. After the three check bytes for $\mathbf{D}_i$ have been formed, they are appended to $\mathbf{D}_i$ to form a codeword $\mathbf{W}_i$, as shown in Fig. 6.17.

The three codewords $\mathbf{W}_1$, $\mathbf{W}_0$, and $\mathbf{W}_{-1}$ are interleaved to form a coded block as shown in Fig. 6.18. Therefore, the overall code is the (174, 171) R–S code interleaved to degree 3. This code is capable of correcting any error burst confined to three consecutive bytes and detecting any error burst confined to six consecutive bytes.

When a coded block is read from the disk, it is decomposed into three subwords, $\mathbf{W}_1'$, $\mathbf{W}_0'$, and $\mathbf{W}_{-1}'$, where

$$\mathbf{W}_i' = \left(C_{i,1}', C_{i,0}', C_{i,-1}', \mathbf{D}_i'\right)$$

$$i = 1, 0, -1$$

Syndrome $S_{i,j}$ ($i = 1, 0 - 1,\ j = 1, 0 - 1$) can be obtained as follows.

$$S_{i,j} = C_{i,j}' + x \cdot \mathbf{D}_i'(x) \qquad \bmod (x + \alpha^j)$$

$$= C_{i,j}' + \alpha^j \cdot \mathbf{D}_i'(\alpha^j)$$

where $\mathbf{D}_i'(x) = D_{i,170}' x^{170} + \cdots + D_{i,1}' x + D_{i,0}'$. If $S_{i,1} = S_{i,0} = S_{i,-1} = 0$, the word is error free. If all syndromes $S_{i,1}$, $S_{i,0}$, and $S_{i,-1}$ are nonzeros, there are single-byte errors in the read word. This is because if error $\alpha^m (0 \le m \le 254)$ is added to the

TABLE 6.3 ERROR INFORMATION BASED ON THE SYNDROMES

$S_{i,1}$	$S_{i,0}$	$S_{i,-1}$	Error Information
0	0	0	Error free
NZ	NZ	NZ	Single-byte errors
NZ	0	0	Errors in $C'_{i,1}$
0	NZ	0	Errors in $C'_{i,0}$
0	0	NZ	Errors in $C'_{i,-1}$
NZ	NZ	0	Errors in $C'_{i,1}$ and $C'_{i,0}$
0	NZ	NZ	Errors in $C'_{i,0}$ and $C'_{i,-1}$
NZ	0	NZ	Double-byte errors

data symbol $D_{i,l}$ $(l = 0, 1, \ldots, 170)$, then the read word is expressed as

$$D'_{i,l} = D_{i,l} + \alpha^m$$

$$D'_{i,k} = D_{i,k} \qquad k \neq l,\ k = 0, 1, \ldots, 170$$

$$C'_{i,j} = C_{i,j}$$

and, hence, not all zero syndromes can be obtained as

$$S_{i,1} = \alpha^{m+l+1}$$

$$S_{i,0} = \alpha^m$$

$$S_{i,-1} = \alpha^{m-(l+1)}$$

In this case, the error pattern can be expressed as $S_{i,0}$, and error position can be determined by the following relation.

$$\frac{S_{i,1}}{S_{i,0}} = \frac{\alpha^{m+l+1}}{\alpha^m} = \alpha^{l+1}$$

$$\frac{S_{i,0}}{S_{i,-1}} = \frac{\alpha^m}{\alpha^{m-(l+1)}} = \alpha^{l+1}$$

Other information regarding errors is given in Table 6.3, where "NZ" shows the nonzero syndrome.

6.2.3 Cross-Interleaved R – S Code (CIRC) for Optical Disk Systems

As mentioned before, errors in optical disk systems are almost always due to the disk surface, and hence with this medium we have not only burst errors but also random errors. Thus we require a code to correct both kinds of errors.

The *C*ross *I*nterleaved *R*eed–Solomon *C*ode (CIRC) is a new class of doubly encoded codes in which the second Reed–Solomon code encodes the delayed and

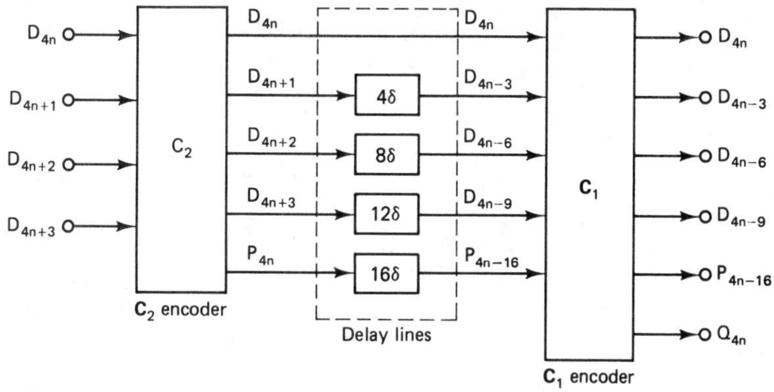

Figure 6.19 Encoder of the CIRC.

dispersed (i.e., *cross-interleaved*) output of the first encoded Reed–Solomon code [DOI 79]. To illustrate the concept behind this class of codes, a simple example is provided.

Example 6-1

Let the two codes that can individually correct single-symbol errors be $\mathbf{C}_1$ and $\mathbf{C}_2$. Fig. 6.19 shows the encoding circuit of the CIRC. Assume that the check symbols, P and Q, are represented as two symbols for the codes $\mathbf{C}_2$ and $\mathbf{C}_1$, respectively.

Check symbols P_{4n} are produced from the consecutive four symbols, D_{4n}, D_{4n+1}, D_{4n+2}, and D_{4n+3} by using the $\mathbf{C}_2$ encoder. The encoded symbols, D_{4n}, D_{4n+1}, D_{4n+2}, D_{4n+3}, and P_{4n}, are delayed by unequal length and then yield to D_{4n}, D_{4n-3}, D_{4n-6}, D_{4n-9}, and P_{4n-16}. These delays are different for each symbol. Check symbols Q_{4n} are produced from the delayed symbols by using the $\mathbf{C}_1$ encoder. The delay lines, which utilize the *cross-interleave* concept, yield an encoding scheme such that check symbols Q_{4n} can be produced from the symbols included in the positive slope shown in Fig. 6.20.

Fig. 6.20 also shows the decoding concept of this code. As a result of the cross-interleaving, even if there are consecutive four-symbol errors, for example, errors in D_7, D_{10}, D_{13}, and D_{16}, that cannot be corrected in $\mathbf{C}_1$ decoding, these four-symbol errors are dispersed into single-symbol errors in each $\mathbf{C}_2$ code, and hence these can be corrected in $\mathbf{C}_2$ decoding. In this case, $\mathbf{C}_i$ decoding, $i = 1, 2$, means the decoding of the code $\mathbf{C}_i$ that may include errors. If there are errors in three symbols, for example, in D_{13}, D_{16}, and D_{17}, shown in Fig. 6.20(b), these errors can also be corrected in sequential steps such that a single-symbol error in D_{13} can be corrected by $\mathbf{C}_2$ decoding, and then a single-symbol error in D_{16} can be corrected by $\mathbf{C}_1$ decoding, and finally a single-symbol error in D_{17} can be corrected by $\mathbf{C}_2$ decoding. In Fig. 6.20(c), however, errors in four symbols, for example, in D_{13}, D_{14}, D_{16}, and D_{17}, cannot be

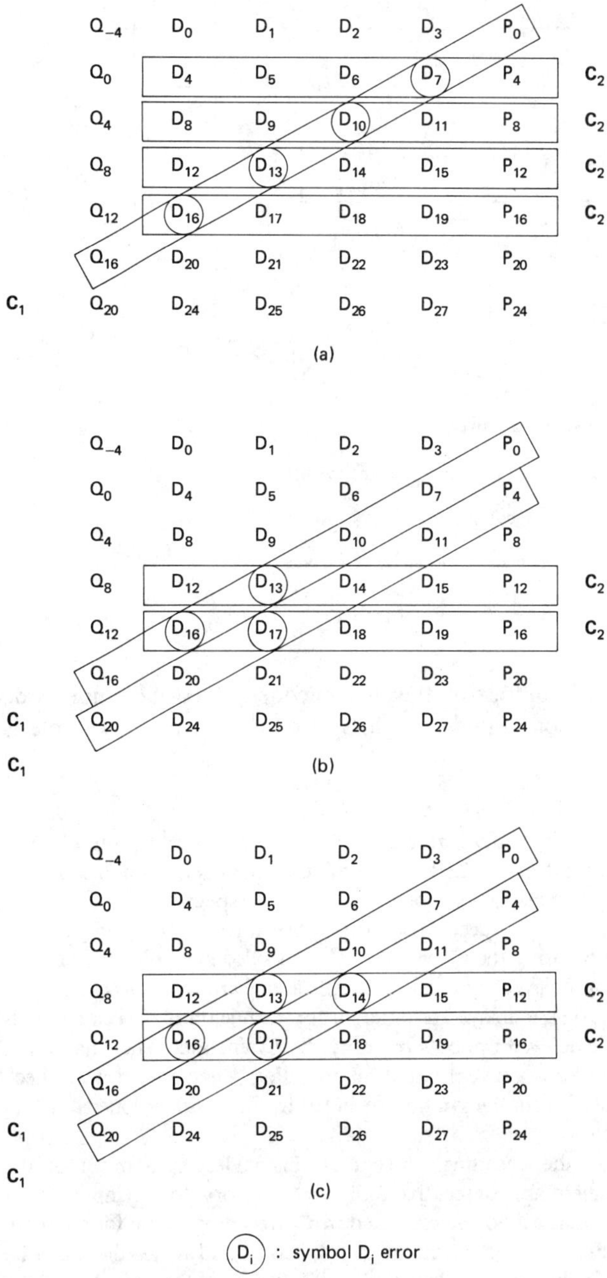

Figure 6.20 Decoding method.

corrected, since there are two-symbol errors in each of $\mathbf{C}_1$ decoding and $\mathbf{C}_2$ decoding at the first stage. In order to correct these four-symbol errors properly, we can make use of the erasure correction technique (see Section 4.1.2) that allows correction of up to two-symbol errors by using the error pointers for the symbol error correcting codes. Therefore, at the first stage, when two-symbol errors are detected in $\mathbf{C}_1$ decoding (i.e., in this case, code $\mathbf{C}_1$ acts as a double-symbol error detecting code), error pointers are set to all symbols included in the positive slopes. At the next stage, $\mathbf{C}_2$ decoding can correct these two-symbol errors by using the error pointers. This is because single-symbol, error correcting codes $\mathbf{C}_1$ and $\mathbf{C}_2$ are distance-3 codes, and therefore can correct up to two-symbol erasures.

The following two distance-5 Reed–Solomon codes (R–S codes) over $GF(2^8)$ are applied to the compact disk (CD) digital audio system [VRIE 80]. The codes $\mathbf{C}_1$ and $\mathbf{C}_2$ are as follows:

$\mathbf{C}_1$: (32, 28) double-symbol error correcting R–S code.
$\mathbf{C}_2$: (28, 24) double-symbol error correcting R–S code.

In this coding scheme, many decoding strategies can be considered. Among these, this compact disk system adopts the following decoding strategy called *super strategy*:

1. $\mathbf{C}_1$ decoding
  (i) All-zero syndrome → error free.
  (ii) Single-symbol errors → single-symbol error correction.
  (iii) Double-symbol errors → double-symbol error correction. Error location pointers are given to the $\mathbf{C}_2$ decoding.
  (iv) More than triple-symbol errors → only error detection. Error location pointers are given to the $\mathbf{C}_2$ decoding.

2. $\mathbf{C}_2$ decoding
  (i) All-zero syndrome → error free.
  (ii) Single-symbol errors → single-symbol error correction.
  (iii) Double-symbol errors →
    (a) Number of error pointers from the $\mathbf{C}_1$ decoding is less than or equal to 4 and at the same time the error locations of the two error pointers are equal to those calculated from the syndrome → double-symbol error correction.
    (b) Others → only error detection.
  (iv) More than triple-symbol errors → only error detection.

Note that when double-symbol errors are corrected in the $\mathbf{C}_1$ decoding, these two error location pointers are given to the $\mathbf{C}_2$ decoding in order to avoid miscorrection of triple-symbol errors as double-symbol errors in the $\mathbf{C}_1$ decoding.

In case even the $\mathbf{C}_2$ decoder cannot correct, it lets pass through 24 data symbols uncorrected but marked only with error pointers originally given out by the $\mathbf{C}_1$ decoder. This way, even if the $\mathbf{C}_2$ decoder cannot decode, most of the symbols are nevertheless probably error free, and the uncorrected marked sample values can be reconstructed via *linear interpolation* [VRIE 80] in digital audio systems. For the marked sample values, this can estimate and interpolate their correct values from both sides of values that haven't been marked with error pointers. The CIRC scheme having super strategy has a maximum fully correctable burst length up to 4,000 bits.

For digital data storage systems, called *compact disk ROMs* (*CD-ROM*), linear interpolation cannot be applied, and therefore another method for increasing data quality should be added. One system adopts both doubly encoded R–S SbEC codes and a cyclic redundancy check (CRC) code for the data already encoded in CIRC. That is, CD-ROM employs such a powerful error correction scheme that the CRC bits are appended to the CIRC encoded data, and then the resulting data are further encoded in doubly encoded R–S SbEC codes. Thus, the data are quadruply encoded. (If CRC is included, they are quintuply encoded.) One disk has about 540-megabyte data capacity.

1. *CRC code.* This code is appended in order to check the miscorrection of the R–S codes, or to detect uncorrectable errors. The CRC code generation polynomial is as follows.

$$\mathbf{g}(x) = (x^{16} + x^{15} + x^2 + 1)(x^{16} + x^2 + x + 1)$$

2. *Doubly encoded R–S codes.* The codes are determined by the following primitive polynomial $\mathbf{g}'(x)$, and α is a primitive element in $GF(2^8)$ (i.e., a root of $\mathbf{g}'(x)$).

$$\mathbf{g}'(x) = x^8 + x^4 + x^3 + x^2 + 1$$

The code includes two R–S codes (i.e., (26, 24) R–S code $\mathbf{C}_1$, and (45, 43) R–S code $\mathbf{C}_2$). Both codes are distance-3 R–S codes.

The check bytes for $\mathbf{C}_1$ are generated from the data included in the vertical direction. The check bytes for $\mathbf{C}_2$ are generated from the data included in the negative slope in the user data (which is 24 bytes $\times$ 43 bytes (= 1032 bytes) in a two-dimensional data format) and the check bytes of code $\mathbf{C}_1$ as can be seen in Fig. 6.21. The $\mathbf{H}$ matrices of code $\mathbf{C}_1$ and code $\mathbf{C}_2$ are as follows.

$$\mathbf{H}_1 = \begin{bmatrix} 1 & 1 & 1 & \cdots & 1 & 1 \\ \alpha^{25} & \alpha^{24} & \alpha^{23} & \cdots & \alpha & 1 \end{bmatrix}$$

$$\mathbf{H}_2 = \begin{bmatrix} 1 & 1 & 1 & \cdots & 1 & 1 \\ \alpha^{44} & \alpha^{43} & \alpha^{42} & \cdots & \alpha & 1 \end{bmatrix}$$

In Fig. 6.21, the code $\mathbf{C}_1$ is generated first, and then code $\mathbf{C}_2$ is generated. Note that the decoding is permitted for either of the sequences, that is, from $\mathbf{C}_1$ decoding to $\mathbf{C}_2$ decoding, or from $\mathbf{C}_2$ decoding to $\mathbf{C}_1$ decoding. In addition, these sequences can be repetitive, that is, for example, $\mathbf{C}_1$ decoding $\rightarrow$ $\mathbf{C}_2$ decoding $\rightarrow$ $\mathbf{C}_1$ decoding $\rightarrow$ $\mathbf{C}_2$

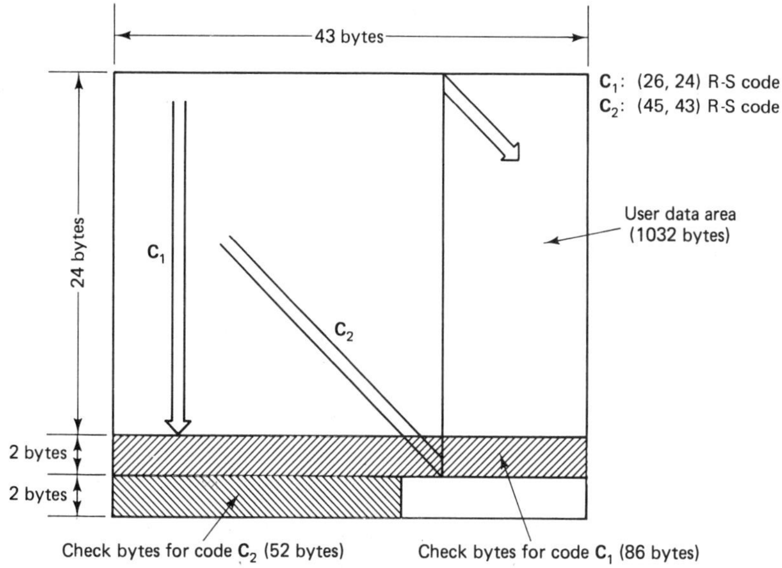

Figure 6.21 Code design format for CD-ROM.

decoding → . . . . Furthermore, we can make use of the results of CIRC decoding. Each code has the following error correction capability.

① Single-byte error correction
② Double-byte erasure correction

Therefore, there are many possible decoding strategies. For example, by using the erasure correction capability of the codes shown as ②, the following decoding can be applicable.

$$\mathbf{C}_1② \rightarrow \mathbf{C}_2② \rightarrow \mathbf{C}_1② \rightarrow \mathbf{C}_2② \rightarrow \cdots$$

In order to guard against miscorrection in ②, the CRC code checks these miscorrections and detects uncorrectable errors. The above decoding strategy can attain the same bit-error rate as the commercial magnetic disk or tape units [SAKO 85, IMAI 88].

Another CD–ROM example system that has 2.6 gigabytes of disk capacity adopts both an interleaved distance-5 R–S code and a cyclic redundancy check (CRC) code for every 512 bytes of user data, called a sector [TSUN 83]. Fig. 6.22 shows one sector of this code design format.

In this system, a (39, 35) distance-5 R–S code **C** over $GF(2^8)$ is adopted, and therefore any double bytes can be corrected. According to Fig. 6.22, the interleaved R–S code can correct up to 30 byte errors in a sector. In addition, this system

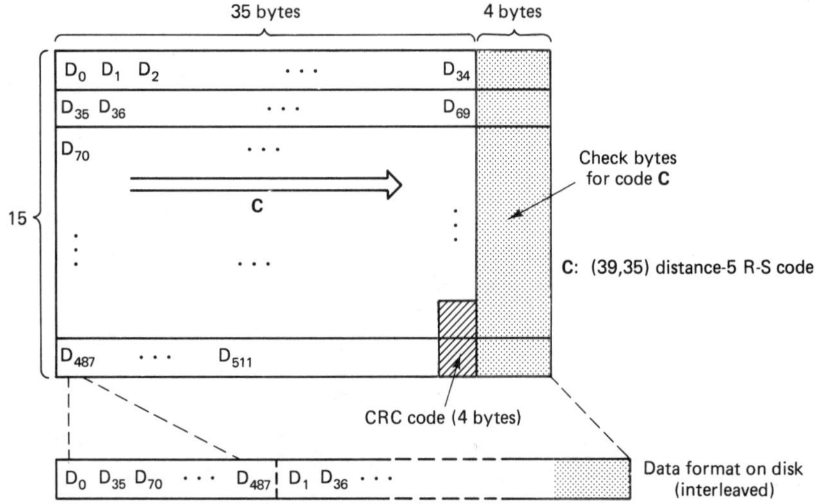

Figure 6.22 Interleaved code design format for CD–ROM.

adopts a CRC code (one with four check bytes) that checks the data corrected by R–S codes, and then guards against miscorrection of the uncorrectable errors that exceed the error correction capability of the R–S codes. The CRC code is appended at the end of the user data shown in Fig. 6.22.

Another type of optical disk system, the *Write Once Read Many optical disk* (*CD-WORM*), with a diameter of 5.25 in, has recently been proposed for application to computer mass memories. With these disks, there are two types of error distribution: one is caused by a short burst error (less than 10 bits) with a high rate and the other by a long burst error (10–100 bits) with a low rate [SAIT 86]. The following strategies have been proposed for correcting these types of errors: the large distance ($d \approx 17$) R–S code with 120 to 140 bytes code length, interleaved to degree 4 to 10, and the product code using two (distance 3 to 5) R–S codes, which result in a distance 15 to 25 code, with 30 to 50 bytes of code length [YAMA 86, KURT 87].

The recently developed *erasable optical disks*, which are a magneto-optical recording type, have similar error characteristics, and therefore large distance R–S codes can be effectively applied to them as well [FUNK 87, ITAO 87, KATO 87].

6.3 BUBBLE MEMORY CODES

In order to increase the reliability of the magnetic bubble memories, some error correction schemes have been applied to the modules that include the high-density bubble memory devices, or to the device as a whole. Some of these use Hamming SEC–DED codes [BOSS 72, CHEN 79, SAIT 82, YOSH 84], and the others use Fire codes that correct up to a 5-bit burst error with 14 check bits in each codeword

[LEE 79] or double-byte error correcting codes [BOUR 73]. Some coding schemes that append error correcting codewords to parallel multiple data are introduced in this section.

Byte error correcting codes [BOUR 73]. The bubble memory organization is such that bubble chips have a bit-per-chip organization and they are installed in basic modules. Therefore, this organization manifests itself as multiple-bit errors in a single b-bit byte of the data word when a single basic module fails. Each b-bit byte in the data word is further subdivided into two $b/2$-bit bytes. Here, we use a double $b/2$-bit byte error correcting code using $2b$ check bits. The **H** matrix of this code is shown as follows:

$$\mathbf{H} = \begin{bmatrix} \mathbf{I} & \mathbf{I} & \cdots & \mathbf{I} & \cdots & \mathbf{I} & \mathbf{I} & \mathbf{0} & \mathbf{0} & \mathbf{0} \\ \mathbf{T} & \mathbf{T}^2 & \cdots & \mathbf{T}^j & \cdots & \mathbf{T}^k & \mathbf{0} & \mathbf{I} & \mathbf{0} & \mathbf{0} \\ \mathbf{T}^2 & \mathbf{T}^4 & \cdots & \mathbf{T}^{2i} & \cdots & \mathbf{T}^{2k} & \mathbf{0} & \mathbf{0} & \mathbf{I} & \mathbf{0} \\ \mathbf{T}^3 & \mathbf{T}^6 & \cdots & \mathbf{T}^{3j} & \cdots & \mathbf{T}^{3k} & \mathbf{0} & \mathbf{0} & \mathbf{0} & \mathbf{I} \end{bmatrix}$$

where

$$k \leq 2^{b/2} - 2, \quad k\text{: even}$$

$\mathbf{I} = (b/2 \times b/2)$ identity matrix.

$\mathbf{T} = (b/2 \times b/2)$ companion matrix defined by the primitive polynomial of degree $b/2$.

Number of check bits used $= 2b$.

Maximum number of information bits $= (b/2)(2^{b/2} - 2)$.

Minimization of circuitry for decoding (i.e., for error byte pointer and error pattern generation) can be achieved by selecting the columns of the **H** matrix with each pair of adjacent columns $(1, 2)$ $(3, 4)$ $\ldots$ $(k - 1, k)$ of the form

$$\begin{bmatrix} \mathbf{I} & \mathbf{I} \\ \mathbf{T}^i & \mathbf{T}^i + \mathbf{I} \\ \mathbf{T}^{2i} & (\mathbf{T}^i + \mathbf{I})^2 \\ \mathbf{T}^{3i} & (\mathbf{T}^i + \mathbf{I})^3 \end{bmatrix}$$

with care being taken to ensure that no two columns of the entire **H** matrix are identical.

Let the syndrome S be expressed as four $b/2$-bit vectors S_1, S_2, S_3, and S_4.

$$S = \begin{bmatrix} S_1 \\ S_2 \\ S_3 \\ S_4 \end{bmatrix}, \quad S_1 = \begin{bmatrix} s_1 \\ \vdots \\ s_{b/2} \end{bmatrix} S_2 = \begin{bmatrix} s_{b/2+1} \\ \vdots \\ s_b \end{bmatrix} S_3 = \begin{bmatrix} s_{b+1} \\ \vdots \\ s_{3b/2} \end{bmatrix} S_4 = \begin{bmatrix} s_{3b/2+1} \\ \vdots \\ s_{2b} \end{bmatrix}$$

It can be shown that if the $b/2$-bit bytes i and j $(i, j < k)$ of the word W are in error (with error pattern E_i and E_j, respectively), then the error-byte-pointer equation for $g_{i,j}$, $(i, j) \in \{(1,2),(3,4),\ldots,(k-1,k)\}$ becomes

$$g_{i,j} = [S_3 = S_2 + \mathbf{B} \cdot S_1] \cdot [S_4 = S_3 + \mathbf{B} \cdot S_2]$$

with

$$\mathbf{B} = \mathbf{T}^i \cdot (\mathbf{T}^i + \mathbf{I})$$

In this case, $g_{i,j} = 1$ only when both relations of $S_3 = S_2 + \mathbf{B} \cdot S_1$ and of $S_4 = S_3 + \mathbf{B} \cdot S_2$ are satisfied. The error patterns for the $b/2$-bit bytes i, j become

$$E_i = (\mathbf{T}^i + \mathbf{I}) \cdot S_1 + S_2$$

$$E_j = E_{i+1} = \mathbf{T}^i \cdot S_1 + S_2, \qquad i < k$$

The error-byte pointers for the check bytes are given by

$$g_{k+1,k+2} = (S_3 = 0) \cap (S_4 = 0)$$

and

$$g_{k+3,k+4} = (S_1 = 0) \cap (S_2 = 0)$$

The error patterns for the check bytes are given by

$$E_{k+1} = S_1$$
$$E_{k+2} = S_2$$
$$E_{k+3} = S_3$$
$$E_{k+4} = S_4$$

These error-byte pointers and the error pattern so obtained have the following properties.

1. In a code space, all $g_{i,j} = 1$ and all $E_l = 0$, $1 \le l \le k + 4$.
2. In a single $b/2$-bit byte error space, exactly one $g_{i,j} = 1$ and either $E_i \ne 0$ or $E_j \ne 0$, E_l's, $(l \ne i, j)$ are zeros.
3. In a single b-bit byte error space, exactly one $g_{i,j} = 1$, and $E_i \ne 0$ and $E_j \ne 0$.
4. In a double $b/2$-bit byte error space, all $g_{i,j} = 0$.

Knowing which group is in error from the error-byte pointers $g_{i,j}$ and the error patterns to be corrected, the correction circuit performs single-byte error correction according to the following equations.

$$\hat{d}_{i,l} = d_{i,l} \oplus g_{i,i+1} \cdot e_{i,l}, \qquad 1 \le l \le b/2$$

$$\hat{d}_{i+1,l} = d_{i+1,l} \oplus g_{i,i+1} \cdot e_{i+1,l}, \qquad i = 1,3,5,\ldots,k+3$$

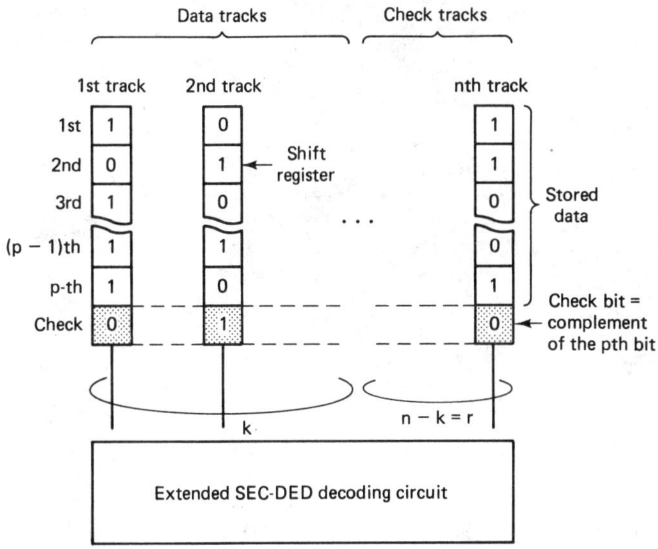

Figure 6.23 Bubble memory error correction scheme.

for the b-bit byte consisting of the $b/2$-bit bytes i, $i + 1$ where

$$E_i = \begin{bmatrix} e_{i,1} \\ \vdots \\ e_{i,l} \\ \vdots \\ e_{i,b/2} \end{bmatrix}$$

and $d_{i,l}$ is the lth bit of the ith $b/2$-bit byte.

SEC-DED codes with extended decoding. Another bubble memory system uses SEC–DED codes. Because bubble memory is a typical shift register type memory, if a defect occurs in a shift register, then the likelihood is very great that *the data stored throughout the register will be erroneous*, because every bit on the register would have to be circulated through the defective point in order to complete one cycle. For example, if there is a stuck-at-1 fault in one of the shift registers, then the readout serial data would be 1 1 1... (i.e., unidirectional errors, see Section 7.3).

We now consider such a type of memory module, shown in Fig. 6.23, that contains k shift registers (i.e., k tracks, for storing k information bits in parallel) and $r = n - k$ shift registers (i.e., r tracks, for r check bits of the SEC–DED code in parallel). These shift registers are shifted cyclically and periodically, and the n-bit word readout is checked and corrected by the SEC–DED decoding circuit.

To determine which tracks are stuck, each track or shift register in Fig. 6.23 contains a check bit immediately succeeding the pth bit. This check bit is a

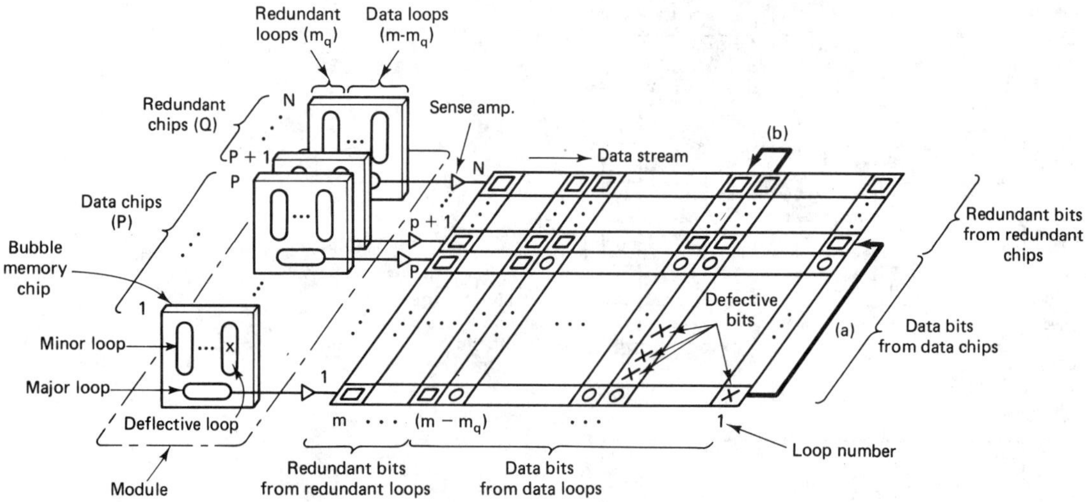

Figure 6.24 Redundancy organization of the bubble memory [SAIT 82]. © 1982 IECE Japan.

complement of the pth bit [BOSS 72]. This check bit may be inserted into the shift register by a technique that involves inverting the binary value of the pth bit and putting this value into the $(p + 1)$th position in the track. This may be accomplished during the workup period, when data is initially loaded into the track. Therefore, as there always is such a check bit in each track, we detect the faulty tracks easily by finding that both pth and $(p + 1)$th bits are "1 1" or "0 0." By this scheme, we can determine faulty track positions, and then this information can be used as error indicators. By using these indicators, two or three errors can be corrected according to the algorithm shown in Fig. 4.7. The "extended SEC–DED decoding circuit" (in Fig. 6.23) includes the circuits for detecting these faulty tracks and generating error indicators. If we read out n bits from the n tracks, this set of n bits should be a codeword of the SEC–DED code. Also, it would be better to use an even-weight-row SEC–DED code because the complement of a codeword is also a codeword (see Section 4.4.3), and hence the word consisting of n $(p + 1)$th bits of the n tracks becomes a codeword.

SEC-DED codes utilizing spare loops and chips. In high-density bubble memory chip, *spare loops* are provided in order to tolerate some faulty loops, and to improve the yield of the chip. In addition to these spare loops in each chip, a large-capacity bubble memory unit may have provision for spare chips, in order to switch the faulty chips out and switch in the spare ones [IIDA 79] (shown in Fig. 6.24).

This redundancy scheme gives the following two-step switching mechanism.

(a) The faulty loop in one of the data chips is exchanged to the loop in the redundant chip that shares its loop number.

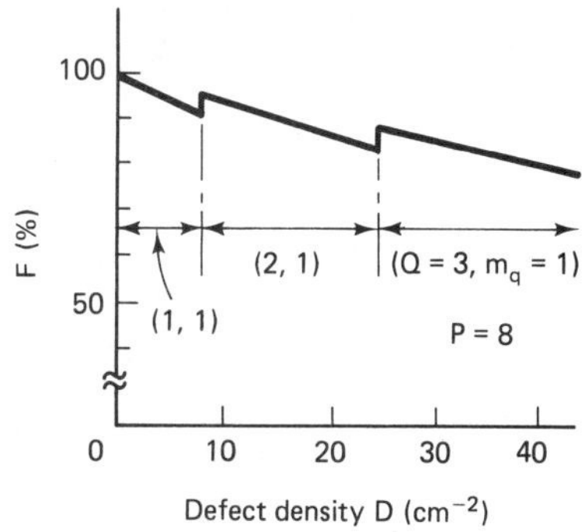

Figure 6.25 Ratio of the unused redundant loops F vs. defect density D [SAIT 82]. © 1982 IECE Japan.

(b) If the faulty loops cannot be tolerated by the above method, then the set of loops having the same loop number and including these faulty loops is exchanged to the adjacent set of loops.

These switching schemes are also shown in Fig. 6.24. In this redundancy organization, there are usually many unused spare loops, because many more are provided at the design stage than the average number of faulty loops encountered during use.

A new idea is to make use of these unused spare loops to store check bits of error correcting codes [SAIT 82]. This would improve reliability with minimum increase in cost. If there are not enough spare loops available for the code, because some spare loops have already been used for exchange with faulty loops, then coding cannot be applied to the place.

One can evaluate the probability that an error correcting code can be applied to the data under specific defect density. This probability is called an *encoding probability* P_c. Before evaluating this, we have to obtain the number of unused spare loops for some specific number of defects. Fig. 6.25 shows this relation for a bubble memory unit that includes eight data chips ($P = 8$), each having 256K-bits capacity, 256 loops, and a chip area of 0.342 cm^2. Here, F shows the ratio of the number of unused spare loops to the total number of spare loops in the spare chips. (Q is the number of spare chips and m_q is the number of spare loops in each chip.) Also, (Q, m_q) shows the redundancy organization that gives the minimum module cost determined by the defect density [SAIT 82]. This figure says that more than 80% of the spare loops are still remaining unused when the defect density D is less than 40 particles/cm^2. We assume that the defects are based on the model of Poisson distribution.

Fig. 6.26 shows the encoding probability P_c versus number of data bits k. Here, it is assumed that the number of data chips P equals 8, and the number of redundant chips Q equals 2. A data block is constructed from some data groups. Each data group is defined as the set of information bits that are read/written at the same timing point. This is shown in Fig. 6.27. Hence, the number of data bits k is equal to ($g \times P$), where g is the number of data groups. A codeword is formed for these k data bits. Fig. 6.27 also shows the use of redundant bits when there are some defective bits. Check bits of the codeword are stored in the remaining redundant

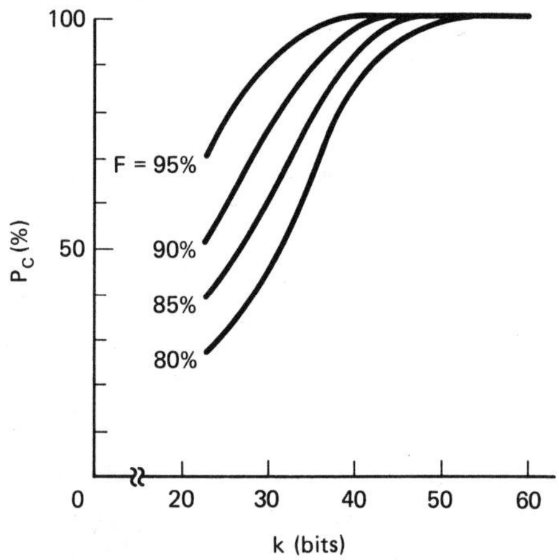

Figure 6.26 Encoding probability P_c vs. number of data bits k [SAIT 82]. © 1982 IECE Japan.

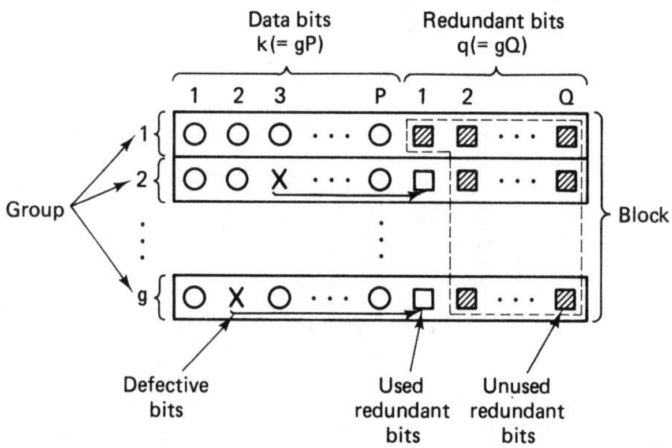

Figure 6.27 Data block [SAIT 82]. © 1982 IECE Japan.

bits. As shown in Fig. 6.26, we can get high encoding probability by increasing k, even when F is 80%.

Fig. 6.28 shows the improvement of the error rate versus ratio of the unused redundant loops. Improvement of error rate is defined as $\log(E_0/E)$, where E_0 is the average error bit rate in the chip, and E is the error bit rate when SEC–DED code is applied to the module. In this figure, E_0 is assumed to be 10^{-12}/bit.

For a bubble memory unit that uses chips each having defect density 8 particles/cm^2, the ratio of unused redundant loops is about 95%. When the SEC–DED code for data bit length $k = 56$ bits is applied to the module, the improvement in error rate is improved by an order of 6. In this case, the module cost increase is only about 2%. For more detailed information, refer to [SAIT 82].

6.4 UNIDIRECTIONAL ERROR CODES FOR MASS MEMORIES

If unidirectional errors are the most dominant type of errors in a mass memory, then unidirectional error detecting/correcting codes are preferable from the standpoint of economics (i.e., they require a low redundancy check bit number and

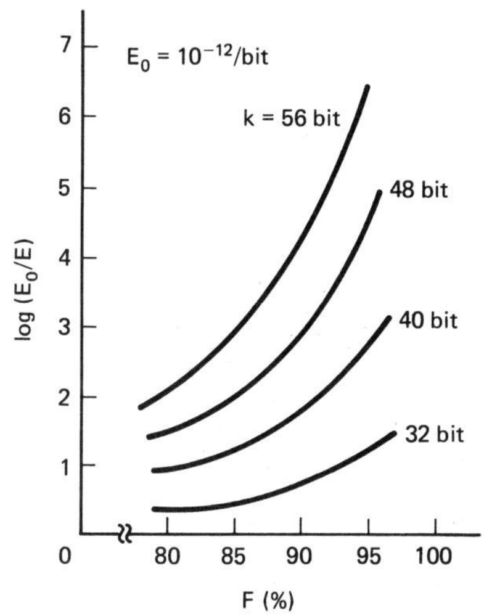

Figure 6.28 Improvement of the error rate vs. ratio of the unused redundant loops [SAIT 82]. © 1982 IECE Japan.

simpler decoding hardware). Such errors are particularly characteristic of the shift register type of memory, such as the magnetic bubble memory or the CCD (charge coupled device) memory, in which a stuck-at-1 or stuck-at-0 fault in a single cell will result in a constant 1 or 0 output from the corresponding shift register. This is because every bit on the track has to be circulated through the defective point in order to complete one shift cycle. In tape or disk memories, burst error due to dust particles, minute scratches, and defects in the coating will also sometimes result in unidirectional errors.

For these memories, arithmetic error codes are extremely effective for detecting unidirectional errors [WAKE 75, PARH 78]. An appropriate code is a two-dimensional one based on an *arithmetic redundancy check* (*ARC*) and a vertical redundancy check (VRC) that provides correction of multiple unidirectional errors in any one track of a large block of characters [GOTO 80, BOSE 84b]. This coding scheme is a modification of the code based on a cyclic redundancy check (CRC) and a VRC [BROW 70]. An extended two-dimensional error correction scheme using ARCs is proposed in [BOSE 84c] and [AVIZ 83, 86]. In ARC, we use arithmetic error codes, and hence we call these codes "*ARC codes*." The improvement attained by using an arithmetic check is that the information rate (i.e., the ratio of the information-bit length to the codeword length) is much higher than that of the CRC code. This scheme is discussed in detail in Section 7.4 of this book.

EXERCISES

6.1. Implement the syndrome (S_2) generation circuit for ORC in the 9-track tape unit by using the backward shifting register. In this case, suppose that the data successively received are C', B_1', B_2', ..., B_6', B_7' bytes in this order, and the syndrome S_2 equation and the matrix $\mathbf{T}^7$ are shown as follows.

$$S_2 = \mathbf{T}^{-7} \cdot (\mathbf{T}^7 \cdot C') \oplus \sum_{i=1}^{7}{}^{\oplus} \mathbf{T}^{i-7} \cdot (\mathbf{T}^7 \cdot B_i')$$

$$\mathbf{T}^7 = \begin{bmatrix} 0 & 1 & 0 & 0 & 1 & 1 & 1 & 1 \\ 0 & 0 & 1 & 0 & 0 & 1 & 1 & 1 \\ 0 & 0 & 0 & 1 & 0 & 0 & 1 & 1 \\ 0 & 1 & 0 & 0 & 0 & 1 & 1 & 0 \\ 0 & 1 & 1 & 0 & 1 & 1 & 0 & 0 \\ 0 & 1 & 1 & 1 & 1 & 0 & 0 & 1 \\ 0 & 0 & 1 & 1 & 1 & 1 & 0 & 0 \\ 1 & 0 & 0 & 1 & 1 & 1 & 1 & 0 \end{bmatrix}$$

6.2. In AXP code, consider the case in which set A is being corrected for errors in a known erroneous track and another unknown track in set A begins to be affected by errors. Show that this second unknown erroneous track can be detected and both erroneous tracks of set A can be corrected, provided that set B has at most one known erroneous track.

6.3. Design the encoding circuit of the MSS code shown in Equation (6.25) with

$$\mathbf{T}^{\lambda} = \mathbf{T}^{68} = \begin{bmatrix} 00001000 \\ 10001100 \\ 01000110 \\ 00101011 \\ 10010101 \\ 01000010 \\ 00100001 \\ 00010000 \end{bmatrix}$$

6.4. Prove that the code adopted in MSS (shown in (6.25)) has the following characteristics.

(a) If the code is used for correction of single-byte errors, then it does not miscorrect any combination of two one-bit errors.

(b) If the code is used for correction of single-bit errors, then it does not miscorrect any combination of a one-byte error with one-bit error in another byte.

6.5. For the Fire code generated by $\mathbf{g}(x) = (x^9 + 1)(x^5 + x^2 + 1)$, do the following.

(a) Obtain the code length of this code.

(b) Obtain the burst error correction length of this code.

(c) Suppose that the error burst $\mathbf{b}(x) = x^6 + x^5 + x^4 + x^3 + x^2$ has occurred. Show the decoding procedure of this case using a high-speed decoding method.

(d) Design the high-speed decoder of this code.

6.6. Design the high-speed decoder for the code generated by $\mathbf{g}(x) = (x^{11} + 1)(x^3 + x + 1)(x^4 + x + 1)$. Determine the error detection and correction capability of this code.

6.7. In CIRC systems, assume that half of the data information shown below are in errors. Indicate the correction procedure by using the codes $\mathbf{C}_1$ and $\mathbf{C}_2$, each having minimum Hamming distance $d_{\min} = 3$.

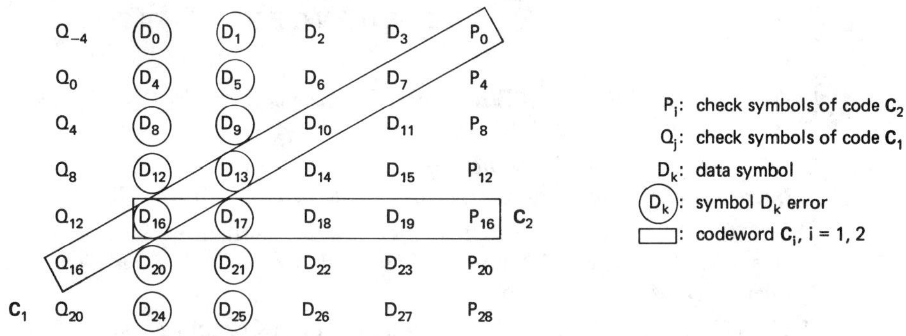

6.8. Determine the error correction capability of the CIRC in which the codes $\mathbf{C}_1$ and $\mathbf{C}_2$ both have a minimum Hamming distance $d_{\text{min}} = 2$.

6.9. Design the extended SEC–DED decoding circuit shown in Fig. 6.23.

6.10. **(1)** Show that the following (20, 12) two-dimensional code with parity check bits 16, 13, 10, 11, 15, 19, 3, 7 can correct any burst error of length up to 3 bits in readout data if the bits are read diagonally instead of horizontally (i.e., readout order: $0 \to 1 \to 2 \to 3 \to \ldots \to 19$). The horizontal syndrome is represented by a vector $(h_0, h_1, h_2, h_3, h_4)$, where h_i is modulo-2 sum of all the received bits in row i. Similarly, the vertical syndrome is represented by a vector (v_0, v_1, v_2, v_3), where v_j is modulo-2 sum of the received bits in column j.

0	17	14	11	h_0
4	1	18	15	h_1
8	5	2	19	h_2
12	9	6	3	h_3
16	13	10	7	h_4
v_0	v_1	v_2	v_3	

(5 × 4, 4 × 3) code

(2) Prove the following generalized relation [BLAU 86]. The $(k_2 + 1) \times (k_1 + 1)$ two-dimensional code, in which the last row and the last column contain parity bits, can correct any burst error of length up to k_1 if and only if bits are read diagonally and $k_2 \geq 2(k_1 - 1)$.

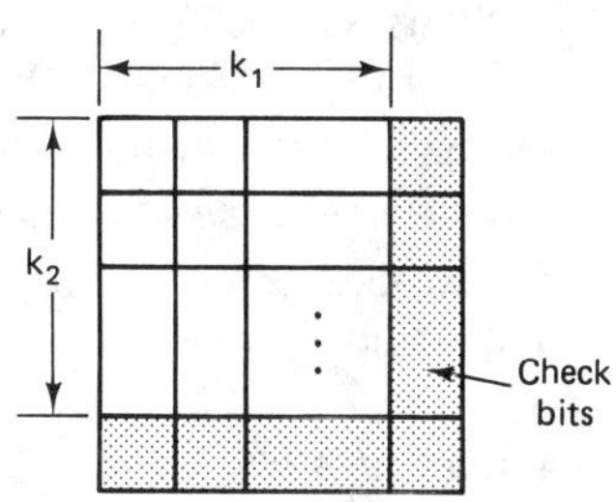

$((k_2 + 1) \times (k_1 + 1), k_1 k_2)$ code

REFERENCES

[ADI 84] W. Adi. "Fast Burst Error-Correction Scheme with Fire Code." *IEEE Transactions on Computers* C-33 (July 1984): 613–18.

[AVIZ 83] A. Avizienis. "Two-Dimensional Low-Cost Arithmetic Error Codes." *Dig., Sixth International Symposium on Comput. Arithmetic* (June 1983): 169–72.

[AVIZ 86] A. Avizienis. "Two-Dimensional Low-Cost Arithmetic Residue Codes: Effectiveness and Arithmetic Algorithms." *Dig., 16th Annual Int. Symposium Fault Tolerant Comput.* (June 1986): 330–36.

[BERL 80] E. R. Berlekamp. "The Technology of Error Correcting Codes." *Proceedings of the IEEE* 68 (May 1980): 564–93.

[BERL 82] E. R. Berlekamp. "Bit-serial Reed-Solomon Encoders." *IEEE Transactions on Information Theory* IT-28, (November 1982): 869–74.

[BLAU 85] M. Blaum and R. J. McEliece. "Coding Protection for Magnetic Tapes: A Generalization of the Patel-Hong Code," *IEEE Transactions on Information Theory* IT-31 (September 1985): 690–93.

[BLAU 86] M. Blaum, P. G. Farrell, and H. C. A. van Tilbory. "A Class of Burst Error-Correcting Array Codes." *IEEE Transactions on Information Theory* IT-32, (November 1986): 836–39.

[BOSE 84b] B. Bose and T. R. N. Rao. "Unidirectional Error Codes for Shift-Register Memories." *IEEE Transactions on Computers* C-33 (June 1984): 575–78.

[BOSE 84c] B. Bose. "Two Dimensional ARC Codes." *Dig., 14th Int. Symposium Fault-Tolerant Comput.* (June 1984): 324–29.

[BOSS 72] D. C. Bossen, R. A. Henle, M. Y. Hsiao, G. A. Maley, and W. D. Pricer. "System for Expanded Detection and Correction of Errors in Parallel Binary Data Produced by Data Tracks." U.S. Patent 3675200 (July 4, 1972).

[BOUR 73] W. G. Bouricius, W. C. Carter, E. P. Hsieh, D. C. Jessep, Jr., and A. B. Wadia. "Modelling of a Bubble-Memory Organization with Self-Checking Translators to Achieve High Reliability." *IEEE Transactions on Computers* C-22 (March 1973): 269–75.

[BREN 84] R. P. Brent and H. T. Kung. "Systolic VLSI Arrays for Polynomial GCD Computation." *IEEE Transactions on Computers* C-33 (August 1984): 731–36.

[BROW 70] D. T. Brown and F. F. Sellers. "Error Correction for IBM 800-bit-per-inch Magnetic Tape." *IBM Journal of Research and Development* 14 (July 1970): 384–89.

[CHEN 79] C. H. Chen. "A Bipolar Microprocessor Based Bubble Memory Controller." *Proceedings of IEEE COMPCON* (Fall 1979): 417–24.

[CHIE 69] R. T. Chien. "Burst-Correcting Codes with High-Speed Decoding." *IEEE Transactions on Information Theory* IT-15 (January 1969): 109–13.

[DENG 87] R. H. Deng and D. J. Costello, Jr. "Decoding of DBEC-TBED Reed-Solomon Codes." *IEEE Transactions on Computers* C-36 (November 1987): 1359–63.

[DOI 79] T. Doi, K. Odaka, G. Fukuda, and S. Furukawa. "Cross Interleave Code for Error Correction of Digital Audio Systems." *Proceedings of the Sixty-Fourth AES Convention* (November 1979).

[FIRE 59] P. Fire. *A Class of Multiple-Error-Correcting Binary Codes for Non-Independent Errors*. Sylvania Report no. RSL-E-2. Mountain View, Calif.: Sylvania Electronic Defense Laboratory, Reconnaissance, Systems Division, 1959.

[FUNK 87] A. W. Funkenbusch, T. A. Rinehart, D. W. Siitari, Y. S. Hwang, and R. N. Gardner. "Magneto-Optics Technology for Mass Storage Systems." *Dig., 8th IEEE Symposium on Mass Storage Systems* (May 1987): 101–6.

[GOTO 80] M. Goto. "Rates of Unidirectional 2-Column Errors Detectable by Arithmetic Codes." *Dig., 10th Annual Int. Symposium Fault-Tolerant Comput.* (October 1980): 21–25.

[HODG 80] P. Hodges, W. J. Schaeuble, and P. L. Shaffer. "Error Correcting System for Serial by Byte Data." U.S. Patent no. 4185269 (January 22, 1980).

[HORI 75b] T. Horiguchi and K. Morita. "A High Performance Burst Correcting System in Peripheral Devices." *Proceedings of the Second USA-Japan Computer Conference* (1975): 118–21.

[HOWE 84] T. D. Howell. "Analysis of Correctable Errors in the IBM3380 Disk File." *IBM Journal of Research and Development* 28 (March 1984): 206–11.

[HSIA 81] M. Y. Hsiao, W. C. Carter, J. W. Thomas, and W. R. Stringfellow. "Reliability, Availability and Serviceability of IBM Computer Systems: A Quarter Century of Progress." *IBM Journal of Research and Development* 25 (September 1981): 453–65.

[HSU 84] I. S. Hsu, I. S. Reed, T. K. Truong, K. Wang, C. S. Yeh, and L. J. Deutsh. "The VLSI Implementation of a Reed-Solomon Encoder Using Berlekamp's Bit-Serial Multiplier Algorithm." *IEEE Transactions on Computers* C-33 (October 1984): 906–11.

[IIDA 79] K. Iida, M. Saito, and K. Furukawa. "An 8 Mbyte Magnetic Bubble Memory." *IEEE Transactions on Magn.* MAG-15 (November 1979): 1892–94.

[IMAI 88] H. Imai, ed. Chaps. 7 & 8 in *Essentials of Error-Correcting Coding Techniques*. New York: Academic Press, 1988.

[INOU 78] T. Inoue, Y. Sugiyama, K. Ohnishi, T. Kanai, and K. Tanaka. "A New Class of Burst-Error-Correcting Codes and Its Application to PCM Tape Recording Systems." *Proc. National Telecommunications Conference* (1978): 20.6.1–20.6.5.

[ITAO 87] K. Itao, A. Yamaji, S. Hara, and N. Izawa. "Magneto-Optical Mass Storage System with 130mm Write-Once Disk Compatibility." *Dig., 8th IEEE Symposium on Mass Storage Systems* (May 1987): 92–97.

[IWAM 88] K. Iwamura, H. Imai, and Y. Dohi. "A Construction Method for Reed-Solomon Codec Suitable for VLSI Design." *Transactions of the IEICE Japan* J71-A (March 1988): 751–59.

[KATO 87] O. Kato, K. Kurosawa, K. Iwakuni, and M. Shimbo. "Development of Error Correction Method and LSI for Optical Disk Data Storage System." *Paper of Technical Group on Computer Architecture*. IPS Japan (September 1987): 67–73.

[KIMU 86] M. Kimura, H. Imai and Y. Doi. "Systolic Decoder for Reed-Solomon Codes" (in Japanese). *Transactions of the IECE of Japan* J69-A (March 1986): 421–28.

[KURT 87] C. Kurtz. "Development of a High-Capacity Performance Optical Storage System." *Dig., 8th IEEE Symposium on Mass Storage Systems* (May 1987): 107–11.

[LEE 79] D. Lee and M. Newman. "A High Density Bubble Memory System." *Proceedings of COMPCON* (September 1979): 412–16.

[LEIS 84] E. L. Leis. "Data Integrity in Digital Optical disks." *IEEE Transactions on Computers* C-33 (September 1984): 818–27.

[LIN 83] S. Lin and D. J. Costello, Jr. Chap. 16.2 in *Error Control Coding: Fundamentals and Applications*. Englewood Cliffs, N.J.: Prentice Hall, 1983.

[OHNI 86] K. Ohnishi, K. Sugiyama, and Y. Ishida. "An LSI for Reed-Solomon Encoder/Decoder." *Proceedings of the Eightieth AES Convention*. (March 1986): no. 2316.

[OKAN 87] H. Okano and H. Imai. "A Construction Method of High-Speed Decoders Using ROMs for Bose-Chaudhuri-Hocquenghem and Reed-Solomon Codes." *IEEE Transactions on Computers* C-36 (October 1987): 1165–71.

[PARH 78] B. Parhami and A. Avizienis. "Detection of Storage Errors in Mass Memories Using Low-Cost Arithmetic Error Codes." *IEEE Transactions on Computers* C-27 (April 1978): 302–8.

[PATE 74] A. M. Patel and S. J. Hong. "Optimal Rectangular Code for High Density Magnetic Tapes." *IBM Journal of Research and Development* 18 (November 1974): 579–88.

[PATE 80] A. M. Patel. "Error Recovery Scheme for the IBM3850 Mass Storage System." *IBM Journal of Research and Development* 24 (January 1980): 32–42.

[PATE 85] A. M. Patel. "Adaptive Cross-Parity (AXP) Code for a High-Density Magnetic Tape Subsystem." *IBM Journal of Research and Development* 29 (November 1985): 546–62.

[PATE 86] A. M. Patel. "On-the-fly Decoder for Multiple Byte Errors." *IBM Journal of Research and Development* 30 (May 1986): 259–69.

[REED 60] I. S. Reed and G. Solomon. "Polynomial Codes over Certain Finite Fields." *Journal Soc. Ind. Appl. Math.* 8 (June 1960): 300–04.

[SAIT 82] M. Saito, S. Furukawa, and M. Nunotani. "Error Correction Using Redundant Loops in a Magnetic Bubble Memory" (in Japanese). *Transactions of the IECE Japan* J65-D (July 1982): 819–25.

[SAIT 86] M. Saito, T. Takeda, and M. Nunotani. "An Evaluation of Error Correcting Codes for Optical Disks" (in Japanese). *Paper of Technical Group* IT86-48. *IECE Japan*, 1986.

[SAKO 85] Y. Sako, T. Suzuki, T. Furuya, and S. Furukawa. "Data Quality of CD-ROM" (in Japanese). *Paper of Technical Group* IT85-31. *IECE Japan*, 1985.

[TANA 80] K. Tanaka, M. Ozaki, T. Inoue, and T. Yamaguchi. "On a Tape Format for Reliable PCM Multi-Channel Tape Recorders." *Proceedings of the Sixty-Sixth AES Convention* (May 1980): no. 1669.

[TSUN 83] Y. Tsunoda, M. Miyazaki, and S. Abe. "Large Capacity Optical Disk File Unit" (in Japanese). *Nikkei Electronics* (November 21, 1983): 189–213.

[VRIE 80] L. B. Vries, K. A. Imink, J. G. Nibor, H. Hoeve, T. Doi, K. Okada, and H. Ogawa. "The Compact Disc Digital Audio System—Modulation and Error Correction." *Proceedings of the Sixty-Seventh AES Convention* (October 1980): no. 1674 (H-8).

[WAKE 75] J. F. Wakerly. "Detection of Unidirectional Multiple Errors Using Low-Cost Arithmetic Codes." *IEEE Transactions on Computers* C-24 (February 1975): 210–12.

[WANG 85] C. C. Wang, T. K. Truong, H. M. Shao, L. J. Deutsh, J. K. Omura, and I. S. Reed. "VLSI Architectures for Computing Multiplications and Inverse in $GF(2^m)$." *IEEE Transactions on Computers* C-34 (August 1985): 709–16.

[YAMA 86] A. Yamagishi. "Encoder and Decoder LSIs for BCH Code and RS Code" (in Japanese). *Proceedings of 1986 Workshop on Coding Theory and Its Applications* WCTA86-2 (August 1986).

[YEH 84] C. S. Yeh, I. S. Reed and T. K. Truong. "Systolic Multipliers for Finite Fields $GF(2^m)$." *IEEE Transactions on Computers* C-33 (April 1984): 357–60.

[YOSH 84] Yoshida and M. Sugie. "A CMOS Bubble Memory Controller" (in Japanese). *Nikkei Electronics* (July 2, 1984): 161–94.

7

Asymmetric and Unidirectional Error Codes

This chapter begins with an examination of the concepts of channel models, asymmetric errors, and unidirectional errors, which are important in many types of memory technologies and logic circuits, such as PLA's and error-tolerant fail-safe designs. Sections 7.1 and 7.2 cover some classic code construction methods.

Section 7.3 covers fundamental theory of unidirectional errors and discusses systematic and nonsystematic types of *all-unidirectional error detecting* (*AUED*) *codes*. The *m-out-of-n codes* and *Berger codes* are introduced in that section. Section 7.4 covers the theory of *t-error correcting and all-unidirectional error detecting* (*tEC–AUED*) *codes*: it discusses code construction and illustrates the special case of *single-error correcting and all-unidirectional error detecting* (*SEC–AUED*) *codes*. These are also shown to be double (bidirectional) error detecting, and thus these are designated the *SEC–DED–AUED* class of codes.

In Section 7.5 a practical application of *t*EC–AUED codes (also called semidistance codes) for address decoder logic of large ROM chips is presented. The code is used to mask single asymmetric errors in the bus lines of the memory address decoder.

Section 7.6 covers a class of codes, *ARC codes*, that enable detection and correction of multiple unidirectional errors confined to one track of multitrack (or two-dimensional array) organized memories, such as magnetic tapes and bubble memories.

7.1 INTRODUCTION

Some semiconductor large-scale integrated (LSI) nonvolatile memory technologies are single-transistor-cell memories and metal-nitride-oxide semiconductor (MNOS) memories. A description of the two types of memories has been given in [COHE 71] and [CRIC 73]. These memories are nonvolatile—they retain information for long periods of time despite power failures or power shutoffs.

Failures in the cells of these memories are most likely caused by leakage of the charge, since a charge cannot be created except by a rewrite process. Therefore, these memory cells are apt to exhibit unidirectional failures. Although the rest of the memory system—the address decoding, the cell selection, the gating logic, and so on—is subject to symmetric failures, for the overall memory system, the probability of "1 → 0" crossover failure (called the 1-error) is significantly greater than the "0 → 1" crossover failure (called the 0-error). Such memories are referred to here as asymmetric memories. The following discussion of asymmetric error codes is derived from the work of Constantin and Rao [CONS 79].

Asymmetric memories are best modeled by the binary asymmetric channel shown in Fig. 7.1, with probability α of the 1-error and probability β of the 0-error, where $\alpha \neq \beta$, $\alpha, \beta < \frac{1}{2}$. For a special case when $1 \gg \alpha \gg \beta$, it is possible to assume β to be 0, particularly for codes of small block length; when $\alpha^2 > \beta$, the probability of erroneous decoding for a single 1-error correcting code is of the same order of magnitude as the one for a single symmetric error correcting code. For the symmetric error model, the binary symmetric channel model is used (i.e., $\alpha = \beta$).

To substantiate this, consider a codeword containing n_1 1's and n_0 0's ($n_1 + n_0 = n$). The probability of erroneous decoding for a single (symmetric) error correcting code (due to undetectable double errors) is given by

$$P_s(e) \approx \binom{n_1}{2}\alpha^2 + \binom{n_0}{2}\beta^2$$

The probability of erroneous decoding for a single 1-error correcting (asymmetric) code is given by

$$P_a(e) \approx \binom{n_1}{2}\alpha^2 + n_0\beta$$

Since $\alpha^2 > \beta > \beta^2$, both $P_s(e)$ and $P_a(e)$ are of the same order of magnitude,

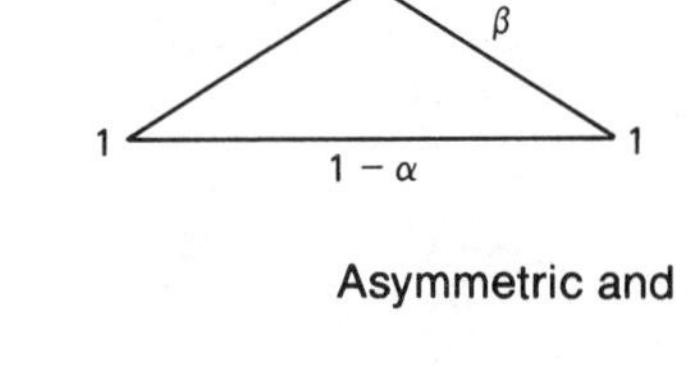

Figure 7.1 The binary asymmetric channel.

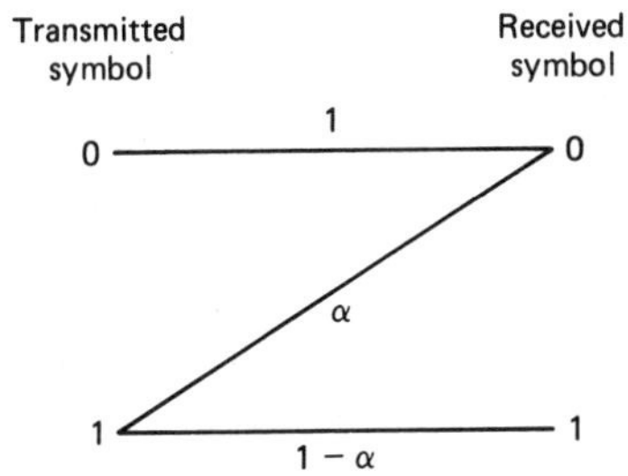

Figure 7.2 The ideal binary asymmetric channel (Z channel).

namely, $O(\alpha^2)$. Thus, it is most appropriate to consider the model of an ideal binary asymmetric channel, shown in Fig. 7.2.

The design of single asymmetric error (1-error or 0-error) correcting codes for the ideal binary asymmetric channel is the topic for this section; the method described involves maximizing the number of codewords in a single 1-error (0-error) correcting code of a given length n.

The asymmetric nature of the new type of channel requires a new concept of distance between two binary vectors. The Hamming distance utilized for the study of the binary symmetric channel, is now replaced by the *asymmetric distance*, defined as follows. This concept has been introduced in Chapter 1 but is repeated here for convenience.

Definition 7-1 [RAO 75, ANDE 71]. The *asymmetric distance*, $d_a(X, Y)$, between two binary n-tuples X and Y is defined as

$$d_a(X, Y) = \max\{N(X, Y), N(Y, X)\} \tag{7.1}$$

where $N(X, Y)$ = number of components of X and Y with $x_i = 1$ and $y_i = 0$, that is,

$$N(X, Y) = \sum_{i=0}^{n-1} x_i \bar{y}_i$$

$$N(Y, X) = \sum_{i=0}^{n-1} y_i \bar{x}_i$$

Using the foregoing notations, the Hamming distance $d(X, Y)$ between two binary n-tuples X and Y can be expressed as $d(X, Y) = N(X, Y) + N(Y, X)$.

The asymmetric distance has in fact the properties of a metric and thus can rightly be called a distance. (See Exercise 7.1 at the end of the chapter.)

The following theorem from [RAO 75] relates the asymmetric distance to the error correcting capabilities of the code.

Theorem 7-1. *A binary code* **C** *of asymmetric distance d is capable of correcting $d - 1$ or fewer 1-errors (or 0-errors). It is therefore called a $(d - 1)$ asymmetric error correcting code.*

Proof. Without loss of generality, we can assume that asymmetric errors are 1-errors. For any codeword $X \in \mathbf{C}$, let $\mathbf{S}_X$ denote the set of vectors obtained from X by introducing t 1-errors, for $0 \le t \le d - 1$. Consider two codewords $X, Y \in \mathbf{C}$; since $d_a(X, Y) \ge d$, without loss of generality we can assume $N(X, Y) \ge d$. Clearly, Y cannot become X by any number of 1-errors. Also $d - 1$ or fewer 1-errors can not take X to Y or into $\mathbf{S}_Y$. That is, $\mathbf{S}_X$ and $\mathbf{S}_Y$ are disjoint and the code can correct up to $d - 1$ asymmetric errors. Q.E.D.

For example, consider a code $\mathbf{C}$ with four codewords $X_1 = 0000$ and $X_2 = 1100$, $X_3 = 0011$, and $X_4 = 1111$. The asymmetric distance of the code is 2. Considering $t = 1$ and the channel as a 1-error channel, we have $\mathbf{S}_{X_1} = \{0000\}$, $\mathbf{S}_{X_2} = \{1100, 0100, 1000\}$, $\mathbf{S}_{X_3} = \{0011, 0001, 0010\}$, $\mathbf{S}_{X_4} = \{1111, 0111, 1011, 1101, 1110\}$, and they are disjoint. For any received vector Z, it is decoded to X_i if and only if $Z \in \mathbf{S}_{X_i}$.

A generalized version of Theorem 7-1 for the binary asymmetric channel can also be obtained.

Theorem 7-2. *A binary code of asymmetric distance d is capable of correcting t_1 or fewer 1-errors and t_0 or fewer 0-errors, where t_1 and t_0 are fixed and $t_1 + t_0 < d$.*

The proof of this theorem is rather long and is not required for an understanding of the rest of this chapter. It is not given here but can be found in [CONS 77].

Single 1-error (0-error) correcting codes are here called single asymmetric error correcting (SAEC) codes. For SAEC codes, the subject of this section, the minimum asymmetric distance required between any two codewords X and Y of the code is, according to Theorem 7-1, $d_a(X, Y) \ge 2$. This is less restrictive than the minimum Hamming distance of 3 required for the single-error correcting codes for the binary symmetric channel. In fact, the following lemma gives a relationship between the asymmetric distance and the Hamming distance and comes easily from the Definition 7-1.

Lemma 7-1. $d(X, Y) \ge d_a(X, Y) = \max(N(X, Y), N(Y, X)) \ge (N(X, Y) + N(Y, X))/2 = d(X, Y)/2$.

Since $d(X, Y) \ge 3$ implies $d_a(X, Y) \ge 2$, we should be able to derive, for any given n, a SAEC code of length n having more codewords (i.e., a higher information rate) than the single-error correcting Hamming code of length n. And indeed, W. K. Kim and C. V. Freiman [KIM 59] obtain slightly higher information rates for most length n codes. Even higher information rates were achieved by R. R. Varshamov (1965, 1966); his technique is based on assigning weights 1 through n to the n positions of a binary vector of length n and then identifying as a single 1-error correcting code those binary vectors V for which the scalar product $V \cdot (1, 2, \ldots, n)$ is equal to a fixed residue mod $(n + 1)$. In particular, Varshamov states that for a given n, the code corresponding to the 0 residue mod $(n + 1)$ has the highest information rate, although he offers no formal proof of this in his paper.

S. D. Constantin and T. R. N. Rao [CONS 79] generalize Varshamov's codes and give a theoretical foundation for a much broader class of codes. The information rates achieved by these codes for a given length n are at least as high as for Varshamov's codes and in many instances are higher.

Other research in this area, as found in [BERG 61], [FREI 61, 63], and [GORD 63], has taken a different direction from that discussed here. Generalizations to multiple error correcting codes were also given in [VARS 73] and [MCEL 73]. Borden has extended some of these results to a q-ary asymmetric channel [BORD 82]. In this section, however, we restrict ourselves to binary single 1-error correcting codes.

7.2 CONSTANTIN – RAO SAEC CODES

The development here relies mainly on the theory of Abelian groups, and their structure is evidently inherited from the structure of the Abelian groups that generated them. These codes are also called *group-theoretic codes* [CONS 79].

Without loss of generality, we assume the Abelian groups we deal with in this chapter to be additive (i.e. the group operation is denoted by "+").

Consider an Abelian group $\mathbf{G}$ of order $n+1$ having elements a_0, $a_1, \ldots, a_n$ ($a_0 = 0$ the identity element). Let $\mathbf{V}$ denote the set of all binary n-tuples. We define a mapping L: $\mathbf{V} \to G$ as follows.

$$\text{For any } V = (\delta_1, \ldots, \delta_n) \in \mathbf{V}, \qquad L(V) = \sum_{i=1}^{n} \delta_i \cdot a_i,\ a_i \in G$$

Here, $L(V)$ is called a linear combination of V (with respect to the nonzero elements of G). It is rather simple to observe that the mapping L is onto G. Furthermore, we define the subsets $\mathbf{V}_i$ $(i = 0, 1, 2, \ldots, n)$ of $\mathbf{V}$ as follows.

$$\mathbf{V}_i = \{U \in \mathbf{V} | L(U) = a_i\}$$

Clearly, $\mathbf{V}_i \cap \mathbf{V}_j = \varnothing$ for $i \neq j$ and $\mathbf{V}_0 \cup \mathbf{V}_1 \cup \cdots \cup \mathbf{V}_n = \mathbf{V}$. Therefore, L partitions $\mathbf{V}$ into $n+1$ disjoint subsets.

Example 7-1

Let G be the group of integers under addition modulo 5. We denote $a_0 = 0$, $a_1 = 1$, $a_2 = 2$, $a_3 = 3$, $a_4 = 4$, and $+$ is addition modulo 5. Also, let $\mathbf{V}$ be the set of all 4-tuples. Then the set $\mathbf{V}$ is partitioned by mapping L as follows.

$$\mathbf{V}_0 = \{(0,0,0,0), (1,0,0,1), (0,1,1,0), (1,1,1,1)\}$$
$$\mathbf{V}_1 = \{(1,0,0,0), (0,1,0,1), (1,1,1,0)\}$$
$$\mathbf{V}_2 = \{(0,1,0,0), (0,0,1,1), (1,1,0,1)\}$$
$$\mathbf{V}_3 = \{(0,0,1,0), (1,1,0,0), (1,0,1,1)\}$$
$$\mathbf{V}_4 = \{(0,0,0,1), (1,0,1,0), (0,1,1,1)\}$$

Since the subsets $\mathbf{V}_i$ $(i = 0, 1, \ldots, n)$ are disjoint and exhaust the set $\mathbf{V}$, we have the following.

Lemma 7-2. *At least one of the subsets* $\mathbf{V}_0, \mathbf{V}_1, \ldots, \mathbf{V}_n$ *has cardinality greater than or equal to* $2^n/(n+1)$, *that is,*

$$|\mathbf{V}_i| \geq 2^n/(n+1) \qquad \textit{for some } i \in \{0,1,2,\ldots,n\}$$

Proof. There are 2^n n-tuples in $\mathbf{V}$, and $\mathbf{V}$ is partitioned into $n+1$ disjoint subsets $\mathbf{V}_0, \mathbf{V}_1, \ldots, \mathbf{V}_n$. Therefore, the average number of elements in these subsets is $2^n/(n+1)$. Therefore, the maximum cardinality of some $\mathbf{V}_i \geq 2^n/n+1$. Q.E.D.

There are other questions one can address with respect to the size of the sets $\mathbf{V}_i$. However, we defer them to a subsequent section, and instead we look at the asymmetric distance between vectors in set $\mathbf{V}_i$, as follows.

Lemma 7-3. *The asymmetric distance between any two vectors* V *and* U *of* $\mathbf{V}_i$ *is greater than or equal to* 2:

$$D_a(V,U) \geq 2,\ U, V \in \mathbf{V}_i, \qquad U \neq V$$

Proof. Suppose there exist two vectors $V, U \in \mathbf{V}_i$, between which there is an asymmetric distance of 1. The following two cases are then possible.

Case (*a*). The two vectors V and U differ in two positions k and h as follows.

$$V = (\delta_1, \delta_2, \ldots, \delta_{k-1}, 1, \delta_{k+1}, \ldots, \delta_{h-1}, 0, \delta_{h+1}, \ldots, \delta_n)$$
$$U = (\delta_1, \delta_2, \ldots, \delta_{k-1}, 0, \delta_{k+1}, \ldots, \delta_{h-1}, 1, \delta_{h+1}, \ldots, \delta_n)$$

Since $V, U \in \mathbf{V}_i$, we have $L(V) = L(U) = a_i$. Also $L(V) - L(U) = a_k - a_h$. Thus, we have $a_k - a_h = a_i - a_i = a_0$. We reach a contradiction, since $a_k \neq a_h$ for $k \neq h$.

Case (*b*). The two vectors differ in only one position k, as follows.

$$V = (\delta_1, \delta_2, \ldots, \delta_{k-1}, 1, \delta_{k+1}, \ldots, \delta_n)$$
$$U = (\delta_1, \delta_2, \ldots, \delta_{k-1}, 0, \delta_{k+1}, \ldots, \delta_n)$$

and this leads to

$$L(V) - L(U) = a_k = a_0$$

Again, we reach a contradiction because $a_k \neq a_0$ for $k = 1, 2, 3, \ldots, n$. Therefore, the asymmetric distance between any two vectors V, U in a set $\mathbf{V}_i$, for any $i = 0, 1, 2, \ldots, n$, is at least 2. Q.E.D.

Thus, from Theorem 7-1 and Lemma 7-3 we can conclude that the sets of vectors $\mathbf{V}_0$, $\mathbf{V}_1, \ldots,$ and $\mathbf{V}_n$, individually, can be used as SAEC codes.

The correction procedure for an erroneous codeword is straightforward. Indeed, if $\mathbf{V}_i$ is selected as the asymmetric code, and if a single 1-error occurs in a codeword $U \in \mathbf{V}_i$, resulting in a vector U', $U' \in \mathbf{V}_j$, then the position k in error is located by the simple calculation $a_k = a_i - a_j$. A fixed order imposed on the elements of an Abelian group G will thus make k easy to find. Once k is obtained, we change the 0 in the kth position of U' into a 1 and we obtain the desired codeword U.

Example 7-2

To illustrate the decoding, consider the set of codewords belonging to the code $\mathbf{V}_0$ of Example 7-1. Now let us assume the received word to be $U' = (0, 0, 0, 1)$. Then

$$L(U') = 0 + 0 + 0 + 4 = 4$$

and hence $U' \in \mathbf{V}_4$. The error position is found from calculating

$$0 - 4 = 1$$

Thus, we learn that the first bit of U' is in error, and hence the transmitted codeword U corresponding to the received word U' is

$$U = (1, 0, 0, 1) \in \mathbf{V}_0$$

A comparison based on the number of codewords in a single-error correcting code is made between the Hamming code, the Kim–Freiman code, the Varshamov code (the group $G = Z_n$) and the Constantin–Rao code. The results are shown in Table 7.1.

In each previous discussion of a group-theoretic code, we have listed the cardinality of the set V_0. Several remarks on the results shown in this table are made in the next sections.

Best SAEC codes. In this section, we are interested in finding the "best" SAEC group-theoretical code(s). The attribute "best" is given to the code that has the largest number of codewords for the given block length n.

This problem is actually threefold; three independent questions can be raised, the answers to which can be found in [MCEL 80].

1. Which Abelian group G (if several exist) of order $(n + 1)$ generates the set $\mathbf{V}_i$ of n-tuples with the largest number of codewords in it?
2. Given that G is the Abelian group of order $(n + 1)$ that generates the set $\mathbf{V}_i$ of largest cardinality, which of the $(n + 1)$ sets, $\mathbf{V}_0, \mathbf{V}_1, \mathbf{V}_2, \ldots, \mathbf{V}_n$, is $\mathbf{V}_i$?
3. What is a general closed form expression for the size of a set $\mathbf{V}_j$, $j = 0, 1, 2, \ldots, n$? More specifically, it would be satisfactory to know just a closed form expression for the size of the set $\mathbf{V}_i$ of the largest cardinality.

Let us consider first the second question, to which a complete solution is given here. This also gives us a better understanding of what is to be done in order to answer the first question.

The answer to the second question is given by the following theorem, whose proof is rather long and not important for understanding the rest of the material presented here; it is therefore omitted. The interested reader may find it in [CONS 79].

TABLE 7.1 NUMBER OF CODEWORDS FOR SAEC CODES [CONS 79]

n	Number of Codewords			Constantin–Rao Code	
Code Length	Hamming Code	Kim–Freiman Code	Varshamov Code[a]	Group	Number of Codewords
2	1	2	2	Z_3	2
3	2	2	2	Z_4 or $Z_2 \times Z_2$	2
4	2	$2 + 2 = 4$	4	Z_5	4
5	$2^2 = 4$	$2^2 + 2 = 6$	6	$Z_6 \equiv Z_2 \times Z_3$	6
6	$2^3 = 8$	$2^3 + 2^2 = 12$	10	Z_7	10
7	$2^4 = 16$	$2^3 + 2^2 = 12$	16	$Z_8 \times Z_2 \times Z_3$	16
8	$2^4 = 16$	$2^4 + 2^3 = 24$	30	$Z_3 \times Z_3$	32[b]
9	$2^5 = 32$	$2^5 + 2^3 = 40$	52	$Z_{10} \equiv Z_2 \times Z_5$	52
10	$2^6 = 64$	$2^4 + 2^4 = 80$	94	Z_{11}	94
11	$2^7 = 128$	$2^7 + 2^4 = 144$	172	$Z_2 \times Z_2 \times Z_5$	172
12	$2^8 = 256$	$2^8 + 2^5 = 288$	316	Z_{13}	316
13	$2^9 = 512$	$2^9 + 2^5 = 544$	586	$Z_{14} \equiv Z_2 \times Z_7$	586
14	$2^{10} = 1024$	$2^{10} + 2^6 = 1088$	1096	$Z_{15} \equiv Z_3 \times Z_5$	1096
15	$2^{11} = 2048$	$2^{10} + 2^6 = 1088$	2048	$Z_2 \times Z_2 \times Z_2 \times Z_2$	2048
16	$2^{11} = 2048$	$2^{11} + 2^7 = 2176$	3856	Z_{17}	3856
17	$2^{12} = 4096$	$2^{12} + 2^7 = 4224$	7286	$Z_3 \times Z_3 \times Z_2$	7296[b]
18	$2^{13} = 8192$	$2^{13} + 2^8 = 8448$	13798	Z_{19}	13798
19	$2^{14} = 16834$	$2^{13} + 2^8 = 8448$	26216	$Z_2 \times Z_2 \times Z_5$	26216
20	$2^{15} = 32768$	$2^{14} + 2^9 = 16896$	49940	$Z_{21} \equiv Z_3 \times Z_7$	49940

[a] The Varshamov code is equivalent to the C–R code generated by $G \equiv Z_{n+1}$.
[b] C–R codes have a better information rate than the Varshamov codes. More information on how these codes can be found is given in the next section.

Theorem 7-3. *For any Abelian group G of order n + 1, the following relation holds.*

$$|\mathbf{V}_0| \geq |\mathbf{V}_i|, \qquad i = 1, 2, \ldots, n$$

1. For a given n, which Abelian group G (when more than one group exists) of order $n + 1$ generates the set $\mathbf{V}_0$ with the most number of vectors (n-tuples) in it?

The question is irrelevant for the case $n + 1 = p$, p prime, since there exists only one Abelian group of order p, namely Z_p. The same is true when $n + 1$, the order of the Abelian group G, is square free. As the Fundamental Theorem of Abelian groups shows, there exists only one Abelian group of order $n + 1$, namely,

$$Z_{p_1} \times Z_{p_2} \times \cdots \times Z_{p_k}$$

where $n + 1 = P_1 \cdot P_2 \ldots P_k$ is the prime decomposition of $n + 1$; $P_i \neq P_j$. $Z_a \times Z_b$ denotes the cross product of the two groups Z_a and Z_b.

There is further discussion on this and other topics in [CONS 79], [MCEL 80], [DELS 81], and [KLOV 81a, 81b].

Notes on Section 7.2. Questions 1 to 3 above concerning the best Constantin–Rao SAEC codes are completely solved by [MCEL80]. The results are rather simple:

1. The size $|\mathbf{V}_0|$ is given by

$$|\mathbf{V}_0| = \frac{1}{2(n+1)} \sum_{o(h)=\text{odd}} 2^{(n+1)/o(h)}$$

the summation in the above expression being extended over all elements $h \in G$ whose order $o(h)$ is odd. Other main results are

$$|\mathbf{V}_g| \le |\mathbf{V}_0|, \quad \text{with equality if and only if } o(g) \text{ is a power of 2.}$$

$$|\mathbf{V}_0| \le (2^n + n2^{(n-2)/3})/(n+1)$$

with the equality if and only if $n + 1$ is a power of 3 and G is an elementary Abelian group.

It is also shown that among all Abelian groups of order $n + 1$, $|\mathbf{V}_0|$ is maximized only by those groups whose odd Sylow subgroups are elementary Abelian.

2. Extensions to the m-ary ($m \ge 2$) SAEC including the enumeration method for the code size have been done by [STAN73] and [HELL81].
3. [DELS81b] has given an extension to m-ary t-asymmetric error correcting codes ($1 \le t < m$). This work includes the definition of m-ary asymmetric distance, an extension of Varshamov's t-asymmetric error correcting code, and the enumeration method for the number of codewords. But it has not succeeded in deriving a simple expression for the number of codewords like in [MCEL80] in the general case.

7.3 UNIDIRECTIONAL ERROR CODES

In this section, we are concerned with unidirectional error detecting codes. The first part will cover all-unidirectional error detecting (AUED) codes. There are two types of codes: one systematic AUED and the other nonsystematic AUED codes. These are discussed in the following section after presentation of some basic theory and the notation used here. In Section 7.3.2, we discuss systematic *d-unidirectional error detecting (dUED) codes*. Following that will be t-error correcting and all-unidirectional error detecting (tEC–AUED) codes. We get some examples of encoding and decoding procedures for single-error correcting and all-unidirectional error detecting (SEC–AUED) codes.

7.3.1 Basic Theory of Unidirectional Error Codes

To recall the notation we stated earlier, $N(X, Y)$ represents the number $1 \to 0$ crossovers from X to Y. That is, $N(X, Y)$ is the number of positions i for which $x_i = 1$ and $y_i = 0$. For example, when $X = (10101)$ and $Y = (10010)$, $N(X, Y) = 2$ and $N(Y, X) = 1$. The asymmetric distance $d_a(X, Y)$ defined earlier for these words is

$$d_a(X, Y) = \max[N(X, Y), N(Y, X)] = 2$$

Definition 7-2. For vectors $X = (x_1, \ldots, x_n)$ and $Y = (y_1, \ldots, y_n)$, X is said to *cover* Y if for all i, $y_i = 1$ implies $x_i = 1$. We can write this as $Y \leq X$.

If $X \leq Y$ and $Y \leq X$, then X and Y are said to be *unordered*. If $X \leq Y$ or $Y \leq X$, then they are an *ordered pair*. For $X_1 = (1011)$ and $Y_1 = (1001)$, then $Y_1 \leq X_1$. Also, $X_2 = (1010)$ and $Y_2 = (0110)$ are unordered. Also, if X and Y are an ordered pair, then their $d_a(X, Y) = d(X, Y)$, the Hamming distance. If they are unordered, $d_a(X, Y) < d(X, Y)$. For detecting unidirectional errors in a code the following theorem from Bose and Rao [BOSE 82a] is easily proved.

Theorem 7-4. *A code* **C** *is capable of detecting all unidirectional errors (i.e., it is a AUED code) if and only if every pair $X, Y \in$* **C** *are unordered.*

The proof is simple and is based on the fact that a codeword X cannot become another codeword Y because of any number of 1-errors (or 0-errors). Two important classes of AUED codes are known: *Berger codes* [BERG 61] and *m*-out-of-*n* (also called constant weight) codes. These are discussed below.

***m*-out-of-*n* codes.** These codes are also called constant weight codes. Early examples of them have been studied as computer number systems (as binary coded decimal systems; see Example 7-3). These codes are nonsystematic, based on the definition given in Chapter 3, and are also nonlinear. But, for any given n, the number of codewords (of weight m) is given by $\binom{n}{m} = n!/((n-m)!m!)$. For the code $m = \lfloor n/2 \rfloor$ or $\lceil n/2 \rceil$ this number is maximized. The class of $\lfloor n/2 \rfloor$-out-of-n codes has the highest possible information rate among all AUED codes and is therefore called an optimal class of AUED codes [ANDE 71]. There is considerable interest in the application of m-out-of-n codes for computer systems. The research in applications and derivation of self-checking checkers using m-out-of-n codes are discussed in Chapters 8 and 9 of this book.

Example 7-3

BCD Digit	2-out-of-7 Code	2-out-of-5 Code
0	01 00001	00011
1	01 00010	00101
2	01 00100	00110
3	01 01000	01001
4	01 10000	01010
5	10 00001	01100
6	10 00010	10001
7	10 00100	10010
8	10 01000	10100
9	10 10000	11000

Berger codes. This class of AUED codes is the systematic type and has been shown to have an advantage in encoding and decoding logic [BERG 61]. We adopt the standard notation of (n, k) block codes here, although Berger used a different notation in his classic paper. For the codeword $[a_0, \ldots, a_{k-1}, a_k, \ldots, a_{n-1}]$, $(a_0 \ldots a_{k-1}) = I$ is the information part, and $(a_k \ldots a_{n-1}) = \beta(I)$ is the check part, which we will call the *Berger check* here. The Berger check, $\beta(I)$, is the binary number representing the number of 0's in I. The number of check bits r required is given by $r = n - k = \lceil \log_2 k + 1 \rceil$, e.g., for a 6-bit ($k = 6$) information, $r = \lceil \log_2 6 + 1 \rceil = 3$.

Alternately, the Berger check $\beta(I)$ can be given as the complement of the number of 1's in I without altering the code's properties. For this chapter, however, we adopt the former definition that $\beta(I)$ is the number of 0's in I.

For example, for information $I = 101101$, the number of 0's is 2, and hence the Berger check $\beta(I) = 010$. Thus, (101101010) is its codeword. Consider a unidirectional error channel with only 1-errors. The number of 0's in the information part may only increase (if errors occur); therefore, the Berger check must increase for the result to be a codeword. However, the check cannot increase due to errors because of the assumption that only 1-errors can occur. Therefore, any number of 1-errors cannot take a codeword into another codeword. Similarly, it is shown that multiple 0-errors are also detected by this code.

Berger check(s) are important and form the basis for the construction of systematic classes of tEC–AUED codes to be covered in Section 7.4. The number of bits in a Berger check is $\lceil \log_2(k + 1) \rceil$, which is smaller than the number of check bits for the Hamming SEC code, which is $\lceil \log_2(n + 1) = \lceil \log_2(k + r + 1) \rceil$. The following theorem will be of interest [BOSE 80, PRAD 86].

Theorem 7-5. *The Berger codes are optimal systematic AUED codes, in the sense that the information rate k/n is the highest possible for any information block length k.*

Proof. We can consider the following k-bit information blocks without any loss of generality.

$$\begin{array}{c} 00\ldots000 \\ 00\ldots001 \\ 00\ldots011 \\ 00\ldots111 \\ \vdots \\ 01\ldots111 \\ 11\ldots111 \end{array}$$

There are $k + 1$ blocks, and no two of these blocks can have the same Berger check, since if they did those two words are ordered and the code is not AUED. Therefore, there has to be at least $k + 1$ different Berger checks and the number of check bits required is $\geq \lceil \log_2(k + 1) \rceil$. That proves the optimality. Q.E.D.

***d*-UED codes.** We discuss a class of codes given by Bose and Lin [BOSE 85] as *d*-unidirectional detecting (*d*-UED) codes. Berger codes are systematic codes that detect all unidirectional errors. For systematic codes that detect up to *d* unidirectional errors, the following theorem applies [BOSE 85].

Theorem 7-6. *A code* **C** *is a d-UED code if and only if for any pair of codewords* $X, Y \in \mathbf{C}$, X, Y *are either unordered or the Hamming distance between them is at least* $d + 1$.

The proof of this theorem is rather simple and is left as an exercise at the end of this chapter.

The code construction for 2-UED and 3-UED codes is a modification of the Berger check. The check symbol (cs) is derived by counting the number of 0's in the k information bits and taking modulo 2^d of that count for $d = 2$ and $d = 3$, respectively. (see Exercise 7.4 at the end of the chapter.) These codes are shown to be optimal in the sense that every systematic *d*-UED code for $d = 2$ or 3 requires at least *d* check bits. [BOSE 85] also derives *d*-UED codes with four check bits capable of detecting up to six unidirectional errors. Improvements in the code construction technique that yield higher efficiencies are given in [JHA 87]. Also given are codes with more than four check bits for larger values of *d*. For further details on code construction and encoding/decoding, the reader is referred to [BOSE 85] and [JHA 87].

7.4 SEC–AUED CODES

The class of codes of practical interest would be single-error correcting and all-unidirectional error detecting (SEC–AUED) codes. These codes can be compared with the popular SEC–DED codes that now dominate applications in computer memories. The early work on SEC–AUED codes is of the nonsystematic type and is by Pradhan and Reddy [PRAD 77], Bose [BOSE 80], and Bose and Rao [BOSE 82a]. Also, systematic SEC–AUED codes and more general *t*EC–AUED (*t*-error correcting and all-unidirectional error detecting) codes have also been reported in [PRAD 80], [BOSE 80], [BOSE 81], and [NICO 86]. Obviously, from the standpoint of applications, the systematic *t*EC–AUED codes will be of greatest interest, although the nonsystematic types have in many cases somewhat superior information rates. We will discuss here some introductory theory and illustrate it with examples. The researcher interested in this topic will be referred to the original papers. The following establishes the necessary and sufficient conditions for codes to be *t*UEC or *t*EC–AUED.

Theorem 7-7. *A code* **C** *can correct t or fewer unidirectional errors* (*i.e.*, **C** *is tUEC*), *if and only if for all* $X, Y \in C$,

$$
\begin{aligned}
d_a(X, Y) &\geq 2t + 1 \qquad \text{for } X, Y \text{ an ordered pair} \\
d_a(X, Y) &\geq t + 1 \qquad \text{for } X, Y \text{ unordered}
\end{aligned}
\tag{7.2}
$$

Proof. Let $\mathbf{S}_{X_0}$ and $\mathbf{S}_{X_1}$ denote the set of all words obtained from a codeword X due to t or fewer (possibly zero) 0-errors and 1-errors, respectively. Then, $\mathbf{S}_X = \mathbf{S}_{X_0} \cup \mathbf{S}_{X_1}$ ($\cup$ denotes union here) is the set of words obtained from X due to t or fewer unidirectional errors. What is then required for the proof is that for all $X, Y \in \mathbf{C}$ the condition (7.2) is equivalent to the condition

$$\mathbf{S}_X \cap \mathbf{S}_Y = \varnothing \qquad (\cap: \text{intersection}, \ \varnothing: \text{empty set}) \tag{7.3}$$

Consider X and Y in **C** satisfying (7.2). If they are ordered, then $d_a(X, Y) = d(X, Y) = 2t + 1$ and, trivially, $\mathbf{S}_X \cap \mathbf{S}_Y = \varnothing$, and therefore the code can correct t unidirectional errors in them. If they are unordered, then $d_a(X, Y) \geq t + 1$. Also, $\mathbf{S}_X \cap \mathbf{S}_Y = (\mathbf{S}_{X_0} \cup \mathbf{S}_{X_1}) \cap (\mathbf{S}_{Y_0} \cup \mathbf{S}_{Y_1}) = (\mathbf{S}_{X_0} \cap \mathbf{S}_{Y_0}) \cup (\mathbf{S}_{X_0} \cap \mathbf{S}_{Y_1}) \cup (\mathbf{S}_{X_1} \cap \mathbf{S}_{Y_0}) \cup (\mathbf{S}_{X_1} \cap \mathbf{S}_{Y_1})$. Each of these intersections can be shown to be empty, and therefore their union is the empty set, giving us once again $\mathbf{S}_X \cap \mathbf{S}_Y = \varnothing$, as required.

Conversely, if any $X, Y \in \mathbf{C}$ is an ordered pair with $d(X, Y) \leq 2t$, then it is easy to show that $\mathbf{S}_X \cap \mathbf{S}_Y \neq \varnothing$. Similarly for the unordered case, $d_a(X, Y) \leq t$, $\mathbf{S}_X \cap \mathbf{S}_Y \neq \varnothing$. Therefore, **C** cannot correct t unidirectional errors and therefore conditions (7.2) are necessary. That completes the proof. Q.E.D.

It is to be noted that if a code is capable of correcting (detecting) t symmetric errors, this implies, trivially, that it can also correct (detect) t unidirectional errors. That is, a tEC code is also a tUEC code. A tUEC code can correct t asymmetric errors (i.e., it is tAEC). The following theorem establishing the necessary and sufficient conditions for tEC–AUED is deemed important.

Theorem 7-8. *A code* **C** *is tEC–AUED if and only if*

$$N(X, Y) \geq t + 1 \qquad \text{for all } X, Y \in \mathbf{C} \tag{7.4}$$

Proof. Let $\mathbf{S}_X$ be the set of all vectors obtained from X due to t symmetric errors, as before, and $\mathbf{R}_X$ be the set of all vectors obtained from X due to $t + 1$ or more unidirectional errors. To prove the theorem, we need to show

$$\mathbf{S}_X \cap \mathbf{S}_Y = \varnothing, \qquad \text{all } X, Y \in \mathbf{C}, \tag{7.5}$$

and

$$\mathbf{S}_X \cap \mathbf{R}_Y = \varnothing \qquad \text{for all } X, Y \in \mathbf{C} \tag{7.6}$$

The proof for (7.5) is the same as in Theorem 7-7. To prove (7.6) consider $X' \in \mathbf{S}_X$ and $Y' \in \mathbf{R}_Y$. If $X' = Y'$, it is easy to show that $N(X, Y)$ or $N(Y, X) \leq t$,

TABLE 7.2 ORDERED AND UNORDERED CODES

Unordered Codes						Ordered Code		
2UEC			SEC–AUED			SEC–DED		
	1000	0111		1100	0011		0000	1111
SEC	0000	1111	SEC	0100	1011	SEC	1000	0111
	1100	0011		1000	0111		0100	1011
	1010	0101		1110	0001		0010	1101
	1001	0110		1101	0010		0001	1110
						DED	1100	
2UEC	1110	0001					1010	
	1101	0010	2UED	0000	1111		1001	
	1011	0100					0101	
							0110	
							0011	

which contradicts (7.4). Therefore, $\mathbf{S}_X$ and $\mathbf{R}_Y$ are disjoint, as to be proved. Conversely, if X and Y are two codewords in $\mathbf{C}$, with $N(X, Y) \leq t$, then there can be a vector Z such that $Z \in \mathbf{S}_X$ and $Z \in \mathbf{R}_Y$. This leads to $\mathbf{S}_X \cap \mathbf{R}_Y \neq \varnothing$ and we cannot detect $t + 1$ or more unidirectional errors; therefore (7.4) is a necessary condition. Q.E.D.

Theorem 7-8 is fundamental to the construction of tEC–AUED codes. Bose and Rao [BOSE 82a] give a theorem even stronger in some sense than Theorem 7-8. With condition (7.4), a tEC–AUED can also detect $t + 1$ symmetric errors; this is fairly easy to prove. To illustrate the theory and for better understanding, consider the following simple examples of binary codes of length 4 having just two codewords.

Example Set 7-4

Consider a code with two codewords {1000, 0111}. The code has Hamming distance 4 but an asymmetric distance 3 between the codewords which are also unordered. Therefore, it satisfies (7.2), and it can correct up to two unidirectional errors. The correction can be based on the decoding table (see Table 7.2). Compare this unordered code with the unordered SEC–AUED code {1100, 0011} and the ordered SEC–DED code {0000, 1111}.

The table for SEC–AUED code above does not contain all 4-tuples because the {1010, 1001, 0110, 0101} cannot occur under a unidirectional error model; they are obtained as a result of two bidirectional errors (a 1-error and a 0-error).

7.4.1 Bose–Rao Construction of SEC–AUED Codes

A general theorem applicable for tEC–AUED code using constant weight codes is stated first.

Theorem 7-9. *A constant weight code* **C**, *with minimum Hamming distance* $2t + 2$, *is a tEC–AUED code.*

Proof. Since **C** is a constant weight code with (Hamming) distance $2t + 2$, it is easy to see that $N(X, Y) = N(Y, X) \geq t + 1$ for all $X, Y \in \mathbf{C}$. Therefore, **C** satisfies (7.4), and by Theorem 7-8 it is a tEC–AUED code. Q.E.D.

One can take any distance-4 code and, by selecting the subset of all its codewords of constant weight, get an SEC–AUED code. Further, if we take an SAEC code such as the constant–Rao code and select a subset of codewords that are of constant weight, then we also get an SEC–AUED code.

A method for increasing information rates is given in [BOSE 82]. We start with an m-out-of-n code and select a subset of the codewords using a construction similar to [CONS 79], as illustrated in the simple example that follows.

Example 7-5

Consider **C** the 3-out-of-6 code that has $\binom{6}{3} = 20$ codewords. If we use weights $\{0,1,\ldots,5\}$ from group Z_6, as in the Constantin–Rao code, we obtain a subset $\mathbf{V}_0 \subseteq \mathbf{C}$.

$$\begin{array}{rcccccc} \textit{weights} & 0 & 1 & 2 & 3 & 4 & 5 \\ \hline \end{array}$$

$$\mathbf{V}_0 = \left\{\begin{matrix} 1 & 1 & 0 & 0 & 0 & 1 \\ 1 & 0 & 1 & 0 & 1 & 0 \\ 0 & 1 & 1 & 1 & 0 & 0 \\ 0 & 0 & 0 & 1 & 1 & 1 \end{matrix}\right.$$

Since $\mathbf{V}_0$ is a constant weight code, the Hamming distance between two codewords is even, and they are unordered. If the Hamming distance is 2 between codewords X, Y, it is easy to show they cannot be in $\mathbf{V}_0$. Therefore, the Hamming distance must be at least 4, and they are unordered. This satisfies Theorem 7-9, and hence the code **C** is SEC–AUED.

Note the two main differences between $\mathbf{V}_0$, of the Constantin–Rao SAEC code over Z_6 and this SEC–AUED code. In the SAEC code, the zero weight is not used, and its length is *5*, whereas the SEC–AUED uses zero weight, and its length is *6*. The second difference is that $\mathbf{V}_0$ consists of all vectors that add to *0* in the SAEC code, but in the SEC–AUED code only those of constant weight (3 in this case) are included.

The above example illustrates the construction procedure, and a formal theorem establishing this class of nonsystematic SEC–AUED codes is given in [BOSE 82a].

7.4.2 Systematic *t*EC – AUED Codes

There are two basic approaches to the construction, which are somewhat similar: one given by Bose and Pradhan [BOSE 82b] and one by Nikolos, Gaitanis, and

Philokyprou [NIKO 86]. These two approaches are here illustrated by examples. For more detail, the reader is referred to the original papers.

Bose – Pradhan codes. The tEC–AUED code **C** has the following form:

$X = [B, B_1, B_2, \ldots, B_{t+1}]$

X: codeword in **C**

B: a systematic $2t + 2$ distance codeword

B_1: Berger check on B (i.e., $B_1 = \beta(B)$)

B_i: Berger check on $(B, B_1, \ldots, B_{i-1})$ for $i = 2, \ldots, t + 1$. $B_i = \beta(B, B_1, \ldots, B_{i-1})$

The information bits are part of B, which also contains parities to make it a codeword in a distance $2t + 2$ systematic code. One may employ here a distance $2t + 2$ BCH code or an equivalent code. To illustrate, we consider 3-bit information $I = 110$, and we construct its SEC–AUED codeword X as follows.

$$X = (B \quad B_1 \quad B_2) = \underbrace{110\,1000}_{B}\ \underbrace{100}_{B_1}\ \underbrace{110}_{B_2}$$

B is a codeword of the (7, 3, 4) Hamming code. B_1 is a Berger check on B, and B_2 is a Berger check on (B, B_1). Since B has four zeros, $B_1 = 100$, and since (B, B_1) has six zeros, $B_2 = 110$. It can easily be seen that B_1 and B_2 both require, at most, 3 bits each and that X is a codeword in a (13, 3) systematic SEC–AUED code.

Let $X' = (B', B_1', B_2')$ denote the word obtained due to errors in $X \in \mathbf{C}$. The syndrome $S(X') = (S_0, S_1, S_2)$ is computed as

$$S_0 = \text{parity check syndrome of the Hamming code}$$

$$S_1 = |B_1 - B_1'| \qquad \text{and} \qquad S_2 = |B_2 - B_2'|$$

where B_1' is the Berger check on B' and B_2' is the Berger check on (B', B_1') ($|Y|$ denotes the absolute value of Y). It is easy to show that for any single error in B', the Hamming code is used to correct that single error. If the single error is in one of the Berger checks, then $S_0 = 0$, and correction of the Berger checks is straightforward. The only case of interest is when multiple (two or more) unidirectional errors occur in B. In such a case it is easy to see that both S_1 and S_2 are 2 or greater, and thus it is detected but not corrected.

The approach to decoding of tEC–AUED is similar and is given in [BOSE 82b]. Other construction methods of SEC–AUED codes can be found in [BOSE 82a] and [PRAD 86].

Nikolos – Gaitanis – Philokyprou (NGP) codes [NIKO 86]. The NGP code construction of systematic tEC–AUED codes utilizes multiple Berger checks on a t–EC systematic parity check code and is similar to the Bose–Pradhan codes.

In [NIKO 86], two methods of construction are given, the second being slightly more efficient. From their second method, we derive a simpler method as follows.

Code construction. A codeword $X = (B \quad B_1 \quad B_2 \quad \cdots \quad B_{t+1})$. The components of X are derived as follows.

B: a systematic parity-check code of distance $D = 2t + 1$ for information I

B_1: Berger check of B, $B_1 = \beta(B)$

B_i: $\lfloor B_1/R_i \rfloor$, for $i = 2, 3, \ldots, t + 1$

where

$$R_i = 2i \quad \text{if } i = 2^j \text{ for some } j$$
$$= 2i - 1 \text{ otherwise}$$

We illustrate this construction by means of an example.

Let $X = (B \quad B_1 \quad B_2 \quad B_3 \quad B_4)$ be a codeword in 3EC–AUED NGP code. B is a codeword in a distance-7 code for information I. Then B_1 is the Berger check on B. The check B_2 is $\lfloor B_1/4 \rfloor$, B_3 is $\lfloor B_1/5 \rfloor$, and B_4 is $\lfloor B_1/8 \rfloor$. Table 7.3 shows (14, 3) distance-7 parity-check codewords for B. The first 3 bits of B are information I. The code is a (23, 3) 3EC–AUED code.

The proof of the error correction capability and the decoding algorithm for the codes are given in [NIKO 86]. These are fairly long and complicated, and we will omit them here.

However, since SEC–AUED codes are the most practical class of codes from the standpoint of applications, we illustrate the encoding and decoding by means of an example. Consider 3 bits of information $I = 110$, and its Hamming (distance-3) codeword $B = 110001$. The check $B_1 = \beta(B) = 011$ and $B_2 = \lfloor B_1/4 \rfloor = 0$ the codeword $X = 110\ 001\ 011\ 0$.

The NGP construction thus yields a (10, 3) SEC–AUED with a better information rate than the Bose–Pradhan construction. The decoding logic is to correct if a single error occurs and detect if two or more unidirectional errors occur in X. Let $X' = (B', B_1', B_2')$ be the (possibly) erroneous word corresponding to X.

TABLE 7.3 3EC–AUED CODES [NIKO 86]

B	B_1	B_2	B_3	B_4
000 00000000000	1110	11	10	1
001 11110011000	0111	01	01	0
010 00001111110	0111	01	01	0
011 11111100110	0100	01	00	0
100 11001100011	0111	01	01	0
101 00111111011	0100	01	00	0
110 11000011101	0110	01	01	0
111 00110000101	0111	01	01	0

Let $S = (S_0, S_1, S_2)$ denote the syndrome of X', to be computed and used to decode as follows.

Decoding algorithm for SEC – AUED code

1. $S_0 = 0$, *if* $B'\,H^T = 0$ (*H is the parity matrix of Hamming distance* 3 *code*).
   $= 1$, *if* $B'\,H^T = h_j$; (h_j *is the column of H indicating a single error*).
   $= 2$ *otherwise* (*uncorrectable error detected*).

   Let B'' *denote the codeword resulting from error correction on* B'.
2. $S_1 = w(B_1' \oplus \beta(B''))$.
3. $S_2 = w(B_2' \oplus \lfloor \beta(B')/4 \rfloor)$.

   "$\oplus$" *is EXOR and* $w(X)$ *is the Hamming weight of X.*
4. *Set* $Q = S_0 + S_1 + S_2$ (+ *is ordinary addition*).
5. *If* $Q = 0$, *then there are no errors* (*multiple bidirectional errors are not detected*).
6. *If* $Q = 1$, *then a single error is detected and is corrected using the code logic.*
7. *If* $Q \geq 2$, *then multiple unidirectional errors are detected.*

Let t denote the number of unidirectional errors in X'. It is trivial to show $Q = 0$ when $t = 0$. If $t = 1$ and the error is in B', then $S_0 = 1$, and the corrected codeword $B'' = B$. This gives $S_1 = S_2 = 0$, and $Q = 1$ exactly. On the other hand, if the error is in B_1' or B_2', then $S_0 = 0$, and only one of S_1 and S_2 will be 1 and the other will be zero, thus giving $Q = 1$. It is trivial to correct X' when $t = 1$.

Let $t = 2$. If the two errors are in B', there are two possible cases. One case is when it is an uncorrectable error and $S_0 = 2$. Since $Q = 2$ for that case, it is detected and not corrected. For the case when it is miscorrected as single error, S_0 will be set to 1, and B'' will then have three errors in it. This would make $S_1 \geq 2$ and consequently $Q \geq 3$, leading to our desired result. If both errors are not in B' but are distributed in X' then Q will also be ≥ 2 and is detected. Let $t \geq 3$. Here, one needs to go over all (too many) possible cases in a tedious manner. In each case, we can show that $Q \geq 2$, and the errors are detected. The one case of interest here may be when some t unidirectional errors are present in B' and still make it a Hamming codeword. Here, S_0 will be 0, but $S_1 + S_2$ will be 2 or greater as required for detection.

The foregoing discussion illustrates the SEC–AUED code encoding and decoding logic. The serious reader is advised to verify these algorithms not only with the example codeword X but also with other codewords and perhaps with longer information blocks.

7.4.3 SEC – DED – AUED Codes

As stated previously, SEC–DED codes are very popular in commercial applications. It would be desirable to have the SEC–AUED codes derived in Section 7.4.2 also be double-error detecting (DED). Here, double errors are the symmetric type. If the two are unidirectional (i.e., both 1-errors or both 0-errors), then these are detected because of the AUED property. If not, they are bidirectional (i.e., one 1-error, the other 0-error). We need to investigate whether the SEC–AUED codes of Section 7.4.2 can detect two bidirectional errors (i.e., whether these codes are SEC–DED–AUED).

We give below a theorem that states that the NGP codes, as constructed in the previous section, are indeed SEC–DED–AUED codes.

Theorem 7-10. *The SEC–AUED codes derived using the NGP construction method (as given in Section 7.4.2) can also detect double (bidirectional) errors.*

Proof. We start with the syndrome $S(X') = (S_0, S_1, S_2)$, as in Section 7.4.2, and $Q = S_0 + S_1 + S_2$. What needs to be shown is that $Q \geq 2$ for double errors in X'. When the two errors are present in B_1' or B_2' it is easy to see $s_1 + s_2 = 2$, $Q = 2$, and therefore these are detected. Assume that the two errors are in B'. There will be two possible cases: (1) these are detected as uncorrectable, and in this case $s_0 = 2$ and $Q \geq 2$, as required; or (2) there is a miscorrection by the SEC decoder, and in this case a third error is introduced to obtain B'', and S_0 will be set to 1. The syndromes S_1 and S_2 will be greater than or equal to 1 due to the miscorrection in B''. The result is $Q \geq 3$, and indeed these are detected.

The last case is when there is one error in B' and another in B_1' or B_2'. Again, $S_0 = 1$, due to a single error in B', and B'' will be error-free. The error in B_1' or B_2' will set s_1 or s_2 to be ≥ 1, and therefore $Q \geq 2$, as to be proved. This completes the proof that NGP codes are indeed SEC–DED–AUED codes. Q.E.D.

Table 7.4 provides some examples of SEC–DED–AUED codes for some selected values of k, the information block length. The information rate (IR) of each code is also given. The block length of the SEC code used to construct the SEC–DED–AUED code is designated as n'. For examples of tEC–AUED codes with $t > 1$, see [NIKO 86].

TABLE 7.4 SEC – DED – AUED CODES

k	n'	n	IR
4	7	11	4/11 = .364
8	12	18	8/18 = .444
11	15	21	11/21 = .524
16	21	29	16/29 = .552
26	31	39	26/39 = .667
32	38	48	32/48 = .667
57	63	73	57/73 = .781
64	71	83	64/83 = .771
120	127	139	120/139 = .863
128	136	150	128/150 = .853

7.5 SEMIDISTANCE CODES AND ERROR-TOLERANT CIRCUITS

We introduce here a new concept called *semidistance* and a class of semidistance codes. These codes are shown to be equivalent to the tEC–AUED codes studied in Section 7.4, but they are applied for *error tolerance* in some logic circuits, such as address decoders for ROM's. Finally, we present some known construction methods for these codes.

7.5.1 Semidistance Code Definition

First, we recall the definition of unordered codes.

Definition 7-3. A code **C** is said to be *unordered* if and only if

$$N(X, Y) \geq 1 \qquad \text{for } all\ X, Y \in \mathbf{C} \tag{7.7}$$

Theorem 7-14 states that a code is all-unidirectional error detecting (AUED) if and only if it is unordered.

Definition 7-4. A code **C** is said to be *t-unordered* (or *t-degree unordered*) if and only if for all $X, Y \in \mathbf{C}$

$$N(X, Y) \geq t \tag{7.8}$$

As a restatement of Theorem 7-8, we can say that a code **C** is t-error correcting and all-unidirectional error detecting (tED–AUED) if and only if **C** is a $(t + 1)$ -unordered code.

Definition 7-5.* The *semidistance* $d_s(X, Y)$ between two binary n-tuples X and Y is given by

$$d_s(X, Y) = \min\{N(X, Y), N(Y, X)\} \tag{7.9}$$

The reader should note the difference between the definitions of asymmetric distance (7.1) and semidistance (7.9). The examples below illustrate these concepts and their correspondence to d, the Hamming distance.

Example 7-6

Let $X = 101101$ and $Y = 100011$. Then we have

$$\begin{aligned} N(X, Y) &= 2 \qquad \text{and} \qquad N(Y, X) = 1 \\ d_a(X, Y) &= \max\{N(X, Y), N(Y, X)\} = 2 \\ d_s(X, Y) &= \min\{N(X, Y), N(Y, X)\} = 1 \\ d(X, Y) &= N(X, Y) + N(Y, X) = d_a(X, Y) + d_s(X, Y) = 3 \end{aligned}$$

The following is easily provable.

*The semidistance definition given here is different from the one given in [IKEN 71], where $d_s(X, Y)$ is the same as $N(X, Y)$. For semi-metric space definition, see also *Modern General Topology* by J. Nagata. Amsterdam: North Holland Publishing Co., 1968.

Theorem 7-11. *In an unordered space* **C**, d_s *is a semi-metric, that is,*

$$d_s(X, Y) \geq 0, \text{ equality if and only if } X = Y \qquad (\textit{Positive definiteness})$$
$$d_s(X, Y) = d_s(Y, X) \qquad (\textit{Symmetry})$$

Definition 7-6. The *minimum semidistance* d_{sm} (or simply semidistance) of a code C is given by

$$d_{sm} = \min\{d_s(X, Y)\} \qquad \text{for all } X, Y \in C \tag{7.10}$$

A code **C** with semidistance $d_{sm} = t$ is written as a $\mathbf{C}(n, d_{sm} = t)$ code (n is understood to be the block length of code throughout). A code **C** with $d_{sm} = t + 1$, by definition is such that for all $X, Y \in \mathbf{C}$, $N(X, Y) \geq t + 1$. Therefore, it is $(t + 1)$-unordered, and hence by Theorem 7-8, it is a tEC–AUED code. Therefore, we can reuse the SEC–AUED code (Example 7-5) as a $\mathbf{C}(6, d_{sm} = 2)$ code, as follows:

$$\left.\begin{aligned} U_0 &= 000111 \\ U_1 &= 011100 \\ U_2 &= 101010 \\ U_3 &= 110001 \end{aligned}\right\} = \mathbf{C}(6, d_{sm} = 2) \textit{ code}$$

To use the full capability of an error correcting code, a decoder (with error detection/correction) logic circuit is required. However an *error-tolerant logic* (or application) is one where the outputs are correct in spite of errors without the explicit use of an error decoder. It was shown in [KITA 80] and [KOHD 86] that unordered (semidistance) codes, when applied to represent address bus lines of the address decoder logic of large-scale ROM, tolerate asymmetric errors. This principle of error tolerance is explained below.

7.5.2 Error-Tolerant Combination Decoders

An error-tolerant design was used for a combination decoder in ROM's [KITA 80, KOHD 86]. The address bus line faults are made electrically high (logic 1), and this results in asymmetric errors (0-errors only). As for open circuits, pull-up transistors render the isolated part of the line electrically high, and for short-circuit faults, the driver or buffer gate is designed to maintain an electrically high level on the line through the current supply from a load transistor. By such a *fail-safe* design, asymmetry in errors is achieved, and the probability of 1-errors, as compared to 0-errors, is extremely small. The word line as specified by the address is correctly selected despite the presence of 0-errors. Also, since the address bus lines are coded in a t-unordered code, no wrong word line is selected for fewer than t 0-errors. An illustration of this is given in Figs. 7.3 and 7.4 by a simple example.

Fig. 7.3 shows a simple 2-bit address decoder (four address bus lines to include true and complement values) and the four word lines W_0, W_1, W_2, and W_3. This nonredundant circuit decoder does not tolerate any line faults. Fig. 7.4 shows a

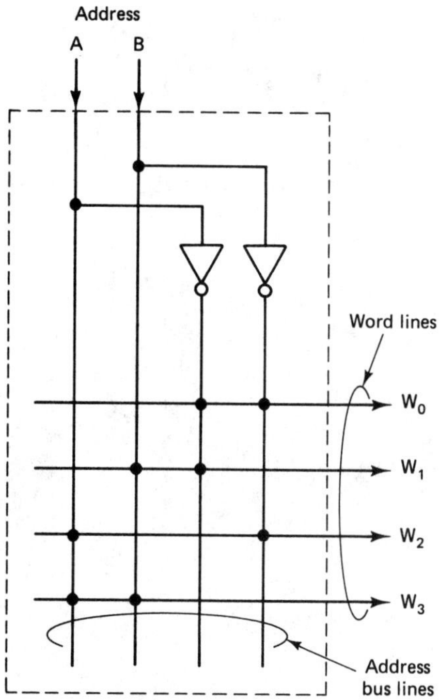

Figure 7.3 A 2-bit address decoder without coding on bus lines.

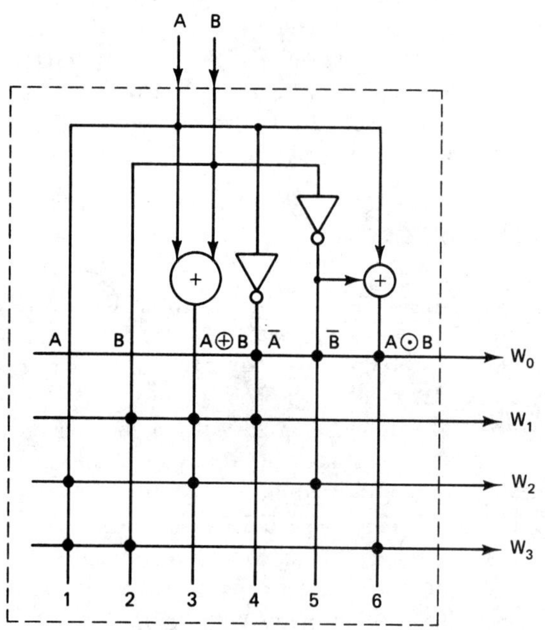

Figure 7.4 A 2-bit address decoder with $d_{sm} = 2$ coding on bus lines.

$\mathbf{C}(6, d_{sm} = 2)$ code on the bus lines of the decoder, and there it tolerates a single 0-error. For instance, if the bus lines (under no faults) have values $U_1 = 011100$, then word line W_1 is selected. Assume there is a line short between bus lines 4 and 5; as a consequence, the bus lines assume values $U_1' = 011110$. Since U_1' covers only U_1 but not others, the correct word, W_1, is selected. This principle extended gives us the following on error-tolerance circuits.

Theorem 7-12 [IKEN 71]. *a code with semidistance t can tolerate $t - 1$ asymmetric errors.*

For a $\mathbf{C}(n, d_{sm} = t)$ code, we use $[\mathbf{C}(n, d_{sm} = t)]$ to denote the number of codewords in it.

Since $N(X, Y) = N(\bar{Y}, \bar{X})$, the complementation of a code $\mathbf{C}$ gives a code $\bar{\mathbf{C}}$ with the same semidistance and the same number of codewords. Particularly, if $\mathbf{C} = \bar{\mathbf{C}}$, then $\mathbf{C}$ is called a *self-complementary code*, and its block length n has to be even. We also can state the following properties of semidistance codes.

For all $X \in C(n, d_{sm})$, let $W(X)$ represent the Hamming weight. Then

$$d_{sm} \leq W(X) \leq n - d_{sm} \tag{7.11}$$

$$d_{sm} \leq \lfloor n/2 \rfloor \tag{7.12}$$

(7.12) represents the necessary and sufficient conditions for the existence of a $C(n, d_{sm})$ code [IKEN 71].

The *coincidence number* λ of the codewords X and Y is defined as

$$\lambda(X, Y) = \sum_{i=0}^{n-1} x_i y_i = \lambda(Y, X)$$

$$W(X) = \lambda(X, Y) + N(X, Y)$$

$$W(Y) = \lambda(X, Y) + N(Y, X)$$

or

$$\lambda(X, Y) = W(X) - N(X, Y) = W(Y) - N(Y, X) \tag{7.13}$$

Example 7-7

Any two codewords in the following code have coincidence number $\lambda = 2$. The code is a semidistance code with constant weight $w = 5$ and $d_{sm} = 3$.

$$V_0 = 1\ 1\ 1\ 1\ 1\ 0\ 0\ 0\ 0\ 0$$

$$V_1 = 1\ 1\ 0\ 0\ 0\ 1\ 1\ 1\ 0\ 0$$

$$V_2 = 1\ 0\ 1\ 0\ 0\ 1\ 0\ 0\ 1\ 1$$

$$V_3 = 0\ 0\ 0\ 1\ 1\ 1\ 1\ 0\ 1\ 0$$

$$V_4 = 0\ 1\ 0\ 1\ 0\ 0\ 0\ 1\ 1\ 1$$

$$V_5 = 0\ 0\ 1\ 0\ 1\ 0\ 1\ 1\ 0\ 1$$

7.5.3 Code Construction

A semidistance code, or its complementary code with constant weight $\lfloor n/2 \rfloor$, is conjectured to be optimal, in the sense that it has a maximum number of codewords [IKEN 71, NAKA 72]. Trivially, when $d_{sm} = 1$, it is the constant weight $\lfloor n/2 \rfloor$ code, and it has been proved to be optimal [FREI 62]. That is, $[C(n, d_{sm} = 1)]_{\max} = \binom{n}{\lfloor n/2 \rfloor}$.

From the practical point of view, let us consider the $d_{sm} = 2$ constant-weight code. This code has the capability of masking single asymmetric errors. Examples of this type of code are shown in Table 7.5 [IKEN 71]. We let $N(n, w, t)$ denote the number of codewords of constant weight w and $d_{sm} = t$.

Theorem 7-13. *The upper bound for $N(n, w, 2)$ with constant weight w (for $w \leq n/2$) is given by*

$$N_{\max}(n, w, 2) = \binom{n}{w} \Big/ (n - w + 1) \tag{7.14}$$

The proof is rather long and is omitted here but can be found in [IKEN 71].

In the above theorem, $N(n, w, 2)$ can be made maximum if $w = \lfloor n/2 \rfloor$. If the equality in (7.14) holds for a code with $w = \lfloor n/2 \rfloor$, then the code is called optimal. To illustrate Theorem 7-13, consider the $(6, w, 2)$ codes below.

$$w = 1,\ N_{\max} = \binom{6}{1} \Big/ (6 - 1 + 1) = 1$$

$$w = 2,\ N_{\max} = \binom{6}{2} \Big/ (6 - 2 + 1) = 3$$

$$w = 3,\ N_{\max} = \binom{6}{3} \Big/ (6 - 2 + 1) = 5$$

While a (6, 2, 2) code with three codewords can be constructed easily, there is no (6, 3, 2) code with five codewords (see Example 7-5.) However, there is a (7, 3, 2) code satisfying the equality of Equation (7.14), and hence it is optimal.

Table 7.6 shows some optimal codes for n and w.

Some systematic implementation methods for the $d_{sm} = 2$ code have been proposed [NAEM 71b]. One type of code is derived from the Hamming code with Hamming distance $d = 4$. Another type of code is constructed from block design.

TABLE 7.6 OPTIMAL CONSTANT-WEIGHT $d_{sm} = 2$ CODES

Code Length (n)	Weight (w)	Number of Codewords (N)
4	2	2
7	3	7
8	4	14
11	5	66
12	6	132

TABLE 7.5 EXAMPLES OF CONSTANT-WEIGHT SEMIDISTANCE CODE WITH d_{sm} = 2 [IKEN 71]

$n = 4$

(1) 1 1 0 0
(2) 0 0 1 1

$n = 5$

(1) 1 1 0 0 0
(2) 0 0 1 1 0

$n = 6$

(1) 1 1 1 0 0 0
(2) 0 0 1 1 1 0
(3) 0 1 0 1 0 1
(4) 1 0 0 0 1 1

$n = 7$

(1) 1 1 1 0 0 0 0
(2) 1 0 0 1 1 0 0
(3) 1 0 0 0 0 1 1
(4) 0 1 0 1 0 1 0
(5) 0 1 0 0 1 0 1
(6) 0 0 1 1 0 0 1
(7) 0 0 1 0 1 1 0

$n = 8$

(1) 1 1 1 1 0 0 0 0
(2) 0 0 0 0 1 1 1 1
(3) 1 1 0 0 1 1 0 0
(4) 0 0 1 1 0 0 1 1
(5) 1 1 0 0 0 0 1 1
(6) 0 0 1 1 1 1 0 0
(7) 1 0 1 0 1 0 1 0
(8) 0 1 0 1 0 1 0 1
(9) 1 0 1 0 0 1 0 1
(10) 0 1 0 1 1 0 1 0
(11) 1 0 0 1 1 0 0 1
(12) 0 1 1 0 0 1 1 0
(13) 1 0 0 1 0 1 1 0
(14) 0 1 1 0 1 0 0 1

$n = 9$

(1) 1 0 0 1 0 0 1 0 1
(2) 0 1 0 0 0 1 1 1 0
(3) 0 0 1 0 1 0 0 1 1
(4) 1 0 0 0 1 1 0 1 0
(5) 0 1 0 1 1 0 0 0 1
(6) 0 0 1 1 0 1 1 0 0
(7) 0 1 1 1 0 0 0 1 0
(8) 1 0 1 0 0 1 0 0 1
(9) 1 1 0 0 1 0 1 0 0
(10) 1 0 1 0 0 0 1 1 0
(11) 1 1 0 1 0 1 0 0 0
(12) 0 0 0 0 1 1 1 0 1
(13) 0 1 1 0 1 1 0 0 0
(14) 0 0 0 1 1 0 1 1 0
(15) 1 1 0 0 0 0 0 1 1
(16) 0 0 0 1 0 1 0 1 1

$n = 9$

(17) 0 1 1 0 0 0 1 0 1
(18) 0 1 1 1 0 0 0 0

$n = 10$

(1) 1 1 0 0 1 0 0 1 0 1
(2) 1 0 1 0 0 0 1 1 1 0
(3) 1 0 0 1 0 1 0 0 1 1
(4) 0 1 1 0 1 1 0 0 1 0
(5) 0 1 0 1 0 1 1 1 0 0
(6) 0 0 1 1 1 0 1 0 0 1
(7) 1 1 0 0 0 1 1 0 1 0
(8) 1 0 1 0 1 1 0 0 0 1
(9) 1 0 0 1 1 0 1 1 0 0
(10) 0 1 1 0 0 0 1 1 0 1
(11) 0 1 0 1 1 0 0 0 1 1
(12) 0 0 1 1 0 1 0 1 1 0
(13) 1 0 1 1 1 0 0 0 1 0
(14) 1 1 0 1 0 0 1 0 0 1
(15) 1 1 1 0 0 1 0 1 0 0
(16) 0 0 0 1 1 1 0 1 0 1
(17) 0 0 1 0 0 1 1 0 1 1
(18) 0 1 0 0 1 0 1 1 1 0
(19) 0 1 1 1 0 1 0 0 0 1
(20) 0 0 0 1 1 1 1 0 1 0
(21) 0 0 1 0 1 0 0 1 1 1
(22) 1 1 0 1 0 0 0 1 1 0
(23) 1 1 1 0 1 0 1 0 0 0
(24) 1 0 0 0 0 1 1 1 0 1
(25) 0 0 0 1 0 0 1 1 1 1
(26) 0 1 1 1 1 0 0 1 0 0
(27) 0 1 0 0 1 1 1 0 0 1
(28) 1 0 1 1 0 1 1 0 0 0
(29) 1 0 0 0 1 1 0 1 1 0
(30) 1 1 1 0 0 0 0 0 1 1
(31) 0 0 1 0 1 1 1 1 0 0
(32) 0 1 0 0 0 1 0 1 1 1
(33) 0 1 1 1 0 0 1 0 1 0
(34) 1 0 0 0 1 0 1 0 1 1
(35) 1 0 1 1 0 0 0 1 0 1
(36) 1 1 0 1 1 1 0 0 0 0

$n = 11$

(1) 1 1 1 1 1 0 0 0 0 0 0
(2) 1 1 0 0 0 1 1 1 0 0 0
(3) 1 0 1 0 0 0 0 1 0 1 1
(4) 1 0 0 1 0 0 1 0 1 0 1
(5) 1 0 0 0 1 1 0 0 1 1 0
(6) 0 1 1 0 0 1 0 0 1 0 1
(7) 0 1 0 1 0 0 0 1 1 1 0
(8) 0 1 0 0 1 0 1 0 0 1 1
(9) 0 0 1 1 0 1 1 0 0 1 0
(10) 0 0 1 0 1 0 1 1 1 0 0
(11) 0 0 0 1 1 1 0 1 0 0 1
(12) 1 1 0 0 0 0 0 0 1 1 1
(13) 1 0 1 0 0 1 1 0 1 0 0

$n = 11$

(14) 1 0 0 1 0 1 0 1 0 1 0
(15) 1 0 0 0 1 0 1 1 0 0 1
(16) 0 1 1 0 0 0 1 1 0 1 0
(17) 0 1 0 1 0 1 1 0 0 0 1
(18) 0 1 0 0 1 1 0 1 1 0 0
(19) 0 0 1 1 0 0 0 1 1 0 1
(20) 0 0 1 0 1 1 0 0 0 1 1
(21) 0 0 0 1 1 0 1 0 1 1 0
(22) 1 0 0 1 1 0 0 1 1 0 0
(23) 1 0 1 0 1 0 1 0 0 1 0
(24) 1 0 1 1 0 1 0 0 0 0 1
(25) 0 1 0 1 1 1 0 0 0 1 0
(26) 0 1 1 0 1 0 0 1 0 0 1
(27) 0 1 1 1 0 0 1 0 1 0 0
(28) 0 0 0 0 1 1 1 0 1 0 1
(29) 0 0 0 1 0 0 1 1 0 1 1
(30) 0 0 1 0 0 1 0 1 1 1 0
(31) 1 1 0 0 1 1 0 0 0 0 1
(32) 1 1 0 1 0 0 1 0 0 1 0
(33) 0 0 1 1 1 0 1 0 0 0 1
(34) 0 0 0 0 1 1 1 1 0 1 0
(35) 0 0 0 1 0 1 0 0 1 1 1
(36) 0 1 1 0 1 0 0 0 1 1 0
(37) 0 1 1 1 0 1 0 1 0 0 0
(38) 0 1 0 0 0 0 1 1 1 0 1
(39) 1 1 1 0 0 0 0 1 1 0 0
(40) 0 0 0 0 1 0 0 1 1 1 1
(41) 0 0 1 1 1 1 0 0 1 0 0
(42) 0 0 1 0 0 1 1 1 0 0 1
(43) 0 1 0 1 1 0 1 1 0 0 0
(44) 0 1 0 0 0 1 1 0 1 1 0
(45) 0 1 1 1 0 0 0 0 0 1 1
(46) 0 0 0 1 0 1 1 1 1 0 0
(47) 0 0 1 0 0 0 1 0 1 1 1
(48) 0 0 1 1 1 0 0 1 0 1 0
(49) 0 1 0 0 0 1 0 1 0 1 1
(50) 0 1 0 1 1 0 0 0 1 0 1
(51) 0 1 1 0 1 1 1 0 0 0 0
(52) 1 1 0 0 1 0 1 0 1 0 0
(53) 1 1 0 1 0 0 0 1 0 0 1
(54) 1 0 1 0 1 1 0 1 0 0 0
(55) 1 0 1 1 0 0 0 0 1 1 0
(56) 1 0 0 0 0 1 1 0 0 1 1
(57) 1 1 1 0 0 1 0 0 0 1 0
(58) 1 0 0 1 1 0 0 0 0 1 1
(59) 1 0 0 0 0 1 0 1 1 0 1
(60) 1 0 1 1 0 0 1 1 0 0 0
(61) 1 0 0 0 0 0 1 1 1 1 0
(62) 1 0 0 1 1 1 1 0 0 0 0
(63) 1 0 1 0 1 0 0 0 1 0 1
(64) 1 1 1 0 0 0 1 0 0 0 1
(65) 1 1 0 1 0 1 0 0 1 0 0
(66) 1 1 0 0 1 0 0 1 0 1 0

TABLE 7.7 NUMBER OF $d = 4$ HAMMING CODEWORDS WITH WEIGHT $\lfloor n/2 \rfloor$ ($d_{sm} = 2$)

n	N_{max}*	$N(n, \lfloor n/2 \rfloor)$
4	2	2
8	14	14
16	1430	820

*From Equation (7.14).

Hamming-type constant-weight code. The number of codewords of the $d = 4$ Hamming code with weight $w = \lfloor n/2 \rfloor$ is given by [PETE 72].

$$N[n, w = \lfloor n/2 \rfloor, 2] = \left\{ \binom{n}{w} + (n-1)\binom{w}{w/2} \right\} \Big/ n.$$

Table 7.7 shows $N(n, w = \lfloor n/2 \rfloor, 2)$ for n. The ratio of $N(n, w = \lfloor n/2 \rfloor, 2)$ to N_{max} tends to 1/2 as n gets larger (i.e., $\lim_{n \to \infty} N(n, w = \lfloor n/2 \rfloor, 2)/N_{max} = \frac{1}{2}$).

Example 7-8

The following **H** matrix gives codewords with Hamming distance $d = 4$.

$$\mathbf{H} = \begin{bmatrix} 1 & 0 & 1 & 1 & 1 & 0 & 0 & 0 \\ 1 & 1 & 0 & 1 & 0 & 1 & 0 & 0 \\ 1 & 1 & 1 & 0 & 0 & 0 & 1 & 0 \\ 0 & 1 & 1 & 1 & 0 & 0 & 0 & 1 \end{bmatrix}$$

Using **H**, the following 16 codewords can be obtained:

$$\begin{array}{l} 00000000 \\ \left.\begin{array}{l} 10001110 \\ 01000111 \\ 11001001 \\ 00101011 \\ 10100101 \\ 01101100 \\ 11100010 \\ 00011101 \\ 10010011 \\ 01011010 \\ 11010100 \\ 00110110 \\ 10111000 \\ 01110001 \end{array}\right\} N(8,4,2) = 14 \\ 11111111 \end{array}$$

If we delete the top and bottom words, we can have the 14 codewords with $d_{sm} = 2$, $n = 8$, and $w = 4$, giving us $N(8, 4, 2) = 14$.

Codes derived from block design. We will investigate the codes derived from a balanced incomplete block design.

Definition 7-7 [HALL 67]. A *balanced incomplete block design* (*BIBD*) is an arrangement of v distinct objects into b blocks such that each block contains exactly k distinct objects, each object occurs in exactly r different blocks, and every pair of distinct objects a_i, a_j occurs together in exactly λ blocks.

There are two elementary relations for the five parameters for the block design, as follows.

$$b \cdot k = v \cdot r$$
$$\lambda v(v - 1) = b \cdot k(k - 1) \tag{7.15}$$

These parameters and the code parameters we used before have the correspondence such that v is the number of codewords $N(n, w, d_s)$, b is codeword length n, r is weight w, and λ is coincidence number. From this design, we have the constant-weight semidistance code with $d_s = r - \lambda$, $n = b$, and $w = r$. From Equation (7.15), the number of codewords v can be expressed as

$$v = \frac{b(r - \lambda)}{b(r - \lambda) - r(b - r)}$$

If we use the code parameters n, w, and d_s, this equation can be rewritten as follows [NAEM 71b].

$$N(n, w, d_s) = \frac{n \cdot d_s}{n \cdot d_s - w(n - w)} \tag{7.16}$$

Example 7-9

An example of the semidistance code derived from BIBD is given for $n = 12$, $w = 4$, and $d_s = 3$, as follows.

$$\left.\begin{array}{ll}
(1) & 100100100100 \\
(2) & 100010010010 \\
(3) & 100001001001 \\
(4) & 010100001010 \\
(5) & 010010100001 \\
(6) & 001010001100 \\
(7) & 001001100010 \\
(8) & 001100010001 \\
(9) & 010001010100
\end{array}\right\} N(12,4,3) = 9$$

In Equation (7.16) $N(n, w, d_s)$ becomes maximum when $w = n/2$. Therefore, the upper bound of the code derived from BIBD is shown as follows [NAKA 72].

$$N'\max = 4 \cdot d_s/(4 \cdot d_s - n)$$

From this, we have the following theorem:

Theorem 7-14. *The upper bound of the constant-weight semidistance code, with minimum semidistance d_s, derived from BIBD, is*

$$N' \max = 4 \cdot d_s/(4 \cdot d_s - n)$$

As for implementation of BIBD, the reader may refer to [HALL 67].

Example 7-10 [NAKA 72]

(1) $n = 6,\ w = 3,\ d_s = 2$

110001
101010
011100
000111

(2) $n = 10,\ w = 5,\ d_s = 3$

1111100000
1100011100
1010010011
0001111010
0101000111
0010101101

Other classes of constant-weight semidistance codes are obtained using Hadamard matrices, finite projective geometries, Mathieu group, orthogonal arrays, and difference sets [NAEM 71b]. Among them, the following example is derived from the Hadamard matrix $\mathbf{H}_8$. (For Hadamard matrices and Hadamard codes, see for instance [MACW 77].)

$$\mathbf{H}_8 = \begin{array}{c|ccccccc} +1 & +1 & +1 & +1 & +1 & +1 & +1 & +1 \\ \hline +1 & -1 & +1 & -1 & +1 & -1 & +1 & -1 \\ +1 & +1 & -1 & -1 & +1 & +1 & -1 & -1 \\ +1 & -1 & -1 & +1 & +1 & -1 & -1 & +1 \\ +1 & +1 & +1 & +1 & -1 & -1 & -1 & -1 \\ +1 & -1 & +1 & -1 & -1 & +1 & -1 & +1 \\ +1 & +1 & -1 & -1 & -1 & -1 & +1 & +1 \\ +1 & -1 & -1 & +1 & -1 & +1 & +1 & -1 \end{array}$$

Deleting the first row and first column from this matrix, and substituting 1 and 0 for $+1$ and -1, respectively, we have the following seven constant-weight semidistance codewords (from the row vectors in the matrix).

(1) 0101010
(2) 1001100
(3) 0011001
(4) 1110000
(5) 0100101
(6) 1000011
(7) 0010110

This is the optimal code with $n = 7$, $w = 3$, and $d_{sm} = 2$.

Another example can be given from orthogonal array $L_s(2^7)$ in the design of experiments, as follows.

$$L_8(2^7) = \begin{bmatrix} 1 & 1 & 1 & 1 & 1 & 1 & 1 \\ 1 & 1 & 1 & 2 & 2 & 2 & 2 \\ 1 & 2 & 2 & 1 & 1 & 2 & 2 \\ 1 & 2 & 2 & 2 & 2 & 1 & 1 \\ 2 & 1 & 2 & 1 & 2 & 1 & 2 \\ 2 & 1 & 2 & 2 & 1 & 2 & 1 \\ 2 & 2 & 1 & 1 & 2 & 2 & 1 \\ 2 & 2 & 1 & 2 & 1 & 1 & 2 \end{bmatrix} \rightarrow \begin{bmatrix} 1 & 1 & 1 & 1 & 1 & 1 & 1 \\ 1 & 1 & 1 & 0 & 0 & 0 & 0 \\ 1 & 0 & 0 & 1 & 1 & 0 & 0 \\ 1 & 0 & 0 & 0 & 0 & 1 & 1 \\ 0 & 1 & 0 & 1 & 0 & 1 & 0 \\ 0 & 1 & 0 & 0 & 1 & 0 & 1 \\ 0 & 0 & 1 & 1 & 0 & 0 & 1 \\ 0 & 0 & 1 & 0 & 1 & 1 & 0 \end{bmatrix}$$

Substituting 2 to 0, we have the array shown above right. From this, we derive the following seven codewords with length 8 from the column vectors in the array.

(1) 11110000
(2) 11001100
(3) 11000011
(4) 10101010
(5) 10100101
(6) 10011001
(7) 10010110

Adding the following complement words to the above words, we have the optimum $d_{sm} = 2$ semidistance code with $n = 8$ and constant-weight $w = 4$.

(8) 00001111
(9) 00110011
(10) 00111100
(11) 01010101
(12) 01011010
(13) 01100110
(14) 01101001

The codes just given are all nonsystematic and nonlinear. The construction of a systematic semidistance code was also proposed [NAEM 71a]. The code length n of this systematic code is approximately $k + d_{sm} \log_2 k$, where k is the information length. As for the constant-weight systematic code, the code length is approximately $2k$ [NAEM 71a]. Another approach to semidistance $(t + 1)$ codes is through NGP construction, as given in Section 7.4 for tEC–AUED codes. The systematic codes will have lower information rates as compared to nonsystematic codes.

7.6 SHIFT-REGISTER TYPE MEMORIES

In shift-register type memories, a permanent failure in one of the cells of the register will result in a constant 0 or 1 output from the shift register. This will cause multiple unidirectional errors in a word [COOK 73, PARH 78]. Mass memories such as CCD's and MBM's, which are of the shift-register type, as well as magnetic tape systems, have use for multiple unidirectional error correction (MUEC) codes.

Brown and Sellers [BROW 70] have given an error correction technique for magnetic tapes. They use vertical overall parity checks and a horizontal cyclic redundancy check to correct any pattern of symmetric errors in a single track. An extension of this coding scheme is given by Hong and Patel [HONG 74]. They show that the new scheme corrects any errors in two tracks if the erroneous tracks are known. More properties of these codes are described by Sloane in [SLOA 76]. Parhami and Avizienis [PARH 78] and Wakerly [WAKE 75] consider detection of unidirectional errors in mass memories using arithmetic checks. They have not discussed correction of unidirectional errors.

The code discussed in this section is obtained from [BOSE 80] and [BOSE 84b]. This code is a modification of the cyclic redundancy check (CRC) used in magnetic tape units [BROW 70, HONG 74, SLOA 76]. An arithmetic redundancy check (ARC) replaces CRC, and the result is a systematic code that provides correction of multiple unidirectional errors in any one track of a large block of characters. These codes are called *ARC codes*. The improvement attained by using an arithmetic check is a considerably larger number of characters included in each block and a much higher information rate as compared to the CRC code.

7.6.1 Code Formats and Memories Organization

We assume that data are transferred byte serially and in blocks between the mass memory and the main memory. Furthermore, we assume that a data block consists of l characters with each character b-bits long.

The shift register memory organization is shown in Fig. 7.5. There are b shift registers. Each bit of a character is in different shift register. Any permanent failure in a shift register results in a constant output of a 0 or 1 [PARH 78]. This can be modeled as multiple unidirectional errors in the bits of that particular shift register.

In the case of magnetic tapes, each bit of a character is stored in a different track. Since there are b bits per character, we have b tracks. Again, we are interested

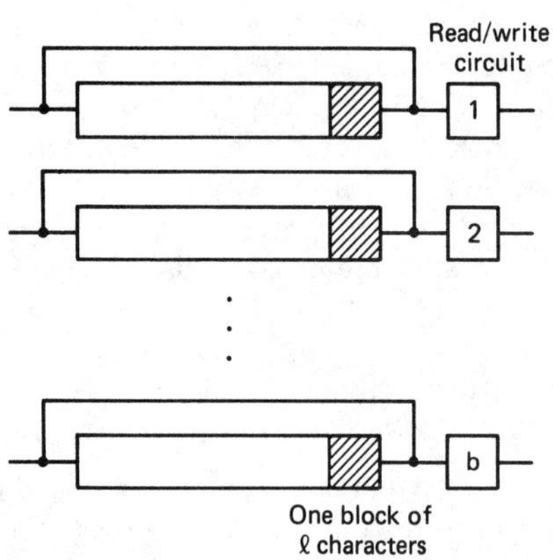

Figure 7.5 Shift register organization [BOSE 84b].

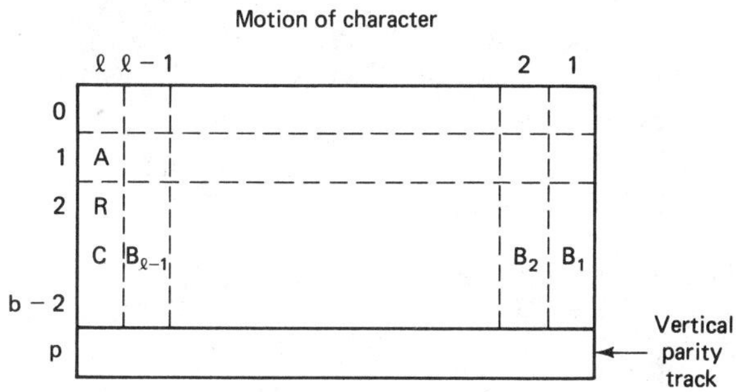

Figure 7.6 Data format of a code block [BOSE 84b].

in correcting multiple unidirectional errors confined to one particular track of the data block. The code discussed here is not intended for the detection or correction of errors in two or more tracks.

From the above discussion we can see that a data block is a two-dimensional array of l columns and b rows. Borrowing from the terminology of magnetic tapes, we will refer to each column as one character and each row as one track. Also, we will refer to the first $b - 1$ rows as information tracks and the last row as a parity track.

Data format and code construction. The data format for this code is shown in Fig. 7.6. Let $B_j = (B_j(b-2), B_j(b-3) \ldots B_j(0))$, where $B_j(i) \in \{0, 1\}$. We give an integer value to each of the B_j's as

$$B_j = B_j(b-2)2^{b-2} + B_j(b-3)2^{b-3} + \cdots B_j(1)2^1 + B_j(0)2^0$$

The last character, B_l, is the arithmetic residue check (ARC), which is equal to the additive inverse of residue modulo A of the sum of the information bytes, where A is an appropriate check base. That is,

$$B_l = -\left|\sum_{j=1}^{l-1} B_j\right|_A$$

Thus we have

$$\left.\begin{aligned} \sum_{j=1}^{l} B_j &\equiv 0 \pmod{A} \\ \text{or} \qquad \left|\sum_{j=1}^{l} B_j\right|_A &= 0 \end{aligned}\right\}$$

The overall vertical parity bits are the even (or odd) parities over each of the characters.

Check base selection and code capabilities. In this section we discuss the condition on check base A of ARC. While reading a data block, assume that k

(unidirectional) errors have occurred in one of the tracks. From vertical parity failures, we can find the vertical positions of the errors and the number of errors. Hence, if we determine the track in error, then we can correct all errors in that track. The ARC is designed to determine the erroneous track. For this we define the arithmetic residue syndrome, or simply syndrome S, as

$$S = \left| \sum_{j=1}^{l} B_j \right|_A$$

If there is no error in any of the information tracks, then $S = 0$. If the k errors are in the vertical parity track, then $S = 0$. On the other hand, if the k errors are in track i, where $0 \le i \le b - 2$, and they are 0-errors, then $S = | + k2^i|_A$. If the errors are of 1-errors, then $S = | - k2^i|_A$.

From the above, we can see that the check base A must satisfy the following two conditions.

1. If k is the number of unidirectional errors in track i, where $1 \le k \le l$ and $0 \le i \le b - 2$, then the syndrome S should not be equal to zero. That is,

$$S \equiv \pm k2^i \not\equiv 0 \pmod{A}$$

2. The syndromes for k unidirectional errors in track i and in track j are not equal; where $i \ne j$ and $1 \le k \le l$. That is,

$$\text{for } i \ne j, \pm k2^i \not\equiv 0 \pmod{A} \qquad i, j \in [0, b-2]$$

Moreover, to obtain a high information rate, we look for as large a value of l as possible.

In order to satisfy these conditions, we will take as the value of the check base A the largest prime less than 2^{b-1}, where b is greater than 3. The largest prime less than 2^{b-1} is always greater than $2^{b-2} + 1$ for $b > 3$ [DICK 71]. The following theorem explains the above condition on A.

Theorem 7-15. *Let A be the largest prime less than 2^{b-1} for $b > 3$. Then for $i, j \in [0, b-2]$ and $1 \le k \le A - 1$, the following conditions hold.*

1. $k2^i \not\equiv 0 \pmod{A}$
2. $\pm k2^i \not\equiv \pm k2^j \pmod{A}$ *for $i \ne j$, that is,* $2^h \not\equiv \pm \pmod{A}$ *for* $1 \le h \le b - 2$.

Proof

1. For some k and i, where $1 \le k \le A - 1$ and $0 \le i \le b - 2$, let $k2^i \equiv 0 \pmod{A}$. Then, $A | k2^i$. Since the greatest common divisor (gcd) of $(A, 2) = 1$, this implies $A | k$. This is a contradiction, because A is a prime and k is a positive integer less than A.
2. Two cases are to be considered for this condition.

Case 1: We have to prove $2^h \not\equiv 1 \pmod A$ for the range $1 \le h \le b-2$. The integers $2^1, 2^2, \ldots, 2^{b-2}$ are all less than A and greater than 1. Hence, none of them is congruent to 1 modulo A.

Case 2: We have to prove $2^h \not\equiv -1 \pmod A$ for the range $1 \le h \le b-2$. For some h, where $1 \le h \le b-2$, let $2^h \equiv -1 \pmod A$. Then, $A | 2^h + 1$. Since A is the largest prime less than 2^{b-1}, $A > 2^h + 1 > 0$ for $1 \le h \le b - 2$, and hence we get a contradiction.

As a consequence of the above theorem, in order to have the largest number of characters in the proposed code, the value of the check base A must be the largest prime less than 2^{b-1}. For the given number of tracks b, ($b \le 17$) the appropriate values of the check base A are given in Table 7.8. It is easy to see that the proposed code is not suitable when b is less than or equal to 3.

Suppose we choose an appropriate prime A satisfying the previously mentioned conditions. Then l, the number of characters in the code block, will be $A - 1$, and b, the number of tracks, will be $\lceil \log_2 A \rceil + 1$. The number of information and check bits will be, respectively, $(l-1)(b-1)$ and $l + b - 1$. Hence, the information rate of the code will be $1 - (l + b - 1/lb)$. Since $l = 2^{b-1}$, the information rate of the code is approximately equal to $1 - 1/b$. For the code given in [BROW 70], [HONG 74], and [SLOA 76], note that the information rate is equal to $1 - (2/b)$.

For example, if we have a 9-track tape, as given in [BROW 70], [HONG 74], and [SLOA 76], we can choose the check base A to be 251. Then the coding scheme developed here can have up to 250 characters, including the arithmetic residue check. The code can correct up to 250 unidirectional errors confined to single track. The number of information bits will be $249 \times 8 = 1992$, and the number of parity bits will be $250 + 8 = 258$. Hence, the information rate will be $[1 - (258/22500)]$

TABLE 7.8 VALUES OF RESIDUE CHECK BASE FOR THE GIVEN NUMBER OF TRACKS [BOSE 84B]

b	Check Base A
4	7
5	13
6	31
7	61
8	127
9	251
10	509
11	1021
12	2039
13	4073
14	8191
15	16381
16	32749
17	65521

$\times$ 100 = 88.5%. On the other hand, the code given in [BROW 70], [HONG 74], and [SLOA 76] has 8 characters, the number of its information bits is 56 and the number of its check bits is 16. Hence, if the errors are of a unidirectional nature, then the code proposed here is much superior to the one discussed in [BROW 70], [HONG 74], and [SLOA 76].

Error correction can be performed as follows. Note that the first consecutive $b - 2$ nonnegative integer powers of 2 modulo A and their additive inverse are all distinct. For example, if $b = 9$ and $A = 251$, then we will have the following congruences modulo 251.

$$\begin{array}{rrr} 2^0 \equiv 1 & 2^3 \equiv 8 & 2^6 \equiv 64 \\ -2^0 \equiv 250 & -2^3 \equiv 243 & -2^6 \equiv 187 \\ 2^0 \equiv 2 & 2^4 \equiv 16 & 2^7 \equiv 128 \\ -2^1 \equiv 249 & -2^4 \equiv 235 & -2^7 \equiv 123 \\ 2^2 \equiv 4 & 2^5 \equiv 32 & \\ -2^2 \equiv 247 & -2^5 \equiv 219 & \end{array}$$

Suppose s ($s \neq 0$) unidirectional errors occur in track j. The number s can be obtained by using an error counter (i.e., by incrementing the error counter whenever there is a failure in the overall vertical parity bits). After reading a word, let the residue be r. Now the track that is in error can be discovered through consideration of the following two cases. (For simplicity, we assume that the unidirectional errors are type 0-errors (i.e., $0 \to 1$ errors). The procedure is valid for 1-errors also.)

Case 1: The number of errors $s \neq 0$, and the residue $r \neq 0$. Then $s2^j \equiv r \pmod{A}$, which implies $2^j \equiv s^{-1}r \pmod{A}$, where s^{-1} is the multiplicative inverse of s in $GF(A)$. For $j = 0, 1, 2, \ldots, b - 2$, the values of $2^j \bmod A$ are all distinct, and thus the above equation holds for a particular value of j. Hence, the track that is in error, j, can be identified.

Case 2: The number of errors, $s \neq 0$, and the residue $r = 0$. In this case the errors are in the last track (i.e., the overall vertical parity check track).

An example is given to illustrate these concepts after describing the encoding and decoding logic. Once the track in error is known, the data can be read again. At this time, whenever there is a failure in the vertical parity bit, the corresponding bit in the erroneous track can be complemented to get the correct data (Alternatively, we can use a buffer register to store the data, and error correction can be carried out by reading the data from this buffer register.)

Encoding and decoding logic. The encoding and decoding procedures are explained as follows.

Encoding. We can use a residue check register (RCR) for finding the residue check. Before writing data into the memory the RCR is cleared. As each character is written, the character (excluding its parity) is added (mod A addition) to the content of the RCR. After all the characters are written, the complement of the RCR with respect to modulo A addition (i.e., the modulo A additive inverse) is written as an arithmetic residue check (ARC). A parity computed on ARC is then loaded as the parity bit of the ARC character.

Decoding. During a read operation, the residue is again calculated in RCR. (We may use a buffer register to store the data that have just been read.) Also, whenever there is a failure in the overall parity check of a character, the error counter register (ECR), which is a modulo A counter, is incremented. If there is an erroneous track, then at the end of the read operation the ECR contains the number of errors in the erroneous track; otherwise, the ECR is zero. If both the RCR and the ECR are zero, then no error has occurred in the data block. If only the RCR is zero, then there are errors in the vertical parity check. The case where the RCR $\neq 0$ and the ECR $= 0$ cannot occur. If both the RCR and the ECR are nonzero, then the erroneous track can be found as follows. The ECR is shifted left till the content of the ECR or its complement with respect to modulo A addition is equal to the contents of the RCR. The number of left shifts j in the ECR gives the position of the track in error. Once the track in error is known, error correction can be easily carried out. An example to illustrate these concepts follows.

Example 7-11

Let the number of tracks including the parity track be equal to 9. Then the check base A will be 251. Suppose 50 0-errors occurred in the third track. Then the contents of the ECR will be 50 and that of the RCR will be $|+50 \times 2^3|_{251} = |400|_{251} = 149$. The contents of the ECR and its complement for the consecutive left shifts will be as follows.

Number of Shifts	ECR	251-ECR
0	50	201
1	100	151
2	200	51
3	149	102

Since the contents of the ECR are equal to those of the RCR after three shifts, it is immediately known that the third track is in error. As another example, let there be 100 $1 \rightarrow 0$ errors in track 4. After reading the data block, the contents of the ECR will be 100 and that of the RCR will be $|-100 \times 2^4|_{251} = |-1600|_{251} = 157$. After shifting the ECR four times, the contents will be 94 and the complement will be $251 - 94 = 157$. Hence, it can be determined that the fourth track is in error.

Note that the maximum number of left shifts required for the ECR to match the RCR is at most $b - 2$. If there is no match between the ECR (or its complement) and the RCR even after $b - 2$ left shifts of ECR, then there is an uncorrectable error pattern (i.e., more than one track may be in error).

In summary, the discussion in this section shows that the replacement of the cyclic redundancy check of the magnetic tape code by an appropriate arithmetic residue check will result in an efficient unidirectional error correcting code. The ARC code has much higher information rate than the CRC code, and the ARC code is simple to implement. Further properties of this code can be found in [BOSE 80].

7.7 ADDITIONAL NOTES ON ASYMMETRIC AND UNIDIRECTIONAL CODES

There has been considerable work in recent years on the theory and application of asymmetric and unidirectional codes. Only selected topics have been covered in the previous section. The following supplemental notes review some recent research and some theoretical bounds on code characteristics.

1. Another construction method for systematic t-error correcting and all-unidirectional error detecting (tEC–AUED) code will be found in [KUND 88]. An SEC–AUED code constructed by this method is optimal in the sense that

$$\lim_{k \to \infty} \frac{r_{act}(k)}{r_{\min}(k)} = 1$$

where k is the information length in bits, $r_{\min}(k)$ is the lower bound on the number of redundant bits required to construct a code of desired ability [BOSE 82a], and $r_{act}(k)$ is the number of redundant bits actually required to construct a particular code of that ability. Also given in [KUND 88] is a construction method for a nonsystematic 2EC–AUED code that has a larger number of codewords for a fixed code length than the codes mentioned in this book.

2. Asymmetric error correcting (or detecting) codes are very useful for photon communication systems, because a photon channel is asymmetric in its nature [UYEN 87]. For such systems, a code having a small average weight is preferred to improve the information efficiency (i.e. information rate per photon). Applications to photon communications can also be found in [MCEL 81] and [HIRO 86].

3. Several researches have been done on the upper bounds on the number of codewords in asymmetric and unidirectional error correcting codes [DELS 81a, b, KLOV 81a, b, SMIT 84, BOSE 86, 87, KNUT 86, WEBE 87].

EXERCISES

7.1. Assuming the code length $n = 20$, and assuming 0's and 1's are likely in each position of a codeword, determine the probabilities of erroneous decoding for the cases in which SAEC and SEC codes are employed. Assume p (1-error) $= 10^{-3}$ and p (0-error) $= 10^{-6}$. Discuss the merits (and demerits) of the two codes.

7.2. If the SAEC code with four codewords $\mathbf{C} = \{0000, 1100, 0011, 1111\}$ is employed over a Z-channel, determine the probability of erroneous decoding. Assume p (1-error) $= 10^{-5}$ and p (0-error) $= 0$.

7.3. Show that the asymmetric distance is a metric. Prove that the semi-distance is not a metric in an arbitrary space of n-tuples.

7.4. Construct a 2-UED code using a modified Berger check for information blocks of length 6. Assuming that p (single error) $= 10^{-3}$ and p (2-UED) $= 10^{-5}$, determine the probability of erroneous decoding for the code you constructed.

7.5. Construct examples of SEC–DED, SEC–AUED, SEC–2UED, 2-UED codes with block length (a) $n = 4$ and (b) $n = 5$.

7.6. Construct examples of SEC–AUED codes for $k = 4$ of (a) systematic form and (b) nonsystematic form. Illustrate how single errors are corrected and unidirectional errors are detected for the two cases.

7.7. Construct a $d_{sm} = 2$ code for

(a) $n = 5$.

(b) $n = 6$.

Show their complement codes are also $d_{sm} = 2$ code.

REFERENCES

[ANDE 71] D. A. Anderson. *Design of Self-Checking Digital Networks Using Coding Techniques*, Coordinated Sci. Lab. Report R-527. Champaign: University of Illinois Press, 1971.

[BERG 61] J. M. Berger. "A Note on Error Detecting Codes for Asymmetric Channels." *Information and Control* 4 (March 1961): 68–73.

[BERG 86] E. E. Bergmann, A. M. Odlyzko and S. H. Sangonl. "Half Weight Block Codes for Optical Communications." *AT&T Technical Journal* 65 (May/June 1986): 85–93.

[BORD 82] J. M. Borden. "Optimal Asymmetric Error Detecting Codes." *Information and Control* 53 (April 1982): 66–73.

[BOSE 80] B. Bose. "Theory and Design of Unidirectional Error Codes." Ph.D. Diss., Dep. Comput. Sci. Eng., Southern Methodist University, Dallas, Texas, May 1980.

[BOSE 81] B. Bose. "On Systematic SEC/MUED Code." *Dig., 11th Annual Int. Symposium Fault-Tolerant Compt.* 11 (June 1981): 265–67.

[BOSE 82a] B. Bose and T. R. N. Rao. "Theory of Unidirectional Error Correcting/Detecting Codes." *IEEE Transactions on Computers* C-31 (June 1982): 521–30.

[BOSE 82b] B. Bose and D. K. Pradhan. "Optimal Unidirectional Error Detecting/Correcting Codes." *IEEE Transactions on Computers* C-31 (June 1982): 564–68.

[BOSE 84b] B. Bose and T. R. N. Rao. "Unidirectional Error Codes for Shift-Register Memories." *IEEE Transactions on Computers* C-33 (June 1984): 575–78.

[BOSE 85] B. Bose and D. J. Lin. "Systematic Unidirectional Error-Detecting Codes." *IEEE Transactions on Computers* C-34 (November 1985): 1026–32.

[BOSE 86a] B. Bose. "Burst Unidirectional Error-Detecting Codes." *IEEE Transactions on Computers* C-35 (April 1986): 350–53.

[BOSE 87] B. Bose. "On Unordered Codes." *Dig. 17th Annual Int. Symposium Fault-Tolerant Comput.* (July 1987): 102–7.

[BROW 70] D. T. Brown and F. F. Sellers. "Error Correction for IBM 800-bit-per-inch Magnetic Tape." *IBM Journal of Research and Development* 14 (July 1970): 384–89.

[COHE 71] L. Cohen, R. Green, K. Smith, and J. L. Seely. "Single-Transistor Cell Makes Room for More Memory on an MOS Chip." *Electronics* 44 (1971): 69–75.

[CONS 77] S. D. Constantin. "Characterization and Design of Error Correcting Codes for Asymmetric Memories." Ph.D. Diss., Southern Methodist University, Dallas, Texas, December 1977.

[CONS 79] S. D. Constantin and T. R. N. Rao. "On the Theory of Binary Asymmetric Error Correcting Codes." *Information and Control* 40 (January 1979): 20–26.

[COOK 73] R. W. Cook, W. H. Sisson, T. G. Stoney, and W. N. Toy. "Design of Self-Checking Microprogram Control." *IEEE Transactions on Computers* C-22 (March 1973): 255–62.

[CRIC 73] J. R. Cricchi, F. C. Blake, and M. D. Fitzpatrick. "The Brain Source Protected MNOS Memory Endurance." *IEEE International Electron Services Meeting, Washington D.C., 1973*, sects. 3–5.

[DELS 81a] P. H. Delsarte and P. H. Piret. "Bounds and Constructions for Binary Asymmetric Error-Correcting Codes." *IEEE Transactions on Information Theory* IT-27 (1981): 125–28.

[DELS 81b] P. H. Delsarte and P. H. Piret. "Spectral Enumerators for Certain Additive-Error-Correcting Codes over Integer Alphabets." *Information and Control* 48 (1981): 193–210.

[DICK 71] L. E. Dickson. *History of the Theory of Numbers*, 435. New York: Chelsea, 1971.

[DONG 84] H. Dong. "Modified Berger Codes for Detection of Unidirectional Errors." *IEEE Transactions on Computers* C-33 (June 1984): 572–75.

[FREI 61] C. V. Freiman. "Protective Block Codes for Asymmetric Binary Channels." Ph.D. Diss., Columbia University, New York, 1981.

[FREI 62] C. V. Freiman. "Optimal Error Detection Codes for Completely Asymmetric Binary Channels." *Information and Control* 5 (1962): 64–71.

[FREI 63] C. V. Freiman. "On the Use of Coset Codes in Asymmetric Channels." *IEEE Transactions on Information Theory* IT-9 (1963): 118.

[GORD 63] T. H. Gordon. "Error Coding Bounds for the Binary Asymmetric Channel." *IEEE Transactions on Information Theory* (1963): 206–8.

[HALL 67] M. Hall. *Combinatorial Theory*. Waltham, Mass.: Blaisdell Publishing Co., 1967.

[HELL 81] T. Helleseth and T. Klove. "On Group-Theoretic Codes for Asymmetric Channels." *Information and Control* 49 (1981): 1–9.

[HIRO 86] O. Hirota, K. Yamazaki, M. Nakagawa, and M. Ohya. "Properties of Error Correcting Code Using Photon Pulse." *Transactions of the IECE Japan* E69 (September 1986): 917–19.

[HONG 74] S. J. Hong and A. M. Patel. "Optimal Rectangular Code for High Density Magnetic Tapes." *IBM Journal of Research and Development* 18 (November 1974): 579–88.

[IKEN 71] N. Ikeno and G. Nakamura. "Constant-Weight Codes" (in Japanese). *Transactions of the IECE Japan* 54-A (July 1971): 410–17.

[ITOH 82a] H. Itoh and M. Nakamichi. "A Construction of Single Error Correcting and Multiple Unidirectional Error-Detecting Codes" (in Japanese). *Transactions of the IECE Japan* J65-A (September 1982): 934–41.

[JHA 87] N. K. Jha and M. B. Vora. "A Systematic Code for Detecting t-Unidirectional Errors." *Dig. 17th Annual Int. Symposium Fault-Tolerant* (July 1987): 96–101.

[KIM 59] W. K. Kim and C. V. Freiman. "Single Error Correction Codes for Asymmetric Channels." *IRE Transactions on Information Theory* IT-5 (June 1959): 62–66.

[KITA 80] Y. Kitano, S. Kohda, H. Kikuchi, and S. Sakai. "A 4-Mbit Full-Wafer ROM." *IEEE Journal of Solid-State Circuits* SC-15 (August 1980): 686–93.

[KLOV 81a] T. Klove. "Upper Bounds on Codes Correcting Asymmetric Errors." *IEEE Transactions on Information Theory* IT-27 (1981): 128–31.

[KLOV 81b] T. Klove. "A Lower Bound for $A(n, 4, w)$." *IEEE Transactions on Information Theory* IT-27 (1981): 257–58.

[KNUT 86] D. E. Knuth. "Efficient Balanced Codes." *IEEE Transactions on Information Theory* IT-32 (January 1986): 51–53.

[KOHD 86] S. Kohda, K. Masuda, K. Matsuzawa, and Y. Kitano. "A Giant Chip Multigate Transistor ROM Circuit Design." *IEEE Journal of Solid-State Circuits* SC-21 (October 1986): 713–19.

[KUND 88] S. Kundu and S. M. Reddy. "On Symmetric Error Correcting and All Unidirectional Error Detecting Codes." *IEEE Transactions on Computers*. Forthcoming.

[MACW 77] F. J. McWilliams and N. J. A. Sloane. *The Theory of Error-Correcting Codes*. New York: North-Holland Publish., 1977.

[MCEL 73] R. J. McEliece. "A Comment on 'A Class of Codes for Asymmetric Channels and a Problem from the Additive Theory of Numbers.'" *IEEE Transactions on Information Theory* IT-19 (January 1973): 137.

[MCEL 80] R. J. McEliece and E. R. Rodemich. "The Constantin-Rao Construction for Binary Asymmetric Error-Correcting Codes." *Information and Control* 44 (1980): 187–96.

[MCEL 81] R. J. McEliece. "Practical Codes for Photon Communication." *IEEE Transactions on Information Theory* IT-27 (July 1981): 393–98.

[NAEM 71a] K. Naemura. *Semi-Distance Systematic Codes* (in Japanese). Paper of Technical Group IT71-31. Tokyo: IECE Japan, 1971.

[NAEM 71b] K. Naemura, G. Nakamura, and N. Ikeno. "Constant-Weight Codes and Block Designs" (in Japanese). *Transactions of the IECE Japan* 54-A (December 1971): 671–78.

[NAKA 72] G. Nakamura, N. Ikeno, and K. Naemura. "Optimality of Constant-Weight Codes" (in Japanese). *Transactions of the IECE Japan* 55-A (July 1972): 354–59.

[NIKO 86] D. Nikolos, N. Gaitanis, and G. Philokyprou. "Systematic t-Error Correcting/All Unidirectional Error Detecting Codes." *IEEE Transactions on Computers* C-35 (1986): 394–402.

[PARH 78] B. Parhami and A. Avizienis. "Detection of Storage Errors in Mass Memories Using Low-Cost Arithmetic Error Codes." *IEEE Transactions on Computers* C-27 (April 1978): 302–8.

[PETE 72] W. W. Peterson and E. J. Weldon, Jr. *Error Correcting Codes*, 2d. ed. Cambridge: MIT Press, 1972.

[PRAD 77] D. K. Pradhan and S. M. Reddy. "Fault-Tolerant Failsafe Logic Networks." *Proceedings of IEEE COMPCON, San Francisco, March 1977*, 363.

[PRAD 80] D. K. Pradhan. "A New Class of Error-Correcting/Detecting Codes for Fault-Tolerant Computer Applications." *IEEE Transactions on Computers* C-29 (June 1980): 471–81.

[PRAD 86] D. K. Pradhan, ed. *Fault-Tolerant Computing, Theory and Techniques*. Englewood Cliffs, N.J.: Prentice-Hall, 1986.

[RAO 75] T. R. N. Rao and A. S. Chawla. "Asymmetric Error Codes for Some LSI Semiconductor Memories." *Proceedings of Annual Southeastern Symposium on System Theory* (March 1975): 170–71.

[SLOA 76] N. J. A. Sloane. "A Simple Description of an Error-Correcting Code for High-Density Magnetic Tape." *Bell Syst. Tech. Journal* 55 (February 1976): 157–65.

[SMIT 84] J. E. Smith. "On Separable Unordered Codes." *IEEE Transactions on Computers* C-33 (August 1984): 741–43.

[STAN 73] R. P. Stanley and M. F. Yoder, "A Study of Varshamov Codes for Asymmetric Channels," *Jet Propulsion Laboratory Technical Report 32–1526* 14 (1973): 117–122.

[UYEM 87] T. Uyematsu et al. "Effect of Asymmetric Error Correcting Code in Photon Communications with Energy Loss." *Proceedings of Symposium on Information Theory and Its Application at Enoshima, Japan, November 1987.*

[VARS 73] R. R. Varshamov. "A Class of Codes for Asymmetric Channels and Problem from Additive Theory of Numbers." *IEEE Transactions on Information Theory* IT-19 (January 1973): 92–95.

[WAKE 75] J. F. Wakerly. "Detection of Unidirectional Multiple Errors Using Low-Cost Arithmetic Codes." *IEEE Transactions on Computers* C-24 (February 1975): 210–12.

[WEBE 87] J. H. Weber, C. D. Vroedt, and D. E. Boekee. "New Upper Bounds on the Size of Codes Correcting Asymmetric Errors." *IEEE Transactions on Information Theory* IT-33, (May 1987): 434–37.

8

Codes for Logic Design I

A number of techniques exist nowadays for improving computer reliability and availability [WINO 63, ANDE 81, SIEW 82]. The general technique of *standby sparing* seems to have found much acceptance in practice. Standby sparing requires a modular design in which several identical modules of each type are present, some being used actively to perform the computing function, the others waiting to be switched in when one of the active modules fails. An ultrareliable computer, the *JPL self-testing and repairing* (*STAR*) *computer* [AVIZ 71], for example, makes extensive use of the techniques of modularity and standby sparing.

The fundamental task of standby sparing is to detect and localize a malfunction so that restructuring of the computer may take place by switching the faulty module out of service. Thus, an important part of the design of a highly reliable computer utilizing the standby sparing technique is an efficient and complete method of error detection and fault location [CART 71a]. Errors caused by faults may be detected by hardware check circuits (i.e., *checkers*). The recently devised diagnostic approach for fault isolation in logic systems also uses checkers extensively to capture errors, interpret their syndromes, and locate the fault positions [BOSS 82]. A circuit whose faults or malfunctions are always checked by itself is said to be *self-checking* [WAKE 78].

Self-checking circuits offer a number of advantages, the most obvious of which is the *immediate detection of errors*. Another is the capability of detecting errors caused by *transient failures*. Further, self-checking circuits are becoming more attractive with the advance in VLSI.

Self-checking circuits rely on redundancy to detect errors. That is, during error-free operation the circuit outputs cannot assume all possible states. This redundancy may be viewed as an encoding of the circuit outputs that must be decoded by a check circuit to determine if they form a proper codeword; if they do not, an error is presumed. Hence, the theory of error detecting codes is important in the design of these circuits.

Some error detecting codes, such as *parity codes*, *check-sum codes*, *low-cost residue codes*, and some unidirectional error detecting codes (e.g., *m-out-of-n codes*, *Berger codes*, and the like), have been studied for application. These applications are for logic circuits, such as the *arithmetic logic unit* (ALU), the *programmable logic array* (PLA), and some kinds of decoding circuits. Considerable literature has appeared on the implementation of these checking circuits. Checkers can no longer be assumed to be error-free in computer systems, because check circuits are constructed from the same components as the circuits that perform the computer operations and hence are subject to the same types of failures. This brings to mind the age-old question: "Who is checking the checker?" The answer is clearly a checker that is self-checking.

This chapter discusses the self-checking concept and how error-correcting/detecting codes are applied to logic circuits (e.g., ALU, PLA, and error checking/correcting (ECC) circuits). An implementation method for a self-checking checker is included in Chapter 9.

8.1 SELF-CHECKING CONCEPT

In order to detect intermittent faults, as well as stuck faults in logic circuits, many kinds of checkers, such as *parity code checkers*, *duplication checkers*, *parity-prediction checkers*, and *residue code checkers*, have already been applied in an adaptive manner to some functional circuits (e.g., adders, multipliers, decoding circuits, data path circuits, and the like [SELL 68]). On the other hand, the theory of self-checking circuits (e.g., *totally self-checking* (*TSC*) circuits, *strongly fault-secure* (*SFS*) circuits, *error-secure* (*ES*) circuits, and so on) has been studied extensively by several researchers [CART 68, 71b, ANDE 71, WAKE 74, SMIT 78, NICO 84, NANY 85b]. Practical design methods for self-checking circuits appear in [CART 77, SMIT 83, NANY 85b].

Here, we study the general concept of self-checking circuits and the checker concept for the self-checking checkers.

8.1.1 General Concept

It would be preferable for the circuits to be designed such that *they will indicate any malfunction during normal operation and will not produce an erroneous result without an error indication*. In these circuits, any fault from a specified set of faults will cause a detectable erroneous output during normal operation, and each fault must not cause an erroneous output without also producing an error signal [CART 68, ANDE 71].

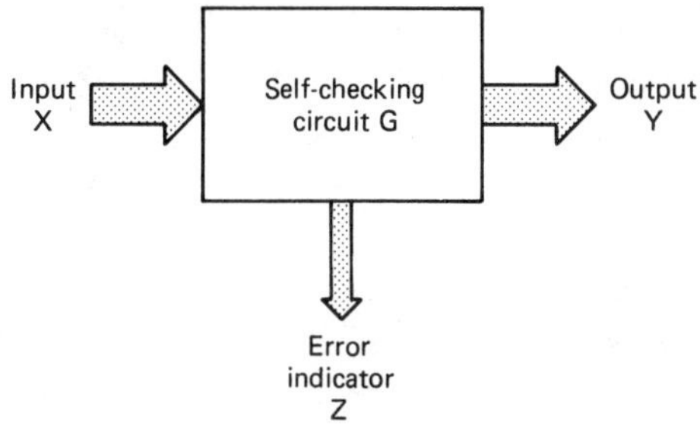

Figure 8.1 Self-checking circuit.

The general structure of these circuits is shown in Fig. 8.1; the *error indicator* output Z must be designed to produce an error signal for some normal circuit input whenever a fault from a specified set of faults occurs within the circuit.

In designing the above circuits, the circuit **G** is considered to be divided into two connected circuit blocks, the functional circuit block **L** and the check circuit block **CK**, as shown in Fig. 8.2.

First, we discuss self-checking functional circuits and then extend that to self-checking functional networks. As for check circuits, they will be covered in a subsequent section.

We will consider a combinational circuit **L** that produces an output vector $Y(X, f)$, which is a function of the input vector X and a fault $f \in F$, a specified set of faults in the circuit. The absence of a fault is called the *null fault* and is denoted by λ. If the circuit **L** has n inputs, then the *input space* $\mathbf{\Omega x}$ of **L** is the set of all 2^n input vectors. Similarly, if **L** has r outputs, then the set of all 2^r output vectors is the *output space* $\mathbf{\Omega y}$ of **L**. In general, logic circuits will receive only a subset of their input space during "normal" (i.e., fault-free) operation; this subset is called the *input codespace* **N**. Then, $\mathbf{\Omega x} - \mathbf{N}$ is the *input noncodespace*. Here, we consider only circuits whose outputs under normal operation are codewords, and therefore we also define for each circuit its *output codespace* **S**. Then, $\mathbf{\Omega y} - \mathbf{S}$ is the *output noncode-*

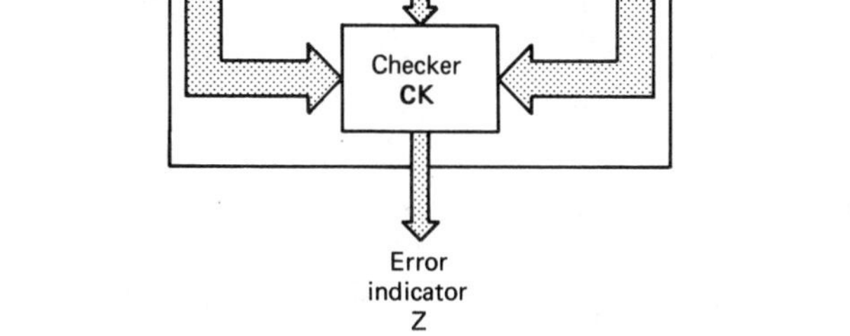

Figure 8.2 A model for a self-checking circuit.

pace. For a given input $X \in \mathbf{N}$, a fault may or may not cause an error in the output. If the fault does cause an error, it may change the output, either to a noncodeword (i.e., a *detectable error*), or to a different codeword (i.e., an *undetectable error*).

Fault secure and self-testing

Definition 8-1. A circuit **L** is *fault secure* (*FS*) for an input set **N** and a fault set F if for any input X in **N** and for any fault f in F, $Y(X, f) = Y(X, \lambda)$, or $Y(X, f) \notin \mathbf{S}$.

That is, the output of a fault-secure circuit is always either the correct codeword or a noncodeword but never a wrong codeword for any fault in F. This is illustrated in Fig. 8.3.

Definition 8-2. A circuit **L** is *self-testing* (*ST*) for an input set **N** and a fault set F if for every fault f in F there is some input X in **N** such that $Y(X, f)$ is not in **S**.

Fig. 8.4 illustrates this definition.

By this definition, an input X for which $Y(X, f)$ is not in **S**, or $Y(X, f) \neq Y(X, \lambda)$, is called a *test pattern* for f. If each input in **N** occurs during the normal course of operations of the circuit, then self-testing guarantees that all faults in F produce detectable errors during normal operation.

The properties of self-testing and fault secureness are further illustrated in Fig. 8.5. This shows the set of all faults and its subsets F, the input space $\mathbf{\Omega x}$ and its subset **N**, and the output space $\mathbf{\Omega y}$ and its subset **S**. For example, F shows the set of single-stuck faults, or the set of unidirectional faults. The outside of F shows all possible faults excluding the faults in F. For input vectors, **N** shows the set of normal *input codewords*, and the outside of **N** shows the set of *input noncodewords*.

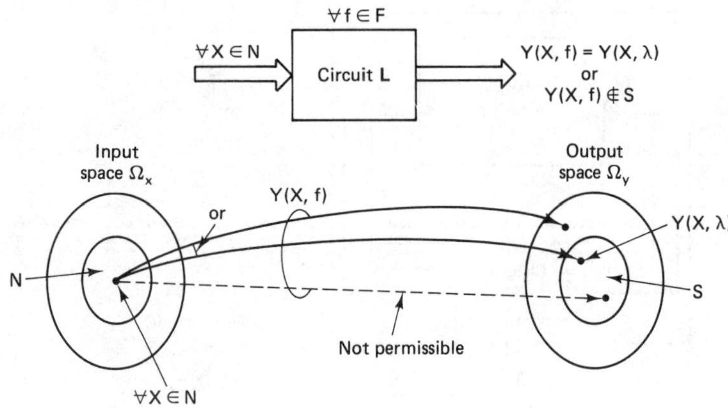

Figure 8.3 Fault-secure circuit.

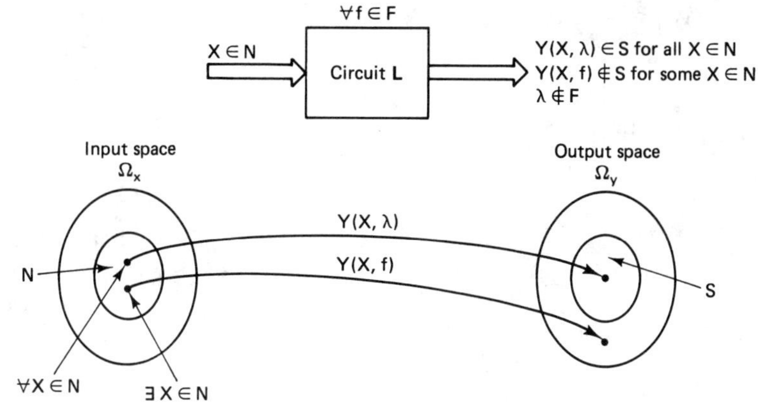

Figure 8.4 Self-testing circuit.

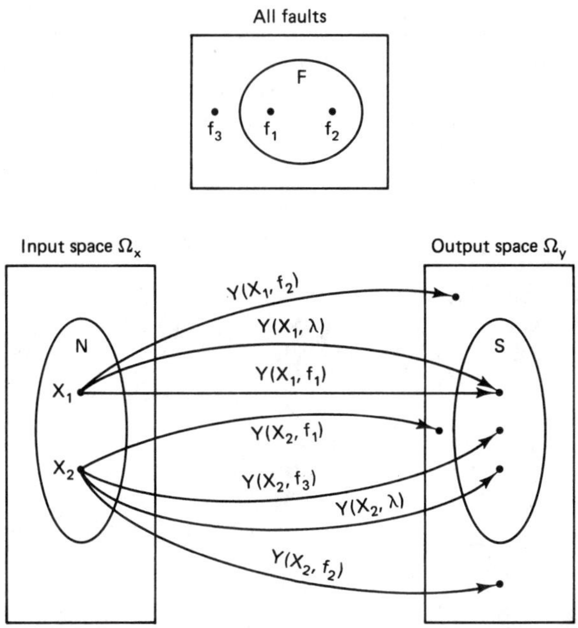

Figure 8.5 Examples of self-testing and fault-secure properties.

For output vectors, **S** shows the set of *output codewords*, and outside of **S** shows the set of *output noncodewords*.

In the absence of faults, inputs from **N** produce outputs in **S**, as shown by the transition $Y(X, \lambda)$ for various X. Self-testing is demonstrated by the existence of a test pattern in **N** for each of the faults f_1 and f_2 in F (X_2 for f_1, and X_1 and X_2 for f_2 are test patterns). Fault-secure property is illustrated by the transition of $Y(X_1, f)$ for various f. In the presence of a fault from F, the output is either correct (e.g., $Y(X_1, f_1)$), or it is a noncodeword (e.g., $Y(X_1, f_2)$). However, faults outside of

F may produce erroneous codeword outputs (e.g., $Y(X_2, f_3)$), which are undetectable.

Definition 8-3. A circuit **L** is *totally self-checking* (TSC) if it is both self-testing and fault-secure.

Self-testing is necessary in addition to fault-secureness because even if the circuit output is always a correct codeword for a single fault in the fault-secure circuit, the second fault may appear after some time has elapsed, and then this circuit may not detect the two faults.

Example 8-1

Fig. 8.6 shows a circuit that computes in parallel the exclusive-or (EX-OR) of two input vectors, $A = [a_0, a_1, \ldots, a_{n-1}, a_p]$ and $B = [b_0, b_1, \ldots, b_{n-1}, b_p]$, where a_p and b_p are even-parity bits. It is apparent that EX-OR of any two even-parity codewords is also an even-parity codeword. That is, an output vector $C = [c_0, c_1, \ldots, c_{n-1}, c_p]$, where c_p is a parity bit, is also an even-parity codeword. This property is called *code preserving*, and the code is said to be *preserved* under this operation. We now consider F to be the set of single faults. Input codespace **N** is defined as the set in which both A and B are even-parity codewords. Output codespace **S** is defined as the set of even-parity codewords (shown in Fig. 8.7).

The even-parity code is a distance-2 linear code, and the circuit of Fig. 8.6 is code preserving. This circuit is also *fault secure* for all single faults, since a single fault produces at most a distance-1 change in the output. That is, single faults produce single errors in the output, or produce masked output (i.e., correct output). Therefore, the output always belongs to noncodespace, or correct output. This satisfies the definition of fault secureness. As for the self-testing property, we can easily find out test patterns for each single fault (see Table 8.1). For example, for a single-stuck fault input in an

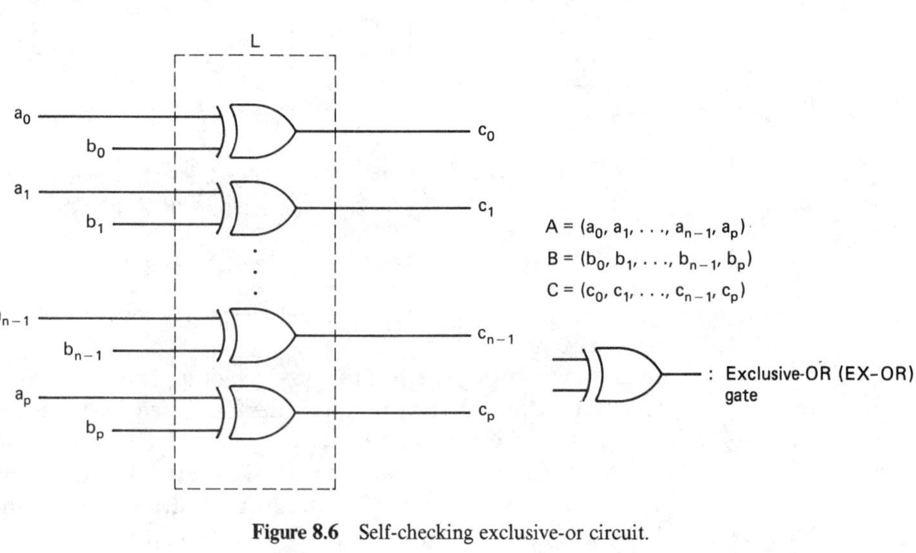

Figure 8.6 Self-checking exclusive-or circuit.

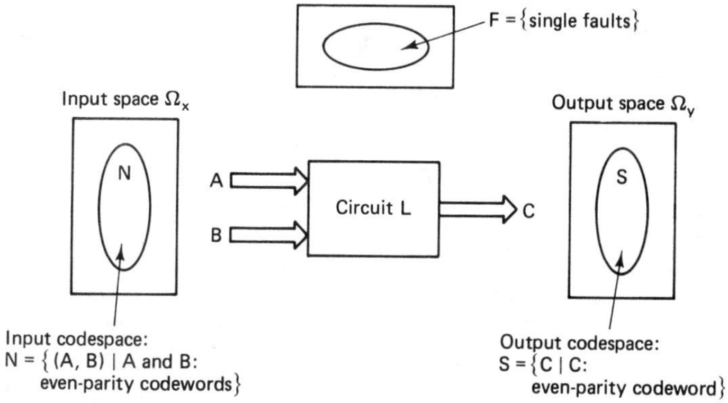

Figure 8.7 Input and output codespaces for the example circuit in Fig. 8.6.

TABLE 8.1 TEST PATTERNS (a_i, b_i) FOR SINGLE FAULTS

Input Single Fault		Output Single Fault	
*s-a-*0,	*s-a-*1	*s-a-*0,	*s-a-*1
(1, 1)	(0, 0)	(1, 0) or (0, 1)	(0, 0) or (1, 1)

EX-OR gate (e.g., stuck-at-0 fault in a_i or b_i input), the codeword inputs A and B that include $(a_i, b_i) = (1, 1)$ are the test patterns.

From the above, the circuit shown in Fig. 8.6 is self-testing and fault secure, and hence is TSC for all codeword inputs under single faults.

From the standpoint of reliability, TSC is ideal. However, in general, self-testing is a rather difficult condition to satisfy perfectly, as compared to fault secureness. This is because there are sometimes not enough inputs **N** to detect every fault in F. With this difficulty in mind, another self-checking concept is proposed in [SMIT 78]. In this conception, a *fault sequence* $\langle f_1, f_2, \ldots, f_n \rangle$, where $f_i \in F$, $1 \le i \le n$, is defined to represent the event where fault f_1 occurs, followed later by f_2 (at which point both f_1 and f_2 are present in the circuit), and so forth until f_n occurs. It is assumed that once a line becomes stuck at 0 or 1, it remains stuck at that value; also assumed is that faults occur one at a time and that between any two fault occurrences there is a time interval sufficient for all input code combinations to be applied to the circuit.

The following definitions are based on [SMIT 78].

Definition 8-4. Assume that circuit **L** always gives correct codewords for a sequence of fewer than m faults (accumulated $m - 1$ faults), $2 \le m \le n$, in F, and for all $X \in \mathbf{N}$. That is,

$$Y(X, \langle f_1, f_2, \ldots, f_{m-1} \rangle) = Y(X, \lambda)$$

Also assume that for m-faults sequence $\langle f_1, f_2, \ldots, f_{m-1}, f_m \rangle$ there is some $X \in \mathbf{N}$ such that

$$Y(X, \langle f_1, f_2, \ldots, f_m \rangle) \notin \mathbf{S}$$

Then **L** is said to be *strongly fault secure* (*SFS*) *for* $\langle f_1, f_2, \ldots, f_m \rangle$.

Definition 8-5. A circuit **L** is *strongly fault secure* (*SFS*) *for* $F = \{f_1, f_2, \ldots, f_m\}$ if it is SFS for all sequences of faults in F.

Fig. 8.8 illustrates the concept of SFS.

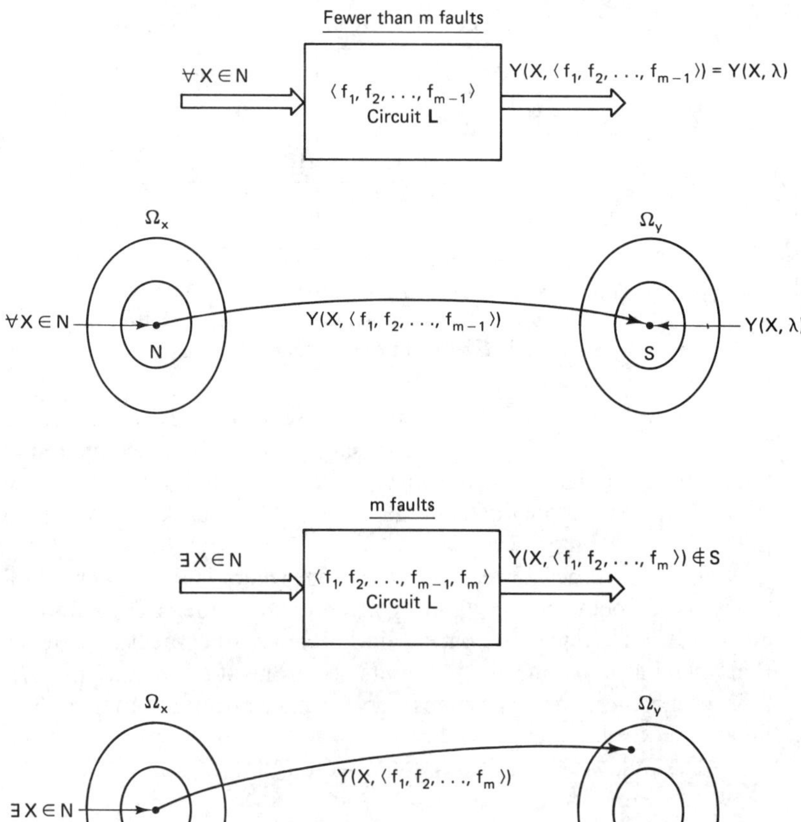

Figure 8.8 SFS circuit for $\langle f_1, f_2, \ldots, f_{m-1}, f_m \rangle$.

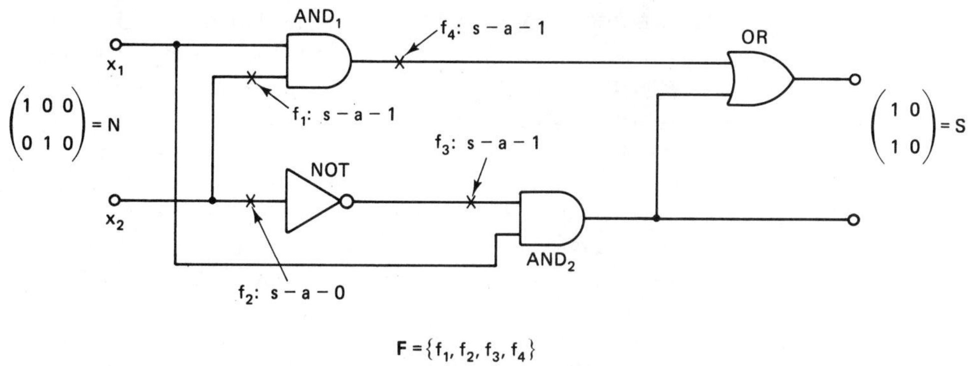

Figure 8.9 Example SFS circuit for $\langle f_1, f_2, f_3, f_4 \rangle$.

Example 8-2

In the circuit **L** given in Fig. 8.9, let faults in F occur in the following sequence.

f_1: stuck-at-1 fault at one input of AND_1 gate.
f_2: stuck-at-0 fault at the input of NOT gate.
f_3: stuck-at-1 fault at one input of AND_2 gate.
f_4: stuck-at-1 fault at the output of AND_1 gate.

In this case, circuit **L** is fault secure for input X, $X \in \mathbf{N}$,

$$\mathbf{N} = \left\{ \begin{pmatrix} x_1 \\ x_2 \end{pmatrix} \right\} = \left\{ \begin{pmatrix} 0 \\ 0 \end{pmatrix} \begin{pmatrix} 0 \\ 1 \end{pmatrix} \begin{pmatrix} 1 \\ 0 \end{pmatrix} \right\}$$

and for the fault sequence $\langle f_1, f_2, f_3 \rangle$, since

$$Y(X, \langle f_1, f_2, f_3 \rangle) = Y(X, \lambda) \quad \text{for all } X \in \mathbf{N}$$

That is, circuit **L** always gives correct output regardless of the fault sequences: $\langle f_1 \rangle$, $\langle f_1, f_2 \rangle$ and $\langle f_1, f_2, f_3 \rangle$.

Next, let stuck-at-1 fault f_4 occur at the output of AND_1 gate. For $X_1 \in \left\{ \begin{pmatrix} 0 \\ 0 \end{pmatrix}, \begin{pmatrix} 0 \\ 1 \end{pmatrix} \right\}$, the circuit manifests itself as

$$Y(X_1, \langle f_1, f_2, f_3, f_4 \rangle) = \begin{pmatrix} 1 \\ 0 \end{pmatrix} \notin \mathbf{S}$$

Therefore the circuit **L** is SFS for the fault sequence $\langle f_1, f_2, f_3, f_4 \rangle$.

It can be shown that any SFS circuit satisfies TSC conditions. Furthermore, if a circuit is not SFS, it is always possible to produce an erroneous code output prior to a noncode output. Hence, SFS circuits form the largest class of circuits to satisfy TSC conditions.

Error secure and error preserving. Note that both fault secureness and self-testing specify only the behavior of the circuit for codeword inputs. That is, inputs are always assumed to be error free. For some circuits, such as self-checking checkers, we are also interested in the behavior of the circuit for noncodeword inputs. When the interconnection of self-checking circuit blocks is considered, it is necessary to examine the mapping of input noncodewords, since under failures in previous circuit blocks a circuit block might receive noncodeword inputs.

Here, we define a pair (X_p, X_q) where X_p is a member of the input codespace of the circuit **L** and X_q is a member of the input noncodespace. The significance of the ordered pair is that X_q represents an erroneous input that may be received by **L** instead of X_p. That is, $X_q = X_p + E$, where $X_p \in N$, $X_q \in \Omega x - \mathbf{N}$, and E expresses an input error. The circuit **L** we consider here is assumed to be fault free, and X_p and X_q are entirely dependent on circuit blocks that are previous to **L**.

Definition 8-6 [SMIT 76]. A circuit **L** with output codespace **S** is *error secure* (ES) for noncodespace (input) $\mathbf{\Omega x - N}$ if for any input X_q in $\mathbf{\Omega x - N}$, where $X_q = X_p + E$, $X_p \in \mathbf{N}$, $E \neq 0$,

$$Y(X_q, \lambda) \notin S, \text{ or } Y(X_q, \lambda) = Y(X_p, \lambda)$$

Fig. 8.10 illustrates this definition.

If the circuit is error secure and receives an erroneous input, then it either passes a noncodeword on to subsequent circuit blocks, or masks (i.e., corrects) the error in the input word.

Definition 8-7 [SMIT 76]. A circuit **L** with output codespace **S** is *error preserving* (EP) for noncodespace $\mathbf{\Omega x - N}$, if for any input X in $\mathbf{\Omega x - N}$,

$$Y(X, \lambda) \notin \mathbf{S}$$

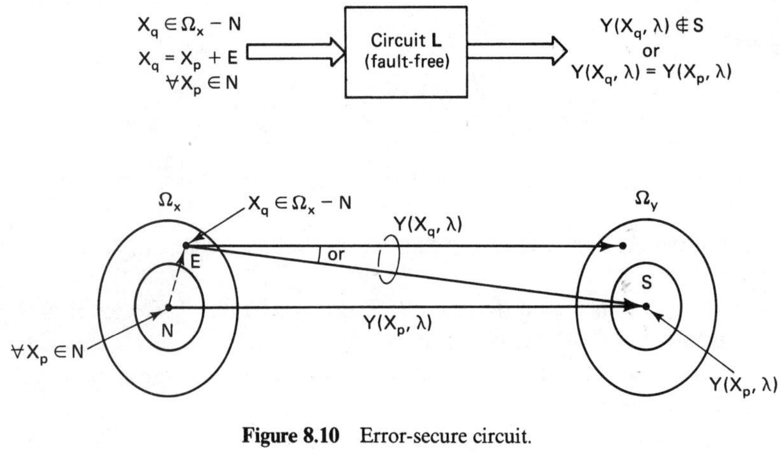

Figure 8.10 Error-secure circuit.

A circuit that is error preserving is error secure, but the converse is not necessarily true. The term *code disjoint* (*CD*) is synonymous with *error preserving* [ANDE 71]. That is, a code-disjoint (or error-preserving) circuit maps all of the members of its input noncodespace to noncodeword outputs, and this concept applies only to circuits under fault-free operation.

Next, we will consider the case in which the circuit **L** has a fault sequence $\langle f_1, f_2, \ldots, f_n \rangle$, where $f_i \in F$, $1 \le i \le n$, in addition to having noncodeword inputs. The following definitions are based on [NICO 84].

Definition 8-8. Before the occurrence of any fault, circuit **L** is code disjoint. Assume that circuit **L** is such that for a sequence of fewer than $m (2 \le m \le n)$ faults in F and for all noncodeword inputs $X \in \mathbf{\Omega x} - \mathbf{N}$,

$$Y(X, \langle f_1, f_2, \ldots, f_{m-1} \rangle) \notin \mathbf{S}$$

Also assume that for the m-fault sequence $\langle f_1, f_2, \ldots, f_m \rangle$, circuit **L** is self-testing. That is,

$$Y(X, \langle f_1, f_2, \ldots, f_m \rangle) \notin \mathbf{S} \quad \text{for some } X \in \mathbf{N}$$

Then **L** is said to be *strongly code disjoint* (*SCD*) for $\langle f_1, f_2, \ldots, f_m \rangle$.

Definition 8-9. A circuit **L** is *strongly code disjoint* (*SCD*) *for* $F = \{f_1, f_2, \ldots, f_m, \ldots, f_n\}$, if it is SCD for all sequences of faults in F.

This is illustrated in Fig. 8.11.

In this definition, an assumption has to be made regarding the occurrence of failures in the circuit such that faults occur one at a time, and between any two fault occurrences there is sufficient interval for all code inputs to be applied to the circuit.

In Definition 8-8, we can also define such that for all inputs $X \in \mathbf{\Omega x} - \mathbf{N}$ and an m-sequence fault $\langle f_1, f_2, \ldots, f_m \rangle$, the circuit satisfies $Y(X, \langle f_1, f_2, \ldots, f_m \rangle) \notin \mathbf{S}$ [NICO 84]. That is, there is no such input $X \in \mathbf{\Omega x} - \mathbf{N}$ that satisfies $Y(X, \langle f_1, f_2, \ldots, f_m \rangle) \in \mathbf{S}$. This definition is stronger than Definition 8-8. Notice that the stronger property is not always necessary, since it is more difficult to implement.

Self-checking networks. We consider a network of circuit blocks as shown in Fig. 8.12.

In this network, we have to consider the faults in the interconnection between circuit blocks as well as those within each circuit block. That is, input noncodewords are given to the circuit block not only by the faults in the previous circuit blocks but also by the faults in the input connection lines.

We divide the network into two subnetworks, one is the subnetwork $\mathbf{L}_{\mathrm{I}}$ of the output interface circuit blocks, whose outputs are primary outputs of the network, and the other one is the subnetwork $\mathbf{L}_{\mathrm{II}}$ of the remaining internal circuit blocks. If the subnetwork $\mathbf{L}_{\mathrm{II}}$ is SFS for a fault set F_{II}, the outputs of $\mathbf{L}_{\mathrm{II}}$ are always correct codewords or noncodewords. Furthermore, if the subnetwork $\mathbf{L}_{\mathrm{I}}$ is SFS and SCD

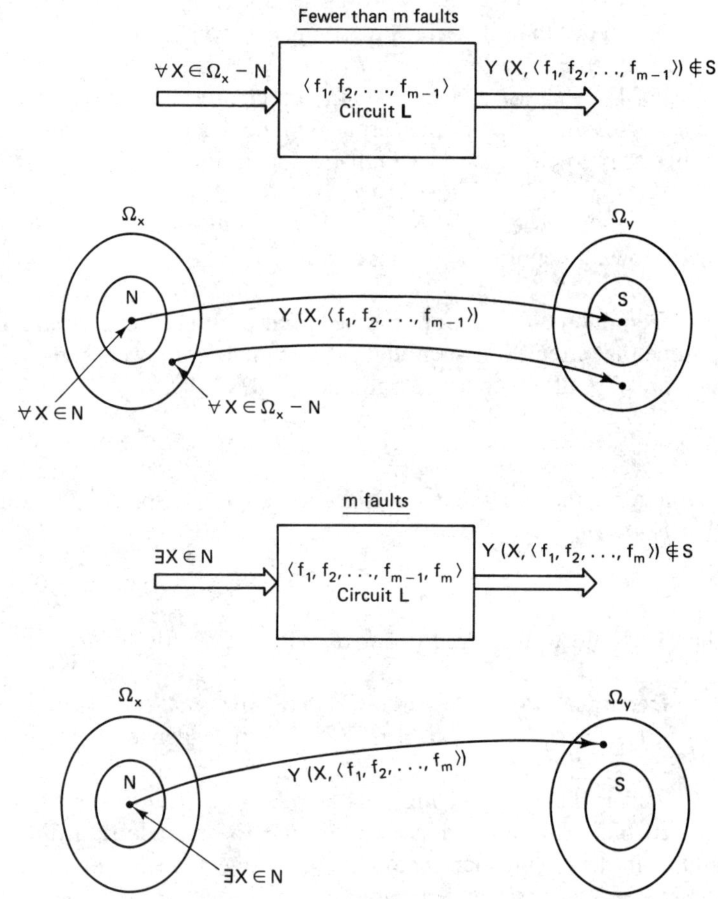

Figure 8.11 Strongly code-disjoint circuit.

for a fault set F_{I}, the outputs of $\mathbf{L}_{\mathrm{I}}$ are always correct codewords or noncodewords. This is because $\mathbf{L}_{\mathrm{I}}$ is SFS for codeword inputs and SCD for noncodeword inputs, and therefore the outputs of $\mathbf{L}_{\mathrm{I}}$ are always correct codewords or noncodewords for all inputs to $\mathbf{L}_{\mathrm{I}}$ (i.e., all outputs of $\mathbf{L}_{\mathrm{II}}$), even if some faults exist in both $\mathbf{L}_{\mathrm{I}}$ and $\mathbf{L}_{\mathrm{II}}$. Hence, the total network is SFS. From the foregoing considerations, an SFS network can be obtained as follows.

Theorem 8-1. *If the subnetwork $\mathbf{L}_{\mathrm{I}}$ consisting of the output interface circuit blocks is SFS and SCD for fault set F_{I}, and the remaining subnetwork $\mathbf{L}_{\mathrm{II}}$ consisting of the internal circuit blocks is SFS for fault set F_{II}, then the total network is SFS for all fault sequences from F_{I} and F_{II}.*

If the faults exist in either $\mathbf{L}_{\mathrm{I}}$ or $\mathbf{L}_{\mathrm{II}}$ but not in both, then the code disjoint (CD) property can replace SCD as a requirement for subnetwork $\mathbf{L}_{\mathrm{I}}$.

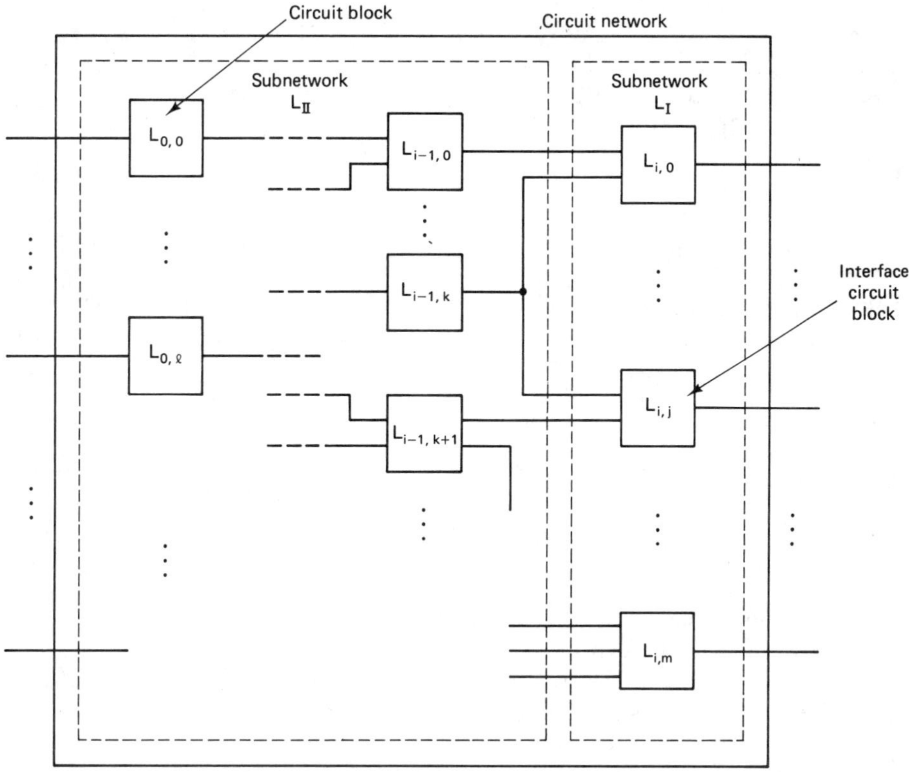

Figure 8.12 Circuit block network.

Corollary 8-1. *If the subnetwork* $\mathbf{L}_{\mathrm{I}}$ *of the output interface block is SFS and CD, and the subnetwork* $\mathbf{L}_{\mathrm{II}}$ *of the remaining internal blocks is SFS, then the total network is SFS for all fault sequences in either* $\mathbf{L}_{\mathrm{I}}$ *or* $\mathbf{L}_{\mathrm{II}}$*, but not in both.*

The SFS network has important advantages: in an SFS network, it may not be necessary to place checkers at every circuit block, but only at the output interface blocks.

Thus checker placement will be determined by mean time between failure (MTBF) of the network. General design methods for SFS networks have not yet been fully established. However, an SFS combinational circuit network can be easily realized if it is inverter free, that is, it contains only AND gates and OR gates, as stated in the following theorem.

Theorem 8-2 [SMIT 78]. *A network that consists of only inverter-free combinational circuit blocks and in which the block input/output interfaces are encoded with unidirectional error detecting codes is SFS with respect to unidirectional faults.*

Proof. It is observed that unidirectional faults in an inverter-free circuit block or in the input interconnection line always cause unidirectional errors. Since every

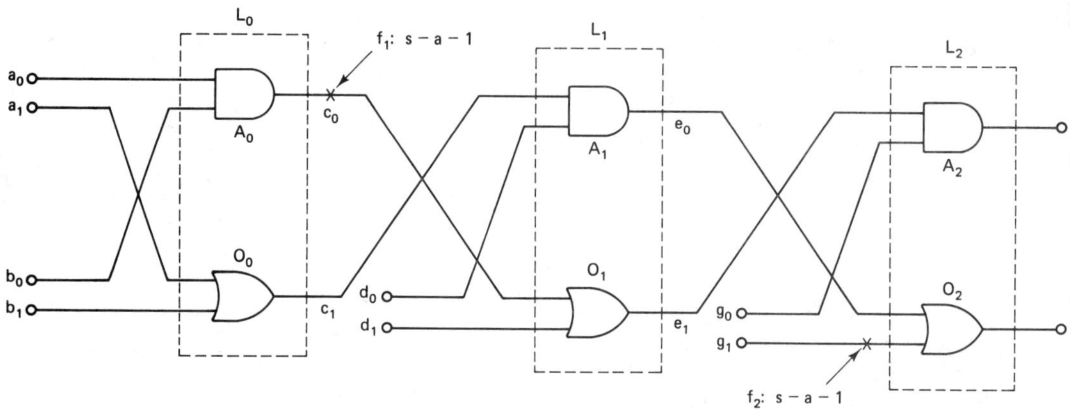

Primary inputs: (a_0, a_1), (b_0, b_1), (d_0, d_1), (g_0, g_1): 1-out-of-2 codes
Observable interface (primary output): (h_0, h_1)
Fault sequence: $\langle f_1, f_2 \rangle$

Figure 8.13 Cascaded inverter-free network.

combinational circuit block has an input and output encoded with a unidirectional error detecting code (e.g., an m-out-of-n code, Berger code (see Chapter 7)), the unidirectional errors always map a codeword to a noncodeword. And unidirectional faults in the inverter-free circuit block never map unidirectional error input to a codeword output. Therefore, these unidirectional errors at some circuit block can be propagated to the output interface of the network and can be detected by a unidirectional error decoder. Q.E.D.

Example 8-3

Let's consider the network that consists of three inverter-free combinational circuit blocks, $\mathbf{L}_0$, $\mathbf{L}_1$, and $\mathbf{L}_2$ interconnected in cascade as shown in Fig. 8.13. The 1-out-of-2 codes are used at all block interfaces as well as at the primary output of the network (i.e., the observable interface).

In this example, two unidirectional faults, stuck-at-1 faults, are assumed to exist at the output of A_0 gate first and then at one input of O_2 gate. Outputs in each block interface are shown in Fig. 8.14, where inputs (a_0, a_1) and (b_0, b_1) are, for example, equal to $(1, 0)$ and $(0, 1)$, respectively. At the first fault stage, which includes only f_1 fault, only case (IV) (Fig. 8.14) has noncodeword output. If there is no such input as case (IV), that is, no such input set as $(a_0, a_1) = (1, 0)$, $(b_0, b_1) = (0, 1)$, $(d_0, d_1) = (1, 0)$, and $(g_0, g_1) = (1, 0)$, this network always has correct codeword outputs. And under these inputs at the second fault stage, which includes f_2 fault as well as f_1 fault, case (II) also has noncodeword outputs. From this, primary output (h_0, h_1) is always correct codeword or noncodeword for these inputs. In case (III) shown in Fig. 8.14, for example, it should be noted that all circuit blocks are not always CD.

The above example shows that the circuit network shown in Fig. 8.13 is SFS for the unidirectional fault sequence $\langle f_1, f_2 \rangle$ and for restricted inputs, even though each circuit block is not always CD. This implies that noncodewords may appear at embedded interfaces of the network before a noncodeword is produced as the first

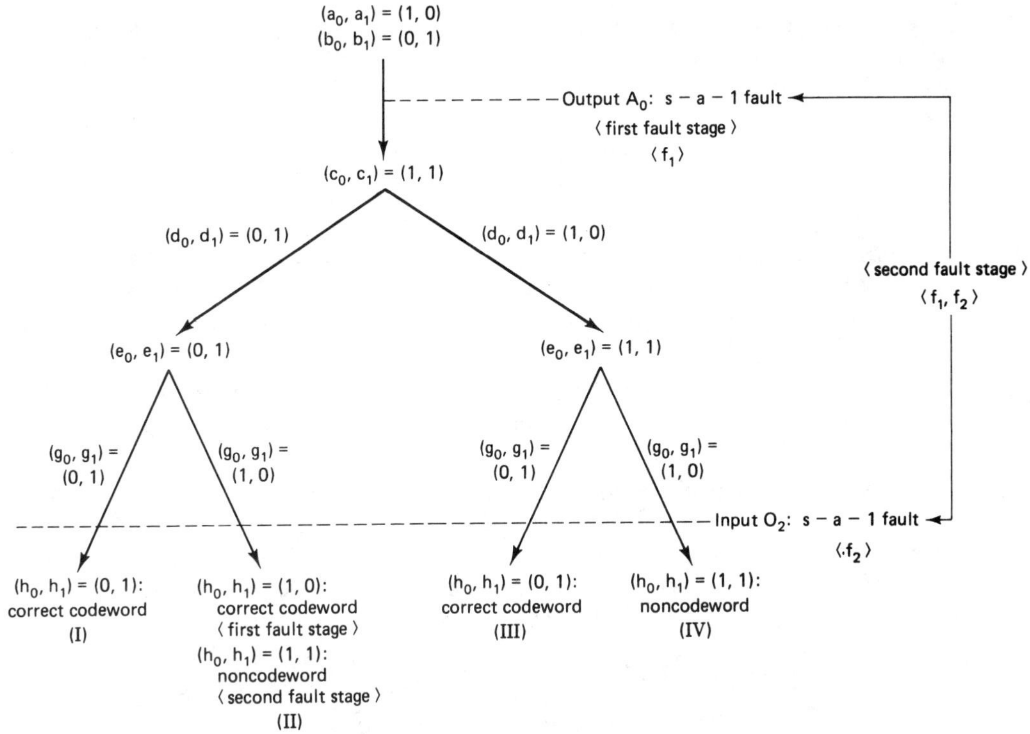

Figure 8.14 Interface outputs in Fig. 8.13 circuit.

erroneous output. From this consideration, new comprehensive concepts of error secure and error propagating are defined for the circuit block interfaces.

Here, let F be the set of all faults in a network consisting of some circuit blocks and $\langle F \rangle$ be the set of all sequences of faults from F. Given a fault sequence from $\langle F \rangle$, the network is assumed to be initially fault free and capable of performing the correct function; once the first fault in the sequence occurs, the network goes into the first fault stage; further on, when the second fault occurs, the system will go into the second fault stage, and so on.

The following definitions and theorem are based on [NANY 85b].

Definition 8-10. A circuit block interface is *error secure* (ES) at a given fault stage if any error that may possibly occur at the interface never causes an incorrect codeword at any observable interface during the fault stage.

Definition 8-11. A circuit block interface is *error propagating* (EP) at a given fault stage if any error that may possibly occur at the interface eventually produces a noncodeword at some observable interface during the fault stage.

It is noted that error secure (ES) in Definition 8-10 and error secure in Definition 8-6 are different in that the former is defined for block interfaces that may include some faults within them while the latter is defined for fault-free circuit blocks. Therefore, the Definition 8-10 covers Definition 8-6, but the converse is not necessarily true.

The concept of error propagating includes both error preserving (i.e., code disjoint) and self-testing. Theorem 8-3 indicates the relation between ES/EP and SFS in a network that consists of some circuit blocks and their interfaces.

Theorem 8-3. *A network is SFS for fault set F if for every fault sequence from $\langle F \rangle$ all the observable interfaces remain error secure (ES) until the earliest fault stage at which at least one observable interface becomes error propagating (EP).*

Based on this theorem, a design method for SFS microprocessor is given in [NANY 85b], and is shown in Section 9.2.2.

8.1.2 Checker Concept

In order to make the functional circuit a TSC or SFS circuit, the error detection circuit (i.e., the checker) must provide an error indicator. Therefore, the circuit **G** consists of the functional circuit under check (**L**) and the checker (**CK**). This is shown in Fig. 8.2.

A model for the error detection circuit can be given as in Fig. 8.2 [SELL 68]. In general, the checker receives inputs X, and also W and Y from the circuit **L**. The line W generated in the process of generating outputs may not be the output Y itself. There have already been many kinds of checkers for special functional circuits [SELL 68]. Some of them are code checkers, such as parity-code checkers, residue-code checkers, m-out-of-n code checkers, and Berger-code checkers. Others are prediction checkers. The self-checking concepts in Section 8.1.1 have been defined for code checkers, that is, for checking the coded output Y. They do not always hold for other types of checkers (e.g., prediction checkers). Here, we will outline two cases:

Case 1: Output *Y* encoded. The checker included in this case is called a *code checker*. The checker's input is always Y, which is the output of the circuit **L**. This is shown in Fig. 8.15.

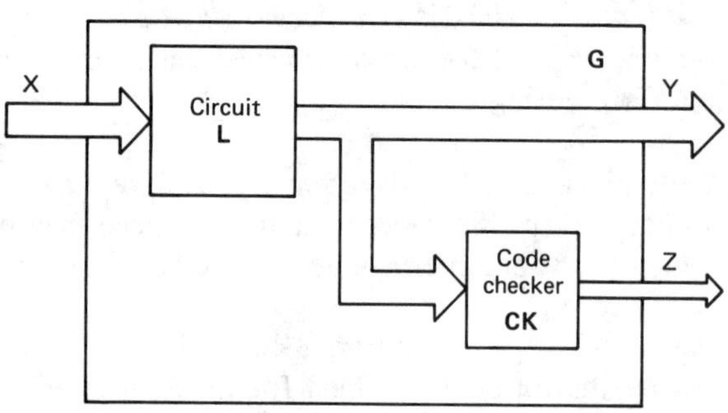

Figure 8.15 Checking by examining outputs—Code checker.

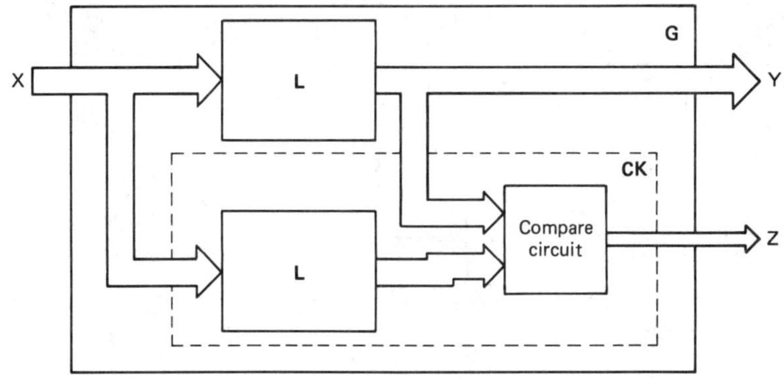

Figure 8.16 Checking by duplication—Duplication checker.

Case 2: Output *Y* nonencoded. Many types of functional circuits, such as control circuits, have their outputs nonencoded. For this type of circuit, *duplication checkers*, *parity prediction checkers*, and *input regeneration checkers* [SELL 68] have already been proposed and are applied to logic systems in existing computers.

Fig. 8.16 describes the concept of the *duplication checker*. The functional circuit **L** is duplicated and the outputs are compared.

Fig. 8.17 describes the concept of the *parity prediction checker* for circuit **L**. A parity bit of the output Y is generated independently by the prediction circuit **P** using input X, while an equivalent output parity bit is generated from output Y, and these parity bits are compared.

Fig. 8.18 describes the concept of the *input regeneration checker*. This checker regenerates the inputs from the outputs by inverse logic $\mathbf{L}^{-1}$ of the original circuit **L** and compares the regenerated inputs with the original inputs. The technique of this

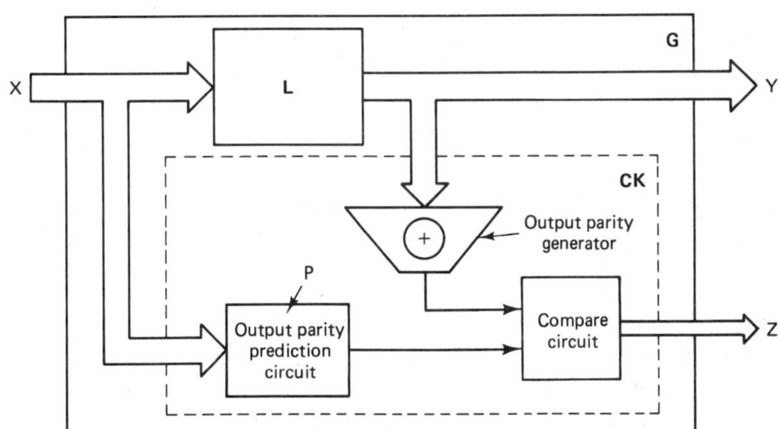

Figure 8.17 Checking by parity prediction—Parity prediction checker.

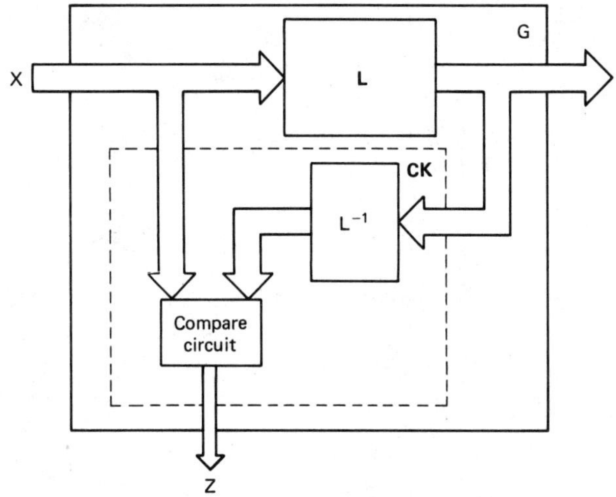

Figure 8.18 Checking by regenerating inputs—Input regeneration checker—[SELL 68]. © 1968 McGraw-Hill Book Company.

checker requires that the functional logic of **L** have a unique inverse operation. Example 8-4 illustrates this principle.

Example 8-4 [SELL 68]

Let **L** be the 3-input (x_0, x_1, x_2), 3-output (y_0, y_1, y_2) combinational circuit defined by the following truth table.

x_0	x_1	x_2	y_0	y_1	y_2
0	0	0	1	1	1
0	0	1	0	0	1
0	1	0	1	0	0
0	1	1	0	1	1
1	0	0	0	0	0
1	0	1	0	1	0
1	1	0	1	1	0
1	1	1	1	0	1

Select x_1 to form a subinverse circuit $\mathbf{L}_1^{-1}$ according to the following equation:

$$x_1 = y_0 \oplus y_1 \cdot y_2$$

Then the error detecting circuit is shown in Fig. 8.19. This checker's ability is limited because not all inputs are checked. This checker will detect if either y_0 or $y_1 \cdot y_2$ is in error, but not both.

The duplication checker and the input regeneration checker can also be considered special cases of the prediction checker, because circuit output Y is exactly "predicted" by the duplicated circuit in the duplication checker and, inversely, circuit input X can be said to be "predicted" from the circuit output Y in the input regeneration checker. This will be discussed in detail in Section 9.1.5. Hence, the checker included in case 2 is called a *prediction checker*.

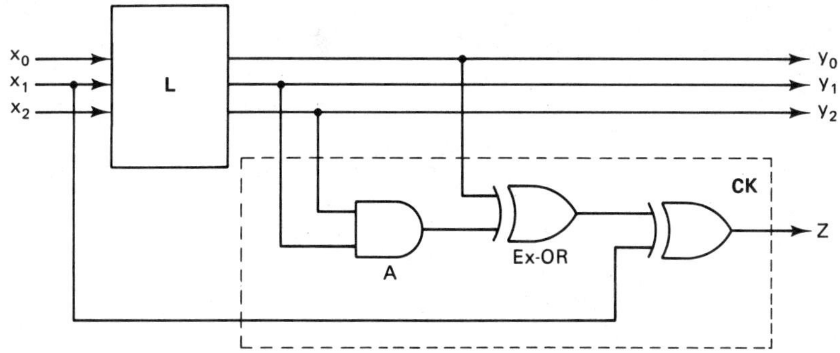

Figure 8.19 Simplified input regeneration checker [SELL 68]. © 1968 McGraw-Hill Book Company.

Note that the use of internal logic signals W shown in Fig. 8.2 sometimes plays a very important role in error detection. In some cases it is difficult to check a logic circuit without such signals. For example, to apply a parity check in adders, it is necessary to have the carries generated during addition (see Section 8.2.1). In such situations, a single fault may cause several outputs to be in error in a manner such that the error is undetectable by examining the output alone.

And we also note that in Case 2 if input X is encoded and this is taken into consideration for checker implementation, then the prediction checker may detect input errors under no fault in both the circuit under check and the checker itself. This satisfies the conditions for circuit **G** being code disjoint. Such cases can be seen in self-checking adders (e.g., full-sum parity checked adders (see Section 8.2.1)).

Next, we have to consider the case when faults exist also in the checkers. In this case, we require a self-checking checker. Here, the input and output codespaces have to be clearly defined and established.

Lemma 8-1 [CART 68]. *Considering single faults, it is necessary that any checker must have at least two outputs and that no output take a constant value.*

The combinational circuit being tested is always monitored by a checker that signals the appearance of a noncodeword. For example, the output of a checker might be 0 whenever a codeword is present in the output of the circuit under test, and 1 when a noncodeword is present. It is also desirable that the checker be self-checking, so that a fault in the checker itself produces an error signal. It is obvious that the simple encoding mentioned above is not sufficient, since a single stuck-at-0 output of the checker would never be detected. Therefore, it is necessary that the checker have at least two outputs and that no output take on a constant value for codespace input. This is a brief proof for the above Lemma 8-1.

In order to make the checker self-checking, its output must be encoded in an error detecting code. The simplest distance-two error detecting codes are the *1-out-of-2 code* (codeword = $\{(0,1),(1,0)\}$), and the *duplication code* (codeword = $\{(0,0),(1,1)\}$). In the 1-out-of-2 code, the outputs $(0,0)$ and $(1,1)$ indicate errors.

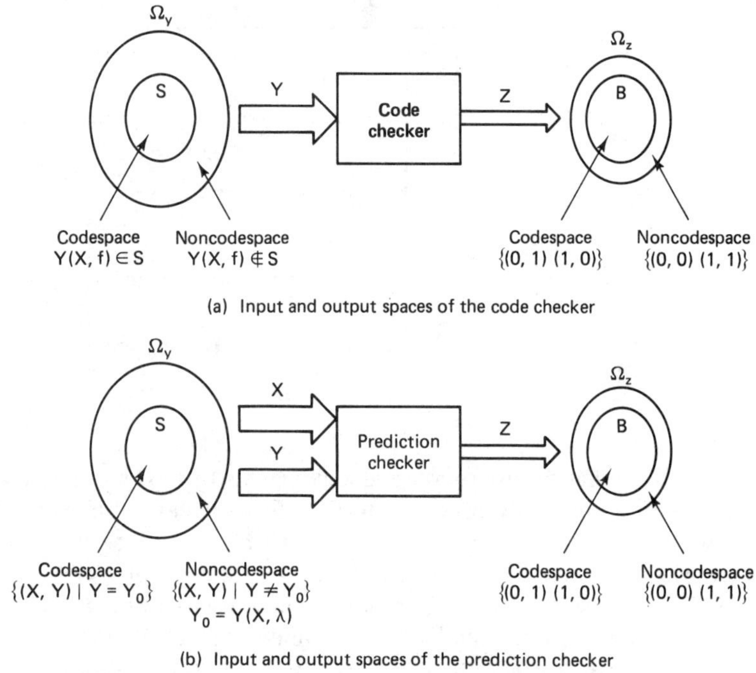

Figure 8.20 Input and output spaces of the checkers.

The 1-out-of-2 code is generally preferred, since it detects unidirectional errors, such as those produced by a loss of power.

From the above consideration, the *checker output space* $\Omega\mathbf{z}$ is defined as the set $\{(0,0)\ (0,1)\ (1,0)\ (1,1)\}$, the *checker output codespace* $\mathbf{B} = \{(1,0)\ (0,1)\}$ and the *checker output noncodespace* $\Omega\mathbf{z} - \mathbf{B} = \{(0,0)\ (1,1)\}$.

Next, we will define the input space for the two types of checkers—the code checker and the prediction checker, shown in Fig. 8.20.

Here, note that in the prediction checker, the input of the checker, that is, the output of the circuit **L**, does not have any redundancy. The output Y is only defined by the input X and the function of the circuit **L** (i.e., $Y(X)$). Since the input of the checker is input X and output Y of the circuit **L**, we can define (X, Y) as the checker input space. Here, let fault-free output Y be $Y_0 = Y(X, \lambda)$, $X \in \mathbf{N}$. Hence the input codespace of the prediction checker can be defined as (X, Y) where $Y = Y_0$, and the input noncodespace as (X, Y) where $Y \neq Y_0$. If signal W is also applied to the checker, then the input space will be defined as (X, Y, W).

As already mentioned, the error-preserving property (i.e., the code-disjoint property) is always necessary for the checker. That is, the checker always maps input codeword in **S** to output codeword in $\{(0,1), (1,0)\}$, and input noncodeword $\notin \mathbf{S}$ to output noncodeword in $\{(0,0), (1,1)\}$.

Definition 8-12. A circuit is a *self-testing checker* if it is self-testing and code disjoint.

Lemma 8-2. *The fault-secure property is not necessary for a checker.*

It is not important for the checker to have some erroneous codewords at the output of the checker. That is, we only are interested in whether or not the checker's output is a codeword or noncodeword, *not* which codeword it is. On the other hand, the self-testing property is a must to ensure the detection of faults inside the checker. Therefore, a *self-testing checker* would be satisfactory. This is the brief proof for the above Lemma 8-2.

If the checker **CK** is a self-testing (ST) checker and the circuit **L** is TSC, then the total circuit **G** shown in Fig. 8.2 is TSC. Note that the checker is an *embedded circuit*, that is, not all input codewords are given to the checker. That is, input to the checker is an output of the circuit **L** that does not always have all codewords. Hence, it is very difficult for the checker to satisfy the self-testing property perfectly without adopting some special design techniques [KHAK 84, JHA 84, HUGH 84, FUJI 87a].

We are interested in preserving the code-disjoint property even in the presence of faults inside the checker. In this case the checker should be *strongly code disjoint* (SCD); (see Definitions 8-8 and 8-9).

If the circuit under check **L** is SFS and the checker **CK** is SCD, then the total circuit **G** is SFS. In this case, note that an assumption has to be made regarding the occurrence of failures in the checker **CK** and the circuit **L**, as follows [NICO 84]:

After the occurrence of a fault affecting the checker, a sufficient time elapses such that all code inputs included in **S** *are applied before a new fault can occur in the checker* **CK** *or in the circuit under check* **L**. *After the occurrence of a fault affecting the circuit under check* **L**, *a sufficient time elapses such that all code inputs included in* **N** *are applied before a new fault can occur in the checker* **CK** *or in the circuit under check* **L**.

8.2 SELF-CHECKING COMBINATIONAL CIRCUITS

Considerable research has already been published on how to check functional circuits, such as adder, multiplier, decoder, *programmable logic array* (*PLA*), error checking/correcting (ECC) circuits, and so on. And a variety of checking circuits have been proposed that use simple error detecting codes and *prediction concepts* [CART 70, LANG 70, AVIZ 71, RAO 77, WANG 79, FUJI 81c, MAK 82].

Here, we study error checking methods for combinational circuits of arithmetic logic unit (ALU), PLA, and ECC circuits. The self-checking implementation of the checker is shown in Section 9.1.

We have to distinguish and understand the relation between faults and errors. In special circuits such as *fan-out-free circuits*, faults and errors are in one-to-one correspondence. That is, single faults always cause single errors. However, in other circuits single faults may cause multiple errors. This depends on the circuit structure. Therefore, in this section, the faults in set F are defined as those that cause detectable errors. That is, for example, if the checker, or output error detecting code, has single-error detection capability, then we can detect faults that cause single errors in the output, and F consists of only such faults.

8.2.1 Self-Checking ALU

Considerable research appears on error detection/correction in ALU. Earlier work on application of parity codes and residue codes to ALU includes [GARN 58, 59, 66, PETE 58, 59, BROW 60, RAO 68b, GADD 70]. Extended residue codes such as *AN codes* [RAO 74], *multiresidue codes* [RAO 70, 71, MAND 72], *systematic AN codes* [RAO 72], and *byte-error correcting AN codes* [NEUM 75], effective parity prediction methods [SELL 68], and *alternate-data retry (ADR)* methods [SHED 78] for application to adder, multiplier, divider, and general logic have been extensively studied [KHOD 79, TAKE 80, FUJI 81c, PATE 83, FURU 83a, 83b, 83c, HUAN 84, TOHM 86].

In other important works, *checksum codes* [WAKE 76] and *combination codes* using both parity checks and residue checks [RAO 77] have been proposed for, respectively, byte error detection in adders and cost-effective error detection and correction in ALU. Effective methods using *Reed–Muller codes* [PRAD 72a, 72b, 74] and residue codes [MONT 72] have been proposed for checking errors in logical operations as well as in arithmetic operations.

Here, we will study the error detection method in adders or ALU's [OBER 79] using parity codes and checksum codes, as well as the error correction method in ALUs using combination codes and *parity-based codes*.

Parity-checked adder. The adders considered here add two operands A and B together to give a resultant sum S. The addition is done on a bit-by-bit basis. The sum bit s_i for the ith stage depends not only on the input bits a_i and b_i for that stage, but also on the carry c_{i-1} from the previous stage.

The following equations express the sum and carry:

$$s_i = a_i \oplus b_i \oplus c_{i-1} \tag{8.1}$$

$$c_i = a_i \cdot b_i + (a_i + b_i) \cdot c_{i-1} \tag{8.2}$$

$$0 \le i \le n-1, \quad c_{-1} = c_{\text{in}}$$

$$A = (a_{n-1}, \ldots, a_i, \ldots, a_1, a_0)$$

$$B = (b_{n-1}, \ldots, b_i, \ldots, b_1, b_0)$$

The following functions are sometimes convenient to express the adder functions.

$$\begin{aligned} \text{Half-sum: } & H_i = a_i \oplus b_i \\ \text{Generate function: } & G_i = a_i \cdot b_i \\ \text{Transmit function: } & T_i = a_i + b_i, \quad 0 \le i \le n-1 \end{aligned}$$

By using these functions, Equations (8.1) and (8.2) can be expressed as follows.

$$
\begin{aligned}
s_i &= G_i \oplus T_i \oplus c_{n-1} \\
&= H_i \oplus c_{n-1} \qquad (8.3) \\
c_i &= G_i + T_i \cdot c_{i-1} \qquad (8.4)
\end{aligned}
$$

Adders are classified into two categories according to how the carries are handled. In the *ripple adder*, shown in Fig. 8.21, each carry bit depends on the preceding carry bit. This requires that the overall carry circuitry form a serial string. The carry equation is given by Equation (8.4).

It can be seen that addition is slow when the carries ripple through the entire adder. Thus, to speed up the addition process, the carry path can be shortened by using the parallel implementation of Equation (8.4), called *look-ahead*.

$$
\begin{aligned}
c_{n-1} &= G_{n-1} + T_{n-1} \cdot c_{n-2} = G_{n-1} + T_{n-1}(G_{n-2} + T_{n-2} \cdot c_{n-3}) = \cdots \\
&= G_{n-1} + T_{n-1}G_{n-2} + T_{n-1}T_{n-2}G_{n-3} + T_{n-1}T_{n-2}T_{n-3}G_{n-4} + \cdots \qquad (8.5)
\end{aligned}
$$

Equation (8.5) shows that each carry bit does not depend on the previous carry but on the transmit and generate function. Fig. 8.22 shows an implementation of an adder using *carry look-ahead*.

Next, we have to refer to the error characteristic of these adders. We call the circuit that satisfies Equations (8.1) or (8.3) a "sum circuit," and the circuit that satisfies Equations (8.2) or (8.4) a "carry circuit." Then we have the following error characteristic.

1. Sum-circuit errors do not propagate and thus cause single errors only.
2. A carry-bit error always propagates to cause an error in the next sum bit.
3. Any failures in the ripple-carry circuit can cause error bursts, whereas only T_i and G_i failures in look-ahead can cause error bursts.
4. In a look-ahead carry circuit, all carries are independent of the previous ones.

Based on the above, we now consider the parity-checked adder. Let p_A and p_B be the parity check bits of the two input operands. The parity of the sum is given by

$$
\begin{aligned}
p_s &= s_{n-1} \oplus s_{n-2} \oplus \cdots \oplus s_1 \oplus s_0 \\
&= (a_{n-1} \oplus b_{n-1} \oplus c_{n-2}) \oplus (a_{n-2} \oplus b_{n-2} \oplus c_{n-3}) \oplus \cdots \oplus (a_0 \oplus b_0 \oplus c_{\text{in}}) \\
&= (a_{n-1} \oplus a_{n-2} \oplus \cdots \oplus a_0) \oplus (b_{n-1} \oplus b_{n-2} \oplus \cdots \oplus b_0) \\
&\quad \oplus (c_{n-2} \oplus c_{n-3} \oplus \cdots \oplus c_{\text{in}}) \\
&= p_A \oplus p_B \oplus p_c \qquad (8.6)
\end{aligned}
$$

Here, p_c denotes the parity of the carries within the adder. The check defined by Equation (8.6) will be referred to as the *full-sum parity check*. The predicted parity $p_A \oplus p_B \oplus p_c$ is compared with the actual parity of the sum p_s (shown in Fig. 8.23).

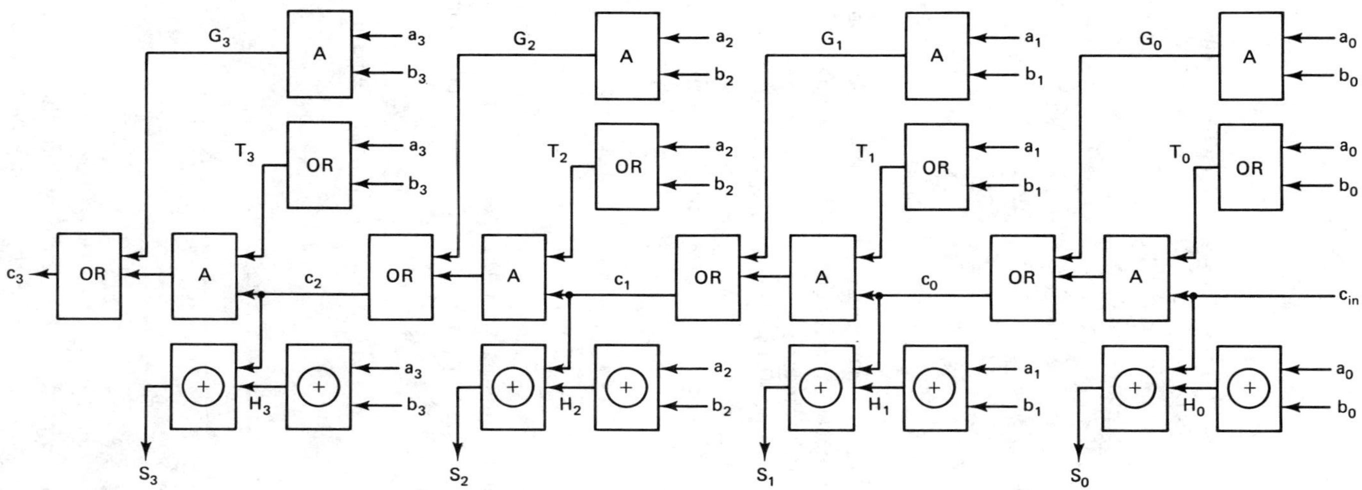

Figure 8.21 Ripple adder [SELL 68]. © 1968 McGraw-Hill Book Company.

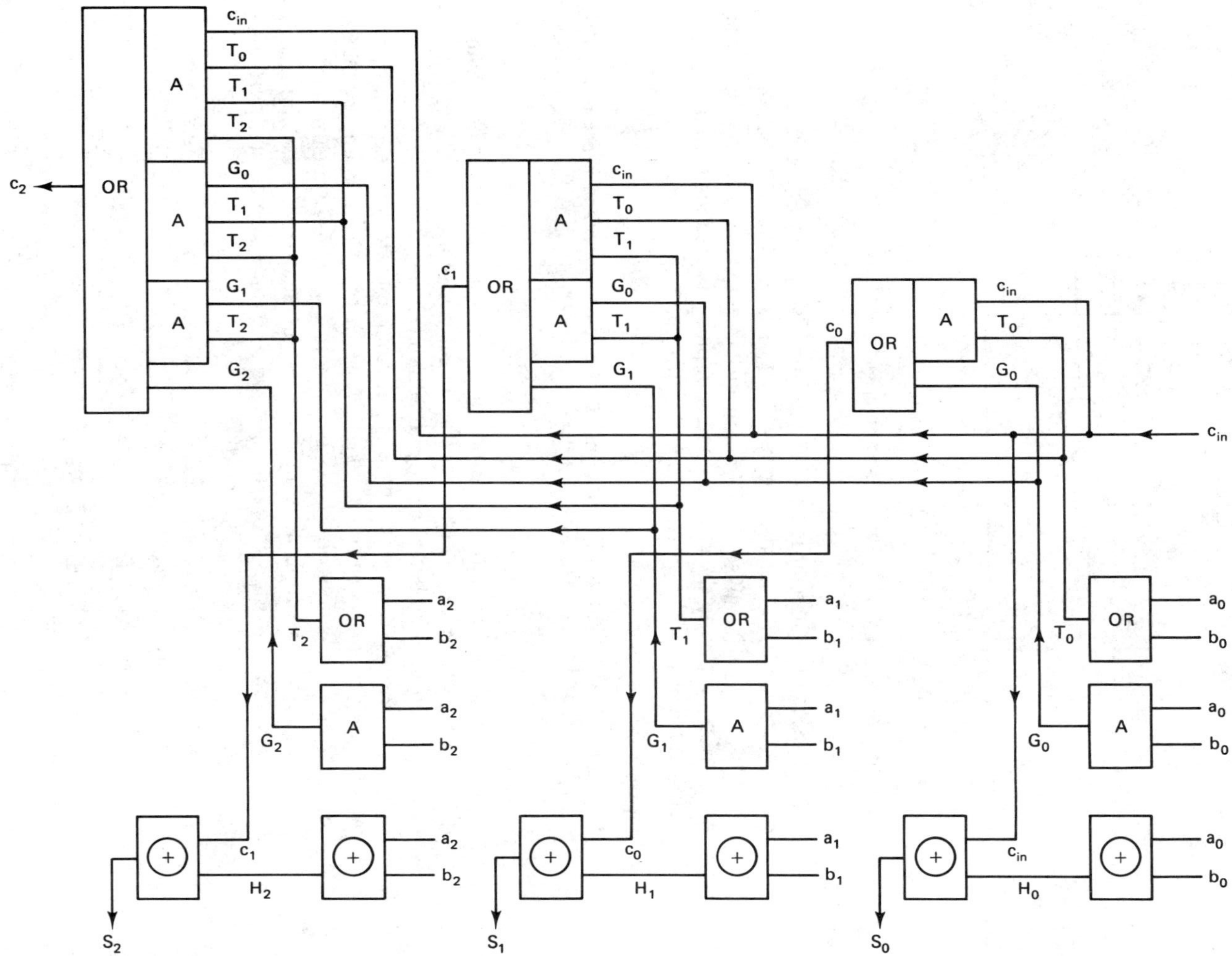

Figure 8.22 Carry-look-ahead adder [SELL 68]. ©1968 McGraw-Hill Book Company.

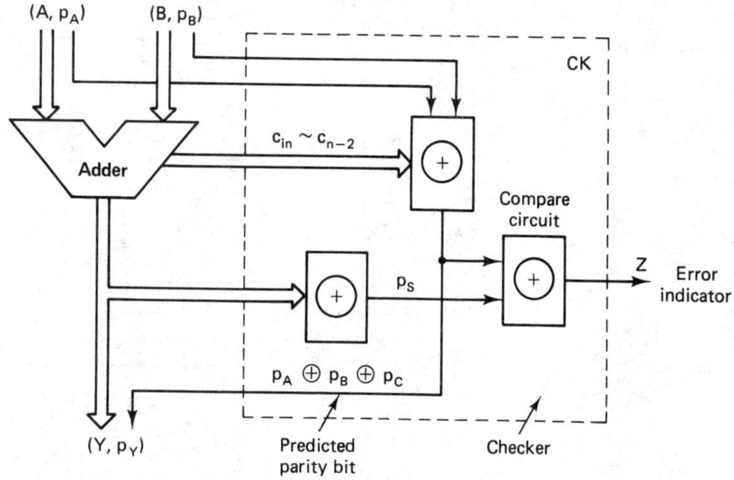

Figure 8.23 Full-sum parity check.

This checking circuit is equal to the circuit shown in Fig. 8.2; that is, the input parities p_A and p_B in the input $X = \{(A, p_A), (B, p_B)\}$, the sum output $S = (s_0, s_1, \ldots, s_{n-1})$, and the internal signals $W = (c_{\text{in}}, c_0, \ldots, c_{n-2})$ (i.e., carry signals) are passed on to the checker, and sum parity is predicted from p_A, p_B, and W and compared with the parity of the output sum.

Example 8-5

Let inputs A and B be (0010) and (0110), respectively, and hence input parities are $p_A = 1$ and $p_B = 0$. Assume that the output sum S equals (1010). Fig. 8.24 shows how to detect sum bit error.

In this checking method, a problem arises because carry errors are undetectable. This is because every carry error also causes a sum-bit error and hence always results in an even number of carry-plus sum-bit errors.

In order to overcome this problem, use of duplicate carries and a carry-dependent sum adder have been proposed [HSIA 63, SELL 68]. An example of the method of *duplicate carry with parity check* is shown in Fig. 8.25. In this method, the carry generation circuit is duplicated and p_{cd} is generated from these duplicated carry bits. Therefore, a parity check using $p_s = p_A \oplus p_B \oplus p_{cd}$ on a ripple adder can

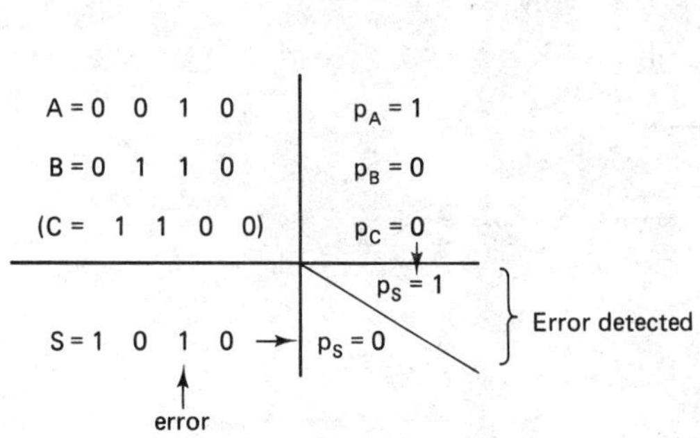

Figure 8.24 Parity checking of addition.

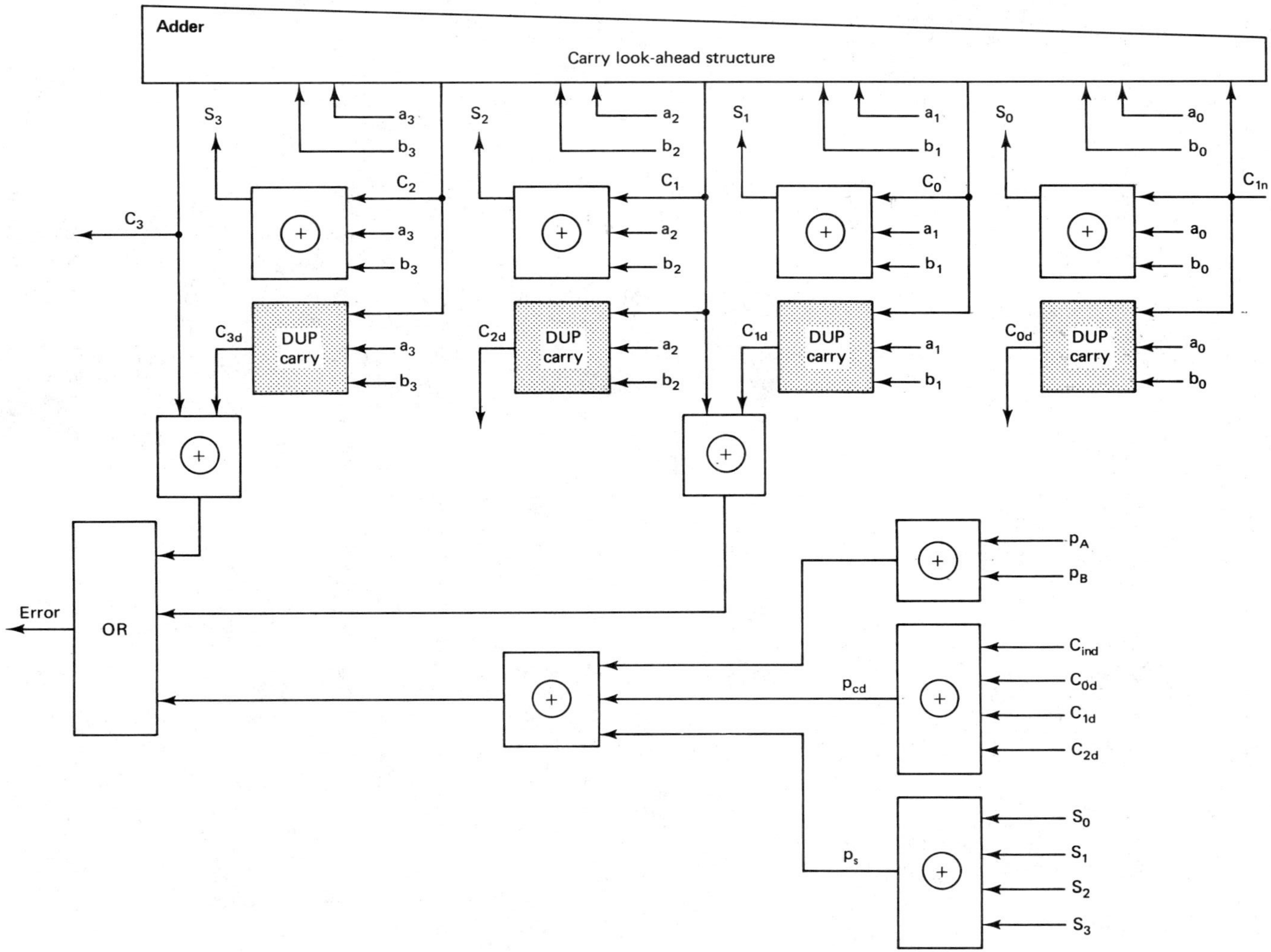

Figure 8.25 Duplicate carry with parity check applied to a carry look-ahead adder [SELL 68]. © 1968 McGraw-Hill Book Company.

detect all carry errors caused by a single fault and on a look-ahead adder can detect all carry errors caused by an error in T_i or G_i.

The next method is the *carry-dependent sum adder* [HSIA 63] (see Fig. 8.26). If a carry error could be made to cause an odd error burst, then parity checking alone could be used for complete adder checking. The adder that satisfies this requirement is called a carry-dependent sum adder. An even error burst $c_i, s_{i+1}, \ldots, c_{i+t-1}, s_{i+t}$ caused by a carry error in c_i can be made "odd" if the carry bit error in c_i also causes the corresponding sum bit s_i to be in error. This can be satisfied by using an equation for the sum of the following form.

$$s_i = f_i \oplus c_i \tag{8.7}$$

where f_i is a function of a_i, b_i, c_{i-1}. The function f_i can be derived from the following table.

a_i	b_i	c_{i-1}	s_i	c_i	$f_i = s_i \oplus c_i$
0	0	0	0	0	0
0	0	1	1	0	1
0	1	0	1	0	1
0	1	1	0	1	1
1	0	0	1	0	1
1	0	1	0	1	1
1	1	0	0	1	1
1	1	1	1	1	0

From this table, f_i can be expressed as the following equation.

$$\begin{aligned} f_i &= \overline{a_i b_i c_{i-1} + \bar{a}_i \bar{b}_i \bar{c}_{i-1}} \\ &= \overline{G_i c_{i-1} + \bar{T}_i \bar{c}_{i-1}} \end{aligned}$$

Therefore, Equation (8.7) becomes

$$s_i = G_i c_{i-1} c_i + \bar{G}_i c_{i-1} \bar{c}_i + T_i \bar{c}_{i-1} \bar{c}_i + \bar{T}_i \bar{c}_{i-1} c_i$$

This type of parity-checked adder is shown in Fig. 8.26.

Let's consider the case in which the error is present in the input but not in the adder. From Equation (8.6), we can predict the parity p_s of the sum output S. Fig. 8.27 shows the circuit whose output is encoded in parity code (i.e., (S, p_s)).

If a single error is in (A, p_A) or (B, p_B), where p_A and p_B are parity bits of the operands A and B, respectively, and we assume there are no faults in circuit **G** shown in Fig. 8.27, then the single input error is always propagated to the output. This is explained as follows. If there is an error in p_A or p_B, this error is always propagated to the output parity p_s, not to S. Therefore, the output (S, p_s) is a noncodeword. Next, we assume that an error is present in A or B. We can assume the error to be in A without loss of generality. Let the ith bit in A (i.e., a_i) be in error. Then, this error is always propagated to s_i, because s_i is a linear function of a_i (i.e., $s_i = a_i \oplus b_i \oplus c_{i-1}$). On the other hand, the error is sometimes propagated and other times not propagated to carry bit c_i. This depends on the value of b_i and

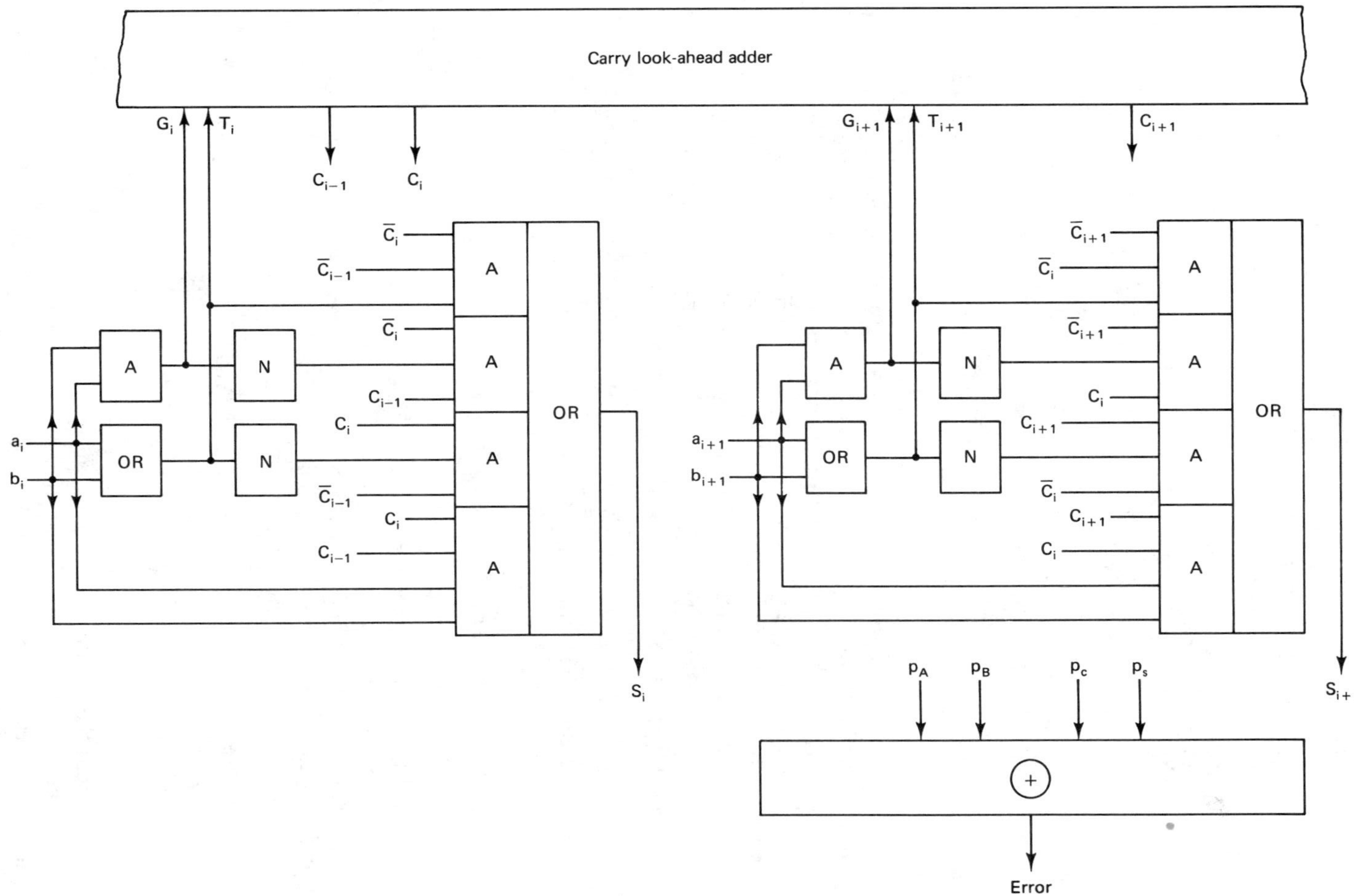

Figure 8.26 Carry-dependent-sum adder [SELL 68]. © 1968 McGraw-Hill Book Company.

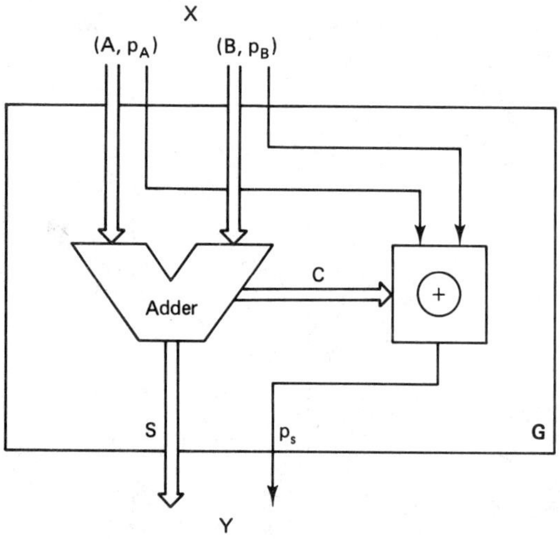

Figure 8.27 Code-disjoint adder.

c_{i-1}. If this error is propagated to c_i, then this is always propagated to sum output s_{i+1} of the next stage. Similarly, if the error is propagated to the carry of another stage (e.g., c_{i+t}), then s_{i+t+1} is always in error. From this, the single input error can be propagated to $s_i, (c_i, s_{i+1}), \ldots, (c_{i+t}, s_{i+t+1}), \ldots$. The result is an odd number of errors in the output sum and carry bits. This means that if an even number of errors occurs in sum, an odd number of errors exists in carries, and vice versa. Therefore, the output (S, p_s) will be a noncodeword. We assume that the input noncodeword space is defined as

$$\Omega_{\mathbf{x}} - \mathbf{N} = \{(A, p_A)(B, p_B) | (A, p_A) \text{ or } (B, p_B) \text{ includes single error}\}$$

Then, the circuit **G** always maps a noncodeword input to a noncodeword output. Therefore we have proved the following theorem.

Theorem 8-4. *The circuit* **G** *shown in Fig.* 8.27 *is code disjoint for single errors in the input space.*

Addition with checksum codes. Checksum codes (also called *digit parity* [GARN 58]) can be used to detect single-byte errors. A checksum code is a set of vectors of $(n + 1)$ symbols from the set Z_q (the integers mod q). Each vector has a component, called the check symbol, that equals the sum mod q of the other components, called the information symbols, of the vector.

Definition 8-13. A *checksum code* [WAKE 76] is the set

$$\left\{(x_c, x_{n-1}, \ldots, x_0) \mid (x_i, x_c \in Z_q), \text{ and } \left(x_c = \sum_{0 \le i \le n-1} x_i \bmod q\right)\right\}$$

From this definition, it is apparent that the minimum Hamming distance of a checksum code is 2. Of particular interest are codes in which q equals 2^b for some integer b greater than 1. (If $b = 1$, it is an even parity code.) In these codes, each symbol from Z_{2^b} may be encoded as a byte of b bits. Hence, each codeword has $n \cdot b$ information bits and b check bits. All errors confined to a single b-bit byte are detected.

We now consider the addition modulo 2^b of vectors with any number of components from Z_{2^b}. In this self-checking adder, we can detect single-byte errors. Therefore, any faults in the adder that cause single-byte errors can be detected. These faults belong to the fault set F.

Let two input vectors in checksum codes have the form

$$A = (a_c, a_{n-1}, a_{n-2}, \ldots, a_0)$$
$$B = (b_c, b_{n-1}, b_{n-2}, \ldots, b_0)$$

where a_c and b_c are the check symbols and $(a_{n-1}, a_{n-2}, \ldots, a_0)$ and $(b_{n-1}, b_{n-2}, \ldots, b_0)$ are the information part,

$$A_d \equiv (a_{n-1}, a_{n-2}, \ldots, a_0)$$
$$B_d \equiv (b_{n-1}, b_{n-2}, \ldots, b_0)$$

The information parts A_d and B_d are understood to be the representation of an integer $[A_d], [B_d]$ such that

$$[A_d] = \sum_{0 \le i \le n-1} a_i 2^{bi}$$
$$[B_d] = \sum_{0 \le i \le n-1} b_i 2^{bi}$$

Ordinary addition of the information parts of codewords is defined so that

$$S_d = A_d + B_d + C$$
$$[S_d] = [A_d] + [B_d] \bmod M$$
$$C = (c_{n-2}, \ldots, c_0, c_{\text{in}})$$
$$c_i = \begin{cases} 0 & \text{if } a_i + b_i + c_{i-1} < 2^b \\ 1 & \text{if } a_i + b_i + c_{i-1} \ge 2^b \end{cases}$$
$$0 \le i \le n-2, \; c_{-1} = c_{\text{in}}$$

In the equations above, M equals 2^{bn} and c_{in} equals 0 for two's complement addition; M equals $2^{bn} - 1$ and c_{in} equals c_{n-1} for one's complement addition.

The check symbol of the sum of two information parts is equal to the result of an addition of the obtained sum symbols, as follows.

$$s_c = \sum_{0 \le i \le n-1} s_i \bmod 2^b \tag{8.9}$$

On the other hand, s_c can be predicted by using the check symbols of the inputs and of the carry as

$$s_c = a_c + b_c + c_c \bmod 2^b. \tag{8.10}$$

Here,

$$c_c = \sum_{0 \le i \le n-1} c_{i-1} \bmod 2^b, \text{ where } c_{-1} = c_{\text{in}}$$

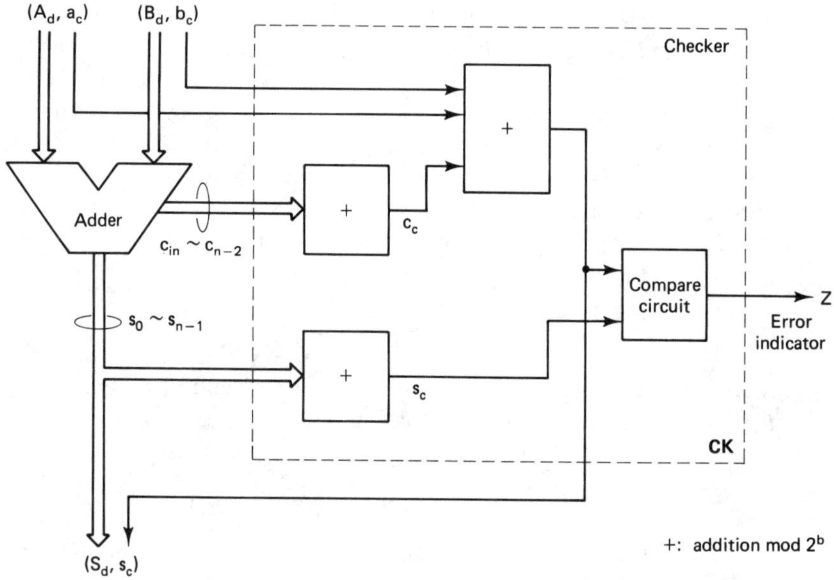

Figure 8.28 Check symbol prediction checker.

Example 8-6

Let $n = 4$, $b = 3$, $A = (7, 2, 2, 4, 7)$, $B = (5, 3, 3, 4, 3)$, and $M = 2^{12}$ (two's complement). Then $C = (0, 1, 1, 0)$ and $S_d = (2, 2, 4, 7) + (3, 3, 4, 3) + (0, 1, 1, 0) = (5, 6, 1, 2)$, from which we get $s_c = (s_3 + s_2 + s_1 + s_0) \bmod 2^3 = 6$. On the other hand, from Equation (8.10) for $a_c = 7$, $b_c = 5$ and $c_c = 2$, s_c can be predicted as $s_c = (a_c + b_c + c_c) \bmod 2^3 = 6$.

As with the full-sum parity check, the obtained check symbols from Equations (8.9) and (8.10) are compared and the result is shown as an error indication (see Fig. 8.28). This checker belongs to the class of prediction checkers. Similar to the result of Theorem 8-4, the circuit including the adder and the check symbol prediction circuit is code disjoint for single symbol errors in an input.

This checker has the same problem as that found in the full-sum parity check. That is, faults in the carry generation circuit are not detected, since they produce compensating errors in both s_c and c_c, and although the output is incorrect, there is no error indication. This problem can also be overcome by using the *duplicated carry logic*, as stated before. This checking scheme can be effectively applied to the adder consisting of byte-sliced adders, as shown in Fig. 8.29.

ALU with combination codes [RAO 77]. The error correcting codes can be broadly divided into two classes: parity-based codes and residue codes. A very commonly used parity code in computer systems is the SEC–DED Hamming code.

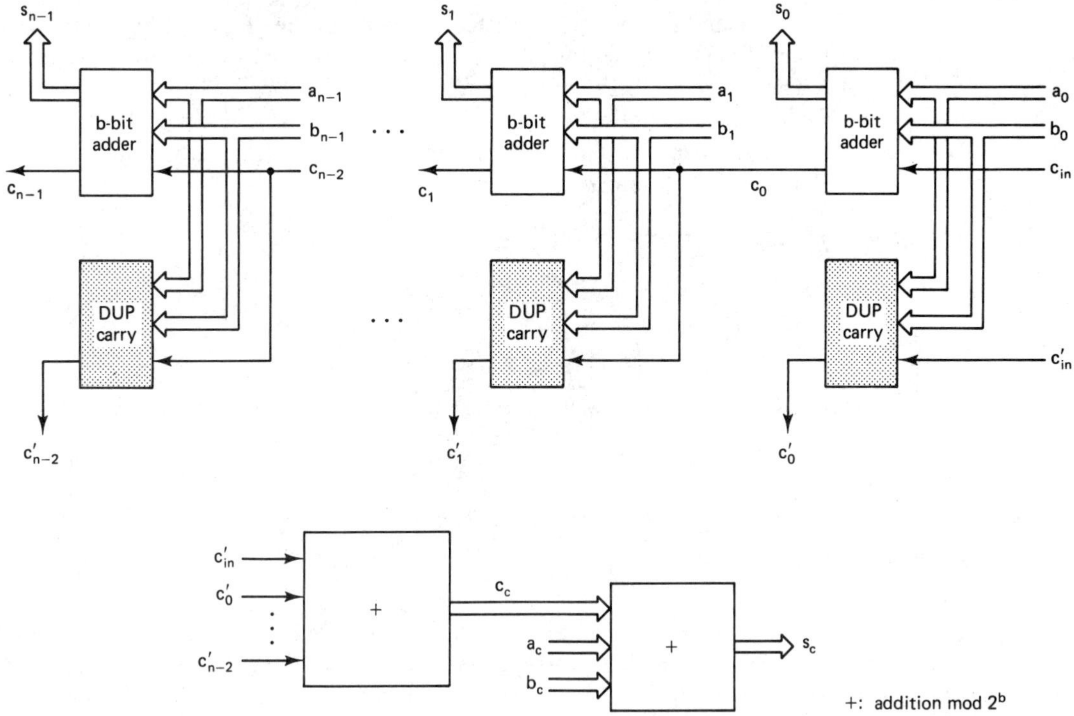

Figure 8.29 Check symbol prediction circuit for checksum code using byte-sliced adders [WAKE 76].

Parity-based codes have proven very efficient and cost effective for memory and data transfer operations. The residue codes, on the other hand, appear very attractive for checking arithmetic operations, such as, ADD, MULTIPLY, and so on.

The concept of combining both parity codes and residue codes, producing what is called a *combination code*, was proposed in [ENGL 66, RAO 77]. This technique can provide efficient error correction for all operations of an arithmetic logic unit (ALU). Here, the concept of a combination code and its error correction mechanism will be discussed. A combination code is a block code of length n, where the information is followed by a group of parity bits and a residue check, as shown in Fig. 8.30. For information X, the corresponding codeword is $[X, P, |X|_m]$, where $|X|_m$ expresses the residue of X modulo m $(= 2^l - 1)$ and P is a group of parities calculated over bytes of X.

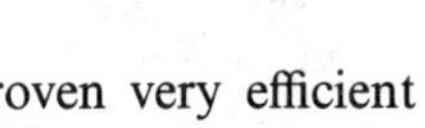

Figure 8.30 The combination codeword. © 1977 IEEE.

The code and its correction mechanism will best be described by the following example [RAO 77]. Let the information X be at most 7 bytes, each byte consists of 3 bits. Three parity check bits P and a residue check $|X|_7$ of these bits are computed over X as follows. Let $X = (x_{20}, x_{19}, \ldots, x_0)$ be divided into 7 bytes $B_6, B_5, \ldots, B_0$. Then the parity check portion $P = (P_2, P_1, P_0)$ is computed from various bytes of X as follows.

$$P_0 = B_0 \oplus B_2 \oplus B_4 \oplus B_6$$

$$= (x_0 \oplus x_1 \oplus x_2) \oplus (x_6 \oplus x_7 \oplus x_8) \oplus (x_{12} \oplus x_{13} \oplus x_{14}) \oplus (x_{18} \oplus x_{19} \oplus x_{20})$$

$$P_1 = B_1 \oplus B_2 \oplus B_5 \oplus B_6$$

$$= (x_3 \oplus x_4 \oplus x_5) \oplus (x_6 \oplus x_7 \oplus x_8) \oplus (x_{15} \oplus x_{16} \oplus x_{17}) \oplus (x_{18} \oplus x_{19} \oplus x_{20})$$

$$P_2 = B_3 \oplus B_4 \oplus B_5 \oplus B_6$$

$$= (x_9 \oplus x_{10} \oplus x_{11}) \oplus (x_{12} \oplus x_{13} \oplus x_{14})$$

$$\oplus (x_{15} \oplus x_{16} \oplus x_{17}) \oplus (x_{18} \oplus x_{19} \oplus x_{20})$$

In this case, the digits chosen to get P_i, $i = 0, 1, 2$, are same as that for the Hamming SEC code. The residue check, $|X|_7$ is obtained by adding all the information bytes $B_0, B_1, \ldots, B_6$ using modulo 7 adders.

Next, the single-error detection and correction capability of the code is determined as follows. Assume that the erroneous word is X' and the erroneous bit is x'_{16}. Also assume that the correct value of $x_{16} = 0$, erroneous value of $x'_{16} = 1$ ($0 \to 1$ type error, i.e., 0-error). Then, by computing the parity check equations over the erroneous word, we get the parity syndrome S_p of (011) pointing to an error in B_5 of X'. To obtain the actual error position we compute the residue syndrome.

$$S_r = |X' - X|_7 = ||X'|_7 - |X|_7|_7$$

This will yield the error magnitude of $|2^{17-1}|_7 = 2$, which determines the error position as the second bit in the byte pointed to by the parity syndrome. On the other hand, if $x_{16} = 1$, $x'_{16} = 0$ ($1 \to 0$ type error, i.e., 1-error) the residue check yields

$$|X' - X|_7 = |-2^{16}|_7 = 5 = |-2|_7$$

This points to the second bit, but to 1-error.

It is to be noted that there is a unique parity syndrome for each one of the seven bytes and a unique residue syndrome for each bit and type error in the byte. Also to be noted is that when the error is in the information part, both parity check and residue check detect this error and together they enable error correction. On the other hand, if error is in P or in $|X|_7$, only one of the two syndromes is nonzero. Therefore, we derive the following error location strategy of Equation (8.11) and the error correction strategy of Equation (8.12).

$$\begin{aligned} &S_p = 0,\ S_r = 0\text{: no error} \\ &S_p = 0,\ S_r \neq 0\text{: error in } |X|_7 \\ &S_p \neq 0,\ S_r = 0\text{: error in } P \\ &S_p \neq 0,\ S_r \neq 0\text{: error in } X \end{aligned} \tag{8.11}$$

$$\begin{aligned} &S_p = i \neq 0,\ S_r = j \neq 0 \rightarrow B_{i-1} \text{ is in error } (i = 1, 2, \ldots, 7) \\ &j = 1\text{: first bit, } 0 \rightarrow 1 \text{ type error} \\ &j = 6\text{: first bit, } 1 \rightarrow 0 \text{ type error} \\ &j = 2\text{: second bit, } 0 \rightarrow 1 \text{ type error} \\ &j = 5\text{: second bit, } 1 \rightarrow 0 \text{ type error} \\ &j = 4\text{: third bit, } 0 \rightarrow 1 \text{ type error} \\ &j = 3\text{: third bit, } 1 \rightarrow 0 \text{ type error} \end{aligned} \tag{8.12}$$

From this, any single-bit error in X can be detected and corrected.

From the point of view of implementation, we resort to one modification that makes the code more attractive. This is to replace the parity byte P by the parity bits, one parity bit for each of the k information bytes of X [RAO 77]. Note that this modification does not alter the error detection/correction properties of the code. However, by this modification, there will be more parity bits (k bits instead of $\log k$) and a lower information rate for the code, but the implementation would be rather straightforward. The modified combination code is illustrated in Fig. 8.31.

We refer to this *modified combination code* as simply a *combination code* hereafter. We illustrate below a schematic for its implementation. For an operand X of n bits ($n = k \cdot l$), we have a corresponding combination codeword $[X, P_X, |X|_m]$ where P_X is k parity bits (one parity bit for each byte of X) and $|X|_m$ is the residue of X modulo m ($= 2^l - 1$).

First let us consider a simple model of an ALU as given in Fig. 8.32.

A is an internal operand, B an input (external) operand, and Φ is the operation code, all specified at time t. We denote the output R as the result of the operation Φ on A and B, which is made available at a unit time later. In this model, we have $R(t+1) = \Phi(A(t), B(t))$. To apply the combination code to the above model we resort to a slightly modified ALU, along with a *residue unit* and a *decoder unit*. This is shown in Fig. 8.33. The operation Φ in Fig. 8.32 is replaced in Fig. 8.33 with combined operation (Φ, Φ_m). For each operation Φ on A and B, parity logic is designed in ALU so that (R, P_R) are generated as outputs. P_R consists of k parity bits called *predicted parity* bits. Also, for each Φ, a corresponding parallel operation Φ_m is designed for the residue unit to operate on the residues $|A|_m$ and $|B|_m$. The

B_{k-1}	P_{k-1}	B_{k-2}	P_{k-2}	B_{k-3} //	B_1	P_1	B_0	P_0	$\lvert X \rvert_m$

Figure 8.31 Modified combination codeword [RAO 77]. © 1977 IEEE.

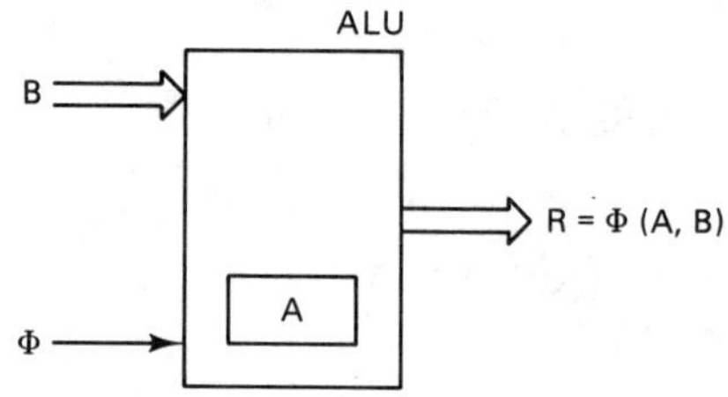

Figure 8.32 A simple model of an ALU [RAO 77]. © 1977 IEEE.

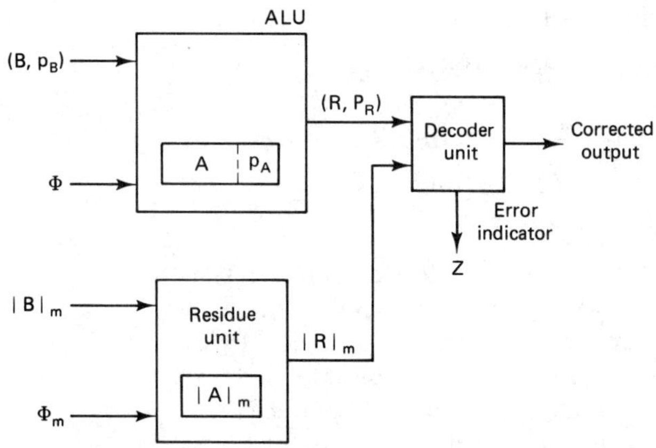

Figure 8.33 A combination code schema for ALU operations [RAO 77]. © 1977 IEEE.

corresponding result is denoted by

$$|R|_m = \Phi_m(|A|_m, |B|_m)$$

By this approach we generate a combined output $[R, P_R, |R|_m]$, a codeword, if there are no errors. However, due to logic faults there could be errors in this combined result. The decoder unit then generates the syndromes (S_p, S_r) and utilizes them to locate and correct those errors.

The foregoing discussion is a general schema of the combination code application to ALUs. For more details on the residue and the decoder units refer to [RAO 77].

ALU with parity-based codes [FUJI 81c]. Parity-based codes have proven very efficient and cost effective for memory and data transfer circuits. If these codes are successfully applied to arithmetic logic units (ALU), a single code can be used throughout a fault-tolerant computer system. This is attractive since it eliminates the need for self-checking code translators and reduces the number of different types of code checkers required.

In general, however, parity-based codes are not preserved in logical operations, except exclusive-or (EX-OR) and exclusive-nor (EX-NOR) operations. The technique given here is based on the idea that the result of an arbitrary operation Φ can be linearly transformed into that of an EX-OR operation. This will enable parity prediction for the operation Φ [FUJI 81c].

Two input data words A and B are given as follows.

$$A = (a_{k-1}, a_{k-2}, \ldots, a_1, a_0)$$
$$B = (b_{k-1}, b_{k-2}, \ldots, b_1, b_0)$$

Parity bits p_A and p_B are generated from the following relation.

$$p_A = \sum_{i=0}^{k-1}{}^{\oplus} a_i$$

$$p_B = \sum_{i=0}^{k-1}{}^{\oplus} b_i$$

where $\Sigma^{\oplus}$ denotes sum mod 2. The circuit model consideration has two inputs, $[A, p_A]$ and $[B, p_B]$, and a single output, $[Y, p_Y]$. In this case, output from ALU is defined as follows.

$$Y = (y_{k-1}, y_{k-2}, \ldots, y_1, y_0)$$

Parity bit p_Y is the parity of Y satisfying the following relation.

$$p_Y = \sum_{i=0}^{k-1}{}^{\oplus} y_i$$

Fig. 8.34 shows this circuit model.

For the EX-OR operation the parity checking (i.e., syndrome S generation) is as follows.

$$S = \left(\sum_{i=0}^{k-1}{}^{\oplus} y_i \right) \oplus p_A \oplus p_B$$

$$y_i = a_i \oplus b_i \quad (i = 0, 1, \ldots, k-1)$$

$$\begin{cases} S = 1: \text{error detection} \\ S = 0: \text{error-free} \end{cases}$$

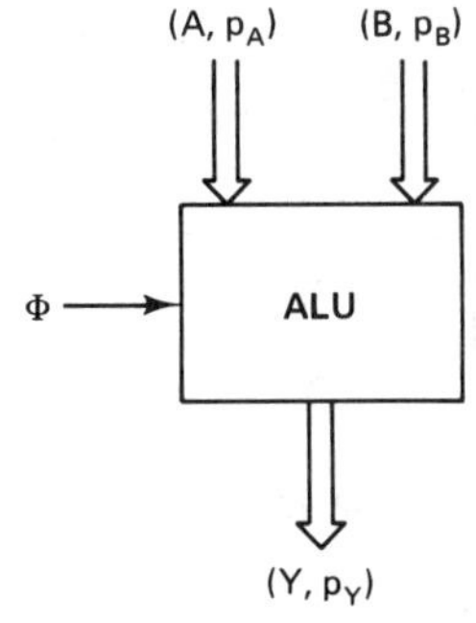

Figure 8.34 ALU circuit model [FUJI 81c]. © 1981 IECE Japan.

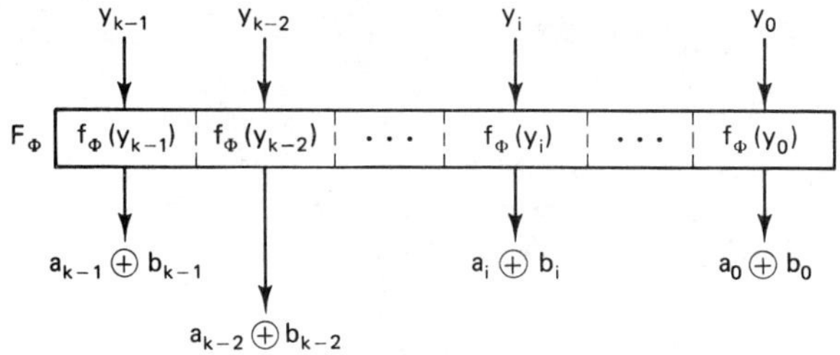

Figure 8.35 Transform function [FUJI 81c]. © 1981 IECE Japan.

The ith transformation function $f_\Phi(y_i)$ expresses the transformation of the ith result of the ALU operation, y_i, into the ith result of the EX-OR operation (i.e., $a_i \oplus b_i$, shown in Fig. 8.35). Hence, the output of the function $f_\Phi(y_i)$ is given as follows: $f_\Phi(y_i) = a_i \oplus b_i$, $i = 0, 1, \ldots, k-1$.

If the function $f_\Phi(y_i)$ satisfies the relation mentioned in the following theorem, an error in y_i is propagated to the output of $f_\Phi(y_i)$, and the parity for the output of ALU can be predicted.

Definition 8-14 [SELL 68]. The *Boolean difference* of a function $F = F(x_0, x_1, \ldots, x_i, \ldots, x_{n-1})$ with respect to x_i is defined as follows.

$$\frac{dF}{dx_i} = F(x_0, x_1, \ldots, x_i, \ldots, x_{n-1}) \oplus F(x_0, x_1, \ldots, \bar{x}_i, \ldots, x_{n-1})$$

Theorem 8-5. *If the following relation relating to the transform function $f_\Phi(y_i)$ is satisfied*

$$\frac{d(f_\Phi(y_i))}{dy_i} = 1, \qquad i = 0, 1, \ldots, k-1 \tag{8.13}$$

$$f_\Phi(y_i) = a_i \oplus b_i \tag{8.14}$$

the parity for the output of ALU, p'_Y, can be predicted as follows:

For $r_i = y_i \oplus a_i \oplus b_i$

$$p'_Y = p_A \oplus p_B \oplus \left(\sum_{i=0}^{k-1}{}^{\oplus}\, r_i \right) \tag{8.15}$$

For $r_i = y_i \oplus \overline{a_i \oplus b_i}$

$$p'_Y = \begin{cases} p_A \oplus p_B \oplus \left(\sum_{i=0}^{k-1}{}^{\oplus}\, r_i \right) \ldots k\text{: even} \\ \overline{p_A \oplus p_B} \oplus \left(\sum_{i=0}^{k-1}{}^{\oplus}\, r_i \right) \ldots k\text{: odd} \end{cases} \tag{8.16}$$

For proving this theorem, the following lemma is useful.

Lemma 8-3. *Let F be the function of two independent variables Y and R. Then,* $F = Y \oplus R$ *and* $\overline{Y \oplus R}$ *are the solutions to satisfy the following relation.*

$$\frac{dF}{dY} = 1 \tag{8.17}$$

Proof of Lemma 8-3. Assume that $F = Y * R$ ($*$ expresses some operation) satisfies Equation (8.17). Then, from Definition 8-14, the following relation can be satisfied.

$$\frac{dF}{dY} = (1 * R) \oplus (0 * R) = 1 \tag{8.18}$$

The following four cases are the only solutions to satisfy Equation (8.18).

Case	$1 * R$	$0 * R$	Solutions
1	1	0	$R = 1$ and $* =$ AND $R = 1$ and $* =$ NAND
2	0	1	$R = 1$ and $* =$ NAND $R = 0$ and $* =$ NOR
3	R	$\overline{R}$	$* =$ exclusive-nor (EX-NOR)
4	$\overline{R}$	R	$* =$ exclusive-or (EX-OR)

Since R is a variable, cases 3 and 4 are the solutions satisfying Equation (8.18). Hence, $F = Y \oplus R$ and $F = \overline{Y \oplus R}$ are the solutions to satisfy Equation (8.17).

Q.E.D.

It is apparent that $F = \overline{Y} * R$, $Y * \overline{R}$, and $\overline{Y} * \overline{R}$, where $* =$ exclusive-or (EX-OR) or $* =$ exclusive-nor (EX-NOR), are also solutions to satisfy Equation (8.17).

Proof of Theorem 8-5. From Lemma 8-3, the following relation satisfies Equation (8.13).

$$f_{\Phi}(y_i) = y_i \oplus r_i \tag{8.19}$$

By Equations (8.14) and (8.19), r_i can always be obtained such that

$$r_i = y_i \oplus a_i \oplus b_i$$

Addition mod 2 with respect to i for both sides of Equations (8.14) and (8.19) produces the following relations.

$$\sum_{i=0}^{k-1}{}^{\oplus} f_\Phi(y_i) = \left(\sum_{i=0}^{k-1}{}^{\oplus} a_i \oplus b_i\right) = p_A \oplus p_B$$

$$\sum_{i=0}^{k-1}{}^{\oplus} f_\Phi(y_i) = \left(\sum_{i=0}^{k-1}{}^{\oplus} y_i \oplus r_i\right)$$

$$= \left(\sum_{i=0}^{k-1}{}^{\oplus} y_i\right) \oplus \left(\sum_{i=0}^{k-1}{}^{\oplus} r_i\right)$$

From these equations, predicted parity p'_Y is obtained.

$$p'_Y = \sum_{i=0}^{k-1}{}^{\oplus} y_i = p_A \oplus p_B \oplus \left(\sum_{i=0}^{k-1}{}^{\oplus} r_i\right)$$

This satisfies Equation (8.15).

On the other hand, from Lemma 8-3, the following relation also satisfies Equation (8.14).

$$f_\Phi(y_i) = \overline{y_i \oplus r_i}$$

In the same manner, for $r_i = y_i \oplus \overline{a_i \oplus b_i}$, the predicted parity p'_Y can be obtained as Equation (8.16). Q.E.D.

TABLE 8.2 FUNCTION r_i

Operation Φ	y_i	r_i: $* =$ EX-OR	r_i: $* =$ EX-NOR
AND	$a_i \cap b_i$	$a_i \cup b_i$	$\overline{a_i} \cap \overline{b_i}$
OR	$a_i \cup b_i$	$a_i \cap b_i$	$\overline{a_i} \cup \overline{b_i}$
EX-OR	$a_i \oplus b_i$	0	1
EX-NOR	$\overline{a_i \oplus b_i}$	1	0
ADD	$a_i + b_i$	c_{i-1}	$\overline{c_{i-1}}$

c_{i-1} in the table is the carry bit that enters into the position i.
Source: [FUJI 81c] © 1981 IECE Japan.

From the definition of the Boolean difference, Equation (8.13) shows apparently that a single y_i error is always propagated to the output of the function $f_\Phi(y_i)$. Equations (8.13) and (8.14) are important equations, not only for giving the predicted parity bits but also for giving the condition for propagating error in y_i to the output of $f_\Phi(y_i)$.

Table 8.2 shows an r_i function for basic arithmetic and logic operations. R is defined as follows.

$$R = (r_{k-1}, r_{k-2}, \ldots, r_1, r_0)$$

Theorem 8-5 gives parity checking for an arbitrary ALU operation by using Equation (8.15) of predicted parity p'_Y as follows.

Theorem 8-6. *For inputs A and B of k bits, parity checking (i.e., syndrome) for an ALU operation Φ becomes*

$$\begin{aligned} S_\Phi &= p_Y \oplus p'_Y \\ &= \left(\sum_{i=0}^{k-1}{}^{\oplus}\, y_i \right) \oplus \left\{ \left(\sum_{i=0}^{k-1}{}^{\oplus}\, r_i \right) \oplus p_A \oplus p_B \right\} \\ &= \left(\sum_{i=0}^{k-1}{}^{\oplus}\, f_\Phi(y_i) \right) \oplus p_A \oplus p_B \end{aligned} \tag{8.20}$$

where

$$\begin{aligned} f_\Phi(y_i) &= y_i \oplus r_i \\ &= a_i \oplus b_i \end{aligned}$$

$$S_\Phi = 1\text{: error detected}$$

$$S_\Phi = 0\text{: error free}$$

Fig. 8.36 shows this parity checking scheme for an ALU operation Φ.

Theorem 8-7. *The parity checking scheme shown in Fig.* 8.36 *detects all single errors in input A or B, if there is no fault in both ALU and the checker.*

Proof. Equation (8.20) can be expressed as follows.

$$\begin{aligned} S_\Phi &= \left(\sum_{i=0}^{k-1}{}^{\oplus}\, f_\Phi(y_i) \right) \oplus p_A \oplus p_B \\ &= \left(\sum_{i=0}^{k-1}{}^{\oplus}\, a_i \oplus b_i \right) \oplus p_A \oplus p_B \end{aligned}$$

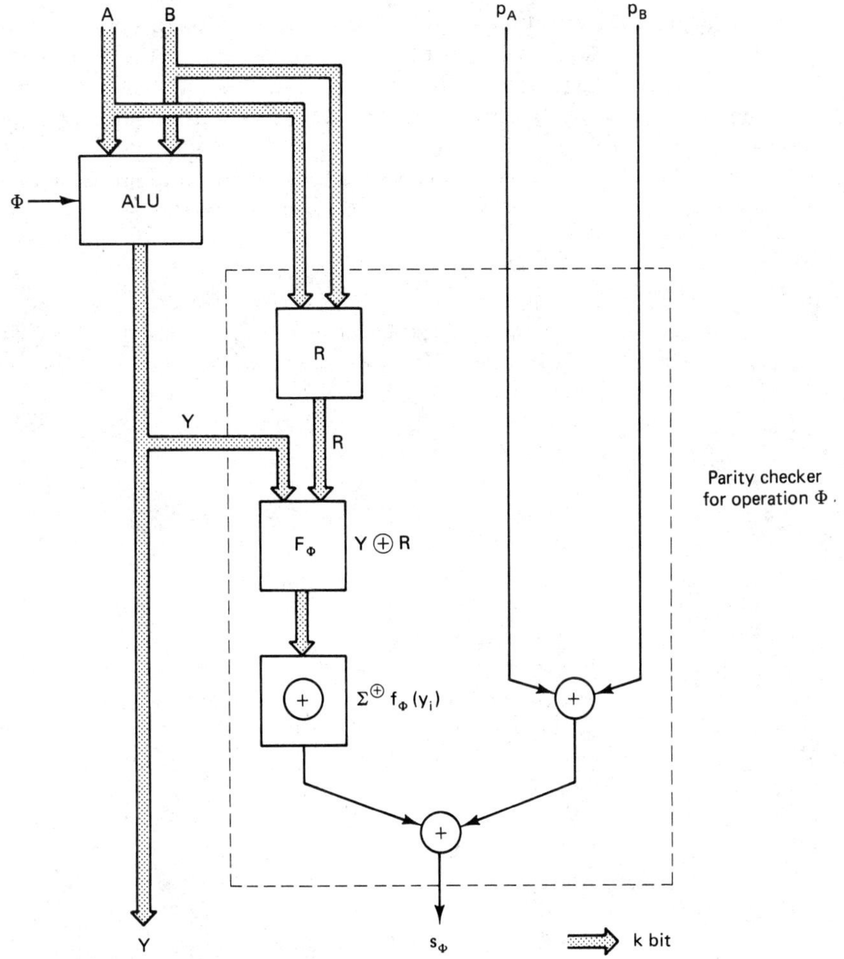

Figure 8.36 Parity checking for an arbitrary operation Φ [FUJI 81c]. © 1981 IECE Japan.

Therefore, we have

$$\frac{dS_\Phi}{da_i} = 1 \text{ and } \frac{dS_\Phi}{db_i} = 1$$

This shows that a single input error can always be detected. Q.E.D.

Next, we consider error correction in ALU operations based on the foregoing results. Parity checking that follows the previous way of thinking can apparently be applied to a check group defined by the row of an **H** matrix. For (n, k) code, there are $n - k = r$ check groups, each of which is the set of bits included in each row of the following **H** matrix:

$$\mathbf{H} = [\mathbf{H}_e \mid \mathbf{I}_r]_{r \times n}$$

Here, $\mathbf{H}_e$ is the $(r \times k)$ encoding matrix and $\mathbf{I}_r$ is the $(r \times r)$ identity matrix. Two input codewords are shown as $[A, C_A]$ and $[B, C_B]$ where C_A and C_B are check-bit groups, such that

$$C_A = (c_{A,0}, c_{A,1}, \ldots, c_{A,r-1})$$
$$C_B = (c_{B,0}, c_{B,1}, \ldots, c_{B,r-1})$$

We also define C such that

$$C = C_A \oplus C_B$$
$$C = (c_0, c_1, \ldots, c_{r-1})$$
$$c_i = c_{A,i} \oplus c_{B,i}$$

The output of ALU is shown as $[Y, C_Y]$, where C_Y is the check-bit group for output Y.,

$$C_Y = (c_{Y,0}, c_{Y,1}, \ldots, c_{Y,r-1})$$

An error correction procedure consists of three major steps: (1) syndrome generation, (2) determination of error location (syndrome decoding), and (3) inversion of the error bit.

Syndrome generation for output Y has the following procedures.

1. Check-bit generation:

$$C_Y = Y \cdot \mathbf{H}_e^T$$

2. Check-bit prediction:

$$C_p = R \cdot \mathbf{H}_e^T \oplus C$$
$$C_p = (c_{p,0}, c_{p,1}, \ldots, c_{p,r-1})$$

3. Syndrome generation:

$$\begin{aligned} S &= C_Y \oplus C_p \\ &= Y \cdot \mathbf{H}_e^T \oplus R \cdot \mathbf{H}_e^T \oplus C \\ &= F_\Phi \cdot \mathbf{H}_e^T \oplus C, \text{ where } F_\Phi = Y \oplus R \end{aligned}$$

Error location is determined from the syndrome, such that

$$W(S) = 0: \text{ No error}$$
$$W(S) = 1: \text{ Error in check-bit part } C_p$$
$$W(S) \geq 2: \text{ Error in ALU output } Y$$

where $W(S)$ means the weight of syndrome. This is determined precisely by the **H** matrix, especially for the case of error correction of output Y.

Error pointer $E = (E_Y, E_c)$ specifies the error pattern to be corrected, where E_Y specifies the output Y error and E_c the check-bit error. Corrected output $[\hat{Y}, \hat{C}_Y]$ is obtained from the foregoing error pointer such that

$$\hat{Y} = Y \oplus E_Y$$

$$\hat{C}_Y = C_p \oplus E_c$$

Fig. 8.37 shows an error correction circuit (**EC**) for ALU. Note particularly that the circuit $\mathbf{EC}_0$ in **EC**, enclosed by the broken line, is the same error decoding circuit as that for high-speed memories.

By using the technique just mentioned, bit-error detecting/correcting codes, or byte-error detecting/correcting codes for memories, as discussed in Chapters 4 and 5, can also be applied to ALU. For more information, refer to [FUJI 81c].

8.2.2 Self-Checking PLA

With very large scale integration (VLSI), the use of programmable logic arrays (PLA's) as components in design has become more widespread because they reduce design time, provide a regular structure, and can be easily tested. The PLA as shown in Fig. 8.38 is a memorylike array structure. Conceptually, the PLA can be modeled as a two-level AND-OR logic network implemented by NOR-NOR, NAND-NAND, or AND-OR logic. Fig. 8.38 shows the circuit diagram of a typical PLA implemented in NOR-NOR logic.

The PLA consists of four main sections: the decoder, the AND array, the OR array, and the output buffers. The decoder section usually consists of a collection of one-input or two-input decoders. Inputs are given to the AND array and then AND terms, called *product terms*, are produced. These vertical lines shown in Fig. 8.39 are called product term lines. On the other hand, in the OR array, OR terms are produced from these product terms. That is, any functions can be expressed in a *disjunctive canonical form* (i.e., sum of products) at the output buffers of the OR array. The user can connect or disconnect n-MOS transistors at any crosspoints according to the prescribed functions, which means the functions are *programmable*. Fig. 8.39 shows the schematic expression of the PLA in which every transistor at crosspoints is expressed in a dotted point. This PLA expresses the same logic functions as that shown in Fig. 8.38.

There are three types of faults that commonly occur in a PLA [OSTA 79, MAK 82, SOME 86].

1. Stuck-at faults caused by line open faults.
2. Short faults between two adjacent lines.
3. Contact faults, which include the missing device faults and the extra device faults.

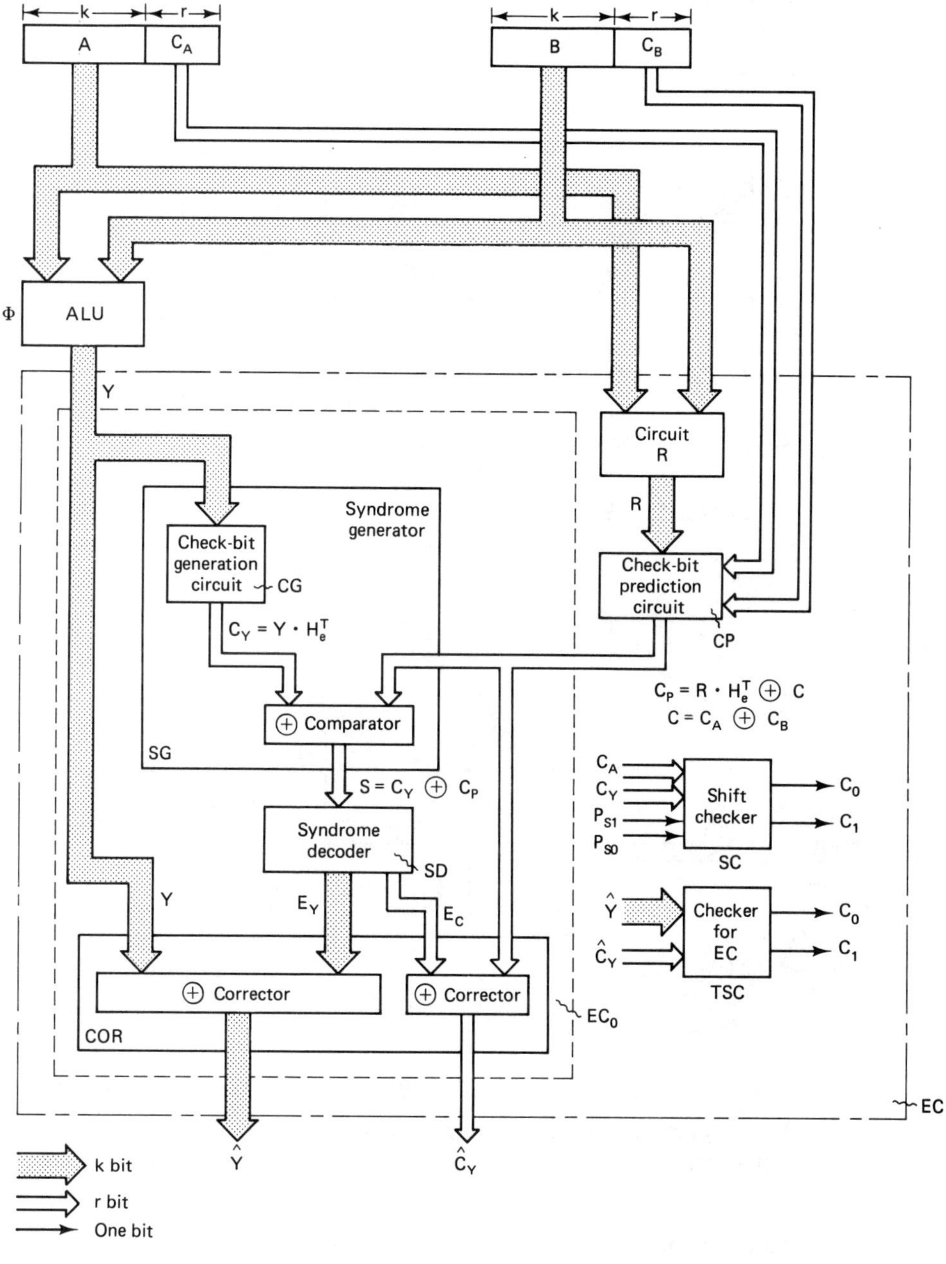

Figure 8.37 Error correction scheme for ALU using $(k + r, k)$ parity-based codes [FUJI 81c]. © 1981 IECE Japan.

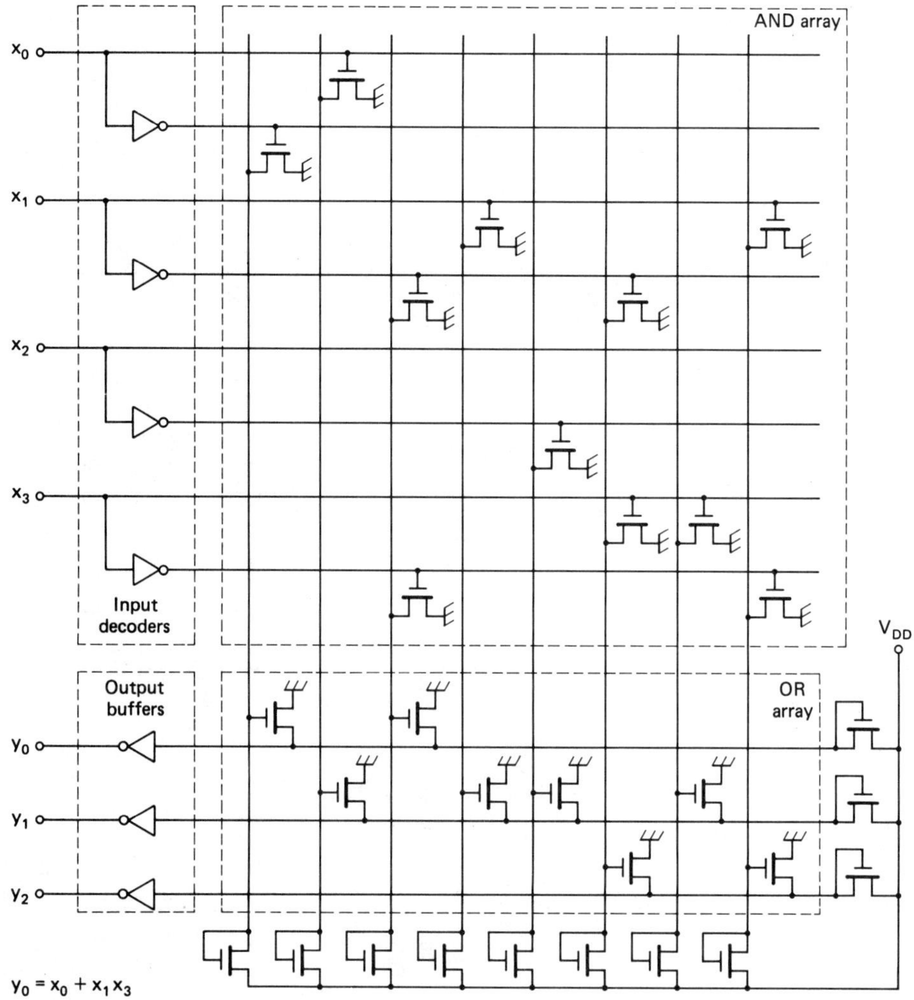

$y_0 = x_0 + x_1 x_3$

$y_2 = \overline{x}_0 + \overline{x}_1 + x_2 + \overline{x}_3$

$y_3 = \overline{x}_1 x_3 + x_1 \overline{x}_3$

Figure 8.38 Circuit diagram of PLA: *n*-MOS NOR-NOR implementation.

We assume that the fault set F consists of all single faults from these three fault types. The effects of these faults on the PLA can be summarized as follows.

1. Faults in the AND array and in the input decoder may cause either the activation of unaddressed product terms, or the deactivation of addressed product terms, or both, or may simply have no effect.
2. Faults in the OR array and in the output inverters may cause either the increment of 1's or the decrement of 1's in the output pattern, or both, or they may have no effect.

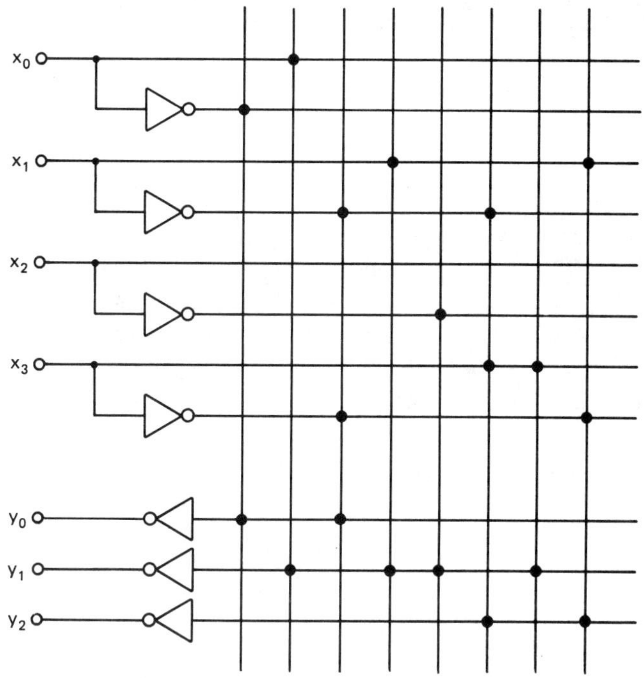

Figure 8.39 Schematic expression of the NOR-NOR PLA. (This expresses the same circuit as that shown in Fig. 8.38.)

For the previously mentioned faults, design methods for self-checking checkers in PLA have been proposed. Some of them are based on the idea that the output is encoded in a parity code, an m-out-of-n code, or a Berger code under activation of a restricted number of product terms [WANG 79, KHAK 82a, MAK 82]. Using code-disjoint (CD) and SFS concepts, further extended checking methods for PLA have been proposed [SON 81, FUCH 87]. Another method proposed is a use of a low-cost residue code with mod 3 and an EX-OR tree [TAO 86].

First, we deal with the checking method based on the idea just mentioned [WANG 79]. Specifically, the following conditions are imposed.

1. One and only one product term is activated by each input pattern.
2. The output pattern belongs to a checkable code.

The design method for this self-checking PLA is as follows.

1. **AND Array**. First, each output function is modified into sum of t disjoint product terms. Let the disjoint product term be p_i, $i = 0, 1, \ldots, t-1$, ($p_0 \cap p_1 \cap \cdots \cap p_{t-1} = \varnothing$). Then, output functions $y_0, y_1, \ldots, y_{k-1}$ are expressed by using these terms. Let the extra product term be q_j, $j = 0, 1, \ldots, s-1$.

These s terms can be determined such that

$$q_0 + q_1 + \cdots + q_{s-1} = \overline{p_0} \cdot \overline{p_1} \cdot \cdots \cdot \overline{p_{t-1}} = \overline{P}, \text{'+': OR, '}\cdot\text{': AND}$$

where $P = p_0 + p_1 + \cdots + p_{t-1}$, and q_j's are also pairwise disjoint (i.e., $q_0 \cap q_1 \cap \cdots \cap q_{s-1} = \varnothing$). It is apparent that the number of these disjoint product terms should be minimized from the practical point of view. Therefore, $W_{\mathrm{I}} = (p_0, p_1, \ldots, p_{t-1}, q_0, q_1, \ldots, q_{s-1})$ covers all cells in the Karnaugh map and these are not overlapped. Since the terms are disjoint with each other, only one term is always activated at a time for an input pattern. Hence, W_{I} is a 1-out-of-N code, where $N = t + s$.

2. OR array. Output of the PLA is encoded, and therefore extra output lines should be included. Let the line be g_i, $i = 0, 1, \ldots, l - 1$. Then, $W_{\mathrm{II}} = (y_0, y_1, \ldots, y_{k-1}, g_0, g_1, \ldots, g_{l-1})$ forms an error detecting code such as a parity code or an m-out-of-n code. If we use an m-out-of-n code, its parameters m and n

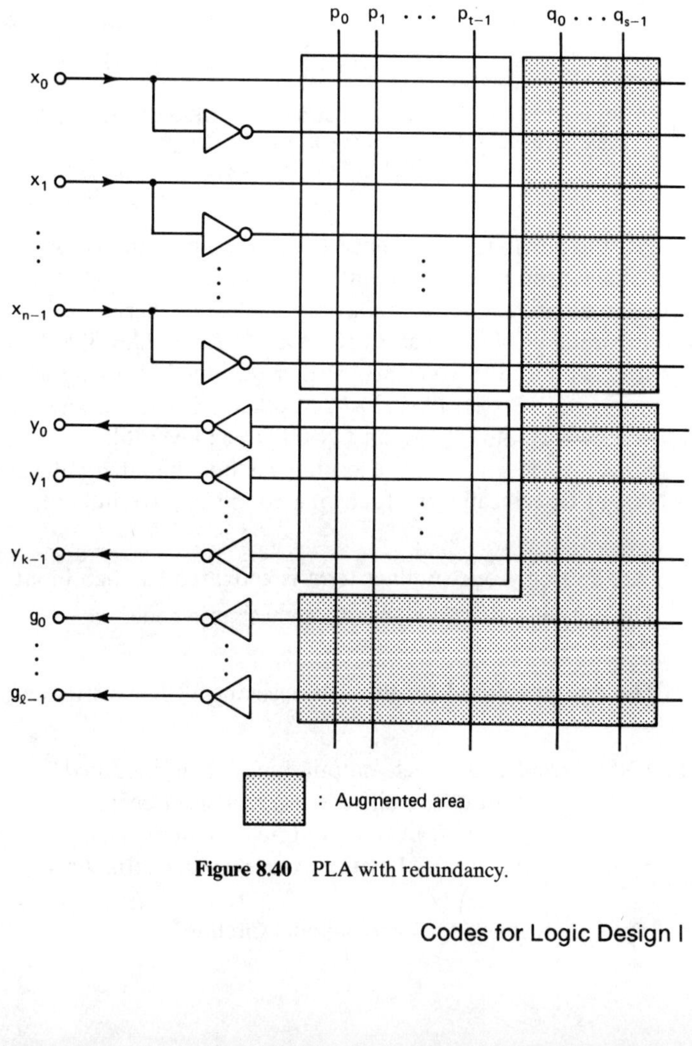

Figure 8.40 PLA with redundancy.

are determined as follows.

$$m = k_{\max}$$
$$n = k + k_{\max} - k_{\min}$$

$k_{\max}$: maximum number of dotted crosspoints on a product term line in an OR array.
$k_{\min}$: minimum number of dotted crosspoints on a product term line in an OR array.

The augmented PLA is shown in Fig. 8.40.

Example 8-7

Let output functions y_0, y_1, and y_2 be expressed as follows.

$$\begin{aligned} y_0 &= \bar{x}_0(x_1 + \bar{x}_2 x_3) \\ y_1 &= \bar{x}_0\bar{x}_1(x_2 + x_3) \\ y_2 &= x_0 + x_1 + x_2 + x_3 \end{aligned} \qquad (8.21)$$

These functions are expressed in Karnaugh maps as follows (Fig. 8.41(a)).

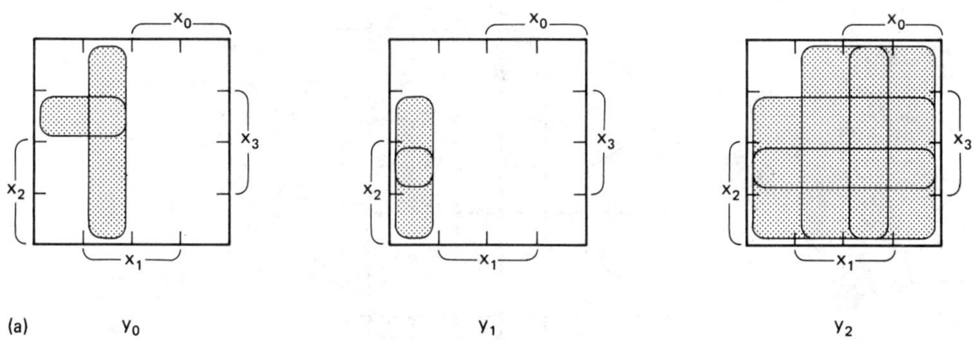

Figure 8.41 (a) Karnaugh maps for functions of Equation (8.21).

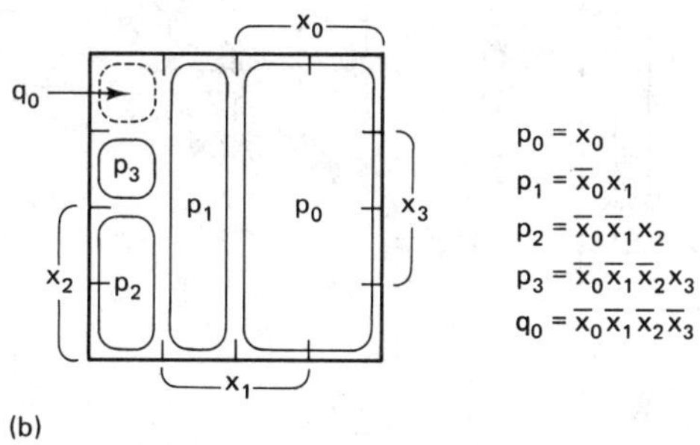

Figure 8.41 (b) Karnaugh maps for disjoint product terms.

From these maps, we can obtain the disjoint product terms, as shown in Fig. 8.41(b). Then, the extra product term is determined as

$$q_0 = \bar{x}_0\bar{x}_1\bar{x}_2\bar{x}_3$$

The output functions in Equation (8.21) are expressed by using the disjoint product terms.

$$y_0 = p_1 + p_3$$

$$y_1 = p_2 + p_3$$

$$y_2 = p_0 + p_1 + p_2 + p_3$$

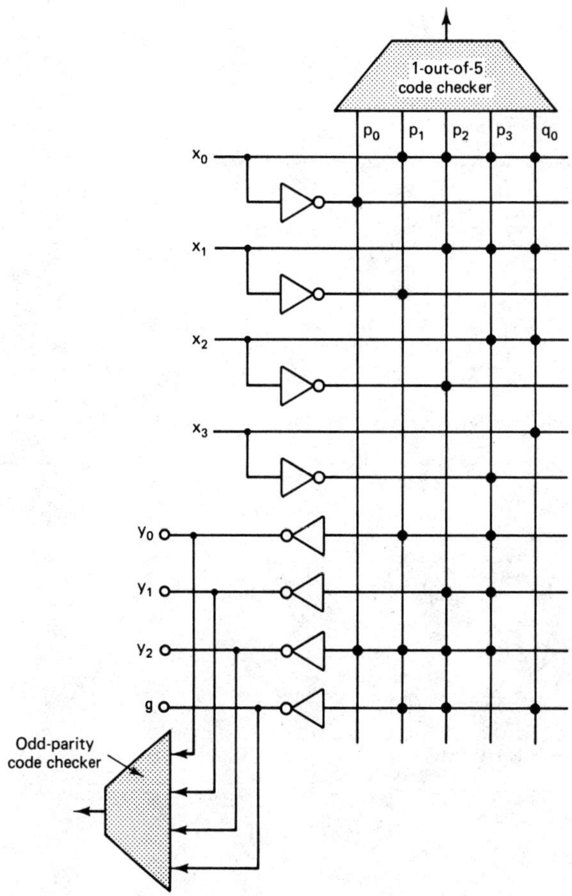

(a) 1-out-of-5 code checker and odd-parity code checker

Figure 8.42 Self-checking PLA.

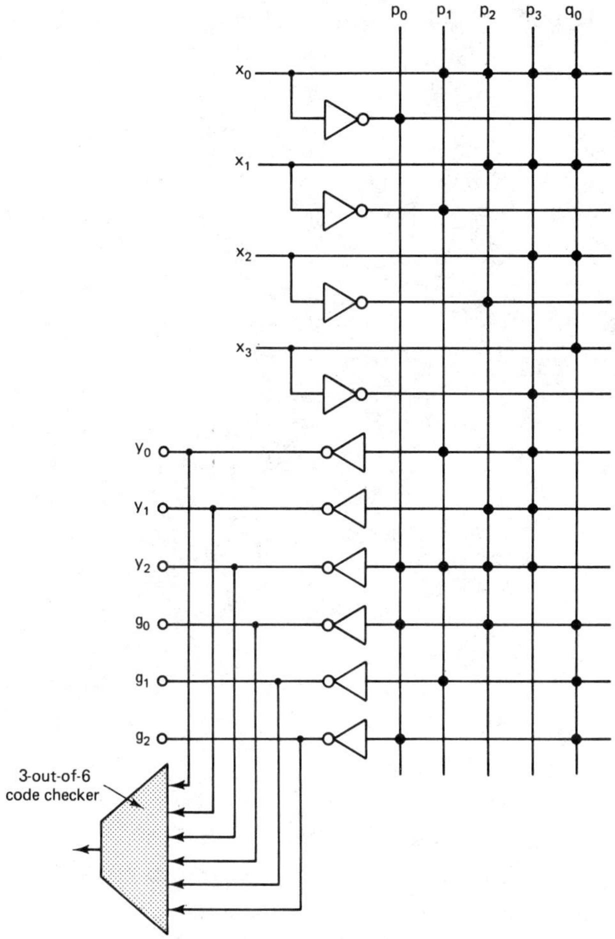

(b) 3-out-of-6 code checker

Figure 8.42 Continued.

Therefore, $W = (p_0, p_1, p_2, p_3, q_0)$ is a 1-out-of-5 code, because always only one product term is activated. Then, product terms can be checked by a 1-out-of-5 code checker.

As for an OR array, the outputs are encoded such as in a parity code, or a 3-out-of-6 code. Fig. 8.42 shows the self-checking PLA. It can be easily proved that the PLA shown in Fig. 8.42 is TSC for prescribed single faults in F and for all codeword inputs.

If we consider the PLA as a circuit that treats the lines after the input decoder as its inputs and the lines before the output inverters in the OR array as the external outputs, then the PLA can be viewed as an *inverter-free circuit*. Therefore, any single fault in F will cause only *unidirectional errors* at the outputs of the PLA. For more details, refer to [MAK 82, ABRA 86]. In this model, to detect all unidirectional errors, either a Berger code or an m-out-of-n code is sufficient for encoding the outputs of the OR array. Similar to the former method of the covering of 1-cells in the Karnaugh map, here each 0-cell must also be covered by some product term. Here, we will have an example of this type of self-checking PLA whose output is encoded in a Berger code.

Example 8-8 [MAK 82]

The truth table for the 4-input (x_0, x_1, x_2, x_3), 3-output (y_0, y_1, y_2) function is shown and is augmented by including a Berger code (codeword = (y_0, y_1, y_2, g_0, g_1)) among the outputs.

x_0	x_1	x_2	x_3	y_0	y_1	y_2	g_0	g_1
0	0	0	0	0	0	0	1	1
0	0	0	1	0	0	0	1	1
0	0	1	0	0	1	0	1	0
0	0	1	1	0	1	1	0	1
0	1	0	0	1	0	1	0	1
0	1	0	1	1	1	1	0	0
0	1	1	0	0	0	1	1	0
0	1	1	1	1	1	1	0	0
1	0	0	0	0	1	0	1	0
1	0	0	1	1	1	1	0	0
1	0	1	0	1	0	0	1	0
1	0	1	1	1	1	0	0	1
1	1	0	0	0	0	0	1	1
1	1	0	1	1	1	1	0	0
1	1	1	0	0	0	0	1	1
1	1	1	1	1	1	1	0	0

The Karnaugh maps for the functions y_0, y_1, y_2, and g_0, g_1 are shown in Fig. 8.43.

From the table, we need two extra output lines for the Berger code. After minimization, there are eleven product terms, which include two (p_0 and p_{10}) redundant product terms and nine original product terms. Fig. 8.44 shows the self-checking PLA using the Berger code.

If we assume that faults occur one at a time and that the time interval between two faults is long enough so that all code inputs are applied to the circuit, the first erroneous output due to a fault in a circuit must be a noncodeword. In this case, for single faults in F, the PLA designed by the above method is SFS [MAK 82].

In the inverter-free circuit defined before in the NOR-NOR PLA, if we apply a systematic unidirectional code (e.g., Berger code) to the PLA, whereby the output check bits are a function of both the output information bits and the input information bits, then the PLA can be made code disjoint and also SFS for all faults in F [FUCH 87]. The codeword transmitted to the PLA as an input X is from the Berger codespace and is composed of information bits, I_i, and check bits, C_i. That is, (I_i, C_i) is a Berger code. The output of the PLA, Y, is composed of information bits, I_0, and check bits, C_0. The function $\beta(Q)$ represents the Berger check bits of

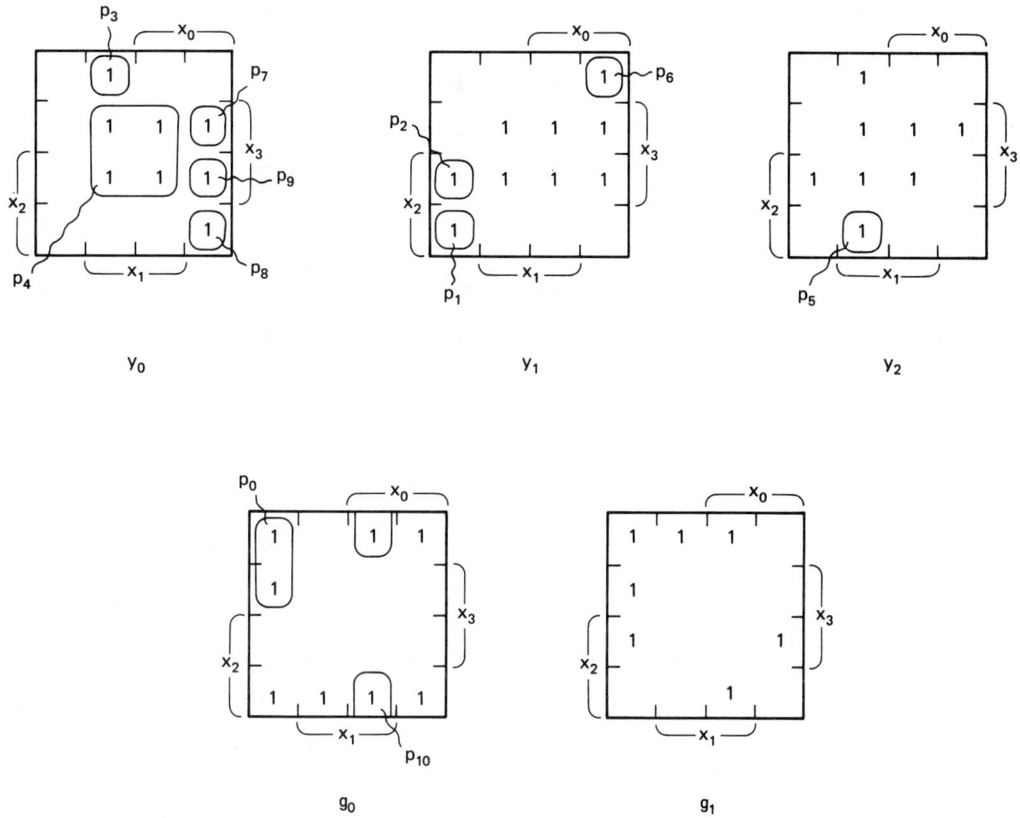

Figure 8.43 Karnaugh maps for functions y_0, y_1, y_2, g_0, and g_1.

the binary vector Q, and the desired function to be implemented by the PLA will be expressed as $I_0 = H(I_i)$. If $C_0 = \overline{\beta(I_i)} + \beta(I_0)$, where + denotes arithmetic addition, then the PLA is proven to be code disjoint and SFS [FUCH 87]. The checker compares the OR array output C_0 with $\overline{C_i} + \beta(I_0)$ and then indicates an error if they are not equal (shown in Fig. 8.45).

The code-disjoint property of the PLA ensures the detectability of errors on inputs I_i without modifying the arrays to include special input codeword checkers. Another code-disjoint PLA, also satisfying the self-testing property, is proposed using m-out-of-n codes that encode both inputs and outputs [PIES 85].

8.2.3 Self-checking ECC Circuit

Error-checking and correcting (ECC) codes are extensively used in recent computer systems. An increase in the memory readout data size will increase the size of the ECC circuit, and therefore increases the probability of circuit failure. Thus the ECC circuit has to withstand failures in itself without transmitting erroneous data.

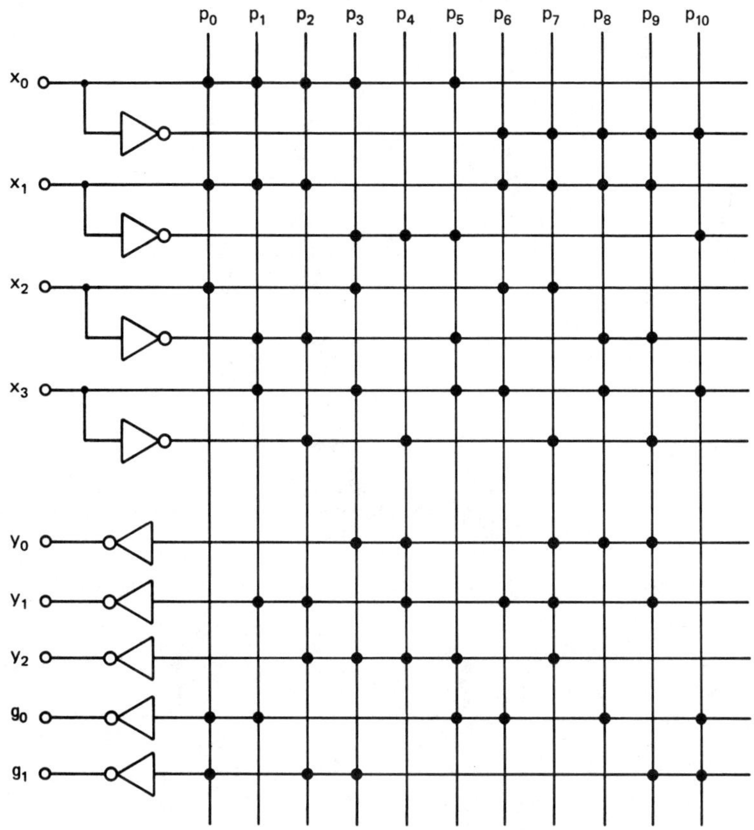

Figure 8.44 Self-checking PLA with Berger code [MAK 82]. © 1982 IEEE.

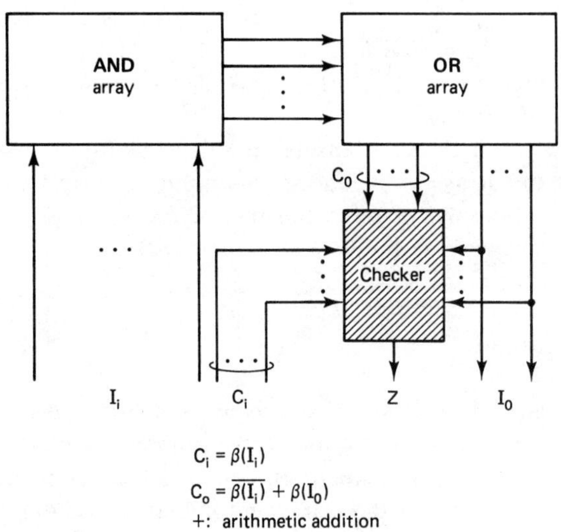

Figure 8.45 Code disjoint and SFS PLA [FUCH 87]. © 1987 IEEE.

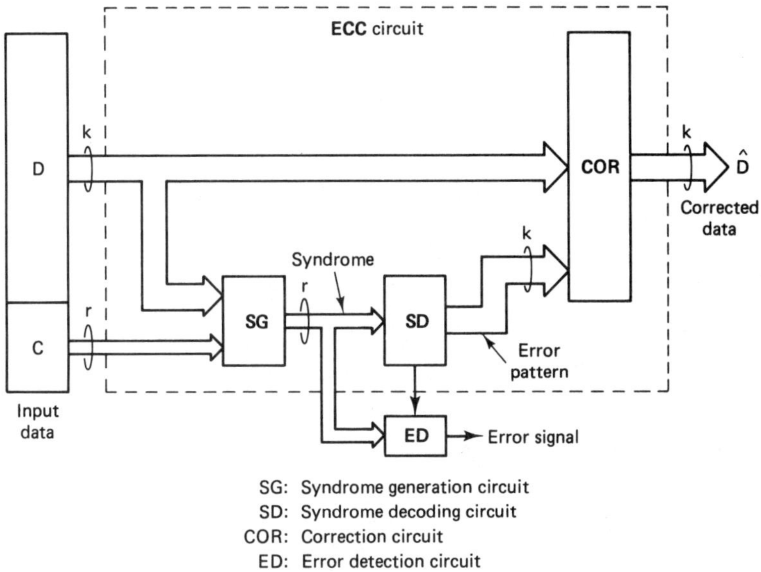

Figure 8.46 ECC circuit.

With such considerations in mind, a design for a self-checking ECC circuit has been proposed [CART 70, BOUR 73, FUJI 79, ITOH 83b, SHIN 86a, 86b, GAIT 88]. Here, we consider the ECC circuit used in high-speed memories; hence it is a combinational circuit.

Fig. 8.46 shows the block diagram of the ECC circuit. This circuit consists of a syndrome generation circuit (**SG**), a syndrome decoding circuit (**SD**), and a correction circuit (**COR**). **SG** generates r syndrome bits from the input data, including k information bits and r check bits. **SD** generates k error patterns that indicate an error in each bit, and **COR** generates the corrected data by using the error patterns. Usually, **COR** does not generate the corrected check bits, but it sometimes generates correct byte parity bits that have been originally generated in the **SG**. The error detection circuit (**ED**) generates the error signal that indicates the error types.

Since this circuit has a large gate amount (e.g., about 1200 gates for $k = 64$), the self-checking techniques are applied to the individual circuits (i.e., **SG**, **SD**, and **COR**) of the ECC circuits [FUJI 79, ITOH 83b, SHIN 86b]. Another method is to apply self-checking techniques to the whole circuit, instead of the individual circuit [CART 70, BOUR 73, SHIN 86a, GAIT 88]. Here, we consider the latter type of self-checking ECC circuit.

The simplest method for checking the ECC circuit is to enter again the corrected output, including corrected check bits, to another syndrome generation circuit; if the syndromes are all zeros, then we assume that the ECC circuit is fault free [BOUR 73]. This checker belongs to the class of code checkers, specifically to the self-checking separate code checkers shown in Section 9.1.4, in which the code adopted is a separate code. In this case, in order to make this circuit (i.e., the circuit

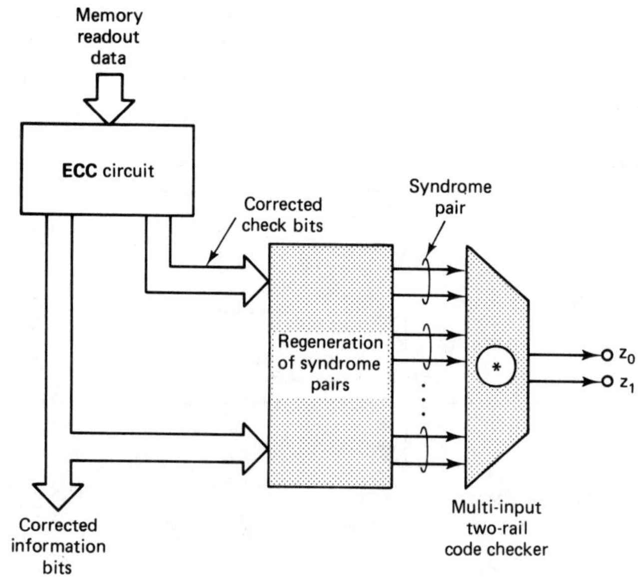

Figure 8.47 Self-checking ECC with regenerated syndrome pair checker.

for regeneration of syndrome pairs) self-checking, it is formed from two-outputs EX-OR trees, as shown in Fig. 8.47. The outputs of the syndrome pairs (i.e., two-rail code pairs) are checked by the multi-input, self-checking, two-rail code checker (see Section 9.1.2).

Next, we consider the self-checking ECC circuit using the odd-weight-column SEC-DED code (see Section 4.1.1), which is most widely used in high-speed memories. This new checking method is based on the principle shown in the following theorem.

Theorem 8-8. *Let $D = (d_0, d_1, \ldots, d_{k-1})$ be the information part and $C = (c_0, c_1, \ldots, c_{r-1})$ be its check part of the codeword $[D, C]$. And let $S = (s_0, s_1, \ldots, s_{r-1})$ be the syndrome. Then the following relation holds for all odd-weight-column codes*:

$$\sum_{l=0}^{r-1}{}^{\oplus} s_l = \left(\sum_{j=0}^{k-1}{}^{\oplus} d_j\right) \oplus \left(\sum_{i=0}^{r-1}{}^{\oplus} c_i\right), \qquad \sum{}^{\oplus} : \textit{mod 2 sum} \tag{8.22}$$

By using the property of the odd-weight-column code mentioned in Section 4.4.2, this can be easily proved. Fig. 8.48 shows the principle of the checker using the idea of this theorem. In this figure, it is apparent that the checker belongs to the prediction checker class.

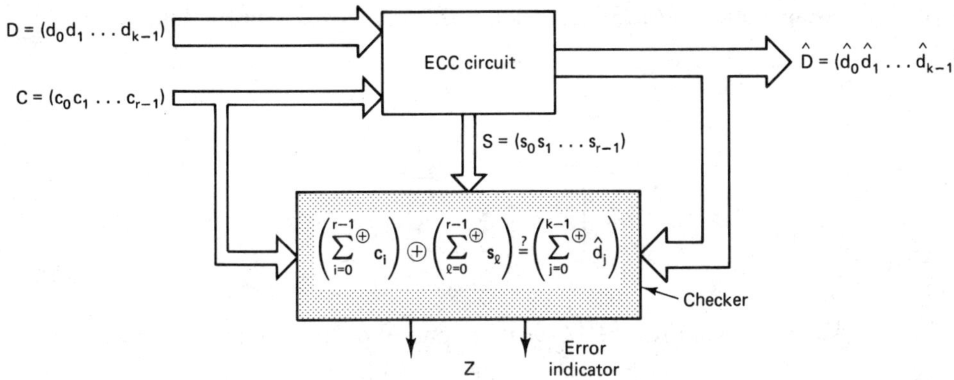

Figure 8.48 Principle of the odd-weight-column ECC code checker.

In order to discriminate the error in the input data and the error due to the ECC circuit fault, the following condition is given to the **H** matrix design [SHIN 86a].

$$\left(h_{l,i} \cdot h_{m,i} \cup h_{m,i} \cdot h_{s,i} \cup h_{s,i} \cdot h_{l,i}\right) \cdot \left(\sum_{j=0}^{r-1}{}^{\oplus}\, h_{j,i}\right) = 1, \quad \cdot : \text{AND}, \cup : \text{OR} \tag{8.23}$$

$h_{l,i}, h_{m,i}, h_{s,i}$: elements in the ith column of the **H** matrix $\in \{0, 1\}$

$$0 \le l, m, s \le r-1, \qquad l \ne m \ne s \ne l, \qquad 0 \le i \le k-1$$

Equation (8.23) shows the logical expression of the **H** matrix column vectors. An example is shown in the following **H** matrix of the odd-weight column (22, 16) SEC–DED code that satisfies Equation (8.23) for the case $l = 0$, $m = 3$, $s = 4$.

$$\mathbf{H} = \left[\begin{array}{cccccccccccccccc|cccccc}
d_0 & d_1 & d_2 & d_3 & d_4 & d_5 & d_6 & d_7 & d_8 & d_9 & d_{10} & d_{11} & d_{12} & d_{13} & d_{14} & d_{15} & c_0 & c_1 & c_2 & c_3 & c_4 & c_5 \\
1 & 1 & 1 & 1 & 0 & 0 & 1 & 1 & 0 & 0 & 1 & 1 & 1 & 1 & 1 & 1 & 1 & 0 & 0 & 0 & 0 & 0 \\
1 & 0 & 1 & 0 & 0 & 1 & 1 & 0 & 0 & 1 & 1 & 0 & 1 & 0 & 1 & 0 & 0 & 1 & 0 & 0 & 0 & 0 \\
1 & 0 & 0 & 1 & 1 & 0 & 1 & 0 & 0 & 1 & 0 & 1 & 1 & 0 & 0 & 1 & 0 & 0 & 1 & 0 & 0 & 0 \\
0 & 0 & 0 & 0 & 1 & 1 & 1 & 1 & 1 & 1 & 1 & 1 & 1 & 1 & 1 & 1 & 0 & 0 & 0 & 1 & 0 & 0 \\
1 & 1 & 1 & 1 & 1 & 1 & 1 & 1 & 1 & 1 & 1 & 1 & 0 & 0 & 0 & 0 & 0 & 0 & 0 & 0 & 1 & 0 \\
1 & 1 & 0 & 0 & 0 & 0 & 0 & 0 & 1 & 1 & 1 & 1 & 1 & 1 & 0 & 0 & 0 & 0 & 0 & 0 & 0 & 1
\end{array}\right]$$

(8.24)*

*[SHIN 86] © 1986 IECE Japan.

Using Equation (8.23), Equation (8.22) is changed into the following:

$$\begin{cases} z_0 = Y_k \oplus \left(\sum_{i=0}^{r-1}{}^{\oplus} c_i \right) \\ z_1 = \left(\overline{\sum_{j=0}^{k-1}{}^{\oplus} \hat{d}_j} \right), \quad \sum{}^{\oplus} : \text{mod 2 sum} \end{cases} \tag{8.25}$$

where $\hat{d}_j$ expresses the ECC circuit output of the jth data and

$$Y_k = \left(\overline{s_l \cdot s_m + s_m \cdot s_s + s_s \cdot s_l} \right) \cdot \left(\sum_{j=0}^{r-1}{}^{\oplus} s_j \right)$$

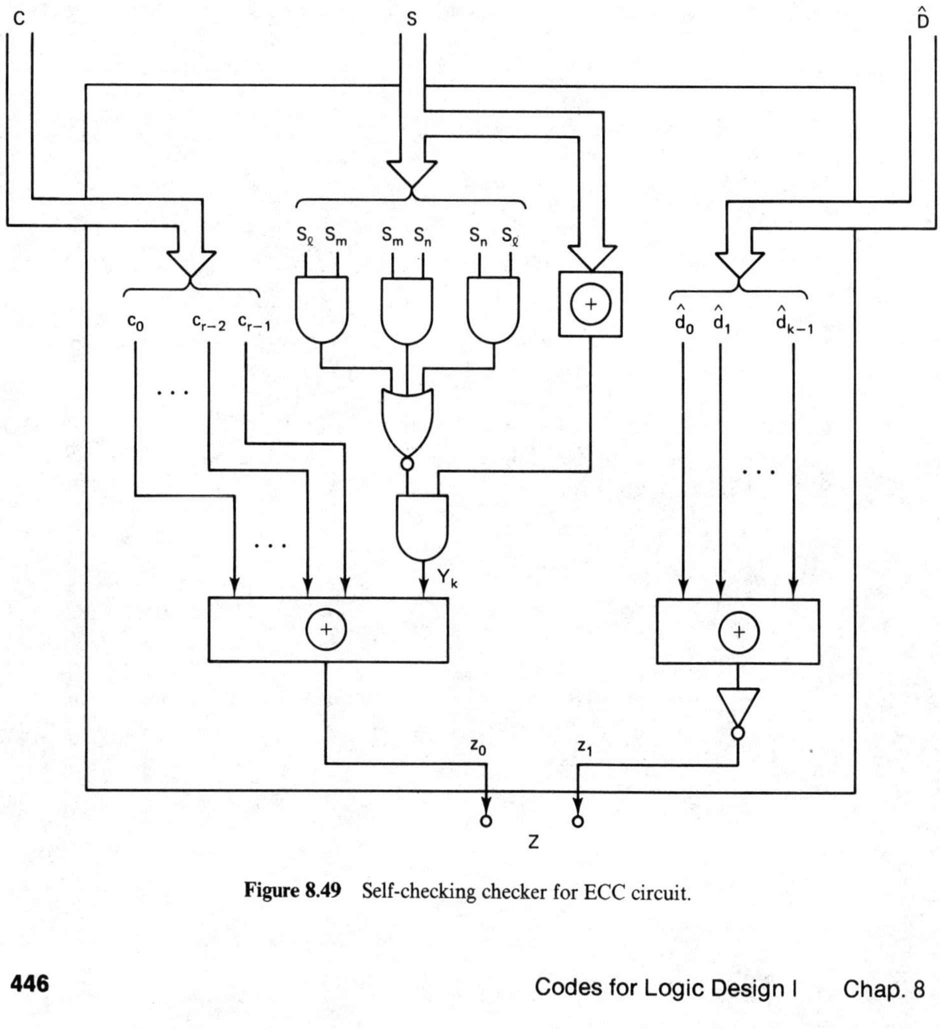

Figure 8.49 Self-checking checker for ECC circuit.

In Equation (8.25), Y_k is always 1 whenever the odd-weight syndrome S indicates the error in check bits (i.e., weight-1 syndrome) or does not equal any **H** matrix column vector. Fig. 8.49 shows the checker implemented from Equation (8.25).

If there is no fault inside the ECC circuit, the checker output is always a 1-out-of-2-code (i.e., $(z_0, z_1) \in \{(0,1)(1,0)\}$). This means that the ECC circuit is fault free. This always holds even if input to the ECC circuit $[D, C]$ includes a single error or double error. The input error is always indicated in the error detection circuit (**ED**).

We now consider the circuit **G** that includes both the ECC circuit and the checker. Input codespace **N** of the circuit **G** includes all codeword inputs, all single-error inputs, and all double-error inputs. Output codespace **S** of the circuit **G** is defined from the ECC circuit output $\hat{D}$, the checker output (z_0, z_1) and the error detection circuit (**ED**) output. Under these conditions, the circuit **G** is proven to be TSC for single faults. For more details regarding the proof, refer to [SHIN 86a]. The circuit **ED** will be duplicated from the self-checking point of view.

Next, we consider the circuit increase due to self-checking of the ECC. The percentage increase is given by

$$p = \left\{ \frac{\text{Self-checking ECC circuit gate count}}{\text{Original ECC circuit gate count}} - 1 \right\} \times 100(\%)$$

where the original ECC circuit means the circuit that does not include the self-checking checker. Table 8.3 shows the percentage increase for information length $k = 16, 32, 64$ bits of the odd-weight-column SEC–DED codes. This is evaluated under the number of transistors of the circuit implemented by CMOS LSI.

8.3 A NOTE ON SELF-CHECKING SEQUENTIAL CIRCUITS

We have studied the self-checking concept and the design approach for the self-checking combinational circuits. Another important class of circuits is sequential circuits, which differ from combinational circuits in having memory cells and/or feedback of some outputs as inputs to the circuit.

TABLE 8.3 CIRCUIT INCREASE FOR SELF-CHECKING ECC CIRCUIT [SHIN 86a]

k(bits)	p(%)
16	45.3
32	33.2
64	31.8

The definitions of the TSC and the SFS sequential circuits have been proposed as extensions of the TSC and the SFS combinational circuits [DIAZ 79, VIAU 80, SMIT 83, NANY 87]. In combinational logic checking, the main problem is to determine whether an output is appropriate for a given input. For sequential logic, the main problem is to determine the appropriateness of a sequence of outputs for a given sequence of inputs. This means checking outputs, the state of the sequential logic, and, if necessary, even the feedback to ensure proper state transition and timing. The state of a sequential circuit can often be checked by choosing the state assignment codes to be members of some error detecting codes [FRAN 66, REED 70]. The codes used for state assignment are m-out-of-n codes, 1-out-of-n codes, parity codes, and Berger codes.

Considerable work appears on self-checking design method for synchronous and asynchronous sequential circuits [TOHM 71, 74, PRAD 73, 76, 78, DIAZ 74a, 74b, 79, MUKA 74, 76, SAWI 74, MAKI 74, OZGU 77, CHUA 78, DAVI 78b, VIAU 80, NANY 79, 87, JANS 85]. These design methods are reported comprehensively in [TOHM 86].

EXERCISES

8.1. Demonstrate that the circuit of Fig. 8.6 is self-testing for all faults affecting fewer than $(n + 1)$ bits if the inputs have an even-parity codeword.

8.2. Obtain the tested and secure fault sets of the exclusive-or circuit of Fig. 8.6 when the inputs are encoded in distance-3 Hamming code.

8.3. Let input codespace of the circuit shown below be $N \in \{(a_0, b_0)(a_1, b_1) | (a_0, b_0), (a_1, b_1) = 1\text{-}out\text{-}of\text{-}2\ codes\}$. And let the output codespace be $S \in \{(c_0, c_1) | (c_0, c_1) = 1\text{-}out\text{-}of\text{-}2\ code\}$. Show that the circuit is a TSC checker for all single faults, provided that it receives all four possible codeword inputs.

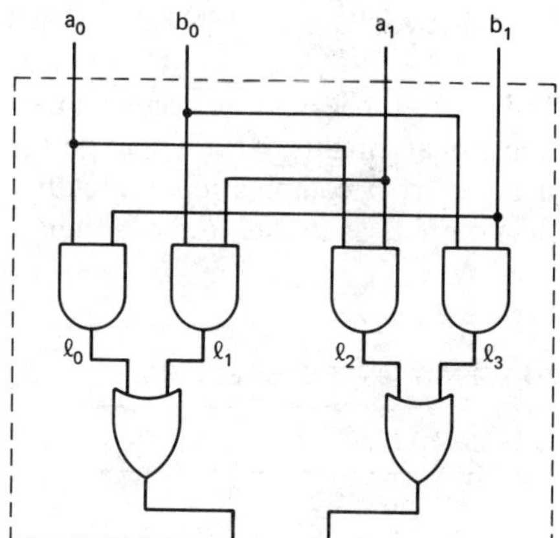

8.4. Verify that the cascaded inverter-free network shown in Fig. 8.13, whose primary inputs are encoded in 1-out-of-2 code, is SFS with respect to unidirectional faults.

8.5. Consider the bit-sliced system each of which consists of three registers and a multiplexer that loads unordered codewords from one of I_1 and I_2, depending on a two-rail encoded load signal $(C, \overline{C})$, into D, as shown below [NANY 85b].
Show that the system is SFS for unidirectional faults, even though it does not satisfy the code-disjoint (CD) property.

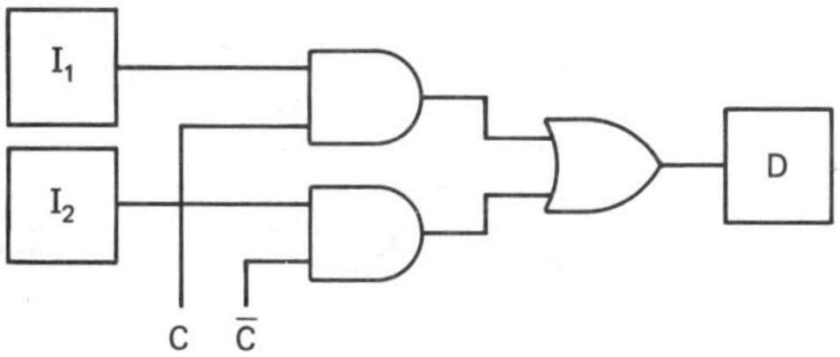

8.6. Show that the system shown in Exercise 8.5 is error secure (ES) in the sense of Definition 8-6 for a fault-free system.

8.7. Perform the following operations relating to the circuit of Fig. 8.19.
(a) Show that this checking circuit can detect any errors in y_0 or $y_1 \cdot y_2$, but not both.
(b) Errors due to y_1 or y_2 can be detected with certain input conditions. Obtain these conditions.

8.8. Design the parity prediction checker for the 3-input (x_0, x_1, x_2), 3-output (y_0, y_1, y_2) combinational circuit defined in the following table.

x_0	x_1	x_2	y_0	y_1	y_2
0	0	0	1	1	1
0	0	1	0	0	1
0	1	0	1	0	0
0	1	1	0	1	1
1	0	0	0	0	0
1	0	1	0	1	0
1	1	0	1	1	0
1	1	1	1	0	1

8.9. Design the input regeneration checker for the 1-out-of-8 decoder.

8.10. Verify that the 1-out-of-8 decoder shown on the next page in (a) is self-testing, while the decoder shown in (b) is not self-testing for all single faults [CART 71b, WAKE 78]. The output codespace is defined as $\{(d_0, d_1, \ldots, d_7)(z_0, z_1) | (d_0, d_1, \ldots, d_7) = \textit{1-out-of-8 code}, \text{ and } (z_0, z_1) = \textit{1-out-of-2 code}\}$.

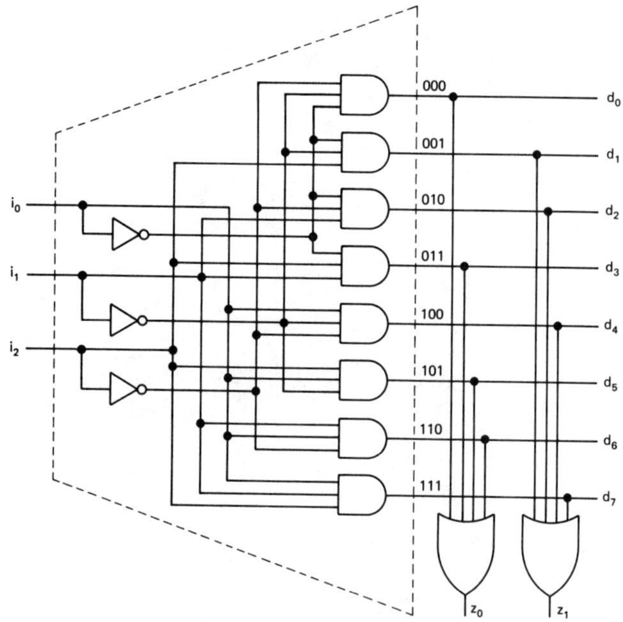

i0
i1
i2
000
001
010
011
100
101
110
111
d0
d1
d2
d3
d4
d5
d6
d7
z0
z1

(a)

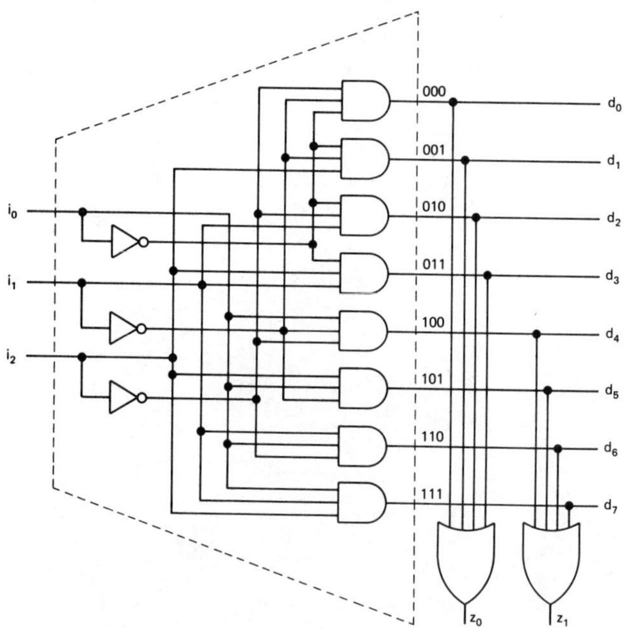

i0
i1
i2
000
001
010
011
100
101
110
111
d0
d1
d2
d3
d4
d5
d6
d7
z0
z1

(b)

8.11. Design the 4-modularized error correction circuit for the 16 bits adder using the following two-dimensional cross-parity code.

$$
\mathbf{H} = \left[\begin{array}{cccc|cccc|cccc|cccc|cccc|cccc}
1&1&1&1& & & & & & & & & & & & &1& & & & & & & \\
 & & & &1&1&1&1& & & & & & & & & &1& & & & & & \\
 & & & & & & & &1&1&1&1& & & & & & &1& & & & & \\
 & & & & & & & & & & & &1&1&1&1& & & &1& & & & \\
\hline
1& & & &1& & & &1& & & &1& & & & & & & &1& & & \\
 &1& & & &1& & & &1& & & &1& & & & & & & &1& & \\
 & &1& & & &1& & & &1& & & &1& & & & & & & &1& \\
 & & &1& & & &1& & & &1& & & &1& & & & & & & &1
\end{array}\right]
$$

8.12. Suppose that two binary operands (a_0, a_1, a_2, a_3) and (b_0, b_1, b_2, b_3), are encoded by the following $\mathbf{H}$ matrix.

$$
\mathbf{H} = \begin{bmatrix} 1 & 1 & 0 & 1 & 1 & 0 & 0 \\ 0 & 1 & 1 & 1 & 0 & 1 & 0 \\ 1 & 0 & 1 & 1 & 0 & 0 & 1 \end{bmatrix}
$$

Design the error correction circuit for the 4-bit binary adder and demonstrate that a single error at an output of the adder can be corrected.

8.13. Show that an adder error can be masked by using an alternate data retry (ADR). ADR is defined as the same operation retried using an alternate data representation (i.e., the bitwise complement of the other (see Section 4.4.3).

8.14. Obtain the necessary and sufficient conditions for the checksum code to be self-complementary. A self-complementing code is defined as one in which the bitwise complement of the codeword is also a codeword [see Definition 4-7 in Section 4.4.3].

8.15. Prove that the circuit shown in Fig. 8.28 is code disjoint.

8.16. Design the decoder for the combination codes with 8 bytes (byte = 3 bits) input. Suppose that the parity check portion is computed according to the following $\mathbf{H}$ matrix.

$$
\mathbf{H} = \begin{bmatrix} 1 & 0 & 1 & 1 & 1 & 0 & 0 & 0 \\ 1 & 1 & 0 & 1 & 0 & 1 & 0 & 0 \\ 1 & 1 & 1 & 0 & 0 & 0 & 1 & 0 \\ 0 & 1 & 1 & 1 & 0 & 0 & 0 & 1 \end{bmatrix}
$$

8.17. Obtain the parity prediction in the AND or OR operation under the condition that input operands are encoded in a simple parity code. Show the difference between the straightforward duplication–comparison scheme and this method.

8.18. By extending the results of Theorem 8-6, obtain the general parity-prediction scheme for general combinational logic.

8.19. Design the self-checking PLA using an m-out-of-n code. The original 3-input (x_0, x_1, x_2), 3-output (y_0, y_1, y_2) function is defined as follows.

x_0	x_1	x_2	y_0	y_1	y_2
0	0	0	1	0	1
0	0	1	0	1	1
0	1	0	1	0	1
0	1	1	0	0	0
1	0	0	0	0	0
1	0	1	0	1	1
1	1	0	1	1	0
1	1	1	1	1	0

8.20. Design the self-checking PLA using the Berger code for the logic function shown in Equation (8.21).

8.21. Prove Theorem 8-8.

8.22. Design the self-checking checker using the method shown in Equation (8.25), where $l = 0$, $m = 3$, and $n = 4$, for the ECC circuit defined by the following **H** matrix of the (13, 8) SEC–DED code.

$$\mathbf{H} = \left[\begin{array}{cccccccc|ccccc} 1 & 1 & 0 & 0 & 1 & 1 & 1 & 1 & 1 & 0 & 0 & 0 & 0 \\ 1 & 0 & 0 & 1 & 1 & 0 & 1 & 0 & 0 & 1 & 0 & 0 & 0 \\ 0 & 1 & 1 & 0 & 1 & 0 & 0 & 1 & 0 & 0 & 1 & 0 & 0 \\ 0 & 0 & 1 & 1 & 1 & 1 & 1 & 1 & 0 & 0 & 0 & 1 & 0 \\ 1 & 1 & 1 & 1 & 1 & 1 & 0 & 0 & 0 & 0 & 0 & 0 & 1 \end{array}\right]$$

Demonstrate that if there is no fault inside the ECC circuit, or even if input to the ECC circuit includes a single-error or a double-error, the checker output is always a 1-out-of-2 code.

8.23. Demonstrate that the self-checking ECC circuit designed in Exercise 8.22 is TSC for all single faults and for all input codewords and all input words including single error or double error.

8.24. Compare the self-checking ability of the (ECC circuit) checker in Fig. 8.47 with that in Fig. 8.48.

REFERENCES

[ABRA 86] J. A. Abraham and W. K. Fuchs. "Fault and Error Models for VLSI." *Proceedings of the IEEE* 74 (May 1986): 639–54.

[ANDE 71] D. A. Anderson. "Design of Self-Checking Digital Networks Using Coding Techniques." Coordinated Science Labs, Rep. R-527. Champaign: University of Illinois, October 1971.

[ANDE 81] T. Anderson and P. A. Lee. *Fault Tolerance, Principle and Practice*. Englewood Cliffs, N.J.: Prentice Hall, 1981.

[AVIZ 71] A. Avizienis, G. C. Gilley, F. P. Mathur, D. A. Rennels, J. A. Rohr, and D. K. Rubin. "The STAR (Self-Testing and Repairing) Computer: An Investigation of the Theory and Practice of Fault-Tolerant Computer Design." *IEEE Transactions on Computers* C-20 (November 1971): 1312–21.

[BOSS 82] D. C. Bossen and M. Y. Hsiao. "Model for Transient and Permanent Error-Detection and Fault-Isolation Coverage." *IBM Journal of Research and Development* 26 (January 1982): 67–77.

[BOUR 73] W. G. Bouricius, W. C. Carter, E. P. Hsieh, D. C. Jessep, Jr., and A. B. Wadia. "Modelling of a Bubble-Memory Organization with Self-Checking Translators to Achieve High Reliability." *IEEE Transactions on Computers* C-22 (March 1973): 269–75.

[BROW 60] D. T. Brown. "Error Detecting and Correcting Binary Codes for Arithmetic Operations." *IEEE Transactions on Elec. Comput.* EC-9 (September 1960): 333–37.

[CART 68] W. C. Carter and P. R. Schneider. "Design of Dynamically Checked Computers." *Proceedings of IFIPS 68, Edinburgh, Scotland, August 1968*, vol. 2, 878–83.

[CART 70] W. C. Carter, D. C. Jessep, and A. Wadia. "Error-Free Decoding for Failure-Tolerant Memories." *Proceedings of IEEE International Computer Group Conference* (June 1970): 229–39.

[CART 71a] W. C. Carter, D. C. Jessep, A. B. Wadia, P. R. Schneider, and W. G. Bouricius. "Logic Design for Dynamic and Interactive Recovery." *IEEE Transactions on Computers* C-20 (November 1971): 1300–5.

[CART 71b] W. C. Carter, K. A. Duke, and D. C. Jessep. "A Simple Self-Testing Decoder Checking Circuit." *IEEE Transactions on Computers* C-20 (November 1971): 1413–14.

[CART 77] W. C. Carter, G. R. Putzolu, A. B. Wadia, W. G. Bouricius, D. C. Jessep, E. P. Hsieh, and C. J. Tan. "Cost Effectiveness of Self-Checking Computer Design." *Dig., 7th Annual Int. Symposium Fault-Tolerant Comput.* (June 1977): 117–23.

[CHUA 78] H. Y. H. Chuang and S. Das. "Design of Fail-Safe Sequential Machines Using Separable Codes." *IEEE Transactions on Computers* C-27 (March 1978): 249–51.

[DAVI 78b] R. David and P. Thevenod-Fosse. "Design of Totally Self-Checking Asynchronous Modular Circuits." *Journal of Design Automation and Fault Tolerant Computing 2* (October 1978): 271–78.

[DIAZ 74a] M. Diaz, J. C. Geffroy, and M. Courooisier. "On-Set Realization of Fail-Safe Sequential Machines." *IEEE Transactions on Computers* C-23 (February 1974): 133–38.

[DIAZ 74b] M. Diaz. "Design of Totally Self-Checking and Fail-Safe Sequential Machines." *Dig., 4th Annual Int. Symposium Fault-Tolerant Comput.* (June 1974): 3–19 to 3–24.

[DIAZ 79] M. Diaz, P. Azema, and J. M. Ayache. "Unified Design of Self-Checking and Fail Safe Combinational Circuits and Sequential Machines." *IEEE Transactions on Computers* C-28 (March 1979): 276–81.

[ENGL 66] W. A. England. "Improving Reliability by the Application of Selected Redundant Techniques." *Proceedings of Workshop on Reliability Technique, UCLA, Los Angeles, April 1966.*

[FRAN 66] H. Frank and S. S. Yau. "Improving Reliability of a Sequential Machine by Error-Correcting State Assignments." *IEEE Transactions on Computers* C-15 (1966): 111–13.

[FUCH 87] W. K. Fuchs and J. A. Abraham. "Concurrent Error Detection in Highly Structured Logic Arrays." *IEEE Journal of Solid-State Circuits* SC-22, (August 1987): 583–94. (Also shown in *Dig., 14th Annual Int. Symposium Fault-Tolerant Comput.* (June 1984): 4–9.)

[FUJI 79] E. Fujiwara and K. Haruta. "Design of Totally Self-Checking Checker for Main Storage Error Checking and Correcting Circuit" (in Japanese). *Transactions of the IECE Japan* 62-D (June 1979): 419–26.

[FUJI 81c] E. Fujiwara and K. Haruta. "Fault-Tolerant Arithmetic Logic Unit Using Parity-Based Codes." *Transactions of the IECE Japan* E64 (October 1981): 653–60.

[FUJI 87a] E. Fujiwara and K. Matsuoka. "A Self-Checking Generalized Prediction Checker and Its Use for Built-In Testing." *IEEE Transactions on Computers* C-36 (January 1987): 86–93. (Also shown in *Dig., 15th Annual Int. Symposium Fault-Tolerant Comput.* (June 1985): 384–89.)

[FURU 83a] K. Furuya, K. Takeda, and Y. Tohma. "Logic Design of Fault-Tolerant Arithmetic Units with Check-Sum Code Based on Alternate-Data-Retry Strategy" (in Japanese). *Transactions of the IECE Japan* J66-D (March 1983): 243–50.

[FURU 83b] K. Furuya, K. Takeda, and Y. Tohma. "Extension of Alternate-Data-Retry Strategy to Adders with Biresidue Code and Estimates of Several Configurations" (in Japanese). *Transactions of the IECE Japan* J66-D (March 1983): 251–58.

[FURU 83c] K. Furuya, Y. Akita, and Y. Tohma. "Logic Design of Fault-Tolerant Dividers Based on Data Complementation Strategy." *Dig., 13th Annual Int. Symposium Fault-Tolerant Comput.* (June 1983): 306–13.

[GADD 70] T. G. Gaddess. "An Error-Detecting Binary Adder: A Hardware-Shared Implementation." *IEEE Transactions on Computers* C-19 (January 1970): 34–38.

[GAIT 88] N. Gaitanis. "The Design of TSC Error C/D Circuits for SEC/DED Codes." *IEEE Transactions on Computers* C-37 (March 1988): 258–265.

[GARN 58] H. L. Garner. "Generalized Parity Checking." *IRE Transactions on Elec. Comput.* EC-7 (September 1958): 207–13.

[GARN 59] H. L. Garner. "The Residue Number System." *IRE Transactions on Elec. Comput.* EC-8 (September 1959): 140–47.

[GARN 66] H. L. Garner. "Error Codes for Arithmetic Operations." *IEEE Transactions on Elec. Comput.*, EC-15 (October 1966): 763–70.

[HSIA 63] M. Y. Hsiao and F. F. Sellers. "The Carry Dependent Sum Adder." *IEEE Transactions on Elec. Comput.* EC-12 (June 1963): 265–68.

[HUAN 84] K. Huang and J. A. Abraham. "Algorithm-Based Fault-Tolerance for Matrix Operations." *IEEE Transactions on Computers* C-33 (June 1984): 518–28.

[HUGH 84] J. L. A. Hughes, E. J. McCluskey, and D. J. Lu. "Design of Totally Self-Checking Comparators with an Arbitrary Number of Inputs." *IEEE Transactions on Computers* C-33 (January 1984): 546–50.

[ITOH 83b] H. Itoh and M. Nakamichi. "A Self-Checking Design of Main Memory Error Checking and Correcting Circuits for Odd-Weight-Column SEC-DED Codes" (in Japanese). *Transactions of the IECE Japan* J66-D (September 1983): 1070–77.

[JANS 85] I. Jansch and B. Courtois. "Strongly Language Disjoint Checking." *Dig., 15th Annual Int. Symposium Fault-Tolerant Comput.* (June 1985): 390–95.

[JHA 84] N. K. Jha and J. A. Abraham. "The Design of Totally Self-Checking Embedded Checkers." *Dig., 14th Annual Int. Symposium Fault-Tolerant Comput.* (June 1984): 265–70.

[KHAK 82a] J. Khakbaz and E. J. McCluskey. "Concurrent Error Detection and Testing for Large PLA's." *IEEE Journal of Solid-State Circuits* SC-17 (April 1982): 386–94.

[KHAK 84] J. Khakbaz and E. J. McCluskey. "Self-Testing Embedded Parity Checkers." *IEEE Transactions on Computers* C-33 (August 1984): 753–56.

[KHOD 79] B. Khodadad-Mostershiry. "Parity Prediction in Combinational Circuit." *Dig., 9th Annual Int. Symposium on Fault-Tolerant Comput.* (June 1979): 185–88.

[LANG 70] G. G. Langdon, Jr. and C. K. Tang. "Concurrent Error Detection for Group Look-Ahead Binary Adders." *IBM Journal of Research and Development* 14 (September 1970): 563–73.

[MAK 82] G. P. Mak, J. A. Abraham, and E. S. Davidson. "The Design of PLAs with Concurrent Error Detection." *Dig., 12th Annual Int. Symposium Fault-Tolerant Comput.* (June 1982): 303–10.

[MAKI 74] G. Maki and D. H. Sawain III. "Fault-Tolerant Asynchronous Sequential Machines." *IEEE Transactions on Computers* C-23 (July 1974): 651–57.

[MAND 72] D. Mandelbaum. "Error Correction in Residue Arithmetic." *IEEE Transactions on Computers* C-21 (June 1972): 538–45.

[MONT 72] P. M. Monteiro and T. R. N. Rao. "A Residue Checker for Arithmetic and Logical Operations." *Dig., 12th Annual Int. Symposium Fault-Tolerant Comput.* (June 1972): 8–13.

[MUKA 74] Y. Mukai and Y. Tohma. "A Method for the Realization of Fail-Safe Asynchronous Sequential Circuits." *IEEE Transactions on Computers* C-23 (July 1974): 736–39.

[MUKA 76] Y. Mukai and Y. Tohma. "A Masked-Fault Free Realization of Fail-Safe Asynchronous Sequential Circuits." *Dig., 6th Annual Int. Symposium Fault-Tolerant Comput.* (June 1976): 69–74.

[NANY 79] T. Nanya and Y. Tohma. "Universal Multicode STT State Assignments for Asynchronous Sequential Machines." *IEEE Transactions on Computers* C-28 (November 1979): 811–18.

[NANY 85b] T. Nanya and T. Kawamura. "Error Secure/Error Propagating Concept and Its Application to the Design of Strongly Fault Secure Processors." *Dig., 15th Annual Int. Symposium Fault-Tolerant Comput.* (June 1985): 396–401. (Also shown in *IEEE Transactions on Computers* C-37 (January 1988): 14–24).

[NANY 87] T. Nanya and T. Kawamura. "A Note on Strongly Fault Secure Sequential Circuits." *IEEE Transactions on Computers* C-36 (September 1987): 1121–23.

[NEUM 75] P. G. Neumann and T. R. N. Rao. "Error-Correcting Codes for Byte-Organized Arithmetic Processors." *IEEE Transactions on Computers* C-24 (March 1975): 226–32.

[NICO 84] M. Nicolaidis, I. Jansch, and B. Courtois. "Strongly Code-Disjoint Checkers." *Dig., 14th Annual Int. Symposium Fault-Tolerant Comput.* (June 1984): 16–21.

[OBER 79] R. M. M. Oberman. *Digital Circuits for Binary Arithmetic.* New York: Macmillan, 1979.

[OSTA 79] D. L. Ostapko and S. J. Hong. "Fault Analysis and Test Generation for Programmable Logic Arrays (PLA's)." *IEEE Transactions on Computers* C-28 (September 1979): 617–27.

[OZGU 77] F. Özgüner. "Design of Totally Self-Checking Asynchronous and Synchronous Sequential Machines." *Dig., 7th Annual Int. Symposium Fault-Tolerant Comput.* (June 1977): 124–29.

[PATE 83] J. H. Patel and L. Y. Fung. "Concurrent Error Detection in Multiply and Divide Arrays." *IEEE Transactions on Computers* C-32 (April 1983): 417–22.

[PETE 58] W. W. Peterson. "On Checking Adder." *IBM Journal* (April 1958): 166–68.

[PETE 59] W. W. Peterson and M. O. Rabin. "On Codes for Checking Logical Operations." *IBM Journal of Research and Development* 3 (1959): 163–68.

[PIES 85] S. J. Piestrak. "PLA Implementations of Totally Self-Checking Circuits Using M-Out-of-N Codes." *Proceedings of IEEE Int. Conference on Computer Design* (October 1985): 777–81.

[PRAD 72a] D. K. Pradhan and S. M. Reddy. "A Design Technique for Synthesis of Fault-Tolerant Adders." *Dig., 12th Annual Int. Symposium Fault-Tolerant Comput.* (June 1972): 20–24.

[PRAD 72b] D. K. Pradhan and S. M. Reddy. "Error Control Techniques for Logic Processors." *IEEE Transactions on Computers* C-21 (December 1972): 1331–37.

[PRAD 73] D. K. Pradhan and S. M. Reddy. "Fault-Tolerant Asynchronous Networks." *IEEE Transactions on Computers* C-22 (July 1973): 662–69.

[PRAD 74] D. K. Pradhan. "Fault-Tolerant Carry-Save Adders." *IEEE Transactions on Computers* (December 1974): 1320–22.

[PRAD 76] D. K. Pradhan and S. M. Reddy. "Techniques to Construct (2, 1) Separating Systems from Linear Error-Correcting Codes." *IEEE Transactions on Computers* C-25 (September 1976): 945–49.

[PRAD 78] D. K. Pradhan. "Asynchronous State Assignments with Unateness Properties and Fault-Secure Design." *IEEE Transactions on Computers* C-27 (May 1978): 396–404.

[RAO 68b] T. R. N. Rao. "Error-Checking Logic for Arithmetic-Type Operations of a Processor." *IEEE Transactions on Computers* C-17 (September 1968): 845–49.

[RAO 70] T. R. N. Rao. "Biresidue Error-Correcting Codes for Computer Arithmetic." *IEEE Transactions on Computers* C-19 (May 1970): 398–402.

[RAO 71] T. R. N. Rao and O. N. Garcia. "Cyclic and Multiresidue Codes for Arithmetic Operations." *IEEE Transactions on Information Theory* IT-17 (January 1971): 85–91.

[RAO 72] T. R. N. Rao. "Error Correction in Adders Using Systematic Subcodes." *IEEE Transactions on Computers* C-21 (March 1972): 254–59.

[RAO 74] T. R. N. Rao. *Error Coding for Arithmetic Processors*. New York: Academic Press, 1974.

[RAO 77] T. R. N. Rao and H. J. Reinheimer. "Fault-Tolerant Modularized Arithmetic Logic Units." *Proceedings of National Computer Conference* AFIPS (1977): 703–10.

[REED 70] I. S. Reed. "Error Tolerant Sequential Circuits." U.S. Patent 3529141 (September 15, 1970).

[SAWI 74] D. H. Sawin, III, and G. K. Maki. "Asynchronous Sequential Machines Designed for Fault Detection." *IEEE Transactions on Computers* C-23 (July 1974): 239–49.

[SELL 68] F. F. Sellers, Jr., M. Y., Hsiao, and L. W. Bearnson. *Error Detecting Logic for Digital Computers*. New York: McGraw-Hill, 1968.

[SHED 78] J. J. Shedletsky. "Error Correction by Alternate-Data Retry." *IEEE Transactions on Computers* C-27 (February 1978): 106–12.

[SHIN 86a] S. Shinmori, M. Hoda, and Y. Koga. "A Realization Method of Totally-Self-Checking Error Checking and Correcting Circuits for Main Memory Systems" (in Japanese). *Transactions of the IECE Japan* J69-D (February 1986): 148–58.

[SHIN 86b] S. Shinmori and Y. Koga. "A Realization Method of Self-Checking SEC-DED-SbED Circuits for Main Memory Systems" (in Japanese). *Transactions of the IECE Japan* J69-D (November 1986): 1583–93.

[SIEW 82] D. P. Siewiorek and R. Swarz. *The Theory and Practice of Reliability Systems*. Bedford, Mass.: Digital Press, 1982.

[SMIT 76] J. E. Smith, "The Design of Totally Self-Checking Combinational Circuits." Coordinated Science Labs, Rep. R-737. Champaign: University of Illinois, February 1976.

[SMIT 78] J. E. Smith and G. Mertze. "Strongly Fault Secure Logic Networks." *IEEE Transactions on Computers* C-27 (June 1978): 495–99.

[SMIT 83] J. E. Smith and P. Lam. "A Theory of Totally Self-Checking System Design." *IEEE Transactions on Computers* C-32 (September 1983): 831–44.

[SOME 86] F. Somenzi and S. Gai. "Fault-Detection in Programmable Logic Arrays." *Proceedings of the IEEE* 74 (May 1986): 655–68.

[SON 81] K. Son and D. K. Pradhan. "Completely Self-Checking Checkers in PLAs." *Proceedings of IEEE International Test Conference* (1981): 231–37.

[TAKE 80] K. Takeda and Y. Tohma. "Logic Design of Fault-Tolerant Arithmetic Units Based on the Data Complementation Strategy." *Dig., 10th Annual Int. Symposium Fault-Tolerant Comput.* (October 1980): 348–50.

[TAO 86] D. L. Tao, P. K. Lala, and C. R. P. Hartmann. "A Concurrent Testing Strategy for PLAs." *Proceedings of IEEE International Test Conference* (1986): 705–9.

[TOHM 71] Y. Tohma, Y. Ohyama, and R. Sakai. "Realization of Fail-Safe Sequential Machines by Using *k*-Out-of-*n* Code." *IEEE Transactions on Computers* C-20 (November 1971): 1270–75.

[TOHM 74] Y. Tohma. "Design Technique of Fail-Safe Sequential Circuits Using Flip-Flops for Internal Memory." *IEEE Transactions on Computers* C-23 (November 1974): 1149–54.

[TOHM 86] Y. Tohma. "Coding Techniques in Fault-Tolerant, Self-Checking and Fail-Safe Circuits." Chap. 5 in *Fault-Tolerant Computing, Theory and Techniques*, ed. D. K. Pradhan, Englewood Cliffs, N.J.: Prentice-Hall, 1986.

[VIAU 80] J. Viaud and R. David. "Sequentially Self-Checking Circuits." *Dig., 10th Annual Int. Symposium Fault-Tolerant Comput.* (October 1980): 263–68.

[WAKE 74] J. F. Wakerly. "Partially Self-Checking Circuits and Their Use in Performing Logical Operations." *IEEE Transactions on Computers* C-23 (July 1974): 658–66.

[WAKE 76] J. F. Wakerly. "Checked Binary Addition with Checksum Codes." *Journal of Design Automation and Fault-Tolerant Computing* 1 (October 1976): 18–27.

[WAKE 78] J. F. Wakerly. *Error Detecting Codes, Self-Checking Circuits, and Applications.* New York: North-Holland Publishing, 1978.

[WANG 79] S. L. Wang and A. Avizienis. "The Design of Totally Self-Checking Circuits Using Programmable Logic Arrays." *Dig., 9th Annual Int. Symposium Fault-Tolerant Comput.* (June 1979): 173–80.

[WINO 63] S. Winograd and F. D. Cowan. *Reliable Computation in the Presence of Noise.* Cambridge: MIT Press, 1963.

9

Codes for Logic Design II

We discussed several types of checkers in Chapter 8. This chapter is concerned with how these checkers are made self-checking, that is, how they can be designed so that if there are faults in the checker, the checker itself detects them. In self-checking checkers, we have to pay attention to the input space of the checker, because as the checker is generally an embedded circuit, not all input codewords are given to the checker.

This chapter provides some examples of self-checking processors and microprocessors in which self-checking checkers are extensively used. We also introduce an interesting error masking technique for logic circuits that improves yield.

9.1 SELF-CHECKING CHECKERS

As we have already seen in Section 8.1.2, the checker should have a code-disjoint property or an error-preserving property. The self-checking checker should satisfy in addition the self-testing property for all faults in the prescribed fault set F in the checker itself. Note that this latter condition is sometimes difficult to satisfy, because the checker is generally an embedded circuit and all input codewords may not be applied to the checker. In other words, the inputs to the checker are the outputs of the circuit under check, and therefore it may not be possible to apply all the input codewords to the checker. This depends on the previous circuits whose outputs are the inputs to the checker.

Considerable literature has appeared on implementing self-checking checkers for all input codewords and for all single faults, or for all unidirectional faults [CART 70, ANDE 71, 73, REDD 74b, SMIT 77, ASHJ 77, MARO 78b, FUJI 87a]. Here, self-checking checkers, such as parity code checkers, two-rail code checkers, m-out-of-n code checkers, separable code checkers, and self-checking generalized prediction checkers are discussed from the standpoint of implementation.

9.1.1 Parity Code Checker

This checker can be constructed using multiple exclusive-or circuits ($\oplus$) in a tree structure. The self-checking parity-tree circuit is easily implemented when the input code vectors have *odd parity*. Two parity-tree circuits are created by dividing the inputs [CART 70]. As a simple example, we implement the self-checking parity code checker with five inputs. Input $Y = (y_0, y_1, y_2, y_3, y_4)$ is divided into two sets, for example, $\{y_0, y_1, y_2\}$ and $\{y_3, y_4\}$, and the two independent parity trees are constructed from these input sets (Fig. 9.1).

Table 9.1 shows the function and lines tested by the parity checker shown in Fig. 9.1. This table shows that all exclusive-or (EX-OR) gates have all possible input pairs $\{(0,0), (1,0), (0,1), (1,1)\}$ and output (z_0, z_1) takes $\{(0,1)\ (1,0)\}$ for all input codewords. For even-parity encoded inputs (i.e., noncodeword inputs), this checker always gives output $(z_0, z_1) = \{(0,0)\ (1,1)\}$. Hence, this circuit is code disjoint. Also, apparently a single fault always causes the output to be noncodeword for some codeword input. Therefore, we have the following theorem.

Theorem 9-1. *The parity circuit that is divided into two independent parity-tree subcircuits is a self-testing checker for all odd-parity encoded inputs and for all single faults.*

When the input code vectors have *even parity*, one subcircuit output is designed to be inverted.

We now consider the case in which not all codeword inputs are given to the checker. Under this condition, it is difficult to satisfy the self-testing property at all

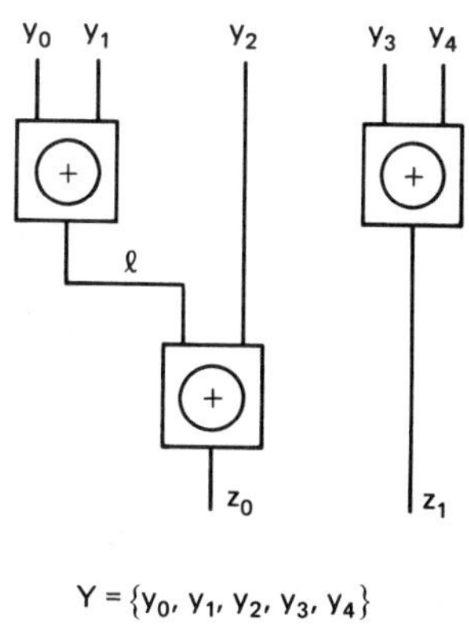

Figure 9.1 Self-checking parity checker.

TABLE 9.1 FUNCTION AND LINES TESTED OF PARITY-TREE CIRCUIT

y_0	y_1	l	y_2	y_3	y_4	z_0	z_1
1	0	1	0	0	0	1	0
0	1	1	0	0	0	1	0
0	0	0	1	0	0	1	0
1	0	1	0	1	1	1	0
0	1	1	0	1	1	1	0
0	0	0	1	1	1	1	0
1	1	0	1	0	0	1	0
1	1	0	1	1	1	1	0
1	1	0	0	1	0	0	1
0	1	1	1	1	0	0	1
1	0	1	1	1	0	0	1
1	1	0	0	0	1	0	1
0	1	1	1	0	1	0	1
1	0	1	1	0	1	0	1
0	0	0	0	0	1	0	1
0	0	0	0	1	0	0	1

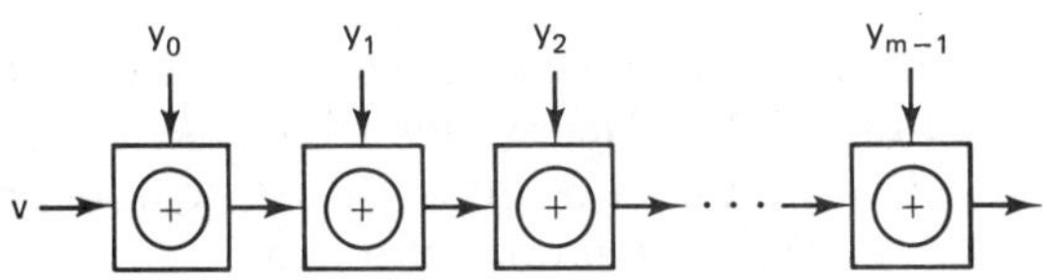

Figure 9.2 Cascaded parity tree circuit with one additional input v.

times.* Some methods for overcoming this difficulty have been proposed in [KHAK 82b, 84, FUJI 87a]. Here, we have a structure whose EX-OR tree circuit is in a cascaded form and which has one extra input v that can take any value in $\{0, 1\}$ [FUJI 87a]. Figure 9.2 shows an example of this type of tree structure.

Theorem 9-2. *If the cascaded EX-OR tree circuit having m EX-OR gates satisfies the following conditions*

1. *Primary input* $y_i \neq const.$ $i = 0, 1, \ldots, m-1$
2. *Independent of* y_i*'s, input* v *can take any value in* $\{0, 1\}$

then every single fault in this circuit can be detected.

Any error due to a fault in this circuit can be propagated to the output, and there exists at least one input pattern to detect this fault. Therefore, each divided tree circuit of Fig. 9.1 can be transformed into a cascaded structure like that shown in Fig. 9.2. Then, the circuit is a self-testing checker for the restricted number of

*Typically, four- or five-input test patterns are necessary to test the multiple-input parity-tree circuits consisting of only two-input EX-OR or EX-NOR gates [BOSS 70b, HONG 81, REDD 85, MOUR 86a, 86b].

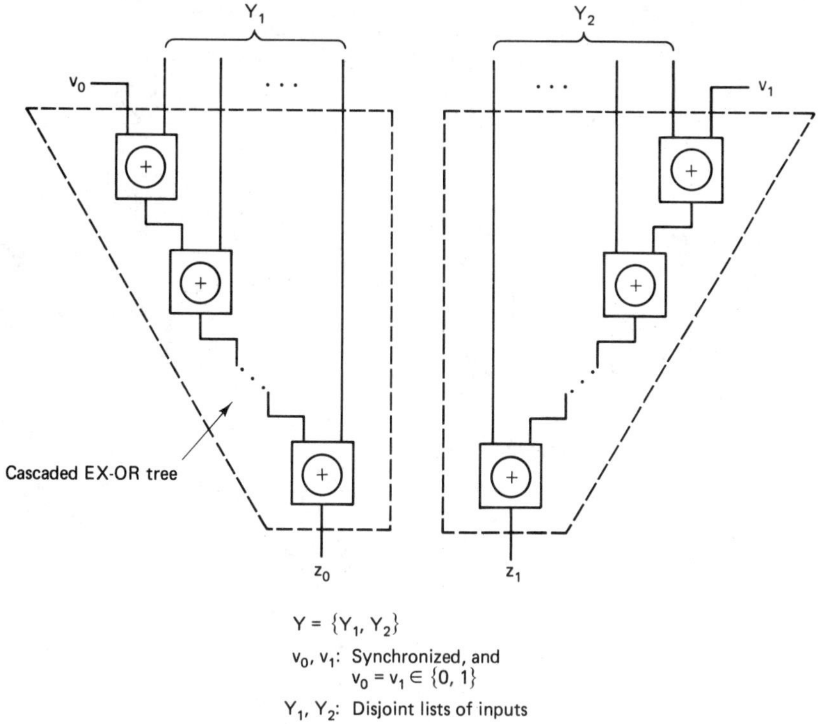

Figure 9.3 Self-testing parity code checker.

input codewords that satisfy condition (1) in Theorem 9-2. This is shown in Fig. 9.3. In this figure, it should be noted that synchronized inputs v_0 and v_1 are applied to each EX-OR tree. This is because the checker can also detect faults in v_0 and v_1. This self-testing checker structure requires, of course, only two more EX-OR gates than the previously given structure.

9.1.2 Two-Rail Code Checker

A two-rail code checker (also called a comparator) is required for a *duplication check* (i.e., for a *comparison check*). This is shown in Fig. 9.4. In order to prevent identical failure states in both the functional circuit and the duplicated circuit, the duplicated one is sometimes designed in a complementary form [SEDM 80b]. In Fig. 9.4, the output of one of the two identical circuits is inverted and fed into a self-checking two-rail code checker, discussed below. In a complementary duplication, no inverter gates are needed, and the outputs from both functional circuits are fed directly to a two-rail code checker.

In a two-rail encoding, bits of information occur as complementary pairs, $(0, 1)$ and $(1, 0)$; the pairs $(0, 0)$ and $(1, 1)$ indicate errors. Thus, the same circuit that checks a two-rail encoding can be used to combine several self-checking checker output pairs into one pair. That is, a self-checking two-rail code

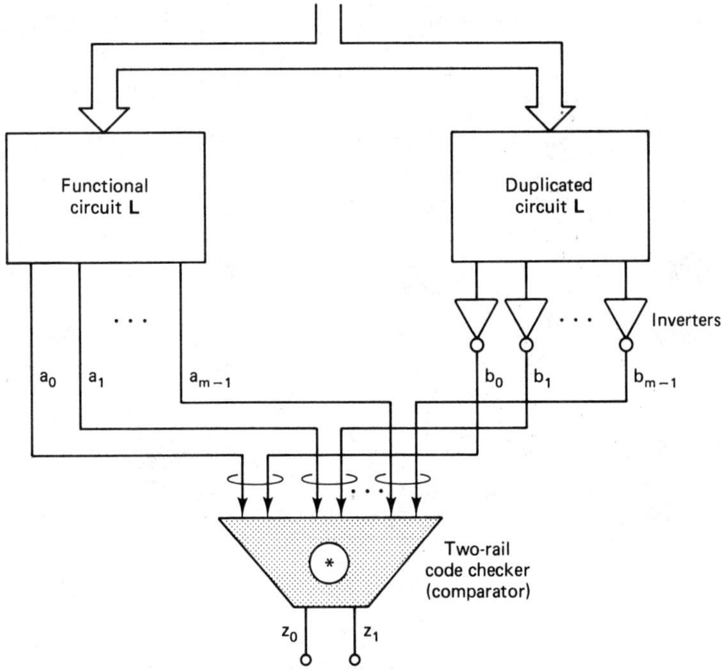

Figure 9.4 Two-rail code checker for duplication check.

checker, i.e., a self-testing comparator, will map m input pairs, referred to as $\{(a_0, b_0), (a_1, b_1), \ldots, (a_{m-1}, b_{m-1})\}$, to one output pair, referred to as (z_0, z_1). The output pair must be complementary if and only if each and every input pair is all complementary [TAMI 84].

A two-rail code checker for $m = 2$ is shown in Fig. 9.5 [CART 70]. This is a two-level AND-OR realization. The table in Fig. 9.5 shows this circuit to be self-testing for single faults and also code disjoint.

Lemma 9-1 [FUJI 87a]. *Let the input to the checker be $A_i = (a_{0,i}, a_{1,i})$ and $B_i = (b_{0,i}, b_{1,i})$, and the output be $C_{i+1} = (c_{0,i+1}, c_{1,i+1})$. In this case, $A_i, B_i, C_{i+1} \in \{\mathbf{0}, \mathbf{1}, \mathbf{W}\}$, where $\mathbf{0} = (0,1)$, $\mathbf{1} = (1,0)$, $\mathbf{W} \in \{(0,0), (1,1)\}$. Then, C_{i+1} can be expressed as the following truth table.*

A_i \ B_i	**0**	**1**	**W**
0	**0**	**1**	**W**
1	**1**	**0**	**W**
W	**W**	**W**	**W**

$C_{i+1} = A_i \circledast B_i$

$\mathbf{0} = (0,1)$
$\mathbf{1} = (1,0)$
$\mathbf{W} = \{(0,0)\ (1,1)\}$

The operation performed in the checker is expressed as $\circledast$ (i.e., $C_{i+1} = A_i \circledast B_i$), defined in the truth table.

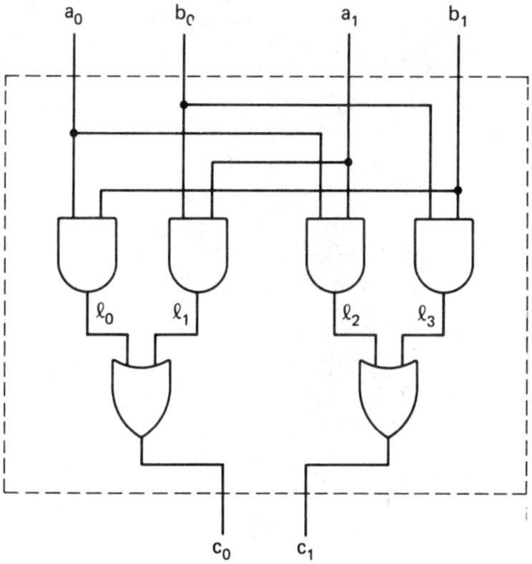

a_0	b_0	a_1	b_1	ℓ_0	ℓ_1	ℓ_2	ℓ_3	c_0	c_1
0	1	0	1	0	0	0	1	0	1
0	1	1	0	0	1	0	0	1	0
1	0	0	1	1	0	0	0	1	0
1	0	1	0	0	0	1	0	0	1
0	0	x	x	0	0	0	0	0	0
x	x	0	0	0	0	0	0	0	0
1	1	1	x	x	1	1	x	1	1
1	1	x	1	1	x	x	1	1	1
1	x	1	1	1	x	1	x	1	1
x	1	1	1	x	1	x	1	1	1

'x' can take any value of 0, 1.

Figure 9.5 A two-rail code checker for $m = 2$ [CART 70]. © 1970 IEEE.

Lemma 9-2. *Every single fault in the checker can be detected, if the inputs A_i and B_i have the following four distinct patterns:*

$$(A_i, B_i) = \{(\mathbf{0},\mathbf{0}), (\mathbf{0},\mathbf{1}), (\mathbf{1},\mathbf{0}), (\mathbf{1},\mathbf{1})\}, \quad \mathbf{0} = (0,1), \mathbf{1} = (1,0)$$

Multi-input two-rail code checker can be implemented by interconnecting such two-level blocks to form multilevel trees of arbitrary size [ITOH 82b]. For example, a tree with eight input pairs formed by interconnecting seven blocks is shown in Fig. 9.6.

Corollary 9-1 [FUJI 87a]

1. *For $A_i, B_i \in \{\mathbf{0}, \mathbf{1}\}$, the two-input two-rail code checker is equal to modulo-2 adder on $\{\mathbf{0}, \mathbf{1}\}$.*
2. *As for the multi-input two-rail code checker implemented with the two-input two-rail code checkers, the output of this checker takes the value* **W** *if at least one input to this checker is equal to* **W**, *where* $\mathbf{W} = \{(0,0), (1,1)\}$.

In general, 2^m test patterns are sufficient to diagnose such multiple-input trees if each two-rail block has no more than m input pairs [ANDE 71]. Therefore, the two-rail tree shown in Fig. 9.6 is completely diagnosed by the *four test patterns*. These test patterns are systematically obtained in [ANDE 71]. Fig. 9.7 shows an example of the four test patterns systematically obtained for the eight-input two-rail code checker. In this test pattern generation, every two-input two-rail code checker has the four distinct input patterns defined in Lemma 9-2.

In normal operation, however, all these patterns may not be applied to the multiple-input tree circuit. This is because these checkers are placed at the output of

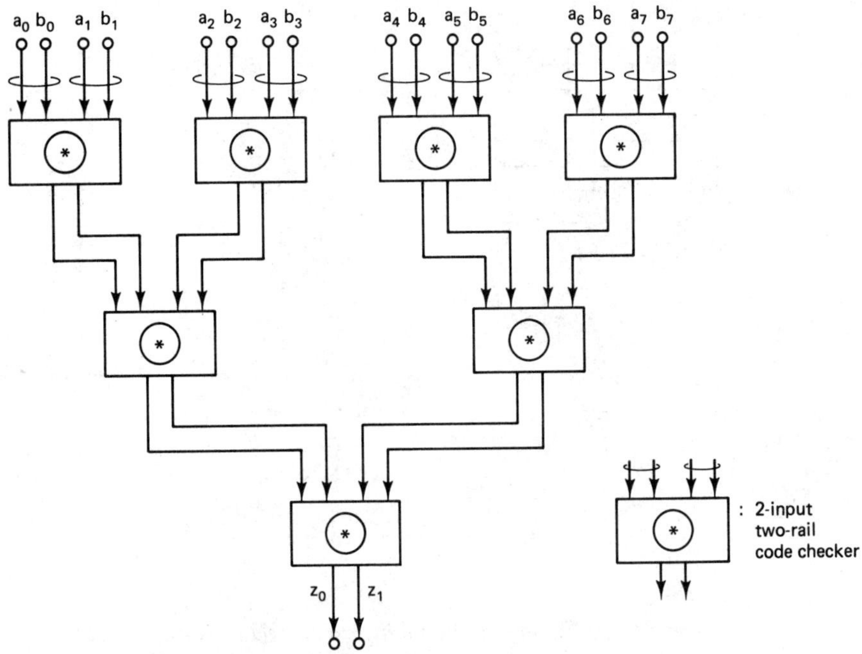

Figure 9.6 Eight-input two-rail code checker.

the circuit under check, as shown in Fig. 9.4; that is, they are embedded, and hence a restricted number of patterns may be given to the checkers. Even for this situation, some techniques have been proposed that satisfy the self-testing condition [HUGH 84, FUJI 87a]. The following theorem deals with the self-testing property of the multi-input two-rail code checkers.

Theorem 9-3 [FUJI 87a]. *If the M-input, cascaded-tree, two-rail code checker having one input V as shown in Fig. 9.8 satisfies the following conditions,*

1. *Primary input* $A_i \neq$ *constant,* $A_i \neq \mathbf{W}$, $i = 0, 1, \ldots, M-1$
2. *Independent of* A_i*'s, input* $V = (v, \bar{v})$ *can take any value in* $\{\mathbf{0}, \mathbf{1}\}$

then every single fault in this checker can be detected.

Proof. The output of the ith level two input two-rail code checker can be expressed as follows.

$$C_{i+1} = A_i \circledast C_i, \quad i = 0, 1, \ldots, M-1,$$

$$C_0 = V$$

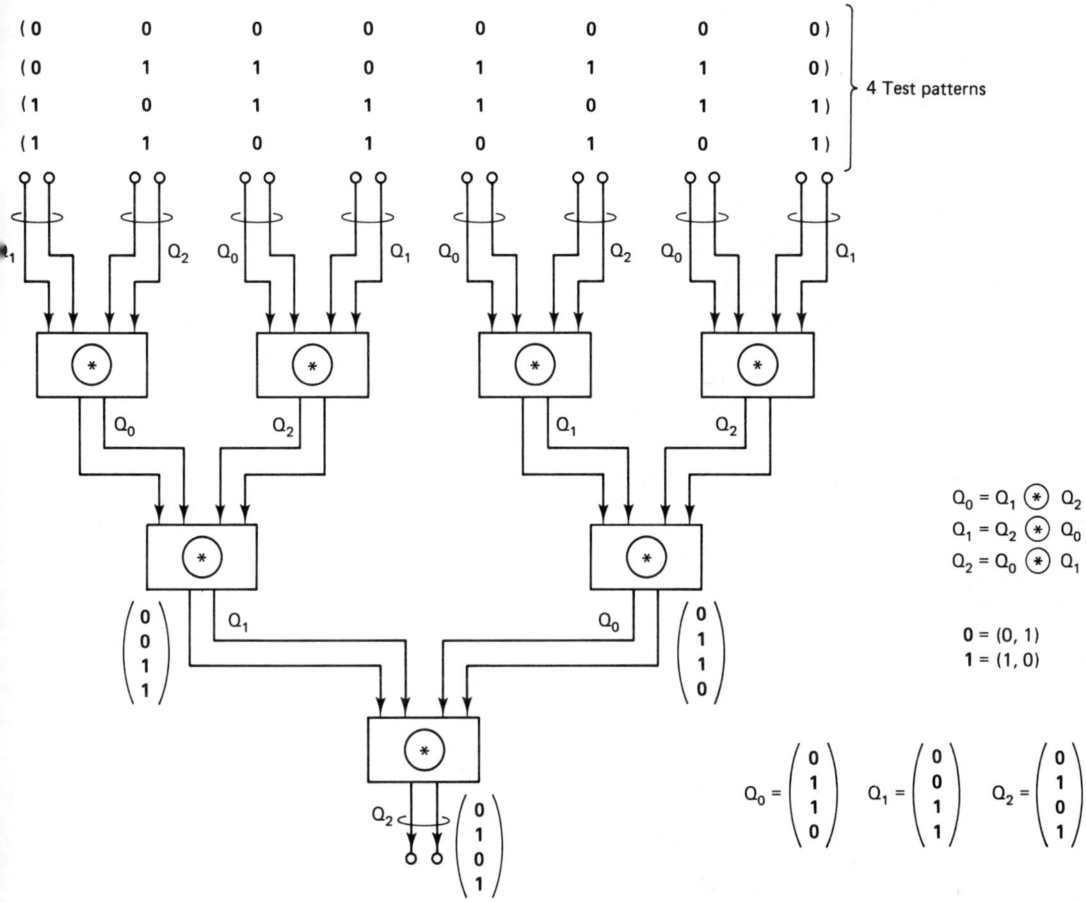

Figure 9.7 An example of the 4 test patterns generated systematically for the 8-input two-rail code checker [ANDE 71].

where ⊛ is defined in Lemma 9-1. This can be expanded as follows.

$$C_{i+1}(V, A_0, A_1, \ldots, A_i) = V \circledast (A_0 \circledast A_1 \circledast \cdots \circledast A_i)$$

$$C_{i+1}(\overline{V}, A_0, A_1, \ldots, A_i) = \overline{V} \circledast (A_0 \circledast A_1 \circledast \cdots \circledast A_i)$$

$$= \overline{C_{i+1}(V, A_0, A_1, \ldots, A_i)}$$

where $C_{i+1}(V, A_0, A_1, \ldots, A_i)$ means that C_{i+1} is the function of $V, A_0, A_1, \ldots,$ and A_i.

Here, $\overline{\mathbf{1}} = \mathbf{0}, \overline{\mathbf{0}} = \mathbf{1}$. Hence, C_{i+1} can take any value in $\{\mathbf{0}, \mathbf{1}\}$ by controlling the value of V. Furthermore, from conditions (1) and (2) in the theorem, (A_i, C_i) can take four distinct patterns such as in Lemma 9-2.

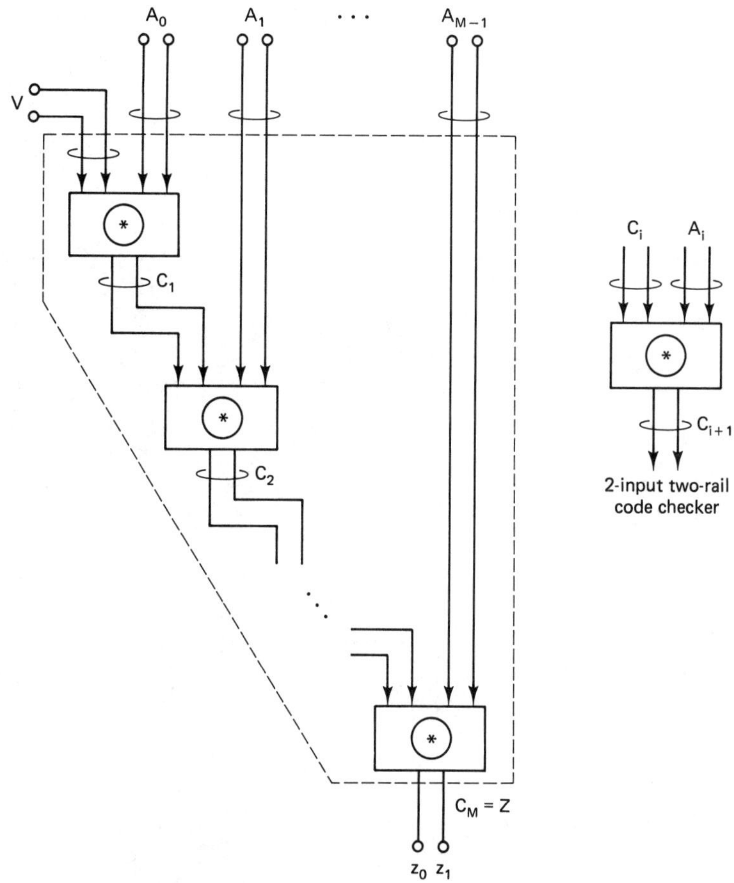

Figure 9.8 Multiinput, cascaded-tree, two-rail code checker.

The output of the tree circuit C_M can also be expressed as follows.

$$C_M(C_{i+1}, A_{i+1}, A_{i+2}, \ldots, A_{M-1}) = C_{i+1} \circledast (A_{i+1} \circledast A_{i+2} \circledast \cdots \circledast A_{M-1})$$

If a single fault in this circuit causes the value of C_{i+1}, A_{i+1}, or C_{i+2} to be **W**, then $C_M = \mathbf{W}$ from the truth table in Lemma 9-1. Therefore, the error due to this fault can be propagated to the output of this circuit.

From this, there exists at least one input satisfying the conditions (1) and (2) that can detect single faults in this checker. Q.E.D.

This input V can be generated from 2 J-K or toggle flip flops whose outputs are inverted with every clock (see Section 9.1.5, Fig. 9.23).

9.1.3 *m*-Out-of-*n* Code Checker

An m-out-of-n code is one in which all valid codewords have exactly m 1's and $(n - m)$ 0's. This code is useful because of its ability to detect all unidirectional errors (see Section 7.3).

The m-out-of-n code checker consists of two independent subcircuits, each having a single output. For normal m-out-of-n code inputs, the checker output is $(0, 1)$ or $(1, 0)$. If the number of 1's at the checker inputs is greater or less than m (i.e., noncodeword inputs), then the output is $(1, 1)$ or $(0, 0)$. Many design methods for implementing m-out-of-n code checkers have been studied [ANDE 73, REDD 74a, 74b, SMIT 77, MARO 78b, PIES 83]. Some of these are presented here.

(1) $n = 2m$ case. In designing an m-out-of-$2m$ code checker, the $2m$ bits are partitioned into two distinct subsets $A = (x_0, x_1, \ldots, x_{m-1})$ and $B = (x_m, x_{m+1}, \ldots, x_{2m-1})$. If the two outputs of the checker are designated as z_0 and z_1, then

$$z_0 = \sum_{i=0}^{m} T(m_A \geq i) \cdot T(m_B \geq m - i): \ i = \textit{odd} \text{ integer}$$

$$z_1 = \sum_{i=0}^{m} T(m_A \geq i) \cdot T(m_B \geq m - i): \ i = \textit{even} \text{ integer}$$

where m_A and m_B are the number of 1's occurring in the subsets A and B, respectively [ANDE 73]. $T(m_A \geq i)$ represents the Boolean function that has the value 1 if and only if the number of 1's in subset A is greater than or equal to the value i; similarly, $T(m_B \geq m - i)$ has the value 1 if and only if the number of 1's in the subset B is greater than or equal to the value $(m - i)$. Σ represents the OR operation.

To show that this design method produces a self-testing checker, we will describe codewords that diagnose the circuit. To test the term $T(m_A \geq i) \cdot T(m_B \geq m - i) = 1$, we must make $T(m_A \geq i)$ and $T(m_B \geq m - i)$ both equal to 1 simultaneously. This is done with codewords containing i 1's in subset A and $(m - i)$ 1's in subset B. These codewords exist because $0 \leq i \leq m$ and $n_A = n_B = m$, where n_A and n_B are the number of bits in A and in B, respectively. Furthermore, $T(m_A \geq i)$ may be implemented by the AND of each different combination of i bits from the n_A available; the results are ORed together. Each combination must be tested separately, and this requires $\binom{n_A}{i} = \binom{m}{i}$ codewords, each containing exactly i 1's in A. Similarly, $T(m_B \geq m - i)$ requires $\binom{n_B}{m-i} = \binom{m}{m-i} = \binom{m}{i}$ codewords, each containing exactly $(m - i)$ 1's in B. Since the bits in A and B are independent except for the constraint that $m_A + m_B = m$ for codewords, these factors can be completely tested with the same $\binom{m}{i}$ codewords. To test all such terms for $0 \le i \le m$ requires a total of

$$\sum_{i=0}^{m} \binom{m}{i} = 2^m$$

tests. If such a test set supplies all 2^m input combinations to A and all 2^m input combinations to B, then the majority functions, such as $T(m_A \ge i)$ or $T(m_B \ge m - i)$, are exhaustively tested, and any nonredundant implementation for them is completely diagnosed. Therefore, the checkers are self-testing for single faults or unidirectional faults if these 2^m codewords are given during normal operation.

Example 9-1 [ANDE 73]

The design of a self-testing 3-out-of-6 code checker ($n = 6,\ m = 3$) is here described. Let $A = (x_0, x_1, x_2)$, $B = (x_3, x_4, x_5)$. The two output functions are given as follows.

$$\begin{aligned} z_0 &= T(m_A \ge 1) \cdot T(m_B \ge 2) + T(m_A \ge 3) \cdot T(m_B \ge 0) \\ &= (x_0 + x_1 + x_2)(x_3x_4 + x_4x_5 + x_5x_3) + x_0x_1x_2 \cdot 1 \\ z_1 &= T(m_A \ge 0) \cdot T(m_B \ge 3) + T(m_A \ge 2) \cdot T(m_B \ge 1) \\ &= 1 \cdot x_3x_4x_5 + (x_0x_1 + x_1x_2 + x_0x_2)(x_3 + x_4 + x_5) \end{aligned}$$

The circuit realizing the above function is shown in Fig. 9.9. The set of $2^3 = 8$ codewords that is sufficient to diagnose the circuit consists of those codewords in which each x_{i+3} is the complement of x_i, where $0 \le i \le 2$.

Other designs for a self-testing m-out-of-$2m$ code checker have been proposed, in particular for the cellular or modular realization of checkers [REDD 74a, 74b, SMIT 77, PASC 88]. Fig. 9.10 illustrates one such construction. These checkers can be tested by $2m$ codewords resulting from a circular shift of m 1's followed by m 0's [SMIT 77]. As an example, the cellular realization of 4-out-of-8 code is shown in Fig. 9.11(a); the test words for the checker are given in Fig. 9.11(b).

The above checkers are self-testing for single faults or unidirectional faults if the specified $2m$ codewords are given during normal operation. For more detailed analysis, refer to [SMIT 77].

(2) $n \ne 2m$ case. The general m-out-of-n code checker, where $n \ne 2m$, can be realized by translating the given code to a 1-out-of-$\binom{n}{m}$ code, which is then converted to a p-out-of-$2p$ code via a TSC translator [ANDE 73]. In this case, p should satisfy the following relation.

$$\binom{2p}{p} \ge \binom{n}{m} \ge 2^p \qquad (9.1)$$

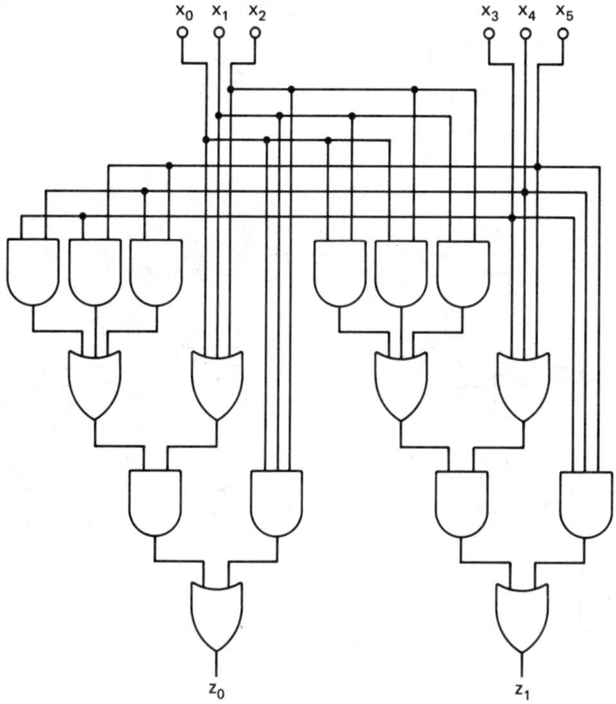

(a) 3-out-of-6 code checker

x_0	x_1	x_2	x_3	x_4	x_5
0	0	0	1	1	1
1	0	0	0	1	1
0	1	0	1	0	1
0	0	1	1	1	0
1	1	0	0	0	1
0	1	1	1	0	0
1	0	1	0	1	0
1	1	1	0	0	0

(b) Test words for the checker

Figure 9.9 Self-testing 3-out-of-6 code checker [ANDE 71].

Figure 9.12 shows the general form of a self-testing checker for an m-out-of-n code, $n \neq 2m$.

In order to make the p-out-of-$2p$ code checker self-testing, input p-out-of-$2p$ codewords should include specified 2^p codewords. That is, these codewords should be selected so that the left-most p bits are complementary to the right-most p bits, as shown in Fig. 9.11(b).

Example 9-2

We here describe the design of a 2-out-of-5 code checker. The design consists of converting the 2-out-of-5 code into a 1-out-of-10 code, which is then translated into a 3-out-of-6 code. Figure 9.13 shows the circuit for decoding the 2-out-of-5 code into a

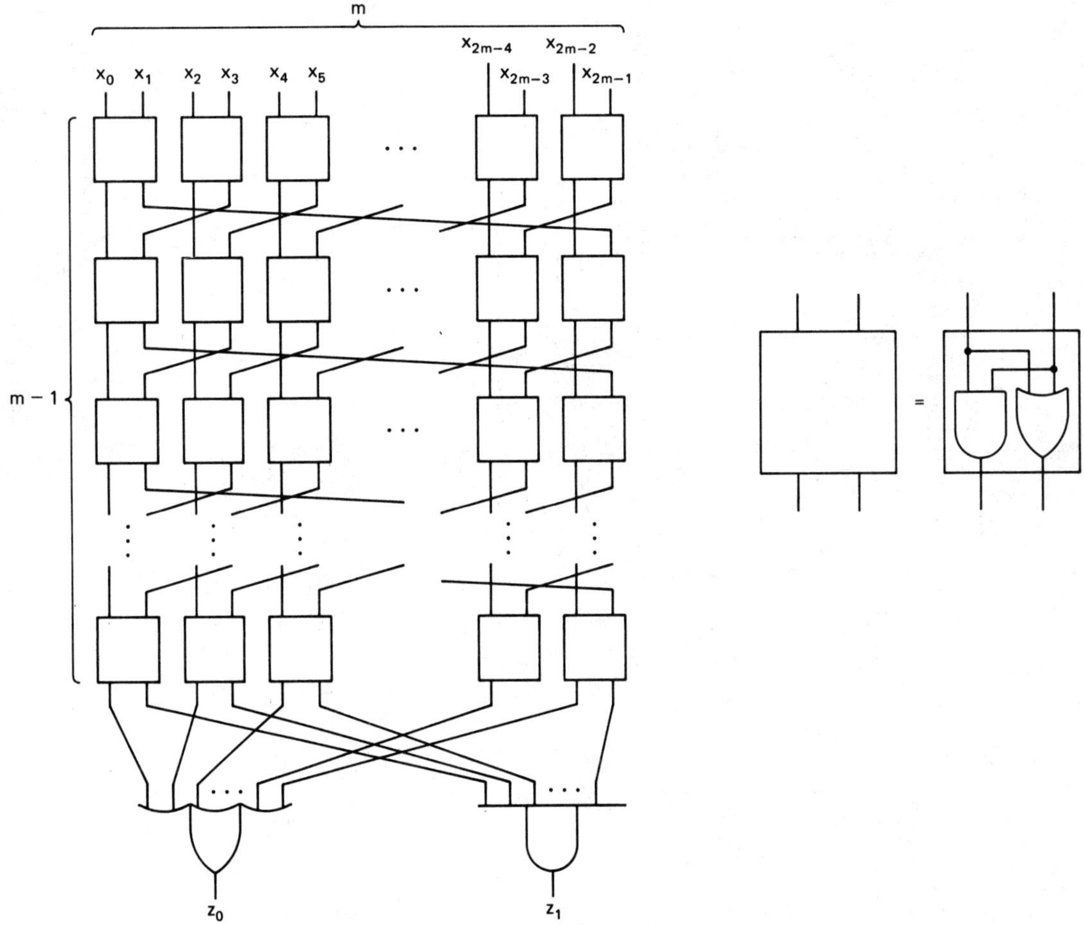

Figure 9.10 A cellular organization of an m-out-of-$2m$ code checker [SMIT 77].

1-out-of-10 code. The decoder is TSC and consists of ten two-input AND gates; each AND gate recognizes only one particular codeword input. The 1-out-of-10 code is translated into a 3-out-of-6 code, which satisfies Equation (9.1), via a single level of OR gates as shown in Fig. 9.13. Furthermore, the output of the 3-out-of-6 code translator can be checked by using the 3-out-of-6 code checkers shown previously, for example, the checker in Fig. 9.9. Equation (9.1) gives unique solution of $p = 3$ for the 2-out-of-5 code checker.

Table 9.2 shows the translation of a 1-out-of-10 code into a 3-out-of-6 code. Note that input to the 3-out-of-6 code checker includes the specified 2^3 (3-out-of-6) code patterns that can test this 3-out-of-6 code checker.

As a special case of the m-out-of-n codes, the 1-out-of-n code occurs quite frequently in computer systems. Such a code may be easily translated into a

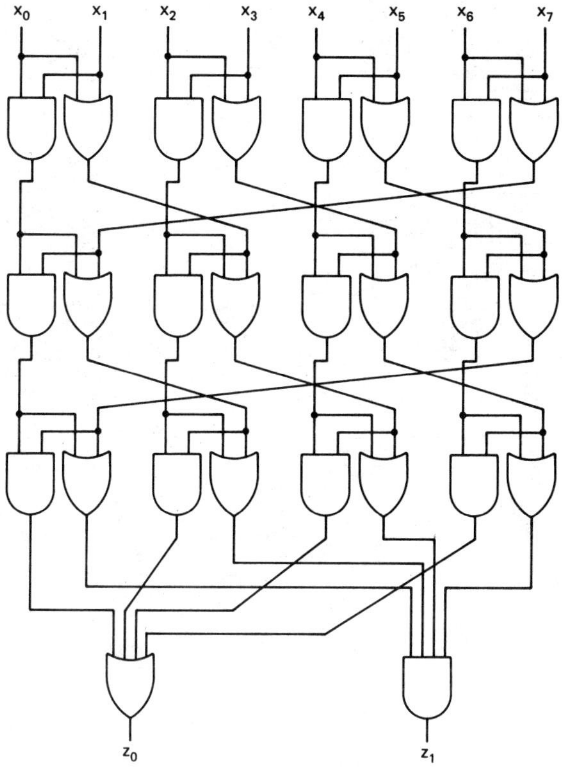

(a) 4-out-of-8 code checker

x_0	x_1	x_2	x_3	x_4	x_5	x_6	x_7
1	1	1	1	0	0	0	0
0	1	1	1	1	0	0	0
0	0	1	1	1	1	0	0
0	0	0	1	1	1	1	0
0	0	0	0	1	1	1	1
1	0	0	0	0	1	1	1
1	1	0	0	0	0	1	1
1	1	1	0	0	0	0	1

(b) Test words for the checker

Figure 9.11 A cellular organized self-testing 4-out-of-8 code checker.

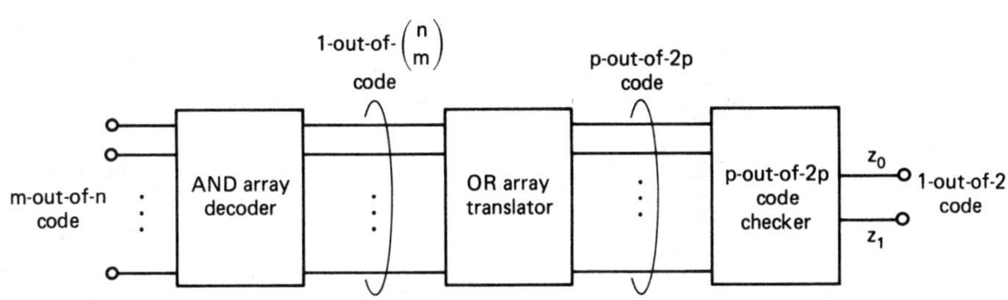

Figure 9.12 A self-testing checker for m-out-of-n codes, $n \neq 2m$.

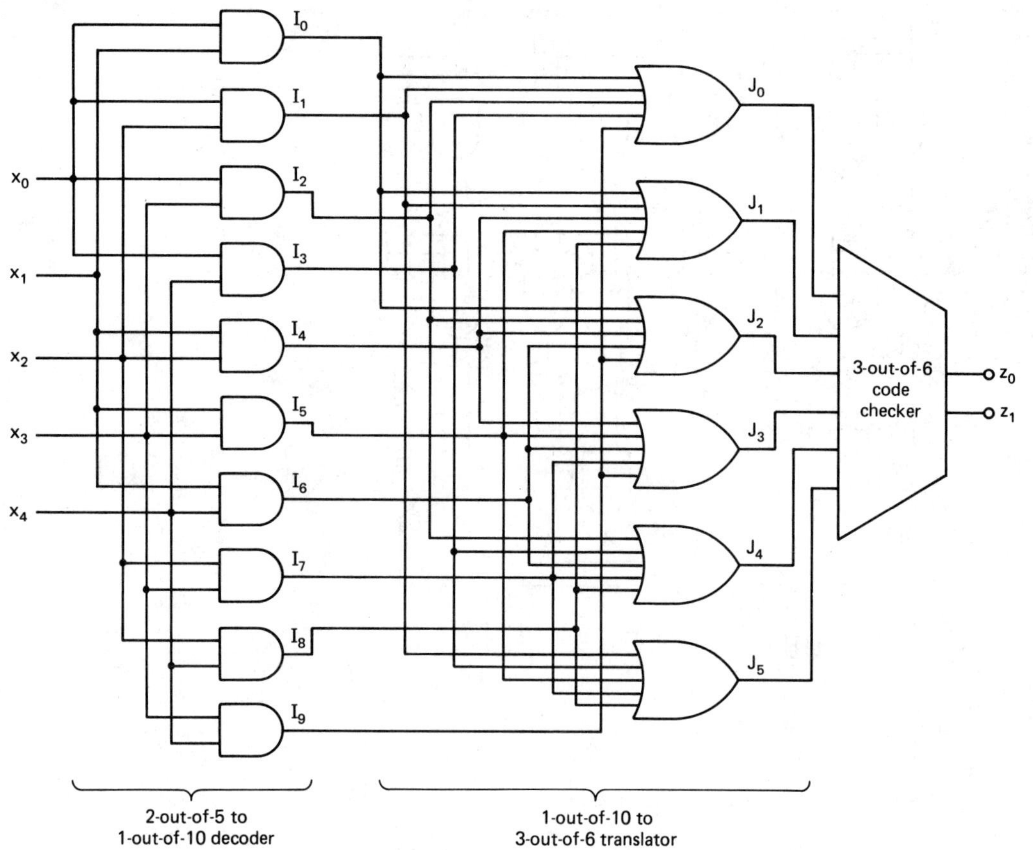

Figure 9.13 A self-testing 2-out-of-5 code checker.

TABLE 9.2 CODE TRANSLATION

1-Out-of-10 Code										3-Out-of-6 Code					
I_0	I_1	I_2	I_3	I_4	I_5	I_6	I_7	I_8	I_9	J_0	J_1	J_2	J_3	J_4	J_5
1	0	0	0	0	0	0	0	0	0	1	1	1	0	0	0
0	1	0	0	0	0	0	0	0	0	1	1	0	0	0	1
0	0	1	0	0	0	0	0	0	0	1	0	1	0	1	0
0	0	0	1	0	0	0	0	0	0	1	0	0	0	1	1
0	0	0	0	1	0	0	0	0	0	0	1	1	1	0	0
0	0	0	0	0	1	0	0	0	0	0	1	0	1	0	1
0	0	0	0	0	0	1	0	0	0	0	0	1	1	1	0
0	0	0	0	0	0	0	1	0	0	0	0	0	1	1	1
0	0	0	0	0	0	0	0	1	0	0	1	0	0	1	1
0	0	0	0	0	0	0	0	0	1	1	0	1	1	0	0

p-out-of-$2p$ code via a single level of OR gates. Note that the output codewords of the translator consist of only n of the possible $\binom{2p}{p}$ codewords of a p-out-of-$2p$ code. On the other hand, 2^p specified codewords should be selected from among these n output codewords of the translator. That is, the following relation is always satisfied from Equation (9.1).

$$\binom{2p}{p} \geq n \geq 2^p \tag{9.2}$$

The following shows the relation between n and p that satisfies Equation (9.2).

n	2	3	4	5	6	7	8	9	···	16	···	20	21	···	70
p	1	—	2	2	2	—	3	3	···	3 or 4	···	3 or 4	4	···	4

From this, it is possible to construct a self-testing 1-out-of-n code checker for any value of n except $n = 3$ and $n = 7$. A 1-out-of-7 code, for example, has too many codewords to be translated to a 2-out-of-4 code and not enough codewords to make a 3-out-of-6 code checker self-testing. However, solutions have been given for these code checkers [REDD 74b, DAVI 78a, ITOH 80, IZAW 81, GOLA 84, LO 87b]. An example of a 1-out-of-7 code checker is shown in Fig. 9.14 [IZAW 81].

Another method of implementing the self-testing 1-out-of-n code checker has been proposed: the 1-out-of-n code is first translated into a two-rail code, and then a self-testing checker for the two-rail output of the translator is used. Such a checker can be designed using a PLA [KHAK 82c].

The above implementation method of the general m-out-of-n code checker sometimes needs a large gate count and many gate levels. From this standpoint, more efficient design methods are proposed for particular n.

For $n = 2m + 1$, $m > 1$, some efficient methods have been proposed by [REDD 74b, MARO 78b], in particular one in which two-level self-testing checkers are introduced [REDD 74b]. Such checkers are basically composed of two subcheckers, an m-out-of-$(2m + 1)$ to 1-out-of-$\binom{2m+1}{m}$ code translator and a 1-out-of-$\binom{2m+1}{m}$ to 1-out-of-2 code translator. The first translator is realized using $\binom{2m+1}{m}$ number of m-input AND gates. The second translator consists of only two OR gates, with a total of $\binom{2m+1}{m}$ inputs. The output of each AND gate is connected to an input of a single OR gate. Hence, the set of AND gates has to be partitioned into two disjoint subsets.

We will use the following notation to indicate the partitioning of the AND gates into two disjoint subsets. Since each AND gate output is 1 for only one input in the m-out-of-$(2m + 1)$ code, we can see that there is a one-to-one correspondence

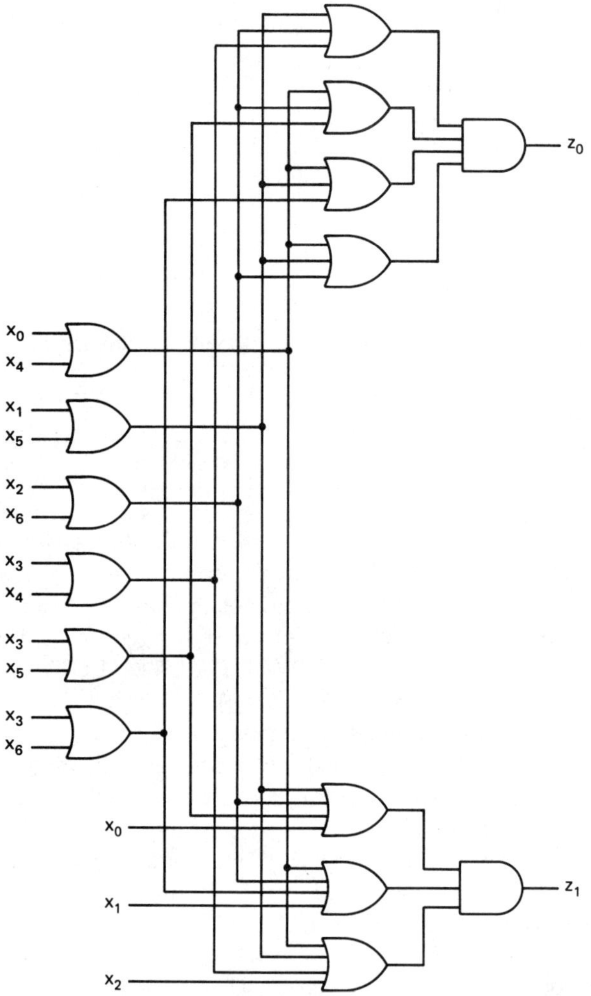

Figure 9.14 Self-testing 1-out-of-7 code checker [IZAW 81].

between the words of this code and the AND gates. The words in this code will be represented in two different ways. In the first representation, we give the indices of the positions in which the word has 1's. For example, 11000 is represented by 12 and 1011010 is represented by 1346. The second representation uses a 3-tuple of integers. Let a binary $(2m + 1)$-tuple be divided into three parts as shown below [REDD 74b].

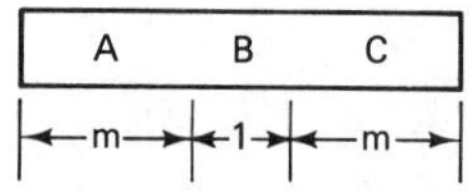

A binary $(2m + 1)$-tuple is then represented by the 3-tuple $(a \mid b \mid c)$ where a, b, and c are the number of ones in the A, B, and C regions, respectively. For example, 11000 is represented by $(2 \mid 0 \mid 0)$ and 1011010 is represented by $(2 \mid 1 \mid 1)$.

We now give the partitioning in terms of the notation given earlier.
Group I:

$$A_i = \{i|0|(m-i),\ i \text{ even, and } 2 \le i \le m\}$$

$$A^+ = \{i(m+i_1)(m+i_2)\cdots(m+i_{m-1}),\ 1 \le i \le m,\ 2 \le i_j \le (m+1), \text{ and } i_j - 1 \ne i\}$$

$$B_i = \{i|1|(m-i-1),\ i \text{ even, and } 0 \le i \le m-1\}$$

Group II:

$$A_i = \{i|0|(m-i),\ i \text{ odd, and } 3 \le i \le m\}$$

$$A^* = \{\text{all elements of } (1|0|(m-1)) \text{ not included in } A^+\}$$

$$A_0 = (0|0|m)$$

$$B_j = \{j|1|(m-1-j),\ j \text{ odd, and } 1 \le j \le m-1\}$$

Note that we are using the second type of representation of the words of the code, except for numbers of A^+, for which we are using the first type of representation.

Example 9-3

We consider the design of a self-testing 2-out-of-5 code checker. The first translator gives 10 two-input AND gates. The set of AND gates is partitioned into two groups.

Group I	Group II
$A_2 = \{1\ 1\ 0\ 0\ 0\}$	$A^* = \{0\ 1\ 0\ 0\ 1,\ 1\ 0\ 0\ 1\ 0\}$
$A^+ = \{15, 24\} = \{1\ 0\ 0\ 0\ 1,\ 0\ 1\ 0\ 1\ 0\}$	$A_0 = \{0\ 0\ 0\ 1\ 1\}$
$B_0 = \{0\ 0\ 1\ 0\ 1,\ 0\ 0\ 1\ 1\ 0\}$	$B_1 = \{1\ 0\ 1\ 0\ 0,\ 0\ 1\ 1\ 0\ 0\}$

Each group represents the subset of AND gates that feed an OR gate. The complete circuit for the 2-out-of-5 code checker is shown in Fig. 9.15.

Next, we discuss an m-out-of-n code checker for $2m+2 \le n \le 4m$ [MARO 78b]. It consists of the following steps:

1. Partition the n bits into two sets A and B such that the number of bits in set A is $n_A = \lfloor n/2 \rfloor$ and the number of bits in set B is $n_B = n - n_A = \lceil n/2 \rceil$. Define two functions f_0 and f_1 as

$$f_0 = \sum_{i=1}^{m-1} T(m_A \ge i) \cdot T(m_B \ge m-i), \quad i\text{: odd}$$

$$f_1 = \sum_{i=1}^{m-1} T(m_A \ge i) \cdot T(m_B \ge m-i), \quad i\text{: even}$$

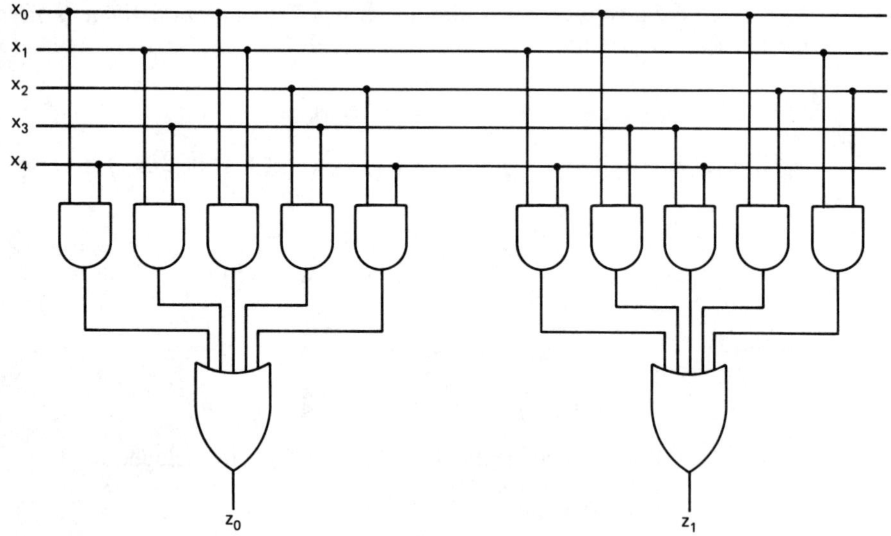

Figure 9.15 A self-testing 2-out-of-5 code checker [REDD 74b]. © 1974 IEEE.

2. Partition the bits of set A into two subsets A_1 and A_2 such that $n_{A_1} = \lfloor n_A/2 \rfloor$ and $n_{A_2} = n_A - n_{A_1} = \lceil n_A/2 \rceil$. Define f_2 and f_3 as

$$f_2 = \sum_{i=m-n_{A_2}}^{n_{A_1}} T(m_{A_1} \geq i) \cdot T(m_{A_2} \geq m - i), \quad i\text{: odd}$$

$$f_3 = \sum_{i=m-n_{A_2}}^{n_{A_1}} T(m_{A_1} \geq i) \cdot T(m_{A_2} \geq m - i), \quad i \text{ even}$$

3. Partition the bits of set B into two subsets B_1 and B_2 such that $n_{B_1} = \lfloor n_B/2 \rfloor$ and $n_{B_2} = n_B - n_{B_1} = \lceil n_B/2 \rceil$. Define f_4 and f_5 as

$$f_4 = \sum_{i=m-n_{B_2}}^{n_{B_1}} T(m_{B_1} \geq i) \cdot T(m_{B_2} \geq m - i), \quad i\text{: odd}$$

$$f_5 = \sum_{i=m-n_{B_2}}^{n_{B_1}} T(m_{B_1} \geq i) \cdot T(m_{B_2} \geq m - i), \quad i\text{: even}$$

4. Design a circuit with n inputs and f_i $(i = 0, 1, \ldots, 5)$ outputs; realize every f_i in sum-of-products form. Call this circuit $\mathbf{L}_0$. It produces a 1-out-of-6 code on its outputs.

5. Feed the outputs of circuit $\mathbf{L}_0$ to the inputs of the circuit $\mathbf{L}_1$, which is a TSC 1-out-of-6 to 2-out-of-4 code translator.

6. Feed the outputs of circuit $\mathbf{L}_1$ to the input of circuit $\mathbf{L}_2$, which is a self-testing checker for a 2-out-of-4 code. The combined circuit $\mathbf{L}$ will have two outputs z_0 and z_1.

The foregoing procedure generates self-testing checkers for m-out-of-n codes, $2m + 2 \le n \le 4m$. The checkers are self-testing for all single and unidirectional faults that can be detected using the following T codeword inputs.

$$T = \sum_{i=1}^{m-1} \max\left[\binom{n_A}{i}, \binom{n_B}{m-i}\right] + \sum_{i=m-n_{A_2}}^{n_{A_1}} \max\left[\binom{n_{A_1}}{i}, \binom{n_{A_2}}{m-i}\right]$$
$$+ \sum_{i=m-n_{B_2}}^{n_{B_1}} \max\left[\binom{n_{B_1}}{i}, \binom{n_{B_2}}{m-i}\right]$$

Example 9-4 [LALA 85]

Let's design a checker for a 2-out-of-6 code defined by the set of inputs $\{x_0, x_1, x_2, x_3, x_4, x_5\}$. Then

$$A = \{x_0, x_1, x_2\}, \qquad B = \{x_3, x_4, x_5\}, \qquad n_A = n_B = 3$$

$$f_0 = \sum_{i=1}^{1} T(m_A \ge i) \cdot T(m_B \ge 2 - i) \qquad i\text{: odd}$$
$$= (x_0 + x_1 + x_2)(x_3 + x_4 + x_5)$$

$$f_1 = \sum_{i=1}^{1} T(m_A \ge i) \cdot T(m_B \ge 2 - i) \qquad i\text{: even}$$
$$= 0$$

$$A_1 = \{x_0\}, \qquad A_2 = \{x_1, x_2\}, \qquad n_{A_1} = 1, \qquad n_{A_2} = 2$$

$$f_2 = \sum_{i=0}^{1} T(m_{A_1} \ge i) \cdot T(m_{A_2} \ge 2 - i) \qquad i\text{: odd}$$
$$= x_0(x_1 + x_2)$$

$$f_3 = \sum_{i=0}^{1} T(m_{A_1} \ge i) \cdot T(m_{A_2} \ge 2 - i) \qquad i\text{: even}$$
$$= x_1 x_2$$

$$B_1 = \{x_3\}, \qquad B_2 = \{x_4, x_5\}, \qquad n_{B_1} = 1, \qquad n_{B_2} = 2$$

$$f_4 = \sum_{i=0}^{1} T(m_{B_1} \ge i) \cdot T(m_{B_2} \ge 2 - i) \qquad i\text{: odd}$$
$$= x_3(x_4 + x_5)$$

$$f_5 = \sum_{i=0}^{1} T(m_{B_1} \ge i) \cdot T(m_{B_2} \ge 2 - i) \qquad i\text{: even}$$
$$= x_4 x_5$$

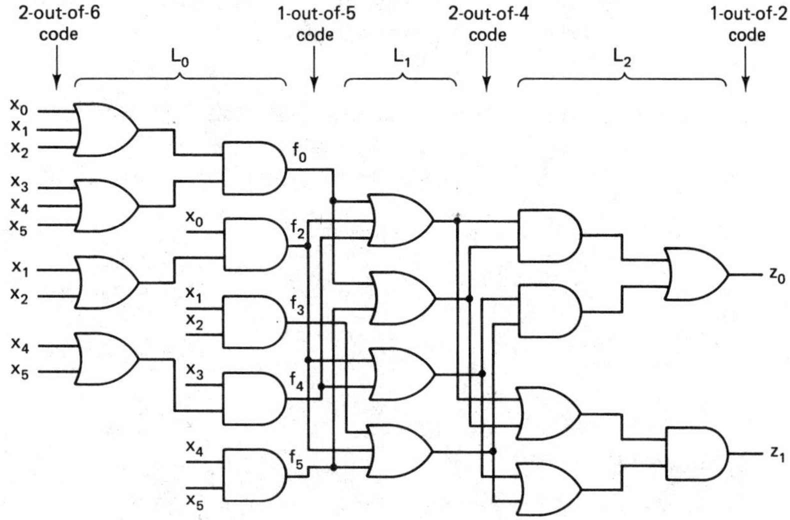

Figure 9.16 A self-testing 2-out-of-6 code checker [LALA 85].

Since $f_1 = 0$, $\mathbf{L}_0$ will have only five outputs, f_0, f_2, f_3, f_4, f_5. Thus $\mathbf{L}_1$ will be 1-out-of-5 to 2-out-of-4 code translator. The final stage circuit $\mathbf{L}_2$ is a 2-out-of-4 code checker. The circuit $\mathbf{L}$ for the checker is shown in Fig. 9.16. The number of codewords required to test the checker is $T = 9$.

Other researches on self-testing m-out-of-n code checkers aim for a general design for *unordered codes*, including m-out-of-n codes and Berger codes [SMIT 77, IZAW 84a, 84b], a modular realization or PLA implementation of self-testing m-out-of-n code checkers [EFST 83, BOSE 84a, PIES 85], or a high speed, gate-level minimized implementation method for these checkers [GAIT 83, HALA 83, NANY 83, IZAW 84a, TAO 87]. There is also research on implementation methods that satisfy the self-testing property even if not all codewords are given to the unordered code checkers, or m-out-of-$2m$ code checkers [IZAW 84a, NANY 85a].

9.1.4 Separable Code Checker

If an error-detecting code is separable (or systematic), then a checker for that code can be constructed from a two-rail code checker and a check-bit generator. As suggested in Fig. 9.17, the two-rail code checker compares the check bits of a codeword with the new check bits generated from the information part of the codeword [ASHJ 77, MARO 78a, ITOH 80, GAIT 84, LO 87a]. We consider the Berger code and the low-cost residue code to be typical separable error-detecting codes.

Berger code checker. For Berger codes, the combinational circuit of the check bits generator shown in Fig. 9.17 generates the binary number corresponding

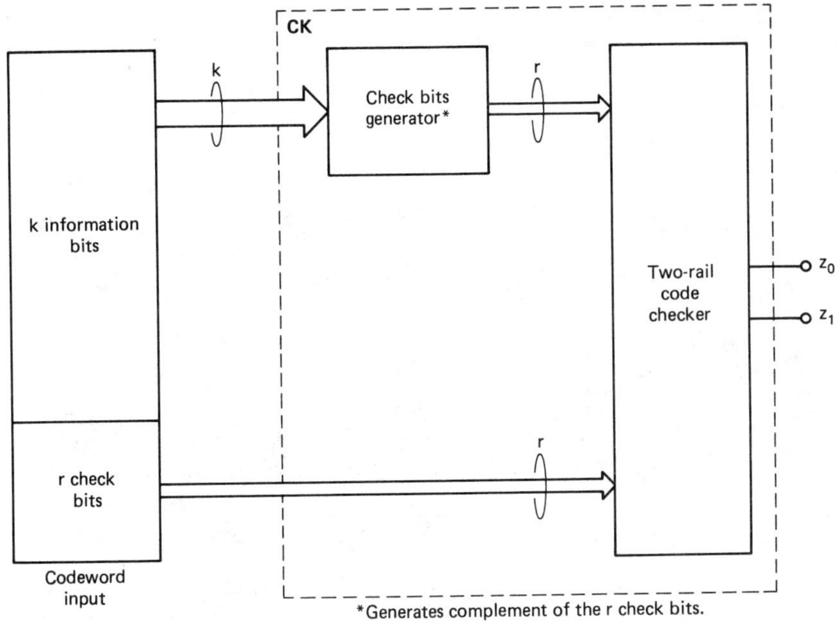

Figure 9.17 A self-testing checker for separable codes.

to the number of 1's in the information bits. It is designed to use a set of full adder modules that add the information bits in parallel and produce the binary number corresponding to the number of 1's in the information bits.

A Berger code is a maximal-length code if and only if the information length $k = 2^r - 1$, where r is the number of check bits. For every non-maximal-length Berger code one can construct an equivalent separable code for which the checker of Fig. 9.17 can be self-testing. The algorithm given below allows one to construct a separable code equivalent to a given non-maximal-length Berger code [ASHJ 77].

Algorithm [ASHJ 77]. *Let W_1 be a non-maximal-length Berger code with length n_1, k_1 information bits and $r = \lceil \log_2(k_1 + 1) \rceil$ check bits, and let W be the maximal-length Berger code with r check bits, $(2^r - 1)$ information bits and length n. Let W' be the code defined as follows.*

$$W' = \{ X | X \in W \textit{ and } (k - k_1 + 1) = (n - n_1 + 1) \textit{ left-most positions of } X \textit{ are either all zeros or all ones} \}$$

Derive W'' from W' according to the defining equation for W'' given as follows:

$$W'' = \{ Y | Y \textit{ is obtained by deleting the left-most } (k - k_1) = (n - n_1) \textit{ positions of some codeword of } W' \}$$

Example 9-5 [ASHJ 77]

Let $W_1 = \{0010, 0101, 1001, 1100\}$, with $r_1 = n_1 - k_1 = 2$. Then $W = \{00011, 00110, 01010, 10010, 01101, 10101, 11001, 11100\}$ with $k = 3$, $n = 5$. Hence, $W' = \{00011, 00110, 11001, 11100\}$ and $W'' = \{0011, 0110, 1001, 1100\}$.

It can be shown that a W'' so constructed can have a self-testing checker of the type shown in Fig. 9.17. However, for Example 9-5, the input to the two-rail code checker should include four specified test patterns that can test this checker completely. The self-testing structure of this checker is demonstrated in [MARO 78a].

Another implementation of self-testing Berger code checkers proceeds from the idea that any Berger code can be constructed from $u = \lceil (k+1)/2 \rceil$ m-out-of-n codes, where k is the number of information bits, $m = 1, 3, 5, \ldots, 2u - 1$, and $n = k + 1$ [PIES 87]. This is called *Berger code partitioning*. Table 9.3 gives an example of the partitioning for a Berger code with $k = 7$ and check bit length $r = 3$, denoted as $C_{(7,3)}$. The above code can be written in the following form.

$$C_{(7,3)} = C_{1/8} \times \{11\} \cup C_{3/8} \times \{10\} \cup C_{5/8} \times \{01\} \cup C_{7/8} \times \{00\}$$

where $C_{m/n}$ shows m-out-of-n code. Therefore, this code can be partitioned into four m-out-of-8 codes, $m = 1, 3, 5, 7$. A major part of a new self-testing checker consists of u self-testing checkers for m-out-of-n codes. All these checkers can be implemented as inverter-free circuits and hence can be self-testing for all unidirectional faults. Compared with the conventional design given above, this checker offers an improvement in delay but with a greater cost in hardware. This implementation is available for codes with $k = 2^r - 1$ or $2^r - 2$, and is useful in fulfilling some conditions of the self-testing property. An improved checker based on this idea of partitioning, like the design shown in Fig. 9.17, which uses one counter circuit consisting of modular adders, is proposed in [LO 87a].

An important design technique, especially for the codes with $k = 2^{r-1}$, provides for use of an additional counter generating two-rail input V (mentioned in

TABLE 9.3 BERGER CODE $C_{(7,3)}$ PARTITIONING. [PIES 87]

Subset	Information Part	Check Part	Partitioning
D_1	0 0 0 0 0 0 0	1 1 1	$C_{1/8} \times \{11\}$
D_2	0 0 0 0 0 0 1	1 1 0	
D_3	0 0 0 0 0 1 1	1 0 1	$C_{3/8} \times \{10\}$
D_4	0 0 0 0 1 1 1	1 0 0	
D_5	0 0 0 1 1 1 1	0 1 1	$C_{5/8} \times \{01\}$
D_6	0 0 1 1 1 1 1	0 1 0	
D_7	0 1 1 1 1 1 1	0 0 1	$C_{7/8} \times \{00\}$
D_8	1 1 1 1 1 1 1	0 0 0	

Theorem 9-3), which makes the embedded two-rail code checker in Fig. 9.17 self-testing [ITOH 80].

Residue code checker. Residue codes are very useful for detecting errors in the results produced by arithmetic operations (see Section 3.4). Like Berger codes, residue codes are also separable. The class of *low-cost residue codes* has been found to be very effective in detecting unidirectional multiple errors. A low-cost residue code is one with the check base

$$m = 2^l - 1, \qquad l \geq 2$$

The check bits for such codes are of length l and obtained by using an l-bit adder with end-around-carry (see Section 3.6).

As shown in Fig. 9.17, the checker compares the check bits of a codeword with the new check bits generated from the information bits of the codeword. A disagreement between the two values is detected as a fault. For this code, the check bits generator is a tree network of modulo-$(2^l - 1)$ adders. Figure 9.18 shows a self-testing checker for low-cost residue codes. However, in certain cases, both two-check values may not agree even under fault-free conditions. This is due to a carry-out bit in 2's complement addition [ASHJ 77]. Therefore, if the carry-out bit of the most significant position of the binary adder is included in the sum bits, then, under fault-free operation, $P_s = P_s^*$ in Fig. 9.18. The checker shown in Fig. 9.18 is

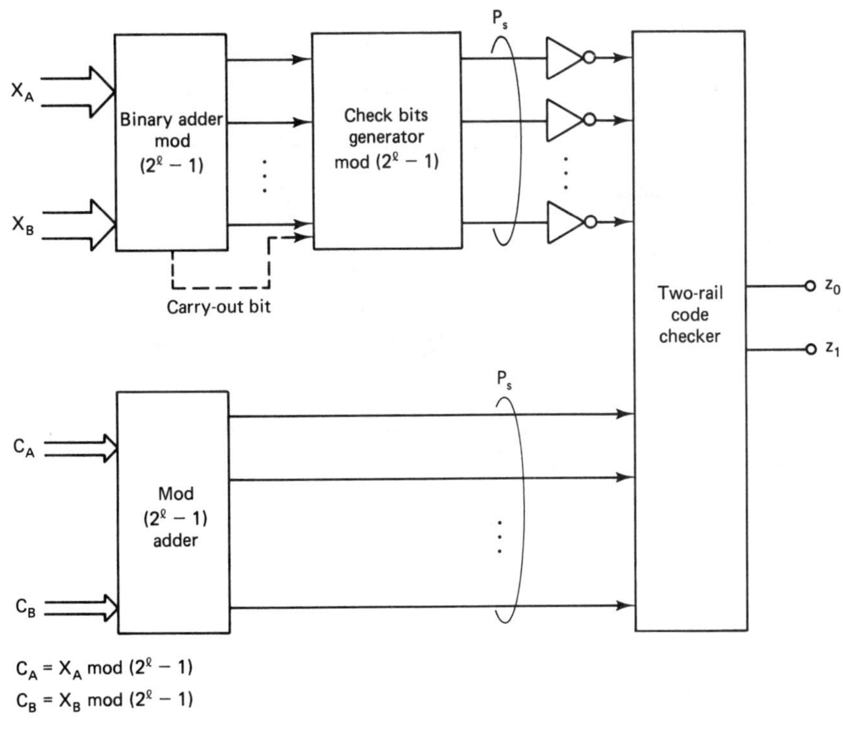

Figure 9.18 A self-testing checker for low-cost residue codes [ASHJ 77].

self-testing only when equality checker input (P_s, P_s^*) includes four specified test patterns that can test this checker completely.

9.1.5 Generalized Prediction Checker (GPC)

We consider a design for a self-checking checker for the combinational circuits having nonencoded inputs and outputs. As stated in Section 8.1, we will have to apply a prediction checking method to these circuits. First, we have a generalized prediction checker, which includes a complementary duplication checker and a parity prediction checker as special cases, and then we have a self-checking prediction checker [FUJI 84, FUJI 87a].

A prediction checker always checks the relation between circuit input and output. The combinational circuit under check **L** is assumed to have a nonencoded n-bit input $X = (x_0, x_1, \ldots, x_{n-1})$ and a nonencoded k-bit output $Y = (y_0, y_1, \ldots, y_{k-1})$. The multi-output combinational circuit can then be expressed in a disjunctive canonical form as

$$Y = \mathbf{A} \cdot U \tag{9.3}$$

where

$$Y = (y_0, y_1, \ldots, y_{k-1})^T$$

$$U = (u_0, u_1, \ldots, u_{2^n-1})^T\text{: vector of minterms}$$

$$= (\bar{x}_0\bar{x}_1 \cdots \bar{x}_{n-1}, x_0\bar{x}_1 \cdots \bar{x}_{n-1}, \ldots, \bar{x}_0 x_1 \cdots x_{n-1}, x_0 x_1 \cdots x_{n-1})^T$$

$$\mathbf{A} = (a_{ij})_{k\times 2^n}, \qquad a_{ij} \in \{0,1\}$$

$$i = 0,1,\ldots,k-1, \;\; j = 0,1,\ldots,2^n-1$$

and the operation $\cdot$ between **A** and U shows

$$y_i = \bigcup_{j=0}^{2^n-1} a_{ij} \cdot u_j \qquad (\cup \text{ and } \cdot \text{ mean logical OR and AND, respectively}),$$

y_i (for $i = 0, \ldots, k-1$): canonical sum of minterms indicated by ith row elements of A.

In this case, Y can also be expressed in a Reed-Muller canonic expansion, which is an easily testable realization [REDD 72a, 72b].

Checker implementation. Compared to the conventional parity prediction checkers, this new checker can be systematically implemented by using the matrix **A**.

Here, we consider a prediction matrix **K**, a $(k \times 2^n)$ matrix, having the same size as that of matrix **A**, and obtain a prediction function (a k-tuple) from the following relation:

$$I = \overline{\mathbf{K} \cdot U} \tag{9.4}$$

By changing the elements of **K**, any desired prediction function can be obtained. We also generate another function, J (a k-tuple)

$$J = Y \oplus (\mathbf{A} \oplus \mathbf{K}) \cdot U \tag{9.5}$$

If there are no errors, then $Y = \mathbf{A} \cdot U$, and J will then be $\mathbf{K} \cdot U$, the complement of I. The circuit Z is thus a two-rail comparator of I and J; a mismatch is signaled by the outputs

$$Z = (z_0, z_1) = \bigcap_{i=0}^{k-1}{}_{\circledast} (I_i, J_i)$$
$$I_i = [I]_i, J_i = [J]_i, \quad i = 0, 1, \ldots, k-1 \tag{9.6}$$

The notations used above are as follows:

$\overline{\mathbf{K} \cdot U}$: logical inversion of $\mathbf{K} \cdot U$. This inversion can be applied either to circuit I or to circuit J.

$[Q]_i$: ith element of vector Q.

$\bigcap_{i=0}^{k-1}{}_{\circledast} (I_i, J_i)$: comparison of k input pairs, $(I_0, J_0), (I_1, J_1), \ldots, (I_{k-1}, J_{k-1})$, which gives output Z as a 1-out-of-2 code only when all k input pairs are 1-out-of-2 codewords.

$\oplus$: EX-OR operation.

The basic structure of the checker is shown as circuit **CK** in Fig. 9.19. When the prediction matrix **K** is equal to **A**, this checker is identical to the complementary duplication checker. This is because circuit **J** does not exist, and hence output Y goes directly to circuit **Z**, and circuit **I** can be expressed as $\overline{\mathbf{A} \cdot U}$, which is the complement of the original circuit output shown in Equation (9.3). Hence, this checker can be said to include the complementary duplication checker as a special case.

The checker has input space (X, Y) and output space Z. Error-free output of the circuit **L** is defined as Y_0 (i.e., $Y_0 = Y(X, \lambda)$, $X \in \mathbf{N}$). The input and the output codespaces for the prediction checkers have already been defined and shown in Fig. 8.20(b).

Theorem 9-4. *The circuit defined by Equations* (9.4) *to* (9.6) *is code disjoint.*

Proof. When circuit **CK** has input codeword $(X, Y_0) \in \mathbf{S}$, it is apparent that this circuit results in output $Z \in \mathbf{B} = \{01, 10\}$. On the other hand, when circuit **CK** has input noncodeword $(X, Y') \notin \mathbf{S}$, where $Y' = Y_0 \oplus E$ and E is a nonzero error vector, the following relation, as given in Equation (9.5), is satisfied.

$$\begin{aligned} J &= Y' \oplus (\mathbf{A} \oplus \mathbf{K}) \cdot U = (Y_0 \oplus E) \oplus (\mathbf{A} \oplus \mathbf{K}) \cdot U \\ &= E \oplus \mathbf{K} \cdot U, \quad \text{because } Y_0 = \mathbf{A} \cdot U \end{aligned}$$

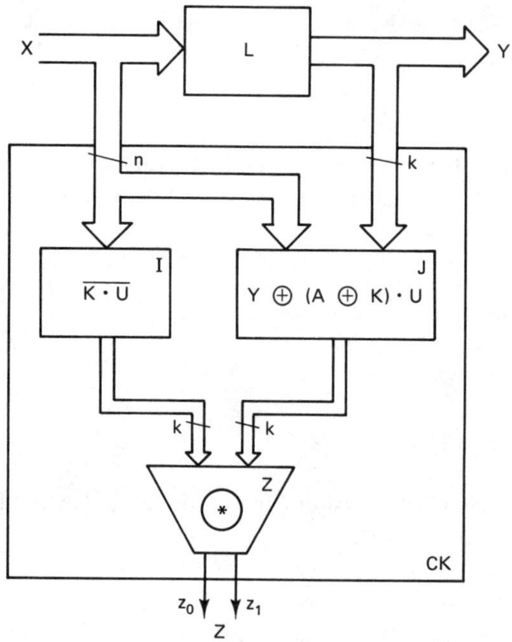

Figure 9.19 Basic structure of the generalized prediction checker [FUJI 87a]. © 1987 IEEE.

When $E \neq 0$, not all pairs of (I_i, J_i), $i = 0, 1, \ldots, k-1$, are 1-out-of-2 code vectors. That is, at least one pair is not equal to a 1-out-of-2 code vector (i.e., $(0, 0)$ or $(1, 1)$). Hence, from the properties of circuit **Z**, the output of circuit **CK** is equal to the vector in $\boldsymbol{\Omega}_z - \mathbf{B}$. That is, the noncodeword inputs are always mapped to the noncodeword outputs. Q.E.D.

Let us now introduce an encoding matrix to the proposed checker. This matrix simplifies the checker, thereby allowing circuit Z to make comparisons using a reduced number of (I_i, J_i) pairs, less than or equal to the number of k pairs; it also gives a wide range of error detection capabilities. The matrix is an r by k matrix denoted as **H**, where $r \leq k$, and is equal to the **H** matrix. Using **H**, the checker shown in Equations (9.4) to (9.6) can be expressed as follows.

$$\text{Circuit } \mathbf{I}\text{: } I = \overline{(\mathbf{H} \cdot \mathbf{K}) \cdot U} \tag{9.7}$$

$$\text{Circuit } \mathbf{J}\text{: } J = \mathbf{H} \cdot Y \oplus \mathbf{H} \cdot (\mathbf{A} \oplus \mathbf{K}) \cdot U \tag{9.8}$$

$$\text{Circuit } \mathbf{Z}\text{: } Z = (z_0, z_1) = \bigcap_{i=0}^{r-1}{}_{\circledast} \, (I_i, J_i) \tag{9.9}$$

In this extended checker, circuit **Z** now compares r $(\leq k)$ pairs. This is shown in Fig. 9.20. The circuit **J** is composed of circuit **J**′, **J**″, and **J**‴, as shown in this

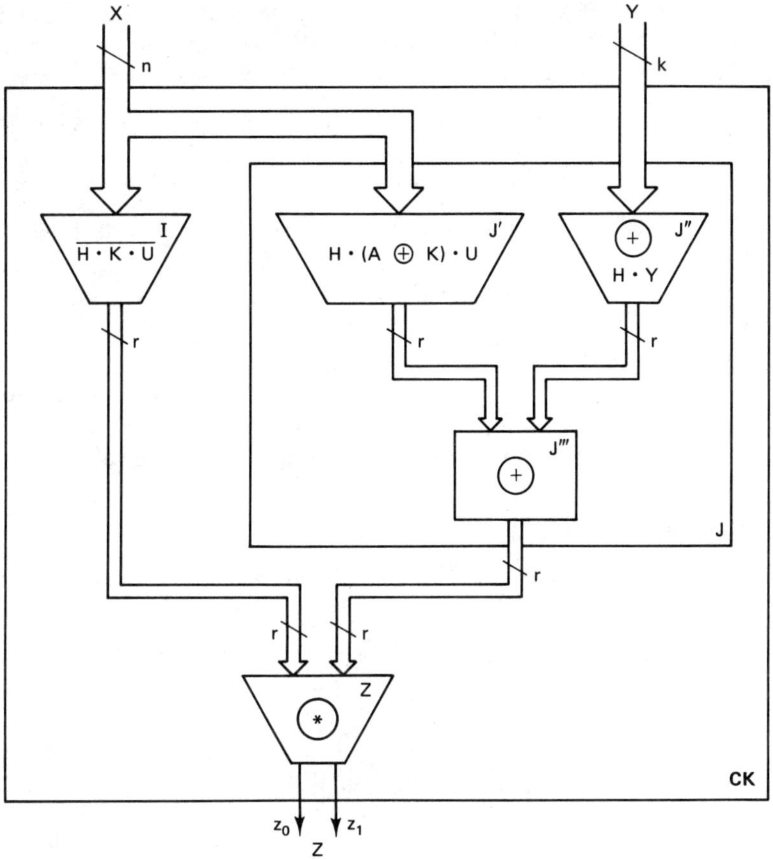

Figure 9.20 Generalized prediction checker [FUJI 87a]. © 1987 IEEE.

figure. The checker is called a *generalized prediction checker* (*GPC*) because it can predict any function, and has a wide range of error detection capabilities.

For the GPC, we have to newly define the input noncodespace, as follows.

Definition 9-1. Input noncodespace of the checker shown in Fig. 9.20 is defined by $\mathbf{\Omega y} - \mathbf{S} = \{(X, Y) \mid \mathbf{H} \cdot Y \neq \mathbf{H} \cdot Y_0\}$, where Y_0 is an error-free output of the circuit under check.

Theorem 9-5. *The circuit defined by Equations* (9.7) *to* (9.9) *is code disjoint for input noncodespace* $\{(X, Y) \mid \mathbf{H} \cdot Y \neq \mathbf{H} \cdot Y_0\}$ *and output noncodespace* $\{(0, 0)\ (1, 1)\}$.

The proof of this theorem is straightforward and is therefore omitted.

Theorem 9-6. *The error detection ability of this checker is determined directly from matrix* **H**.

Proof. In general, the checker's error detection ability can be expressed in terms of syndrome F. When error E exists and output Y is expressed as $Y = Y_0 \oplus E$, then the syndrome F of the checker can be expressed as follows.

$$F = \bar{I} \oplus J = \mathbf{H} \cdot \mathbf{K} \cdot U \oplus \{\mathbf{H} \cdot (Y_0 \oplus E) \oplus \mathbf{H} \cdot (\mathbf{A} \oplus \mathbf{K}) \cdot U\}$$

$$= \mathbf{H} \cdot E, \text{ because } Y_0 = \mathbf{A} \cdot U$$

Errors can be detected only when $F \neq 0$. When $E \neq 0$, then F is determined directly from **H**. If $F = 0$, checker output Z equals a 1-out-of-2 code, and if $F \neq 0$, output Z does not equal a 1-out-of-2 code. Hence, the error detection ability of this checker is determined directly from **H**. Q.E.D.

Although we can use **H** matrices of any error detecting and correcting codes, the **H** matrices of parity codes, double-error detecting codes (i.e., SEC codes), and triple-error detecting codes (i.e., SEC–DED codes) are suitable from the practical point of view.

Example 9-6 [FUJI 87a]

Let us implement the GPC for the following 4-input, 3-output function. The output functions of the circuit, y_0, y_1, and y_2, can be expressed as follows.

$$y_0 = \bar{x}_0(x_1 + \bar{x}_2 x_3)$$

$$y_1 = \bar{x}_0 \bar{x}_1 (x_2 + x_3)$$

$$y_2 = x_0 + x_1 + x_2 + x_3$$

Matrix **A** and vectors U and Y can be expressed as below.

$$\mathbf{A} = \begin{bmatrix} 0 & 0 & 1 & 0 & 0 & 0 & 1 & 0 & 1 & 0 & 1 & 0 & 0 & 0 & 1 & 0 \\ 0 & 0 & 0 & 0 & 1 & 0 & 0 & 0 & 1 & 0 & 0 & 0 & 1 & 0 & 0 & 0 \\ 0 & 1 & 1 & 1 & 1 & 1 & 1 & 1 & 1 & 1 & 1 & 1 & 1 & 1 & 1 & 1 \end{bmatrix}$$

$$U = (\bar{x}_0 \bar{x}_1 \bar{x}_2 \bar{x}_3, x_0 \bar{x}_1 \bar{x}_2 \bar{x}_3, \ldots, \bar{x}_0 x_1 x_2 x_3, x_0 x_1 x_2 x_3)^T$$

$$Y = (y_0, y_1, y_2)^T = \mathbf{A} \cdot U$$

As an example, let the prediction functions be AND, OR, and the parity function of the inputs for y_0, y_1, and y_2, respectively. In this case, **K** can be expressed as follows.

$$\mathbf{K} = \begin{bmatrix} 0 & 0 & 0 & 0 & 0 & 0 & 0 & 0 & 0 & 0 & 0 & 0 & 0 & 0 & 0 & 1 \\ 0 & 1 & 1 & 1 & 1 & 1 & 1 & 1 & 1 & 1 & 1 & 1 & 1 & 1 & 1 & 1 \\ 0 & 1 & 1 & 0 & 1 & 0 & 0 & 1 & 1 & 0 & 0 & 1 & 0 & 1 & 1 & 0 \end{bmatrix}$$

That is, the prediction function $x_0 x_1 x_2 x_3$ is adopted for y_0, $x_0 + x_1 + x_2 + x_3$ for y_1, and $x_0 \oplus x_1 \oplus x_2 \oplus x_3$ for y_2.

Next, let the encoding matrix **H** be as follows.

$$\mathbf{H} = \begin{bmatrix} 0 & 1 & 0 \\ 1 & 0 & 1 \end{bmatrix}$$

This matrix can be shown to detect double errors, such as y_0 and y_1 errors and y_1 and y_2 errors, as well as single and triple errors in Y.

Given the above conditions, the checking logic can be formulated systematically as follows:

Circuit **I**:

$$\mathbf{H}\cdot\mathbf{K}=\begin{bmatrix}0&1&1&1&1&1&1&1&1&1&1&1&1&1&1&1\\0&1&1&0&1&0&0&1&1&0&0&1&0&1&1&1\end{bmatrix}$$

$$I=\overline{\mathbf{H}\cdot\mathbf{K}\cdot U}=\begin{bmatrix}\overline{x_0+x_1+x_2+x_3}\\ \overline{x_0\oplus x_1\oplus x_2\oplus x_3\oplus x_0x_1x_2x_3}\end{bmatrix}=\begin{bmatrix}I_0\\I_1\end{bmatrix}$$

Circuit **J**:

$$\mathbf{H}\cdot(\mathbf{A}\oplus\mathbf{K})=\begin{bmatrix}0&1&1&1&0&1&1&1&0&1&1&1&0&1&1&1\\0&0&1&1&0&1&0&0&1&1&0&0&1&0&1&0\end{bmatrix}$$

$$\begin{aligned}J&=\mathbf{H}\cdot Y\oplus\mathbf{H}\cdot(\mathbf{A}\oplus\mathbf{K})\cdot U\\&=\begin{bmatrix}y_1\oplus(x_0+x_1)\\ y_0\oplus y_2\oplus(x_0\bar{x}_1x_2\bar{x}_3+x_1\bar{x}_2\bar{x}_3+\bar{x}_0\bar{x}_1x_3+\bar{x}_0x_2x_3+\bar{x}_1\bar{x}_2x_3)\end{bmatrix}\\&=\begin{bmatrix}J_0\\J_1\end{bmatrix}\end{aligned}$$

Circuit **Z**:

$$Z=(z_0,z_1)=(I_0,J_0)\circledast(I_1,J_1).$$

Operation " $\circledast$ " is defined in Lemma 9-1.

Figure 9.21 shows the GPC having ability to detect some double errors as well as single and triple errors.

If $\mathbf{K}=\mathbf{A}$, then circuits **I** and **J** can be expressed as follows.

Circuit **I**: $I=\overline{\mathbf{H}\cdot\mathbf{K}\cdot U}=\overline{\mathbf{H}\cdot\mathbf{A}\cdot U}$

Circuit **J**: $J=\mathbf{H}\cdot Y$

Next, we adopt **H** as a parity code.

$$\mathbf{H}=[1\ 1\ 1]$$

Then, the circuits **I** and **J** can be expressed as follows.

Circuit **I**: $\overline{\mathbf{H}\cdot\mathbf{A}\cdot U}=\overline{(0101010111010101)}\cdot U=\bar{x}_0(x_1+x_2+x_3)$

Circuit **J**: $y_0\oplus y_1\oplus y_2$

Figure 9.22 shows the checker just equal to the parity prediction checker.

We consider now the method for reducing the number of gates in this checker under the given matrix **H**. Circuit **Z** and circuit **J**″ are determined from **H**. Let $\mathbf{K}=\mathbf{A}$, then the circuit **J**′ does not exist (i.e., $\mathbf{H}\cdot(\mathbf{A}\oplus\mathbf{K})\cdot U=0$), and therefore circuit **J**‴ is left out. (Circuits **J**′, **J**″, and **J**‴ are shown in Fig. 9.20.) This reduces the number of gates in circuit **J** to a minimum. In this case, this checker is equivalent to the parity-based prediction checker determined from **H**. In general, for $\mathbf{K}\neq\mathbf{A}$, reducing the number of gates in the checker, especially in circuit **I** and circuit **J**′, is basically a problem of logic minimization. For the example circuit shown in Fig. 9.21, the number of gates can be reduced from 44 to 18 when **K** is equal to **A**, given the same matrix **H**.

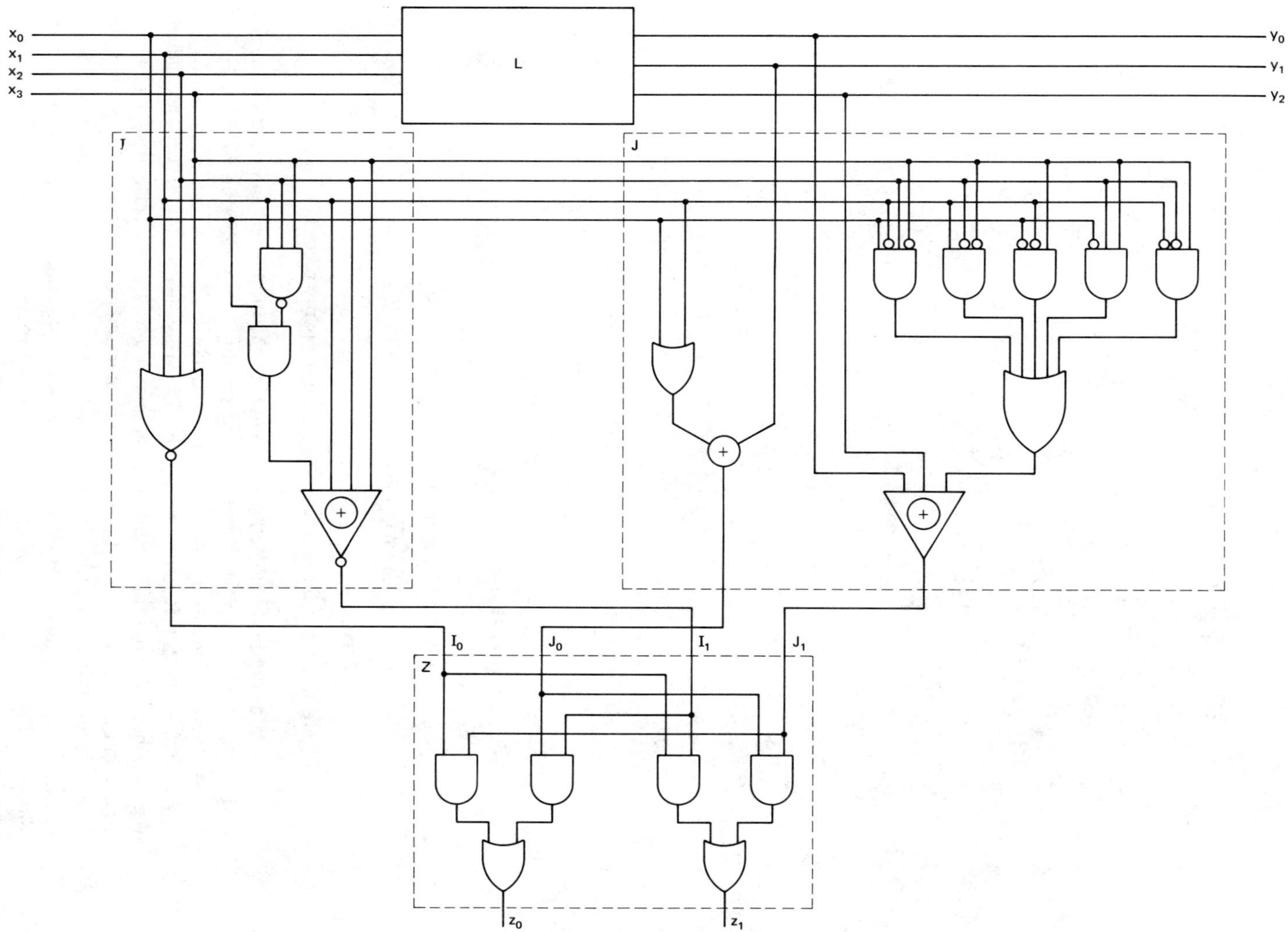

Figure 9.21 An example of the generalized prediction checker (GPC) [FUJI 87a]. © 1987 IEEE.

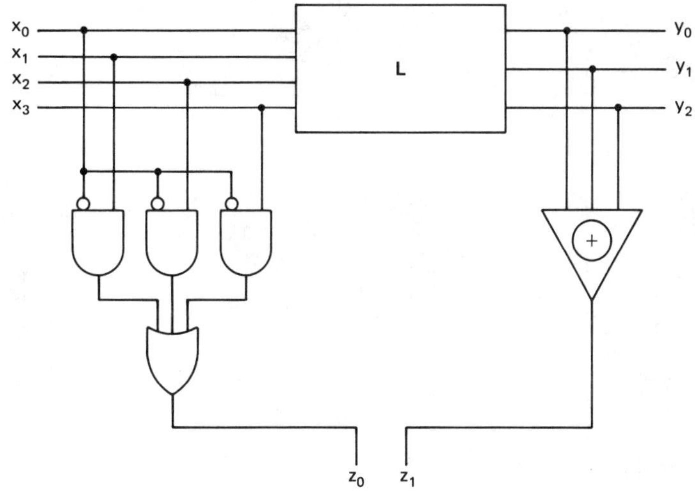

Figure 9.22 An example of the GPC (equal to parity prediction checker).

Self-testing GPC. Next, we consider a self-testing GPC. The checker will operate correctly when single faults occur in both the circuit **L** and the checker **CK**. To make the checker self-checking, an input v that can take any value in $\{0,1\}$ is added to the checker, as follows.

$$\text{Circuit } \mathbf{I}\text{: } I_i = \left[\overline{\mathbf{H} \cdot \mathbf{K} \cdot U}\right]_i \oplus v \tag{9.10}$$

$$\text{Circuit } \mathbf{J}\text{: } J_i = [\mathbf{H} \cdot \mathbf{Y}]_i \oplus [\mathbf{H} \cdot (\mathbf{A} \oplus \mathbf{K}) \cdot U]_i \oplus v \tag{9.11}$$

$$\text{Circuit } \mathbf{Z}\text{: } Z = (z_0, z_1) = \left[\bigcap_{i=0}^{r-1}{}_{\circledast} (I_i, J_i)\right] \circledast (v, \bar{v}) \tag{9.12}$$

$$v \in \{0,1\}, \quad i = 0,1,\ldots, r-1$$

Theorem 9-7. *The circuit prescribed by Equations* (9.10) *to* (9.12) *is code disjoint.*

Input v is equally added to both circuit **I** and circuit **J**, and therefore this does not affect any checking logic defined by Equations (9.7) to (9.9). From this, Theorem 9-7 can be easily proved.

Circuit **Z** consists of two-input, two-rail code checkers. According to Theorem 9-3, if these are connected in a cascaded-tree structure having $(r+1)$ input pairs (i.e., $(I_0, J_0)(I_1, J_1) \cdots (I_{r-1}, J_{r-1})$, and $(v, \bar{v})$), then the circuit **Z** is self-testing for single faults, provided that every input does not have constant value and $V = (v, \bar{v})$ can take any value in $\{0,1\}$ during normal operation.

Circuit **J** is constructed from circuits **J**′, **J**″, and **J**‴ shown in Fig. 9.20 and is realized from r subcircuits $\mathbf{J}_0, \mathbf{J}_1, \ldots, \mathbf{J}_{r-1}$. Circuits **J**″ and **J**‴ are implemented by

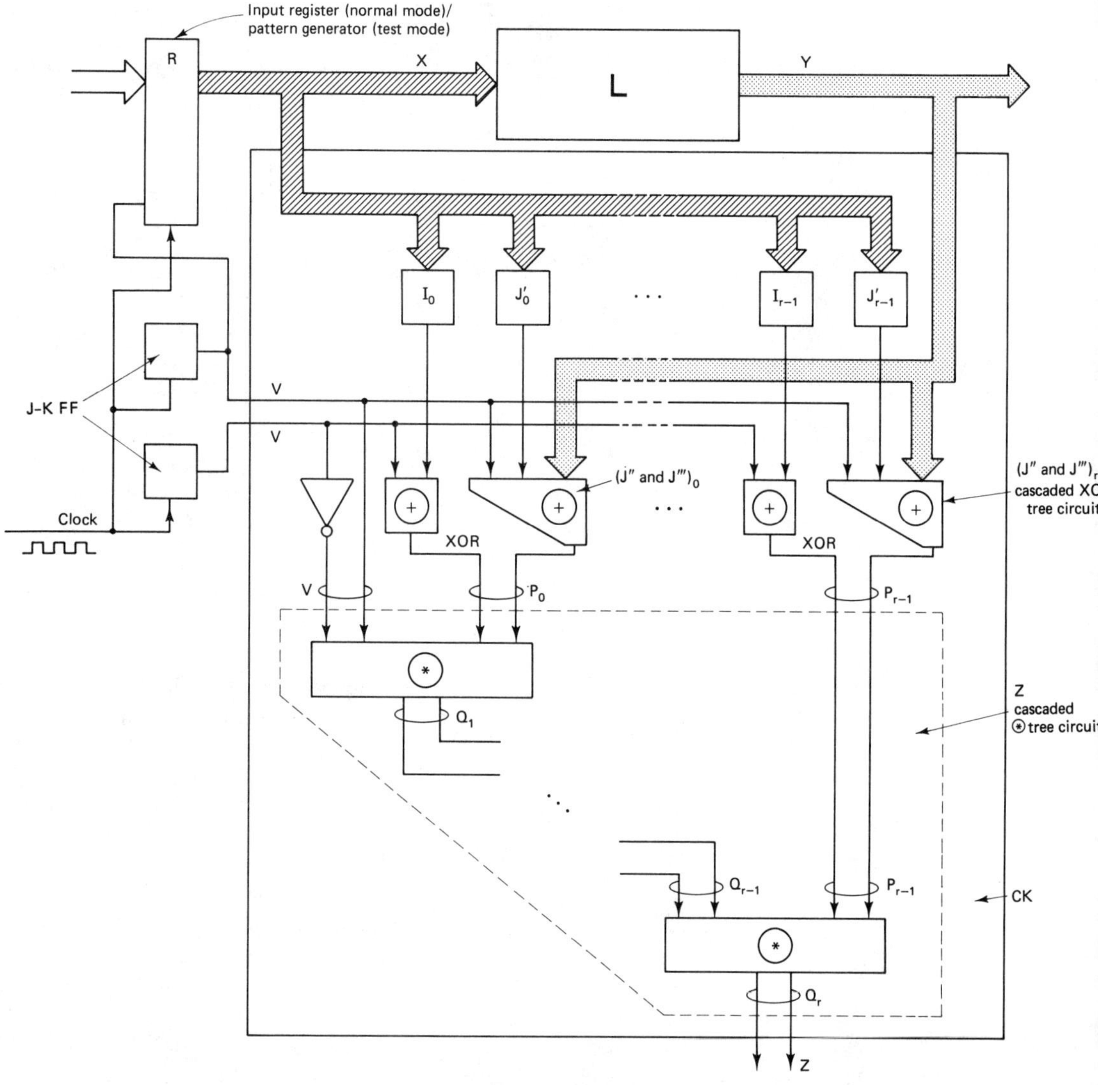

Figure 9.23 Self-testing generalized prediction checker [FUJI 87a]. © 1987 IEEE.

using exclusive-or gates. From Theorem 9-2, if these circuits are also constructed in cascaded-tree structure having input v that can take any value in $\{0, 1\}$ in normal operation, then this cascaded exclusive-or circuit is self-testing for single-faults. Circuit **J**′ has the input X, the same as in circuit **L**.

Circuit **I** is also realized from r subcircuits $\mathbf{I}_0, \mathbf{I}_1, \ldots, \mathbf{I}_{r-1}$, and each subcircuit has the input X, the same as in circuit **L**. The resulting self-testing prediction checker can be shown in Fig. 9.23.

The control input v is generated from a J-K flip-flop, or a toggle flip-flop whose output is inverted with every clock input during concurrent or on-line error detection. Furthermore, the same two flip-flops operate simultaneously with the same clock and are connected one each for circuit **I** and circuit **J**, as shown in Fig. 9.23. The input vector V to circuit **Z** is also produced from the outputs of the flip-flops. With this structure, the checker can detect faults related to the cascaded EX-OR tree circuits, as well as to one of these flip-flops, or input faults to the EX-OR gates. This is because these faults cause at least one **W** in circuit **Z** inputs, where **W** is defined as in Lemma 9-1, which can then be detected according to (2) in Corollary 9-1.

Theorem 9-8. *Circuit* **CK** *in Fig.* 9.23, *is a self-testing checker for single faults if input X can take all patterns.*

Proof. The circuit **CK** shown in Fig. 9.23 is implemented from Equations (9.10) to (9.12). Hence, this circuit is code disjoint from Theorem 9-3. Circuits **I** and **J′** are self-testing for single faults because input X to these circuits can take all patterns from the assumption. It is apparent from Theorem 9.2 that the multi-input EX-OR tree circuit having cascaded structure and one control input v can satisfy the self-testing property for single faults. This is because we can assume that circuit output Y does not have constant value. The cascaded-tree circuit (i.e., circuit **Z**) satisfies conditions (1) and (2) of Theorem 9-3, and therefore it is self-testing. Then, the noncodeword output of circuits **I** and **J** always cause the noncodeword output, that is, **W**, in the cascaded circuit **Z**. Therefore, circuit **CK** is a self-testing checker. Q.E.D.

Applications to built-in testing. On-line error detection can be combined with off-line functional testing of combinational circuits by using the same checker

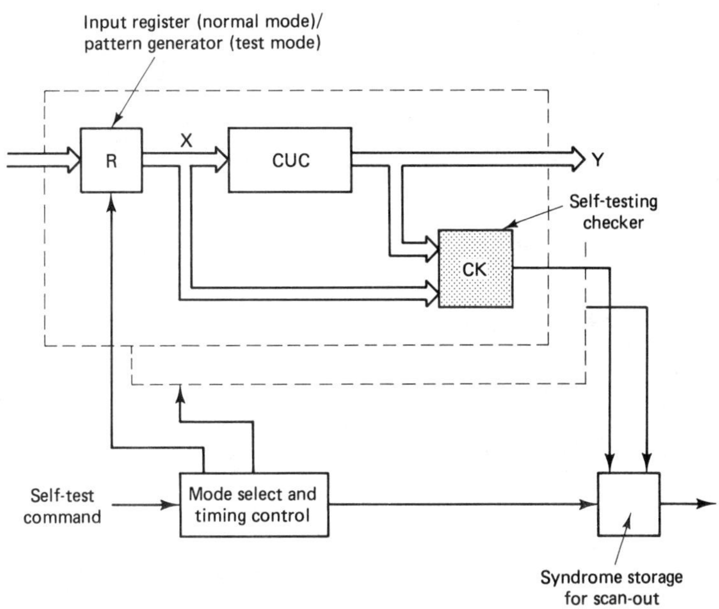

Figure 9.24 Testing scheme using self-testing checker [FUJI 87a]. © 1987 IEEE.

hardware for both purposes [SEDM 79, 80a, KHAK 82a, FUJI 84, FUJI 87a]. This built-in testing method takes advantage of the checker's fault detection capability and eliminates the need for sophisticated test systems and precalculated test patterns or signatures [KONE 80, WILL 82, MACC 85, CART 86]. It also allows testing at on-line operation speeds. In Fig. 9.23, the circuit **R** is an input register in the normal mode and a pattern generator (which generates 2^n patterns for an n-input vector X) in the test mode. One of the J-K flip-flops or toggle flip-flops can be connected to the lowest level of the pattern generator, resulting in an $(n + 1)$-bit pattern generator. The faults in the circuit **L** and the checker **CK** can be detected only when the output of the checker $Z \in \{(0,0)\ (1,1)\}$. It is important in this test scheme that if we use such a self-testing checker, *the faults in the checker itself or in the circuit L can be detected in the test mode as well as in the normal mode*. Fig. 9.24 shows the built-in testing scheme using a self-testing checker.

9.2 SELF-CHECKING PROCESSORS AND MICROPROCESSORS

9.2.1 Self-Checking Processor [SIEW 82, RENN 84]

Original concepts for the design of self-checking computers are presented in [CART 68]. Design methods for TSC system or SFS networks are proposed in [SMIT 78, 83]. Designs for self-checking processors have been applied to practical systems. Some of these are introduced here. Self-checking microprocessors are included in the succeeding subsection.

STAR computer. As a special purpose ultrareliable computer, the Jet Propulsion Lab's self-testing and repair (STAR) computer makes extensive use of the technique of modularity and standby sparing, as well as error detection methods [AVIZ 71]. For example, low-cost arithmetic error detecting codes are used in a data word or an instruction word. Modulo 15 arithmetic checking is especially effective for a byte-organized computer with four-bit bytes. All words are encoded as shown in Fig. 9.25.

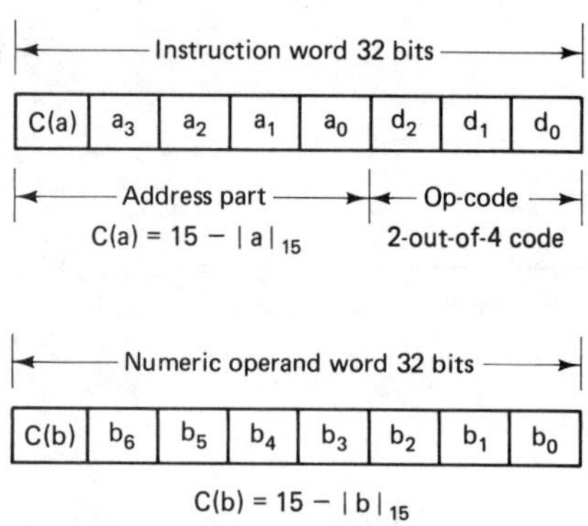

Figure 9.25 STAR Instruction word and operand word format [AVIZ 71]. © 1971 IEEE.

The 32-bit numeric operand word consists of a 28-bit binary number b and a 4-bit check byte $C(b)$. The check byte is a binary number that has the value

$$C(b) = 15 - |b|_{15}$$

where $|b|$ means the modulo-15 residue of b. The 32-bit instruction word consists of a 12-bit operation code and a 20-bit residue-coded address part. The 16-bit address is encoded in the same residue code as the operands. The operation code is divided into three bytes, and each byte is encoded in a 2-out-of-4 code. This code permits each byte to be checked individually.

Electronic switching systems. In electronic switching systems (ESS), self-checking hardware has been integrated into the design to detect faults during normal system operation [TOY 78]. For example, in microprogram control, an efficient nonsystematic check-code (4-out-of-8 code) is applied to the control information in order to detect all multiple unidirectional errors. A TSC 4-out-of-8 checker is designed and adapted.

(4, 2) Concept. An interesting and important concept, the *(4, 2) concept*, is proposed in [KROL 86]. This concept has been applied in the digital telephone exchange system [GEEL 85]. The system consists of four modules. The processor part is quadrupled as compared with the nonredundant computer, in which the memory consists of four parts, each with a word length of half a data word. So the memory hardware is only doubled. The information stored in the memories of the four modules is protected by means of a symbol-error correcting code having additional bit-error correcting capability. This code consists of four 8-bit symbols, two of which are to be regarded as information symbols, while the other two are check symbols. The basic (4, 2)-concept architecture is shown in Fig. 9.26. In this example, we assume a data word length of 16 bits. Each module comprises a complete microprocessor with a 16-bit data-word length and a memory with a word length of 8-bits. The memory contents are protected by a symbol-error correcting code of four 8-bit symbols. Each symbol is stored in a different module. The four processors contain identical information and run synchronously. This system basically tolerates any failures in one of the four modules.

The code adopted is built up from two interleaved codes, both consisting of four symbols of four bits per symbol. The code can correct any single-symbol errors and any double-bit errors even if these bit errors are in different modules. (Double-bit errors and single-symbol errors cannot be corrected simultaneously.) This code was found by means of an exhaustive computer search. The code is given in the following **H** matrix.

$$\mathbf{H} = \begin{bmatrix} \mathbf{T}^7 & \mathbf{T}^{11} & \mathbf{I} & \mathbf{0} \\ \mathbf{T}^{11} & \mathbf{T}^7 & \mathbf{0} & \mathbf{I} \end{bmatrix} \tag{9.13}$$

where $\mathbf{T}$ is a companion matrix of α, a root of the primitive polynomial $\mathbf{g}(x) = x^4 + x + 1$ (see Section 5.1).

Based on this concept, the extended work on combined symbol-and-bit error control codes is shown in [GILS 86a, 86b, 87].

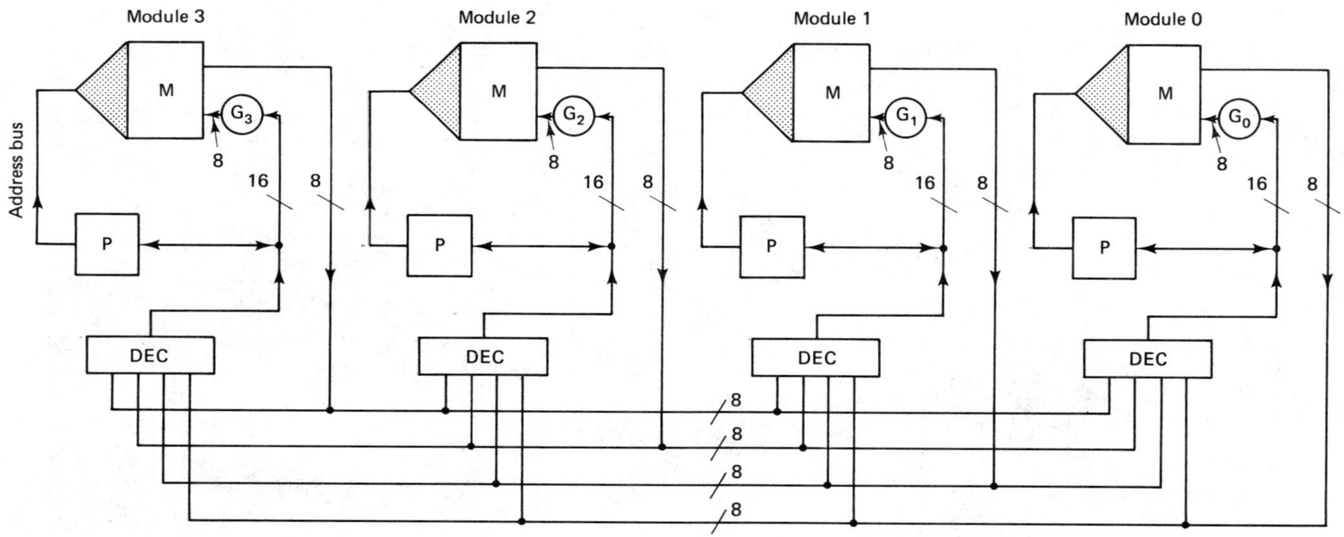

P: Processor
M: Memory
DEC: Decoder of the (4, 2) symbol-error correcting code
G_i: Encoder of the error correcting code

Figure 9.26 The (4, 2) concept [KROL 86]. © 1986 IEEE.

This concept can generally be expanded to an (n, k) concept, in which (n, k) symbol-error correcting code is used [KROL 86]. In the (n, k) concept the processor data are encoded into an $(n, 1)$ symbol-error correcting code, i.e., an n-fold repetition code; however, the memory data are encoded into an (n, k) symbol-error correcting code. Note that the symbol size of the (n, k) code is k times smaller than the symbol size of the $(n, 1)$ code. The applied (n, k) symbol-error correcting code is capable of correcting up to $(n - k)/2$ randomly failing symbols and requires a factor of $(n - k)/k$ additional memory hardware.

General-purpose computer. Carter [CART 77] has studied the cost-effectiveness of self-checking computer designs, with the IBM S/360 general-purpose computer as a target. The target machine would be constructed with a small number (say 10) of LSI chip types. Prior to design, the following objectives were settled and achieved:

1. To make the processing unit (PU) design completely checkable and self-testing, and to investigate hardware trade-off.
2. To modify the processing unit to achieve a retry capability without speed degradation and without significant additional hardware.

The conclusions are that complete checking of a PU is relatively inexpensive (35% additional hardware over the unchecked PU and 6.5% over a S/360-checked PU, with only one additional new chip type) and that simple instruction retry can be achieved with one additional chip and with no apparent speed degradation.

Duplicate VLSI processor. Sedmak [SEDM 80b] also studied the fault-tolerance of a general-purpose computer utilizing very large-scale integration. A major method of achieving fault-tolerance is by internal redundancy using *duplicate complementary logic*. This kind of complementary duplication is used in the VLSI chips shown in Figs. 9.27 and 9.28. From these figures it is easy to see that for a given combination logic element in the functional portion, the signals into and out of the gate will be of polarities opposite to those of the complementary portion. This technique serves two purposes. First, it eliminates a problem associated with applying the same mask or cell type twice internally. The problem is that failures (design, process, and wearout) undetected by the comparators could occur in noncomplementary duplication where a mask or cell fault might materialize in both the functional and duplicate circuits and thus create an identical failure state. Second, the design with complementary duplication will be much less susceptible to bridging faults than noncomplementary duplication. This is because there will be far fewer occurrences of long nets of metalization with the same Boolean function and the same polarity signal, which if bridged might result in an undetected error should a subsequent failure occur.

Each of the code checkers and comparators is implemented using a self-checking design approach. The self-checking comparators shown in Figs. 9.5 and 9.6 are extensively used.

As a result of the cost effectiveness of the design, the logic overhead that consists of duplicate complementary gates, comparators, and other fault detection

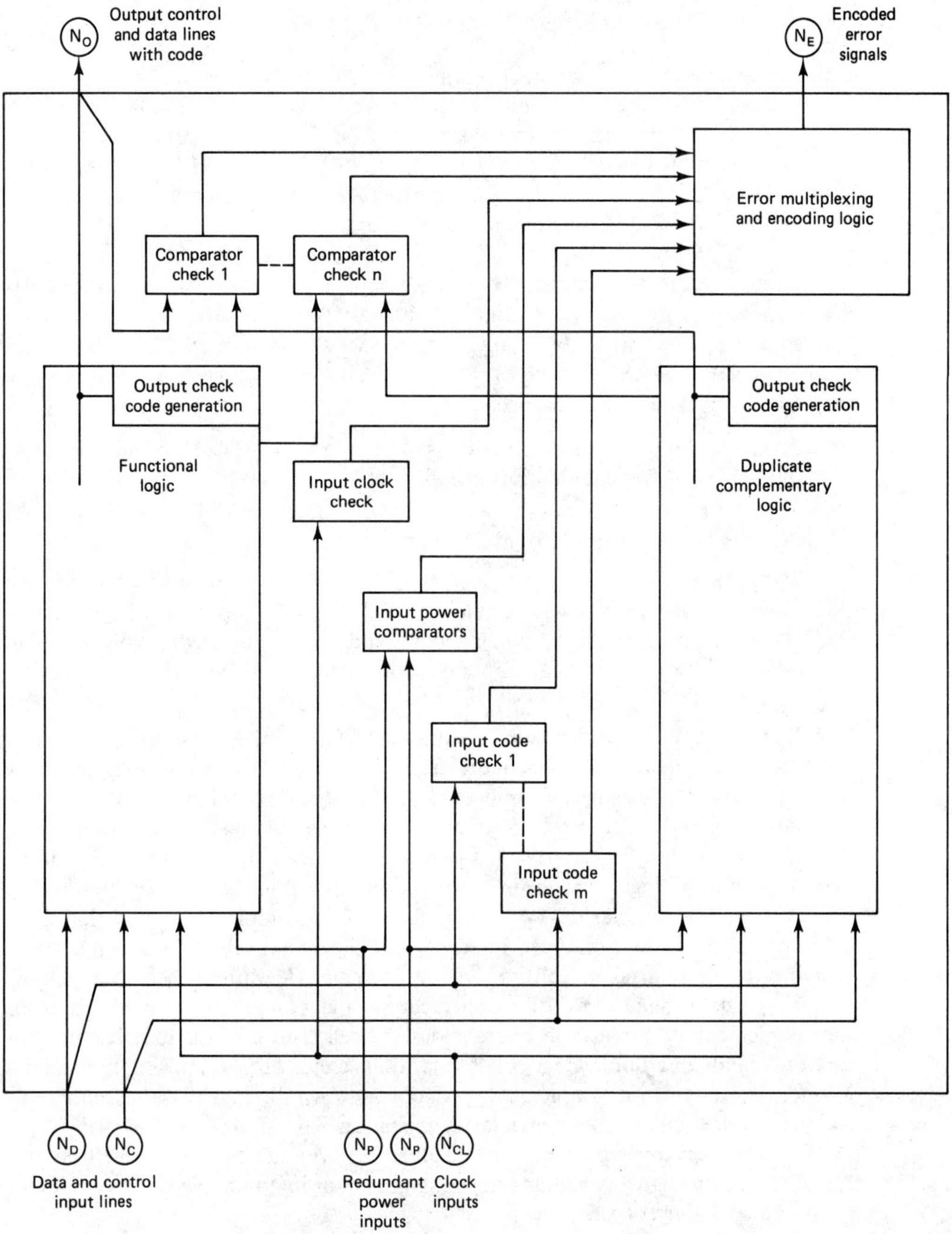

Figure 9.27 Generalized VLSI chip [SEDM 80b]. © 1980 IEEE.

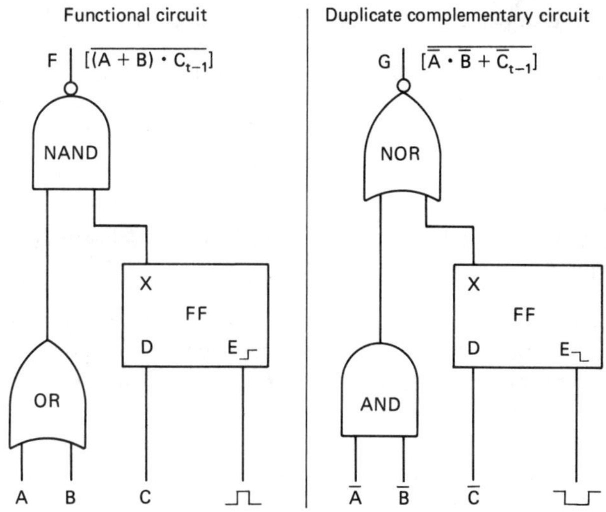

Truth table

Inputs			Outputs	
A_t	B_t	C_{t-1}	F_t	G_t
L	L	L	H	L
L	L	H	H	L
L	H	L	H	L
L	H	H	L	H
H	L	L	H	L
H	L	H	L	H
H	H	L	H	L
H	H	H	L	H

Symbol	Meaning
–	NOT
·	Logical AND
+	Logical INCLUSIVE OR
subscript t	Time period t
subscript t−1	Time period t−1
E (low-to-high clock edge)	Enable on low to high transition of clock
E (high-to-low clock edge)	Enable on high to low transition of clock

Figure 9.28 Example of functional versus duplicate complementary circuits [SEDM 80b]. © 1980 IEEE.

circuits comprises approximately 55% of the total gates in the CPU. As compared to the conventionally checked VLSI machine, the increase in chip count is only 5.5%. (A conventionally checked VLSI machine is assumed to have parity code for memories and complete checking for single faults in data paths, but no fault detection in the control logic.)

9.2.2 Self-Checking Microprocessor

Microprocessors have been extensively used in digital systems. They are also sometimes used in ultrareliable process controls for industry and medicine. A considerable body of work on a self-checking version of the commercial microprocessors or microprogram control unit has been done, which can be found in [DISP 81, TSAO 82, WONG 83, HALB 84, NICO 85a, NANY 85b, YEN 87].

The techniques adopted commonly are classified as follows:

1. Duplication of circuits (such as a control circuit (or ALU)) and an output comparison check using a self-checking comparator (or self-checking two-rail code checker).
2. Coding for control signals (encoded in two-rail codes, or Berger codes) and for address and data signals (encoded in simple parity codes, or m-out-of-n codes).
3. Extensive use of PLA's together with the self-checking techniques covered in Section 8.2.

A diagram of a VLSI self-checking microprocessor is given in Fig. 9.29 [DISP 81]. The hardware overhead in these self-checking microprocessors is 30% to 60% greater as compared to those without self-checking capability.

We will study an SFS microprocessor whose target architecture is Intel's i8080 8-bit microprocessor [NANY 85b]. This design is based on Theorem 8-3 relating to the error-secure/error-propagating (ES/EP) concepts (Definitions 8-10, 8-11). This new design for the SFS processors requires only a few TSC checkers (i.e., four checkers at embedded interfaces) and no duplicated subsystems except a few registers. Therefore, a hardware overhead of only 38% more gates is required for the SFS version, as compared with the non-SFS version, of the i8080.

The design approach includes the following features.

1. A complete set of functional building blocks for SFS processors has been defined, and the ES and EP properties for all the interfaces of each block have been investigated. Each section of the processor consists of only these building blocks. This feature facilitates the verification of the SFS property in each section and drastically reduces the number of TSC checkers required for the SFS processor as a whole.

2. Every interface of the blocks is encoded in an *unordered code* that detects unidirectional errors. For cost-effectiveness, the Berger code is used for the register section and the microprogram section, and the two-rail code is used for the ALU section, the timing controller and the external control signals.

3. The PLA's, one of the building blocks in the SFS design, are used extensively for implementing SFS combinational and sequential circuits. The use of an inverter-free PLA for the microprogram control storage, in particular, significantly reduces the hardware overhead requirement for the SFS capability.

4. No subsystems are duplicated, except for registers that hold two-rail encoded data.

The modeled faults in the processor are

1. the single stuck-at faults in gate outputs,
2. the single stuck-at line faults, the single crosspoint faults, and the bridging faults between adjacent lines in PLA's,
3. the single-bit slice faults in registers, and
4. the unidirectional faults in buses.

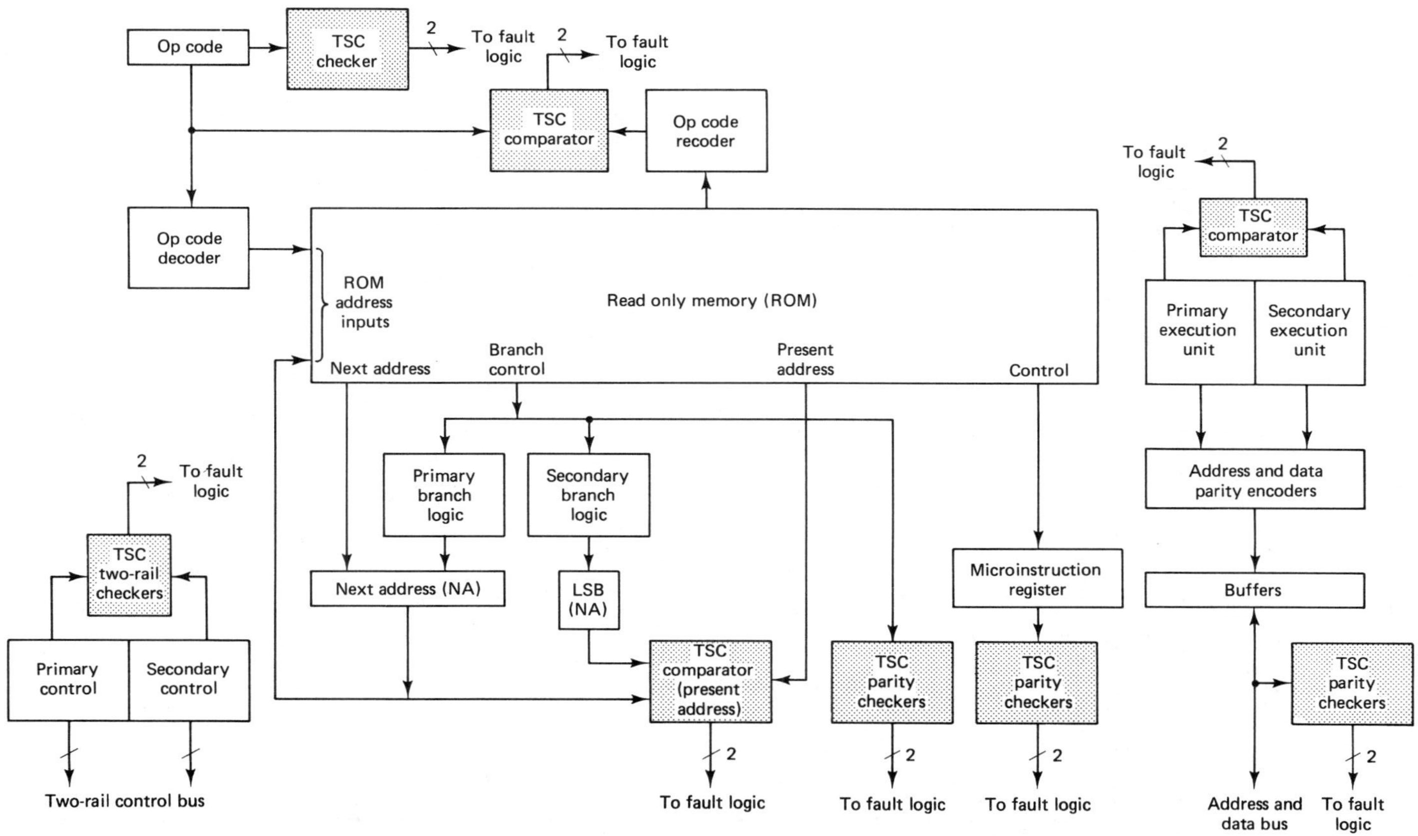

Figure 9.29 An example of a self-checking microprocessor [DISP 81]. © 1981 IEEE.

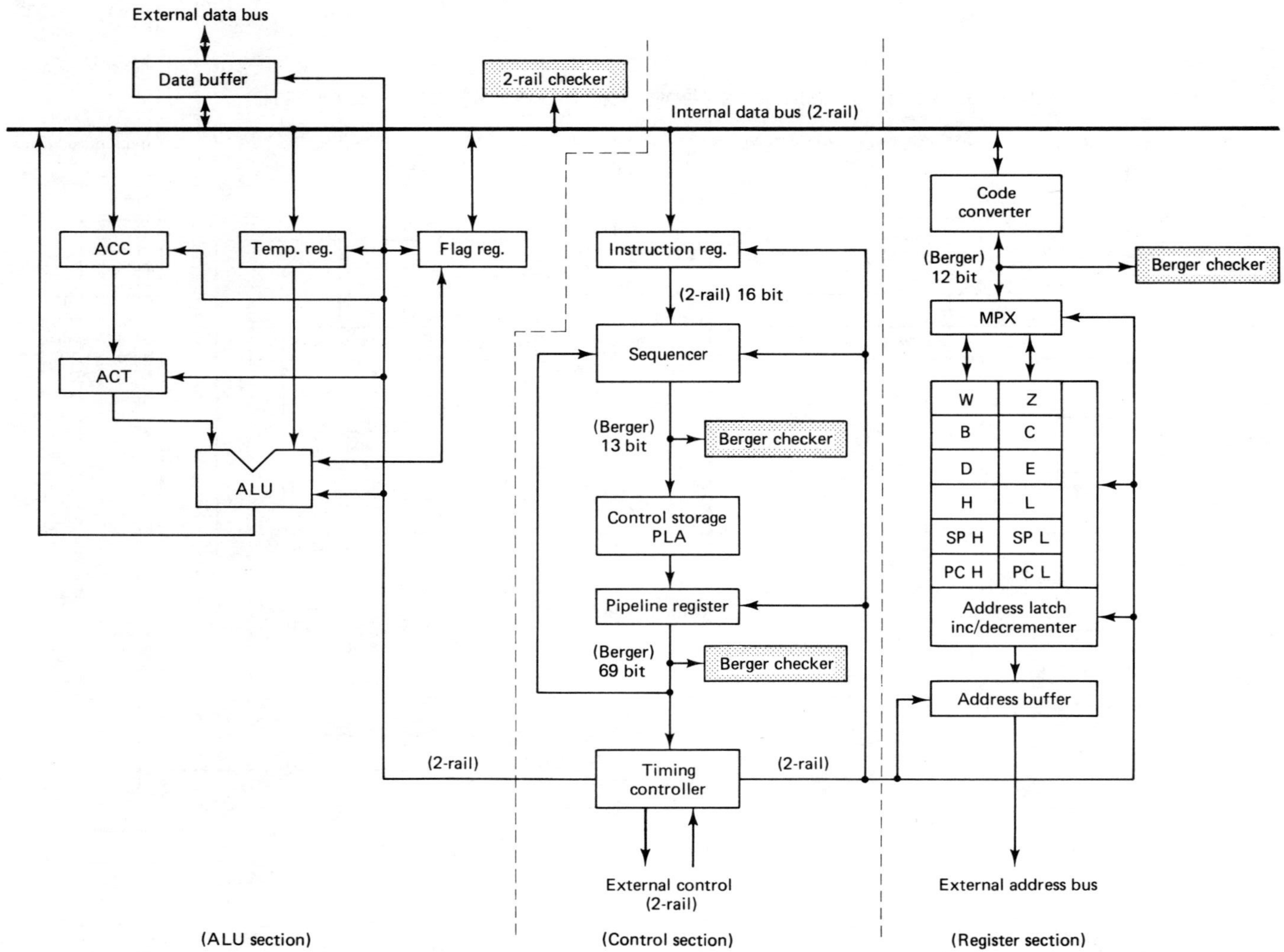

Figure 9.30 SFS processor organization [NANY 85b]. © 1985 IEEE.

Some new design techniques are applied to every building block in order to satisfy the error-secure (ES) and error-propagating (EP) properties at each interface. A unique design is utilized for a sequential circuit with its next-state function d and output function w such that for unidirectional faults in d and w the circuit is SFS if the outputs of w are encoded in an unordered code and d and w are implemented with inverter-free circuits. This brings a significant advantage to the practical design of complex SFS systems [NANY 87]. For further details, refer to [NANY 85b].

The overall organization of the SFS processor is shown in Fig. 9.30. It consists basically of an ALU section, a control section, a register section, and an internal data bus. Four TSC checkers are used as indicated.

9.3 ERROR MASKING FOR YIELD IMPROVEMENT

In producing VLSI chips, it is very important for manufacturers to consider the *production yield* as a factor in determining their cost, function, and size. The production yield is defined as the number of good chips divided by the expected number of chips. The production yield can be expected to be improved by the *restoring function* [MANG 82, 84a, 84b, CARL 86]. In memory VLSI's, some defect-tolerant techniques (e.g., *N-modular redundancy*, *m-out-of-n modular redundancy* and *address reallocation*) have been proposed and practically applied (see Section 4.3.2). But since logic circuits are generally not in regular structure and have many varieties of functions, not much work has been done on *defect tolerance* in logic systems. Several techniques have been proposed for gate-level fault masking. Among these are Von Neumann's designs for circuits with interspersed *restoring organs* [NEUM 56], *quadded logic* [TRYO 62], and *interwoven logic* [PIER 65]. Recent work has dealt with the reconfigurable processor arrays, or *systolic arrays* based on the m-out-of-n redundancy techniques [FINN 77, KORE 81, LEIG 82, SAMI 83, 86, KART 83, 84, KAWA 86, TSUD 87, SHIM 87, FUJI 87b, 87c, YAMA 87a, HARD 88]. Note that defect-tolerant techniques are also useful and available for fault-tolerance during on-line operation modes [KORE 86].

Here, we present a novel approach to defect-tolerant and fault-tolerant logic by using an error correcting code [TAKE 82]. The design calls for a gate-function module, called a *fault-tolerant gate* (*FTG*), which consists of a gate formed from conventional gates; the reliability of the gate-function module is higher than that of a single gate. In this FTG, correct logical operations are performed, even if inputs have some errors. Since redundancy is applied to the input, input errors are always masked, and therefore FTG can produce correct output.

The concept of the FTG is best explained by an example. Figure 9.31 shows an example of a two-input NOR-FTG. We consider the single-error correction for FTG's. In order to correct single errors, it is apparent that at least three bits—one bit for information and two bits for check—are necessary. Thus the input and output are codewords in a (3, 1) code. The generator polynomial $\mathbf{g}(x) = x^2 + x + 1$ is used to determine the check bits from the information bit. This generator polynomial gives us the advantage that the same circuit as the one that generates the

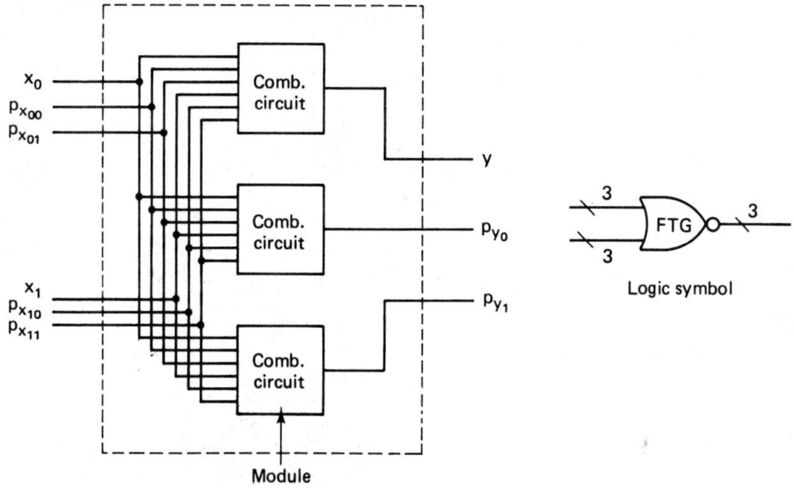

Figure 9.31 Basic structure of a two-input NOR fault-tolerant gate (FTG) and its logic symbol [TAKE 82]. © 1982 IEEE.

output information bit can be used for check-bit generation. This will be shown later in Equations (9.14) and (9.15).

A logic diagram of a two-input NOR-FTG and its mode of error correction are shown in Fig. 9.31 and Table 9.4, respectively. By using the generator polynomial $\mathbf{g}(x) = x^2 + x + 1$, the vectors (0 0 0) and (1 1 1) become codewords. In FTG's, a correct output can be produced even if each vector includes up to one erroneous bit. Hence, the input/output vectors have the following words.

$$\left.\begin{array}{l}(\textcircled{1}\ \ 0\ \ 0)\\(0\ \ \textcircled{1}\ \ 0)\\(0\ \ 0\ \ \textcircled{1})\end{array}\right\}\quad \text{These words are regarded as a } (0\ \ 0\ \ 0) \text{ vector}$$

$$\left.\begin{array}{l}(\textcircled{0}\ \ 1\ \ 1)\\(1\ \ \textcircled{0}\ \ 1)\\(1\ \ 1\ \ \textcircled{0})\end{array}\right\}\quad \text{These words are regarded as a } (1\ \ 1\ \ 1) \text{ vector}$$

Note that "○" designates an erroneous bit. Even if any combination of these six input vectors, each including one erroneous bit, is applied to an FTG, the FTG will produce a correct output vector. By using Table 9.4, the output of the two-input NOR-FTG can be expressed as follows.

$$y = p_{y_0} = p_{y_1} \tag{9.14}$$

$$y = (\bar{x}_0\bar{p}_{x_{00}} + \bar{x}_0\bar{p}_{x_{01}} + \bar{p}_{x_{00}}\bar{p}_{x_{01}})(\bar{x}_1\bar{p}_{x_{10}} + \bar{x}_1\bar{p}_{x_{11}} + \bar{p}_{x_{10}}\bar{p}_{x_{11}}) \tag{9.15}$$

In order to reduce the number of gates required to realize the FTG, Equation (9.15)

TABLE 9.4 OUTPUT (y, p_{y_0}, p_{y_1}) OF A TWO-INPUT NOR-FTG [TAKE 82]

$x_0 P_{x_{00}} P_{x_{01}}$ \ $x_1 P_{x_{10}} P_{x_{11}}$	[0 0 0]	0 0 (1)	(0) 1 1	0 (1) 0	1 1 (0)	[1 1 1]	1 (0) 1	(1) 0 0
[0 0 0]	1 1 1	1 1 1	0 0 0	1 1 1	0 0 0	0 0 0	0 0 0	1 1 1
0 0 (1)	1 1 1	1 1 1	0 0 0	1 1 1	0 0 0	0 0 0	0 0 0	1 1 1
(0) 1 1	0 0 0	0 0 0	0 0 0	0 0 0	0 0 0	0 0 0	0 0 0	0 0 0
0 (1) 0	1 1 1	1 1 1	0 0 0	1 1 1	0 0 0	0 0 0	0 0 0	1 1 1
1 1 (0)	0 0 0	0 0 0	0 0 0	0 0 0	0 0 0	0 0 0	0 0 0	0 0 0
[1 1 1]	0 0 0	0 0 0	0 0 0	0 0 0	0 0 0	0 0 0	0 0 0	0 0 0
1 (0) 1	0 0 0	0 0 0	0 0 0	0 0 0	0 0 0	0 0 0	0 0 0	0 0 0
(1) 0 0	1 1 1	1 1 1	0 0 0	1 1 1	0 0 0	0 0 0	0 0 0	1 1 1

1. x_0 and x_1 are input information bits, and $p_{x_{00}}, p_{x_{01}}$ are check bits for x_0, and $p_{x_{10}}, p_{x_{11}}$ are check bits for x_1.
2. y is output information bit, and p_{y_0}, p_{y_1} are check bits for y.
3. '○' means error bit.
4. □ indicates codewords.

is transformed into

$$y = (\bar{x}_0 + \bar{p}_{x_{00}})(\bar{x}_0 + \bar{p}_{x_{01}})(\bar{p}_{x_{00}} + \bar{p}_{x_{01}}) \\ \times (\bar{x}_1 + \bar{p}_{x_{10}})(\bar{x}_1 + \bar{p}_{x_{11}})(\bar{p}_{x_{10}} + \bar{p}_{x_{11}})$$

Each subcircuit that produces an element of an output vector will be called a

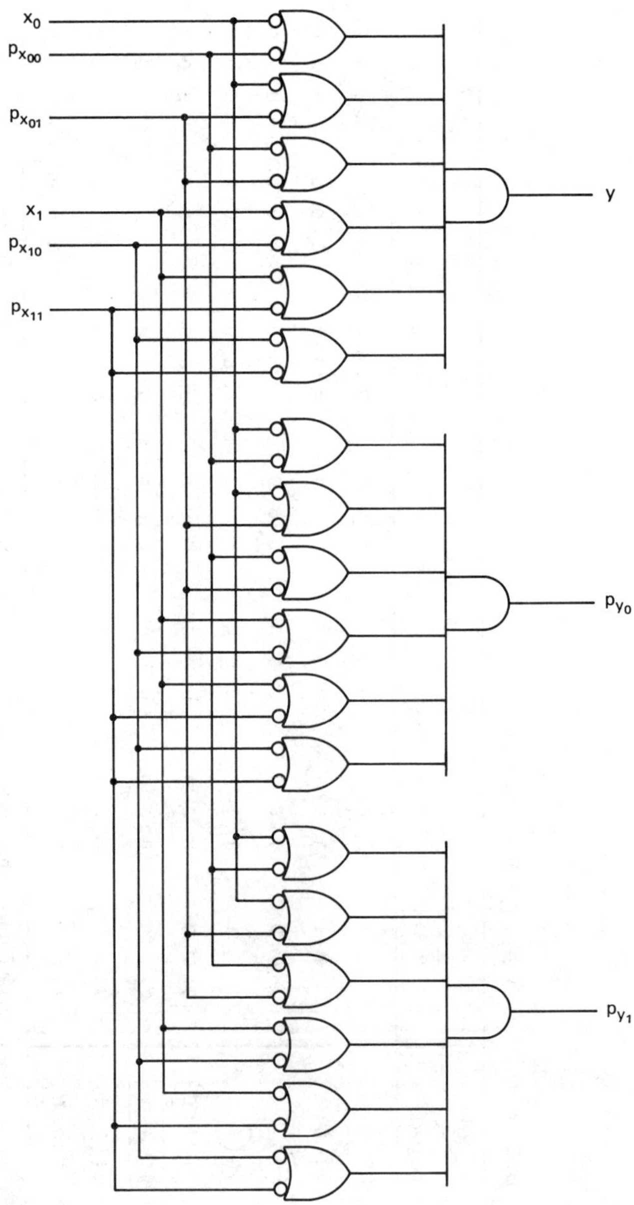

Figure 9.32 Two-input NOR-FTG [TAKE 82]. © 1982 IEEE.

TABLE 9.5 NUMBER OF GATES FOR FTG's (GATE)

2-input AND-FTG	2-input OR-FTG	NOT-FTG	2-input NAND-FTG	2-input NOR-FTG	2-input EX-OR-FTG
21	21	12	21	21	33

module. As in Fig. 9.31, an FTG is composed of three identical modules. The two-input NOR-FTG is shown in Fig. 9.32. If the two-input NOR-FTG is implemented in MOS transistors, a hardware redundancy of a factor of 13 relative to the nonredundant NOR gate is needed (NOR-FTG: 39 transistors; nonredundant NOR gate: 3 transistors). For the FTG shown in Fig. 9.32, a correct NOR function output can be produced even if there is up to one error in each of the inputs $(x_0, p_{x_{00}}, p_{x_{01}})$ and $(x_1, p_{x_{10}}, p_{x_{11}})$. If there are faults or defects in one of the modules, only one bit error is produced in the output vector (y_0, p_{y_0}, p_{y_1}), and this single-error output is masked in the next FTG's.

Table 9.5 shows the number of gates required for realizing the FTGs.

Next, we will estimate the yield improvement of the FTG's. As mentioned before, in order to realize NOR logic circuits by using two-input NOR-FTG's, a hardware redundancy of a factor of 13 is needed. That is, the area of a chip consisting of FTGs is 13 times that of a chip consisting of nonredundant gates. Since an FTG having a self-restoring function can correct the faults or ignore the defects occurring on a wafer, it does not follow that the increasing area of a chip exponentially reduces the yield of the chip. The yield of chips consisting of FTGs

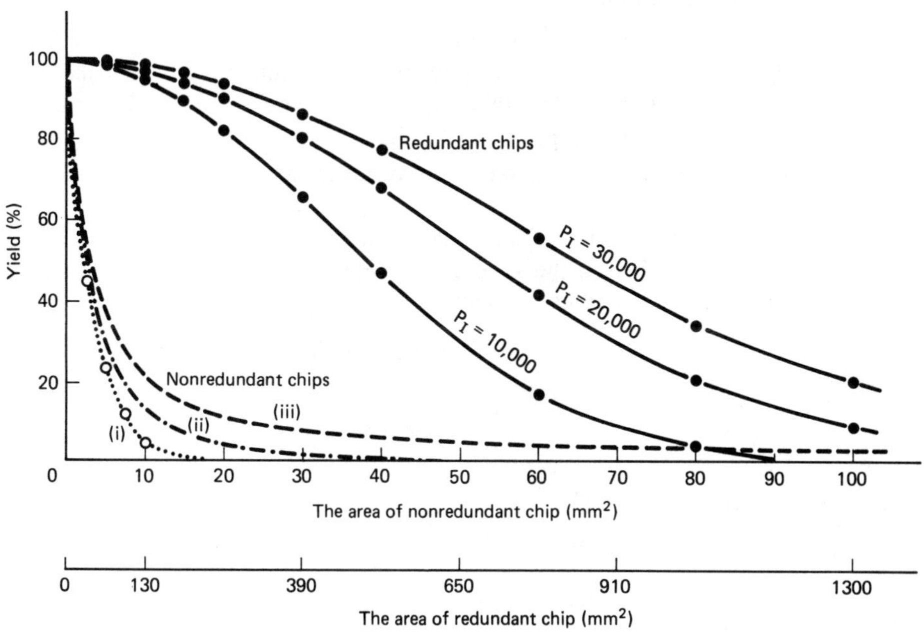

Figure 9.33 Yield vs. chip area (P_D = 30) [TAKE 82]. © 1982 IEEE.

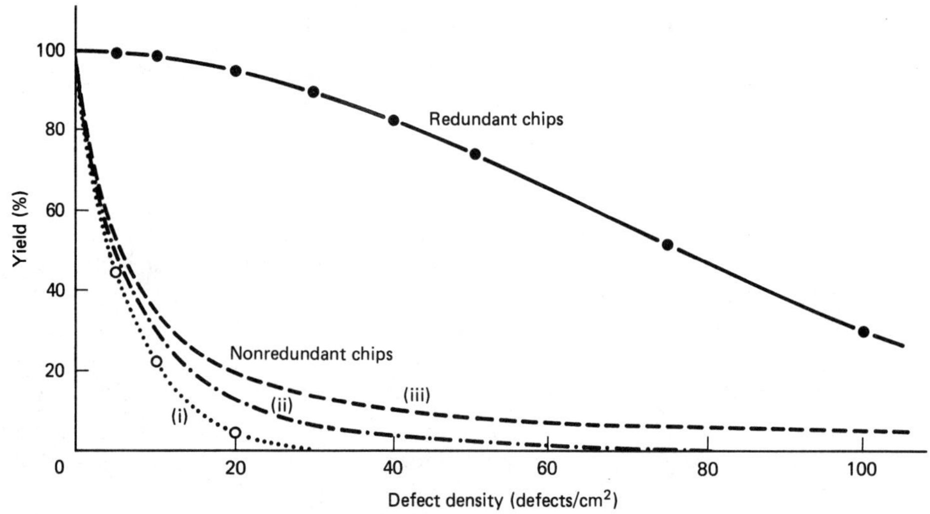

Figure 9.34 Yield vs. defect density ($P_A = 100$, $P_I = 10{,}000$, $P_R = 0.2$) [TAKE 82].

and containing defects on a wafer could be higher. Let us call a chip consisting of normal gates a nonredundant chip and a chip consisting of FTGs a redundant chip.

In order to estimate the yield improvement, the following is assumed.

1. The defects are uniformly distributed.
2. A defect causes a failure of a single transistor.
3. A chip consists of NOR gates in a nonredundant chip and NOR-FTG's in a redundant chip. The function of a redundant chip is the same as that of a nonredundant chip.
4. A wafer area of redundant chips is the same as that of nonredundant chips.

The simulation results are shown in Figs. 9.33 and 9.34.

In these figures, the yield Y of nonredundant chips is evaluated according to three different functions as follows [TAKE 82].

D_m: maximum defect density
A: chip area
D: average defect density

(i) $Y = e^{-AD}$

(ii) $Y = (1 + \frac{AD}{3})^{-3}$

(iii) $Y = (-2)\frac{(1 - e^{-AD_m} - AD_m)}{(AD_m)^2}$

The following parameters are introduced to obtain the yield.

P_A: the area of one transistor (μm^2)

P_D: the average defect density (defects/cm^2)

P_I: the integration degree (gates/chip or FTG's/chip)

P_R: the ratio of area required for wires to that required for transistors

From these results, the yield of redundant chips is superior to that of nonredundant chips.

EXERCISES

9.1. Obtain the test patterns sufficient to test the self-checking (odd) parity checker shown in Fig. 9.1.

9.2. Prove Theorem 9-1.

9.3. Prove Theorem 9-2.

9.4. Design the complementary duplication checker for the circuit **L** shown in Equation (8.21). Also show the circuit designed in a complementary form of **L**.

9.5. Verify that the two-rail code checker of Fig. 9.5 is self-testing for all unidirectional multiple faults.

9.6. Obtain the sufficient test patterns for the following two-rail code checker.

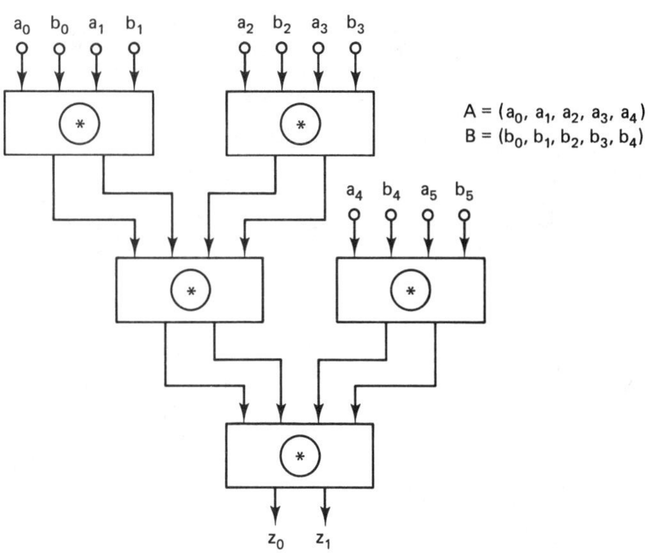

9.7. Verify the code disjointness of a m-out-of-$2m$ code checker expressed by the equations z_0 and z_1 on p. 467.

9.8. Construct the self-testing 4-out-of-8 code checker and also obtain the test words of this checker.

9.9. Construct the self-testing 3-out-of-7 code checker having two gate levels.

9.10. Construct the self-testing 3-out-of-8 and 3-out-of-9 code checkers and obtain the number of test words in each checker.

9.11. Demonstrate that the circuit of Fig. 9.14 is self-testing.

9.12. Design the self-testing checker for a Berger code with length $k = 4,\ n = 7$.

9.13. Design the self-testing checker for Berger code with $k = 7$, based on the code partitioning shown in Table 9.3.

9.14. Design a self-testing checker that is capable of checking whether greater than or equal to k input variables in n inputs have 1.

9.15. Design the GPC's with the following prediction function and **H** matrix for the four-input, three-output combinational circuit shown in Equation (8.21).

(a) Prediction function: $\mathbf{K} \cdot U$ = simple parity function of inputs

$$\mathbf{K} = \begin{bmatrix} 0110100010000000 \\ 0110100010000000 \\ 0110100010000000 \end{bmatrix}$$

$$\mathbf{H} = [1 \quad 1 \quad 1]$$

(b) Prediction function: $\mathbf{K} \cdot U$ = OR function of inputs

$$\mathbf{K} = \begin{bmatrix} 0111111111111111 \\ 0111111111111111 \\ 0111111111111111 \end{bmatrix}$$

$$\mathbf{H} = [1 \quad 1 \quad 1]$$

9.16. Design the GPC for the four-input, six-output decoding circuit (shown on p. 509) expressed by the following matrix **A** under the condition $\mathbf{K} = \mathbf{A}$ and $\mathbf{H} = \begin{bmatrix} 111000 \\ 000111 \end{bmatrix}$.

$$\mathbf{A} = \begin{bmatrix} 0110110111101011 \\ 0001101101010010 \\ 0001000100111110 \\ 1001011110110100 \\ 1100000000000011 \\ 0101010100100010 \end{bmatrix}$$

Next, make this GPC self-testing.

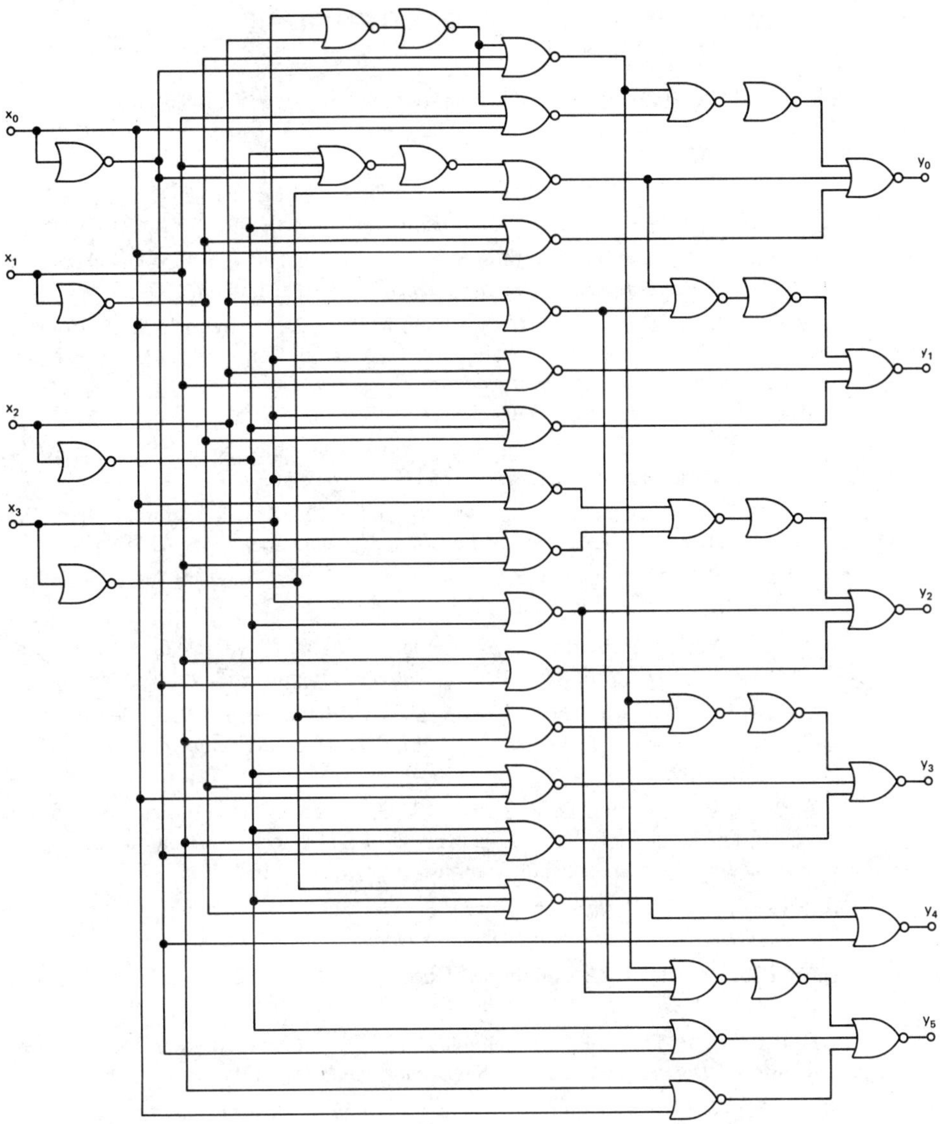

9.17. Verify that the code shown in Equation (9.13) corrects any single-symbol errors and any double-bit errors. (Note that double-bit errors and single-symbol errors cannot be corrected simultaneously.) Also verify that this code corrects any single-bit errors in the presence of a symbol erasure.

9.18. Construct the NOT-FTG, two-input AND-FTG, and two-input EX-OR-FTG.

REFERENCES

[ANDE 71] D. A. Anderson. "Design of Self-Checking Digital Networks Using Coding Techniques." Coordinated Science Labs, Rep. R-527. Champaign: University of Illinois, October 1971.

[ANDE 73] D. A. Anderson and G. Metze. "Design of Totally Self-Checking Check Circuits for m-Out-of-n Codes." *IEEE Transactions on Computers* C-22 (March 1973): 263–69.

[ASHJ 77] M. J. Ashjaee and S. M. Reddy. "On Totally Self-Checking Checkers for Separable Codes." *IEEE Transactions on Computers* C-26 (August 1977): 737–44.

[AVIZ 71] A. Avizienis, G. C. Gilley, F. P. Mathur, D. A. Rennels, J. A. Rohr, and D. K. Rubin. "The STAR (Self-Testing and Repairing) Computer: An Investigation of the Theory and Practice of Fault-Tolerant Computer Design." *IEEE Transactions on Computers* C-20 (November 1971): 1312–21.

[BOSE 84a] B. Bose and D. J. Lin. "PLA Implementation of k-Out-of-n Code TSC Checker." *IEEE Transactions on Computers* C-33 (June 1984): 583–88.

[BOSS 70b] D. C. Bossen, D. L. Ostapko, and A. M. Patel. "Optimum Test Patterns for Parity Networks." *Proceedings of Fall Joint Comput. Conference* AFIPS (1970): 63–68.

[CARL 86] R. O. Carlson and C. A. Neugebauer. "Future Trends in Wafer Scale Integration." *Proceedings of the IEEE* 74 (December 1986): 1741–52.

[CART 68] W. C. Carter and P. R. Schneider. "Design of Dynamically Checked Computers." *Proceedings in IFIPS 68, Edinburgh, Scotland, August 1968*, vol. 2, 878–83.

[CART 70] W. C. Carter, D. C. Jessep, and A. Wadia. "Error-Free Decoding for Failure-Tolerant Memories." *Proceedings of IEEE International Computer Group Conference* (June 1970): 229–39.

[CART 77] W. C. Carter, G. R. Putzolu, A. B. Wadia, W. G. Bouricius, D. C. Jessep, E. P. Hsieh, and C. J. Tan. "Cost Effectiveness of Self-Checking Computer Design." *Dig., 7th Annual Int. Symposium Fault-Tolerant Comput.* (June 1977): 117–23.

[CART 86] W. C. Carter. "Improved Parallel Signature Checker/Analyzers." *Dig., 16th Annual Int. Symposium Fault-Tolerant Comput.* (June 1986): 416–21.

[DAVI 78a] R. David. "A Totally Self-Checking 1-Out-of-3 Checker." *IEEE Transactions on Computers* C-27 (June 1978): 570–72.

[DISP 81] C. P. Disparte. "A Self-Checking VLSI Microprocessor for Electronic Engine Control." *Dig. 11th Annual Int. Symposium Fault-Tolerant Comput.* (June 1981): 253.

[EFST 83] C. Efstathiou and C. Halatsis. "Modular Realization of Totally Self-Checking Checkers for m-Out-of-n Codes." *Dig., 13th Annual Int. Symposium Fault-Tolerant Comput.* (June 1983): 154–61.

[FINN 77] C. A. Finnila and H. H. Love, Jr. "The Associative Linear Array Processor." *IEEE Transactions on Computers* C-26 (February 1977): 112–25.

[FUJI 84] E. Fujiwara, N. Mutoh, and K. Matsuoka. "A Self-Testing Group-Parity Prediction Checker and Its Use for Built-In Testing." *IEEE Transactions on Computers* C-33 (June 1984): 578–83.

[FUJI 87a] E. Fujiwara, and K. Matsuoka. "A Self-Checking Generalized Prediction Checker and Its Use for Built-In Testing." *IEEE Transactions on Computers* C-36 (January 1987): 86–93. (Also shown in *Dig., 15th Annual Int. Symposium Fault-Tolerant Comput.* (June 1985): 384–89.)

[FUJI 87b] E. Fujiwara and K. Matsuoka. "Fault-Tolerant k-Out-of-n Logic Unit Networks" (in Japanese). *Transactions of the IECE Japan* J70-D (September 1987): 1791–1800.

[FUJI 87c] E. Fujiwara and K. Matsuoka. "A Hardware Implementation of Permuter" (in Japanese). *Transactions of the IECE Japan* J70-D (October 1987): 1995–98.

[GAIT 83] N. Gaitanis and C. Halatsis. "A New Design Method for m-Out-of-n TSC Checkers." *IEEE Transactions on Computers* C-32 (March 1983): 273–83.

[GAIT 84] N. Gaitanis. "Totally Self-Checking Checkers for Low Cost Arithmetic Codes." *Dig., 14th Annual Int. Symposium Fault-Tolerant Comput.* (June 1984): 260–64.

[GEEL 85] M. B. Geelhoed and M. J. Jordan. "SOPHO S2500, The Heigh Range Communication Switch." *Philips Telecommunication Review* 43, no. 2 (June 1985): 92–113.

[GILS 86a] W. J. van Gils. "An Error-Control Coding System for Storage of 16-bit Words in Memory Arrays Composed of Three 9-bit Wide Units." *Philips Journal Research* 41 (1986): 391–9.

[GILS 86b] W. J. van Gils. "A Triple Modular Redundancy Technique Providing Multiple-Bit Error Protection Without Using Extra Redundancy." *IEEE Transactions on Computers* C-35 (July 1986): 623–31.

[GILS 87] W. J. van Gils and J.-P. Boly. "On Combined Symbol-and-Bit Error-Control [4, 2] Codes over $\{0,1\}^8$ To be Used in the (4, 2) Concept Fault-Tolerant Computer." *IEEE Transactions on Information Theory* IT-33 (November 1987): 911–7.

[GOLA 84] P. Golan. "Design of Totally Self-Checking Checker for 1-Out-of-3 Code." *IEEE Transactions on Computers* C-33 (March 1984): 285.

[HALA 83] C. Halatsis, N. Gaitanis, and M. Sigala. "Fast and Efficient Totally Self-Checking Checkers for m-Out-of-$(2m \pm 1)$ Codes." *IEEE Transactions on Computers* C-32 (May 1983): 507–11.

[HALB 84] M. P. Halbert and S. M. Bose. "Design Approach for a VLSI Self-Checking MIL-STD-1750A Microprocessor." *Dig., 14th Annual Int. Symposium Fault-Tolerant Comput.* (June 1984): 254–59.

[HARD 88] J. C. Harden and N. R. Strader II. "Architecture Yield Optimization for WSI." *IEEE Transactions on Computers* C-37 (January 1988): 88–110.

[HONG 81] S. J. Hong and D. L. Ostapko. "A Simple Procedure to Generate Optimum Test Patterns for Parity Logic Networks." *IEEE Transactions on Computers* C-30 (May 1981): 356–58.

[HUGH 84] J. L. A. Hughes, E. J. McCluskey, and D. J. Lu. "Design of Totally Self-Checking Comparators with an Arbitrary Number of Inputs." *IEEE Transactions on Computers* C-33 (January 1984): 546–50.

[ITOH 80] H. Itoh and M. Nakamichi. "Design of Self-Checking Checkers for Berger Code and m-Out-of-n Code" (in Japanese). *Transactions of IECE Japan* J63-D (April 1980): 326–31.

[ITOH 82b] H. Itoh and M. Nakamichi. "Self-Checking Checker Designs for Various 2-Rail Codes." *Transactions of IECE Japan* E65 (November 1982): 665–71.

[IZAW 81] N. Izawa. "3-Level Realization of Self-Checking 1-Out-of-n Code Checkers" (in Japanese). *Dig., 1981 IECE Nat. Conv. Inf. Syst., IECE of Japan*, (October 1981): no. 504.

[IZAW 84a] N. Izawa. "Design of Totally Self-Checking Checkers for Unordered Codes" (in Japanese). *Transactions of the IECE Japan* J67-D (May 1984): 585–92.

[IZAW 84b] N. Izawa. "Reduced-Gate Design of Totally Self-Checking Checkers for Unordered Codes" (in Japanese). *Transactions of the IECE Japan* J67-D (December 1984): 1395–1402.

[KART 83] S. P. Kartashev and S. I. Kartashev. "Reconfigurable Fault-Tolerant Multicomputer Network." *Proceedings of National Computer Conference IFIPS* (1983): 595–610.

[KART 84] S. P. Kartashev and S. I. Kartashev. "Efficient Internode Communications in Reconfigurable Binary Trees." *IEEE Transactions on Computers* C-33 (November 1984): 977–90.

[KAWA 86] T. Kawada, Y. Takahashi, N. Tsuda, M. Waki, and N. Hagiwara. "A Pattern Matching Processor Array with Defect Tolerance." *Dig., 1986 IEEE Solid-State Circuit Conference* (February 1986): WPM 8.4, 90–91.

[KHAK 82a] J. Khakbaz and E. J. McCluskey. "Concurrent Error Detection and Testing for Large PLA's." *IEEE Journal of Solid-State Circuits* SC-17 (April 1982): 386–94.

[KHAK 82b] J. Khakbaz. "Self-Testing Embedded Parity Trees." *Dig., 12th Annual Int. Symposium Fault-Tolerant Comput.* (June 1982): 109–16.

[KHAK 82c] J. Khakbaz. "Totally Self-Checking Checker for 1-Out-of-*n* Code Using Two-Rail Codes." *IEEE Transactions on Computers* C-13 (July 1982); 667–81.

[KHAK 84] J. Khakbaz and E. J. McCluskey. "Self-Testing Embedded Parity Checkers." *IEEE Transactions on Computers* C-33 (August 1984): 753–56.

[KONE 80] B. Könemann, J. Mucha, and G. Zwiehoff. "Built-in Test for Complex Digital Integrated Circuits." *IEEE Journal of Solid-State Circuits* SC-15 (June 1980): 315–19.

[KORE 81] I. Koren. "A Reconfigurable and Fault-Tolerant VLSI Multiprocessor Array." *Proceedings of the IEEE Annual Symposium on Computer Architecture* (1981): 425–42.

[KORE 86] I. Koren and D. K. Pradhan. "Yield and Performance Enhancement Through Redundancy in VLSI and WSI Multiprocessor Systems." *Proceedings of the IEEE* 74 (May 1986): 699–711.

[KROL 86] T. Krol. "(N, K) Concept Fault Tolerance." *IEEE Transactions on Computers* C-35 (April 1986): 339–49.

[LALA 85] P. K. Lala. *Fault Tolerant & Fault Testable Hardware Design*. Englewood Cliffs, N.J.: Prentice-Hall, 1985.

[LEIG 82] F. T. Leighton and C. E. Leiserson. "Wafer Scale Integration of Systolic Arrays." *Proceedings of the Twenty-Third Annual Symposium on Foundation of Computer Science, Chicago, 1982*, 297–311.

[LO 87a] J. C. Lo and S. Thanawastien. "The Design of Fast Totally Self-Checking Berger Codes Checkers Based on Berger Code Partitioning." Research paper, University of Southwestern Louisiana, Lafayette, March 25, 1987. (Also shown in *Dig., 18th Annual Int. Symposium Fault-Tolerant Comput.* (June 1988).)

[LO 87b] J. C. Lo and S. Thanawastien. "On the Design of Combinational Totally Self-Checking 1-Out-of-3 Code Checkers." Research paper, University of Southwestern Louisiana, Lafayette, May 25, 1987.

[MACC 85] E. J. McCluskey. "Built-In Self-Test Techniques, Built-In Self-Test Structures." *IEEE Design & Test* 2 (April 1985): 21–28, 29–36.

[MANG 82] T. E. Mangir and A. Avizienis. "Fault-Tolerant Design for VLSI: Effect of Interconnect Requirement on Yield Improvement of VLSI Designs." *IEEE Transactions on Computers* C-31 (July 1982): 609–15.

[MANG 84a] T. E. Mangir. "Sources of Failures and Yield Improvement for VLSI and Restructurable Interconnects for RVLSI and WSI: Part I—Sources of Failures and Yield Improvement for VLSI." *Proceedings of the IEEE* 72 (June 1984): 690–708.

[MANG 84b] T. E. Mangir. "Sources of Failures and Yield Improvement for VLSI and Restructurable Interconnects for RVLSI and WSI: Part II—Restructurable Interconnects for RVLSI and WSI." *Proceedings of the IEEE* 72 (December 1984): 1687–94.

[MARO 78a] M. A. Marouf and A. D. Friedman. "Design of Self-Checking Checkers for Berger Codes." *Dig., 8th Annual Int. Symposium Fault-Tolerant Comput.* (1978): 179–84.

[MARO 78b] M. A. Marouf and A. D. Friedman. "Efficient Design of Self-Checking Checker for Any *m*-Out-of-*n* Code." *IEEE Transactions on Computers* C-27 (June 1978): 482–90.

[MOUR 86a] S. Mourad, J. L. A. Hughes, and E. J. McCluskey. "Multiple Fault Detection in Parity Trees." *Proceedings of IEEE Compcon Spring* (1986): 441–44.

[MOUR 86b] S. Mourad, J. L. A. Hughes, and E. J. McCluskey. "Stuck-at Fault Detection in Parity Trees." *Proceedings of Fall Joint Computer Conference* (September 1986): 836–40.

[NANY 83] T. Nanya and Y. Tohma. "A 3-Level Realization of Totally Self-Checking Checkers for *m*-Out-of-*n* Codes." *Dig., 13th Annual Int. Symposium Fault-Tolerant Comput.* (1983): 173–76.

[NANY 85a] T. Nanya and T. Hamamatsu. "Totally Self-Checking Checkers for Subsets of m-Out-of-2m Codes" (in Japanese). *Transactions of the IECE Japan* J68-D (March 1985): 229–36.

[NANY 85b] T. Nanya and T. Kawamura. "Error Secure/Error Propagating Concept and Its Application to the Design of Strongly Fault Secure Processors." *Dig., 15th Annual Int. Symposium Fault-Tolerant Comput.* (June 1985): 396–401. [Also in *IEEE Transactions on Computers* C-37 (January 1988): 14–24.]

[NANY 87] T. Nanya and T. Kawamura. "A Note on Strongly Fault Secure Sequential Circuits." *IEEE Transactions on Computers* C-36 (September 1987): 1121–23.

[NEUM 56] J. von Neumann. "Probabilistic Logic and Synthesis of Reliable Organisms." In *Automa Studies*, 43–98. Princeton, N.J.: Princeton University Press, 1956.

[NICO 85a] M. Nicolaidis. "Evaluation of a Self-Checking Version of the MC68000 Microprocessor." *Dig., 15th Annual Int. Symposium Fault-Tolerant Comput.* (June 1985): 350–356.

[PASC 88] A. M. Paschalis, D. Nikolos, and C. Halatsis," Efficient Modular Design of TSC Checkers for *m*-out-of-2*m* Codes." *IEEE Transactions on Computers* C-37 (March 1988): 301–9.

[PIER 65] W. H. Pierce. "Interconnection Structure for Redundant Logic (the Theory of Interwoven Redundant Logic)". Chap. 5 in *Failure-Tolerant Computer Design*. New York: Academic Press, 1965.

[PIES 83] S. J. Piestrak. "Design Method of Totally Self-Checking Checkers for *m*-Out-of-*n* Codes." *Dig., 13th Annual Int. Symposium on Fault-Tolerant Comput.* (June 1983): 162–68.

[PIES 85] S. J. Piestrak. "PLA Implementation of Totally Self-Checking Circuits Using *m*-Out-of-*n* Codes." *Proceedings of IEEE. Int. Conference on Computer Design* (October 1985): 777–781.

[PIES 87] S. J. Piestrak. "Design of Fast Self-Testing Checkers for a Class of Berger Codes." *IEEE Transactions on Computers* C-36 (May 1987): 629–34.

[REDD 72a] S. M. Reddy. "Easily Testable Realization for Logic Functions." *IEEE Transactions on Computers* C-21 (November 1972): 1183–88.

[REDD 72b] S. M. Reddy. "Easily Testable Realization for Logic Functions." *IEEE Transactions on Computers* C-21 (December 1972): 1421–26.

[REDD 72c] S. M. Reddy. "A Design Procedure for Fault-Locatable Switching Circuits." *IEEE Transactions on Computers* C-21 (December 1972): 1421–26.

[REDD 74a] S. M. Reddy and J. R. Wilson. "Easily Testable Cellular Realization for the (Exactly p)-out-of-n and (p or More)-out-of-n Logic Functions." *IEEE Transactions on Computers* C-23 (January 1974): 98–100.

[REDD 74b] S. M. Reddy. "A Note on Self-Checking Checkers." *IEEE Transactions on Computers* C-23 (October 1974): 1100–1102.

[REDD 85] S. M. Reddy, K. K. Saluja, and M. Karpovsky. "A Data Compression Technique for Built-in Self-Test." *Dig., 15th Annual Int. Symposium Fault-Tolerant Comput.* (June 1985): 294–99.

[RENN 84] D. A. Rennels. "Fault-Tolerant Computing—Concepts and Examples." *IEEE Transactions on Computers* C-33 (December 1984): 1116–29.

[SAMI 83] M. Sami and R. Stefanelli. "Reconfigurable Architecture for VLSI Processing Arrays." *Proceedings of National Computer Conference IFIPS* (1983): 565–77.

[SAMI 86] M. Sami and R. Stefanelli. "Reconfigurable Architecture for VLSI Processing Arrays." *Proceedings of the IEEE* 74 (May 1986): 712–22.

[SEDM 79] R. M. Sedmak. "Design for Self-Verification: An Approach for Dealing with Testability Problems in VLSI-Based Designs." *Proceedings of IEEE International Test Conference* (1979): 112–20.

[SEDM 80a] R. M. Sedmak. "Implementation Techniques for Self-Verification." *Proceedings of IEEE International Test Conference* (1980): 267–78.

[SEDM 80b] R. M. Sedmak and H. L. Liebergot. "Fault Tolerance of a General Purpose Computer Implemented by Very Large Scale Integration." *IEEE Transactions on Computers* C-29 (June 1980): 492–500.

[SHIM 87] S. Shimada and T. Ishikawa. "A Note on Reliability Improvement of a Highly Parallel Computer" (in Japanese). *Transactions of the IECE Japan* J70-D (January 1987): 91–98.

[SIEW 82] D. P. Siewiorek and R. Swarz. *The Theory and Practice of Reliable System.* Bedford, Mass.: Digital Press, 1982.

[SMIT 77] J. E. Smith. "The Design of Totally Self-Checking Check Circuits for a Class of Unordered Codes." *Journal of Design Automation and Fault-Tolerant Computing* 1 (August 1977): 321–42.

[SMIT 78] J. E. Smith and G. Metze. "Strongly Fault-Secure Logic Networks." *IEEE Transactions on Computers* C-27 (June 1978): 495–499.

[SMIT 83] J. E. Smith and P. Lam. "A Theory of Totally Self-Checking System Design." *IEEE Transactions on Computers* C-32 (September 1983): 831–44.

[TAKE 82] Y. Takefuji, Y. Adachi, and H. Aiso. "A Novel Approach to Fault-Tolerant Logic and Yield Enhancement." *Proceedings of IEEE Compcon Fall* (1982): 56–64.

[TAMI 84] Y. Tamir and C. H. Sequin. "Design and Application of Self-Testing Comparators Implemented with MOS PLA's." *IEEE Transactions on Computers* (June 1984): 494–506.

[TANG 83] D. T. Tang and L. S. Woo. "Exhaustive Test Pattern Generation with Constant Weight Vectors." *IEEE Transactions on Computers* C-32 (December 1983): 1145–50.

[TANG 84] D. T. Tang and C. L. Chen. "Logic Test Pattern Generation Using Linear Codes." *IEEE Transactions on Computers* C-33 (September 1984): 845–50.

[TAO 87] D. L. Tao and P. K. Lala. "Three Level Totally Self-Checking Checker for 1-Out-of-n Code." *Dig., 17th Annual Int. Symposium Fault-Tolerant Comput.* (July 1987): 108–13.

[TOY 78] W. N. Toy. "Fault-Tolerant Design of Local ESS Processor." *Proceedings of IEEE* 66 (October 1978): 1126–45.

[TRYO 62] J. G. Tryon. "Quadded Logic." In *Redundancy Techniques for Computing Systems*, eds. Wilcox and Mann, 205–28. Washington, D.C.: Spartan Books, 1962.

[TSAO 82] M. M. Tsao, A. W. Wilson, R. C. McGarity, C. T. Tseng, and D. P. Siewiorek. "The Design of C. Fast: Single Chip Fault Tolerant Microprocessor." *Dig., 12th Annual Int. Symposium Fault-Tolerant Comput.* (June 1982): 63–69.

[TSUD 87] N. Tsuda, T. Satoh, and T. Kawada. "A Pipeline Sorting Chip." *Dig., 1987 IEEE Int. Solid-State Circuit Conference* (February 1987): FAM20.1, 270–71.

[WILL 82] T. W. Williams and K. P. Parker. "Design for Testability—A Survey." *IEEE Transactions on Computers* C-31 (January 1982): 2–5.

[WONG 83] C. Y. Wong, W. K. Fuchs, J. A. Abraham, and E. S. Davidson. "The Design of a Microprogram Control Unit with Concurrent Error Detection." *Dig., 13th Annual Int. Symposium Fault-Tolerant Comput.* (June 1983): 476–83.

[YAMA 87a] K. Yamashita, A. Kanasugi, S. Hijiya, G. Goto, N. Matsumura, and T. Shirato. "A Wafer-Scale 170,000-Gate FFT Processor with Built-In Test Circuits." *Proceedings of IEEE 1987 Custom Integrated Circuits Conference* (May 1987): 207–10.

[YEN 87] M. M. Yen, W. K. Fuchs, and J. A. Abraham. "Designing for Concurrent Error Detection in VLSI: Application to a Microprogram Control Unit." *IEEE Journal of Solid-State Circuits* SC-22 (August 1987): 595–605.

Index

D

E

M